core
SERVLETS AND
JAVASERVER PAGES

VOLUME 2–ADVANCED TECHNOLOGIES

SECOND EDITION

core
SERVLETS AND JAVASERVER PAGES
VOLUME 2–ADVANCED TECHNOLOGIES

SECOND EDITION

MARTY HALL
LARRY BROWN
YAAKOV CHAIKIN

PRENTICE
HALL

Upper Saddle River, NJ • Boston • Indianapolis • San Francisco
New York • Toronto • Montreal • London • Munich • Paris • Madrid
Capetown • Sydney • Tokyo • Singapore • Mexico City

Many of the designations used by manufacturers and sellers to distinguish their products are claimed as trademarks. Where those designations appear in this book, and the publisher was aware of a trademark claim, the designations have been printed with initial capital letters or in all capitals.

The authors and publisher have taken care in the preparation of this book, but make no expressed or implied warranty of any kind and assume no responsibility for errors or omissions. No liability is assumed for incidental or consequential damages in connection with or arising out of the use of the information or programs contained herein.

The publisher offers excellent discounts on this book when ordered in quantity for bulk purchases or special sales, which may include electronic versions and/or custom covers and content particular to your business, training goals, marketing focus, and branding interests. For more information, please contact:

U.S. Corporate and Government Sales

(800) 382-3419
corpsales@pearsontechgroup.com
For sales outside the United States please contact:

International Sales

international@pearsoned.com

This Book Is Safari Enabled

The Safari® Enabled icon on the cover of your favorite technology book means the book is available through Safari Bookshelf. When you buy this book, you get free access to the online edition for 45 days.

Safari Bookshelf is an electronic reference library that lets you easily search thousands of technical books, find code samples, download chapters, and access technical information whenever and wherever you need it.

To gain 45-day Safari Enabled access to this book:

- Go to http://www.prenhallprofessional.com/safarienabled
- Complete the brief registration form
- Enter the coupon code HLJ5-S0UK-WUI6-TPLD-DC7K

If you have difficulty registering on Safari Bookshelf or accessing the online edition, please e-mail customer-service@safaribooksonline.com.

Visit us on the Web: www.prenhallprofessional.com

Library of Congress Control Number: 2003058100

ISBN-13:   978-0-13-148260-9
ISBN-10:   0-13-148260-2

Text printed in the United States on recycled paper at Courier in Stoughton, Massachusetts.

First printing, December 2007

Contents

Introduction

Suppose your company wants to sell products online. You have a database that gives the price and inventory status of each item. However, your database doesn't speak HTTP, the protocol that Web browsers use. Nor does it output HTML, the format Web browsers need. What can you do? Once users know what they want to buy, how do you gather that information? You want to customize your site for visitors' preferences and interests, but how? You want to keep track of user's purchases as they shop at your site, but what techniques are required to implement this behavior? When your Web site becomes popular, you might want to compress pages to reduce bandwidth. How can you do this without causing your site to fail for those visitors whose browsers don't support compression? In all these cases, you need a program to act as the intermediary between the browser and some server-side resource. This book is about using the Java platform for this type of program.

"Wait a second," you say. "Didn't you already write a book about that?" Well, yes. In May of 2000, Sun Microsystems Press and Prentice Hall released Marty Hall's second book, *Core Servlets and JavaServer Pages*. It was successful beyond everyone's wildest expectations, selling approximately 100,000 copies, getting translated into Bulgarian, Chinese simplified script, Chinese traditional script, Czech, French, German, Hebrew, Japanese, Korean, Polish, Russian, and Spanish, and being chosen by Amazon.com as one of the top five computer programming books of 2001. What fun!

Since then, use of servlets and JSP has continued to grow at a phenomenal rate. The Java 2 Platform has become the technology of choice for developing e-commerce applications, dynamic Web sites, and Web-enabled applications and service. Servlets and JSP continue to be the foundation of this platform—they provide the link between Web clients and server-side applications. Virtually all major

Web servers for Windows, UNIX (including Linux), Mac OS, VMS, and mainframe operating systems now support servlet and JSP technology either natively or by means of a plug-in. With only a small amount of configuration, you can run servlets and JSP in Microsoft IIS, the Apache Web Server, IBM WebSphere, BEA WebLogic, Oracle Application Server 10g, and dozens of other servers. Performance of both commercial and open-source servlet and JSP engines has improved significantly.

To no one's surprise, this field continues to grow at a rapid rate. As a result, we could no longer cover the technology in a single book. *Core Servlets and JavaServer Pages, Volume 1: Core Technologies*, covers the servlet and JSP capabilities that you are likely to use in almost every real-life project. This book, *Volume 2: Advanced Technologies*, covers features that you may use less frequently but are extremely valuable in robust applications. For example,

- **Deployment descriptor file.** Through the proper use of the deployment descriptor file, web.xml, you can control many aspects of the Web application behavior, from preloading servlets, to restricting resource access, to controlling session time-outs.
- **Web application security.** In any Web application today, security is a must! The servlet and JSP security model allows you to easily create login pages and control access to resources.
- **Custom tag libraries.** Custom tags significantly improve the design of JSPs. Custom tags allow you to easily develop your own library of reusable tags specific to your business applications. In addition to creating your own tags, we cover the Standard Tag Library (JSTL).
- **Event handling.** With the events framework, you can control initialization and shutdown of the Web application, recognize destruction of HTTP sessions, and set application-wide values.
- **Servlet and JSP filters.** With filters, you can apply many pre- and post-processing actions. For instance, logging incoming requests, blocking access, and modifying the servlet or JSP response.
- **Apache Struts.** This framework greatly enhances the standard model-view-controller (MVC) architecture available with servlets and JSPs. More importantly, Apache Struts still remains one of the most common frameworks used in industry.

Who Should Read This Book

The main audience is developers who are familiar with basic servlet and JSP technologies, but want to make use of advanced capabilities. As we cover many topics in this book—the deployment descriptor file, security, listeners, custom tags, JSTL, Struts,

Ant—you may want to first start with the technologies of most interest, and then later read the remaining material. Most commercial servlet and JSP Web applications take advantage of the technologies presented throughout, thus, at some point you may want to read the complete book.

If you are new to servlets and JSPs, you will want to read *Core Servlets and Java-Server Pages, Volume 1: Core Technologies*. In addition to teaching you how to install and configure a servlet container, Volume 1 provides excellent coverage of the servlet and JSP specifications. Volume 1 provides the foundation material to this book.

Both books assume that you are familiar with basic Java programming. You don't have to be an expert Java developer, but if you know nothing about the Java programming language, this is not the place to start. After all, servlet and JSP technology is an application of the Java programming language. If you don't know the language, you can't apply it. So, if you know nothing about basic Java development, start with a good introductory book like *Thinking in Java, Core Java*, or *Core Web Programming*, all from Prentice Hall.

Conventions

Throughout the book, concrete programming constructs or program output are presented in a monospaced font. For example, when abstractly discussing server-side programs that use HTTP, we might refer to "HTTP servlets" or just "servlets," but when we say `HttpServlet` we are talking about a specific Java class.

User input is indicated in boldface, and command-line prompts are either generic (`Prompt>`) or indicate the operating system to which they apply (`DOS>`). For instance, the following indicates that "`Some Output`" is the result when "`java SomeProgram`" is executed on any platform.

```
Prompt> java SomeProgram
Some Output
```

URLs, file names, and directory names are presented in a sans serif font. So, for example, we would say "the `StringTokenizer` class" (monospaced because we're talking about the class name) and "Listing such and such shows SomeFile.java" (sans-serif because we're talking about the file name). Paths use forward slashes as in URLs unless they are specific to the Windows operating system. So, for instance, we would use a forward slash when saying "look in *install_dir*/bin" (OS neutral), but use backslashes when saying "see C:\Windows\Temp" (Windows specific).

Important standard techniques are indicated by specially marked entries, as in the following example.

Core Approach

*Pay particular attention to items in Core Approach sections. They
indicate techniques that should always or almost always be used.*

Core Notes and Core Warnings are called out in a similar manner.

About the Web Site

The book has a companion Web site at http://volume2.coreservlets.com/. This free
site includes:

- Documented source code for all examples shown in the book, which
  can be downloaded for unrestricted use.
- Links to all URLs mentioned in the text of the book.
- Up-to-date download sites for servlet and JSP software.
- Information on book discounts.
- Book additions, updates, and news.

Acknowledgments

Many people helped us with this book. Without their assistance, we would still be on the second chapter. Chuck Cavaness (Cypress Care, Inc.), Bob Evans (JHU Applied Physics Laboratory), Randal Hanford (Boeing), Kalman Hazins (JHU Applied Physics Laboratory), Michael Kolodny (Raba Technologies), Kyong Park (Raba Technologies), Eric Purcell (Lockheed-Martin), Ylber Ramadani (George Brown College), and Richard Slywczak (NASA Glenn Research Center) provided valuable technical feedback on many different chapters. Their recommendations improved the book considerably.

Teresa Horton spotted our errant commas, awkward sentences, typographical errors, and grammatical inconsistencies. She improved the result immensely. Vanessa Moore designed the book layout and produced the final version; she did a great job despite our many last-minute changes. Greg Doench of Prentice Hall believed in the concept from before the first edition and encouraged us to write a second edition. Thanks to all.

Most of all, Marty would like to thank B.J., Lindsay, and Nathan for their patience and encouragement. Larry would like to thank Lee for her loving and unfailing support. Yaakov would like to thank the Almighty for shining His grace and mercy upon him every day; his parents, Mr. Ilia and Mrs. Galina Khaikin, who in the '80s had the vision to take him to his first programming class when he was just 13 years old; his children, Moshe and Esther Miriam, who bring challenge and joy into his life; and of course his wife, Perel, for her constant loving support and encouragement. God has blessed us with great families.

About the Authors

Marty Hall is president of coreservlets.com, Inc., a small company that provides training courses and consulting services related to server-side Java technology. He also teaches Java and Web programming in the Johns Hopkins University part-time graduate program in Computer Science, where he directs the Distributed Computing and Web Technology concentration areas. Marty is the author of five books from Prentice Hall and Sun Microsystems Press: the first and second editions of *Core Servlets and JavaServer Pages*, *More Servlets and JavaServer Pages*, and the first and second editions of *Core Web Programming*. You can reach Marty at hall@coreservlets.com.

Larry Brown is a Network and Systems manager at a U.S. Navy Research and Development laboratory. He is the co-author of the second editions of *Core Web Programming*, also from Prentice Hall and Sun Microsystems Press. You can reach Larry at larry@lmbrown.com.

Yaakov Chaikin is a senior consultant at a software development company based in Columbia, MD. Besides his day job, he teaches Web development technologies at the graduate Computer Science program of Loyola College in Maryland, where he heads the Web Development track. At times, he also helps his wife with her Web/graphic design business, tbiq.com. Yaakov can be reached at yaakov.chaikin@gmail.com.

core SERVLETS AND JAVASERVER PAGES

VOLUME 2 – ADVANCED TECHNOLOGIES

SECOND EDITION

USING AND DEPLOYING WEB APPLICATIONS

Topics in This Chapter

- The purpose of Web applications
- The structure of Web applications
- Web application registration
- Development and deployment strategies
- WAR files
- Web application data sharing

Chapter 1

Web applications (or "Web apps") let you bundle a set of servlets, JavaServer Pages (JSP) pages, tag libraries, Hypertext Markup Language (HTML) documents, images, style sheets, and other Web content into a single collection that can be used on any server compatible with the servlet specification. When designed carefully, Web apps can be moved from server to server or placed at different locations on the same server, all without making any changes to any of the servlets, JSP pages, or HTML files in the application.

This capability lets you move complex applications around with a minimum of effort, streamlining application reuse. In addition, because each Web app has its own directory structure, sessions, `ServletContext`, and class loader, using a Web app simplifies even the initial development because it reduces the amount of coordination needed among various parts of your overall system.

1.1 Purpose of Web Applications

Web applications help you in three main ways: organizing your resources, portably deploying your applications, and keeping different applications from interfering with each other. Let's look at each benefit in a bit more detail.

Organization

The first advantage of Web applications is that you know where everything goes: Web apps have a standard location for each type of resource. Individual Java class files always go in the directory called WEB-INF/classes, JAR files (bundles of Java class files) always go in WEB-INF/lib, the web.xml configuration file always goes in the WEB-INF directory, and so on. Files directly accessible to clients (e.g., Web browsers) go into the top-level directory of your Web app or any subdirectory under the top-level directory except WEB-INF.

In addition, it's very common for developers to move from one project to another. Having a standard way of organizing your application's resources saves you from having to come up with an application structure every time you start a new project and it also saves a new developer joining your project from having to learn your particular file organization.

Portability

Because the servlet specification provides a specific file organization, any compliant server should be able to deploy and run your application immediately. This affords you much freedom in choosing the vendor of your Web server. As long as a server is compliant, you can pick up your application and, with almost no changes, deploy and run it on a server from a different vendor, thus avoiding the dreaded "vendor lock-in." For example, you could start developing your applications using a free Web server and move to a more established, vendor-supported server closer to deployment time.

Separation

Different Web applications deployed on the same server do not interfere with each other. Each application has its own uniform resource locator (URL) with which it can be accessed, its own ServletContext object, and so on. Two Web applications deployed on the same server act as if they were deployed on separate servers. Neither needs to know about the other.

This further simplifies development and deployment of Web applications. The developer doesn't have to be concerned with how the application will integrate with the existing applications already deployed on the server. Now, as we will see later in this chapter, there are a few ways in which Web applications can deliberately interact with each other. However, for the most part, they can be developed independently.

1.2   Structure of Web Applications

As mentioned earlier, a Web application has a standardized format and is portable across all compliant Web or application servers. The top-level directory of a Web application is simply a directory with a name of your choosing. Within that directory, certain types of content go in designated locations. This section provides details on the type of content and the locations in which it should be placed.

Locations for Various File Types

Figure 1–1 shows a representative example of a Web application hierarchy. For a step-by-step example of creating your own Web application, download the app-blank Web app from http://volume2.coreservlets.com/ and follow the instructions in Section 1.6 (Building a Simple Web Application).

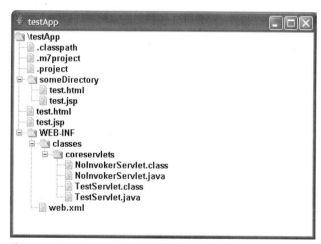

Figure 1–1   A representative Web application.

JSP Pages

JSP pages should be placed in the top-level Web application directory or in a subdirectory with any name other than WEB-INF or META-INF. Servers are prohibited from serving files from WEB-INF or META-INF to the user. When you register a Web application (see Section 1.3), you tell the server the URL prefix that designates the Web app and define where the Web app directory is located. It is common, but by no means mandatory, to use the name of the main Web application directory as the URL prefix. Once you register a prefix, JSP pages are then accessed with URLs of the form http://*host/*

webAppPrefix/filename.jsp (if the pages are in the top-level directory of the Web application) or http://*host*/*webAppPrefix*/subdirectory/filename.jsp (if the pages are in a subdirectory).

It depends on the server whether a default file such as index.jsp can be accessed with a URL that specifies only a directory (e.g., http://*host*/*webAppPrefix*/) without the developer first making an entry in the Web app's WEB-INF/web.xml file. If you want index.jsp to be the default file name, we strongly recommend that you make an explicit `welcome-file-list` entry in your Web app's web.xml file. For example, the following web.xml entry specifies that if a URL specifies a directory name but no file name, the server should try index.jsp first and index.html second. If neither is found, the result is server specific (e.g., a directory listing).

```
<welcome-file-list>
  <welcome-file>index.jsp</welcome-file>
  <welcome-file>index.html</welcome-file>
</welcome-file-list>
```

On the use of web.xml, see Chapter 2 (Controlling Web Application Behavior with web.xml).

HTML Documents, Images, and Other Regular Web Content

As far as the servlet and JSP engine is concerned, HTML files, GIF and JPEG images, style sheets, and other Web documents follow exactly the same rules as do JSP pages. They are placed in exactly the same locations and accessed with URLs of exactly the same form.

Individual Servlets, Beans, and Helper Classes

Servlets and other .class files are placed either in WEB-INF/classes or in a subdirectory of WEB-INF/classes that matches their package name.

To access one of these servlets, you need to designate the specific URL for it by specifying the `servlet-mapping` element in the web.xml deployment descriptor file that is located within the WEB-INF directory of the Web application. See Section 1.3 (Registering Web Applications with the Server) for details.

There is a second way to access servlets without having to specify a custom URL. It is with URLs of the form http://*host*/*webAppPrefix*/servlet/packageName.Servlet-Name. Using this way of accessing servlets is fine if you want to try capabilities or make a quick test case. However, we recommend you do *not* use this approach for real-world applications. There are several reasons for this advice. First, if you also specify a `servlet-mapping` for this servlet, you will have two different ways of accessing the same servlet. This side effect could quickly grow to be a maintenance headache. Second, because declarative security depends on the URL with which the resource is accessed, it could also be a potential security hole in your application. Third, the user is forced to type in a URL that contains the fully qualified name of your servlet. This name includes the entire package structure with the class name. Such URLs look ugly and users find them hard to remember. Therefore, this approach would score very low on the Web application usability meter. Fourth, if you ever decide to change the name of your class or to repackage your classes, the URL must change, forcing you to update every place in your entire application where this URL was used. Besides the maintenance problem, this will also confuse users who have already bookmarked the original URL, once again hurting usability of your application.

In fact, we recommend that you explicitly block the user from accessing the servlets in your Web application without mapping a custom URL. The mapping could be specified with the help of the `servlet-mapping` element of web.xml. See web.xml of the app-blank sample application for an example of this. You can download app-blank from http://volume2.coreservlets.com/.

Servlets, Beans, and Helper Classes (Bundled in JAR Files)

If the servlets or other .class files are bundled inside JAR files, then the JAR files should be placed in WEB-INF/lib. If the classes are in packages, then within the JAR file they should be in a directory that matches their package name. On most servers, JAR files can also be shared across multiple Web applications. However, this feature is not standardized, and the details vary from server to server. On Tomcat, you place shared JAR files in *tomcat_dir*/shared/lib.

Deployment Descriptor

The deployment descriptor file, web.xml, should be placed in the WEB-INF subdirectory of the main Web application directory. For details on using web.xml, see Chapter 2 (Controlling Web Application Behavior with web.xml). Note that a few servers have a global web.xml file that applies to all Web applications. For example, Tomcat uses *tomcat_dir*/conf/web.xml for global configuration settings. That file is entirely server specific; the *only* standard web.xml file is the per-application one that is placed within the WEB-INF directory of the Web app.

Tag Library Descriptor Files

Tag Library Descriptor (TLD) files should be placed inside of the WEB-INF directory or any subdirectory of WEB-INF. However, we recommend that you put them in a tlds directory within WEB-INF. Grouping them in a common directory (e.g., tlds) simplifies their management. JSP pages can access TLD files that are in WEB-INF using a `taglib` directive as follows:

```
<%@ taglib uri="/WEB-INF/tlds/myTaglibFile.tld" ...%>
```

Because it is the server, not the client (e.g., Web browser), that accesses the TLD file, the prohibition that content inside of WEB-INF is not Web accessible does not apply.

When deployed inside a JAR file, the .tld file should be placed inside the META-INF directory or any subdirectory of META-INF. The switch in location from WEB-INF to META-INF is because JAR files are not Web application archives and thus don't contain a WEB-INF directory. See Chapter 7 (Tag Libraries: The Basics) for a more detailed discussion of TLD files.

Tag Files

Tag files should be placed in the WEB-INF/tags directory or a subdirectory of WEB-INF/tags. As with TLD files, tag files are still accessible to JSP pages even though they are located inside of the protected WEB-INF directory. Tag files are also declared inside a JSP page through the taglib directive. However, instead of uri, they use the tagdir attribute. For example, if we placed the myTagFile.tag file inside of the WEB-INF/tags directory of our Web application, the taglib directive of a JSP page would look something like this:

```
<%@ taglib tagdir="/WEB-INF/tags" ...%>
```

In this scenario, the server automatically generates the TLD for the tag files, so no custom mapping is necessary.

You can also include tag files bundled in a JAR file. The JAR file itself would have to be placed inside of the WEB-INF/lib directory as we mentioned earlier. However, within the JAR file, the tag files should be placed inside of the META-INF/tags directory. In this case, the server does not automatically generate the TLD. You must declare the tag file and its path within a .tld file. Note that the .tld file can contain declarations of other types of custom tags as well. See Chapter 7 (Tag Libraries: The Basics) for a more detailed coverage of tag files.

WAR Manifest File

When you create a WAR file (see Section 1.5), a MANIFEST.MF file is placed in the META-INF subdirectory. Normally, the jar utility automatically creates MANIFEST.MF and places it into the META-INF directory, and you ignore it if you unpack the WAR file. Occasionally, however, you modify MANIFEST.MF explicitly, so it is useful to know where it is stored.

1.3 Registering Web Applications with the Server

As we explained earlier, Web applications are portable. Regardless of the server, you store files in the same directory structure and access them with URLs of the same form. For example, Figure 1–2 summarizes the directory structure and URLs that would be used for a simple Web application called myWebApp. This section illustrates how to install and execute this simple Web application on different platforms.

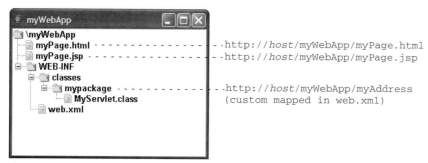

Figure 1–2   Structure of the myWebApp Web application.

Although Web applications themselves are completely portable, the registration process is server specific. For example, to move the myWebApp application from server to server, you don't have to modify anything inside any of the directories shown in Figure 1–2. However, the location in which the top-level directory (myWebApp in this case) is placed will vary from server to server. Similarly, you use a server-specific process to tell the system that URLs that begin with http://*host*/myWebApp/ should apply to the Web application.

This section assumes that you already went through the steps of installing and setting up your server. For information on setting up your server, read your server's documentation, see the introductory chapter of the first volume of this book, or (for Tomcat users) refer to the continually updated Tomcat setup and configuration guide at http://www.coreservlets.com/. Here, we present a brief example, then give explicit details for Tomcat in one of the following subsections. For a complete step-by-step example of developing and deploying a simple Web application on Tomcat, see Section 1.6 (Building a Simple Web Application).

As we show in Section 1.4 (Development and Deployment Strategies), the usual strategy is to build Web applications in a personal development environment and periodically copy them to various deployment directories for testing on different servers. We recommend that you avoid placing your development directory directly within a server's deployment directory—doing so makes it hard to deploy on multiple servers, hard to develop while a Web application is executing, and hard to organize the files. Instead, use a separate development directory and deploy by means of one of the strategies outlined in Section 1.4 (Development and Deployment Strategies). The simplest approach is to keep a shortcut (Windows) or symbolic link (UNIX/Linux) to the deployment directories of various servers, and simply copy the entire development directory whenever you want to deploy. For example, on Windows you can use the right mouse button to drag the development folder onto the shortcut, release the button, and select Copy.

Registering a Web Application with Tomcat

With Tomcat, creating a Web application consists of creating the appropriate directory structure and copying that directory structure into the *tomcat_dir*/webapps directory. Tomcat will take care of the rest. The ability to deploy a Web app by simply copying its directory structure into some server directory is usually referred to as *hot-deployment* or *auto-deployment*. The directory within the server that allows this functionality is referred to as a *hot-deploy directory* or an *auto-deploy directory*. Most, if not all modern Web servers provide this feature. For extra control over the process, you can modify *tomcat_dir*/conf/server.xml (a Tomcat-specific file) to refer to the Web application.

The following steps walk you through what is required to create a Web app that is accessed by means of URLs that start with http://*host*/myWebApp/.

1. **Create a Web application directory structure with the top-level directory called myWebApp.** Because this is your personal development directory structure, it can be located at any place you find convenient. This directory structure should be organized as we showed in Section 1.2 (Structure of Web Applications). You can reduce the amount of manual work you have to do in this step by simply downloading the app-blank Web application from http://volume2.coreservlets.com/. It already contains all the required directories and a sample web.xml deployment descriptor. All you have left to do is rename the top-level directory from app-blank to myWebApp.

   However, if you decide to create these directories by hand, here is what you will need to do. Create a directory called myWebApp anywhere on your system outside of your server's installation directory. Right under it, create a directory called WEB-INF. Under WEB-INF, create a directory called classes. Create the deployment descriptor file, web.xml, and place it into the WEB-INF directory. We discuss the deployment descriptor in detail in Chapter 2 (Controlling Web Application Behavior with web.xml). For now, however, just copy the existing web.xml file from *tomcat_dir*/webapps/ROOT/WEB-INF or use the version that is bundled with app-blank.

Once you have created the proper directory structure, place a simple JSP page called myPage.jsp into the myWebApp directory. Put a simple servlet called MyServlet.class into the WEB-INF/classes directory.

2. **Declare the servlet and map it to a URL by editing the web.xml deployment descriptor file.** Unlike JSP files, servlets need to be explicitly declared. We need to tell the server that it exists by providing the fully qualified class name of the servlet. In addition, we need to inform the server which URLs requested by the client should invoke MyServlet.class. Both of these steps can be accomplished by adding the following entries in web.xml:

```
<servlet>
  <servlet-name>MyName</servlet-name>
  <servlet-class>mypackage.MyServlet</servlet-class>
</servlet>
<servlet-mapping>
  <servlet-name>MyName</servlet-name>
  <url-pattern>/MyAddress</url-pattern>
</servlet-mapping>
```

The servlet element and its subelements inform the server of the name we want to use for declaring our servlet as well as the fully qualified name of the servlet class. The servlet-mapping element and its subelements tell the server which servlet should be invoked when the client requests a URL that matches the pattern provided by the value of the url-pattern element. Thus, the servlet declared as MyName can be invoked with http://*host*/myWebApp/MyAddress.

3. **Copy the myWebApp directory to *tomcat_dir*/webapps.** For example, suppose you installed Tomcat in C:*tomcat_dir*. You would then copy the myWebApp directory to the webapps directory, resulting in C:*tomcat_dir*\webapps\myWebApp\HelloWebApp.jsp, C:*tomcat_dir*\webapps\myWebApp\WEB-INF\classes\HelloWebApp.class, and C:*tomcat_dir*\webapps\myWebApp\WEB-INF\web.xml. You could also wrap the directory inside a WAR file (Section 1.5) and simply drop the WAR file into C:*tomcat_dir*\webapps.

4. **Optional: Add a Context entry to *tomcat_dir*/conf/server.xml.** By default, Tomcat configures your Web application to have a URL prefix that exactly matches the name of the top-level directory of your Web app. If you are satisfied with these default settings you can omit this step. However, if you want a bit more control over the Web app registration process, you can supply a Context element in *tomcat_dir*/conf/server.xml. If you do edit server.xml, be sure to make a backup copy first; a small syntax error in server.xml can

completely prevent Tomcat from running. However, for the later versions of Tomcat, the recommended approach is to place the Context element (and its subelements) by itself into the context.xml file. Then, place context.xml alongside the web.xml deployment descriptor into the WEB-INF directory of your Web application.

The Context element has several possible attributes that are documented at http://jakarta.apache.org/tomcat/tomcat-5.0-doc/config/context.html. For instance, you can decide whether to use cookies or URL rewriting for session tracking, you can enable or disable servlet reloading (i.e., monitoring of classes for changes and reloading servlets whose class file changes on disk), and you can set debugging levels. However, for basic Web apps, you just need to deal with the two required attributes: path (the URL prefix) and docBase (the base installation directory of the Web application, relative to *tomcat_dir/* webapps.) This entry should look like the following snippet.

```
<Context path="/some-web-app" docBase="myWebApp" />
```

Note that you should not use /examples as the URL prefix; Tomcat already uses that prefix for a sample Web application.

Core Warning

Do not use /examples as the URL prefix of a Web application in Tomcat.

5. **Access the JSP page and the servlet.** The URL http://*host*/myWebApp/myPage.jsp invokes the JSP page, and http://*host*/myWebApp/MyAddress invokes the servlet. During development, you probably use localhost for the host name. These URLs assume that you have modified the Tomcat configuration file (*tomcat_dir/*conf/server.xml) to use port 80 as recommended in the Tomcat setup and configuration guide at http://www.coreservlets.com/. If you haven't made this change, use http://*host:**8080***/myWebApp/myPage.jsp and http://*host:**8080***/myWebApp/MyAddress.

Registering a Web Application with Other Servers

The first two steps described earlier deal with creating the portable part of a Web application. These steps would be identical for any compliant server. The steps for the actual registration are specific to Tomcat. However, registering a Web app with

other servers is very similar. In this subsection we summarize the server-specific registration process for some of the more popular servers today.

BEA WebLogic

Like Tomcat, WebLogic provides an auto-deploy directory used to register and
deploy Web applications. First, if you haven't done so already, create a new domain
called myDomain. This can be done by running WebLogic's configuration wizard
config.cmd on Windows or config.sh on UNIX/Linux, both located in the bea/
weblogic_dir/common/bin directory, and following its instructions. Once this is done,
simply copy your entire Web application directory structure (including the top-level
directory) or a WAR file to the bea/user_projects/domains/myDomain/applications
directory. You can also use WebLogic's Web console application to deploy a Web app.
Log into the console by going to http://localhost:7001/console/. (Note that this
assumes you left the default settings for the port number unchanged and that
you are running the server on your local machine.) In the left pane, expand the
Deployments node and click Web Application Modules. Then, click Deploy a
New Web Application Module. This starts a browser-based deployment wizard.
Simply follow the step-by-step instructions for the wizard. After you deploy the
Web application, the JSP page can be accessed by going to http://local-
host:7001/myWebApp/myPage.jsp and the servlet by going to http://local-
host:7001/myWebApp/MyAddress.

JBoss

In JBoss, registering a Web application is almost as easy as in Tomcat. In fact, by
default, JBoss uses Tomcat as its embedded Web server. To register your Web application, start by first renaming your top-level directory myWebApp to myWebApp.war.
Note that you are not actually creating a WAR file, but simply renaming the top-level
directory to end with .war. JBoss insists that to be deployable, not only should WAR
file names end in .war, which is required by the servlet specification, but the
top-level directory name of your Web app should end in .war as well. Once this is
done, copy the myWebApp.war directory to the jboss_dir/server/default/deploy
directory. Assuming you didn't change any default configuration settings when
installing JBoss, you can invoke the JSP page by going to http://localhost:8080/
myWebApp/myPage.jsp and invoke the servlet by going to http://localhost:8080/
myWebApp/MyAddress. If you do package your Web application into a WAR file, you
should place myWebApp.war into the same JBoss directory to deploy it.

Caucho Resin

To use the auto-deployment feature of Caucho Resin server, copy your entire
Web application directory structure (including the top-level directory) or a WAR
file to the resin_dir/webapps directory. Assuming you didn't change any default

configuration settings of the server, you can access the JSP page by going to
http://localhost:8080/myWebApp/myPage.jsp and the servlet by going to
http://localhost:8080/myWebApp/MyAddress.

1.4   Development and Deployment Strategies

Whenever you are ready to start developing a new Web application, follow these
three steps:

1. **Create the Web app directory structure.** In your development
   directory, make a new directory structure that follows the Web application structure (including the web.xml file within WEB-INF) discussed earlier in this chapter. The easiest way to do this is to copy and rename the
   app-blank application. (Remember, you can download app-blank and all
   the other code from the book at http://volume2.coreservlets.com/.)
2. **Create your code.** Place HTML and JSP pages into the top-level
   directory or into subdirectories other than WEB-INF or META-INF. Place
   individual Java class files into WEB-INF/classes/*subdirectory-match-
   ing-package-name*. Place JAR files into WEB-INF/lib. Place .tag and
   .tagx files into WEB-INF/tags and so on.
3. **Deploy the app.** Copy the entire Web application directory structure
   (including the top-level directory) to your server's auto-deploy directory. There are a number of strategies you can use to simplify this third
   step, but here are the most popular ones:
   • Copying to a shortcut or symbolic link
   • Using deployment features specific to an integrated development
     environment (IDE)
   • Using Ant or a similar tool
   • Using an IDE in combination with Ant

If you are just beginning with servlets and JSP, you should probably start with the
first option. Learning how to use Ant or a specific IDE could get in the way of you
getting comfortable with the servlet and JSP technology itself. Note, however, that
we do *not* list the option of putting your code directly in the server's deployment
directory. Although this is one of the most common choices among beginners, it
scales so poorly to advanced tasks that we recommend you steer clear of it from the
start.

Details on these four options are given in the following subsections.

Copying to a Shortcut or Symbolic Link

On Windows, go to the directory that is one above the server's auto-deployment directory. On Tomcat, this would position you inside the root installation directory, *tomcat_dir*. Right-click the auto-deploy directory (e.g., webapps on Tomcat), and select Copy. Then go to the directory that is one above your top-level development directory (e.g., one above myWebApp), right-click, and select Paste Shortcut (not just Paste). Now, whenever you are ready to deploy your Web app, click and hold the right mouse button on your development directory (e.g., myWebApp), then drag onto the deployment directory shortcut, and release the button. A pop-up menu will appear. Select the Copy Here option. Figure 1–3 shows an example setup that simplifies testing of this chapter's examples on Tomcat, WebLogic, JBoss, and Resin. On UNIX, you can use symbolic links (created with ln -s) in a manner similar to that for Windows shortcuts.

Figure 1–3   Using shortcuts to simplify deployment.

An advantage of this approach is that it is simple. Therefore, it is good for beginners who want to concentrate on learning servlets and JSP technology, not deployment tools or IDEs.

One disadvantage of this approach is that it requires repeated copying if you use multiple servers. For example, we keep several different servers (Tomcat, Resin, etc.) on our development system and regularly test the code on all servers. A second disadvantage is that this approach copies both the Java source code files and the class files to the server, although only the class files are needed. This may not matter much on your desktop server, but when you get to the "real" deployment server, you won't want to include the source code files.

Using IDE-Specific Deployment Features

Most servlet- and JSP-savvy development environments (e.g., IBM WebSphere Studio Application Developer, Sun ONE Studio, NetBeans, Oracle JDeveloper, Borland JBuilder, Eclipse with MyEclipseIDE or NitroX plug-ins) let you configure your environment so you can deploy your Web application to a test, development, or production server with the click of a button.

With all the clear advantages of IDEs, there are a number of disadvantages as well. Most worthwhile IDEs have a steep learning curve. This prevents you from concentrating on real development, at least at the beginning. In addition, it's very common for developers to switch projects and for projects to have one specific IDE everyone must use to have one common development environment on the team. If you switch, and the new project uses a different IDE for compilation and deployment than the one you are used to, you will be forced to learn and get used to yet another IDE. This wastes additional time.

Using Ant, Maven, or a Similar Tool

Developed by the Apache Foundation, ant is a tool similar to the UNIX make utility. However, ant is written in the Java programming language (and thus is portable) and is touted to be both simpler to use and more powerful than make. Many servlet and JSP developers use ant for compiling and deploying. The usage of ant is discussed in the Appendix (Developing Applications with Apache Ant).

For general information on using ant, see http://jakarta.apache.org/ant/manual/. See http://jakarta.apache.org/tomcat/tomcat-5.5-doc/appdev/processes.html for specific guidance on using ant with Tomcat.

The main advantage of this approach is flexibility: ant is powerful enough to handle everything from compiling the Java source code to copying files to producing Web archive (WAR) files (see Section 1.5).

Another tool that is attracting a lot of attention in the Java world is maven. Maven extends ant, so it is very similar to ant in some respects and drastically different in another. Although maven is just as flexible as ant, its focus is on simplicity of use. It accomplishes this simplicity by utilizing conventions. For example, maven can compile the code without the developer ever specifying where the code is located with the project folder. This is because maven assumes, by convention, that the Java code is located in the src/main/java folder. Of course, this assumption can be reconfigured, but why bother? Unlike ant, these conventions allow maven configuration files to be very short and easy to understand. You can learn more about maven at http://maven.apache.org.

The disadvantage of both ant and maven is the overhead of learning to use them; there is a steeper learning curve with ant and maven than the previous two techniques in this section. However, the big difference between investing time into learning a particular IDE and learning ant or maven is that more and more projects are adapting the usage of ant or maven as their standard, non-IDE-specific deployment tool, so chances are high that learning ant or maven will pay off in the future.

Using an IDE in Combination with Ant

IDEs help us be more productive by helping us write the code, but restrict us in terms of portability. ant lets us develop portably, but doesn't help at all with actual code writing. What should we do?

One way to bridge the gap a little between the two options is to adapt the use of an IDE that integrates with ant. This way you can still use your favorite IDE to help you write code and with the click of a button invoke ant scripts to compile and deploy your application. Even if your favorite IDE is not integrated with ant (most modern IDEs are), you can still use this approach, but you'll have to switch between the command prompt and your IDE quite a bit.

This approach works really well in a real-world project. The developers get to keep using their favorite IDEs, which helps them be most productive, and the project doesn't suffer from deployment inconsistencies because the compilation and deployment is done by the same portable ant script. We have participated in projects where several IDEs were used by different developers on the team working on the same Web applications; some even used different operating systems for their environments. The application deployment stayed consistent and the developers were happy to be able to use whatever made each one personally more productive. Isn't a happy developer what this is all about?

1.5   The Art of WAR: Bundling Web Applications into WAR Files

Web archive (WAR) files provide a convenient way of bundling Web apps in a single file. Having a single large file instead of many small files makes it easier to transfer the Web application from server to server.

A WAR file is really just a JAR file with a .war extension, and you use the regular jar command to create it. For example, to bundle the entire some-web-app application into a WAR file named some-web-app.war, you would navigate to the some-web-app directory and execute the following command:

```
jar cvf some-web-app.war *
```

There is no special relationship between the jar command and WAR files. jar is just one tool among others to use for bundling files together. If you so choose, you can use WinZip (or tar on UNIX) to do the exact same thing. Just specify the file name to end with .war instead of .zip.

Of course, you can use other `jar` options (e.g., to digitally sign classes) with WAR files just as you can with regular JAR files. For details, see http://java.sun.com/j2se/ 1.5.0/docs/tooldocs/windows/jar.html (Windows) or http://java.sun.com/j2se/ 1.5.0/docs/tooldocs/solaris/jar.html (UNIX/Linux).

1.6 Building a Simple Web Application

Well, enough talk. Let's get down to it and build our first Web application. We'll be using Tomcat as our server, but similar steps could be applied to other servers as well. See Section 1.3 (Registering Web Applications with the Server) for more details.

Here is the outline of steps we'll be following.

1. Download and rename app-blank to testApp (http://volume2.coreservlets.com/).
2. Download test.html, test.jsp, and TestServlet.java (http://volume2.coreservlets.com/).
3. Add test.html, test.jsp to the testApp Web application.
4. Place TestServlet.java into the testApp/WEB-INF/classes/coreservlets directory.
5. Compile TestServlet.java.
6. Declare TestServlet.class and the URL that will invoke it in web.xml.
7. Copy testApp to *tomcat_dir*/webapps.
8. Start Tomcat.
9. Access testApp with the URL of the form http://localhost/testApp/ someResource.

The following subsections will walk you through these steps in some detail.

Download and Rename app-blank to testApp

This step is pretty easy. Simply download app-blank.zip from http://volume2.core-servlets.com/. This file contains the proper directory structure every J2EE-compliant Web application needs. It also contains a starting point for your application's deployment descriptor, web.xml, with a servlet mapping that disables the invoker servlet. We'll look at servlet mapping in a little more detail when we get to mapping our TestServlet to a URL. For now, just unzip app-blank.zip to a directory of your choosing and rename it testApp. Remember to place testApp somewhere on your system outside of Tomcat directories.

Download test.html, test.jsp, and TestServlet.java

As in the previous step, these files can be downloaded from http://volume2.coreservlets.com/. You can either download them one by one or bundled into testApp-Files.zip and unzip them into a directory of your choice.

Add test.html, test.jsp to the testApp Web Application

Put test.html, test.jsp into the testApp directory, create someDirectory inside the testApp directory, put a copy of test.html, test.jsp into testApp/someDirectory. The test.html file contains a static message, and test.jsp contains a scriptlet that outputs the URL used to access the page. Listings 1.1 and 1.2 show the complete code of these files.

Listing 1.1   test.html

```
<!DOCTYPE HTML PUBLIC "-//W3C//DTD HTML 4.0 Transitional//EN">
<HTML>
<HEAD><TITLE>HTML Test</TITLE></HEAD>
<BODY BGCOLOR="#FDF5E6">
<H1>HTML Test</H1>
Hello.
</BODY></HTML>
```

Listing 1.2   test.jsp

```
<!DOCTYPE HTML PUBLIC "-//W3C//DTD HTML 4.0 Transitional//EN">
<HTML>
<HEAD><TITLE>JSP Test</TITLE></HEAD>
<BODY BGCOLOR="#FDF5E6">
<H1>JSP Test</H1>
URL you used:
<%= request.getRequestURL() %>
</BODY></HTML>
```

Place TestServlet.java into the testApp/WEB-INF/classes/coreservlets Directory

TestServlet.java declares that it belongs to the `coreservlets` package. Therefore, you have to place TestServlet.java into it before compiling. As with test.jsp, TestServlet.class contains code that outputs the URL used to access the servlet. See Listing 1.3 for the complete code of TestServlet.java.

Listing 1.3 TestServlet.java

```java
package coreservlets;

import java.io.*;
import javax.servlet.*;
import javax.servlet.http.*;

public class TestServlet extends HttpServlet {
  public void doGet(HttpServletRequest request,
                    HttpServletResponse response)
      throws ServletException, IOException {
    response.setContentType("text/html");
    PrintWriter out = response.getWriter();
    String docType =
      "<!DOCTYPE HTML PUBLIC \"-//W3C//DTD HTML 4.0 " +
      "Transitional//EN\">\n";
    out.println
      (docType +
      "<HTML>\n" +
      "<HEAD><TITLE>Servlet Test</TITLE></HEAD>\n" +
      "<BODY BGCOLOR=\"#FDF5E6\">\n" +
      "<H1>Servlet Test</H1>\n" +
      "URL you used: " + request.getRequestURL() + "\n" +
      "</BODY></HTML>");
  }
}
```

Compile TestServlet.java

Remember that your CLASSPATH should include the servlet application programming interface (API). Tomcat bundles it into the servlet-api.jar file, which is located in the *tomcat_dir*/common/lib directory. On Windows you can set your CLASSPATH by going to the DOS command prompt and typing the following command:

```
set CLASSPATH=tomcat_dir\common\lib\servlet-api.jar
```

On UNIX/Linux compatible systems, you can set the CLASSPATH by opening a console and typing the following command:

```
CLASSPATH=tomcat_dir/common/lib/servlet-api.jar
```

Once the CLASSPATH is set, you can compile TestServlet.java by navigating to the testApp/WEB-INF/classes/coreservlets directory and typing the following command:

```
javac TestServlet.java
```

After compilation, TestServlet.class should reside in the testApp/WEB-INF/classes/ coreservlets directory.

Declare TestServlet.class and the URL That Will Invoke It in web.xml

Navigate to the testApp/WEB-INF directory and open web.xml with your favorite Extensible Markup Language (XML) or text editor. To declare TestServlet.class, you need to add the following lines right after the <!-- Your entries go here. --> XML comment:

```
<servlet>
  <servlet-name>Test</servlet-name>
  <servlet-class>coreservlets.TestServlet</servlet-class>
</servlet>
```

In these few lines, we declared a servlet with the name Test to represent our TestServlet.class. Note that the <servlet-class> element lists the fully qualified name of the servlet class, which has the form *packageName.className* (without the *.class* ending.)

Now, we need to tell Tomcat which URLs will invoke the declared Test servlet. This can be accomplished by adding the following lines to web.xml, right after the ending </servlet> element:

```
<servlet-mapping>
  <servlet-name>Test</servlet-name>
  <url-pattern>/test</url-pattern>
</servlet-mapping>
```

These lines tell Tomcat that a client request to the testApp Web application with the URL of the form http://*host*/testApp/test should result in the invocation of the previously declared Test servlet. See Listing 1.4 for the complete code of web.xml.

Listing 1.4   web.xml

```xml
<?xml version="1.0" encoding="ISO-8859-1"?>
<!-- web.xml from the app-blank template Web app
     from http://courses.coreservlets.com/Course-Materials/.
     Includes two standard elements: welcome-file list
     and a servlet-mapping to disable the invoker servlet.
-->
<web-app xmlns="http://java.sun.com/xml/ns/j2ee"
         xmlns:xsi="http://www.w3.org/2001/XMLSchema-instance"
         xsi:schemaLocation=
           "http://java.sun.com/xml/ns/j2ee
            http://java.sun.com/xml/ns/j2ee/web-app_2_4.xsd"
         version="2.4">

  <!-- Your entries go here. -->
  <servlet>
    <servlet-name>Test</servlet-name>
    <servlet-class>coreservlets.TestServlet</servlet-class>
  </servlet>
  <servlet-mapping>
    <servlet-name>Test</servlet-name>
    <url-pattern>/test</url-pattern>
  </servlet-mapping>


  <!-- Disable the invoker servlet. -->
  <servlet>
    <servlet-name>NoInvoker</servlet-name>
    <servlet-class>coreservlets.NoInvokerServlet</servlet-class>
  </servlet>
  <servlet-mapping>
    <servlet-name>NoInvoker</servlet-name>
    <url-pattern>/servlet/*</url-pattern>
  </servlet-mapping>

  <!-- If URL gives a directory but no file name, try index.jsp
       first and index.html second. If neither is found,
       the result is server-specific (e.g., a directory
       listing).
  -->
  <welcome-file-list>
    <welcome-file>index.jsp</welcome-file>
    <welcome-file>index.html</welcome-file>
  </welcome-file-list>
</web-app>
```

See Chapter 2 (Controlling Web Application Behavior with web.xml) for a detailed discussion of web.xml.

Copy testApp to tomcat_dir/webapps

In this step, we are copying the entire directory structure starting with the top-level directory (testApp) to the Tomcat's auto-deploy directory *tomcat_dir*/webapps. We can likewise choose to zip testApp into a WAR file (either with the jar command, WinZip, tar, or a similar bundling tool) and then copy just the WAR file into tomcat_dir/webapps. Whether you choose to copy testApp in its "exploded" or in its WAR file version, the end result will be the same.

Start Tomcat

You can start Tomcat by executing *tomcat_dir*/bin/startup.bat on Windows and *tomcat_dir*/bin/startup.sh on UNIX/Linux. Tomcat detects a new directory in its auto-deploy directory and automatically registers and deploys the testApp Web application.

Access testApp with the URL of the Form http://localhost/testApp/someResource

The URLs http://localhost/testApp/test.html and http://localhost/testApp/someDirectory/test.html retrieve test.html, http://localhost/testApp/test.jsp and http://localhost/testApp/someDirectory/test.jsp invoke test.jsp, and http://localhost/testApp/test invokes TestServlet.class.

These URLs assume that you have modified the Tomcat configuration file (*tomcat_dir*/conf/server.xml) to use port 80 as recommended in Volume 1 of this book. If you haven't made this change, simply replace localhost with localhost:8080 in the URL. See Figures 1–4 through 1–8 for screenshots of what should appear in your browser as results of accessing these resources.

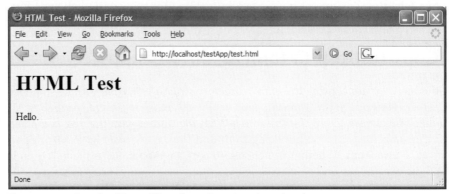

Figure 1–4   Result of http://localhost/testApp/test.html.

Figure 1–5   Result of http://localhost/testApp/test.jsp.

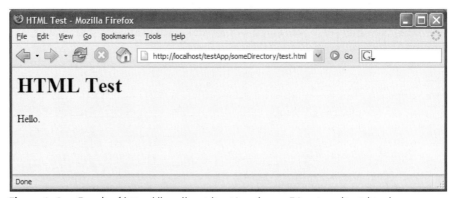

Figure 1–6   Result of http://localhost/testApp/someDirectory/test.html.

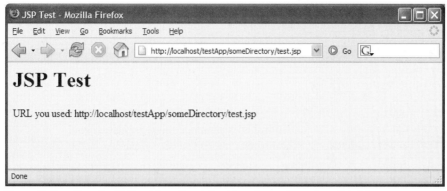

Figure 1–7   Result of http://localhost/testApp/someDirectory/test.jsp.

Figure 1–8   Result of http://localhost/testApp/test.

1.7   Sharing Data Among Web Applications

One of the major purposes of Web applications is to keep data and functionality separate. Each Web application maintains its own table of sessions and its own servlet context. Each Web application also uses its own class loader; this behavior eliminates problems with name conflicts but means that static methods and fields can't be used to share data among applications. However, it *is* still possible to share data with cookies or by using `ServletContext` objects that are associated with specific URLs. These approaches are viable options for sharing minimal information between Web applications, but if you are striving to achieve a lot of sharing, you should consider keeping the apps as one Web application. The two approaches for sharing data are summarized next.

- **Cookies.** Cookies are maintained by the browser, not by the server. Consequently, cookies can be shared across multiple Web applications as long as they are set to apply to any path on the server. By default, the browser sends cookies only to URLs that have the same prefix as the one from which it first received the cookies. For example, if the server sends a cookie from the page associated with http://*host/* path1/SomeFile.jsp, the browser sends the cookie back to http://*host/* path1/SomeOtherFile.jsp and http://*host/*path1/path2/Anything, but not to http://*host/*path3/Anything. Because Web applications always have unique URL prefixes, this behavior means that default-style cookies will never be shared between two different Web applications.

  However, as described in Chapter 8 of Volume 1, you can use the setPath method of the Cookie class to change this behavior. Supplying a value of "/", as shown here, instructs the browser to send the cookie to *all* URLs at the host from which the original cookie was received:

  ```
  Cookie c = new Cookie("name", "value");
  c.setMaxAge(...);
  c.setPath("/");
  response.addCookie(c);
  ```

- **ServletContext objects associated with a specific URL.** In a servlet, you obtain the Web application's servlet context by calling the getServletContext method of the servlet itself (inherited from GenericServlet). In a JSP page, you use the predefined application variable. Either way, you get the servlet context associated with the servlet or JSP page that is making the request. However, you can also call the getContext method of ServletContext to obtain a servlet context—not necessarily your own—associated with a particular URL. This approach is illustrated here.

  ```
  ServletContext myContext = getServletContext();
  String url = "/someWebAppPrefix";
  ServletContext otherContext = myContext.getContext(url);
  Object someData = otherContext.getAttribute("someKey");
  ```

Neither of these two data-sharing approaches is perfect.

The drawback to cookies is that only limited data can be stored in them. Each cookie value is a string, and the length of each value is limited to 4 kilobytes. So, robust data sharing requires a database: You use the cookie value as a key into the database and store the real data in the database.

One drawback to sharing servlet contexts is that you have to know the URL prefix that the other Web application is using. You normally want the freedom to change a Web application's prefix without changing any associated code. Use of the get-Context method restricts this flexibility. A second drawback is that, for security reasons, servers are permitted to prohibit access to the ServletContext of certain Web applications. In such cases, calls to getContext return null. For example, in some Tomcat versions, context sharing is enabled by default, whereas in others you have to explicitly enable it. For instance, in Tomcat 5.5.7 you can add the attribute crossContext="true" as part of the Context element in *tomcat_dir/* conf/context.xml, enabling context sharing as the default behavior for all deployed applications. Leaving out the crossContext attribute altogether causes Tomcat to use its default behavior, which is to prohibit sharing of ServletContext between Web applications.

These two data-sharing approaches are illustrated by the SetSharedInfo and ShowSharedInfo servlets shown in Listings 1.5 and 1.6. These servlets are mapped to URLs in the deployment descriptor as shown in Listing 1.7. The SetShared-Info servlet creates custom entries in the session object and the servlet context. It also sets two cookies: one with the default path, indicating that the cookie should apply only to URLs with the same URL prefix as the original request, and one with a path of "/", indicating that the cookie should apply to all URLs on the host. Finally, the SetSharedInfo servlet redirects the client to the ShowSharedInfo servlet, which displays the names of all session attributes, all attributes in the current servlet context, all attributes in the servlet context that applies to URLs with the prefix /shareTest1, and all cookies.

Listing 1.5	SetSharedInfo.java

```
package coreservlets;

import java.io.*;
import javax.servlet.*;
import javax.servlet.http.*;

public class SetSharedInfo extends HttpServlet {
  public void doGet(HttpServletRequest request,
                    HttpServletResponse response)
    throws ServletException, IOException {
```

Listing 1.5   SetSharedInfo.java *(continued)*

```java
    HttpSession session = request.getSession(true);
    session.setAttribute("sessionTest", "Session Entry One");
    ServletContext context = getServletContext();
    context.setAttribute("servletContextTest",
                         "Servlet Context Entry One");
    Cookie c1 = new Cookie("cookieTest1", "Cookie One");
    c1.setMaxAge(3600);      // One hour
    response.addCookie(c1); // Default path
    Cookie c2 = new Cookie("cookieTest2", "Cookie Two");
    c2.setMaxAge(3600);      // One hour
    c2.setPath("/");         // Explicit path: all URLs
    response.addCookie(c2);
    String url = request.getContextPath() +
                 "/servlet/coreservlets.ShowSharedInfo";
    // In case session tracking is based on URL rewriting.
    url = response.encodeRedirectURL(url);
    response.sendRedirect(url);
  }
}
```

Listing 1.6   ShowSharedInfo.java

```java
package coreservlets;

import java.io.*;
import javax.servlet.*;
import javax.servlet.http.*;
import java.util.*;

public class ShowSharedInfo extends HttpServlet {
  public void doGet(HttpServletRequest request,
                    HttpServletResponse response)
      throws ServletException, IOException {
    response.setContentType("text/html");
    PrintWriter out = response.getWriter();
    String title = "Shared Info";
    out.println("<!DOCTYPE HTML PUBLIC \"-//W3C//DTD HTML 4.0 " +
                "Transitional//EN\">" +
                "<HTML>\n" +
                "<HEAD><TITLE>" + title + "</TITLE></HEAD>\n" +
                "<BODY BGCOLOR=\"#FDF5E6\">\n" +
                "<H1 ALIGN=\"CENTER\">" + title + "</H1>\n" +
                "<UL>\n" +
                "  <LI>Session:");
```

Listing 1.6   ShowSharedInfo.java *(continued)*

```
HttpSession session = request.getSession(true);
Enumeration attributes = session.getAttributeNames();
out.println(getAttributeList(attributes));
out.println("  <LI>Current Servlet Context:");
ServletContext application = getServletContext();
attributes = application.getAttributeNames();
out.println(getAttributeList(attributes));
out.println("  <LI>Servlet Context of /shareTest1:");
application = application.getContext("/shareTest1");
if (application == null) {
   out.println("Context sharing disabled");
} else {
   attributes = application.getAttributeNames();
   out.println(getAttributeList(attributes));
}
out.println("  <LI>Cookies:<UL>");
Cookie[] cookies = request.getCookies();
if ((cookies == null) || (cookies.length == 0)) {
   out.println("    <LI>No cookies found.");
} else {
   Cookie cookie;
   for(int i=0; i<cookies.length; i++) {
      cookie = cookies[i];
      out.println("    <LI>" + cookie.getName());
   }
}
out.println("    </UL>\n" +
              "</UL>\n" +
              "</BODY></HTML>");
  }
private String getAttributeList(Enumeration attributes) {
   StringBuffer list = new StringBuffer("  <UL>\n");
   if (!attributes.hasMoreElements()) {
      list.append("    <LI>No attributes found.");
   } else {
      while(attributes.hasMoreElements()) {
         list.append("    <LI>");
         list.append(attributes.nextElement());
         list.append("\n");
      }
   }
   list.append("  </UL>");
   return(list.toString());
  }
}
```

Listing 1.7   web.xml

```
<?xml version="1.0" encoding="ISO-8859-1"?>
<!-- web.xml from the app-blank template Web app
     from http://courses.coreservlets.com/Course-Materials/.
     Includes two standard elements: welcome-file list
     and a servlet-mapping to disable the invoker servlet.
-->
<web-app xmlns="http://java.sun.com/xml/ns/j2ee"
         xmlns:xsi="http://www.w3.org/2001/XMLSchema-instance"
         xsi:schemaLocation=
           "http://java.sun.com/xml/ns/j2ee
            http://java.sun.com/xml/ns/j2ee/web-app_2_4.xsd"
         version="2.4">

  <!-- Your entries go here. -->
  <servlet>
    <servlet-name>setSharedInfoServlet</servlet-name>
    <servlet-class>coreservlets.SetSharedInfo</servlet-class>
  </servlet>
  <servlet-mapping>
    <servlet-name>setSharedInfoServlet</servlet-name>
    <url-pattern>/setSharedInfo</url-pattern>
  </servlet-mapping>
  <servlet>
    <servlet-name>showSharedInfoServlet</servlet-name>
    <servlet-class>coreservlets.ShowSharedInfo</servlet-class>
  </servlet>
  <servlet-mapping>
    <servlet-name>showSharedInfoServlet</servlet-name>
    <url-pattern>/showSharedInfo</url-pattern>
  </servlet-mapping>

  <!-- Disable the invoker servlet. -->
  <servlet>
    <servlet-name>NoInvoker</servlet-name>
    <servlet-class>coreservlets.NoInvokerServlet</servlet-class>
  </servlet>
  <servlet-mapping>
    <servlet-name>NoInvoker</servlet-name>
    <url-pattern>/servlet/*</url-pattern>
  </servlet-mapping>

  <!-- If URL gives a directory but no file name, try index.jsp
       first and index.html second. If neither is found,
       the result is server-specific (e.g., a directory
       listing).
  -->
```

Listing 1.7	web.xml *(continued)*

```
<welcome-file-list>
  <welcome-file>index.jsp</welcome-file>
  <welcome-file>index.html</welcome-file>
</welcome-file-list>
</web-app>
```

When running this example, make sure you invoke the `SetSharedInfo` servlet of the **shareTest1** application only. After that, invoke the `ShowSharedInfo` servlet of the **shareTest1** and **shareTest2** applications. Do not invoke the `ShowSharedInfo` servlet of **shareTest2** as this will not illustrate data sharing between the two applications.

Figure 1–9 shows the result after the user visits the `SetSharedInfo` and `ShowSharedInfo` servlets from within the Web application that is assigned **/shareTest1** as a URL prefix. The `ShowSharedInfo` servlet sees:

- The custom session attribute.
- The custom (explicitly created by the `SetSharedInfo` servlet) and standard (automatically created by the server) attributes that are contained in the default servlet context.
- The custom and standard attributes that are contained in the servlet context that is found by means of `getContext("/shareTest1")`, which in this case is the same as the default servlet context.
- The two explicitly created cookies and the system-created cookie used behind the scenes by the session tracking API.

Figure 1–10 shows the result when the user later visits an identical copy of the `ShowSharedInfo` servlet that is installed in a Web application that has **/shareTest2** as the URL prefix. The servlet sees:

- The standard attributes that are contained in the default servlet context.
- The custom and standard attributes that are contained in the servlet context that is found by means of `getContext("/shareTest1")`, which in this case is different from the default servlet context.
- Two cookies: the explicitly created one that has its path set to `"/"` and the system-created one used behind the scenes for session tracking (which also uses a custom path of `"/"`).

The servlet does *not* see:

- Any attributes in its session object.
- Any custom attributes contained in the default servlet context.
- The explicitly created cookie that uses the default path.

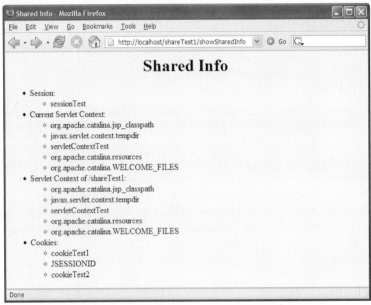

Figure 1–9   Result of visiting the `SetSharedInfo` and `ShowSharedInfo` servlets from within the same Web application.

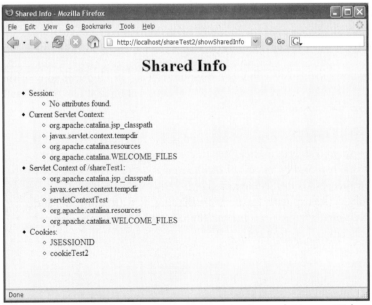

Figure 1–10   Result of visiting the `SetSharedInfo` servlet in one Web application and the `ShowSharedInfo` servlet in a different Web application.

CONTROLLING
WEB APPLICATION
BEHAVIOR WITH
WEB.XML

Topics in This Chapter

- Understanding the purpose of web.xml
- Customizing URLs
- Turning off default URLs
- Initializing servlets and JSP pages
- Preloading servlets and JSP pages
- Declaring filters
- Designating welcome pages and error pages
- Restricting access to Web resources
- Controlling session timeouts
- Documenting Web applications
- Specifying MIME types
- Locating tag library descriptors
- Configuring JSP pages
- Configuring character encoding
- Declaring event listeners
- Developing for the clustered environment
- Accessing J2EE resources

Chapter 2

This chapter describes the makeup of the deployment descriptor file, web.xml, which is placed in the WEB-INF directory within each Web application.

We'll summarize all the legal elements here; for the formal specification see http://java.sun.com/xml/ns/j2ee/web-app_2_4.xsd (for version 2.4 of the servlet API) or http://java.sun.com/dtd/web-app_2_3.dtd (for version 2.3).

Most of the servlet and JSP examples in this chapter assume that they are part of a Web application named deployDemo. For details on how to set up and register Web applications, please see Chapter 1 (Using and Deploying Web Applications).

2.1 Purpose of the Deployment Descriptor

The deployment descriptor, web.xml, is used to control many facets of a Web application. Using web.xml, you can assign custom URLs for invoking servlets, specify initialization parameters for the entire application as well as for specific servlets, control session timeouts, declare filters, declare security roles, restrict access to Web resources based on declared security roles, and so on.

The deployment descriptor is not part of the Java compilation process. Therefore, changes in web.xml don't force you to recompile your code. In addition, the separation between the configuration mechanism, web.xml, and the Java code allows for the division between the development and deployment roles within the development process. The Java developer is relieved of having to know about the specific operational environment while writing code; this facilitates code reuse. By editing web.xml, the person deploying the application has the power to affect application behavior without ever having to deal with Java code. For example, a company might decide to deploy the same Web application at several office locations. Even within one company, different offices might have slightly different needs and therefore would need to customize the application. The exact same compiled Java code could be shipped to all locations. The web.xml file would then be used to customize the behavior of the application based on the particular office location.

2.2   Defining the Header and the Root Element

The deployment descriptor, like all XML files, must begin with an XML header. This header declares the version of XML that is in effect, and gives the character encoding for the file.

The top-level (root) element for the deployment descriptor is web-app. Remember that XML elements, unlike HTML elements, are case sensitive. Consequently, Web-App and WEB-APP are not legal; you must use web-app in lowercase.

Core Warning

XML elements are case sensitive.

You must declare an XML Schema instance as part of the web-app element. This declaration tells the server the version of the servlet specification (e.g., 2.4) that applies and specifies the XML Schema location that governs the syntax of the rest of the file. All subelements of web-app are optional.

Thus, the web.xml file should be structured as follows:

```
<web-app xmlns="http://java.sun.com/xml/ns/j2ee"
         xmlns:xsi="http://www.w3.org/2001/XMLSchema-instance"
         xsi:schemaLocation=
         "http://java.sun.com/xml/ns/j2ee
          http://java.sun.com/xml/ns/j2ee/web-app_2_4.xsd"
         version="2.4">
<!-- Your entries go here. All are optional. -->
</web-app>
```

Note that http://java.sun.com/xml/ns/j2ee/web-app_2_4.xsd is the only URL that must actually exist, pointing to the location of the XML Schema file. The rest of the URLs in the declaration of web.xml are namespaces. Namespaces are just unique identifiers for a particular Schema syntax and could be any unique string. The server never connects to the namespace URLs.

You can download a blank web.xml file from http://volume2.coreservlets.com/. Or, if you start your Web applications by copying and renaming app-blank, a legal web.xml file is already included.

If you are using an earlier version of the servlet specification (e.g., 2.3), instead of declaring an XML Schema inside of the web-app element, a DOCTYPE declaration must appear immediately after the header declaration (but before the web-app element). Similar to the XML Schema, this declaration tells the server the version of the servlet specification (e.g., 2.3) that applies and specifies the Document Type Definition (DTD) that governs the syntax of the rest of the file. However, with version 2.3, the elements must appear in the DTD-defined order.

```
<?xml version="1.0" encoding="ISO-8859-1"?>
<!DOCTYPE web-app PUBLIC
    "-//Sun Microsystems, Inc.//DTD Web Application 2.3//EN"
    "http://java.sun.com/dtd/web-app_2_3.dtd">
<web-app>
  <!-- Your entries go here. All are optional. -->
</web-app>
```

Servers compliant with servlet specification version 2.4 are required to correctly deploy Web applications compliant with version 2.3. However, if you declare web.xml with version 2.3, even if the server used for deployment complies with servlet specification 2.4, the 2.4-specific features will not be enabled for your Web application. For example, the JSP Expression Language Code (introduced in version 2.4) will be treated as regular text in your JSP pages.

2.3   The Elements of web.xml

In this section we look at the main elements of web.xml that appear directly under web-app and briefly discuss their purpose. For detailed treatment of each of these subelements, see later sections in this chapter.

Because there are just a few differences between web.xml version 2.4 and 2.3, we first discuss the elements of web.xml declared with the latest servlet specification, version 2.4, and then briefly cover version 2.3.

Even though version 2.4 is the current version of the servlet specification, version 2.3 is still important. A project may have a requirement to run on multiple servers, some of which are older or only comply with version 2.3. It's also important for maintaining preexisting Web apps. For example, the web.xml file in the struts-blank application that comes with Jakarta Struts uses web.xml version 2.2.

Version 2.4

The order of web-app subelements does not matter if you are using version 2.4. This is one of the major differences between web.xml of version 2.4 and earlier versions.

The following list shows all legal elements that can appear directly within the web-app element. Remember that all these elements are optional.

- **servlet and servlet-mapping.** Before you assign initialization parameters or custom URLs to servlets or JSP pages, you must first name the servlet or JSP page. You use the servlet element for that purpose. Once you have declared a servlet (using the servlet element), you can designate one or more URL patterns that allow the clients to invoke the servlet. See Section 2.4 (Assigning Names and Custom URLs).

- **context-param.** The context-param element declares application-wide initialization parameters. See Section 2.6 (Initializing and Preloading Servlets and JSP Pages).

- **filter and filter-mapping.** The filter element associates a name with a class that implements the javax.servlet.Filter interface. Once you have named a filter, you associate it with one or more servlets or JSP pages by means of the filter-mapping element. See Section 2.7 (Declaring Filters).

- **welcome-file-list.** The welcome-file-list element tells the server what file to use when the server receives URLs that refer to a directory name but not a file name. See Section 2.8 (Specifying Welcome Pages).

- **error-page.** The error-page element lets you designate the pages that will be displayed when certain HTTP status codes are returned or when certain types of exceptions are thrown. See Section 2.9 (Designating Pages to Handle Errors).

- **security-constraint.** The security-constraint element lets you designate URLs that should be protected from unauthorized users. It goes hand-in-hand with the login-config element. See Section 2.10 (Providing Security).

- **login-config.** You use the login-config element to specify how the server should authenticate users who attempt to access protected pages. It goes hand-in-hand with the security-constraint element. See Section 2.10 (Providing Security).

- **security-role.** The security-role element must declare explicit role names used in the role-name subelements of the auth-constraint element inside every security-constraint element in web.xml. It could also list security role names that will appear in the role-name subelements of the security-role-ref element inside the `servlet` element. See Section 2.10 (Providing Security).

- **session-config.** If a session has not been accessed for a certain period of time, the server can throw it away to save memory. You can explicitly set the timeout for individual session objects by using the `setMaxInactiveInterval` method of `HttpSession`, or you can use the `session-config` element to designate a default timeout. See Section 2.11 (Controlling Session Timeouts).

- **icon.** The `icon` element designates the location of either one or two image files that an IDE can use to represent the Web application. See Section 2.12 (Documenting Web Applications).

- **display-name.** The `display-name` element provides a name that graphical user interface (GUI) tools might use to label the Web application. See Section 2.12 (Documenting Web Applications).

- **description.** The `description` element gives explanatory text about the Web application. See Section 2.12 (Documenting Web Applications).

- **mime-mapping.** If your Web application has unusual files that you want to guarantee are assigned certain MIME types, the `mime-mapping` element can provide this guarantee. See Section 2.13 (Associating Files with MIME Types).

- **jsp-config.** The `jsp-config element` is used to provide configuration information for the JSP pages in a Web application. It has two subelements, `taglib` and `jsp-property-group`. The `taglib` element assigns aliases to Tag Library Descriptor (TLD) files. This capability lets you change the location of the TLD files without editing the JSP pages that use those files. The `jsp-property-group` element is used to configure property information for a group of files that match a URL pattern. See Section 2.14 (Configuring JSP Pages).

- **locale-encoding-mapping-list.** This element sets the default locale character encodings using one or more `locale-encoding-mapping` elements. See Section 2.15 (Configuring Character Encoding).

- **listener.** The `listener` element designates an event listener class. Listener classes are notified when a particular Web application life-cycle event occurs. For example, it can be notified when the `ServletContext` or `HttpSession` is first initialized or destroyed. See Section 2.16 (Designating Application Event Listeners).

- **distributable.** The `distributable` element tells the system that it is safe to distribute the Web application across multiple servers in a cluster. See Section 2.17 (Developing for the Clustered Environment).

- **env-entry.** The `env-entry` element declares the Web application's environment entry. See Section 2.18 (J2EE Elements).

- **ejb-ref.** The `ejb-ref` element declares a reference to the home interface of an enterprise bean. See Section 2.18 (J2EE Elements).
- **ejb-local-ref.** The `ejb-local-ref` element declares a reference to the local home interface of an enterprise bean. See Section 2.18 (J2EE Elements).
- **service-ref.** The `service-ref` element declares a reference to a Web service. See Section 2.18 (J2EE Elements).
- **resource-ref.** The `resource-ref` element declares a reference to an external resource used with a resource factory. See Section 2.18 (J2EE Elements).
- **resource-env-ref.** The `resource-env-ref` element declares a reference to an administered object associated with a resource. See Section 2.18 (J2EE Elements).
- **message-destination-ref.** The `message-destination-ref` element declares a reference to a message destination associated with a resource. See Section 2.18 (J2EE Elements).
- **message-destination.** The `message-destination` element specifies a logical (e.g., portable) message destination name. See Section 2.18 (J2EE Elements).

Version 2.3

As we mentioned, web.xml version 2.3 mandates the ordering of elements under `web-app`. Servers are not required to enforce this order, but they are permitted to, and some do so in practice, completely refusing to run Web applications that contain elements that are out of order. This means that web.xml files that use nonstandard element ordering are not portable.

Core Approach

If you are using web.xml declared with version 2.3, be sure to correctly order the elements that appear within web-app.

The following list gives the required ordering of all legal elements that can appear directly within the web-app element for version 2.3. For example, the list shows that all `servlet` elements must appear before any `servlet-mapping` elements. If there are any mime-mapping elements, they must go after any `servlet` and `servlet-mapping` elements but before `welcome-file-list`.

For example, suppose your Web application has several servlets. The natural approach would be to declare the first servlet and give it a URL, then declare the second servlet and give it a URL, and so on, as follows:

```
<servlet>
  <servlet-name>Name1</servlet-name>
  <servlet-class>somepackage.Servlet1</servlet-class>
</servlet>
<servlet-mapping>
  <servlet-name>Name1</servlet-name>
  <url-pattern>/pattern1</url-pattern>
<servlet-mapping>
...
<servlet>
  <servlet-name>NameN</servlet-name>
  <servlet-class>somepackage.ServletN</servlet-class>
</servlet>
<servlet-mapping>
  <servlet-name>NameN</servlet-name>
  <url-pattern>/patternN</url-pattern>
<servlet-mapping>
```

However, if you use web.xml version 2.3 or earlier, you have to first declare all the servlets, then give them all a URL, as follows.

```
<servlet>
  <servlet-name>Name1</servlet-name>
  <servlet-class>somepackage.Servlet1</servlet-class>
</servlet>
...
<servlet>
  <servlet-name>NameN</servlet-name>
  <servlet-class>somepackage.ServletN</servlet-class>
</servlet>
...
<servlet-mapping>
  <servlet-name>Name1</servlet-name>
  <url-pattern>/pattern1</url-pattern>
<servlet-mapping>
...
<servlet-mapping>
  <servlet-name>NameN</servlet-name>
  <url-pattern>/patternN</url-pattern>
<servlet-mapping>
```

Remember that all these elements are optional, so you can omit any element, but you cannot place it in a nonstandard location.

The servlet specification version 2.3 defines fewer features than version 2.4, thus web.xml version 2.3 has fewer elements than version 2.4. However, the purpose and usage of identically named elements is the same, so we do not list their meaning again. For details about these elements, please see the relevant sections in this chapter. Also note that the taglib element appears directly under the web-app element because there is no jsp-config element in version 2.3.

- **icon.** See Section 2.12 (Documenting Web Applications).
- **display-name.** See Section 2.12 (Documenting Web Applications).
- **description.** See Section 2.12 (Documenting Web Applications).
- **distributable.** See Section 2.6 (Initializing and Preloading Servlets and JSP Pages).
- **context-param.** See Section 2.6 (Initializing and Preloading Servlets and JSP Pages).
- **filter.** See Section 2.7 (Declaring Filters).
- **filter-mapping.** See Section 2.7 (Declaring Filters).
- **listener.** See Section 2.15 (Configuring Character Encoding).
- **servlet.** See Section 2.4 (Assigning Names and Custom URLs).
- **servlet-mapping.** See Section 2.4 (Assigning Names and Custom URLs) and Section 2.6 (Initializing and Preloading Servlets and JSP Pages).
- **session-config.** See Section 2.11 (Controlling Session Timeouts).
- **mime-mapping.** See Section 2.13 (Associating Files with MIME Types).
- **welcome-file-list.** See Section 2.8 (Specifying Welcome Pages).
- **error-page.** See Section 2.9 (Designating Pages to Handle Errors).
- **taglib.** See Section 2.14 (Configuring JSP Pages).
- **resource-env-ref.** See Section 2.18 (J2EE Elements).
- **resource-ref.** See Section 2.18 (J2EE Elements).
- **security-constraint.** See Section 2.10 (Providing Security).
- **login-config.** See Section 2.10 (Providing Security).
- **security-role.** See Section 2.10 (Providing Security).
- **env-entry.** See Section 2.18 (J2EE Elements).
- **ejb-ref.** See Section 2.18 (J2EE Elements).
- **ejb-local-ref.** See Section 2.18 (J2EE Elements).

2.4   Assigning Names and Custom URLs

One of the most common tasks that you perform in web.xml is declaring names and mapping custom URLs to your servlets or JSP pages. You use the servlet element to assign names; you use the servlet-mapping element to associate custom URLs with the names just assigned.

Assigning Names

To provide initialization parameters, define a custom URL, or assign a logical (portable) security role to a servlet or JSP page, you must first give the servlet or page a name. You assign a name by means of the servlet element. The most common format includes servlet-name and servlet-class subelements (inside the web-app element), as follows:

```
<servlet>
  <servlet-name>Test</servlet-name>
  <servlet-class>coreservlets.TestServlet</servlet-class>
</servlet>
```

This means that the servlet at WEB-INF/classes/coreservlets/TestServlet is now known by the registered name Test. Giving a servlet a name has the following major implications: Initialization parameters, custom URL patterns, and other customizations refer to the servlet by the registered name, not by the class name. We see how to take advantage of these features later on in this chapter.

For example, Listing 2.1 shows a simple servlet called TestServlet1 that resides in the coreservlets package. Because the servlet is part of a Web application rooted in a directory named deployDemo, TestServlet1.class is placed in deployDemo/WEB-INF/classes/coreservlets. Listing 2.2 shows a portion of the web.xml file that would be placed in deployDemo/WEB-INF. This web.xml file uses the servlet-name and servlet-class elements to associate the name Test1 with TestServlet1.class.

Listing 2.1   TestServlet1.java

```
package coreservlets;

import java.io.*;
import javax.servlet.*;
import javax.servlet.http.*;

/** Simple servlet used to illustrate servlet naming
 *  and custom URLs.
 */

public class TestServlet1 extends HttpServlet {
  public void doGet(HttpServletRequest request,
                    HttpServletResponse response)
      throws ServletException, IOException {
    response.setContentType("text/html");
    PrintWriter out = response.getWriter();
    String uri = request.getRequestURI();
    out.println("<!DOCTYPE HTML PUBLIC \"-//W3C//DTD HTML 4.0 " +
                "Transitional//EN\">" + "\n" +
                "<HTML>\n" + "<HEAD><TITLE>" +
                "Test Servlet 1" + "</TITLE></HEAD>\n" +
                "<BODY BGCOLOR=\"#FDF5E6\">\n" +
                "<H2>" + "Servlet Name: Test1" + "</H2>\n" +
                "<H2>URI: " + uri + "</H2>\n" +
                "</BODY></HTML>");
  }
}
```

| Listing 2.2 | web.xml (Excerpt showing servlet name) |

```
<?xml version="1.0" encoding="ISO-8859-1"?>
<web-app xmlns="http://java.sun.com/xml/ns/j2ee"
         xmlns:xsi="http://www.w3.org/2001/XMLSchema-instance"
         xsi:schemaLocation=
         "http://java.sun.com/xml/ns/j2ee
          http://java.sun.com/xml/ns/j2ee/web-app_2_4.xsd"
         version="2.4">

  <!-- Register the name "Test1" for TestServlet1. -->
  <servlet>
    <servlet-name>Test1</servlet-name>
    <servlet-class>coreservlets.TestServlet1</servlet-class>
  </servlet>
  <!-- ... -->
</web-app>
```

Defining Custom URLs

To assign a custom URL, you use the `servlet-mapping` element along with its `servlet-name` and `url-pattern` subelements. The `servlet-name` element specifies the name that was assigned to the servlet using the `servlet-name` subelement of the `servlet` element; `url-pattern` describes a URL relative to the Web application root. The value of the `url-pattern` element must begin with either a slash (`/`) or an asterisk and period combination (`*.`).

Core Approach

The value of `url-pattern` must begin with either `/` or `*.`.

The specification allows you to map a servlet to a particular custom URL. For example, here is a simple **web.xml** excerpt that lets you use the URL http://*host*/*webApp-Prefix*/UrlTest1 to invoke `TestServlet1` declared with the name `Test1`. Figure 2–1 shows the result of invoking `TestServlet1` with the exact-matching URL.

```
  <servlet>
    <servlet-name>Test1</servlet-name>
    <servlet-class>coreservlets.TestServlet1</servlet-class>
  </servlet>
```

```
<servlet-mapping>
  <servlet-name>Test1</servlet-name>
  <url-pattern>/UrlTest1</url-pattern>
</servlet-mapping>
```

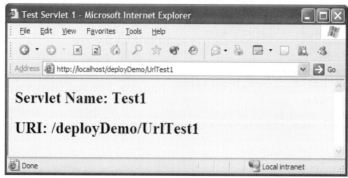

Figure 2–1   `TestServlet1` invoked with http://localhost/deployDemo/UrlTest1.

Exact-Match Patterns

The previous example showed an exact-match pattern: the `url-pattern` element specified an address beginning with a slash that did not contain `*`. The associated servlet will be invoked when the part of the incoming URL that is after the Web application prefix (but before the attached GET data, if any) exactly matches the URL pattern.

Here are a couple more examples using exact matching. Listing 2.3 shows an excerpt from web.xml declaring and mapping `TestServlet2` and `TestServlet3` using exact-matching URL patterns. Figures 2–2 and 2–3 show the results of invoking these servlets with their respective URLs.

Listing 2.3	web.xml (Excerpt showing exact matching)

```
<?xml version="1.0" encoding="ISO-8859-1"?>
<web-app xmlns="http://java.sun.com/xml/ns/j2ee"
         xmlns:xsi="http://www.w3.org/2001/XMLSchema-instance"
         xsi:schemaLocation=
         "http://java.sun.com/xml/ns/j2ee
          http://java.sun.com/xml/ns/j2ee/web-app_2_4.xsd"
         version="2.4">
```

Listing 2.3 web.xml (Excerpt showing exact matching) *(continued)*

```
<!-- Register the name "Test2" for TestServlet2. -->
<servlet>
  <servlet-name>Test2</servlet-name>
  <servlet-class>coreservlets.TestServlet2</servlet-class>
</servlet>
<!-- Use the URL http://host/webAppPrefix/UrlTest2/ -->
<servlet-mapping>
  <servlet-name>Test2</servlet-name>
  <url-pattern>/UrlTest2/</url-pattern>
</servlet-mapping>

<!-- Register the name "Test3" for TestServlet3. -->
<servlet>
  <servlet-name>Test3</servlet-name>
  <servlet-class>coreservlets.TestServlet3</servlet-class>
</servlet>
<!-- Use the URL http://host/webAppPrefix/UrlTest3.asp -->
<servlet-mapping>
  <servlet-name>Test3</servlet-name>
  <url-pattern>/UrlTest3.asp</url-pattern>
</servlet-mapping>
<!-- ... -->
</web-app>
```

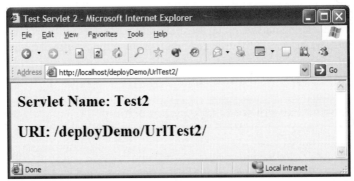

Figure 2–2 TestServlet2 invoked with http://localhost/deployDemo/UrlTest2/.

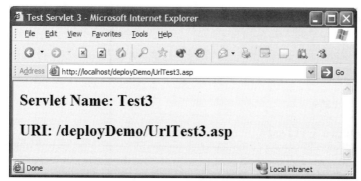

Figure 2–3   `TestServlet3` invoked with `http://localhost/deployDemo/`
`UrlTest3.asp`.

Multimapping Patterns

In the majority of cases, you want to assign one URL to each servlet. Once in a while, however, you want multiple URLs to invoke the same servlet. There are two ways you can accomplish this multimapping:

- By giving a `url-pattern` of `/directoryName/*`, you can specify that all URLs of the form `http://host/webAppPrefix/directoryName/blah` are handled by the designated servlet.
- By giving a `url-pattern` of `*.foo`, you can specify that all URLs of the form `http://host/webAppPrefix/.../blah.foo` are handled by the designated servlet.

Details follow.

Here is an excerpt from web.xml showing a mapping that lets you use URLs like `http://host/webAppPrefix/UrlTest4`, `http://host/webAppPrefix/UrlTest4/` (note the slash at the end), `http://host/webAppPrefix/UrlTest4/foo/bar` to invoke `TestServlet4` declared with the name `Test4`. Figures 2–4, 2–5, and 2–6 show the results of invoking `TestServlet4` with these URLs, respectively.

```
<servlet>
  <servlet-name>Test4</servlet-name>
  <servlet-class>coreservlets.TestServlet4</servlet-class>
</servlet>
<servlet-mapping>
  <servlet-name>Test4</servlet-name>
  <url-pattern>/UrlTest4/*</url-pattern>
</servlet-mapping>
```

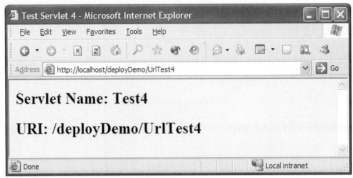

Figure 2–4 `TestServlet4` invoked with http://localhost/deployDemo/UrlTest4.

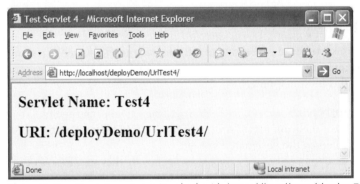

Figure 2–5 `TestServlet4` invoked with http://localhost/deployDemo/UrlTest4/.

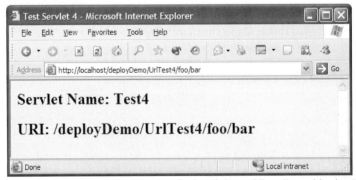

Figure 2–6 `TestServlet4` invoked with http://localhost/deployDemo/UrlTest4/foo/bar.

Likewise, you can use * if you want all URLs ending with a certain extension to invoke a particular servlet. For example, here is an excerpt from web.xml that lets you use URLs like http://*host/webAppPrefix*/foo/bar/baz.urlTest5, http://*host/webAppPrefix*/foo.urlTest5 to invoke TestServlet5 declared with the name Test5. Figures 2–7 and 2–8 show the results of invoking TestServlet5 with these URLs, respectively.

```
<servlet>
  <servlet-name>Test5</servlet-name>
  <servlet-class>coreservlets.TestServlet5</servlet-class>
</servlet>
<servlet-mapping>
  <servlet-name>Test5</servlet-name>
  <url-pattern>*.urlTest5</url-pattern>
</servlet-mapping>
```

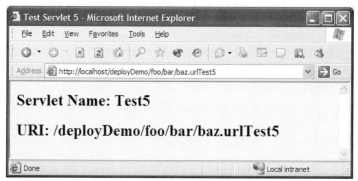

Figure 2–7   TestServlet5 invoked with http://localhost/deployDemo/foo/bar/baz.urlTest5.

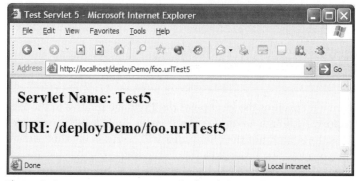

Figure 2–8   TestServlet5 invoked with http://localhost/deployDemo/foo.urlTest5.

Matching Overlapping Patterns

When mapping a servlet to a URL, the specification does not allow the same value of url-pattern to appear twice within the same web.xml file. Thus, there can never be an overlap between two patterns that map exact matches. However, if one or more servlet mappings use "*", an overlap could occur.

Compliant servers are required to use the following rules to resolve these overlaps.

- **Exact matches are handled first.** Thus, if /foo/bar and /foo/* were both url-pattern entries, the first would take precedence for a request URL of http://*host/webAppPrefix*/foo/bar. Similarly, /foo/bar.html would win over *.html for an incoming URL of http://*host/webAppPrefix*/foo/bar.html.
- **Directory mappings are preferred over extension mappings.** Thus, if /foo/* and *.html were both url-pattern entries, the first would take precedence for a request URL of http://*host/ webAppPrefix*/foo/bar.html.
- **For overlapping directory mappings, the longest path is preferred.** Thus, if /foo/bar/* and /foo/* were both url-pattern entries, the first would take precedence for a request URL of http://*host/webAppPrefix*/foo/bar/baz.html.

Naming JSP Pages

Because JSP pages get translated into servlets, it is natural to expect that you can name JSP pages just as you can name servlets. After all, JSP pages might benefit from initialization parameters, security settings, or custom URLs, just as regular servlets do. Although it is true that JSP pages are really servlets behind the scenes, there is one key difference: You don't know the actual class name of JSP pages (because the system picks the name). So, to name JSP pages, you substitute the jsp-file element for the servlet-class element, as follows:

```
<servlet>
  <servlet-name>PageName</servlet-name>
  <jsp-file>/WEB-INF/jspPages/TestPage.jsp</jsp-file>
</servlet>
```

The jsp-file element specifies the location of the JSP page relative to the Web application root directory. Although anything placed inside of WEB-INF is protected from direct access, it is the server, not the client, that will be resolving this path, so you are allowed to specify a location inside WEB-INF.

Generally, JSP pages do not need to be declared inside web.xml. They can be invoked like any other static resource (e.g., somePage.html), provided you place them outside of WEB-INF. However, there are times when you might still want to declare a name for a JSP page. Declaring a name for a JSP page allows you to provide a name to use with customization settings (e.g., initialization parameters and security settings) and so that you can change the URL that invokes the JSP page (e.g., so that multiple URLs get handled by the same page or to remove the .jsp extension from the URL). However, when setting initialization parameters, remember that JSP pages read initialization parameters by using the `jspInit` method, not the `init` method. See Section 2.6 (Initializing and Preloading Servlets and JSP Pages) for details.

For example, Listing 2.4 is a simple JSP page named TestPage.jsp that just prints out the local part of the URL used to invoke it. Listing 2.5 shows a portion of the web.xml file (i.e., deployDemo/WEB-INF/web.xml) used to assign a registered name of `PageName` and then to associate that registered name with URLs of the form http://*host*/*webAppPrefix*/UrlTest7/anything. Figure 2–9 shows the result for the URL http://localhost/deployDemo/UrlTest7/foo.

Listing 2.4   TestPage.jsp

```
<!DOCTYPE HTML PUBLIC "-//W3C//DTD HTML 4.0 Transitional//EN">
<HTML>
<HEAD><TITLE>JSP Test Page</TITLE></HEAD>
<BODY BGCOLOR="#FDF5E6">
<H2>TestPage.jsp<br/>
  URI: <%= request.getRequestURI() %></H2>
</BODY></HTML>
```

Listing 2.5   web.xml (Excerpt illustrating the naming of JSP pages)

```
<?xml version="1.0" encoding="ISO-8859-1"?>
<web-app xmlns="http://java.sun.com/xml/ns/j2ee"
         xmlns:xsi="http://www.w3.org/2001/XMLSchema-instance"
         xsi:schemaLocation=
         "http://java.sun.com/xml/ns/j2ee
          http://java.sun.com/xml/ns/j2ee/web-app_2_4.xsd"
         version="2.4">

  <!-- Register the name "PageName" for TestPage.jsp -->
  <servlet>
    <servlet-name>PageName</servlet-name>
    <jsp-file>/WEB-INF/jspPages/TestPage.jsp</jsp-file>
  </servlet>
  <!-- Use the URL http://host/webAppPrefix/UrlTest7/foo -->
  <servlet-mapping>
    <servlet-name>PageName</servlet-name>
    <url-pattern>/UrlTest7/*</url-pattern>
  </servlet-mapping>
  <!-- ... ->
</web-app>
```

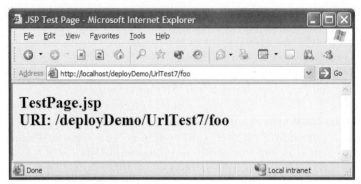

Figure 2–9   TestPage.jsp invoked with http://localhost/deployDemo/UrlTest7/foo.

2.5   Disabling the Invoker Servlet

One reason for setting up a custom URL for a servlet or JSP page is so that you can register initialization parameters to be read from the `init` (servlets) or `jspInit` (JSP pages) methods. However, as discussed in Section 2.6 (Initializing and Preloading Servlets and JSP Pages), the initialization parameters are available only when the servlet or JSP page is accessed by means of a custom URL pattern, not when it is accessed with the default URL of http://*host*/*webAppPrefix*/servlet/*package.Servlet-Class*. Consequently, you might want to turn off the default URL so that nobody accidentally calls the uninitialized servlet. This process is sometimes known as disabling *the invoker servlet*, because most servers have a standard servlet that is registered with the default servlet URLs and simply invokes the real servlet.

There are two main approaches for disabling the default URL:

- Remapping the /servlet/ pattern in each Web application.
- Globally turning off the invoker servlet.

It is important to note that, although remapping the /servlet/ pattern in each Web application is more work than disabling the invoker servlet in one fell swoop, remapping can be done in a completely portable manner. In contrast, the process for globally disabling the invoker servlet is entirely server specific. The first following subsection discusses the per-Web-application strategy of remapping the /servlet/ URL pattern. The next subsection provides details on globally disabling the invoker servlet in Tomcat.

Remapping the /servlet/ URL Pattern

It is quite straightforward to disable processing of URLs that begin with http://*host*/ *webAppPrefix*/servlet/ in a particular Web application. All you need to do is create an error message servlet and use the `url-pattern` element discussed in the previous section to direct all matching requests to that servlet. Simply use

```
<url-pattern>/servlet/*</url-pattern>
```

as the pattern within the `servlet-mapping` element.

For example, Listing 2.6 shows a portion of the deployment descriptor that associates the `NoInvokerServlet` servlet (Listing 2.7) with all URLs that begin with http://*host*/*webAppPrefix*/servlet/. Figure 2–10 illustrates an attempt to access the `TestServlet1` servlet (Listing 2.1 in Section 2.4) with the default URL.

Listing 2.6   web.xml (Excerpt showing how to disable default URLs)

```
<?xml version="1.0" encoding="ISO-8859-1"?>
<web-app xmlns="http://java.sun.com/xml/ns/j2ee"
         xmlns:xsi="http://www.w3.org/2001/XMLSchema-instance"
         xsi:schemaLocation=
         "http://java.sun.com/xml/ns/j2ee
          http://java.sun.com/xml/ns/j2ee/web-app_2_4.xsd"
         version="2.4">

  <!-- Disable the invoker servlet. -->
  <servlet>
    <servlet-name>NoInvoker</servlet-name>
    <servlet-class>coreservlets.NoInvokerServlet</servlet-class>
  </servlet>
  <servlet-mapping>
    <servlet-name>NoInvoker</servlet-name>
    <url-pattern>/servlet/*</url-pattern>
  </servlet-mapping>
  <!-- ... -->
</web-app>
```

Listing 2.7   NoInvokerServlet.java

```
package coreservlets;

import java.io.*;
import javax.servlet.*;
import javax.servlet.http.*;

/** Simple servlet used to give error messages to
 *   users who try to access default servlet URLs
 *   (i.e., http://host/webAppPrefix/servlet/ServletName)
 *   in Web applications that have disabled this
 *   behavior.
 */

public class NoInvokerServlet extends HttpServlet {
  public void doGet(HttpServletRequest request,
                    HttpServletResponse response)
      throws ServletException, IOException {
    response.setContentType("text/html");
    PrintWriter out = response.getWriter();
    String docType =
      "<!DOCTYPE HTML PUBLIC \"-//W3C//DTD HTML 4.0 " +
      "Transitional//EN\">\n";
    String title = "Invoker Servlet Disabled.";
    out.println
      (docType +
       "<HTML>\n" +
       "<HEAD><TITLE>" + title + "</TITLE></HEAD>\n" +
       "<BODY BGCOLOR=\"#FDF5E6\">\n" +
       "<H2>" + title + "</H2>\n" +
       "Sorry, access to servlets by means of\n" +
       "URLs that begin with\n" +
       "http://host/webAppPrefix/servlet/\n" +
       "has been disabled.\n" +
       "</BODY></HTML>");
  }

  public void doPost(HttpServletRequest request,
                     HttpServletResponse response)
      throws ServletException, IOException {
    doGet(request, response);
  }
}
```

Figure 2–10 Unsuccessful attempt to invoke the `TestServlet1` servlet by means of the default URL. The invoker servlet is disabled.

Globally Disabling the Invoker: Tomcat

Tomcat 5 turns off the invoker servlet by default. It does this in the same way that we turned it off in the previous section: by means of a `url-mapping` element in web.xml. The difference is that Tomcat uses a server-specific global web.xml file that is stored in *install_dir*/conf, whereas we used the standard web.xml file that is stored in the WEB-INF directory of each Web application.

Thus, to turn off the invoker servlet in Tomcat 5, you simply comment out the `/servlet/*` URL mapping entry in *install_dir*/conf/web.xml, as shown here.

```
<!--
<servlet-mapping>
  <servlet-name>invoker</servlet-name>
  <url-pattern>/servlet/*</url-pattern>
</servlet-mapping>
-->
```

Again, note that this entry is in the Tomcat-specific web.xml file that is stored in *install_dir*/conf, not the standard web.xml file that is stored in the WEB-INF directory of each Web application.

Figure 2–11 shows the result when the `TestServlet1` (Listing 2.1 from Section 2.4) is invoked with the default URL in a version of Tomcat that has the invoker servlet globally disabled. The default URL fails.

Please see http://www.coreservlets.com/ for more information on setting up Tomcat.

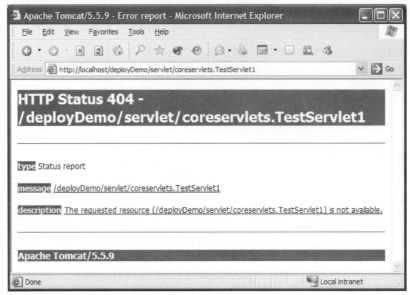

Figure 2–11 `TestServlet1` when invoked with the default URL in a server that has globally disabled the invoker servlet.

2.6 Initializing and Preloading Servlets and JSP Pages

This section discusses methods for controlling the startup behavior of servlets and JSP pages. In particular, it explains how you can assign initialization parameters and how you can change the point in the server life cycle at which servlets and JSP pages are loaded.

Assigning Servlet Initialization Parameters

You provide servlets with initialization parameters by means of the `init-param` element, which has `param-name` and `param-value` subelements. For instance, in the following example, if the `InitServlet` servlet is accessed by means of a URL in the form of `http://host/webAppPrefix/showInitValues`, it could call `getServletConfig().getInitParameter("firstName")` from its init method to get `"Larry"` and could call `getServletConfig().getInitParameter("emailAddress")` to get `"ellison@microsoft.com"`.

```
<servlet>
  <servlet-name>InitTest</servlet-name>
  <servlet-class>coreservlets.InitServlet</servlet-class>
  <init-param>
    <param-name>firstName</param-name>
    <param-value>Larry</param-value>
  </init-param>
  <init-param>
    <param-name>emailAddress</param-name>
    <param-value>ellison@microsoft.com</param-value>
  </init-param>
</servlet>
<servlet-mapping>
  <servlet-name>InitTest</servlet-name>
  <url-pattern>/showInitValues</url-pattern>
</servlet-mapping>
```

There are a few common gotchas that are worth keeping in mind when dealing with initialization parameters:

- **Return values.** The return value of `getInitParameter` is always a `String`. So, for integer parameters you might use `Integer.parseInt` to obtain an `int`.
- **Nonexistent values.** If the key passed into the `getInitParameter` method does not appear inside the servlet's `init-param` declarations, `null` will be returned. Because someone other than the Java developer can modify web.xml, you should always check for `null` inside your code.
- **Initialization in JSP.** JSP pages use `jspInit`, not `init`. JSP pages also require use of the `jsp-file` element in place of `servlet-class`, as described in Section 2.4 (Assigning Names and Custom URLs). Initializing JSP pages is discussed in the next subsection.
- **Default URLs.** Initialization parameters are only available when servlets are accessed through custom URL patterns associated with their registered names. So, in this example, the `firstName` and `emailAddress` init parameters would be available when you used the URL http://*host*/*webAppPrefix*/showInitValues, but not when you used the URL http://*host*/*webAppPrefix*/servlet/coreservlets.InitServlet.

Core Warning

Initialization parameters are not available in servlets that are accessed by their default URL.

For example, Listing 2.8 shows a simple servlet called `InitServlet` that uses the `init` method to set the `firstName` and `emailAddress` fields. Listing 2.9 shows the excerpt from the **web**.xml file that assigns the custom URL pattern /`showInitValues` to the servlet. Figures 2–12 and 2–13 show the results when the servlet is accessed with the custom URL (correct) and the default URL (incorrect), respectively.

It is simply too hard to remember which URL works and which doesn't. In real Web apps, disable the invoker servlet so that there is only one URL for each servlet. Reserve the invoker servlet exclusively for quick tests of capabilities in separate (test-only) Web applications.

Listing 2.8 InitServlet.java

```
package coreservlets;

import java.io.*;
import javax.servlet.*;
import javax.servlet.http.*;

/** Simple servlet used to illustrate servlet
 *  initialization parameters.
 */

public class InitServlet extends HttpServlet {
  private String firstName = "First name is missing.";
  private String emailAddress = "Email address is missing";

  public void init() {
    ServletConfig config = getServletConfig();
    if (config.getInitParameter("firstName") != null) {
      firstName = config.getInitParameter("firstName");
    }
    if (config.getInitParameter("emailAddress") != null) {
      emailAddress = config.getInitParameter("emailAddress");
    }
  }

  public void doGet(HttpServletRequest request,
                    HttpServletResponse response)
      throws ServletException, IOException {
    response.setContentType("text/html");
    PrintWriter out = response.getWriter();
    String uri = request.getRequestURI();
```

Listing 2.8   InitServlet.java *(continued)*

```
    out.println("<!DOCTYPE HTML PUBLIC \"-//W3C//DTD HTML 4.0 " +
                "Transitional//EN\">" + "\n" +
                "<HTML>\n" + "<HEAD><TITLE>" +
                "Init Servlet" + "</TITLE></HEAD>\n" +
                "<BODY BGCOLOR=\"#FDF5E6\">\n" +
                "<H2>Init Parameters:</H2>\n" +
                "<UL>\n" +
                "<LI>First name: " + firstName + "\n" +
                "<LI>Email address: " + emailAddress + "\n" +
                "</UL>\n" +
                "</BODY></HTML>");
  }
}
```

Listing 2.9   web.xml (Excerpt illustrating initialization parameters)

```
<?xml version="1.0" encoding="ISO-8859-1"?>
<web-app xmlns="http://java.sun.com/xml/ns/j2ee"
         xmlns:xsi="http://www.w3.org/2001/XMLSchema-instance"
         xsi:schemaLocation=
         "http://java.sun.com/xml/ns/j2ee
          http://java.sun.com/xml/ns/j2ee/web-app_2_4.xsd"
         version="2.4">

  <servlet>
    <servlet-name>InitTest</servlet-name>
    <servlet-class>coreservlets.InitServlet</servlet-class>
    <init-param>
      <param-name>firstName</param-name>
      <param-value>Larry</param-value>
    </init-param>
    <init-param>
      <param-name>emailAddress</param-name>
      <param-value>ellison@microsoft.com</param-value>
    </init-param>
  </servlet>
  <servlet-mapping>
    <servlet-name>InitTest</servlet-name>
    <url-pattern>/showInitValues</url-pattern>
  </servlet-mapping>
  <!-- ... -->
</web-app>
```

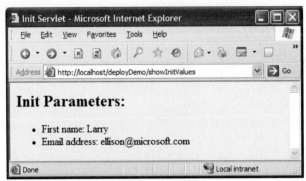

Figure 2–12 The `InitServlet` when correctly accessed with its custom URL.

Figure 2–13 The `InitServlet` when incorrectly accessed with the default URL. Disable the invoker servlet to avoid this problem.

Assigning JSP Initialization Parameters

Although the servlet specification provides a mechanism for assigning JSP initialization parameters, in practice, this is discouraged and thus very rare. A much better approach to loading initialization parameters is to use the Model-View-Controller (MVC) architecture and do the initialization inside the `init` method of a servlet.

Providing initialization parameters to JSP pages differs in three ways from providing them to servlets.

1. **You use `jsp-file` instead of `servlet-class`.** The servlet element of the WEB-INF/web.xml file would look something like this:

```
<servlet>
  <servlet-name>InitPage</servlet-name>
  <jsp-file>/InitPage.jsp</jsp-file>
```

```
<init-param>
  <param-name>...</param-name>
  <param-value>...</param-value>
</init-param>
...
</servlet>
```

2. **You should assign the original URL of the JSP page as its custom URL pattern.** With servlets, it is moderately common to use a custom URL pattern that differs from the name of the servlet. There wouldn't be anything technically illegal in doing the same for JSP pages as well. However, many users dislike URLs that appear to refer to regular servlets when used for JSP pages. Furthermore, if the JSP page is in a directory for which the server provides a directory listing (e.g., a directory with neither an index.html nor an index.jsp file), the user might get a link to the JSP page, click it, and thus accidentally invoke the uninitialized page. Therefore, a good strategy is to use url-pattern (Section 2.4) to associate the original URL of the JSP page with the registered servlet name. That way, clients can use the normal name for the JSP page but still invoke the customized version. For example, given the servlet definition from item 1, you might use the following servlet-mapping definition:

```
<servlet-mapping>
  <servlet-name>InitPage</servlet-name>
  <url-pattern>/InitPage.jsp</url-pattern>
</servlet-mapping>
```

3. **The JSP page uses `jspInit`, not `init`.** The servlet that is automatically built from a JSP page may already be using the init method. Consequently, it is illegal to use a JSP declaration to provide an init method. You must name the method jspInit instead.

To illustrate the process of initializing JSP pages, Listing 2.10 shows a JSP page called InitPage.jsp that contains a jspInit method and is placed at the top level of the deployDemo Web page hierarchy. Normally, a URL of http://localhost/deployDemo/InitPage.jsp would invoke a version of the page that has no access to initialization parameters and would thus return null for the firstName and emailAddress parameters. However, the web.xml file (Listing 2.11) assigns a registered name and then associates that registered name with the URL pattern /InitPage.jsp. As Figure 2–14 shows, the result is that the normal URL for the JSP page now invokes the version of the page that has access to the initialization parameters.

Listing 2.10 InitPage.jsp

```
<!DOCTYPE HTML PUBLIC "-//W3C//DTD HTML 4.0 Transitional//EN">
<HTML>
<HEAD><TITLE>JSP Init Test</TITLE></HEAD>
<BODY BGCOLOR="#FDF5E6">
<H2>Init Parameters:</H2>
<UL>
  <LI>First name: <%= firstName %>
  <LI>Email address: <%= emailAddress %>
</UL>
</BODY></HTML>
<%!
private String firstName = "First name is missing.";
private String emailAddress = "Email address is missing";

public void jspInit() {
  ServletConfig config = getServletConfig();
  if (config.getInitParameter("firstName") != null) {
    firstName = config.getInitParameter("firstName");
  }
  if (config.getInitParameter("emailAddress") != null) {
    emailAddress = config.getInitParameter("emailAddress");
  }
}
%>
```

Listing 2.11 web.xml (Excerpt showing init params for JSP pages)

```
<?xml version="1.0" encoding="ISO-8859-1"?>
<web-app xmlns="http://java.sun.com/xml/ns/j2ee"
         xmlns:xsi="http://www.w3.org/2001/XMLSchema-instance"
         xsi:schemaLocation=
         "http://java.sun.com/xml/ns/j2ee
          http://java.sun.com/xml/ns/j2ee/web-app_2_4.xsd"
         version="2.4">

  <servlet>
    <servlet-name>InitPage</servlet-name>
    <jsp-file>/InitPage.jsp</jsp-file>
    <init-param>
      <param-name>firstName</param-name>
      <param-value>Bill</param-value>
    </init-param>
```

| Listing 2.11 | web.xml (Excerpt showing init params for JSP pages) *(continued)* |

```
    <init-param>
      <param-name>emailAddress</param-name>
      <param-value>gates@oracle.com</param-value>
    </init-param>
  </servlet>
  <servlet-mapping>
    <servlet-name>InitPage</servlet-name>
    <url-pattern>/InitPage.jsp</url-pattern>
  </servlet-mapping>
  <!-- ... -->
</web-app>
```

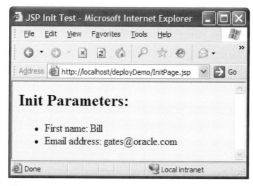

Figure 2–14 Mapping a JSP page's original URL to the registered custom URL pattern prevents users from accidentally accessing the uninitialized version.

Supplying Application-Wide Initialization Parameters

Normally, you assign initialization parameters to individual servlets or JSP pages. The designated servlet or JSP page reads the parameters by means of the getInit-Parameter method of Servlet**Config**. However, in some situations you want to supply system-wide initialization parameters that can be read by any servlet or JSP page by means of the getInitParameter method of Servlet**Context**.

You use the context-param element to declare these system-wide initialization values. The context-param element should contain param-name, param-value, and, optionally, description subelements, as shown here.

```
<context-param>
  <param-name>support-email</param-name>
  <param-value>blackhole@mycompany.com</param-value>
</context-param>
```

Loading Servlets When the Server Starts

Suppose the LoadInitServlet has an init method that reads an initialization parameter, companyName, and stores it in the ServletContext object. The doGet method of the LoadInitServlet retrieves companyName from the ServletContext and displays it to the client. After the LoadInitServlet has been invoked at least once, two different JSP pages, ShowInitLoaded1.jsp and ShowInitLoaded2.jsp, are invoked with ${companyName} somewhere on both pages. The JSP pages will retrieve the previously stored companyName from the ServletContext and display it to the client. In this case, everything works as we would expect it to. For the complete code of LoadInitServlet.java, ShowInitLoaded1.jsp, and ShowInitLoaded2.jsp, see Listings 2.12 through 2.14, respectively. Figures 2–15 through 2–17 show the result of invoking LoadInitServlet (with <url-pattern>/showLoadInit</url-pattern>), ShowInitLoaded1.jsp, and ShowInitLoaded2.jsp, respectively.

Listing 2.12 LoadInitServlet.java

```
package coreservlets;

import java.io.*;
import javax.servlet.*;
import javax.servlet.http.*;

/** Simple servlet used to illustrate loading init-param
 *  into ServletContext.
 */

public class LoadInitServlet extends HttpServlet {
  private String companyName = "Company name is missing";

  public void init() {
    ServletConfig config = getServletConfig();
    if (config.getInitParameter("companyName") != null) {
      companyName = config.getInitParameter("companyName");
    }
    ServletContext context = getServletContext();
    context.setAttribute("companyName", companyName);
  }
```

Listing 2.12 LoadInitServlet.java *(continued)*

```java
public void doGet(HttpServletRequest request,
                  HttpServletResponse response)
    throws ServletException, IOException {
  response.setContentType("text/html");
  PrintWriter out = response.getWriter();
  out.println("<!DOCTYPE HTML PUBLIC \"-//W3C//DTD HTML 4.0 " +
              "Transitional//EN\">" + "\n" +
              "<HTML>\n" + "<HEAD><TITLE>" +
              "Load Init Servlet" + "</TITLE></HEAD>\n" +
              "<BODY BGCOLOR=\"#FDF5E6\">\n" +
              "<H2>Init Parameter:</H2>\n" +
              "Company name: " +
              getServletContext().getAttribute("companyName") +
              "\n" + "</BODY></HTML>");
  }
}
```

Listing 2.13 ShowInitLoaded1.jsp

```
<!DOCTYPE HTML PUBLIC "-//W3C//DTD HTML 4.0 Transitional//EN">
<HTML>
<HEAD><TITLE>Current Company Name</TITLE></HEAD>
<BODY BGCOLOR="#FDF5E6">
<H2>Welcome to ${companyName}!</H2>
We changed our name to serve you better!
</BODY></HTML>
```

Listing 2.14 ShowInitLoaded2.jsp

```
<!DOCTYPE HTML PUBLIC "-//W3C//DTD HTML 4.0 Transitional//EN">
<HTML>
<HEAD><TITLE>Init Parameter from ServletContext</TITLE></HEAD>
<BODY BGCOLOR="#FDF5E6">
<H2>Init Parameter: ${companyName}</H2>
</BODY></HTML>
```

Figure 2–15   Result of invoking `LoadInitServlet` with http://localhost/deployDemo/showLoadInit. The servlet loads a company name using `getInitParameter`, stores it in `ServletContext`, and displays it in the `doGet` method.

Figure 2–16   Result of invoking http://localhost/deployDemo/ShowInitLoaded1.jsp. This page retrieves the name of the company previously stored in the `ServletContext` by the `LoadInitServlet`.

Figure 2–17   Result of invoking http://localhost/deployDemo/ShowInitLoaded2.jsp. This page retrieves the name of the company previously stored in the `ServletContext` by the `LoadInitServlet`.

But what happens if we reboot the server and then the JSP pages are accessed before the `LoadInitServlet` is invoked? At this point, because the `LoadInitServlet` has not yet been loaded into memory, its `init` method has not been called, and the attribute `companyName` is not present in the `ServletContext`. The JSP pages would therefore not produce expected results. Figure 2–18 shows the result of invoking ShowInitLoaded1.jsp after rebooting the server but before invoking the `LoadInitServlet`.

Figure 2–18   Result of invoking http://localhost/deployDemo/ShowInitLoaded1.jsp after rebooting the server but before invoking the `LoadInitServlet`. The company name was never loaded into the `ServletContext`, thus the page shows blank for the name of the company.

We could easily solve the problem by declaring `companyName` in con-text-param, but then we would have Java code in the JSP pages and we would have to repeat the check for `null` everywhere. So, we use `load-on-startup` to guarantee that the `LoadInitServlet`'s init method is run when the Web application is first loaded as follows:

```
<servlet>
    <servlet-name>LoadInit</servlet-name>
    <servlet-class>
      coreservlets.LoadInitServlet
    </servlet-class>
    <init-param>
      <param-name>companyName</param-name>
      <param-value>Doozilch Daley Inc.</param-value>
    </init-param>
    <load-on-startup>0</load-on-startup>
</servlet>
```

At server startup, the `LoadInitServlet` will be loaded into memory and its init method called. If we invoke ShowInitLoad1.jsp as the very first thing at server reboot, it will now show the name of the company because the `LoadInitServlet`'s init method is guaranteed to have been called.

You can have more than one servlet or JSP page configured to load at server startup. The integer 0 in the `load-on-startup`'s element body tells the server that this servlet should be loaded into memory at server startup before any other servlet or JSP page. The idea is that the server should load lower numbered servlets or JSP pages before higher numbered ones. For example, the following `servlet` entries (placed within the `web-app` element in the web.xml file that goes in the WEB-INF directory of your Web application) would instruct the server to first load and initialize the `SearchServlet`, then load and initialize the servlet resulting from the index.jsp file that is in the Web app's results directory.

```
<servlet>
  <servlet-name>Search</servlet-name>
  <servlet-class>myPackage.SearchServlet</servlet-class>
  <load-on-startup>0</load-on-startup>
</servlet>
<servlet>
  <servlet-name>Results</servlet-name>
  <jsp-file>/results/index.jsp</jsp-file>
  <load-on-startup>1</load-on-startup>
</servlet>
```

If you specify two different servlets with the same `load-on-startup` number, the server is free to choose which of the same-numbered servlets is loaded first. Loading the servlet at startup is not guaranteed if you specify a negative number in the body of the `load-on-startup` element.

The `load-on-startup` feature is also convenient if the `init` (servlet) or `jspInit` (JSP) method takes a long time to execute. For example, suppose that the `init` or `jspInit` method looks up constants from a database or `ResourceBundle`. In such a case, the default behavior of loading the servlet at the time of the first client request results in a significant delay for that first client. So, you can use the `load-on-startup` subelement of `servlet` to stipulate that the server load the servlet when the server first starts. However, a much better approach to this problem is to place the slow-loading initialization into the `ServletContextListener`'s `contextInitialized` method. This method is guaranteed to be called by the container before any other resources are loaded. For more details on listeners, please see Chapter 6 (The Application Events Framework).

2.7   Declaring Filters

Filters are discussed in detail in Chapter 5 (Servlet and JSP Filters), but the basic idea is that filters can intercept and modify the request coming into or the response going out of a servlet or JSP page. Before a servlet or JSP page is executed, the `doFilter` method of the first associated filter is executed. When that filter calls doFilter on its FilterChain object, the next filter in the chain is executed. If there is no other filter, the servlet or JSP page itself is executed. Filters have full access to the incoming ServletRequest object, so they can check the client's hostname, look for incoming cookies, and so forth. To access the output of the servlet or JSP page, a filter can wrap the response object inside a stand-in object that, for example, accumulates the output into a buffer. After the call to the doFilter method of the FilterChain object, the filter can examine the buffer, modify it if necessary, and then pass it on to the client.

For example, Listing 2.15 defines a simple filter that intercepts requests and prints a report on the standard output (available with most servers when you run them on your desktop during development) whenever the associated servlet or JSP page is accessed.

Listing 2.15	ReportFilter.java

```java
package coreservlets;

import java.io.*;
import javax.servlet.*;
import javax.servlet.http.*;
import java.util.*;

/** Simple filter that prints a report on the standard output
 *  whenever the associated servlet or JSP page is accessed.
 */

public class ReportFilter implements Filter {
  public void doFilter(ServletRequest request,
                       ServletResponse response,
                       FilterChain chain)
      throws ServletException, IOException {
    HttpServletRequest req = (HttpServletRequest)request;
    System.out.println(req.getRemoteHost() +
                       " tried to access " +
                       req.getRequestURL() +
                       " on " + new Date() + ".");
    chain.doFilter(request,response);
  }

  public void init(FilterConfig config)
      throws ServletException {
  }

  public void destroy() {}
}
```

Once you have created a filter, you declare it in the web.xml file by using the filter element along with the filter-name (arbitrary name), filter-class (fully qualified class name), and, optionally, init-params subelements.

For instance, given the ReportFilter class just shown, you could make the following filter declaration in web.xml. It associates the name Reporter with the actual class ReportFilter (which is in the coreservlets package).

```
<filter>
  <filter-name>Reporter</filter-name>
  <filter-class>coreservlets.ReportFilter</filter-class>
</filter>
```

Once you have named a filter, you associate it with one or more servlets or JSP pages by means of the filter-mapping element. You have two choices in this regard.

First, you can use filter-name and servlet-name subelements to associate the filter with a specific servlet name (which must be declared with a servlet element in the same web.xml file). For example, the following snippet instructs the system to run the filter named Reporter whenever the servlet or JSP page named SomeServletName is accessed by means of a custom URL.

```
<filter-mapping>
  <filter-name>Reporter</filter-name>
  <servlet-name>SomeServletName</servlet-name>
</filter-mapping>
```

Second, you can use the filter-name and url-pattern subelements to associate the filter with groups of servlets, JSP pages, or static content. For example, the following snippet instructs the system to run the filter named Reporter when any URL in the Web application is accessed.

```
<filter-mapping>
  <filter-name>Reporter</filter-name>
  <url-pattern>/*</url-pattern>
</filter-mapping>
```

For example, Listing 2.16 shows a portion of a web.xml file that associates the ReportFilter filter with the servlet named PageName. The name PageName, in turn, is associated with a JSP file named TestPage.jsp and URLs with the pattern /UrlTest/*. The source code for TestPage.jsp and a discussion of the naming of JSP pages were given earlier in Section 2.4 (Assigning Names and Custom URLs). In fact, the servlet and servlet-name entries in Listing 2.16 are taken unchanged from that section. Given these web.xml entries, you see debugging reports in the standard output of the following sort (line breaks added for readability):

```
audit.irs.gov tried to access
http://mycompany.com/deployDemo/UrlTest7/business/tax-plan.html
on Tue Dec 25 13:12:29 EDT 2005.
```

Listing 2.16 web.xml (Excerpt showing filter usage)

```
<?xml version="1.0" encoding="ISO-8859-1"?>
<web-app xmlns="http://java.sun.com/xml/ns/j2ee"
         xmlns:xsi="http://www.w3.org/2001/XMLSchema-instance"
         xsi:schemaLocation=
         "http://java.sun.com/xml/ns/j2ee
          http://java.sun.com/xml/ns/j2ee/web-app_2_4.xsd"
         version="2.4">

  <servlet>
    <servlet-name>PageName</servlet-name>
    <jsp-file>/WEB-INF/jspPages/TestPage.jsp</jsp-file>
  </servlet>
  <servlet-mapping>
    <servlet-name>PageName</servlet-name>
    <url-pattern>/UrlTest7/*</url-pattern>
  </servlet-mapping>
  <filter>
    <filter-name>Reporter</filter-name>
    <filter-class>coreservlets.ReportFilter</filter-class>
  </filter>
  <filter-mapping>
    <filter-name>Reporter</filter-name>
    <servlet-name>PageName</servlet-name>
  </filter-mapping>
  <!-- ... -->
</web-app>
```

2.8   Specifying Welcome Pages

Suppose a user supplies a URL like http://*host*/*webAppPrefix*/*directoryName*/ that contains a directory name but no file name. What happens? Does the user get a directory listing? An error? The contents of a standard file? If so, which one—index.html, index.jsp, default.html, default.htm, or what?

The welcome-file-list element, along with its subsidiary welcome-file element, resolves this ambiguity. For example, the following web.xml entry specifies that if a URL gives a directory name but no file name, the server should try index.jsp first and index.html second. If neither is found, the result is server specific (e.g., a directory listing).

```
<welcome-file-list>
  <welcome-file>index.jsp</welcome-file>
  <welcome-file>index.html</welcome-file>
</welcome-file-list>
```

Although many servers follow this behavior by default, they are not required to do so. As a result, it is good practice to explicitly use welcome-file-list to ensure portability.

Core Approach

*Make welcome-file-list a standard entry in your **web.xml** files.*

2.9   Designating Pages to Handle Errors

Now, we realize that you never make any mistakes when developing servlets and JSP pages and that all of your pages are so clear that no rational person could be confused by them. Still, the world is full of irrational people, and users could supply illegal parameters, use incorrect URLs, or fail to provide values for required form fields. Besides, other developers might not be as careful as you are, and they should have some tools to overcome their deficiencies.

The error-page element is used to handle problems. It has two possible subelements: error-code and exception-type. The first of these, error-code, designates what URL to use when a designated Hypertext Transfer Protocol (HTTP) error code occurs. (If you aren't familiar with HTTP error codes, they are discussed in Chapter 6 of Volume I of *Core Servlets and JavaServer Pages*.) The second of these subelements, exception-type, designates what URL to use when a designated Java exception is thrown but not caught. Both error-code and exception-type use the location element to designate the URL. This URL must begin with /, making it relative to the Web application root directory. The page at the place designated by location can access information about the error by looking up two special-purpose attributes of the HttpServletRequest object: javax.servlet.error.status_code and javax.servlet.error.message.

The error-code Element

To better understand the value of the `error-code` element, consider what happens at most sites when you type the file name incorrectly. You typically get a 404 error message that tells you that the file can't be found but provides little useful information. On the other hand, try typing unknown file names at www.microsoft.com, www.ibm.com, or www.bea.com. There, you get useful messages that provide alternative places to look for the page of interest. Providing such useful error pages is a valuable addition to your Web application. In fact, http://www.plinko.net/404/ has an entire site devoted to the topic of 404 error pages. This site includes examples of the best, worst, and funniest 404 pages from around the world.

Listing 2.17 shows the web.xml file that designates Listing 2.18 as the page that gets displayed when a 404 error code is returned. Listing 2.18 shows the JSP page that could be returned to clients that provide unknown file names. Figure 2–19 shows a typical result. Note that the URL displayed in the browser remains the one supplied by the client; the error page is a behind-the-scenes implementation technique; the system uses `RequestDispatcher.forward` to access it, not `response.sendRedirect`. Also note the location of NotFound.jsp. Because it is the server, not the client (e.g., browser), that resolves the path specified by the `location` subelement, you are allowed to place NotFound.jsp inside of the WEB-INF directory.

Listing 2.17 web.xml (Excerpt designating error pages for HTTP error codes)

```
<?xml version="1.0" encoding="ISO-8859-1"?>
<web-app xmlns="http://java.sun.com/xml/ns/j2ee"
         xmlns:xsi="http://www.w3.org/2001/XMLSchema-instance"
         xsi:schemaLocation=
         "http://java.sun.com/xml/ns/j2ee
          http://java.sun.com/xml/ns/j2ee/web-app_2_4.xsd"
         version="2.4">

  <error-page>
    <error-code>404</error-code>
    <location>/WEB-INF/jspPages/NotFound.jsp</location>
  </error-page>
  <!-- ... -->
</web-app>
```

Listing 2.18   NotFound.jsp

```
<!DOCTYPE HTML PUBLIC "-//W3C//DTD HTML 4.0 Transitional//EN">
<HTML>
<HEAD><TITLE>404: Not Found</TITLE></HEAD>
<BODY BGCOLOR="#FDF5E6">
<H2>Error!</H2>
I'm sorry, but I cannot find a page that matches
<%= request.getAttribute("javax.servlet.forward.request_uri") %>
on the system. Maybe you should try one of the following:
<UL>
  <LI>Go to the server's <A HREF="/">home page</A>.
  <LI>Search for relevant pages.<BR>
      <FORM ACTION="http://www.google.com/search">
      <CENTER>
      Keywords: <INPUT TYPE="TEXT" NAME="q"><BR>
      <INPUT TYPE="SUBMIT" VALUE="Search">
      </CENTER>
      </FORM>
  <LI>Admire a random multiple of 404:
      <%= 404*((int)(1000*Math.random())) %>.
  <LI>Try the amazing and amusing plinko.net
  <A HREF="http://www.plinko.net/404/">404 archive</A>.
</UL>
</BODY></HTML>
```

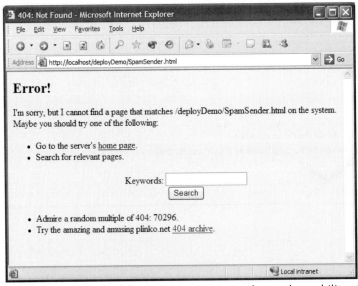

Figure 2–19   Use of helpful 404 messages can enhance the usability of your site.

The exception-type Element

The `error-code` element handles the case when a request results in a particular HTTP status code. But what about the equally common case when the servlet or JSP page returns 200 but generates a runtime exception? That's the situation that can be handled by the `exception-type` element. However, in real Web applications you should rarely if ever rely on this mechanism to catch exceptions. All exceptions should be caught explicitly in your code.

To use the web.xml way of catching exceptions, you only need to supply two things: a fully qualified exception class and a location, as shown here.

```
<error-page>
  <exception-type>package.ClassName</exception-type>
  <location>/SomeURL</location>
</error-page>
```

Then, if any servlet or JSP page in the Web application generates an uncaught exception of the specified type, the designated URL is used. The exception type can be a standard one like `javax.ServletException` or `java.lang.OutOf-MemoryError`, or it can be an exception specific to your application.

For instance, Listing 2.19 shows an exception class named `DumbDeveloper-Exception` that might be used to flag particularly bad mistakes by clueless programmers (not that you have any of those types on your development team). The class also contains a static method called `dangerousComputation` that sometimes generates this type of exception. Listing 2.20 shows a JSP page that calls `dangerous-Computation` on random integer values. When the exception is thrown, DDE.jsp (Listing 2.21) is displayed to the client, as designated by the `exception-type` entry shown in the web.xml version of Listing 2.22. Figures 2–20 and 2–21 show lucky and unlucky results, respectively.

Listing 2.19 DumbDeveloperException.java

```
package coreservlets;

/** Exception used to flag particularly onerous
    programmer blunders. Used to illustrate the
    exception-type web.xml element.
*/

public class DumbDeveloperException extends Exception {
  public DumbDeveloperException() {
    super("Duh. What was I *thinking*?");
  }
```

Listing 2.19   DumbDeveloperException.java *(continued)*

```
public static int dangerousComputation(int n)
    throws DumbDeveloperException {
  if (n < 5) {
    return(n + 10);
  } else {
    throw(new DumbDeveloperException());
  }
 }
}
```

Listing 2.20   RiskyPage.jsp

```
<!DOCTYPE HTML PUBLIC "-//W3C//DTD HTML 4.0 Transitional//EN">
<HTML>
<HEAD><TITLE>Risky JSP Page</TITLE></HEAD>
<BODY BGCOLOR="#FDF5E6">
<H2>Risky Calculations</H2>
<%@ page import="coreservlets.*" %>
<% int n = ((int)(10 * Math.random())); %>
<UL>
  <LI>n: <%= n %>
  <LI>dangerousComputation(n):
      <%= DumbDeveloperException.dangerousComputation(n) %>
</UL>
</BODY></HTML>
```

Listing 2.21   DDE.jsp

```
<!DOCTYPE HTML PUBLIC "-//W3C//DTD HTML 4.0 Transitional//EN">
<HTML>
<HEAD><TITLE>Dumb</TITLE></HEAD>
<BODY BGCOLOR="#FDF5E6">
<H2>Dumb Developer</H2>
We're brain dead. Consider using our competitors.
</BODY></HTML>
```

Listing 2.22   web.xml (Excerpt designating error pages for exceptions)

```
<?xml version="1.0" encoding="ISO-8859-1"?>
<web-app xmlns="http://java.sun.com/xml/ns/j2ee"
        xmlns:xsi="http://www.w3.org/2001/XMLSchema-instance"
        xsi:schemaLocation=
        "http://java.sun.com/xml/ns/j2ee
         http://java.sun.com/xml/ns/j2ee/web-app_2_4.xsd"
        version="2.4">

  <error-page>
    <exception-type>
      coreservlets.DumbDeveloperException
    </exception-type>
    <location>/WEB-INF/jspPages/DDE.jsp</location>
  </error-page>
  <!-- ... -->
</web-app>
```

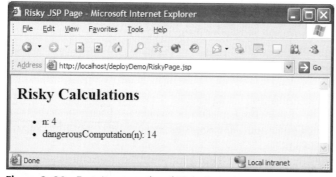

Figure 2–20   Fortuitous results of RiskyPage.jsp.

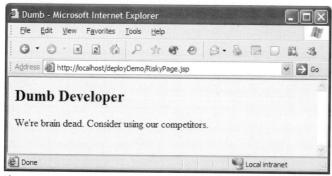

Figure 2–21   Unlucky results of RiskyPage.jsp.

2.10 Providing Security

Use of the server's built-in capabilities to manage security is discussed in Chapter 3 (Declarative Security). This section summarizes the web.xml elements that relate to this topic.

Designating the Authentication Method

You use the login-config element to specify how the server should authenticate users who attempt to access protected pages. It contains three possible subelements: auth-method, realm-name, and form-login-config.

auth-method

This subelement of login-config lists the specific authentication mechanism that the server should use. Legal values are BASIC, DIGEST, FORM, and CLIENT-CERT. Servers are only required to support BASIC and FORM.

BASIC specifies that standard HTTP authentication should be used, in which the server checks for an Authorization header, returning a 401 status code and a WWW-Authenticate header if the header is missing. This causes the client to pop up a dialog box that is used to populate the Authorization header. Details of this process are discussed in Section 3.3 (BASIC Authentication). Note that this mechanism provides little or no security against attackers who are snooping on the Internet connection (e.g., by running a packet sniffer on the client's subnet) because the username and password are sent with the easily reversible base64 encoding. All compliant servers are required to support BASIC authentication.

DIGEST indicates that the client should transmit the username and password using the encrypted Digest Authentication form. This provides more security against network intercepts than does BASIC authentication, but the encryption can be reversed more easily than the method used in Secure Sockets Layer (SSL; HTTPS). The point is somewhat moot, however, since few browsers currently support Digest Authentication, and consequently servlet containers are not required to support it.

FORM specifies that the server should check for a reserved session cookie and should redirect users who do not have it to a designated login page. That page should contain a normal HTML form to gather the username and password. After logging in, users are tracked by means of the reserved session-level cookie. Although in and of itself, FORM authentication is no more secure against network snooping than is BASIC authentication, additional protection such as SSL or network-level security (e.g., IPSec or VPN) can be layered on top if necessary. All compliant servers are required to support FORM authentication.

CLIENT-CERT stipulates that the server must use HTTPS (HTTP over SSL) and authenticate users by means of their public key certificate. This provides strong security against network intercept, but only fully J2EE-compliant servers are required to support it.

realm-name

This element applies only when the auth-method is BASIC. It designates the name of the security realm that is used by the browser in the title of the dialog box and as part of the Authorization header.

form-login-config

This element applies only when the auth-method is FORM. It designates two pages: the page that contains the HTML form that collects the username and password (by means of the form-login-page subelement), and the page that should be used to indicate failed authentication (by means of the form-error-page subelement). As discussed in Chapter 3 (Declarative Security), the HTML form given by the form-login-page must have an ACTION attribute of j_security_check, a username text field named j_username, and a password field named j_password.

For example, Listing 2.23 instructs the server to use form-based authentication. A page named login.jsp in the top-level directory of the Web app should collect the username and password, and failed login attempts should be reported by a page named login-error.jsp in the same directory.

Listing 2.23 web.xml (Excerpt showing login-config)

```xml
<?xml version="1.0" encoding="ISO-8859-1"?>
<web-app xmlns="http://java.sun.com/xml/ns/j2ee"
         xmlns:xsi="http://www.w3.org/2001/XMLSchema-instance"
         xsi:schemaLocation=
         "http://java.sun.com/xml/ns/j2ee
          http://java.sun.com/xml/ns/j2ee/web-app_2_4.xsd"
         version="2.4">

  <security-constraint>...</security-constraint>
  <login-config>
    <auth-method>FORM</auth-method>
    <form-login-config>
      <form-login-page>/login.jsp</form-login-page>
      <form-error-page>/login-error.jsp</form-error-page>
    </form-login-config>
  </login-config>
  <!-- ... -->
</web-app>
```

Restricting Access to Web Resources

So, you can tell the server which authentication method to use. "Big deal," you say, "that's not much use unless I can designate the URLs that should be protected." Right. Designating these URLs and describing the protection they should have is the purpose of the `security-constraint` element. This element contains four possible subelements: `web-resource-collection`, `auth-constraint`, `user-data-constraint`, and `display-name`. Each of these is described in the following subsections.

web-resource-collection

This element identifies the resources that should be protected. All `security-constraint` elements must contain at least one `web-resource-collection` entry. This element consists of a `web-resource-name` element that gives an arbitrary identifying name, a `url-pattern` element that identifies the URLs that should be protected, an optional `http-method` element that designates the HTTP commands to which the protection applies (`GET`, `POST`, etc.; the default is all methods), and an optional `description` element that provides documentation. For example, the following `web-resource-collection` entry (within a `security-constraint` element) designates that all documents in the **proprietary** directory of the Web application should be protected.

```
<security-constraint>
  <web-resource-collection>
    <web-resource-name>Proprietary</web-resource-name>
    <url-pattern>/proprietary/*</url-pattern>
  </web-resource-collection>
  <!-- ... -->
</security-constraint>
```

It is important to note that the `url-pattern` applies only to clients that access the resources directly. In particular, it does not apply to pages that are accessed through the MVC architecture with a `RequestDispatcher` or by the similar means of `jsp:forward`. This asymmetry is good if used properly. For example, with the MVC architecture a servlet looks up data, places it in beans, and forwards the request to a JSP page that extracts the data from the beans and displays it. You want to ensure that the JSP page is never accessed directly but instead is accessed only through the servlet that sets up the beans the page will use. The `url-pattern` and `auth-constraint` (see next subsection) elements can provide this guarantee by declaring that no user is permitted direct access to the JSP page. However, this asymmetric behavior can catch developers off guard and allow them to accidentally provide unrestricted access to resources that should be protected.

Core Warning

These protections apply only to direct client access. The security model does not apply to pages accessed by means of a RequestDispatcher or jsp:forward.

auth-constraint

Whereas the web-resource-collection element designates which URLs should be protected, the auth-constraint element designates which users should have access to protected resources. It should contain one or more role-name elements identifying the class of users that have access and, optionally, a description element describing the role. All role names that appear in web.xml specified with the role-name subelement of the auth-constraint element must be globally declared under the secu-rity-role element. The security-role element goes directly under the web-app element. It contains one or more role-name subelements. For instance, the following part of the security-constraint element in web.xml states that only users who are designated as either Administrators or Big Kahunas (or both) should have access to the designated resource.

```
<security-constraint>
  <web-resource-collection>...</web-resource-collection>
  <auth-constraint>
    <role-name>administrator</role-name>
    <role-name>kahuna</role-name>
  </auth-constraint>
</security-constraint>
<security-role>
  <role-name>administrator</role-name>
  <role-name>kahuna</role-name>
</security-role>
```

It is important to realize that this is the point at which the portable portion of the process ends. How a server determines which users are in which roles and how it stores user passwords is completely system dependent. See Section 3.1 (Form-Based Authentication) for the details on the approach used by Tomcat.

For example, by default Tomcat uses *install_dir*/conf/tomcat-users.xml to associate usernames with role names and passwords, as in the following example that designates users joe (with password bigshot) and jane (with password enaj) as belonging to the administrator and/or kahuna roles.

```
<tomcat-users>
  <user name="joe"
        password="bigshot" roles="administrator,kahuna" />
```

```
<user name="jane"
      password="enaj" roles="kahuna" />
<!-- ... -->
</tomcat-users>
```

Core Warning

Container-managed security requires a significant server-specific component. In particular, you must use nonportable methods to associate passwords with usernames and to map usernames to role names.

user-data-constraint

This optional element indicates which transport-level protections should be used when the associated resource is accessed. It must contain a transport-guarantee subelement (with legal values NONE, INTEGRAL, or CONFIDENTIAL) and may optionally contain a description element. A value of NONE (the default) for transport-guarantee puts no restrictions on the communication protocol used. A value of INTEGRAL means that the communication must be of a variety that prevents data from being changed in transit without detection. A value of CONFIDENTIAL means that the data must be transmitted in a way that prevents anyone who intercepts it from reading it. Although in principle (and in future HTTP versions) there may be a distinction between INTEGRAL and CONFIDENTIAL, in current practice they both simply mandate the use of SSL. For example, the following instructs the server to only permit HTTPS connections to the associated resource:

```
<security-constraint>
  <!-- ... -->
  <user-data-constraint>
    <transport-guarantee>CONFIDENTIAL</transport-guarantee>
  </user-data-constraint>
</security-constraint>
```

display-name

This rarely used subelement of security-constraint gives a name to the security constraint entry that might be used by a GUI tool.

Assigning Role Names

Up to this point, the discussion has focused on security that was completely managed by the container (server). Servlets and JSP pages, however, can also manage their own security. For details, see Chapter 4 (Programmatic Security).

For example, the container might let users from either the `bigwig` or `bigcheese` role access a page showing executive perks, but permit only the `bigwig` users to modify the page's parameters. One common way to accomplish this more fine-grained control is to call the `isUserInRole("someRoleName")` method of `HttpServletRequest` and modify access accordingly (for an example, see Section 4.1). The `someRoleName` role used in the `isUserInRole` method usually refers to one of the role names declared inside the `security-role` element. However, it can also refer to the value of the `role-name` subelement of the `security-role-ref` element.

The `security-role-ref` is a subelement of `servlet`, which provides an alias for a security role name that appears in the list of security role names under the `security-role` element. For instance, suppose you acquired a precompiled third-party servlet that was written to call `request.isUserInRole("boss")`. However, in your Web application you've declared and have been using `"manager"` to refer to the same concept. The following would permit the third-party servlet to use `"boss"` to refer to the `"manager"` role declared in your Web app.

```
<servlet>
  <!-- ... -->
  <security-role-ref>
    <role-name>boss</role-name>     <!-- New alias -->
    <role-link>manager</role-link>  <!-- Declared name -->
  </security-role-ref>
</servlet>
<security-role>
  <role-name>manager</role-name>
</security-role>
```

2.11 Controlling Session Timeouts

If a session has not been accessed for a certain period of time, the server can throw it away to save memory. You can explicitly set the timeout for individual session objects by using the `setMaxInactiveInterval` method of `HttpSession`. If you do not use this method, the default timeout is server specific. However, the `session-config` and `session-timeout` elements can be used to give an explicit timeout that will apply on all servers. The units are minutes, so the following example sets the default session timeout to three hours (180 minutes).

```
<session-config>
  <session-timeout>180</session-timeout>
</session-config>
```

There are two small inconsistencies between the `session-config` method of setting the session timeout and using the `setMaxInactiveInterval` method of `HttpSession`. First, the value of the `session-timeout` subelement is specified in minutes, whereas the value of `setMaxInactiveInterval` is specified in seconds. Second, if `session-timeout` is specified as either 0 or a negative number, the session will never expire, but only the negative number passed to `setMaxInac-tiveInterval` will accomplish the same result.

2.12 Documenting Web Applications

More and more development environments are starting to provide explicit support for servlets and JSP. Examples include Borland JBuilder Enterprise Edition, Oracle JDeveloper, Dreamweaver, MyEclipseIDE, NitroX, Sun Java Studio Creator, WebLogic Workshop, and others.

A number of the web.xml elements are designed not for the server, but for the visual development environment. These include `icon`, `display-name`, and `description`.

icon

The `icon` element designates the location of either one or two image files that the GUI tool can use to represent the Web application. A 16 × 16 GIF or JPEG image can be specified with the `small-icon` element, and a 32 × 32 image can be specified with `large-icon`. Here is an example:

```
<icon>
  <small-icon>/WEB-INF/images/small-book.gif</small-icon>
  <large-icon>/WEB-INF/images/tome.jpg</large-icon>
</icon>
```

Because these images are only used by the IDEs, they are never served to the client (e.g., a browser), you are allowed to store them inside the protected WEB-INF directory.

display-name

The `display-name` element provides a name that the GUI tools might use to label this particular Web application. Here is an example:

```
<display-name>Rare Books</display-name>
```

description

The description element provides explanatory text, as shown here:

```
<description>
This Web application represents the store developed for
rare-books.com, an online bookstore specializing in rare
and limited-edition books.
</description>
```

2.13 Associating Files with MIME Types

Servers typically have a way for Webmasters to associate file extensions with media types. So, for example, a file named mom.jpg would automatically be given a MIME type of image/jpeg. However, suppose that your Web application has unusual files that you want to guarantee are assigned a certain MIME type when sent to clients. The mime-mapping element, with extension and mime-type subelements, can provide this guarantee. For example, the following code instructs the server to assign a MIME type of application/x-fubar to all files that end in .foo.

```
<mime-mapping>
  <extension>foo</extension>
  <mime-type>application/x-fubar</mime-type>
</mime-mapping>
```

Or, perhaps your Web application wants to override standard mappings. For instance, the following would tell the server to designate .ps files as plain text (text/plain) rather than as PostScript (application/postscript) when sending them to clients.

```
<mime-mapping>
  <extension>ps</extension>
  <mime-type>text/plain</mime-type>
</mime-mapping>
```

For more information on MIME types, see http://www.iana.org/assignments/media-types/.

2.14 Configuring JSP Pages

The `jsp-config` element is used to provide configuration information for the JSP pages in a Web application. It has two subelements, `taglib` and `jsp-property-group`. Both subelements can appear zero or more times under the `jsp-config` element, but any of the `taglib` subelements must appear before any of the `jsp-property-group` subelements. Each one is discussed in the following subsections.

Locating Tag Library Descriptors

The JSP `taglib` directive has a required `uri` attribute that gives the location of a TLD file relative to the Web application root. The actual name of the TLD file might change when a new version of the tag library is released, but you might want to avoid changing all the existing JSP pages. Furthermore, you might want to use a short `uri` to keep the `taglib` directives concise. That's where the deployment descriptor's `taglib` element comes in. It contains two subelements: `taglib-uri` and `taglib-location`. The `taglib-uri` element should exactly match whatever is used for the `uri` attribute of the JSP `taglib` directive. The `taglib-location` element gives the real location of the TLD file. For example, suppose that you place the file chart-tags-1.3beta.tld in *yourWebApp*/WEB-INF/tlds. Now, suppose that web.xml contains the following within the web-app element:

```
<jsp-config>
  <taglib>
    <taglib-uri>/charts</taglib-uri>
    <taglib-location>
      /WEB-INF/tlds/chart-tags-1.3beta.tld
    </taglib-location>
  </taglib>
</jsp-config>
```

Given this specification, JSP pages can now make use of the tag library by means of the following simplified form:

```
<% taglib uri="/charts" prefix="somePrefix" %>
```

When the next version of the charts tag becomes available, you will only have to update the `taglib-location` element. The `taglib` directive used in your JSP pages can stay unchanged.

Also note that the `taglib` element appears inside the `jsp-config` element in web.xml version 2.4, whereas version 2.3 of web.xml requires this element to be directly under the web-app root element.

Configuring JSP Page Properties

JSP page properties are configured using one or more `jsp-property-group` elements. The properties specified within each `jsp-property-group` apply only to the URLs matched by the `url-pattern` subelement mapping. You can list more than one `url-pattern` subelement, but all of them have to appear before any other subelement of `jsp-property-group`. The rest of the `jsp-property-group` subelements are optional. The following is a list of all `jsp-property-group` subelements and their usages. These subelements have to appear (if at all) in the following order.

url-pattern

The `url-pattern` element contains the mapping used to match URLs to JSP pages. All other configuration properties specified within `jsp-property-group` apply only to the JSP pages matched by the `url-pattern` element. Recall that there can be more than one `url-pattern` element specified as long as all of them appear before any other `jsp-property-group` subelements. Here, the `url-pattern` element works exactly the same way it works when used as a subelement of the `servlet-mapping` element discussed in Section 2.4 (Assigning Names and Custom URLs). Note that the URLs specified by this element are not resolved by the client, but the server. Thus, it's perfectly legal to specify a URL containing the protected WEB-INF directory. For example, the following web.xml snippet will apply configuration properties to all JSP pages found inside the WEB-INF/myjsps folder.

```
<jsp-config>
  <jsp-property-group>
    <url-pattern>/WEB-INF/myjsps/*</url-pattern>
    <!-- ... -->
  </jsp-property-group>
</jsp-config>
```

el-ignored

The `el-ignored` element can be set to either `true` or `false` (e.g., `<el-ignored>true</el-ignored>`).When set to `true`, the affected pages turn off JSP Expression Language (EL) processing and treat JSP EL as regular text. This could be useful if some of the pages are inherited from a Web application compliant with the servlet 2.3 or earlier specification. Such pages could have unintentionally used $ { and \ $ as regular text. If you wish to turn off JSP EL for just a few pages, it might be more convenient to use the `isELIgnored` attribute of the page directive as follows:

```
<%@ page isELIgnored="true" %>
```

The page directive's isELIgnored attribute value overrides the value speci-fied in jsp-property-group. The default value for el-ignored is false.

page-encoding

The page-encoding element specifies the character encoding to be used by the JSP pages in this property group (e.g., <page-encoding>ISO-8859-1 </page-encoding>).The valid values for this element are the same as the values for the pageEncoding attribute of the page directive. It is a transla-tion time error to specify a different encoding through the jsp-property-group element than any other means. For example, if the character encoding specified inside the jsp-property-group element is ISO-8859-1, but inside the JSP page you specify UTF-8, the server will not be able to translate this JSP page into Java code, reporting an error. If you need to specify page encoding for just a few pages, it might be more convenient to use the pageEncoding attribute as follows:

```
<%@ page pageEncoding="UTF-8" %>
```

The default encoding is ISO-8859-1.

scripting-invalid

The scripting-invalid element can be set to either true or false (e.g., <scripting-invalid>true</scripting-invalid>).When set to true, the server will produce a translation time error if any JSP page in this property group uses scripting declarations, scriptlets, or scripting expressions. Because using MVC and the JSP 2.0 EL generally produces cleaner JSP page code than does explicit JSP scripting, the scripting-invalid element can be used to enforce this practice across the development team. The default value is false.

is-xml

The is-xml element can be set to either true or false (e.g., <is-xml> true</is-xml>). If set to true, this tells the server that the group of resources that match the URL pattern of this property group are to be treated as JSP Documents. A JSP Document is a JSP page that contains only valid XML code. If the server encounters a resource within this property group that is not a JSP Document, it will not be able to parse it. A regular JSP page con-tains JSP as well as HTML code. Even if your HTML code is not correct (e.g., some end tag is missing), the server will still successfully parse it and produce the Java code to output the erroneous HTML code to the client. You will not be able to detect your error until the page displays in a browser and you notice that something is visually wrong. On the other hand, enforcing a set of JSP pages to contain valid XML avoids this problem. If false, the resources are assumed to not be JSP documents, unless there is another property group that indicates otherwise. The default is `false`.

include-prelude

The `include-prelude` element contains a context-relative path that must correspond to a resource in the Web application. When the resource is present, the given path will be automatically included, using the static `include` directive, at the beginning of each JSP page in the `jsp-property-group`. This capability can be useful if you want to provide a standard header in multiple pages of your application. Rather than having to specify `<%@ include file="header.jsp" %>` for each page, you can use the `include-prelude` element to specify this header for the entire group of JSP pages. For an example of this, please see Listings 2.24 through 2.28 and Figure 2–22.

include-coda

The `include-coda` element contains a context-relative path that must correspond to a resource in the Web application. When the resource is present, the given path will be automatically included, using the static `include` directive, at the end of each JSP page in this `jsp-property-group`. Similar to the `include-prelude` element, this can be useful if you want to provide a standard footer across multiple pages in your application. Rather than having to specify `<%@ include file="footer.jsp" %>` for each page, you can use the `include-coda` element to specify this footer for the entire group of JSP pages. For an example of this, please see Listings 2.24 through 2.28 and Figure 2–22.

Here is an example of a typical configuration. Listing 2.24 shows an excerpt from the web.xml file. The excerpt indicates that the configurations will apply to all files located in the /WEB-INF/jspPages/ustm directory. In this configuration we are instructing the server to include a header and a footer with every resource served from that directory. Listings 2.25 and 2.26 show the complete code for USTM-Header.jsp and USTMFooter.jsp, respectively. Listing 2.27 shows the complete code for the target of our configuration, USTMBody.jsp, which is located in the /WEB-INF/jspPages/ustm directory. Note that USTMHeader.jsp, USTMBody.jsp, and USTM-Footer.jsp do not produce valid HTML code by themselves. Each one is a snippet of code that only makes sense in the context of all three, and only in the proper order—USTMHeader.jsp, USTMBody.jsp, and then USTMFooter.jsp. Figure 2–22 shows the result of the custom mapped URL invoking the USTMBody.jsp page. Also note that because we configured JSP EL to be ignored, `${money}` is interpreted as regular text. Finally, Listing 2.28 shows the generated HTML code as the result of our invocation.

Listing 2.24   web.xml (Excerpt showing jsp-property-group)

```xml
<?xml version="1.0" encoding="ISO-8859-1"?>
<web-app xmlns="http://java.sun.com/xml/ns/j2ee"
         xmlns:xsi="http://www.w3.org/2001/XMLSchema-instance"
         xsi:schemaLocation=
         "http://java.sun.com/xml/ns/j2ee
          http://java.sun.com/xml/ns/j2ee/web-app_2_4.xsd"
         version="2.4">

  <servlet>
    <servlet-name>USTMHomePage</servlet-name>
    <jsp-file>
      /WEB-INF/jspPages/ustm/USTMBody.jsp
    </jsp-file>
  </servlet>
  <servlet-mapping>
    <servlet-name>USTMHomePage</servlet-name>
    <url-pattern>/ustm</url-pattern>
  </servlet-mapping>

  <!-- Every page inside WEB-INF/jspPages/ustm should
       include USTMHeader.jsp at the top and
       USTMFooter.jsp at the bottom -->
  <jsp-config>
    <jsp-property-group>
      <url-pattern>/WEB-INF/jspPages/ustm/*</url-pattern>
      <el-ignored>true</el-ignored>
      <include-prelude>
        /WEB-INF/jspPages/USTMHeader.jsp
      </include-prelude>
      <include-coda>
        /WEB-INF/jspPages/USTMFooter.jsp
      </include-coda>
    </jsp-property-group>
  </jsp-config>
  <!-- ... -->
</web-app>
```

Listing 2.25   USTMHeader.jsp

```
<!DOCTYPE HTML PUBLIC "-//W3C//DTD HTML 4.01 Transitional//EN">
<HTML>
<HEAD><TITLE>USTM Commission Home Page</TITLE></HEAD>

<BODY BGCOLOR="#FDF5E6">
<CENTER><H2 style="display:inline;">
Welcome to the USTM Commission Home Page!</H2><BR />
No tax dollars will be spared to save your hard-earned money!
&trade;</CENTER><P />
```

Listing 2.26   USTMFooter.jsp

```
<HR />
<CENTER><H4 style="display: inline;">&copy; 2005 USTM Commission
(United States Tax Misuse Commission)</H4></CENTER>
</BODY>
</HTML>
```

Listing 2.27   USTMBody.jsp

```
<B>This year's agenda:</B>
<UL>
<LI>Finish hearing countless expert testimonies on the concept of
"The more of your ${money} we spend, the less you have.
Why?"</LI>
<LI>Schedule hearings on the topic of "No matter what we do it's
bad for the economy."</LI>
<LI>Why it's crucial that we double the budget of this
commission to prolong hearings on these topics, which are
extremely important to every American.</LI>
</UL><P />
```

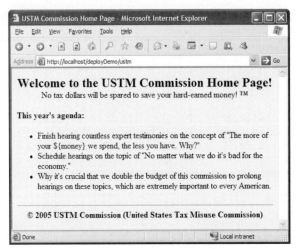

Figure 2–22   Result of invoking /WEB-INF/jspPages/ustm/USTMBody.jsp through a custom URL. **USTMHeader.jsp** is prepended and **USTMFooter.jsp** is appended per our **web**.xml configuration. The string $\{money\}$ shows up as text because we disabled EL processing.

Listing 2.28   Generated HTML from invoking /ustm

```
<!DOCTYPE HTML PUBLIC "-//W3C//DTD HTML 4.01 Transitional//EN">
<HTML>
<HEAD><TITLE>USTM Commission Home Page</TITLE></HEAD>

<BODY BGCOLOR="#FDF5E6">
<CENTER><H2 style="display:inline;">
Welcome to the USTM Commission Home Page!</H2><BR />
No tax dollars will be spared to save your hard-earned money!
&trade;</CENTER><P />
<B>This year's agenda:</B>
<UL>
<LI>Finish hearing countless expert testimonies on the concept of
"The more of your ${money} we spend, the less you have.
Why?"</LI>
<LI>Schedule hearings on the topic of "No matter what we do it's
bad for the economy."</LI>
<LI>Why it's crucial that we double the budget of this
commission to prolong hearings on these topics, which are
extremely important to every American.</LI>
</UL><P /><HR />
<CENTER><H4 style="display: inline;">&copy; 2005 USTM Commission
(United States Tax Misuse Commission)</H4></CENTER>
</BODY>
</HTML>
```

2.15 Configuring Character Encoding

The locale and character encoding of the servlet response can be set explicitly by calling `setLocale` in combination with the `setContentType` and `setCharacterEncoding` methods of the `HttpServletResponse` object. If only the `setLocale` method is called, the character encoding used for the explicitly set locale is server dependent. For portability and convenience, the character encoding to be used for the particular locale can be specified in **web.xml** with the use of `locale-encoding-mapping-list`. The `locale-encoding-mapping-list` element is a subelement of the root web-app element, and contains one or more `locale-encoding-mapping` elements. The `locale-encoding-mapping` element contains the `locale` and `encoding` elements as follows:

```
<locale-encoding-mapping-list>
  <locale-encoding-mapping>
    <locale>ja</locale>
    <encoding>Shift_JIS</encoding>
  </locale-encoding-mapping>
  <locale-encoding-mapping>
    <locale>he</locale>
    <encoding>windows-1255</encoding>
  </locale-encoding-mapping>
</locale-encoding-mapping-list>
```

2.16 Designating Application Event Listeners

Application event listeners are classes that are notified when some event in the Web application life cycle occurs. Examples of life-cycle events would include a notification when the servlet context or a session object is created or modified. There are other life-cycle events that have listener classes associated with them. They are discussed in detail in Chapter 6 (The Application Events Framework). Here, though, we just want to briefly illustrate the use of the **web.xml** elements that are used to register a listener with the Web application.

Registering a listener involves simply placing a `listener` element inside the web-app element of **web.xml**. Inside the `listener` element, a `listener-class` element lists the fully qualified class name of the listener, as follows:

```
<listener>
  <listener-class>package.ListenerClass</listener-class>
</listener>
```

For example, Listing 2.29 shows a simple listener called `ContextReporter` that prints a message on the standard output whenever the Web application's `Servlet-Context` is created (e.g., the Web application is loaded) or destroyed (e.g., the server is shut down). Listing 2.30 shows the portion of the web.xml file that is required for registration of the listener.

Listing 2.29 ContextReporter.java

```
package coreservlets;

import javax.servlet.*;
import java.util.*;

/** Simple listener that prints a report on the standard output
 *  when the ServletContext is created or destroyed.
 */

public class ContextReporter implements ServletContextListener {
  public void contextInitialized(ServletContextEvent event) {
    System.out.println("Context created on " +
                       new Date() + ".");
  }

  public void contextDestroyed(ServletContextEvent event) {
    System.out.println("Context destroyed on " +
                       new Date() + ".");
  }
}
```

Listing 2.30 web.xml (Excerpt declaring a listener)

```
<?xml version="1.0" encoding="ISO-8859-1"?>
<web-app xmlns="http://java.sun.com/xml/ns/j2ee"
         xmlns:xsi="http://www.w3.org/2001/XMLSchema-instance"
         xsi:schemaLocation=
         "http://java.sun.com/xml/ns/j2ee
          http://java.sun.com/xml/ns/j2ee/web-app_2_4.xsd"
         version="2.4">

  <!-- Turn on the ContextReporter. -->
  <listener>
    <listener-class>coreservlets.ContextReporter</listener-class>
  </listener>
  <!-- ... -->
</web-app>
```

2.17 Developing for the Clustered Environment

Enterprise-level Web applications are required to handle tens of thousands of concurrent user activities. It would be close to impossible to have a machine powerful enough to process that many requests by itself. It would certainly be extremely expensive to purchase such a machine. In addition, if that enormously powerful machine broke, it would mean downtime for the Web site hosted on that machine. For high-traffic Web sites like Amazon or eBay, this downtime would amount to millions of dollars of lost revenue an hour.

To address this problem, enterprise-level applications are deployed in a clustered environment. A clustered environment usually consists of many machines connected through the local area network (LAN) and sometimes even through the wide area network (WAN). Usually, a hardware load balancer is placed in front of all of these machines. The load balancer receives a request from the client and decides which machine in the cluster to forward this request to based on a preconfigured set of algorithms. In general, this keeps each machine in the cluster equally loaded, so no single machine's resources are exhausted. Software-based load balancers exist as well. For example, Tomcat comes bundled with a software-based load balancer, which resides as a Web application in *tomcat_dir*/webapps/balancer.

In this environment, it is quite possible for a client to be served by different machines from one request to another. Yet, to the client, it all looks like a single Web application. For example, you can be served by *machine A* to display a list of items in your online shopping cart. When you click the Complete Purchase button, it might be *machine B* that sends the Payment Options screen to your browser. The information about who you are as a user as well as your session data is shared between *machine A* and *machine B*.

This behavior is achieved by sharing the `HttpSession` among the machines in the cluster. Even though each machine in the cluster has its own Java Virtual Machine (JVM), the `HttpSession` object gets copied and shared among the cluster.

Because clustered Web applications run in multiple JVMs, you may not rely on the usual mechanisms of sharing data used in regular Web applications. The following is a list of the things you should remember when developing a Web application that might be deployed in a clustered environment.

1. **Avoid instance variables and static data (such as singletons) for shared data.** Each JVM in a cluster will have its own copy of the instance variables and static data. Changes to this data in one JVM will leave all other JVMs unaffected. However, if you are certain that the static data never changes throughout the execution of your Web app, it's perfectly fine to use static data (and singletons) to share data

among the resources in your Web application (not different deployments on different machines in the cluster). In this case, it doesn't matter that each JVM has its own copy of this data because it would be the same on all machines in the cluster.

2. **Don't store data in the `ServletContext`.** Each JVM in a cluster has its own copy of the `ServletContext`. Therefore, if you store an attribute in the `ServletContext`, the `ServletContext` object of other servers (JVMs) will not contain this attribute. However, you can use the `ServletContext` to share data that is guaranteed to stay unchanged among the resources in your Web application (not different deployments on different machines in the cluster). This data would have to be placed into the `ServletContext` immediately at startup of the Web application. This initialization can be accomplished with a servlet that is guaranteed to be loaded at server startup by the `load-on-startup` element of web.xml (see Section 2.6). The initialization can also be accomplished with the `ServletContextListener`'s `contextInitialized` method. For example, if several pages in your application need a drop-down box with a prefilled list of countries that are stored in a database, you can initialize and store this list in the `ServletContext` inside the `contextInitialized` method of the `ServletContextListener`. For a detailed discussion of listeners, please see Chapter 6 (The Application Events Framework).

3. **Objects stored in `HttpSession` must implement Serializable.** The servlet specification requires compliant Web containers to support migration of objects stored in the `HttpSession` that implement the `Serializable` interface. If the objects stored in the `HttpSession` do not implement the `Serializable` interface, the container may fail to migrate the session. If this failure happens, the container will throw an `IllegalArgumentException`. Also note that the class implementing the `Serializable` interface has to follow regular serialization guidelines. For more information, please go to http://java.sun.com/j2se/1.5.0/docs/guide/serialization/.

4. **Only minimal information should be stored in `HttpSession`.** For a clustered environment to function as a single Web application, the data stored in the `HttpSession` must be kept in sync with the other servers in the cluster. This is achieved by sending the data back and forth between the servers. Naturally, this consumes a lot of resources. Therefore, storing a lot of data in the `HttpSession` could considerably degrade the performance of your Web application even when the request load is not very high.

In the deployment descriptor, web.xml, the `distributable` element indicates that the Web application is programmed in such a way that servers that support clustering can safely distribute the Web application across multiple servers. The `distributable` element contains no subelements or data—it is simply a flag (as follows):

```
<distributable />
```

One of the prime features of a J2EE application is its scalability. The idea of scalability is that the same code written to serve 100 users per day can serve tens of thousands of users per second. Think of a music CD. The same music CD that you use in your portable CD player with headphones can be inserted into a huge amplifying system with many speakers and played for an entire stadium containing thousands of people. All that's changed is the hardware you plugged the CD into. If there is a possibility that your Web application will need to handle many more users in the future, and you don't take the previously mentioned guidelines into account, the result might be an expensive rewrite of your application.

2.18 J2EE Elements

This section describes the web.xml elements that are used for Web applications that are part of a full J2EE environment. We provide a brief summary here; for details, see Chapter 5 of the Java 2 Platform Enterprise Edition version 1.4 specification at http://java.sun.com/j2ee/j2ee-1_4-fr-spec.pdf.

resource-env-ref
The `resource-env-ref` element declares an administered object associated with a resource. It consists of an optional `description` element, a `resource-env-ref-name` element (a Java Naming and Directory Interface [JNDI] name relative to the `java:comp/env` context), and a `resource-env-type` element (the fully qualified class designating the type of the resource), as follows:

```
<resource-env-ref>
  <resource-env-ref-name>
    jms/StockQueue
  </resource-env-ref-name>
  <resource-env-ref-type>
    javax.jms.Queue
  </resource-env-ref-type>
</resource-env-ref>
```

resource-ref

The `resource-ref` element declares an external resource used with a resource factory. It consists of an optional `description` element, a `res-ref-name` element (the resource manager connection-factory reference name), a `res-type` element (the fully qualified class name of the factory type), a `res-auth` element (the type of authentication used—`Application` or `Container`), and an optional `res-sharing-scope` element (a specification of the shareability of connections obtained from the resource—`Shareable` or `Unshareable`.) Here is an example:

```
<resource-ref>
  <res-ref-name>jdbc/EmployeeAppDB</res-ref-name>
  <res-type>javax.sql.DataSource</res-type>
  <res-auth>Container</res-auth>
  <res-sharing-scope>Shareable</res-sharing-scope>
</resource-ref>
```

env-entry

The `env-entry` element declares the Web application's environment entry. It consists of an optional `description` element, an `env-entry-name` element (a JNDI name relative to the `java:comp/env` context), an `env-entry-value` element (the entry value), and an `env-entry-type` element (the fully qualified class name of a type). Valid values for `env-entry-type` are `java.lang.Boolean`, `java.lang.Byte`, `java.lang.Character`, `java.lang.String`, `java.lang.Short`, `java.lang.Integer`, `java.lang.Long`, `java.lang.Float`, and `java.lang.Double`. Here is an example:

```
<env-entry>
  <env-entry-name>minAmount</env-entry-name>
  <env-entry-value>100.00</env-entry-value>
  <env-entry-type>java.lang.Double</env-entry-type>
</env-entry>
```

ejb-ref

The `ejb-ref` element declares a reference to the home interface of an enterprise bean. It consists of an optional `description` element, an `ejb-ref-name` element (the name of the EJB reference relative to `java:comp/env`), an `ejb-ref-type` element (the type of the bean—`Entity` or `Session`), a `home` element (the fully qualified name of the bean's home interface), a `remote` element (the fully qualified name of the bean's remote interface), and an optional `ejb-link` element (the name of another bean, from a different jar file, to which the current bean is linked). The path name specified by the `ejb-link` element has to be relative to the location of the WAR file of your Web application followed by "#" and the registered name of the bean. Here is an example:

```
<ejb-ref>
  <ejb-ref-name>ejb/FireEveryoneRemoteHome</ejb-ref-name>
  <ejb-ref-type>Session</ejb-ref-type>
  <home>humanresources.FireEveryoneRemoteHome</home>
  <remote>humanresources.FireEveryoneRemote</remote>
  <ejb-link>cheating.jar#SellCEOStockEJB</ejb-link>
</ejb-ref>
```

ejb-local-ref

The `ejb-local-ref` element declares a reference to the local home interface of an enterprise bean. It has the same attributes and is used in the same way as the `ejb-ref` element, with the exception that `local-home` is used in place of home as follows:

```
<ejb-local-ref>
  <ejb-ref-name>ejb/CutSalaryLocal</ejb-ref-name>
  <ejb-ref-type>Session</ejb-ref-type>
  <local-home>humanresources.CutSalaryLocalHome</local-home>
  <local>humanresources.CutSalaryLocal</local>
  <ejb-link>uppermanagement.jar#BeanCounterLocal</ejb-link>
</ejb-local-ref>
```

service-ref

The `service-ref` element declares a reference to a Web Service as follows:

```
<service-ref>
  <description>Weather Forecast Service Client</description>
  <display-name>Weather Service Client</display-name>
  <icon>
    <small-icon>weather16x16.gif</small-icon>
    <large-icon>weather32x32.gif</large-icon>
  </icon>
  <service-ref-name>services/myWeather</service-ref-name>
  <service-interface>
    javax.xml.rpc.Service
  </service-interface>
  <wsdl-file>WEB-INF/wsdl/weatherForecast.wsdl</wsdl-file>
  <jaxrpc-mapping-file>
    WEB-INF/weatherServiceMapping.xml
  </jaxrpc-mapping-file>

  <service-qname>
    <namespaceURI>
      http://ws.myweatherservice.com
```

```
      </namespaceURI>
      <localpart>MyWeatherService</localpart>
    </service-qname>

    <port-component-ref>
      <service-endpoint-interface>
        com.myweatherservice.ws.beans.endpoint.MyWeather
      </service-endpoint-interface>
      <port-component-link>
        nationalWeather.jar#LocalizedWeather
      </port-component-link>
    </port-component-ref>

    <handler>
      <handler-name>MyWeatherHandler</handler-name>
      <handler-class>
        com.mycentralportal.handlers.MyWeatherHandler
      </handler-class>
      <init-param>
        <param-name>localState</param-name>
        <param-value>OH</param-value>
      </init-param>
      <soap-header>
        <namespaceURI>
          http://ws.myweatherservice.com
        </namespaceURI>
        <localpart>MyWeatherHeader</localpart>
      </soap-header>
      <soap-role>
        http://actor.soap.myweatherservice.com
      </soap-role>
      <port-name>myWeatherPort</port-name>
    </handler>
  </service-ref>
```

The optional `description`, `display-name`, and `icon` elements are there for IDEs and documentation. The JNDI name that will be used in your code to look up the Web Service is specified by the `service-ref-name` element (relative to the `java:comp/env` context). The `service-interface` element specifies the fully qualified JAX-RPC interface name that your Web application depends on. Usually, this will be `javax.xml.rpc.Service`. The optional `wsdl-file` element contains the location (relative to the root directory of the Web app) of the Web Services Description Language (WSDL) file. This file has to be placed inside of the WEB-INF/wsdl directory.

The optional `jaxrpc-mapping-file` element contains the location of the file that maps the WSDL definition to the Service Endpoint Interface and Service Interface.

The optional `service-qname` element and its two subelements
(`namespaceURI` and `localpart`) declare the specific WSDL Service element that is being referred to. It is omitted if the `wsdl-file` element is not
specified or if the WSDL file contains only one service.

The `port-component-ref` element declares a client dependency on the
container for resolving a Service Endpoint Interface to a WSDL port. It optionally associates the Service Endpoint Interface with a particular port-component.
It contains the `service-endpoint-interface` element and the optional
`port-component-link` element. The `service-endpoint-interface`
element defines a fully qualified name of the class that represents the Service
Endpoint Interface of a WSDL port. The `port-component-link` element
links a `port-component-ref` to a specific port component required to be
made available by the service reference.

The optional `handler` element declares the handler for the port component. It contains the required elements `handler-name` and `handler-
class`, and the optional elements `init-param`, `soap-header`, `soap-role`,
and `port-name`. The `handler-name` element defines the name of the handler (unique within web.xml). The `handler-class` element defines the fully
qualified class name of the handler implementation. The `init-param` element contains `param-name` and `param-value` elements that define parameters that the handler can retrieve and use during its initialization process. The
`soap-header` element defines the QName of the Simple Object Access Protocol (SOAP) header that will be processed by the handler. The `soap-role`
element contains the SOAP actor definition that the handler will play as a role.
The `port-name` element defines the WSDL port name with which the handler should be associated.

message-destination-ref

The `message-destination-ref` element contains a declaration of a reference to a message destination associated with a resource declared in web.xml.
It consists of optional `description` and required `message-destination-
ref-name`, `message-destination-type`, and `message-destination-
usage`, and optional `message-destination-link` elements. The `message-
destination-ref-name` element specifies the JNDI name (relative to the
`java:comp/env` context) of a message destination reference. This name must
be unique within web.xml. The `message-destination-type` element
specifies the type of the destination, which can be either `javax.jms.Queue`
or `javax.jms.Topic`. The `message-destination-usage` specifies the
use of the message destination indicated by the reference. Its value indicates
whether messages are consumed from the message destination, produced
for the destination, or both (valid values are `Consumes`, `Produces`, or
`ConsumesProduces`). The `message-destination-link` is used to link
a message destination reference to a message destination. Its value must be

declared by the `message-destination-name` element of the `message-destination` element in the same web.xml file or in another deployment descriptor in the same J2EE application unit. Here is an example:

```
<message-destination-ref>
  <message-destination-ref-name>
    jms/StockQueue
  </message-destination-ref-name>
  <message-destination-type>
    javax.jms.Queue
  </message-destination-type>
  <message-destination-usage>
    Consumes
  </message-destination-usage>
  <message-destination-link>
    CorporateStocks
  </message-destination-link>
</message-destination-ref>
```

message-destination

The `message-destination` specifies a logical message destination that is mapped to a physical destination in the server-specific deployment descriptor. It contains three optional elements (`description`, `display-name`, and `icon`) and one required element—`message-destination-name`. The `message-destination-name` element specifies a unique (within web.xml) name for a message destination. There should be a `message-destination` declared for every destination used in this web.xml file. Here is an example:

```
<message-destination>
  <message-destination-name>
    CorporateStocks
  </message-destination-name>
</message-destination>
```

DECLARATIVE
SECURITY

Topics in This Chapter

- Understanding the major aspects of Web application security
- Authenticating users with HTML forms
- Using BASIC HTTP authentication
- Defining passwords in Tomcat
- Designating protected resources with the `security-constraint` element
- Using `login-config` to specify the authentication method
- Mandating the use of SSL
- Configuring Tomcat to use SSL
- Talking to Web servers interactively
- Creating your own Certificate Authority
- Signing a server certificate

Chapter 3

There are two major aspects to securing Web applications:

1. **Preventing unauthorized users from accessing sensitive data.**
   This process involves *access restriction* (identifying which resources
   need protection and who should have access to them) and *authentication* (identifying users to determine if they are one of the authorized
   ones). Simple authentication involves the user entering a username
   and password in an HTML form or a dialog box; stronger authentication involves the use of X.509 certificates sent by the client to the
   server. The first aspect of Web security applies to virtually all secure
   applications. Even intranets at locations with physical access controls
   usually require some sort of user authentication.

2. **Preventing attackers from stealing network data while it is in
   transit.** This process involves the use of Secure Sockets Layer (SSL)
   to encrypt the traffic between the browser and the server. This capability is generally reserved for particularly sensitive applications or for
   particularly sensitive pages within a larger application. After all, unless
   the attackers are on your local subnet, it is exceedingly difficult for
   them to gain access to your network traffic.

These two security aspects are mostly independent. The approaches to access
restriction are the same regardless of whether or not you use SSL. With the exception of client certificates (which apply only to SSL), the approaches to authentication
are also identical whether or not you use SSL.

Within the Web application framework, there are two general approaches to this type of security:

1. **Declarative security.** With declarative security, the topic of this chapter, none of the individual servlets or JSP pages need any security-aware code. Instead, both of the major security aspects are handled by the server.

   To prevent unauthorized access, you use the Web application deployment descriptor (web.xml) to declare that certain URLs need protection, and which categories of users should have access to them. You also designate the authentication method that the server should use to identify users. At request time, the server automatically prompts users for usernames and passwords when they try to access restricted resources, automatically checks the results against a pre-defined set of usernames and passwords, and automatically keeps track of which users have previously been authenticated. This process is completely transparent to the servlets and JSP pages.

   To safeguard network data, you use the deployment descriptor to stipulate that certain URLs should only be accessible with SSL. If users try to use a regular HTTP connection to access one of these URLs, the server automatically redirects them to the HTTPS (SSL) equivalent.

2. **Programmatic security.** With programmatic security, the topic of the next chapter, protected servlets and JSP pages at least partially manage their own security.

   To prevent unauthorized access, each servlet or JSP page must either authenticate the user or verify that the user has been authenticated previously.

   To safeguard network data, each servlet or JSP page has to check the network protocol used to access it. If users try to use a regular HTTP connection to access one of these URLs, the servlet or JSP page must manually redirect them to the HTTPS (SSL) equivalent.

3.1   Form-Based Authentication

The most common type of declarative security uses regular HTML forms. The developer uses the deployment descriptor to identify the protected resources and to designate a page that has a form to collect usernames and passwords. A user who attempts to access protected resources is redirected to the page containing the form. When the form is submitted, the server checks the username and password against a list of usernames, passwords, and roles (categories of users). If the login is successful and the user belongs to a role that is permitted access to the page, the user is sent to the page originally requested. If the login is unsuccessful, the user is sent to a designated error page. Behind the scenes, the system uses some variation of session tracking to remember which users have already been validated.

The whole process is automatic: redirection to the login page, checking of usernames and passwords, redirection back to the original resource, and tracking of already authenticated users are all performed by the container (server) in a manner that is completely transparent to the individual resources. However, there is one major caveat: The servlet specification explicitly says that form-based authentication is not guaranteed to work when the server is set to perform session tracking based on URL rewriting instead of cookies (the default session-tracking mechanism).

Core Warning

Depending on your server, form-based authentication might fail when you use URL rewriting as the basis of session tracking.

This type of access restriction and authentication is completely independent of the protection of the network traffic. You can stipulate that SSL be used for all, some, or none of your application, but doing so does not change the way you restrict access or authenticate users, nor does the use of SSL require your individual servlets or JSP pages to participate in the security process; redirection to the URL that uses SSL and encryption/decryption of the network traffic are all performed by the server in a manner that is transparent to the servlets and JSP pages.

Eight basic steps are required to set up your system to use this type of form-based security. We summarize the steps here, then give details on each step in the following subsections. All the steps except for the first are standardized and portable across all servers that support version 2.2 or later of the servlet API. Section 3.2 (Example: Form-Based Authentication) illustrates the concepts with a small application.

1. **Set up usernames, passwords, and roles.** In this step, you designate a list of users and associate each with a password and one or more abstract roles (e.g., normal user or administrator). This is a completely server-specific process. In general, you'll have to read your server's documentation, but we summarize the process for Tomcat.
2. **Tell the server that you are using form-based authentication. Designate the locations of the login and login-failure page.** This process uses the `web.xml` `login-config` element with an `auth-method` subelement of `FORM` and a `form-login-config` subelement that gives the locations of the two pages.

3. **Create a login page.** This page must have a form with an ACTION of j_security_check, a METHOD of POST, a text field named j_username, and a password field named j_password.

4. **Create a page to report failed login attempts.** This page can simply say something like "username and password not found" and perhaps give a link back to the login page.

5. **Specify which URLs should be password protected.** For this step, you use the security-constraint element of web.xml. This element, in turn, uses web-resource-collection and auth-constraint subelements. The first of these (web-resource-collection) designates the URL patterns to which access should be restricted, and the second (auth-constraint) specifies the abstract roles that should have access to the resources at the given URLs.

6. **List all possible abstract roles (types of users) that will be grated access to *any* resource.** Each abstract role is declared using the security-role element. The security-role element contains the required role-name element, which contains the name of the abstract role.

7. **Specify which URLs should be available only with SSL.** If your server supports SSL, you can stipulate that certain resources are available *only* through encrypted HTTPS (SSL) connections. You use the user-data-constraint subelement of security-constraint for this purpose.

8. **Turn off the invoker servlet.** Security settings are based on URLs, so you protect servlets by listing their URLs within the web-resource-collection element. The servlet URLs, in turn, are normally defined with the url-pattern element of servlet-mapping. However, many servers also have a default servlet URL of the form http://*host*/*webAppPrefix*/servlet/*ServletName*. If you have this capability enabled, there are now two URLs that can invoke each servlet: the URL registered in servlet-mapping and the default (invoker servlet) URL. Remembering to protect both addresses is too hard. Instead, disable the invoker servlet, either globally for your server, or by mapping the /servlet/* pattern within your Web application.

Details follow.

Setting Up Usernames, Passwords, and Roles

When a user attempts to access a protected resource in an application that is using form-based authentication, the system automatically sends the user to an HTML form to ask for a username and password, verifies that the password matches the user, determines what abstract roles (regular user, administrator, executive, etc.) that user belongs to, and sees whether any of those roles has permission to access the resource. If so, the server redirects the user to the originally requested page. If not, the server redirects the user to an error page.

The good news regarding this process is that the server (container) does a lot of the work for you. The bad news is that the task of associating users with passwords and logical roles is server specific. So, although you would not have to change the web.xml file or any of the actual servlet and JSP code to move a secure Web application from system to system, you would still have to make custom changes on each system to set up the users and passwords.

In general, you will have to read your server's documentation to determine how to assign passwords and role membership to users. However, we summarize the process for Tomcat.

Setting Passwords with Tomcat

Tomcat permits advanced developers to configure custom username and password management schemes (e.g., accessing a database, looking in the UNIX /etc/passwd file, checking the Windows User Account settings, or making a Kerberos call). For details, see http://jakarta.apache.org/tomcat/tomcat-5.5-doc/realm-howto.html. However, this configuration is a lot of work, so Tomcat also provides a default mechanism for use in testing. With this mechanism, Tomcat stores usernames, passwords, and roles in *tomcat_dir*/conf/tomcat-users.xml. This file should contain an XML header followed by a tomcat-users element containing any number of role and user elements. Each role element should have a rolename attribute. Each user element should have three attributes: username, password (the plain text password), and roles (a comma-separated list of logical role names). Listing 3.1 presents a simple example that defines four users (valjean, bishop, javert, thenardier), each of whom belongs to two logical roles.

Note that the default Tomcat strategy of storing unencrypted passwords is a poor one for real deployed applications. First, an intruder who gains access to the server's file system can obtain all the passwords. Second, even system administrators who are authorized to access server resources should not be able to obtain users' passwords. In fact, because many users reuse passwords on multiple systems, passwords should never be stored in clear text. Instead, they should be encrypted with an algorithm that cannot easily be reversed. Then, when a user supplies a password, it is encrypted and the encrypted version is compared with the stored encrypted password. Nevertheless, the default Tomcat approach makes it easy to set up and test secure Web applications. Just keep in mind that for real applications you'll want to replace the simple file-based password scheme with something more robust (e.g., a database or a system call to Kerberos or the Windows User Account system).

| Listing 3.1 | *tomcat_dir*/conf/tomcat-users.xml (Sample) |

```
<?xml version='1.0' encoding='utf-8'?>
<tomcat-users>
  <role rolename="lowStatus" />
  <role rolename="highStatus" />
  <role rolename="nobleSpirited" />
  <role rolename="meanSpirited" />

  <user username="valjean" password="forgiven"
        roles="lowStatus,nobleSpirited" />
  <user username="bishop" password="mercy"
        roles="lowStatus,nobleSpirited" />
  <user username="javert" password="strict"
        roles="highStatus,meanSpirited" />
  <user username="thenardier" password="grab"
        roles="lowStatus,meanSpirited" />
</tomcat-users>
```

Telling the Server You Are Using Form-Based Authentication; Designating Locations of Login and Login-Failure Pages

You use the login-config element in the deployment descriptor (web.xml) to control the authentication method. Recall from Chapter 1 (Using and Deploying Web Applications) that this file goes in the WEB-INF directory of your Web application. Although a few servers support nonstandard web.xml files (e.g., Tomcat has one in *tomcat_dir*/conf that provides defaults for multiple Web applications), those files are entirely server specific. We are addressing only the standard version that goes in the Web application's WEB-INF directory.

To use form-based authentication, supply a value of FORM for the auth-method subelement and use the form-login-config subelement to give the locations of the login (form-login-page) and login-failure (form-error-page) pages. In the next sections we explain exactly what these two files should contain. For now, however, note that nothing mandates that they use dynamic content. Thus, these pages can consist of either JSP or ordinary HTML.

For example, Listing 3.2 shows part of a web.xml file that stipulates that the container use form-based authentication. Unauthenticated users who attempt to access protected resources will be redirected to http://*host*/*webAppPrefix*/login.jsp. If they log in successfully, they will be returned to whatever resource they first attempted to access. If their login attempt fails, they will be redirected to http://*host*/*webAppPrefix*/login-error.html.

web.xml (Excerpt designating form-based authentication)

```
<?xml version="1.0" encoding="ISO-8859-1"?>
<web-app xmlns="http://java.sun.com/xml/ns/j2ee"
         xmlns:xsi="http://www.w3.org/2001/XMLSchema-instance"
         xsi:schemaLocation=
         "http://java.sun.com/xml/ns/j2ee
          http://java.sun.com/xml/ns/j2ee/web-app_2_4.xsd"
         version="2.4">
  <security-constraint>...</security-constraint>
  <login-config>
    <auth-method>FORM</auth-method>
    <form-login-config>
      <form-login-page>/login.jsp</form-login-page>
      <form-error-page>/login-error.html</form-error-page>
    </form-login-config>
  </login-config>
</web-app>
```

Creating the Login Page

The login-config element tells the server to use form-based authentication and to redirect unauthenticated users to a designated page. Fine. But what should you put *in* that page? The answer is surprisingly simple: All the login page requires is a form with an ACTION of j_security_check, a text field named j_username, and a password field named j_password. And, because using GET defeats the whole point of password fields (protecting the password from prying eyes looking over the user's shoulder), all forms that have password fields should use a METHOD of POST. You never use GET with password fields because the password would show up in clear text in the browser's address bar. Note that j_security_check is a "magic" name; you don't preface it with a slash even if your login page is in a subdirectory of the main Web application directory. Listing 3.3 gives an example.

Listing 3.3   login.jsp

```
<!DOCTYPE HTML PUBLIC "-//W3C//DTD HTML 4.0 Transitional//EN">
<HTML><HEAD><TITLE>...</TITLE></HEAD>
<BODY>
...
<FORM ACTION="j_security_check" METHOD="POST">
<TABLE>
```

Listing 3.3	login.jsp *(continued)*

```
<TR><TD>User name: <INPUT TYPE="TEXT" NAME="j_username">
<TR><TD>Password: <INPUT TYPE="PASSWORD" NAME="j_password">
<TR><TH><INPUT TYPE="SUBMIT" VALUE="Log In">
</TABLE>
</FORM>
. . .
</BODY></HTML>
```

That was the page for logging *in*. What about a page for logging *out*? The session should time out eventually, but what if users want to log out immediately without closing the browser? The servlet specification mandates that invalidating the `HttpSession` should log users out and cause them to be reauthenticated the next time they try to access a protected resource. So, you could create a logout page by making a servlet or JSP page that looks up the session and calls `invalidate` on it. This is in contrast to BASIC authentication (see Section 3.3), where logging out is not supported without the user quitting and restarting the browser.

Restricting Direct Access to the Login Page

As we explained, when an unauthenticated user tries to access a protected resource, the server automatically redirects to the login page. Unfortunately, the servlet specification does not force compliant servers to use the "behind-the-scenes" redirecting (i.e., using the `RequestDispatcher.forward` method) to the JSP page specified in the `form-login-page` element. The servers are free to use the `HttpServlet-Response.sendRedirect` method, and some modern servers do. The containers that use the `sendRedirect` method expose the full URL of the login page to the client. The unsuspecting user can later invoke this URL, attempting to either log in to the application for the first time (the user would not be authenticated yet), log in under a different username while already logged in, or by simply hitting the browser back button.

Neither does the servlet specification dictate what compliant servers should do if the user tries to access the login page directly, as in the outlined scenarios. Therefore, the outcome is highly server specific. The server might forward the user to a nonexisting page, resulting in an HTTP 404 error, or produce some other result not expected by the user. Obviously, neither of these outcomes is good.

We can partially avoid this unpredictable behavior by placing some logic into the login page (see Figure 3–1). The logic would need to protect two types of users from directly accessing the login page: an *unauthenticated* user (has not logged in yet) and an *authenticated* user (tries to access the login page having been logged in already).

To protect a user who has already logged in, we would place the following code into our login.jsp.

```
<%
response.setHeader("Cache-Control",
                   "no-store, no-cache, must-revalidate");
response.setHeader("Pragma", "no-cache");
response.setDateHeader("Expires", -1);
// Check if user is already logged in
if (request.getRemoteUser() != null) {
  response.sendRedirect("logout-confirmation.jsp");
}
%>
```

The first line, which sets the HTTP version 1.1 response header Cache-Control to "no-store, no-cache, must-revalidate", ensures that the user will never see the browser-cached version of the login page. Similarly, to satisfy HTTP version 1.0, we also set the Pragma and Expires headers. The next few lines use the getRemoteUser method, which returns the username of the currently logged-in user. If the user is not logged in, it returns null. Thus, if getRemoteUser does, in fact, return a non-null value, we can be sure that this user has already been logged in and is invoking the login page directly. In this case, we simply redirect the user to some logout-confirmation.jsp, which gives the user the option to formally logout.

Figure 3–1   When the client tries to access a protected resource, Weblogic 8.1 uses the response.sendRedirect method to send the client to the login page, exposing the login page's URL.

There isn't really a clean and easy way to protect the unauthenticated user from directly accessing the login page. One unclean way would be to blindly redirect every request for the login page to a protected resource (e.g., /protectedA.jsp), causing the server to trigger the authentication process, and "re-serving" the login page to the client as part of that process. This approach would solve the problem of an unauthenticated user directly invoking the login page. However, it would also introduce some side effects. What would happen if an unauthenticated user attempts to invoke another protected resource, /protectedB.jsp? The server would serve the login page, and if the login is successful, the user would be forwarded to /protectedA.jsp. However, the user asked to go to /protectedB.jsp! The logged in but frustrated user would now be forced to once again navigate through your Web site to get to /protectedB.jsp.

So, if your Web application is to be deployed on a server that uses send-Redirect to forward the user to the login page, you have to decide which side effect is more detrimental to your application and adjust accordingly.

More important, the problem with all the discussed approaches is that they are forcing you to write security-related code, which is antithetical to the declarative security model.

Creating the Page to Report Failed Login Attempts

The login page must contain a form with a special-purpose ACTION (j_security_check), a text field with a special name (j_username), and a password field with yet another reserved name (j_password). When the user attempts to access a protected resource, the server automatically presents the login page. The user fills out the login form and submits it. If the presented credentials (e.g., username and password) are those of a legal user but the user does not belong to the category of users able to access the requested resource, the server will reject the request with an HTTP error code 403 Forbidden. Remember that using the deployment descriptor, you can specify a custom page to be displayed when an HTTP error occurs. For details see Section 2.9 (Designating Pages to Handle Errors).

However, if the username and password are not those of a legal user, the server will automatically send the user to the login-failure page specified in the form-error-page element.

So, what is required to be in the login-failure page? Nothing! This page is arbitrary; it can contain a link to an unrestricted section of the Web application or a simple "login failed" message.

Specifying URLs That Should Be Password Protected

The `login-config` element tells the server which authentication method to use. Good, but how do you designate the specific URLs to which access should be restricted? Designating restricted URLs and describing the protection they should have is the purpose of the `security-constraint` element.

The `security-constraint` element contains four possible subelements: `display-name` (an optional element giving a name for IDEs to use), `web-resource-collection` (a required element that specifies the URLs that should be protected), `auth-constraint` (an optional element that designates the abstract roles that should have access to the URLs), and `user-data-constraint` (an optional element that specifies whether SSL is required). Note that multiple `web-resource-collection` entries are permitted within `security-constraint`.

For a quick example of the use of `security-constraint`, Listing 3.4 instructs the server to require passwords for all URLs of the form http://*host*/*webAppPrefix*/sensitive/*blah*. Users who supply passwords and belong to the `administrator` or `executive` logical roles should be granted access; all others should be denied access. The rest of this subsection provides details on the `web-resource-collection`, `auth-constraint`, and `display-name` elements. The role of `user-data-constraint` is explained in a later subsection (Specifying URLs That Should Be Available Only with SSL).

Listing 3.4 web.xml (Excerpt specifying protected URLs)

```
<?xml version="1.0" encoding="ISO-8859-1"?>
<web-app xmlns="http://java.sun.com/xml/ns/j2ee"
         xmlns:xsi="http://www.w3.org/2001/XMLSchema-instance"
         xsi:schemaLocation=
         "http://java.sun.com/xml/ns/j2ee
          http://java.sun.com/xml/ns/j2ee/web-app_2_4.xsd"
         version="2.4">
  <security-constraint>
    <web-resource-collection>
      <web-resource-name>Sensitive</web-resource-name>
      <url-pattern>/sensitive/*</url-pattern>
    </web-resource-collection>
    <auth-constraint>
      <role-name>administrator</role-name>
      <role-name>executive</role-name>
    </auth-constraint>
  </security-constraint>
  <login-config>...</login-config>
</web-app>
```

web-resource-collection

This subelement of `security-constraint` identifies the resources that should be protected. Each `security-constraint` element must contain one or more `web-resource-collection` entries; all other `security-constraint` subelements are optional. The `web-resource-collection` element consists of a `web-resource-name` element that gives an arbitrary identifying name, a `url-pattern` element that identifies the URLs that should be protected, an optional `http-method` element that designates the HTTP commands to which the protection applies (`GET`, `POST`, etc.; the default is all methods), and an optional `description` element providing documentation. For example, the following `web-resource-collection` entries (within a `security-constraint` element) specify that password protection should be applied to all documents in the **proprietary** directory (and subdirectories thereof) and to the **delete-account.jsp** page in the **admin** directory. Because security constraints apply to request the URL, not the physical directory, this security constraint would equally apply to any servlets mapped to URLs that contain the **proprietary** directory in them. For example, a servlet mapped with a pattern `/proprietary/CompanySecretOfTheDayServlet` would likewise be protected by the following security constraint:

```
<security-constraint>
  <web-resource-collection>
    <web-resource-name>Proprietary</web-resource-name>
    <url-pattern>/proprietary/*</url-pattern>
  </web-resource-collection>
  <web-resource-collection>
    <web-resource-name>Account Deletion</web-resource-name>
    <url-pattern>/admin/delete-account.jsp</url-pattern>
  </web-resource-collection>
  <!-- ... -->
</security-constraint>
```

When protecting form submissions, it's important that you protect the page that has the form as well as the servlet that the form submits to. A common mistake is to protect only the form and leave the servlet unprotected. This oversight lets the users bypass the form, either deliberately or accidentally (e.g., by following a bookmark), and access the servlet without being authenticated.

Core Warning

When protecting form submissions, make sure to protect the servlet that the form submits to in addition to the form page itself.

It is also important to note that the `url-pattern` applies only to clients that access the resources directly. In particular, it does not apply to pages that are accessed through the MVC architecture with a `RequestDispatcher` (see Chapter 15 of Volume 1) or by the similar means of `jsp:forward` or `jsp:include` (see Chapter 13 of Volume 1). This asymmetry is good if used properly. For example, with the MVC architecture a servlet looks up data, places it in beans, and forwards the request to a JSP page that extracts the data from the beans and displays it. You want to ensure that the JSP page is never accessed directly but instead is accessed only through the servlet that sets up the beans the page will use. The `url-pattern` and `auth-constraint` (see next subsection) elements can provide this guarantee by declaring that no user is permitted direct access to the JSP page. Note, however, that the simpler approach to this problem is to place the JSP pages inside the WEB-INF directory. This asymmetric behavior can catch developers off guard and allow them to accidentally provide unrestricted access to resources that should be protected.

Core Warning

These protections apply only to direct client access. The security model does not apply to pages accessed by means of a `RequestDispatcher,` `jsp:forward,` *or* `jsp:include.`

auth-constraint

Whereas the `web-resource-collection` element designates the URLs that should be protected, the `auth-constraint` element designates the users who should have access to these resources. It should contain one or more `role-name` elements identifying the class of users that have access and, optionally, a `description` element describing the role. For instance, the following part of the `security-constraint` element in web.xml states that only users who are designated as either Administrators or Big Kahunas (or both) should have access to the designated resource.

```
<security-constraint>
  <web-resource-collection>...</web-resource-collection>
  <auth-constraint>
    <role-name>administrator</role-name>
    <role-name>kahuna</role-name>
  </auth-constraint>
</security-constraint>
```

If you want all authenticated users to have access to a resource, use * as the
role-name. To restrict anyone from accessing a group of resources, use an
empty auth-constraint element (e.g., <auth-constraint/>). The
empty auth-constraint element means that no roles have access. Although
at first glance it appears pointless to deny access to all users, remember that
these security restrictions apply only to direct client access. So, for example,
suppose you had a JSP snippet that is intended to be inserted into another file
with jsp:include (see Chapter 13 of Volume 1). Or, suppose you have a JSP
page that is the forwarding destination of a servlet that is using a Request-
Dispatcher as part of the MVC architecture (see Chapter 15 of Volume 1).
In both cases, users should be prohibited from directly accessing the JSP page.
A security-constraint element with an empty auth-constraint element would enforce this restriction. However, as we mentioned, placing such
resources inside the WEB-INF directory is the simpler solution.

display-name

This rarely used optional subelement of security-constraint gives a
name to the security constraint entry. This name might be used by an IDE or
other graphical tool.

Listing All Possible Abstract Roles

The servlet specification requires that all possible abstract roles are listed within the
web.xml file. This means that any role used within any of the security-constraint
elements must be separately declared. You declare the abstract roles using one or
more security-role elements. Each security-role element contains an
optional description element and a required role-name element. For example,
suppose you had one security-constraint element with auth-constraint
entries for teacher and student, another security-constraint element
with auth-constraint entries for teacher and principal, and a third
security-constraint element with auth-constraint entries for principal,
administrator, and dean. You would then use security-role elements to list
the unique names as follows:

```
<security-role>
  <role-name>teacher</role-name>
</security-role>
<security-role>
  <role-name>student</role-name>
</security-role>
<security-role>
  <role-name>principal</role-name>
</security-role>
<security-role>
```

```
    <role-name>administrator</role-name>
  </security-role>
  <security-role>
    <role-name>dean</role-name>
  </security-role>
```

Specifying URLs That Should Be Available Only with SSL

Suppose your servlet or JSP page collects credit card numbers. User authentication keeps out unauthorized users but does nothing to protect the network traffic. So, for instance, an attacker who runs a packet sniffer on the end user's LAN could see that user's credit card number. This scenario is exactly what SSL protects against—it encrypts the traffic between the browser and the server.

Use of SSL does not change the basic way that form-based authentication works. Regardless of whether you are using SSL, you use the `login-config` element to indicate that you are using form-based authentication and to identify the login and login-failure pages. With or without SSL, you designate the protected resources with the `url-pattern` subelement of `web-resource-collection`. None of your servlets or JSP pages need to be modified or moved to different locations when you enable or disable SSL. That's the beauty of declarative security.

The `user-data-constraint` subelement of `security-constraint` can mandate that certain resources be accessed only with SSL. So, for example, attempts to access https://*host*/*webAppPrefix*/specialURL are handled normally, whereas attempts to access http://*host*/*webAppPrefix*/specialURL are redirected to the https URL. This behavior does not mean that you cannot supply an explicit https URL for a hypertext link or the ACTION of a form; it just means that you aren't required to. You can stick with the simpler and more easily maintained relative URLs and still be assured that certain URLs will only be accessed with SSL.

The `user-data-constraint` element, if used, must contain a `transport-guarantee` subelement (with legal values NONE, INTEGRAL, or CONFIDENTIAL) and can optionally contain a `description` element. A value of NONE for `transport-guarantee` puts no restrictions on the communication protocol used. Because NONE is the default, there is little point in using `user-data-constraint` or `transport-guarantee` if you specify NONE. A value of INTEGRAL means that the communication must be of a variety that prevents data from being changed in transit without detection. A value of CONFIDENTIAL means that the data must be transmitted in a way that prevents anyone who intercepts it from reading it. Although in principle (and perhaps in future HTTP versions) there may be a distinction between INTEGRAL and CONFIDENTIAL, in current practice they both simply mandate the use of SSL.

For example, the following instructs the server to permit only https connections to the associated resource:

```
<security-constraint>
  <!-- ... -->
  <user-data-constraint>
    <transport-guarantee>CONFIDENTIAL</transport-guarantee>
  </user-data-constraint>
</security-constraint>
```

In addition to simply requiring SSL, the servlet API provides a way to stipulate that users must authenticate themselves with client certificates. You supply a value of CLIENT-CERT for the auth-method subelement of login-config (discussed earlier in this section). However, only servers that have full J2EE support are required to support this capability.

Now, although the method of prohibiting non-SSL access is standardized, servers that are compliant with the servlet 2.4 and JSP 2.0 specifications are not required to support SSL. So, Web applications that use a transport-guarantee of CONFIDENTIAL (or, equivalently, INTEGRAL) are not necessarily portable. For example, JRun and ServletExec are usually used as plug-ins in Web servers like Apache or Internet Information Server (IIS). In this scenario, the network traffic between the client and the Web server is encrypted with SSL, but the local traffic from the Web server to the servlet/JSP container is not encrypted. Consequently, a CONFIDENTIAL transport-guarantee will fail. Tomcat, however, can be set up to use SSL directly. Details on this process are given in Section 3.5 (Configuring Tomcat to Use SSL). Some server plug-ins maintain SSL even on the local connection between the main Web server and the servlet/JSP engine; for example, the BEA WebLogic plug-in for IIS, Apache, and Netscape Enterprise Server does so. Furthermore, integrated application servers like the standalone version of WebLogic have no "separate" servlet and JSP engine, so SSL works exactly as described here. Nevertheless, it is important to realize that these features, although useful, are not mandated by the servlet and JSP specifications.

Core Warning

Web applications that rely on SSL are not necessarily portable.

Turning Off the Invoker Servlet

When you restrict access to certain resources, you do so by specifying the URL patterns to which the restrictions apply. This pattern, in turn, matches a pattern that you set with the servlet-mapping web.xml element. See Section 2.4 (Assigning

Names and Custom URLs). However, most servers use an "invoker servlet" that provides a default URL for servlets: http://*host*/*webAppPrefix*/servlet/ServletName. You need to make sure that users don't access protected servlets with this URL, thus bypassing the access restrictions that were set by the url-pattern subelement of web-resource-collection.

For example, suppose that you use security-constraint, web-resource-collection, and url-pattern to say that the URL /admin/DeclareChapter3 should be protected. You also use the auth-constraint and role-name elements to say that only users in the director role can access this URL. Next, you use the servlet and servlet-mapping elements to say that the servlet BankruptcyServlet.class in the disaster package should correspond to /admin/DeclareChapter3. Now, the security restrictions are in force when clients use the URL http://*host*/*webAppPrefix*/admin/DeclareChapter3. No restrictions apply to http://*host*/*webAppPrefix*/servlet/disaster.BankruptcyServlet. Oops.

Section 2.5 (Disabling the Invoker Servlet) discusses server-specific approaches to turning off the invoker. The most portable approach, however, is to simply remap the /servlet/* pattern in your Web application so that all requests that include the pattern are sent to the same servlet. To remap the pattern, you first create a simple servlet that prints an error message or redirects users to the top-level page. Then, you use the servlet and servlet-mapping elements (Section 2.4) to send requests that include the /servlet/* pattern to that servlet. Listing 3.5 gives a brief example.

Listing 3.5 web.xml (Excerpt redirecting requests from default servlet URLs to an error-message servlet)

```xml
<?xml version="1.0" encoding="ISO-8859-1"?>
<web-app xmlns="http://java.sun.com/xml/ns/j2ee"
         xmlns:xsi="http://www.w3.org/2001/XMLSchema-instance"
         xsi:schemaLocation=
         "http://java.sun.com/xml/ns/j2ee
          http://java.sun.com/xml/ns/j2ee/web-app_2_4.xsd"
         version="2.4">
  <servlet>
    <servlet-name>NoInvoker</servlet-name>
    <servlet-class>coreservlets.NoInvokerServlet</servlet-class>
  </servlet>
  <servlet-mapping>
    <servlet-name>NoInvoker</servlet-name>
    <url-pattern>/servlet/*</url-pattern>
  </servlet-mapping>
</web-app>
```

3.2 Example: Form-Based Authentication

In this section we work through a small Web site for a fictional company called hot-dot-com.com. We'll start by showing the home page, then list the web.xml file, summarize the various protection mechanisms, show the password file, present the login and login-failure pages, and give the code for each of the protected resources.

The Home Page

Listing 3.6 shows the top-level home page for the Web application. The application is registered with a URL prefix of /hotdotcom so the home page can be accessed with the URL http://*host*/hotdotcom/index.jsp as shown in Figure 3–2. If you've forgotten how to assign URL prefixes to Web applications, review Section 2.4 (Assigning Names and Custom URLs).

Now, the main home page has no security protections and consequently does not absolutely require an entry in web.xml. However, many users expect URLs that list a directory but no file to invoke the default file from that directory and index.jsp is not absolutely guaranteed to be used as one of the default file names. So, we put a `welcome-file-list` entry in web.xml (see Listing 3.7 in the next section) to ensure that http://*host*/hotdotcom/ would invoke index.jsp.

Listing 3.6   index.jsp (Top-level home page)

```
<!DOCTYPE HTML PUBLIC "-//W3C//DTD HTML 4.0 Transitional//EN">
<HTML>
<HEAD>
<TITLE>hot-dot-com.com!</TITLE>
<LINK REL=STYLESHEET
      HREF="company-styles.css"
      TYPE="text/css">
</HEAD>
<BODY>
<TABLE BORDER=5 ALIGN="CENTER">
  <TR><TH CLASS="TITLE">hot-dot-com.com!</TABLE>
<P>
<H3>Welcome to the ultimate dot-com company!</H3>
Please select one of the following:
```

Listing 3.6	index.jsp (Top-level home page) *(continued)*

```
<UL>
  <LI><A HREF="investing/">Investing</A>.
      Guaranteed growth for your hard-earned dollars!
  <LI><A HREF="business/">Business Model</A>.
      New economy strategy!
  <LI><A HREF="history/">History</A>.
      Fascinating company history.
</UL>
</BODY></HTML>
```

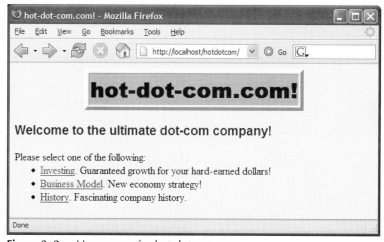

Figure 3–2   Home page for hot-dot-com.com.

The Deployment Descriptor

Listing 3.7 shows the complete deployment descriptor used with the `hotdotcom`
Web application.

The `hotdotcom` deployment descriptor specifies several things:

- URLs that give a directory but no filename result in the server first
  trying to use index.jsp and next trying index.html. If neither file is
  available, the result is server specific (e.g., a directory listing).
- URLs that use the default servlet mapping (i.e., http://*host*/
  hotdotcom/servlet/*ServletName*) invoke the NoInvokerServlet and
  display a message telling the user that the invoker servlet has been
  disabled.

- Requests to http://*host*/hotdotcom/ssl/buy-stock.jsp are redirected to https://*host*/hotdotcom/ssl/buy-stock.jsp. Requests directly to https://*host*/hotdotcom/ssl/buy-stock.jsp require no redirection. Similarly, requests to http://*host*/hotdotcom/ssl/FinalizePurchase are redirected to https://*host*/hotdotcom/ssl/FinalizePurchase. See Section 3.5 (Configuring Tomcat to Use SSL) for information on setting up Tomcat to use SSL.
- URLs in the investing "directory" (really incoming URL pattern) can be accessed only by users in the `registered-user` or `administrator` roles.
- The delete-account.jsp page in the admin directory can be accessed only by users in the `administrator` role.
- Requests for restricted resources by unauthenticated users are redirected to the login.jsp page in the admin directory. Users who are authenticated successfully get sent to the page they tried to access originally. Users who fail authentication are sent to the login-error.jsp page in the admin directory.

Listing 3.7	WEB-INF/web.xml (Complete version for hot-dot-com.com)

```xml
<?xml version="1.0" encoding="ISO-8859-1"?>
<web-app xmlns="http://java.sun.com/xml/ns/j2ee"
         xmlns:xsi="http://www.w3.org/2001/XMLSchema-instance"
         xsi:schemaLocation=
         "http://java.sun.com/xml/ns/j2ee
          http://java.sun.com/xml/ns/j2ee/web-app_2_4.xsd"
         version="2.4">

  <!-- Give name to FinalizePurchaseServlet. This servlet
       is mapped to the URL /ssl/FinalizePurchase
       (by means of servlet-mapping and url-pattern).
       Then, that URL will later be designated as one requiring
       SSL (by means of security-constraint and
       transport-guarantee). -->
  <servlet>
    <servlet-name>
      FinalizePurchaseServlet
    </servlet-name>
    <servlet-class>
      hotdotcom.FinalizePurchaseServlet
    </servlet-class>
  </servlet>
```

Listing 3.7	WEB-INF/web.xml (Complete version for hot-dot-com.com) *(continued)*

```xml
<servlet-mapping>
   <servlet-name>
     FinalizePurchaseServlet
   </servlet-name>
   <url-pattern>
     /ssl/FinalizePurchase
   </url-pattern>
 </servlet-mapping>

 <!-- Servlet to logout the user. -->
 <servlet>
   <servlet-name>Logout</servlet-name>
   <servlet-class>hotdotcom.LogoutServlet</servlet-class>
 </servlet>
 <servlet-mapping>
   <servlet-name>Logout</servlet-name>
   <url-pattern>/admin/logout</url-pattern>
 </servlet-mapping>

 <error-page>
   <error-code>403</error-code>
   <location>/WEB-INF/jspPages/forbidden.jsp</location>
 </error-page>

 <!-- Protect everything within the "investing" directory. -->
 <security-constraint>
   <web-resource-collection>
     <web-resource-name>Investing</web-resource-name>
     <url-pattern>/investing/*</url-pattern>
   </web-resource-collection>
   <auth-constraint>
     <role-name>registered-user</role-name>
     <role-name>administrator</role-name>
   </auth-constraint>
 </security-constraint>

 <!-- URLs of the form http://host/webAppPrefix/ssl/blah
      require SSL and are thus redirected to
      https://host/webAppPrefix/ssl/blah. -->
 <security-constraint>
   <web-resource-collection>
     <web-resource-name>Purchase</web-resource-name>
     <url-pattern>/ssl/*</url-pattern>
   </web-resource-collection>
```

```
<auth-constraint>
    <role-name>registered-user</role-name>
  </auth-constraint>
  <user-data-constraint>
    <transport-guarantee>CONFIDENTIAL</transport-guarantee>
  </user-data-constraint>
</security-constraint>
<!-- Only users in the administrator role can access
     the delete-account.jsp page within the admin
     directory. -->
<security-constraint>
  <web-resource-collection>
    <web-resource-name>Account Deletion</web-resource-name>
    <url-pattern>/admin/delete-account.jsp</url-pattern>
  </web-resource-collection>
  <auth-constraint>
    <role-name>administrator</role-name>
  </auth-constraint>
</security-constraint>

<!-- Declare security roles used in this app. -->
<security-role>
  <role-name>administrator</role-name>
</security-role>
<security-role>
  <role-name>registered-user</role-name>
</security-role>

<!-- Tell the server to use form-based authentication. -->
<login-config>
  <auth-method>FORM</auth-method>
  <form-login-config>
    <form-login-page>/admin/login.jsp</form-login-page>
    <form-error-page>/admin/login-error.jsp</form-error-page>
  </form-login-config>
</login-config>

<!-- Disable the invoker servlet. -->
<servlet>
  <servlet-name>NoInvoker</servlet-name>
  <servlet-class>coreservlets.NoInvokerServlet</servlet-class>
</servlet>
<servlet-mapping>
  <servlet-name>NoInvoker</servlet-name>
  <url-pattern>/servlet/*</url-pattern>
</servlet-mapping>
```

<table>
<tr><td>**Listing 3.7**</td><td>WEB-INF/web.xml
(Complete version for hot-dot-com.com) *(continued)*</td></tr>
</table>

```
    <!-- If URL gives a directory but no filename, try index.jsp
        first and index.html second. If neither is found,
        the result is server specific (e.g., a directory
        listing). -->
  <welcome-file-list>
    <welcome-file>index.jsp</welcome-file>
    <welcome-file>index.html</welcome-file>
  </welcome-file-list>
</web-app>
```

The Password File

With form-based authentication, the server (container) performs a lot of the work for you. That's good. However, shifting so much work to the server means that there is a server-specific component: the assignment of passwords and roles to individual users (see Section 3.1).

Listing 3.8 shows the password file used by Tomcat for this Web application. It defines four users: john (in the registered-user role), jane (also in the registered-user role), juan (in the administrator role), and juana (in the registered-user and administrator roles).

<table>
<tr><td>**Listing 3.8**</td><td>install_dir/conf/tomcat-users.xml (First four users)</td></tr>
</table>

```
<?xml version='1.0' encoding='utf-8'?>
<tomcat-users>
  <role rolename="registered-user" />
  <role rolename="administrator" />

  <user username="john" password="nhoj"
        roles="registered-user" />
  <user username="jane" password="enaj"
        roles="registered-user" />
  <user username="juan" password="nauj"
        roles="administrator" />
  <user username="juana" password="anauj"
        roles="administrator,registered-user" />
</tomcat-users>
```

The Login and Login-Failure Pages

This Web application uses form-based authentication. Attempts by not-yet-authenticated users to access any password-protected resource will be sent to the login.jsp page in the admin directory. This page, shown in Listing 3.9, collects the username in a field named j_username and the password in a field named j_password. The results are sent by POST to a resource called j_security_check. Successful login attempts are redirected to the page that was originally requested. Failed attempts are redirected to the login-error.jsp page in the admin directory (Listing 3.10). Note that the login.jsp page also contains the code to prevent an already logged-in user from accessing the login page directly. This code is discussed in Section 3.1 (Form-Based Authentication).

Listing 3.9   admin/login.jsp

```
<%
response.setHeader("Cache-Control",
                   "no-store, no-cache, must-revalidate");
response.setHeader("Pragma", "no-cache");
response.setDateHeader("Expires", -1);

// Check if user is already logged in
if (request.getRemoteUser() != null) {
  response.sendRedirect("logoutConfirmation.jsp");
}
%>
<!DOCTYPE HTML PUBLIC "-//W3C//DTD HTML 4.0 Transitional//EN">
<HTML>
<HEAD>
<TITLE>Log In</TITLE>
<LINK REL=STYLESHEET
      HREF="../company-styles.css"
      TYPE="text/css">
</HEAD>
<BODY>
<TABLE BORDER=5 ALIGN="CENTER">
  <TR><TH CLASS="TITLE">Log In</TABLE>
<P>
<H3>Sorry, you must log in before accessing this resource.</H3>
<FORM ACTION="j_security_check" METHOD="POST">
```

Listing 3.9   admin/login.jsp *(continued)*

```
<TABLE>
<TR><TD>User name: <INPUT TYPE="TEXT" NAME="j_username">
<TR><TD>Password: <INPUT TYPE="PASSWORD" NAME="j_password">
<TR><TH><INPUT TYPE="SUBMIT" VALUE="Log In">
</TABLE>
</FORM>
</BODY>
</HTML>
```

Listing 3.10   admin/login-error.jsp

```
<!DOCTYPE HTML PUBLIC "-//W3C//DTD HTML 4.0 Transitional//EN">
<HTML>
<HEAD>
<TITLE>Begone!</TITLE>
<LINK REL=STYLESHEET
      HREF="../company-styles.css"
      TYPE="text/css">
</HEAD>
<BODY>
<TABLE BORDER=5 ALIGN="CENTER">
  <TR><TH CLASS="TITLE">Begone!</TABLE>

<H3>Begone, ye unauthorized peon.</H3>
</BODY></HTML>
```

The investing Directory

The web.xml file for the hotdotcom Web application (Listing 3.7) specifies that all URLs that begin with http://*host*/hotdotcom/investing/ should be password protected, accessible only to users in the registered-user role. So, the first attempt by any user to access the home page of the investing directory (see Listing 3.11) results in the login form shown earlier in Listing 3.9. Figure 3–3 shows the initial result, Figure 3–4 shows the result of an unsuccessful login attempt, and Figure 3–5 shows the investing home page—the result of a successful login.

Once authenticated, a user can browse other pages and return to a protected page without reauthentication. Selecting the link to the account status page (see Listing 3.12) does not result in reauthentication, even if the user has accessed other pages since being authenticated. Figure 3–6 shows the successful access to the account status page, without being asked for the username and password again. The system uses some variation of session tracking to remember which users have previously been authenticated.

Listing 3.11   investing/index.html

```
<!DOCTYPE HTML PUBLIC "-//W3C//DTD HTML 4.0 Transitional//EN">
<HTML>
<HEAD>
<TITLE>Investing</TITLE>
<LINK REL=STYLESHEET
      HREF="../company-styles.css"
      TYPE="text/css">
</HEAD>
<BODY>
<TABLE BORDER=5 ALIGN="CENTER">
  <TR><TH CLASS="TITLE">Investing</TABLE>
<H3><I>hot-dot-com.com</I> welcomes the discriminating investor!
</H3>
Please choose one of the following:
<UL>
  <LI><A HREF="../ssl/buy-stock.jsp">Buy stock</A>.
      Astronomic growth rates!
  <LI><A HREF="account-status.jsp">Check account status</A>.
      See how much you've already earned!
</UL>
</BODY></HTML>
```

Listing 3.12   investing/account-status.jsp

```
<!DOCTYPE HTML PUBLIC "-//W3C//DTD HTML 4.0 Transitional//EN">
<HTML>
<HEAD>
<TITLE>Account Status</TITLE>
<LINK REL=STYLESHEET
      HREF="../company-styles.css"
      TYPE="text/css">
</HEAD>
<BODY>
<TABLE BORDER=5 ALIGN="CENTER">
  <TR><TH CLASS="TITLE">Account Status</TABLE>
<P>
<H3>Your stock is basically worthless now.</H3>
But, hey, that makes this a buying opportunity.
Why don't you <A HREF="../ssl/buy-stock.jsp">buy
some more</A>?
</BODY></HTML>
```

Figure 3–3   Users who are not yet authenticated get redirected to the login page when they attempt to access the investing page.

Figure 3–4   Failed login attempts result in the login-error.jsp page.

Figure 3–5 Successful login attempts result in redirection back to the originally requested page.

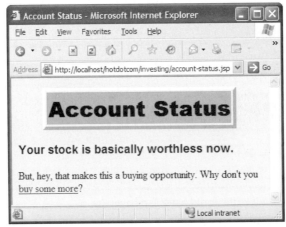

Figure 3–6 Selecting the Account Status link on the investing home page does not result in reauthentication, even if the user has accessed other pages since being authenticated. The system uses a variation of session tracking to remember which users have already been authenticated.

The ssl Directory

The stock purchase page (Listings 3.13 and 3.14) submits data to the purchase finalization servlet (Listing 3.15), which, in turn, dispatches to the confirmation page (Listing 3.16).

Note that the purchase finalization servlet is not really in the **ssl** directory; it is in **WEB-INF/classes/hotdotcom**. However, the deployment descriptor (Listing 3.7) uses `servlet-mapping` to assign a URL that makes the servlet appear (to the client) to be in the **ssl** directory. This mapping serves two purposes.

First, it lets the HTML form of Listing 3.13 use a simple relative URL to refer to the servlet. This is convenient because absolute URLs require modification every time your hostname or URL prefix changes. However, if you use this approach, it is important that both the original form and the servlet it talks to are accessed with SSL. If the original form used a relative URL for the `ACTION` and was accessed with a normal HTTP connection, the browser would first submit the data by HTTP and then get redirected to HTTPS. Too late: An attacker with access to the network traffic could have obtained the data from the initial HTTP request. On the other hand, if the `ACTION` of a form is an absolute URL that uses **https**, it is not necessary for the original form to be accessed with SSL.

Core Warning

When using SSL with relative URLs, secure the URL of the form page besides the URL of the servlet.

Second, using `servlet-mapping` in this way guarantees that SSL will be used to access the servlet, even if the user tries to bypass the HTML form and access the servlet URL directly. This guarantee is in effect because the `transport-guarantee` element (with a value of `CONFIDENTIAL`) applies to the pattern `/ssl/*`. Figures 3–7 through 3–9 show the results.

We already explained that absolute URLs specifying **https** are significantly harder to maintain. However, if you are concerned about overloading your SSL server (HTTPS connections are much slower than HTTP connections), you could use this approach to gain some efficiency.

Listing 3.13 ssl/buy-stock.jsp

```
<!DOCTYPE HTML PUBLIC "-//W3C//DTD HTML 4.0 Transitional//EN">
<HTML>
<HEAD>
<TITLE>Purchase</TITLE>
<LINK REL=STYLESHEET
      HREF="../company-styles.css"
      TYPE="text/css">
</HEAD>
<BODY>
```

Listing 3.13 ssl/buy-stock.jsp *(continued)*

```
<TABLE BORDER=5 ALIGN="CENTER">
  <TR><TH CLASS="TITLE">Purchase</TABLE>
<P>
<H3><I>hot-dot-com.com</I> congratulates you on a wise
investment!</H3>
<jsp:useBean id="stock" class="hotdotcom.StockInfo" />
<UL>
  <LI>Current stock value: ${stock.currentValue}
  <LI>Predicted value in one year: ${stock.futureValue}
</UL>
<FORM ACTION="FinalizePurchase" METHOD="POST">
  <DL>
    <DT>Number of shares:
    <DD><INPUT TYPE="RADIO" NAME="numShares" VALUE="1000">
        1000
    <DD><INPUT TYPE="RADIO" NAME="numShares" VALUE="10000">
        10000
    <DD><INPUT TYPE="RADIO" NAME="numShares" VALUE="100000"
              CHECKED>
        100000
  </DL>
  Full name: <INPUT TYPE="TEXT" NAME="fullName"><BR>
  Credit card number: <INPUT TYPE="TEXT" NAME="cardNum"><P>
  <CENTER><INPUT TYPE="SUBMIT" VALUE="Confirm Purchase"></CENTER>
</FORM>
</BODY></HTML>
```

Listing 3.14 WEB-INF/classes/hotdotcom/StockInfo.java (Bean used by buy-stock.jsp)

```
package hotdotcom;

public class StockInfo {
  public String getCurrentValue() {
    return("$2.00");
  }

  public String getFutureValue() {
    return("$200.00");
  }
}
```

Listing 3.15 WEB-INF/classes/hotdotcom/FinalizePurchaseServlet.java

```java
package hotdotcom;

import java.io.*;
import javax.servlet.*;
import javax.servlet.http.*;

/** Servlet that reads credit card information,
 *  performs a stock purchase, and displays confirmation page.
 */

public class FinalizePurchaseServlet extends HttpServlet {

  /** Use doPost for non-SSL access to prevent
   *  credit card number from showing up in URL.
   */

  public void doPost(HttpServletRequest request,
                     HttpServletResponse response)
      throws ServletException, IOException {
    String fullName = request.getParameter("fullName");
    String cardNum = request.getParameter("cardNum");
    confirmPurchase(fullName, cardNum);
    String destination = "/investing/sucker.jsp";
    RequestDispatcher dispatcher =
      request.getRequestDispatcher(destination);
    dispatcher.forward(request, response);
  }

  /** doGet calls doPost. Servlets that are
   *  redirected to through SSL must have doGet.
   */

  public void doGet(HttpServletRequest request,
                    HttpServletResponse response)
      throws ServletException, IOException {
    doPost(request, response);
  }

  private void confirmPurchase(String fullName,
                               String cardNum) {
    // Details removed to protect the guilty.
  }
}
```

Listing 3.16	investing/sucker.jsp (Dispatched to from FinalizePurchaseServlet.java)

```
<!DOCTYPE HTML PUBLIC "-//W3C//DTD HTML 4.0 Transitional//EN">
<HTML>
<HEAD>
<TITLE>Thanks!</TITLE>
<LINK REL=STYLESHEET
      HREF="../company-styles.css"
      TYPE="text/css">
</HEAD>
<BODY>
<TABLE BORDER=5 ALIGN="CENTER">
  <TR><TH CLASS="TITLE">Thanks!</TABLE>
<H3><I>hot-dot-com.com</I> thanks you for your purchase.</H3>
You'll be thanking yourself soon!
</BODY></HTML>
```

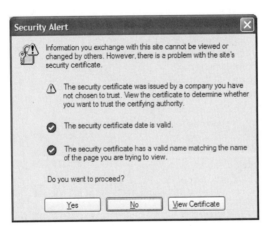

Figure 3–7   Warning when user first accesses `FinalizePurchaseServlet` when Tomcat is using a self-signed certificate. Self-signed certificates result in warnings and are for test purposes only. See Section 3.5 (Configuring Tomcat to Use SSL) for details on creating them for use with Tomcat and for information on suppressing warnings for future requests.

Figure 3–8   The stock purchase page must be accessed with SSL. Because the form's ACTION uses a simple relative URL, the initial form submission uses the same protocol as the request for the form itself.

Figure 3–9   To protect the credit card number in transit, you must use SSL to access the Finalize-Purchase servlet. Although FinalizePurchaseServlet dispatches to sucker.jsp, no web.xml entry is needed for that JSP page. Access restrictions apply to the client's URL, not to the behind-the-scenes file locations.

The admin Directory

URLs in the admin directory are not uniformly protected as are URLs in the investing directory. We already discussed the login and login-failure pages (Listings 3.9 and 3.10, Figures 3–3 and 3–4). This just leaves the Delete Account page (Listing 3.17). This page has been designated as accessible only to users in the administrator role. So, when users that are only in the registered-user role attempt to access the page, they are denied permission (see Figure 3–10). Note that the permission-denied page of Figure 3–10 can generated automatically by the server. Because it's more user-friendly, we configure our application to send the custom forbidden.jsp page instead of the Tomcat's standard permission-denied page. We can accomplish this configuration using the error-page element like so:

```
<error-page>
  <error-code>403</error-code>
  <location>/WEB-INF/jspPages/forbidden.jsp</location>
</error-page>
```

For more detail on setting up error pages see Section 2.9 (Designating Pages to Handle Errors). The code for the custom error page forbidden.jsp is shown in Listing 3.18.

This scenario applies to authenticated users whose roles do not match any of the required ones—it is not the same as the login error page that applies to users who cannot be authenticated.

A user in the administrator role can access the page without difficulty (Figure 3–11).

Listing 3.17   admin/delete-account.jsp

```
<!DOCTYPE HTML PUBLIC "-//W3C//DTD HTML 4.0 Transitional//EN">
<HTML>
<HEAD>
<TITLE>Delete Account</TITLE>
<LINK REL=STYLESHEET
      HREF="../company-styles.css"
      TYPE="text/css">
</HEAD>
<BODY>
<TABLE BORDER=5 ALIGN="CENTER">
  <TR><TH CLASS="TITLE">Delete Account</TABLE>
<P>
<FORM ACTION="confirm-deletion.jsp">
  Username: <INPUT TYPE="TEXT" NAME="userName"><BR>
  <CENTER><INPUT TYPE="SUBMIT" VALUE="Confirm Deletion"></CENTER>
</FORM>
</BODY></HTML>
```

Listing 3.18	WEB-INF/jspPages/forbidden.jsp

```
<!DOCTYPE HTML PUBLIC "-//W3C//DTD HTML 4.0 Transitional//EN">
<HTML>
<HEAD>
<TITLE>FORBIDDEN!</TITLE>
<LINK REL=STYLESHEET
    HREF="${pageContext.request.contextPath}/company-styles.css"
    TYPE="text/css">
</HEAD>
<BODY>
<TABLE BORDER=5 ALIGN="CENTER">
  <TR><TH CLASS="TITLE">FORBIDDEN!</TABLE>
<H3 style="text-align: center;">Who do you think you are?!</H3>
</BODY></HTML>
```

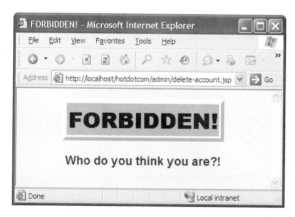

Figure 3–10 When John and Jane attempt to access the Delete Account page, they are denied (even though they are authenticated). That's because they belong to the `registered-user` role and the **web**.xml file stipulates that only users in the `administrator` role should be able to access this page.

Figure 3–11 Once authenticated, Juan or Juana (in the `administrator` role) can access the Delete Account page.

The NoInvoker Servlet

Web applications that have protected servlets should always disable the invoker serv-let so that users cannot bypass security by using http://*host*/*webAppPrefix*/servlet/ *ServletName* when the access restrictions are assigned to a custom servlet URL. In the hotdotcom application, we used the servlet and servlet-mapping ele-ments to register the NoInvokerServlet with requests to http://*host*/hotdotcom/ servlet/*anything*. This servlet, shown in Listing 3.19, simply displays a message to the user that the invoker servlet has been disabled.

Listing 3.19	WEB-INF/classes/coreservlets/ NoInvokerServlet.java

```java
package coreservlets;

import java.io.*;
import javax.servlet.*;
import javax.servlet.http.*;

/** Simple servlet used to give error messages to
 *  users who try to access default servlet URLs
 *  (i.e., http://host/webAppPrefix/servlet/ServletName)
 *  in Web applications that have disabled this
 *  behavior.
 */

public class NoInvokerServlet extends HttpServlet {
  public void doGet(HttpServletRequest request,
                    HttpServletResponse response)
      throws ServletException, IOException {
    response.setContentType("text/html");
    PrintWriter out = response.getWriter();
    String docType =
      "<!DOCTYPE HTML PUBLIC \"-//W3C//DTD HTML 4.0 " +
      "Transitional//EN\">\n";
    String title = "Invoker Servlet Disabled.";
    out.println
      (docType +
      "<HTML>\n" +
      "<HEAD><TITLE>" + title + "</TITLE></HEAD>\n" +
      "<BODY BGCOLOR=\"#FDF5E6\">\n" +
      "<H2>" + title + "</H2>\n" +
      "Sorry, access to servlets by means of\n" +
      "URLs that begin with\n" +
      "http://host/webAppPrefix/servlet/\n" +
```

Listing 3.19 WEB-INF/classes/coreservlets/ NoInvokerServlet.java *(continued)*

```
        "has been disabled.\n" +
        "</BODY></HTML>");
  }

  public void doPost(HttpServletRequest request,
                     HttpServletResponse response)
      throws ServletException, IOException {
    doGet(request, response);
  }
}
```

Unprotected Pages

The fact that *some* pages in a Web application have access restrictions does not imply that *all* pages in the application need such restrictions. Resources that have no access restrictions need no special handling regarding security. There are two points to keep in mind, however.

First, if you use default pages such as index.jsp or index.html, you should have an explicit welcome-file-list entry in web.xml. Without a welcome-file-list entry, servers are not required to use those files as the default file when a user supplies a URL that gives only a directory. See Section 2.8 (Specifying Welcome Pages) for details on the welcome-file-list element.

Second, you should use relative URLs to refer to images or style sheets so that your pages don't need modification if the Web application's URL prefix changes. The application of these points is demonstrated in Listing 3.20 and Figure 3–12 and in Listing 3.21 and Figure 3–13.

Listing 3.20 business/index.html

```
<!DOCTYPE HTML PUBLIC "-//W3C//DTD HTML 4.0 Transitional//EN">
<HTML>
<HEAD>
<TITLE>Business Model</TITLE>
<LINK REL=STYLESHEET
      HREF="../company-styles.css"
      TYPE="text/css">
</HEAD>
<BODY>
```

Listing 3.20 business/index.html *(continued)*

```
<TABLE BORDER=5 ALIGN="CENTER">
  <TR><TH CLASS="TITLE">Business Model</TABLE>
<P>
<H3>Who needs a business model?</H3>
Hey, this is the new economy. We don't need a real business
model, do we?
<P>
OK, ok, if you insist:
<OL>
  <LI>Start a dot-com.
  <LI>Have an IPO.
  <LI>Get a bunch of suckers to work for peanuts
      plus stock options.
  <LI>Retire.
</OL>
Isn't that what many other dot-coms did?
</BODY></HTML>
```

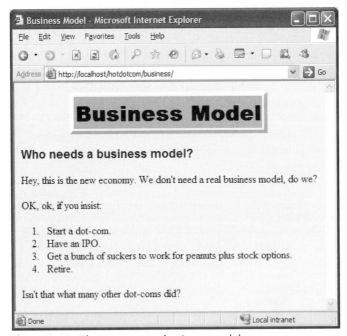

Figure 3–12   The hotdotcom business model.

Listing 3.21	history/index.html

```
<!DOCTYPE HTML PUBLIC "-//W3C//DTD HTML 4.0 Transitional//EN">
<HTML>
<HEAD>
<TITLE>History</TITLE>
<LINK REL=STYLESHEET
      HREF="../company-styles.css"
      TYPE="text/css">
</HEAD>
<BODY>
<TABLE BORDER=5 ALIGN="CENTER">
  <TR><TH CLASS="TITLE">History</TABLE>
<P>
<H3>None yet...</H3>
</BODY></HTML>
```

Figure 3–13   The distinguished `hotdotcom` heritage.

3.3   BASIC Authentication

The most common type of container-managed security is built on form-based authentication, discussed in Section 3.1 (Form-Based Authentication). There, the server automatically redirects unauthenticated users to an HTML form, checks their username and password, determines which logical roles they are in, and sees whether any of those roles is permitted to access the resource in question. Then, it uses a variation of session tracking to remember the users that have already been authenticated.

This approach has the advantage that the login form can have the same look and feel as the rest of the Web site. However, it has a few disadvantages. For example, if the client's browser has cookies disabled, session tracking would fail. Or, the server might be configured to always use URL rewriting. The servlet specification explicitly states that form-based authentication is not guaranteed to work in such a case.

So, another approach is to use the standard HTTP BASIC security. With BASIC security, the browser uses a dialog box instead of an HTML form to collect the user-name and password. Then, the `Authorization` request header is used to remember which users have already been authenticated. As with form-based security, you must use SSL if you are concerned with protecting the network traffic. However, doing so neither changes the way BASIC authentication is set up nor necessitates changes in the individual servlets or JSP pages.

Because there is no login or login-error page to create and configure, another advantage of BASIC authentication is that it's easier to set up. The absence of the login page also means not with having to handle the user trying to access the login page directly as discussed in Section 3.1 (Form-Based Authentication). In reality, most Web sites intended for external customers (e.g., e-commerce sites) use form-based authentication, whereas intranet applications often use BASIC.

There is also DIGEST security and security based on client certificates. However, few browsers or servers support DIGEST, and only fully J2EE-compliant servers are required to support client certificates.

Compared to form-based authentication, the two main disadvantages of BASIC authentication are that the input dialog box looks glaringly different than the rest of your application and it is very difficult to log in as a different user once you are authenticated. In fact, once authenticated, you have to quit the browser and restart if you want to log in as a different user! Now, in principle it is possible to write a "relogin" servlet that sends a 401 (`Unauthorized`) status code and a `WWW-Authenticate` header containing the appropriate realm. But, that is hardly "declarative" security!

Use of BASIC security involves six steps, as shown next. Each of the steps except for the second is identical to the corresponding step used in form-based authentication.

1. **Set up usernames, passwords, and roles.** In this step, you designate a list of users and associate each with a password and one or more abstract roles (e.g., normal user, administrator, etc.). This is a completely server-specific process.
2. **Tell the server that you are using BASIC authentication. Designate the realm name.** This process uses the web.xml `login-config` element with an `auth-method` subelement of `BASIC` and a `realm-name` subelement that specifies the realm (which is generally used as part of the title of the dialog box that the browser opens).

3. **Specify which URLs should be password protected.** For this step, you use the `security-constraint` element of `web.xml`. This element, in turn, uses `web-resource-collection` and `auth-constraint` subelements. The first of these designates the URL patterns to which access should be restricted, and the second specifies the abstract roles that should have access to the resources at the given URLs.

4. **List all possible abstract roles (types of users) that will be granted access to *any* resource.** Each abstract role is declared using the `security-role` element. The `security-role` element contains a required `role-name` element, which contains the name of the abstract role.

5. **Specify which URLs should be available only with SSL.** If your server supports SSL, you can stipulate that certain resources are available only through encrypted `https` (SSL) connections. You use the `user-data-constraint` subelement of `security-constraint` for this purpose.

6. **Turn off the invoker servlet.** If your application restricts access to servlets, the access restrictions are placed only on the custom URL that you associate with the servlet. To prevent users from bypassing the security settings, disable default servlet URLs of the form `http://host/webAppPrefix/servlet/ServletName`. To disable these URLs, use the `servlet-mapping` element with a `url-pattern` subelement that designates a pattern of `/servlet/*`.

Details on these steps are given in the following sections.

Setting Up Usernames, Passwords, and Roles

This step is exactly the same when BASIC authentication is used as when form-based authentication is used. See Section 3.1 (Form-Based Authentication) for details. For a quick summary, recall that this process is completely server specific. Tomcat lets you use *tomcat_dir*/conf/tomcat-users.xml simple test applications.

Telling the Server You Are Using BASIC Authentication; Designating Realm

You use the `login-config` element in the deployment descriptor to control the authentication method. To use BASIC authentication, supply a value of `BASIC` for the `auth-method` subelement and use the `realm-name` subelement to designate the realm that will be used by the browser in the pop-up dialog box and in the `Authorization` request header. Listing 3.22 gives an example.

Listing 3.22 web.xml (Excerpt designating BASIC authentication)

```xml
<?xml version="1.0" encoding="ISO-8859-1"?>
<web-app xmlns="http://java.sun.com/xml/ns/j2ee"
         xmlns:xsi="http://www.w3.org/2001/XMLSchema-instance"
         xsi:schemaLocation=
         "http://java.sun.com/xml/ns/j2ee
          http://java.sun.com/xml/ns/j2ee/web-app_2_4.xsd"
         version="2.4">
  <security-constraint>...</security-constraint>
  <login-config>
    <auth-method>BASIC</auth-method>
    <realm-name>Some Name</realm-name>
  </login-config>
</web-app>
```

Specifying URLs That Should Be Password Protected

You designate password-protected resources in the same manner with BASIC authentication as you do with form-based authentication. See Section 3.1 (Form-Based Authentication) for details. For a quick summary, you use the security-constraint element to specify restricted URLs and the roles that should have access to them. The security-constraint element contains four possible subelements: display-name (an optional element giving a name for IDEs to use), web-resource-collection (a required element that specifies the URLs that should be protected), auth-constraint (an optional element that designates the abstract roles that should have access to the URLs), and user-data-constraint (an optional element that specifies whether SSL is required). Multiple web-resource-collection entries are permitted within security-constraint.

Listing All Possible Abstract Roles

You have to declare all possible abstract roles in the same manner with BASIC authentication as you do with form-based authentication. See Section 3.1 (Form-Based Authentication) for details. For a quick summary, you use one or more security-role elements for this purpose. Each security-role element contains an optional description element and a required role-name element.

Specifying URLs That Should Be Available Only with SSL

You designate SSL-only resources in the same manner with BASIC authentication as you do with form-based authentication. See Section 3.1 (Form-Based Authentication) for details. To summarize, use the `user-data-constraint` subelement of `security-constraint` with a `transport-guarantee` subelement specifying `INTEGRAL` or `CONFIDENTIAL`.

In addition to simply requiring SSL, the servlet API provides a way for stipulating that users must authenticate themselves with client certificates. You supply a value of `CLIENT-CERT` for the `auth-method` subelement of `login-config` (see "Specifying URLs That Should Be Password Protected" in Section 3.1). However, only application servers that have full J2EE support are required to support this capability.

3.4   Example: BASIC Authentication

In Section 3.2 (Example: Form-Based Authentication), we showed the external Web site for a fictional company named hot-dot-com.com. In this section, we show their intranet. Because applications that use form-based authentication vary only slightly from those that use BASIC authentication, we just concentrate on the differences here. We start by showing the home page, then list the web.xml file, summarize the various protection mechanisms, show the password file, and give the code for each of the protected resources.

The Home Page

Listing 3.23 shows the top-level home page for the Web application. The application is registered with a URL prefix of /hotdotcom-internal so the home page can be accessed with the URL http://*host*/hotdotcom-internal/index.jsp as shown in Figure 3–14. If you've forgotten how to assign URL prefixes to Web applications, review Section 1.3 (Registering Web Applications with the Server).

Now, the main home page has no security protections and consequently does not absolutely require an entry in web.xml. However, many users expect URLs that list a directory but no file to invoke the default file from that directory. So, we put a `welcome-file-list` entry in web.xml (see Listing 3.24 in the next section) to ensure that http://*host*/hotdotcom-internal/ invokes index.jsp.

Listing 3.23 index.jsp (Top-level home page)

```
<!DOCTYPE HTML PUBLIC "-//W3C//DTD HTML 4.0 Transitional//EN">
<HTML>
<HEAD>
<TITLE>hot-dot-com.com!</TITLE>
<LINK REL=STYLESHEET
      HREF="company-styles.css"
      TYPE="text/css">
</HEAD>
<BODY>
<TABLE BORDER=5 ALIGN="CENTER">
  <TR><TH CLASS="TITLE">hot-dot-com.com!</TABLE>
<P>
<H3>Welcome to the hot-dot-com intranet</H3>
Please select one of the following:
<UL>
  <LI><A HREF="financial-plan.html">Financial Plan</A>.
      Available to all employees.
  <LI><A HREF="business-plan.html">Business Plan</A>.
      Available only to corporate executives.
  <LI><A HREF="employee-pay.jsp">Employee Compensation Plans</A>.
      Available to all employees.
</UL>
</BODY></HTML>
```

Figure 3–14   Home page for the hot-dot-com.com intranet.

The Deployment Descriptor

Listing 3.24 shows the complete deployment descriptor used with the hotdot-com-internal Web application.

The deployment descriptor specifies several things:

- URLs that give a directory but no file name result in the server first trying to use index.jsp and next trying index.html. If neither file is available, the result is server specific (e.g., a directory listing).
- URLs that use the default servlet mapping (i.e., http://*host*/hotdotcom/ servlet/*ServletName*) invoke the NoInvokerServlet and display a message telling the user that the invoker servlet has been disabled.
- The financial-plan.html page can be accessed only by company employees or executives.
- The business-plan.html page can be accessed only by company executives.

Listing 3.24   WEB-INF/web.xml (Complete version for hot-dot-com.com intranet)

```xml
<?xml version="1.0" encoding="ISO-8859-1"?>
<web-app xmlns="http://java.sun.com/xml/ns/j2ee"
         xmlns:xsi="http://www.w3.org/2001/XMLSchema-instance"
         xsi:schemaLocation=
         "http://java.sun.com/xml/ns/j2ee
          http://java.sun.com/xml/ns/j2ee/web-app_2_4.xsd"
         version="2.4">
  <error-page>
    <error-code>400</error-code>
    <location>/WEB-INF/jspPages/failed-login.jsp</location>
  </error-page>

  <error-page>
    <error-code>403</error-code>
    <location>/WEB-INF/jspPages/forbidden.jsp</location>
  </error-page>

  <!-- Protect financial plan. Employees or executives. -->
  <security-constraint>
    <web-resource-collection>
      <web-resource-name>Financial Plan</web-resource-name>
      <url-pattern>/financial-plan.html</url-pattern>
    </web-resource-collection>
    <auth-constraint>
      <role-name>employee</role-name>
      <role-name>executive</role-name>
    </auth-constraint>
  </security-constraint>
</security-constraint>
```

Listing 3.24   WEB-INF/web.xml (Complete version for hot-dot-com.com intranet) *(continued)*

```xml
<!-- Protect business plan. Executives only. -->
<security-constraint>
  <web-resource-collection>
    <web-resource-name>Business Plan</web-resource-name>
    <url-pattern>/business-plan.html</url-pattern>
  </web-resource-collection>
  <auth-constraint>
    <role-name>executive</role-name>
  </auth-constraint>
</security-constraint>
<!-- Protect compensation plan. Employees or executives. -->
<security-constraint>
  <web-resource-collection>
    <web-resource-name>Compensation Plan</web-resource-name>
    <url-pattern>/employee-pay.jsp</url-pattern>
  </web-resource-collection>
  <auth-constraint>
    <role-name>employee</role-name>
    <role-name>executive</role-name>
  </auth-constraint>
</security-constraint>

<!-- Tell the server to use BASIC authentication. -->
<login-config>
  <auth-method>BASIC</auth-method>
  <realm-name>Intranet</realm-name>
</login-config>

<security-role>
<role-name>employee</role-name>
</security-role>
<security-role>
<role-name>executive</role-name>
</security-role>

<!-- Disable the invoker servlet. -->
<servlet>
  <servlet-name>NoInvoker</servlet-name>
  <servlet-class>coreservlets.NoInvokerServlet</servlet-class>
</servlet>
<servlet-mapping>
  <servlet-name>NoInvoker</servlet-name>
  <url-pattern>/servlet/*</url-pattern>
</servlet-mapping>
```

| Listing 3.24 | WEB-INF/web.xml (Complete version for hot-dot-com.com intranet) *(continued)* |

```
<!-- If URL gives a directory but no file name, try index.jsp
     first and index.html second. If neither is found,
     the result is server specific (e.g., a directory
     listing). -->
<welcome-file-list>
  <welcome-file>index.jsp</welcome-file>
  <welcome-file>index.html</welcome-file>
</welcome-file-list>
</web-app>
```

The Password File

Tomcat password files are not specific to Web applications; they are general to the server. Listing 3.25 shows the password file used by Tomcat for this Web application. It defines three new users: `gates` and `ellison` in the `employee` role and `mcnealy` in the `executive` role.

| Listing 3.25 | install_dir/conf/tomcat-users.xml (Three new users) |

```
<?xml version='1.0' encoding='utf-8'?>
<tomcat-users>
  <role rolename="registered-user" />
  <role rolename="administrator" />
  <role rolename="employee" />
  <role rolename="executive" />

  <user username="juan" password="nauj"
        roles="administrator" />
  <user username="john" password="nhoj"
        roles="registered-user" />
  <user username="juana" password="anauj"
        roles="administrator,registered-user" />
  <user username="jane" password="enaj"
        roles="registered-user" />
  <user username="gates" password="llib"
        roles="employee" />
  <user username="ellison" password="yrral"
        roles="employee" />
  <user username="mcnealy" password="ttocs"
        roles="executive" />
</tomcat-users>
```

The Financial Plan

Listing 3.26 shows the first of the protected pages at the `hotdotcom-internal` site. Figure 3–15 shows the dialog box presented by Microsoft Internet Explorer to unauthenticated users who attempt to access the page. If authentication fails, the same dialog box will be redisplayed to the user up to three times. If the third try is likewise unsuccessful, the login-failure page will be displayed. We also place the `error-page` element into the `web.xml` file to direct the server to display our custom 401 page (e.g., `failed-login.jsp`) instead of the Tomcat's generated one like so:

```
<error-page>
  <error-code>401</error-code>
  <location>/WEB-INF/jspPages/failed-login.jsp</location>
</error-page>
```

For more detail on setting up error pages see Section 2.9 (Designating Pages to Handle Errors). Figure 3–16 shows an unsuccessful login (after three tries) and Figure 3–17 shows a successful login attempt.

Listing 3.26   financial-plan.html

```
<!DOCTYPE HTML PUBLIC "-//W3C//DTD HTML 4.0 Transitional//EN">
<HTML>
<HEAD>
<TITLE>Financial Plan</TITLE>
<LINK REL=STYLESHEET
      HREF="company-styles.css"
      TYPE="text/css">
</HEAD>
<BODY>
<TABLE BORDER=5 ALIGN="CENTER">
  <TR><TH CLASS="TITLE">Financial Plan</TABLE>
<P>
<H3>Steps:</H3>
<OL>
  <LI>Make lots of money.
  <LI>Increase value of stock options.
  <LI>Make more money.
  <LI>Increase stock option value further.
</OL>
</BODY></HTML>
```

Figure 3–15 Unauthenticated users who attempt to access protected resources are presented with a dialog box. If the authentication fails, the same dialog box will be redisplayed to the user up to three times.

Figure 3–16 If the user tries to log in three times in a row and fails, the unsuccessful login page will be displayed.

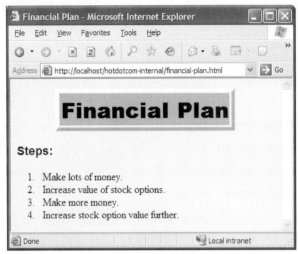

Figure 3–17   A successful login attempt.

The Business Plan

The financial plan of the previous section is available to all employees and executives. The business plan (Listing 3.27), in contrast, is available only to executives. Thus, it is possible for an authenticated user to be denied access to it. Figure 3–18 shows this result. You have access to more than one username/password combination. You were authenticated as a user with restricted privileges. You now want to log in as a user with additional privileges. How do you do so? Unfortunately, the answer is to quit the browser and restart. That's one of the downsides of BASIC authentication.

Figure 3–19 shows the result after the browser is restarted and the client logs in as a user in the executive role (mcnealy in this case).

Listing 3.27	business-plan.html

```
<!DOCTYPE HTML PUBLIC "-//W3C//DTD HTML 4.0 Transitional//EN">
<HTML>
<HEAD>
<TITLE>Business Plan</TITLE>
<LINK REL=STYLESHEET
      HREF="company-styles.css"
      TYPE="text/css">
</HEAD>
```

| Listing 3.27 | business-plan.html *(continued)* |

```
<BODY>
<TABLE BORDER=5 ALIGN="CENTER">
  <TR><TH CLASS="TITLE">Business Plan</TABLE>
<P>
<H3>Steps:</H3>
<OL>
  <LI>Inflate name recognition by buying meaningless ads
      on high-profile TV shows.
  <LI>Decrease employee pay by promising stock options instead.
  <LI>Increase executive pay with lots of perks and bonuses.
  <LI>Get bought out before anyone notices we have no
      business plan.
</OL>
</BODY>
</HTML>
```

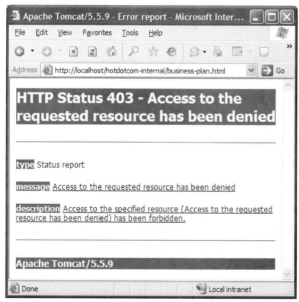

Figure 3–18 Attempt to access the business plan by an authenticated user who is not in the `executive` role. This result is different from that of failed authentication, which is shown in Figure 3–16.

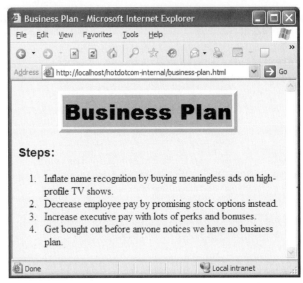

Figure 3–19   Attempt to access the business plan by an authenticated user who is in the `executive` role.

The NoInvoker Servlet

As it currently stands, the `hotdotcom-internal` application has no protected servlets, so it is not absolutely necessary to disable the invoker servlet for the requests that are sent to http://*host*/hotdotcom-internal/servlet/something. However, it is a good idea to plan ahead and disable the invoker servlet as a matter of course in all Web applications that have restricted resources.

This application uses the same `NoInvokerServlet` (Listing 3.19) and `url-pattern` entry in web.xml (Listing 3.24) as does the external `hotdotcom` application.

3.5   Configuring Tomcat to Use SSL

Servlet and JSP containers are not required to support SSL, even in fully J2EE-compliant application servers or with version 2.4 of the servlet specification. There are servlet containers that don't support SSL and function as a plug-in to the Web server. Even if the communication between the client and the Web server is encrypted, the communication between the Web server and the servlet container might not be. Thus, if you declare that some URLs in your application must use SSL, you would not be able to deploy your application on such a server. Therefore, Web applications that rely on SSL are not necessarily portable.

Nevertheless, SSL is extremely useful, and many applications make use of it. For example, many application servers are self-contained; they do not have a servlet/JSP plug-in that is separate from the main Web server. In addition, some server plug-ins use SSL even for the communication between the Web server and the plug-in. The BEA WebLogic plug-in and IBM WebSphere support this very useful capability, for example.

In Tomcat, the support for SSL is present, but disabled by default. This section summarizes the steps necessary to enable the SSL support in Tomcat. For more details, see http://jakarta.apache.org/tomcat/tomcat-5.0-doc/ssl-howto.html.

1. **Create a self-signed public key certificate.** SSL-based servers use X.509 certificates to validate to clients that they (i.e., the servers) are who they claim to be. This prevents attackers from hacking Domain Name System (DNS) servers to redirect SSL requests to their site. For real-world use, the certificate needs to be signed by a trusted authority like VeriSign or Thawte. For testing purposes, however, a self-signed certificate is sufficient. To generate one that will be valid for two years (730 days), execute the following:

   ```
   keytool -genkey -alias tomcat -keyalg RSA -validity 730
   ```

   The system will prompt you for a variety of information starting with your first and last name. For a server certificate, this should be the server's name, not your name! For example, with a server that will be accessed from multiple machines, respond with the hostname (www.yourcompany.com) or the Internet Protocol (IP) address (207.46.230.220) when asked "What is your first and last name?" For a development server that will run on your desktop, use localhost. Remember that, for deployment purposes, self-signed certificates are not sufficient. You would need to get your certificate signed by a trusted Certificate Authority. You can use certificates from keytool for this purpose also; it just requires a lot more work. For testing purposes, however, self-signed certificates are just as good as trusted ones.

Core Approach

Supply the server's hostname or IP address when asked for your first and last name. Use localhost for a desktop development server.

The system will also prompt you for your organization, your location, a keystore password, and a key password. Be sure to use the same value for both passwords. The system will then create a file called .keystore in your home directory (e.g., /home/username on UNIX or C:\Documents and Settings\username on Windows XP). You can also use the -keystore argument to change where this file is created.

For more details on keytool (including information on creating trusted certificates that are signed by a standard Certificate Authority), see http://java.sun.com/j2se/1.5.0/docs/tooldocs/windows/keytool.html.

2. **Copy the keystore file to the Tomcat installation directory.** Copy the .keystore file just created from your home directory to *tomcat_dir*.

3. **Uncomment and edit the SSL connector entry in *tomcat_dir/* conf/server.xml.** Look for a commented-out Connector element that has the port attribute set to 8443. Remove the enclosing comment tags (<!--...-->). Change the port from 8443 to the default SSL value of 443. Add a keystoreFile attribute designating the location and name of the keystore file relative to the tomcat_dir installation directory. Add a keystorePass attribute designating the password (used when you created the .keystore file). Here is an example:

```
<Connector port="443" maxHttpHeaderSize="8192"
           maxThreads="150" minSpareThreads="25"
           maxSpareThreads="75" enableLookups="false"
           disableUploadTimeout="true" acceptCount="100"
           scheme="https" secure="true" clientAuth="false"
           sslProtocol="TLS" keystoreFile=".keystore"
           keystorePass="mypassword"/>
```

4. **Change the main connector entry in *tomcat_dir*/conf/ server.xml to use port 443 for SSL redirects.** Use the redirectPort attribute to specify this. Here is an example:

```
<Connector port="80" maxHttpHeaderSize="8192"
           maxThreads="150" minSpareThreads="25"
           maxSpareThreads="75" enableLookups="false"
           redirectPort="443" acceptCount="100"
           connectionTimeout="20000"
           disableUploadTimeout="true"/>
```

5. **Restart the server.**
6. **Access https://localhost/.** (Note that this URL starts with https, not http.) With Firefox, you should see an initial warning like that of Figure 3–20. If you click the Examine Certificate button, you should see a dialog box like the one shown in Figure 3–21. You can suppress the warnings on Firefox by choosing the "Accept this certificate permanently" option in the original warning dialog box. Once you have accepted the certificate, you should see the Tomcat home page (Figure 3–22). With Internet Explorer, you will see an initial warning like that shown in Figure 3–23. To view the certificate information, click the View Certificate button. You should see something close to Figure 3–24. For future requests, you can suppress the warnings by clicking the Install Certificate button and importing the certificate (Figures 3–25 through 3–29). The next time you access http://localhost/, you should see the Tomcat home page without any warnings as in Figure 3–30.

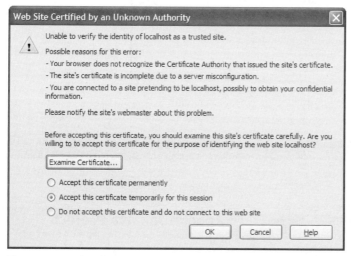

Figure 3–20 Certificate warning dialog box supplied by Firefox. You can view the certificate information by clicking Examine Certificate.

Figure 3–21   Certificate information presented on Firefox.

Figure 3–22   After the certificate has been accepted, accessing Tomcat's home page with HTTPS does not produce any warnings (Firefox shown).

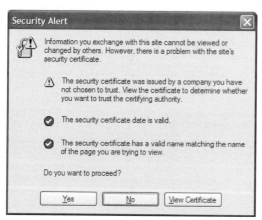

Figure 3–23 Certificate warning dialog box supplied by Internet Explorer. You can view the certificate information by clicking View Certificate.

Figure 3–24 Certificate information presented by Internet Explorer. View different types of certificate information by clicking the General, Details, and Certification Path tabs at the top of this dialog box. To suppress future warnings, you can import the certificate by clicking the Install Certificate button and starting the Certificate Import Wizard shown in Figure 3–25.

Figure 3–25   First screen of the Certificate Import Wizard in Internet Explorer.

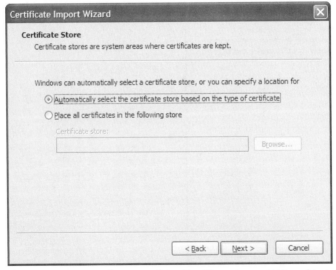

Figure 3–26   Second screen of the Certificate Import Wizard in Internet Explorer. You can let Internet Explorer place the certificate in its default certificate store or choose your own.

Figure 3–27 Third screen of the Certificate Import Wizard in Internet Explorer.

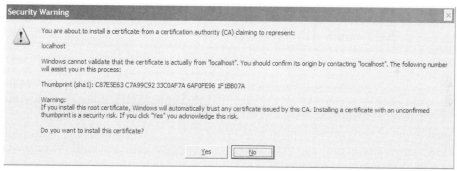

Figure 3–28 Warning dialog box in Internet Explorer making sure you understand that once the certificate is imported, Windows will no longer pop up a warning dialog box, automatically trusting this certificate.

Figure 3–29 Internet Explorer Certificate Import Wizard success dialog box.

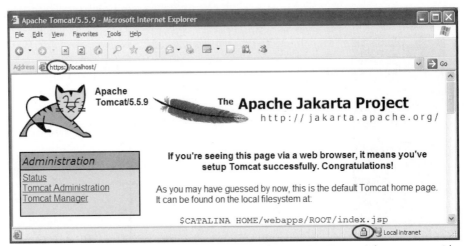

Figure 3–30   After the certificate has been accepted, accessing Tomcat's home page with HTTPS does not produce any warnings (Internet Explorer shown).

3.6   WebClient: Talking to Web Servers Interactively

Sometimes, debugging Web-based applications is fairly difficult. Is the problem with the code, the browser, or the networking? To help debug Web applications, we wrote WebClient, a standalone Swing application to interactively connect to Web servers, send requests, and receive replies. Essentially, WebClient is a simple browser from which you can send custom HTTP requests to the server and see both the response headers and returned document.

The code for WebClient is available at http://www.coreservlets.com/ and is bundled as an executable JAR file. To run this program as a JAR file, enter the following line at the command prompt:

```
PROMPT> java -jar webclient.jar
```

WebClient supports the following options:

- **GET or POST.** You can select either a GET or POST request. For a GET request, you need to append any query data to the URL after a question mark, ?. For a POST request, you would enter the query data in the Query Data text area. Remember that for a POST request you need to add a Content-Length header to the request.

- **HTTP/1.0 or HTTP/1.1.** You can select either the HTTP/1.0 or HTTP/1.1 protocol version for the request. Remember that for HTTP/1.1 a HOST header is also required (e.g., Host: *hostname*, where *hostname* is the host server from which to request the page).
- **Request headers.** You can specify one or more request headers. If you are uncertain which headers your browser normally sends to a server, you can use the EchoServer program to see them. EchoServer simply sends back the complete HTTP request, wrapped in an HTML document. You can find EchoServer in Chapter 19 of Volume 1 or online at http://www.coreservlets.com/.
- **Query data.** You can send POST data to the server. When sending name/value pairs, you must encode the value in the application/x-www-form-urlencoded format. See http://www.w3.org/TR/html40/appendix/notes.html#non-ascii-chars for encoding details. If you are unfamiliar with this encoding, WebClient provides a button, Encode Data, to encode the data for you. Note that WebClient assumes a UTF-8 character set.
- **Secure Sockets Layer (SSL).** You can send a request either as HTTP or HTTPS (SSL 3.0). For a secure connection, WebClient obtains a socket from an SSLSocketFactory by using a code similar to the following:

```
SocketFactory factory = SSLSocketFactory.getDefault();
Socket secureClient = factory.createSocket(host, port);
```

Before establishing an SSL connection, Java uses the default keystore at *JRE_HOME*/lib/security/cacerts to determine whether to trust the signed server certificate. This file contains a number of standard Certificate Authorities (CAs).

If you digitally sign your own certificates (see Section 3.7) and need to use a different keystore that knows about your CA, specify the location and type of the keystore through the javax.net.ssl.trustStore and javax.net.ssl.trustStoreType system properties, respectively. For example, if the name of the keystore is .keystore and the keystore type is JKS, start WebClient with the following command:

```
PROMPT> java -Djavax.net.ssl.trustStore=.keystore
             -Djavax.net.ssl.trustStoreType=JKS
             -jar webclient.jar
```

Common keystore types are JKS, JCEKS, and PKCS12.
- **Proxy servers.** If your network environment uses a proxy server, you can specify both a proxy host and proxy port to use with WebClient.

When a request is sent to a proxy server, the complete URL is sent, instead of just the URI. For example, if you request the page http://java.sun.com/reference/api/, `WebClient` sends the following request to the proxy server:

```
GET http://java.sun.com/reference/api/ HTTP/1.0
```

In this example, the proxy server, in turn, then sends the standard request to java.sun.com:

```
GET /reference/api/ HTTP/1.0
```

Be aware that some proxy servers may use special proxy headers, for instance, `Proxy-Connection` and `Proxy-Authorization`. Contact the administrator of the proxy server if you have questions.

A representative conversation of `WebClient` with www.google.com is shown in Figure 3–31. Here, the URL is http://www.google.com/search, and the query data for the `GET` request is q=Olympics+Torino—a Google search for documents on the 2006 Winter Olympics in Torino, Italy.

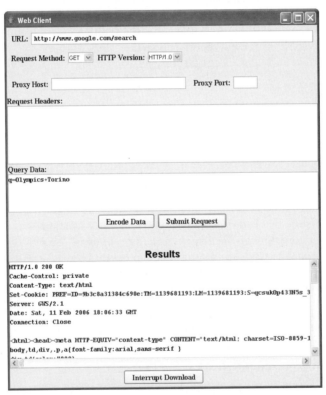

Figure 3–31 Conversation with www.google.com, where the user can completely customize the request. The captured server response shows both the response headers and document.

3.7   Signing a Server Certificate

In Section 3.5 (Configuring Tomcat to Use SSL) we show you how to configure a self-signed public key certificate for a server. Self-signed certificates are suitable for development and testing; however, to simulate a production environment, you may want a trusted certificate signed by a CA.

You can submit a certificate signing request to many recognized commercial CAs (for instance, http://www.thawte.com/ and http://www.entrust.com/). However, purchasing a signed digital certificate from a commercial company is relatively expensive, so many corporations choose to set themselves up as their own CA.

In this section, we illustrate signing a server certificate as a CA. Much of the detail for setting up a CA is beyond the scope of this book, so instead, we use the Java Security Tool Kit (JSTK), written by Pankaj Kumar. The JSTK is available for educational purposes under the Open Source License v2.0 at http://www.j2ee-security.net/.

Next, we cover the steps to sign your own CA and server certificates. The steps we present are for the Java Developer's Kit (JDK) 1.4.2_09 on a Windows platform. If you are using an earlier JDK or a different operating system, please check the JSTK documentation for specific information.

1. **Download and install the JSTK.** The JSTK is available at
    http://www.j2ee-security.net/book/dnldsrc/ as a ZIP file,
    jstk-1_0_1.zip. Unzip the JSTK into the default directory,
    C:\jstk-1.0.1, and from a DOS window set both the JAVA_HOME
    and the JSTK_HOME environment variables as shown:

    ```
    C:\jstk-1.0.1> set JAVA_HOME=C:\j2sdk1.4.2_09
    C:\jstk-1.0.1> set JSTK_HOME=C:\jstk-1.0.1
    ```

    The JAVA_HOME variable refers to the install directory of the JDK, and the JSTK_HOME variable refers to the install directory of the JSTK.

    The JSTK contains numerous scripts, of which we use only the certtool script to set up a CA and sign certificates. For more information on the other tools available in the JSTK, we recommend reading the security book, *J2EE Security for Servlets, EJBs, and Web Services*, by Pankaj Kumar.

2. **Set up the CA.** Use the JSTK certtool script to establish a public key infrastructure (PKI) for your CA. Enter the following command to set up a keystore for your CA:

    ```
    C:\jstk-1.0.1> bin\certtool.bat setupca -dn "CN=MyCompany
               Root CA, OU=J2EE Division, O=MyCompany Inc., C=US"
            -storetype jks -password certauth
    ```

```
CA setup successful: cadir
```

This command creates a CA keystore, ca.ks, in the subdirectory cadir. The keystore type is jks (Java KeyStore) and the CA keystore password is certauth.

For a complete description of the options when setting up a Root CA, enter

```
C:\jstk-1.0.1> bin\certtool.bat setupca -h
```

3. **Create a self-signed public key certificate.** Issue the Java keytool command shown here to generate a public–private key pair and self-signed server certificate. Following, we show an example input to the questions generated by the keytool command.

```
C:\jstk-1.0.1> keytool -alias tomcat -genkey -keyalg RSA
                       -validity 730 -keystore .keystore
                       -storepass srvrpass
What is your first and last name?
  [Unknown]:  localhost
What is the name of your organizational unit?
  [Unknown]:  Consulting
What is the name of your organization?
  [Unknown]:  LMBrown.com, Inc.
What is the name of your City or Locality?
  [Unknown]:  Manassas
What is the name of your State or Province?
  [Unknown]:  VA
What is the two-letter country code for this unit?
  [Unknown]:  US
Is CN=localhost, OU=Consulting, O="LMBrown.com, Inc.",
L=Manassas, ST=VA, C=US correct?
  [no]:  yes

Enter key password for <tomcat>
          (RETURN if same as keystore password): srvrpass
```

The command creates a public–private key pair, with the public key wrapped in an X.509 v3 self-signed certificate and stored as a single certificate chain. Both the certificate chain and private key are stored in the keystore identified by the alias tomcat. The name of the keystore is .keystore (located in the working directory) with a password of srvrpass. The certificate is considered valid for 730 days (two years).

4. **Generate a certificate signing request (CSR).** Use the keytool to generate a CSR in the PKCS#10 format, suitable for signing by your CA. The following command creates a CSR for the self-signed certificate identified by the alias tomcat in .keystore:

```
C:\jstk-1.0.1> keytool -certreq -alias tomcat
               -keystore .keystore -storepass srvrpass
               -file server.csr
```

The generated CSR is stored in the file server.csr.

5. **Sign the server certificate by the JSTK Test CA.** Use the following JSTK `certtool` command to sign the CSR by the JSTK Test CA:

```
C:\jstk-1.0.1> bin\certtool.bat issue -csrfile server.csr
               -cerfile server.cer -password certauth

Issued Certificate written to file: server.cer
```

The command accepts the CSR, server.csr, signs the request by the CA, and places the signed certificate in the file server.cer. The password is the CA keystore password, `certauth`.

6. **Import the trusted certificate into the server keystore.** The last step is to enter the following `keytool` command to import the CA-signed server certificate back into the server keystore:

```
C:\jstk-1.0.1> keytool -import -alias tomcat
               -keystore .keystore -storepass srvrpass
               -file server.cer
Top-level certificate in reply:

Owner: CN=MyCompany Root CA, OU=J2EE Division,
       O=MyCompany Inc., C=US
Issuer: CN=MyCompany Root CA, OU=J2EE Division,
       O=MyCompany Inc., C=US
Serial number: 64
Valid from: Sun Nov 13 08:26:00 GMT-05:00 2005
       until: Sat Aug 09 08:26:00 GMT-05:00 2008
Certificate fingerprints:
       MD5: B9:68:45:17:86:38:62:BC:36:E3:89:E7:25:5B:49:56
       SHA1: 85:54:FE:B3:CA:43:BF:00:D6:62:BC:B7:36:62:
             0A:39:F6:9F:4A:F5

... is not trusted. Install reply anyway? [no]: yes
Certificate reply was installed in keystore
```

Once you've completed this last step, you should have a certificate, signed by MyCompany Root CA, for your server located in .keystore. If you'd like to test this certificate with Apache Tomcat, see Section 3.5 (Configuring Tomcat to Use SSL) for configuring the server for a certificate. Just be certain to specify `srvrpass` for the password of the server keystore.

Exporting the CA Certificate

To install your CA certificate into your browser as a Trusted Root Certificate, you can export the certificate with the following command:

```
C:\jstk-1.0.1> keytool -export -alias cakey -file ca.cer
                    -keystore cadir\ca.ks
                    -storetype jks -storepass certauth
Certificate stored in file <ca.cer>
```

The command exports the CA certificate to the file ca.cer.

To import the CA certificate as a Trusted Root Certificate in Internet Explorer, select Tools, Internet Options, then click the Content tab (Figure 3–32).

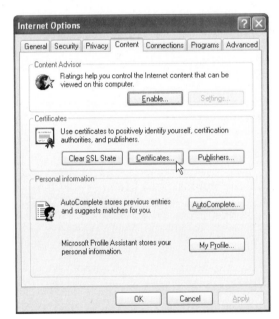

Figure 3–32   Content tab for Internet Options in Internet Explorer 6.0.

Click the Certificates button to open the Certificates dialog box and click the Trusted Root Certification Authorities tab (Figure 3–33).

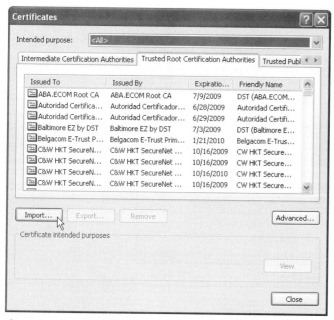

Figure 3–33   Trusted Root Certification Authorities tab in the Certificates dialog box.

Click Import to open the Certificate Import Wizard (Figure 3–34) and then click Next to display the window for selecting the CA certificate (Figure 3–35). Browse to the ca.cer file located in the C:\jstk-1.0.1 directory and click Next.

Figure 3–34   Initial Certificate Import Wizard to import a new CA certificate.

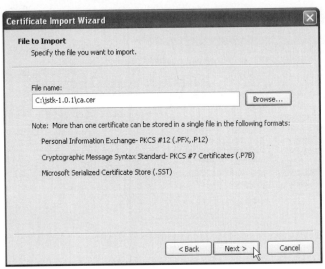

Figure 3–35   Selection of the `ca.cer` file issues by JSTK Test Root CA.

When presented with the option to choose the certificate store (Figure 3–36), accept the default option of "Place all certificates in the following store," and then click Next.

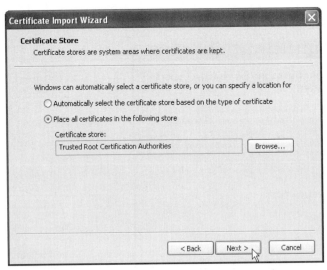

Figure 3–36   Available options for choosing the certificate store for the new CA certificate.

At this point, you should see a summary of the settings to complete the import (Figure 3–37). Click Finish.

Figure 3–37   Summary of configuration settings before completion of the certificate import.

When prompted to add the certificate to the Root Store (Figure 3–38), click Yes. The MyCompany Root CA should now be listed as one of the Trusted Root Certification Authorities (Figure 3–39). Click Close.

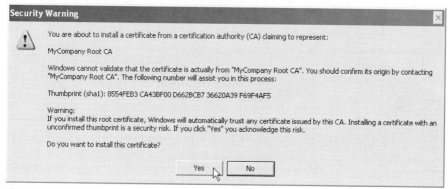

Figure 3–38   Dialog box to choose whether to add the certificate to the Root Store. Click Yes.

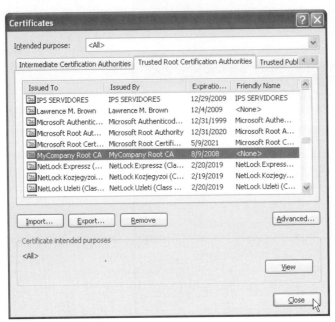

Figure 3–39 Certificates dialog box showing the MyCompany Root CA added to the Trusted Root Certification Authorities list.

If you configured Apache Tomcat on your localhost to use the .keystore created earlier (see Section 3.5), then you can successfully load https://localhost/ into the browser without a warning message (see Figure 3–40).

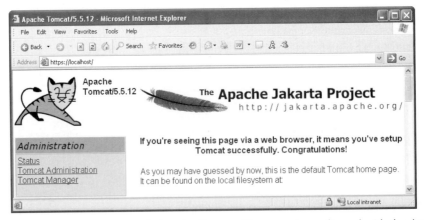

Figure 3–40 Using SSL with Apache Tomcat. The server is configured with the .keystore containing the server certificate signed by the CA and the browser is configured to trust the signing CA.

Using WebClient with Tomcat and SSL

In Section 3.6 (WebClient: Talking to Web Servers Interactively), we presented WebClient, a simple browser to help you debug your Web applications over SSL connections and through proxy servers. WebClient permits you to examine both the server response headers and the returned document.

If you configure Tomcat for SSL and use the default keystore for the Java Runtime Environment (JRE), WebClient will throw an SSLHandshakeException "No trusted certificate found." exception when you request a secure Web page, for example, https://localhost/.

This exception occurs because the JRE, by default, uses the keystore located at *JRE_HOME*/jre/lib/security/cacerts to determine whether to trust the server certificate and establish the SSL connection. The keystore, cacerts, contains many common root CA certificates (see http://java.sun.com/j2se/1.4.2/docs/tooldocs/windows/keytool.html#Certificates); however, if you established your own CA, the JRE has no knowledge of the CA that signed your server certificate.

To specify a different keystore containing information about your CA when starting WebClient, provide a system property for the keystore location javax.net.ssl.trustStore and a system property for the keystore type javax.net.ssl.trustStoreType.

The following command starts WebClient with the keystore of the CA created earlier:

```
Prompt> java -jar
  -Djavax.net.ssl.trustStore=C:\jstk-1.0.1\cadir\ca.ks
  -Djavax.net.ssl.trustStoreType=jks
  webclient.jar
```

Figure 3–41 shows a typical SSL communication with Tomcat through WebClient. The page requested is https://localhost/.

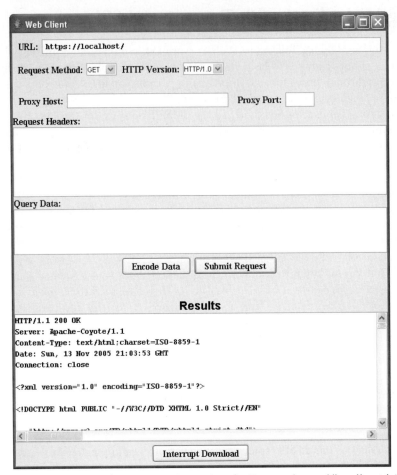

Figure 3–41   Test of SSL connection to Apache Tomcat, `https://localhost/`. When starting `WebClient`, command-line system properties specify information about the Root CA (for the returned SSL server certificate).

PROGRAMMATIC SECURITY

Topics in This Chapter

- Combining container-managed and programmatic security
- Using the `isUserInRole` method
- Using the `getRemoteUser` method
- Using the `getUserPrincipal` method
- Programmatically controlling all aspects of security
- Using SSL with programmatic security

Chapter 4

Chapter 3 (Declarative Security) introduced two fundamental aspects of Web application security:

1. **Preventing unauthorized users from accessing sensitive data.**
   This process involves *access restriction* (identifying which resources need protection and who should have access to them) and *authentication* (identifying users to determine if they are one of the authorized ones). Simple authentication involves the user entering a username and password in an HTML form or a dialog box; stronger authentication involves the use of X.509 certificates sent by the client to the server. The first aspect of Web security applies to virtually all secure applications. Even intranets at locations with physical access controls usually require some sort of user authentication.
2. **Preventing attackers from stealing network data while it is in transit.** This process involves the use of SSL to encrypt the traffic between the browser and the server. This capability is generally reserved for particularly sensitive applications or for particularly sensitive pages within a larger application. After all, unless the attackers are on your local subnet, it is exceedingly difficult for them to gain access to your network traffic.

There are two general strategies for implementing these security aspects: *declarative security* and *programmatic security*.

With declarative security, the topic of the previous chapter, none of the individual servlets or JSP pages need any security-aware code. Instead, both of the major security aspects are handled by the server. To prevent unauthorized access, you use the Web application deployment descriptor (web.xml) to declare that certain URLs need protection, and which categories of users should have access to them. You also designate the authentication method that the server should use to identify users. At request time, the server automatically prompts users for usernames and passwords when they try to access restricted resources, automatically checks the results against a predefined set of usernames and passwords, and automatically keeps track of which users have previously been authenticated. This process is completely transparent to the servlets and JSP pages. To safeguard network data, you use the deployment descriptor to stipulate that certain URLs should only be accessible with SSL. If users try to use a regular HTTP connection to access one of these URLs, the server automatically redirects them to the HTTPS (SSL) equivalent.

Declarative security is all well and good. In fact, it is by far the most common approach to Web application security. But what if you want your servlets to be completely independent of any server-specific settings such as password files? Or, what if you want to let users in various roles access a particular resource but customize the data depending on the role that they are in? Or, what if you want to authenticate users other than by requiring an exact match from a fixed set of usernames and passwords? That's where programmatic security comes in.

With programmatic security, the topic of this chapter, protected servlets and JSP pages at least partially manage their own security. To prevent unauthorized access, each servlet or JSP page must either authenticate the user or verify that the user has been authenticated previously. Even after the servlet or JSP page grants access to a user, it can still customize the results for different individual users or categories of users. To safeguard network data, each servlet or JSP page has to check the network protocol used to access it. If users try to use a regular HTTP connection to access one of these URLs, the servlet or JSP page must manually redirect them to the HTTPS (SSL) equivalent.

4.1   Combining Container-Managed and Programmatic Security

Declarative security is very convenient: you set up usernames, passwords, access mechanisms (HTML forms vs. BASIC authentication) and transport-layer requirements (SSL vs. normal HTTP), all without putting any security-related code in any of the individual servlets or JSP pages. However, declarative security provides only two levels of access for each resource: allowed and denied. Declarative security provides no options to permit resources to customize their output depending on the username or role of the client that accesses them.

It would be nice to provide this customization without giving up the convenience of container-managed security for the usernames, passwords, and roles as would be required if a servlet or JSP page completely managed its own security (as in Section 4.3). To support this type of hybrid security, the servlet specification provides three methods in `HttpServletRequest`:

- **isUserInRole.** This method determines if the currently authenticated user belongs to a specified role. For example, given the usernames, passwords, and roles of Listing 4.1, if the client has successfully logged in as user `valjean`, the following two expressions would return `true`:

  ```
  request.isUserInRole("lowStatus")
  request.isUserInRole("nobleSpirited")
  ```

  Tests for all other roles would return `false`. If no user is currently authenticated (e.g., if authorization failed or if `isUserInRole` is called from an unrestricted page and the user has not yet accessed a restricted page), `isUserInRole` returns `false`. In addition to the standard security roles given in the password file, you can use the `security-role-ref` element to define aliases for the standard roles. See the next subsection for details.

- **getRemoteUser.** This method returns the name of the current user. For example, if the client has successfully logged in as user `valjean`, `request.getRemoteUser()` would return `"valjean"`. If no user is currently authenticated (e.g., if authorization failed or if `isUserInRole` is called from an unrestricted page and the user has not yet accessed a restricted page), `getRemoteUser` returns `null`.

- **getUserPrincipal.** This method returns the current username wrapped inside a `java.security.Principal` object. The `Principal` object contains little information beyond the username (available with the `getName` method). So, the main reason for using `getUserPrincipal` in lieu of `getRemoteUser` is to be compatible with preexisting security code (the `Principal` class is not specific to the servlet and JSP API and has been part of the Java platform since version 1.1). If no user is currently authenticated, `getUserPrincipal` returns `null`.

It is important to note that this type of programmatic security does not negate the benefits of container-managed security. With this approach, you can still set up usernames, passwords, and roles by using your server's mechanisms. You still use the `login-config` element to tell the server whether you are using form-based or BASIC authentication. If you choose form-based authentication, you still use an HTML form with an `ACTION` of `j_security_check`, a text field named j_username, and a password field named j_password. Unauthenticated users are still automatically sent to the page containing this form, and the server still automatically keeps track of which users have been authenticated. You still use the security-constraint element to designate the URLs to which the access restrictions apply. You still use the user-data-constraint element to specify that certain URLs require SSL. For details on all of these topics, see Section 3.1 (Form-Based Authentication). However, you *also* add code to some of your resources to customize their behavior based on who is accessing them.

Security Role References

The security-role-ref subelement of servlet lets you define servlet-specific synonyms for existing role names. This element should contain three possible subelements: description (optional descriptive text), role-name (the new synonym), and role-link (the existing security role).

For instance, suppose that you are creating an online bookstore and your server's user information store (e.g., Tomcat lets you use a password file as we describe in Section 3.1) stipulates that user rowling is in role author. However, you want to reuse a servlet of type BookInfo (in the catalog package) that was created elsewhere. The problem is that this servlet calls the role writer, not author. Rather than modifying the user information store, you can use security-role-ref to provide writer as an alias for author.

Suppose further that you have a servlet of class EmployeeData (in the hr package) that provides one type of information to a goodguy and another type to a meanie. You want to use this servlet with the password file (i.e., Tomcat's specific user information store) defined in Listing 3.1 that assigns users to the nobleSpirited and meanSpirited roles. To accomplish this task, you can use security-role-ref to say that isUserInRole("goodguy") should return true for the same users that isUserInRole("nobleSpirited") already would. Similarly, you can use security-role-ref to say that isUserInRole("meanie") should return true for the same users that isUserInRole("meanSpirited") would.

Listing 4.1 shows a deployment descriptor that accomplishes both of these tasks.

Listing 4.1   web.xml (Excerpt illustrating security role aliases)

```
<?xml version="1.0" encoding="ISO-8859-1"?>
<web-app xmlns="http://java.sun.com/xml/ns/j2ee"
        xmlns:xsi="http://www.w3.org/2001/XMLSchema-instance"
        xsi:schemaLocation=
        "http://java.sun.com/xml/ns/j2ee
         http://java.sun.com/xml/ns/j2ee/web-app_2_4.xsd"
        version="2.4">
```

Listing 4.1   web.xml (Excerpt illustrating security role aliases) *(continued)*

```
<servlet>
  <servlet-name>BookInformation</servlet-name>
  <servlet-class>catalog.BookInfo</servlet-class>
  <security-role-ref>
    <role-name>writer</role-name> <!-- New alias. -->
    <role-link>author</role-link> <!-- Preexisting role. -->
  </security-role-ref>
</servlet>
<servlet>
  <servlet-name>EmployeeInformation</servlet-name>
  <servlet-class>hr.EmployeeData</servlet-class>
  <security-role-ref>
    <role-name>goodguy</role-name>        <!-- New. -->
    <role-link>nobleSpirited</role-link> <!-- Preexisting. -->
  </security-role-ref>
  <security-role-ref>
    <role-name>meanie</role-name>        <!-- New. -->
    <role-link>meanSpirited</role-link> <!-- Preexisting. -->
  </security-role-ref>
</servlet>
<security-constraint>...</security-constraint>
<login-config>...</login-config>
</web-app>
```

4.2   Example: Combining Container-Managed and Programmatic Security

Listing 4.2 presents a JSP page that augments the internal Web site for hot-dot-com.com that was introduced in Section 3.4 (Example: BASIC Authentication). The page shows plans for employee pay. Because of entries in web.xml (Listing 4.3), the page can be accessed only by users in the employee or executive roles. Although both groups can access the page, they see substantially different results. In particular, the planned pay scales for executives are hidden from the normal employees.

Figure 4–1 shows the page when it is accessed by user gates or ellison (both in the employee role; see Listing 3.25). Figure 4–2 shows the page when it is accessed by user mcnealy (in the executive role). Remember that BASIC security provides no simple mechanism for changing your username once you are validated (see Section 3.3). So, for example, switching from user gates to user mcnealy requires you to quit and restart your browser.

Listing 4.2   employee-pay.jsp

```
<!DOCTYPE HTML PUBLIC "-//W3C//DTD HTML 4.0 Transitional//EN">
<HTML>
<HEAD>
<TITLE>Compensation Plans</TITLE>
<LINK REL=STYLESHEET
      HREF="company-styles.css"
      TYPE="text/css">
</HEAD>
<BODY>
<TABLE BORDER=5 ALIGN="CENTER">
  <TR><TH CLASS="TITLE">Compensation Plans</TABLE>
<P>
Due to temporary financial difficulties, we are scaling
back our very generous plans for salary increases. Don't
worry, though: your valuable stock options more than
compensate for any small drops in direct salary.
<H3>Regular Employees</H3>
Pay for median-level employee (Master's degree, eight year's
experience):
<UL>
  <LI><B>2004:</B> $50,000.
  <LI><B>2005:</B> $30,000.
  <LI><B>2006:</B> $25,000.
  <LI><B>2007:</B> $20,000.
</UL>
<% if (request.isUserInRole("executive")) { %>
<H3>Executives</H3>
Median pay for corporate executives:
<UL>
  <LI><B>2004:</B> $500,000.
  <LI><B>2005:</B> $600,000.
  <LI><B>2006:</B> $700,000.
  <LI><B>2007:</B> $800,000.
</UL>
<% } %>
</BODY></HTML>
```

Listing 4.3	web.xml (For augmented hotdotcom intranet)

```xml
<?xml version="1.0" encoding="ISO-8859-1"?>
<web-app xmlns="http://java.sun.com/xml/ns/j2ee"
         xmlns:xsi="http://www.w3.org/2001/XMLSchema-instance"
         xsi:schemaLocation=
         "http://java.sun.com/xml/ns/j2ee
          http://java.sun.com/xml/ns/j2ee/web-app_2_4.xsd"
         version="2.4">
  <!-- Protect compensation plan. Employees or executives. -->
  <security-constraint>
    <web-resource-collection>
      <web-resource-name>Compensation Plan</web-resource-name>
      <url-pattern>/employee-pay.jsp</url-pattern>
    </web-resource-collection>
    <auth-constraint>
      <role-name>employee</role-name>
      <role-name>executive</role-name>
    </auth-constraint>
  </security-constraint>

  <!-- Protect financial plan. Employees or executives. -->
  <security-constraint>
    <web-resource-collection>
      <web-resource-name>Financial Plan</web-resource-name>
      <url-pattern>/financial-plan.html</url-pattern>
    </web-resource-collection>
    <auth-constraint>
      <role-name>employee</role-name>
      <role-name>executive</role-name>
    </auth-constraint>
  </security-constraint>

  <!-- Protect business plan. Executives only. -->
  <security-constraint>
    <web-resource-collection>
      <web-resource-name>Business Plan</web-resource-name>
      <url-pattern>/business-plan.html</url-pattern>
    </web-resource-collection>
    <auth-constraint>
      <role-name>executive</role-name>
    </auth-constraint>
  </security-constraint>
```

Listing 4.3   web.xml (For augmented hotdotcom intranet) *(continued)*

```xml
<!-- Tell the server to use BASIC authentication. -->
  <login-config>
    <auth-method>BASIC</auth-method>
    <realm-name>Intranet</realm-name>
  </login-config>

  <security-role>
    <role-name>employee</role-name>
  </security-role>
  <security-role>
    <role-name>executive</role-name>
  </security-role>

  <!-- Disable the invoker servlet. -->
  <servlet>
    <servlet-name>NoInvoker</servlet-name>
    <servlet-class>coreservlets.NoInvokerServlet</servlet-class>
  </servlet>
  <servlet-mapping>
    <servlet-name>NoInvoker</servlet-name>
    <url-pattern>/servlet/*</url-pattern>
  </servlet-mapping>

  <!-- If URL gives a directory but no file name, try index.jsp
       first and index.html second. If neither is found,
       the result is server specific (e.g., a directory
       listing). -->
  <welcome-file-list>
    <welcome-file>index.jsp</welcome-file>
    <welcome-file>index.html</welcome-file>
  </welcome-file-list>
 </web-app>
```

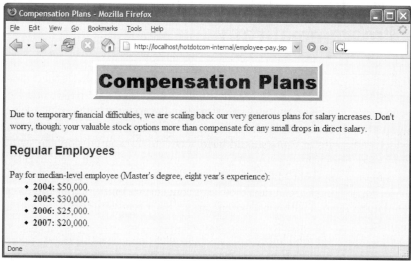

Figure 4–1   The employee-pay.jsp page when accessed by a user who is in the employee role.

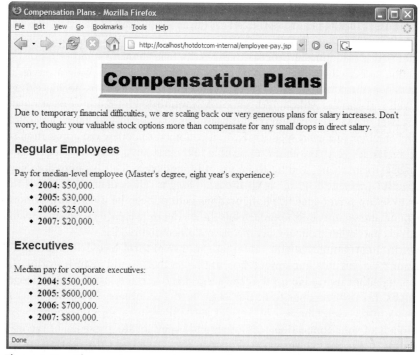

Figure 4–2   The employee-pay.jsp page when accessed by a user who is in the executive role.

4.3   Handling All Security Programmatically

Declarative security (see Chapter 3) offers a number of advantages to the developer. Chief among them is the fact that individual servlets and JSP pages need no security-conscious code: The container (server) handles authentication in a manner that is completely transparent to the individual resources. For example, you can change which categories of users should have access to a resource, you can switch from form-based authentication to BASIC authentication, or from regular HTTP connections to encrypted HTTPS connections, all without any changes to the individual servlets or JSP pages. The developer can concentrate on the application logic and which data to display without worrying about what type of user might end up seeing the data.

Even when you want a bit more control than just "access allowed" or "access denied," it is convenient to let the server maintain and process the usernames and passwords, as discussed in Section 4.1 (Combining Container-Managed and Programmatic Security).

However, the convenience of container-managed security comes at a price: It requires a server-specific component. The method for setting up usernames, passwords, and user roles is not standardized and thus is not portable across different servers. In most situations, this disadvantage is outweighed by the faster and simpler servlet and JSP development process that results from leaving some or all of the authorization tasks to the server. In some cases, however, you might want a servlet or JSP page to be entirely self-contained with no dependencies on server-specific settings or even web.xml entries. Although this approach requires a lot more work, it means that the servlet or JSP page can be ported from server to server with much less effort than with container-managed security. Even if you need to deploy the application on the same server, it's very convenient to be able to bundle up a WAR file (see Section 1.5), e-mail it to someone, and let them use it immediately. This is impossible with declarative security because the WAR file is no longer self-contained. It needs the deployer to set up server-specific configurations before it can be used. Furthermore, the programmatic security only approach lets the servlet or JSP page use username and password schemes other than an exact match to a preconfigured list.

It's worth mentioning that you can create your own form-based authentication mechanism. One possible implementation of this method would involve storing the user ID (e.g., either username itself or the session ID) and the names of the categories of users this user belongs to in the HttpSession object. For example, you might use a filter—see Chapter 5 (Servlet and JSP Filters)—to intercept every request to any of your application's resources and check for the presence of the user information in the HttpSession. You can then use the information in the HttpSession to decide if this user is allowed to have access to the requested resource. If the user information is absent, you can forward the user's request to the login page. The action of the login page form would then evaluate username and password for validity. If valid, the user's information would be loaded into the `HttpSession` object. The main advantage of this approach is that you still get to present a custom login page with the look and feel of the rest of the application and at the same time achieve complete portability. However, creating such a security module would mean a lot of work. In this section, we'll concentrate on the native HTTP authentication.

HTTP supports two varieties of authentication: BASIC and DIGEST. Few browsers support DIGEST, so we focus on BASIC here.

Here is a summary of the steps involved for BASIC authentication:

1. **Check whether there is an `Authorization` request header.** If there is no such header, go to Step 5.
2. **Get the encoded username/password string.** If there is an `Authorization` header, it should have the following form:

   Authorization: Basic *encodedData*

   Skip over the word `Basic` and the following space—the remaining part is the username and password represented in base64 encoding.
3. **Reverse the base64 encoding of the username/password string.** Use the `decodeBuffer` method of the `BASE64Decoder` class. This method call results in a string of the form `username:password`. The `BASE64Decoder` class is bundled with the JDK; in JDK 1.3 or later it can be found in the `sun.misc` package in *jdk_dir*/jre/lib/rt.jar.
4. **Check the username and password.** The most common approach is to use a database or a file to obtain the real usernames and passwords. For simple cases, it is also possible to place the password information directly in the servlet. In such a case, remember that access to the servlet source code or class file provides access to the passwords. If the incoming username and password match one of the reference username/password pairs, return the page. If not, go to Step 5. With this approach you can provide your own definition of "match." With container-managed security, you cannot.
5. **When authentication fails, send the appropriate response to the client.** Return a 401 (`Unauthorized`) response code and a header of the following form:

   WWW-Authenticate: BASIC realm="some-name"

   This response instructs the browser to pop up a dialog box telling the user to enter a name and password for `some-name`, then to reconnect with that username and password embedded in a single base64 string inside the `Authorization` header.

If you care about the details, base64 encoding is explained in RFC 1521. To retrieve Requests for Comments (RFCs), start at http://www.rfc-editor.org/ to get a current list of the RFC archive sites. However, there are probably only two things you need to know about base64 encoding.

First, it is not intended to provide security, as the encoding can be easily reversed. So, base64 encoding does not obviate the need for SSL (see Section 3.3) to thwart attackers who might be able to snoop on your network connection (no easy task unless they are on your local subnet). SSL is a variation of HTTP where the entire stream is encrypted. It is supported by many commercial servers and is generally invoked by use of https in the URL instead of http. Servlets can run on SSL servers just as easily as on standard servers, and the encryption and decryption are handled transparently before the servlets are invoked. See Chapter 3 (Declarative Security) for examples.

The second point you should know about base64 encoding is that Sun provides the `sun.misc.BASE64Decoder` class, distributed with JDK 1.1 and later, to decode strings that were encoded with base64. In JDK 1.3 or later it can be found in the `sun.misc` package in jdk_install_dir/jre/lib/rt.jar. Just be aware that classes in the `sun` package hierarchy are not part of the official language specification and thus are not guaranteed to appear in all implementations. So, if you use this decoder class, make sure that you explicitly include the class file when you distribute your application. One possible approach is to make the JAR file available to all Web applications on your server and then to explicitly record the fact that your applications depend on it.

4.4   Example: Handling All Security Programmatically

Listing 4.4 shows a servlet that generates hot stock recommendations. If it were made freely available on the Web, it would put half the financial advisors out of business. So, it needs to be password protected, available only to people who have paid the very reasonable $2000 access fee.

Furthermore, the servlet needs to be as portable as possible because ISPs keep shutting it down (they claim fraud, but no doubt they are really being pressured by the financial services companies that the servlet outperforms). So, it uses complete programmatic security and is entirely self-contained: Absolutely no changes or server-specific customizations are required to move the servlet from system to system.

Finally, requiring an exact match against a static list of usernames and passwords (as is required in container-managed security) is too limiting for this application. So, the servlet uses a custom algorithm (see the `areEqualReversed` method) for determining if an incoming username and password are legal.

Figure 4–3 shows what happens when the user first tries to access the servlet. Figure 4–4 shows the result of a failed authorization attempt. Figure 4–5 shows the result of successful authorization. Listing 4.5 shows the complete web.xml file used to deploy the servlet.

Listing 4.4	StockTip.java

```java
package stocks;

import java.io.*;
import javax.servlet.*;
import javax.servlet.http.*;
import sun.misc.BASE64Decoder;

/** Servlet that gives very hot stock tips. So hot that
 *  only authorized users (presumably ones who have paid
 *  the steep financial advisory fee) can access the servlet.
 */

public class StockTip extends HttpServlet {

  /** Denies access to all users except those who know
   *  the secret username/password combination.
   */

  public void doGet(HttpServletRequest request,
                    HttpServletResponse response)
      throws ServletException, IOException {
    String authorization = request.getHeader("Authorization");
    if (authorization == null) {
      askForPassword(response);
    } else {
      // Authorization headers looks like "Basic blahblah",
      // where blahblah is the base64 encoded username and
      // password. We want the part after "Basic ".
      String userInfo = authorization.substring(6).trim();
      BASE64Decoder decoder = new BASE64Decoder();
      String nameAndPassword =
        new String(decoder.decodeBuffer(userInfo));
      // Decoded part looks like "username:password".
      int index = nameAndPassword.indexOf(":");
      String user = nameAndPassword.substring(0, index);
      String password = nameAndPassword.substring(index+1);
```

Listing 4.4   StockTip.java *(continued)*

```java
      // High security: username must be reverse of password.
      if (areEqualReversed(user, password)) {
        showStock(request, response);
      } else {
        askForPassword(response);
      }
    }
  }

  // Show a Web page giving the symbol of the next hot stock.

  private void showStock(HttpServletRequest request,
                         HttpServletResponse response)
      throws ServletException, IOException {
        response.setContentType("text/html");
    PrintWriter out = response.getWriter();
    String docType =
      "<!DOCTYPE HTML PUBLIC \"-//W3C//DTD HTML 4.0 " +
      "Transitional//EN\">\n";
    out.println(docType +
                "<HTML>\n" +
                "<HEAD><TITLE>Hot Stock Tip!</TITLE></HEAD>\n" +
                "<BODY BGCOLOR=\"#FDF5E6\">\n" +
                "<H1>Today's Hot Stock:");
    for(int i=0; i<3; i++) {
      out.print(randomLetter());
    }
    out.println("</H1>\n" +
                "</BODY></HTML>");
  }

  // If no Authorization header was supplied in the request.

  private void askForPassword(HttpServletResponse response) {
    // Send HTTP 401
    response.setStatus(HttpServletResponse.SC_UNAUTHORIZED);
    response.setHeader("WWW-Authenticate",
                       "BASIC realm=\"Insider-Trading\"");

  }

  // Returns true if s1 is the reverse of s2.
  // Empty strings don't count.
```

Listing 4.4	StockTip.java *(continued)*

```java
    private boolean areEqualReversed(String s1, String s2) {
      s2 = (new StringBuffer(s2)).reverse().toString();
      return((s1.length() > 0) && s1.equals(s2));
    }

    private final String ALPHABET = "ABCDEFGHIJKLMNOPQRSTUVWXYZ";

    // Returns a random number from 0 to n-1 inclusive.

    private int randomInt(int n) {
      return((int)(Math.random() * n));
    }

    // A random letter from the alphabet.

    private char randomLetter() {
      return(ALPHABET.charAt(randomInt(ALPHABET.length())));
    }
}
```

Listing 4.5	web.xml (from stocks Web app)

```xml
<?xml version="1.0" encoding="ISO-8859-1"?>
<web-app xmlns="http://java.sun.com/xml/ns/j2ee"
    xmlns:xsi="http://www.w3.org/2001/XMLSchema-instance"
    xsi:schemaLocation=
    "http://java.sun.com/xml/ns/j2ee
    http://java.sun.com/xml/ns/j2ee/web-app_2_4.xsd"
    version="2.4">
    <servlet>
        <servlet-name>StockTip</servlet-name>
        <servlet-class>stocks.StockTip</servlet-class>
    </servlet>
    <servlet-mapping>
        <servlet-name>StockTip</servlet-name>
        <url-pattern>/stockTip</url-pattern>
    </servlet-mapping>
</web-app>
```

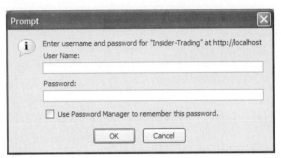

Figure 4–3   When the browser first receives the 401 (Unauthorized) status code, it opens a dialog box to collect the username and password.

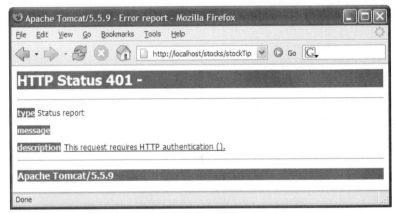

Figure 4–4   Result of cancelled authorization attempt with Tomcat—Tomcat returns an error page along with the 401 (Unauthorized) status code.

Figure 4–5   Result of successful authorization attempt. Invest now!

4.5 Using Programmatic Security with SSL

SSL can be used with security that is entirely servlet managed, just as it can be with container-managed security (see Section 3.3). As is typical with servlet-managed security, this approach is more portable but requires significantly more effort.

The use of SSL in programmatic security may require one or more of the following capabilities not needed in normal programmatic security:

- Determining if SSL is in use.
- Redirecting non-SSL requests.
- Discovering the number of bits in the key.
- Looking up the encryption algorithm.
- Accessing client X.509 certificates.

Details on these capabilities follow.

Determining If SSL Is in Use

The `ServletRequest` interface provides two methods that let you find out if SSL is in use. The `getScheme` method returns `"http"` for regular requests and `"https"` for SSL requests. The `isSecure` method returns `false` for regular requests and `true` for SSL requests.

Redirecting Non-SSL Requests

With container-managed security, you can use the `transport-guarantee` sub-element of `user-data-constraint` to ensure that the server redirects regular (http) requests to the SSL (https) equivalent. See Section 3.5 (Configuring Tomcat to Use SSL) for details.

In programmatic security, you might want to explicitly do what the server automatically does with container-managed security. Once you have a URL, redirection is straightforward: use `response.sendRedirect`.

The difficulty is in generating the URL in the first place. Unfortunately, there is no built-in method that says "give me the complete incoming URL with http changed to https." So, you have to call `request.getRequestURL` to get the main URL, change http to https manually, then tack on any form data by using `request.get-QueryString`. You pass that result to `response.sendRedirect`.

Even this tedious manual approach runs some portability risks. For example, what if the server is running SSL on a port other than 443 (the default SSL port)? In such a case, the approach outlined here redirects to the wrong port. Unfortunately, there is no general solution to this problem; you simply have to know something about how the server is configured to redirect to a nonstandard SSL port. However, because you have to know that the server supports SSL in the first place, this additional burden is not too onerous.

Discovering the Number of Bits in the Key

Suppose that you have a servlet or JSP page that lets authorized users access your company's financial records. You might want to ensure that the most sensitive data is only sent to users that have a strong (128-bit) level of encryption. Users whose browsers use comparatively weak 40-bit keys should be denied access. To accomplish this task, you need to be able to discover the level of encryption being used.

In version 2.3 and later of the servlet API, SSL requests automatically result in an attribute named `javax.servlet.request.key_size` being placed in the request object. You can access it by calling `request.getAttribute` with the specified name. The value is an `Integer` that tells you the length of the encryption key. However, because the return type of `getAttribute` is `Object`, you have to perform a typecast to `Integer`. Be sure to check if the result is `null` to handle non-SSL requests. Here is a simple example:

```
String keyAttribute = "javax.servlet.request.key_size";
Integer keySize =
  (Integer)request.getAttribute(keyAttribute);
if (keySize != null) { ... }
```

Looking Up the Encryption Algorithm

In version 2.3 and later of the servlet API, SSL requests also result in an attribute named `javax.servlet.request.cipher_suite` being placed in the request object. You can access it by calling `request.getAttribute` with the specified name. The value is a `String` that describes the encryption algorithm being used. However, because the return type of `getAttribute` is `Object`, you have to perform a typecast to `String`. Be sure to check if the result is `null` to handle non-SSL requests. Here is a simple example:

```
String cipherAttribute = "javax.servlet.request.cipher_suite";
String cipherSuite =
  (String)request.getAttribute(cipherAttribute);
if (cipherSuite != null) { ... }
```

Accessing Client X.509 Certificates

Rather than using a simple username and password, some browsers permit users to authenticate themselves with X.509 certificates. X.509 certificates are discussed in RFC 1421. To retrieve RFCs, start at http://www.rfc-editor.org/ to get a current list of the RFC archive sites.

If the client is authenticated with an X.509 certificate, that certificate is available by means of the `javax.servlet.request.X509Certificate` attribute of the request object. The value is an object of type `java.security.cert.X509Certificate` that contains exhaustive information about the certificate. However, because the return type of `getAttribute` is `Object`, you have to perform a typecast to `X509Certificate`. Be sure to check if the result is `null` to handle non-SSL requests and SSL requests that include no certificate. A simple example follows.

```
String certAttribute = "javax.servlet.request.X509Certificate";
X509Certificate certificate =
  (X509Certificate)request.getAttribute(certAttribute);
if (certificate != null) { ... }
```

Once you have an X.509 certificate, you can look up the issuer's distinguished name, the serial number, the raw signature value, the public key, and a number of other pieces of information. For details, see http://java.sun.com/j2se/1.5.0/docs/api/java/security/cert/X509Certificate.html.

4.6 Example: Programmatic Security and SSL

Listing 4.6 presents a servlet that redirects non-SSL requests to a URL that is identical to the URL of the original request except that http is changed to https. When an SSL request is received, the servlet presents a page that displays information on the URL, query data, key size, encryption algorithm, and client certificate. Figures 4–6 and 4–7 show the results. Listing 4.7 shows the complete web.xml file used to deploy the servlet.

In a real application, make sure that you redirect users when they access the servlet or JSP page that contains the form that collects the data. Once users submit sensitive data to an ordinary non-SSL URL, it is too late to redirect the request: Attackers with access to the network traffic could have already obtained the data.

Listing 4.6 SecurityInfo.java

```java
package coreservlets;

import java.io.*;
import javax.servlet.*;
import javax.servlet.http.*;
import java.security.cert.*; // For X509Certificate

/** Servlet that prints information on SSL requests. Non-SSL
 *  requests get redirected to SSL.
 */

public class SecurityInfo extends HttpServlet {
  public void doGet(HttpServletRequest request,
                    HttpServletResponse response)
      throws ServletException, IOException {
    // Redirect non-SSL requests to the SSL equivalent.
    if (request.getScheme().equalsIgnoreCase("http")) {
      String origURL = request.getRequestURL().toString();
      String newURL = httpsURL(origURL);
      String formData = request.getQueryString();
      if (formData != null) {
        newURL = newURL + "?" + formData;
      }
      response.sendRedirect(newURL);
    } else {
      String currentURL = request.getRequestURL().toString();
      String formData = request.getQueryString();
      PrintWriter out = response.getWriter();
      String docType =
        "<!DOCTYPE HTML PUBLIC \"-//W3C//DTD HTML 4.0 " +
        "Transitional//EN\">\n";
      String title = "Security Info";
      out.println
        (docType +
         "<HTML>\n" +
         "<HEAD><TITLE>" + title +
         "</TITLE></HEAD>\n" +
         "<BODY BGCOLOR=\"#FDF5E6\">\n" +
         "<H1>" + title + "</H1>\n" +
         "<UL>\n" +
         "  <LI>URL: " + currentURL + "\n" +
         "  <LI>Data: " + formData);
      boolean isSecure = request.isSecure();
```

Listing 4.6   SecurityInfo.java *(continued)*

```java
      if (isSecure) {
        String keyAttribute =
          "javax.servlet.request.key_size";
        // Available only with servlets 2.3
        Integer keySize =
          (Integer)request.getAttribute(keyAttribute);
        String sizeString =
          replaceNull(keySize, "Unknown");
        String cipherAttribute =
          "javax.servlet.request.cipher_suite";
        // Available only with servlets 2.3
        String cipherSuite =
          (String)request.getAttribute(cipherAttribute);
        String cipherString =
          replaceNull(cipherSuite, "Unknown");
        String certAttribute =
          "javax.servlet.request.X509Certificate";
        // Available with servlets 2.2 and 2.3
        X509Certificate certificate =
          (X509Certificate)request.getAttribute(certAttribute);
        String certificateString =
          replaceNull(certificate, "None");
        out.println
          ("   <LI>SSL: true\n" +
           "   <UL>\n" +
           "      <LI>Key Size: " + sizeString + "\n" +
           "      <LI>Cipher Suite: " + cipherString + "\n" +
           "      <LI>Client Certificate: " +
           certificateString + "\n" +
           "   </UL>");
      }
      out.println
        ("</UL>\n" +
         "</BODY></HTML>");
    }
  }

  // Given http://blah, return https://blah.

  private String httpsURL(String origURL) {
    int index = origURL.indexOf(":");
    StringBuffer newURL = new StringBuffer(origURL);
    newURL.insert(index, 's');
    return(newURL.toString());
  }
```

Listing 4.6 SecurityInfo.java *(continued)*

```
// If the first argument is null, return the second argument.
// Otherwise, convert first argument to a String and
// return that String.

private String replaceNull(Object obj, String fallback) {
  if (obj == null) {
    return(fallback);
  } else {
    return(obj.toString());
  }
}
}
```

Listing 4.7 web.xml (from securityInfo Web app)

```
<?xml version="1.0" encoding="ISO-8859-1"?>
<web-app xmlns="http://java.sun.com/xml/ns/j2ee"
    xmlns:xsi="http://www.w3.org/2001/XMLSchema-instance"
    xsi:schemaLocation=
    "http://java.sun.com/xml/ns/j2ee
    http://java.sun.com/xml/ns/j2ee/web-app_2_4.xsd"
    version="2.4">
    <servlet>
        <servlet-name>SecurityInfo</servlet-name>
        <servlet-class>coreservlets.SecurityInfo</servlet-class>
    </servlet>
    <servlet-mapping>
        <servlet-name>SecurityInfo</servlet-name>
        <url-pattern>/securityInfo</url-pattern>
    </servlet-mapping>
</web-app>
```

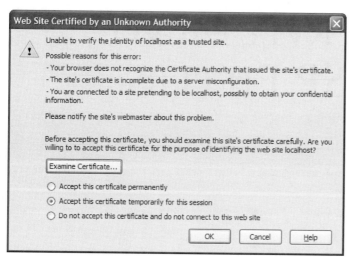

Figure 4–6 New certificate page for Firefox. Examine and accept the certificate permanently to suppress future warnings. For details on creating self-signed certificates for use with Tomcat, see Section 3.7 (Signing a Server Certificate). Again, self-signed certificates would not be trusted in real-world applications; they are for testing purposes only.

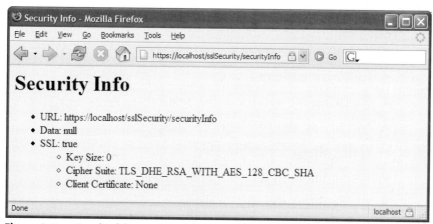

Figure 4–7 Result of the `SecurityInfo` servlet.

SERVLET AND JSP FILTERS

Topics in This Chapter

- Designing basic filters
- Reading request data
- Accessing the servlet context
- Initializing filters
- Blocking the servlet or JSP response
- Modifying the servlet or JSP response
- Using filters for debugging and logging
- Using filters to monitor site access
- Using filters to replace strings
- Using filters to compress the response
- Configuring filters for different request types

A filter is a program that runs on the server before the servlet or JSP page with which it is associated. A filter can be attached to one or more servlets or JSP pages and can examine the request information going into these resources. After doing so, it can choose among the following options:

- Invoke the resource (i.e., the servlet or JSP page) in the normal manner.
- Invoke the resource with modified request information.
- Invoke the resource but modify the response before sending it to the client.
- Prevent the resource from being invoked and instead redirect to a different resource, return a particular status code, or generate replacement output.

This capability provides several important benefits.

First, it lets you encapsulate common behavior in a modular and reusable manner. Do you have 30 different servlets or JSP pages that need to compress their content to decrease download time? No problem: Make a single compression filter (Section 5.11) and apply it to all 30 resources.

Second, it lets you separate high-level access decisions from presentation code. This is particularly valuable with JSP, where you usually want to keep the page almost entirely focused on presentation, not processing business logic. For example, do you want to block access from certain sites without modifying the individual pages to which these access restrictions apply? No problem: Create an access restriction filter (Section 5.8) and apply it to as many or few pages as you like.

Finally, filters let you apply wholesale changes to many different resources. Do you have a bunch of existing resources that should remain unchanged except that the company name should be changed? No problem: Make a string replacement filter (Section 5.10) and apply it wherever appropriate.

5.1   Creating Basic Filters

Creating a filter involves five basic steps:

1. **Create a class that implements the `Filter` interface.** Your class will need three methods: doFilter, init, and destroy. The doFilter method contains the main filtering code (see Step 2), the init method performs setup operations, and the destroy method does cleanup.

2. **Put the filtering behavior in the `doFilter` method.** The first argument to the doFilter method is a ServletRequest object. This object gives your filter full access to the incoming information, including form data, cookies, and HTTP request headers. The second argument is a ServletResponse; it is mostly ignored in simple filters. The final argument is a FilterChain; it is used to invoke the servlet, JSP page, or the next filter in the chain as described in the next step.

3. **Call the `doFilter` method of the `FilterChain` object.** The doFilter method of the Filter interface takes a FilterChain object as one of its arguments. When you call the doFilter method of that object, the next associated filter is invoked. If no other filter is associated with the servlet or JSP page, then the servlet or page itself is invoked.

4. **Register the filter with the appropriate servlets and JSP pages.** Use the filter and filter-mapping elements in the deployment descriptor (web.xml).

5. **Disable the invoker servlet.** Prevent users from bypassing filter settings by using default servlet URLs.

Details follow.

Create a Class That Implements the Filter Interface

All filters must implement `javax.servlet.Filter`. This interface comprises three methods: `doFilter`, `init`, and `destroy`.

public void doFilter(ServletRequest request,
ServletResponse response,
FilterChain chain)
throws ServletException, IOException

The `doFilter` method is executed each time a filter is invoked (i.e., once for each request for a servlet or JSP page with which the filter is associated). It is this method that contains the bulk of the filtering logic.

The first argument is the `ServletRequest` associated with the incoming request. For simple filters, most of your filter logic is based on this object. Cast the object to `HttpServletRequest` if you are dealing with HTTP requests and you need access to methods such as `getHeader` or `getCookies` that are unavailable in `ServletRequest`.

The second argument is the `ServletResponse`. In simple filters you often ignore this argument, but there are two cases when you use it. First, if you want to completely block access to the associated servlet or JSP page, you can call `response.getWriter` and send a response directly to the client. Section 5.7 (Blocking the Response) gives details; Section 5.8 (Example: A Prohibited-Site Filter) gives an example. Second, if you want to modify the output of the associated servlet or JSP page, you can wrap the response inside an object that collects all output sent to it. Then, after the servlet or JSP page is invoked, the filter can examine the output, modify it if appropriate, and then send it to the client. See Section 5.9 (Modifying the Response) for details.

The final argument to `doFilter` is a `FilterChain` object. You call `doFilter` on this object to invoke the next filter that is associated with the servlet or JSP page. If no other filters are in effect, then the call to `doFilter` invokes the servlet or JSP page itself.

public void init(FilterConfig config)
throws ServletException

The `init` method is executed only when the filter is first initialized. It is not executed each time the filter is invoked. For simple filters you can provide an empty body to this method, but there are two common reasons for using `init`. First, the `FilterConfig` object provides access to the servlet context and to the name of the filter that is assigned in the web.xml file. So, it is common to use init to store the FilterConfig object in a field so that the doFilter method can access the servlet context or the filter name. This process is described in Section 5.3 (Accessing the Servlet Context from Filters). Second, the FilterConfig object has a getInitParameter method that lets you access filter initialization parameters that are assigned in the deployment descriptor (web.xml). Use of initialization parameters is described in Section 5.5 (Using Filter Initialization Parameters).

public void destroy()

This method is called when a server is permanently finished with a given filter object (e.g., when the server is being shut down). Most filters simply provide an empty body for this method, but it can be used for cleanup tasks like closing files or database connection pools that are used by the filter.

Put the Filtering Behavior in the doFilter Method

The doFilter method is the key part of most filters. Each time a filter is invoked, doFilter is executed. With most filters, the steps that doFilter performs are based on the incoming information. So, you will probably make use of the ServletRequest that is supplied as the first argument to doFilter. This object is frequently typecast to HttpServletRequest to provide access to the more specialized methods of that class.

Call the doFilter Method of the FilterChain Object

The doFilter method of the Filter interface takes a FilterChain object as its third argument. When you call the doFilter method of that object, the next associated filter is invoked. This process normally continues until the last filter in the chain is invoked. When the final filter calls the doFilter method of its FilterChain object, the servlet or page itself is invoked.

However, any filter in the chain can interrupt the process by omitting the call to the doFilter method of its FilterChain. In such a case, the servlet or JSP page is never invoked and the filter is responsible for providing output to the client. For details, see Section 5.7 (Blocking the Response).

Register the Filter with the Appropriate Servlets and JSP Pages

The deployment descriptor provides two elements for use with filters: `filter` and `filter-mapping`. The `filter` element registers a filtering object with the system. The `filter-mapping` element specifies the URLs to which the filtering object applies.

The filter Element

The `filter` element contains six possible subelements:

- **icon.** This is an optional element that declares an image file that an IDE can use.
- **filter-name.** This is a required element that assigns a name of your choosing to the filter.
- **display-name.** This is an optional element that provides a short name for use by IDEs.
- **description.** This is another optional element that gives information for IDEs. It provides textual documentation.
- **filter-class.** This is a required element that specifies the fully qualified name of the filter implementation class.
- **init-param.** This is an optional element that defines an initialization parameter that can be read with the `getInitParameter` method of `FilterConfig`. A single filter element can contain multiple `init-param` elements.

Here is a simple example:

```
<?xml version="1.0" encoding="ISO-8859-1"?>
<web-app ... version="2.4">
  <filter>
    <filter-name>MyFilter</filter-name>
    <filter-class>myPackage.FilterClass</filter-class>
  </filter>
  <filter-mapping>...</filter-mapping>
  ...
</web-app>
```

The filter-mapping Element

The `filter-mapping` element contains four possible subelements:

- **filter-name.** This required element must match the name you gave to the filter when you declared it with the `filter` element.
- **url-pattern.** This element declares a pattern starting with either a slash (/) or a `*.` that designates the URLs to which the filter applies. The same rules apply to `url-pattern` of `filter-mapping` as to `url-pattern` of `servlet-mapping`. For more detail see Section 2.4 (Assigning Names and Custom URLs). You must supply `url-pattern` or `servlet-name` in all `filter-mapping` elements. You cannot provide multiple `url-pattern` entries with a single `filter-mapping` element, however. If you want the filter to apply to multiple patterns, repeat the entire `filter-mapping` element.
- **servlet-name.** This element gives a name that must match a name given to a servlet or JSP page by means of the `servlet` element. For details on the `servlet` element, see Section 2.4 (Assigning Names and Custom URLs). You cannot provide multiple `servlet-name` elements entries with a single `filter-mapping` element. If you want the filter to apply to multiple servlet names, repeat the entire `filter-mapping` element.
- **dispatcher.** This optional element specifies what type of request this filter mapping should apply to. Possible values are REQUEST, FORWARD, INCLUDE, and ERROR. If no dispatcher element is specified, REQUEST is assumed. To allow the same filter to apply to different types of requests, several `dispatcher` elements may be used. For more information on the `dispatcher` element, see Section 5.12 (Configuring Filters to Work with RequestDispatcher).

Here is a simple example:

```
<?xml version="1.0" encoding="ISO-8859-1"?>
<web-app ... version="2.4">

  <filter>
    <filter-name>MyFilter</filter-name>
    <filter-class>myPackage.FilterClass</filter-class>
  </filter>
  <filter-mapping>
    <filter-name>MyFilter</filter-name>
    <url-pattern>/someDirectory/SomePage.jsp</url-pattern>
  </filter-mapping>
  ...
</web-app>
```

Disable the Invoker Servlet

When you apply filters to resources, you do so by specifying the URL pattern or servlet name to which the filters apply. If you supply a servlet name, that name must match a name given in the `servlet` element of web.xml. If you use a URL pattern that applies to a servlet, the pattern must match a pattern that you specified with the `servlet-mapping` web.xml element—see Section 2.4 (Assigning Names and Custom URLs). However, most servers use an "invoker servlet" that provides a default URL for servlets: http://*host*/*webAppPrefix*/servlet/*ServletName*. You need to make sure that users don't access servlets with this URL, thus bypassing the filter settings.

Section 2.5 (Disabling the Invoker Servlet) discusses server-specific approaches to turning off the invoker. The most portable approach, however, is to simply remap the `/servlet/*` pattern in your Web application so that all requests that include the pattern are sent to the same servlet. To remap the pattern, you first create a simple servlet that prints an error message. Then, you use the `servlet` and `servlet-mapping` elements (Section 2.3) to send requests that include the `/servlet/*` pattern to that servlet. Listing 5.1 gives a brief example.

Listing 5.1 | web.xml (Excerpt that blocks default servlet URLs)

```
<?xml version="1.0" encoding="ISO-8859-1"?>
<web-app xmlns="http://java.sun.com/xml/ns/j2ee"
         xmlns:xsi="http://www.w3.org/2001/XMLSchema-instance"
         xsi:schemaLocation=
         "http://java.sun.com/xml/ns/j2ee
          http://java.sun.com/xml/ns/j2ee/web-app_2_4.xsd"
         version="2.4">
  <!-- Disable the invoker servlet. -->
  <servlet>
    <servlet-name>NoInvoker</servlet-name>
    <servlet-class>coreservlets.NoInvokerServlet</servlet-class>
  </servlet>
  <servlet-mapping>
    <servlet-name>NoInvoker</servlet-name>
    <url-pattern>/servlet/*</url-pattern>
  </servlet-mapping>
  ...
</web-app>
```

5.2 Example: A Reporting Filter

Just to warm up, let's try a simple filter that merely prints a message to standard output whenever the associated servlet or JSP page is invoked. To accomplish this task, we implement the following capabilities.

1. **A class that implements the `Filter` interface.** This class is called `ReportFilter` and is shown in Listing 5.2. The class provides empty bodies for the `init` and `destroy` methods.

2. **Filtering behavior in the `doFilter` method.** Each time a servlet or JSP page associated with this filter is invoked, the `doFilter` method generates a printout that lists the requesting host and the URL that was invoked. Because the `getRequestURL` method is in `HttpServletRequest`, not `ServletRequest`, we cast the `ServletRequest` object to `HttpServletRequest`.

3. **A call to the `doFilter` method of the `FilterChain`.** After printing the report, the filter calls the `doFilter` method of the `FilterChain` to invoke the servlet or JSP page (or the next filter in the chain, if there is one).

4. **Registration with the Web application home page and the servlet that displays the daily special.** First, the `filter` element associates the name `Reporter` with the class `coreservlets.filters.ReportFilter`. Then, the `filter-mapping` element uses a `url-pattern` of `/index.jsp` to associate the filter with the home page. Finally, the `filter-mapping` element uses a `servlet-name` of `TodaysSpecial` to associate the filter with the daily special servlet (the name `TodaysSpecial` is declared in the `servlet` element). See Listing 5.3.

5. **Disablement of the invoker servlet.** First, we create `NoInvokerServlet` (Listing 5.6) that generates an error message stating that the invoker servlet has been disabled. Next, we use the `servlet` and `servlet-mapping` elements (Listing 5.3) to specify that all URLs that begin with http://*host*/*webAppPrefix*/servlet/ should invoke the `NoInvokerServlet`.

Given these settings, the filter is invoked each time a client requests the Web application home page (Listing 5.4 and Figure 5–1) or the daily special servlet (Listing 5.5 and Figure 5–2).

Listing 5.2	ReportFilter.java

```java
package coreservlets.filters;

import java.io.*;
import java.util.*;
import javax.servlet.*;
import javax.servlet.http.*;

/** Simple filter that prints a report on the standard output
 *  each time an associated servlet or JSP page is accessed.
 */
public class ReportFilter implements Filter {
  public void doFilter(ServletRequest request,
                       ServletResponse response,
                       FilterChain chain)
      throws ServletException, IOException {
    HttpServletRequest req = (HttpServletRequest)request;
    System.out.println(req.getRemoteHost() +
                       " tried to access " +
                       req.getRequestURL() +
                       " on " + new Date() + ".");
    chain.doFilter(request,response);
  }

  public void init(FilterConfig config) {}

  public void destroy() {}
}
```

Listing 5.3	web.xml (Excerpt for reporting filter)

```xml
<?xml version="1.0" encoding="ISO-8859-1"?>
<web-app xmlns="http://java.sun.com/xml/ns/j2ee"
  xmlns:xsi="http://www.w3.org/2001/XMLSchema-instance"
  xsi:schemaLocation=
  "http://java.sun.com/xml/ns/j2ee
  http://java.sun.com/xml/ns/j2ee/web-app_2_4.xsd"
  version="2.4">

  <!-- Register the name "Reporter" for ReportFilter. -->
  <filter>
    <filter-name>Reporter</filter-name>
    <filter-class>
      coreservlets.filters.ReportFilter
    </filter-class>
```

Listing 5.3   web.xml (Excerpt for reporting filter) *(continued)*

```xml
</filter>
<!-- Apply the Reporter filter to home page. -->
<filter-mapping>
  <filter-name>Reporter</filter-name>
  <url-pattern>/index.jsp</url-pattern>
</filter-mapping>
<!-- Also apply the Reporter filter to the servlet named
     "TodaysSpecial". -->
<filter-mapping>
  <filter-name>Reporter</filter-name>
  <servlet-name>TodaysSpecial</servlet-name>
</filter-mapping>
...

<!-- Give a name to the Today's Special servlet so that filters
     can be applied to it. -->
<servlet>
  <servlet-name>TodaysSpecial</servlet-name>
  <servlet-class>
    coreservlets.TodaysSpecialServlet
  </servlet-class>
</servlet>
<!-- Make /TodaysSpecial invoke the servlet
     named TodaysSpecial (i.e., coreservlets.TodaysSpecial).
     -->
<servlet-mapping>
  <servlet-name>TodaysSpecial</servlet-name>
  <url-pattern>/TodaysSpecial</url-pattern>
</servlet-mapping>
<!-- Disable the invoker servlet. -->
<servlet>
  <servlet-name>NoInvoker</servlet-name>
  <servlet-class>coreservlets.NoInvokerServlet</servlet-class>
</servlet>
<servlet-mapping>
  <servlet-name>NoInvoker</servlet-name>
  <url-pattern>/servlet/*</url-pattern>
</servlet-mapping>

</web-app>
```

Figure 5–1 Home page for the filter company. After the page is deployed on an external server and the reporting filter is attached, each client access results in a printout akin to "purchasing.sun.com tried to access http://www.filtersrus.com/filters/index.jsp on Fri Oct 27 13:19:14 EDT 2006."

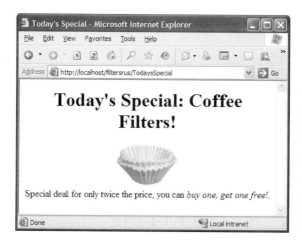

Figure 5–2 Page advertising a special sale. After the page is deployed on an external server and the reporting filter is attached, each client access results in a printout akin to "admin.microsoft.com tried to access http://www.filtersrus.com/filters/TodaysSpecial on Fri Oct 27 13:21:56 EDT 2006."

Listing 5.4   index.jsp

```
<!DOCTYPE HTML PUBLIC "-//W3C//DTD HTML 4.0 Transitional//EN">
<HTML>
<HEAD>
<TITLE>Filters 'R' Us</TITLE>
<LINK REL=STYLESHEET
      HREF="filter-styles.css"
      TYPE="text/css">
</HEAD>
<BODY>
<CENTER>
<TABLE BORDER=5>
  <TR><TH CLASS="TITLE">Filters 'R' Us</TABLE>
<P>
<TABLE>
  <TR>
    <TH><IMG SRC="images/air-filter.jpg" ALT="Air Filter">
    <TH><IMG SRC="images/coffee-filter.gif" ALT="Coffee Filter">
    <TH><IMG SRC="images/pump-filter.jpg" ALT="Pump Filter">
</TABLE>
<H3>We specialize in the following:</H3>
<UL>
  <LI>Air filters
  <LI>Coffee filters
  <LI>Pump filters
  <LI>Camera lens filters
  <LI>Image filters for Adobe Photoshop
  <LI>Web content filters
  <LI>Kalman filters
  <LI>Servlet and JSP filters
</UL>
Check out <A HREF="TodaysSpecial">Today's Special</A>.
</CENTER>
</BODY></HTML>
```

Listing 5.5 TodaysSpecialServlet.java

```java
package coreservlets;

import java.io.*;
import javax.servlet.*;
import javax.servlet.http.*;

/** Sample servlet used to test the simple filters.
 */
public class TodaysSpecialServlet extends HttpServlet {
  private String title, picture;
  public void doGet(HttpServletRequest request,
                    HttpServletResponse response)
      throws ServletException, IOException {
    updateSpecials();
    response.setContentType("text/html");
    PrintWriter out = response.getWriter();
    String docType =
      "<!DOCTYPE HTML PUBLIC \"-//W3C//DTD HTML 4.0 " +
      "Transitional//EN\">\n";
    out.println
      (docType +
       "<HTML>\n" +
       "<HEAD><TITLE>Today's Special</TITLE></HEAD>\n" +
       "<BODY BGCOLOR=\"WHITE\">\n" +
       "<CENTER>\n" +
       "<H1>Today's Special: " + title + "s!</H1>\n" +
       "<IMG SRC=\"images/" + picture + "\"\n" +
       "     ALT=\"" + title + "\">\n" +
       "<BR CLEAR=\"ALL\">\n" +
       "Special deal: for only twice the price, you can\n" +
       "<I>buy one, get one free!</I>.\n" +
       "</BODY></HTML>");
  }
   // Rotate among the three available filter images.
  private void updateSpecials() {
    double num = Math.random();
    if (num < 0.333) {
      title = "Air Filter";
      picture = "air-filter.jpg";
    } else if (num < 0.666) {
      title = "Coffee Filter";
      picture = "coffee-filter.gif";
    } else {
      title = "Pump Filter";
      picture = "pump-filter.jpg";
    }
  }
}
```

Listing 5.6 NoInvokerServlet.java

```
package coreservlets;

import java.io.*;
import javax.servlet.*;
import javax.servlet.http.*;

/** Simple servlet used to give error messages to
 *  users who try to access default servlet URLs
 *  (i.e., http://host/webAppPrefix/servlet/ServletName)
 *  in Web applications that have disabled this
 *  behavior.
 */
public class NoInvokerServlet extends HttpServlet {
  public void doGet(HttpServletRequest request,
                    HttpServletResponse response)
      throws ServletException, IOException {
    response.setContentType("text/html");
    PrintWriter out = response.getWriter();
    String docType =
      "<!DOCTYPE HTML PUBLIC \"-//W3C//DTD HTML 4.0 " +
      "Transitional//EN\">\n";
    String title = "Invoker Servlet Disabled.";
    out.println
      (docType +
       "<HTML>\n" +
       "<HEAD><TITLE>" + title + "</TITLE></HEAD>\n" +
       "<BODY BGCOLOR=\"#FDF5E6\">\n" +
       "<H2>" + title + "</H2>\n" +
       "Sorry, access to servlets by means of\n" +
       "URLs that begin with\n" +
       "http://host/webAppPrefix/servlet/\n" +
       "has been disabled.\n" +
       "</BODY></HTML>");
  }

  public void doPost(HttpServletRequest request,
                     HttpServletResponse response)
      throws ServletException, IOException {
    doGet(request, response);
  }
}
```

5.3 Accessing the Servlet Context from Filters

The `ReportFilter` of the previous section prints a report on the standard output whenever the designated servlet or JSP page is invoked. A report on the standard output is fine during development: When you run a server on your desktop, you typically have a window that displays the standard output. During deployment, however, you are unlikely to have access to this window. A natural enhancement is to write the reports into the servlet log file instead of the standard output.

The servlet API provides two `log` methods: one that takes a simple `String` and another that takes a `String` and a `Throwable`. These two methods are available from either the `GenericServlet` or `ServletContext` classes. Check your server's documentation for the exact location of the log files that these methods use. For example, Tomcat stores the log files in the *tomcat_dir*/logs directory. The problem is that the `doFilter` method executes before the servlet or JSP page with which it is associated, so you don't have access to the servlet instance and thus can't call the `log` methods that are inherited from `GenericServlet`. Furthermore, the Filter API provides no simple way to access the `ServletContext` from the `doFilter` method. The only filter-related class that has a method to access the `ServletContext` is `FilterConfig` with its `getServletContext` method. A `FilterConfig` object is passed to the `init` method but is not automatically stored in a location that is available to `doFilter`.

So, you have to store the `FilterConfig` yourself. Simply create a field (instance variable) of type `FilterConfig`, then override `init` to assign its argument to that field. Because you typically use the `FilterConfig` object only to access the `ServletContext` and the filter name, you can store the `ServletContext` and name in fields as well. Here is a simple example:

```
public class SomeFilter implements Filter {
  protected FilterConfig config;
  private ServletContext context;
  private String filterName;

  public void init(FilterConfig config)
      throws ServletException {
    this.config = config; // In case it is needed by subclass.
    context = config.getServletContext();
    filterName = config.getFilterName();
  }

  // doFilter and destroy methods...
}
```

5.4   Example: A Logging Filter

Let's update the `ReportFilter` (Listing 5.2) so that messages go in the log file instead of to the standard output. To accomplish this task, we implement the following capabilities.

1. **A class that implements the `Filter` interface.** This class is called `LogFilter` and is shown in Listing 5.7. The `init` method of this class stores the `FilterConfig`, `ServletContext`, and filter name in fields of the filter. The class provides an empty body for the `destroy` method.

2. **Filtering behavior in the `doFilter` method.** There are two differences between this behavior and that of the `ReportFilter`: The report is placed in the log file instead of the standard output and the report includes the name of the filter.

3. **A call to the `doFilter` method of the `FilterChain`.** After printing the report, the filter calls the `doFilter` method of the `FilterChain` to invoke the next filter in the chain (or the servlet or JSP page if there are no more filters).

4. **Registration with all URLs.** First, the `filter` element associates the name `LogFilter` with the class `coreservlets.filters.LogFilter`. Next, the `filter-mapping` element uses a `url-pattern` of `/*` to associate the filter with *all* URLs in the Web application. See Listing 5.8.

5. **Disablement of the invoker servlet.** This operation is shown in Section 5.2 (Example: A Reporting Filter) and is not repeated here.

After the Web application is deployed on an external server and the logging filter is attached, a client request for the Web application home page results in an entry in the log file like "audits.irs.gov tried to access http://www.filtersrus.com/filters/index.jsp on Fri Apr 14 15:16:15 EDT 2001. (Reported by Logger.)" On Tomcat, the log file is located in the *tomcat_dir*/logs directory. For example, Listing 5.9 shows partial contents of the localhost.2006-04-14.log file.

Listing 5.7   LogFilter.java

```java
package coreservlets.filters;

import java.io.*;
import java.util.*;
import javax.servlet.*;
import javax.servlet.http.*;

/** Simple filter that prints a report in the log file
 *  whenever the associated servlets or JSP pages
 *  are accessed.
 */
public class LogFilter implements Filter {
  protected FilterConfig config;
  private ServletContext context;
  private String filterName;

  public void doFilter(ServletRequest request,
                       ServletResponse response,
                       FilterChain chain)
      throws ServletException, IOException {
    HttpServletRequest req = (HttpServletRequest)request;
    context.log(req.getRemoteHost() +
                " tried to access " +
                req.getRequestURL() +
                " on " + new Date() + ". " +
                "(Reported by " + filterName + ".)");
    chain.doFilter(request,response);
  }

  public void init(FilterConfig config)
      throws ServletException {
    this.config = config; // In case it is needed by subclass.
    context = config.getServletContext();
    filterName = config.getFilterName();
  }

  public void destroy() {}
}
```

Listing 5.8 web.xml (Excerpt for logging filter)

```
<?xml version="1.0" encoding="ISO-8859-1"?>
<web-app xmlns="http://java.sun.com/xml/ns/j2ee"
  xmlns:xsi="http://www.w3.org/2001/XMLSchema-instance"
  xsi:schemaLocation=
  "http://java.sun.com/xml/ns/j2ee
  http://java.sun.com/xml/ns/j2ee/web-app_2_4.xsd"
  version="2.4">

  <!-- Register the name "Logger" for LogFilter. -->
  <filter>
    <filter-name>Logger</filter-name>
    <filter-class>
      coreservlets.filters.LogFilter
    </filter-class>
  </filter>
  <!-- Apply the Logger filter to all servlets and
       JSP pages. -->
  <filter-mapping>
    <filter-name>Logger</filter-name>
    <url-pattern>/*</url-pattern>
  </filter-mapping>
</web-app>
```

Listing 5.9 Partial contents of localhost.2006-04-14.log on Tomcat

```
Apr 14, 2006 3:22:14 PM org.apache.catalina.core.ApplicationCon-
text log
INFO: 127.0.0.1 tried to access http://localhost/filtersrus/ on
Fri Apr 14 15:22:14 EDT 2006. (Reported by Logger.)
Apr 14, 2006 3:22:15 PM org.apache.catalina.core.ApplicationCon-
text log
INFO: 127.0.0.1 tried to access http://localhost/filtersrus/fil-
ter-styles.css on Fri Apr 14 15:22:15 EDT 2006. (Reported by Log-
ger.)
Apr 14, 2006 3:22:15 PM org.apache.catalina.core.ApplicationCon-
text log
INFO: 127.0.0.1 tried to access http://localhost/filtersrus/
images/air-filter.jpg on Fri Apr 14 15:22:15 EDT 2006. (Reported
by Logger.)
Apr 14, 2006 3:22:15 PM org.apache.catalina.core.ApplicationCon-
text log
```

Listing 5.9	Partial contents of localhost.2006-04-14.log on Tomcat *(continued)*

```
INFO: 127.0.0.1 tried to access http://localhost/filtersrus/
images/coffee-filter.gif on Fri Apr 14 15:22:15 EDT 2006.
(Reported by Logger.)
Apr 14, 2006 3:22:25 PM org.apache.catalina.core.ApplicationCon-
text log
INFO: 127.0.0.1 tried to access http://localhost/filtersrus/Secu-
rityHole on Fri Apr 14 15:22:25 EDT 2006. (Reported by Logger.)
Apr 14, 2006 3:22:30 PM org.apache.catalina.core.ApplicationCon-
text log
INFO: 127.0.0.1 tried to access http://localhost/filtersrus/Today-
sSpecial on Fri Apr 14 15:22:30 EDT 2006. (Reported by Logger.)
Apr 14, 2006 3:22:32 PM org.apache.catalina.core.ApplicationCon-
text log
INFO: 127.0.0.1 tried to access http://localhost/filtersrus/Today-
sSpecial on Fri Apr 14 15:22:32 EDT 2006. (Reported by Logger.)
...
```

5.5 Using Filter Initialization Parameters

With servlets and JSP pages, you can customize the initialization behavior by supplying initialization parameters. For details, see Section 2.6 (Initializing and Preloading Servlets and JSP Pages). The reason this capability is useful is that there are three distinct groups that might want to customize the behavior of servlets or JSP pages:

1. **Developers.** They customize the behavior by changing the code of the servlet or JSP page itself.
2. **End users.** They customize the behavior by entering values in HTML forms.
3. **Deployers.** This third group is the one served by initialization parameters. Members of this group are people who take existing Web applications (or individual servlets or JSP pages) and deploy them in a customized environment. They are not necessarily developers, so it is not realistic to expect them to modify the servlet and JSP code. Besides, you often omit the source code when distributing servlets. So, developers need a standard way to allow deployers to change servlet and JSP behavior.

If these capabilities are useful for servlets and JSP pages, you would expect them to also be useful for the filters that apply to servlets and JSP pages. Indeed they are. However, because filters execute before the servlets or JSP pages to which they are attached, it is not normally possible for end users to customize filter behavior. Nevertheless, it is still useful to permit deployers (not just developers) to customize filter behavior by providing initialization parameters. This behavior is accomplished with the following steps.

1. **Define initialization parameters.** Use the `init-param` subelement of `filter` in web.xml along with `param-name` and `param-value` subelements, as follows:

```
<filter>
  <filter-name>SomeFilter</filter-name>
  <filter-class>somePackage.SomeFilterClass</filter-class>
  <init-param>
    <param-name>param1</param-name>
    <param-value>value1</param-value>
  </init-param>
  <init-param>
    <param-name>param2</param-name>
    <param-value>value2</param-value>
  </init-param>
</filter>
```

2. **Read the initialization parameters.** Call the `getInitParameter` method of `FilterConfig` from the `init` method of your filter, as follows:

```
public void init(FilterConfig config)
    throws ServletException {
  String val1 = config.getInitParameter("param1");
  String val2 = config.getInitParameter("param2");
  ...
}
```

3. **Parse the initialization parameters.** Like servlet and JSP initialization parameters, each filter initialization value is of type `String`. So, if you want a value of another type, you have to convert it yourself. For example, you would use `Integer.parseInt` to turn the `String` `"7"` into the `int` 7. When parsing, don't forget to check for missing and malformed data. Missing initialization parameters result in `null` being returned from `getInitParameter`. Even if the parameters exist, you should consider the possibility that the deployer formatted the value improperly. For example, when converting a `String` to an `int`, you should enclose the `Integer.parseInt` call within a try/catch block that catches `NumberFormatException`. This handles `null` and incorrectly formatted values in one fell swoop.

5.6   Example: An Access Time Filter

The `LogFilter` of Section 5.4 (Example: A Logging Filter) prints an entry in the log file every time the associated servlet or JSP page is accessed. Suppose you want to modify it so that it only notes accesses that occur at unusual times. Because "unusual" is situation dependent, the servlet should provide default values for the abnormal time ranges and let deployers override these values by supplying initialization parameters. To implement this functionality, we implement the following capabilities.

1. **A class that implements the `Filter` interface.** This class is called `LateAccessFilter` and is shown in Listing 5.10. The `init` method of this class reads the `startTime` and `endTime` initialization parameters. It attempts to parse these values as type `int`, using default values if the parameters are `null` or not formatted as integers. It then stores the start and end times, the `FilterConfig`, the `Servlet-Context`, and the filter name in fields (instance variables) of the filter. Finally, `LateAccessFilter` provides an empty body for the `destroy` method.

2. **Filtering behavior in the `doFilter` method.** This method looks up the current time, sees if it is within the range given by the start and end times, and prints a log entry if so.

3. **A call to the `doFilter` method of the `FilterChain`.** After printing the report, the filter calls the `doFilter` method of the `Filter-Chain` to invoke the next filter in the chain (or the servlet or JSP page if there are no more filters).

4. **Registration with the Web application home page; definition of initialization parameters.** First, the `filter` element associates the name `LateAccessFilter` with the class `coreservlets.filters.LateAccessFilter`. The `filter` element also includes two `init-param` subelements: one that defines the `startTime` parameter and another that defines `endTime`. Because the people that will be accessing the filtersRus home page are programmers, an abnormal range is considered to be between 2:00 a.m. and 10:00 a.m. Finally, the `filter-mapping` element uses a `url-pattern` of `/index.jsp` to associate the filter with the Web application home page. See Listing 5.11.

5. **Disablement of the invoker servlet.** This operation is shown in Section Section 5.2 (Example: A Reporting Filter) and is not repeated here.

After the Web application is deployed on an external server and the logging filter is attached, a client request for the Web application home page results in an entry in the log file like "WARNING: hacker6.filtersrus.com accessed http://www.filtersrus.com/filters/index.jsp on Oct 30, 2006 9:22:09 AM."

Listing 5.10   LateAccessFilter.java

```java
package coreservlets.filters;

import java.io.*;
import java.text.*;
import java.util.*;
import javax.servlet.*;
import javax.servlet.http.*;

/** Filter that keeps track of accesses that occur
 *  at unusual hours.
 */
public class LateAccessFilter implements Filter {
  private FilterConfig config;
  private ServletContext context;
  private int startTime, endTime;
  private DateFormat formatter;

  public void doFilter(ServletRequest request,
                       ServletResponse response,
                       FilterChain chain)
      throws ServletException, IOException {
    HttpServletRequest req = (HttpServletRequest)request;
    GregorianCalendar calendar = new GregorianCalendar();
    int currentTime = calendar.get(Calendar.HOUR_OF_DAY);
    if (isUnusualTime(currentTime, startTime, endTime)) {
      context.log("WARNING: " +
                  req.getRemoteHost() +
                  " accessed " +
                  req.getRequestURL() +
                  " on " +
                  formatter.format(calendar.getTime()));
    }
    chain.doFilter(request,response);
  }
```

Listing 5.10 LateAccessFilter.java *(continued)*

```java
public void init(FilterConfig config)
      throws ServletException {
    this.config = config;
    context = config.getServletContext();
    formatter =
      DateFormat.getDateTimeInstance(DateFormat.MEDIUM,
                             DateFormat.MEDIUM);
    try {
      startTime =
        Integer.parseInt(config.getInitParameter("startTime"));
      endTime =
        Integer.parseInt(config.getInitParameter("endTime"));
    } catch(NumberFormatException nfe) { // Malformed or null
      // Default: access at or after 10 p.m. but before 6 a.m.
      // is considered unusual.
      startTime = 22; // 10:00 p.m.
      endTime = 6;    //  6:00 a.m.
    }
  }

  public void destroy() {}

  // Is the current time between the start and end
  // times that are marked as abnormal access times?
  private boolean isUnusualTime(int currentTime,
                               int startTime,
                               int endTime) {
    // If the start time is less than the end time (i.e.,
    // they are two times on the same day), then the
    // current time is considered unusual if it is
    // between the start and end times.
    if (startTime < endTime) {
      return((currentTime >= startTime) &&
            (currentTime < endTime));
    }
    // If the start time is greater than or equal to the
    // end time (i.e., the start time is on one day and
    // the end time is on the next day), then the current
    // time is considered unusual if it is NOT between
    // the end and start times.
    else {
      return(!isUnusualTime(currentTime, endTime, startTime));
    }
  }
}
```

Listing 5.11 web.xml (Excerpt for access time filter)

```
<?xml version="1.0" encoding="ISO-8859-1"?>
<web-app xmlns="http://java.sun.com/xml/ns/j2ee"
  xmlns:xsi="http://www.w3.org/2001/XMLSchema-instance"
  xsi:schemaLocation=
  "http://java.sun.com/xml/ns/j2ee
  http://java.sun.com/xml/ns/j2ee/web-app_2_4.xsd"
  version="2.4">
  <!-- Register the name "LateAccessFilter" for
       coreservlets.filter.LateAccessFilter.
       Supply two initialization parameters:
       startTime and endTime. -->
  <filter>
    <filter-name>LateAccessFilter</filter-name>
    <filter-class>
      coreservlets.filters.LateAccessFilter
    </filter-class>
    <init-param>
      <param-name>startTime</param-name>
      <param-value>2</param-value>
    </init-param>
    <init-param>
      <param-name>endTime</param-name>
      <param-value>10</param-value>
    </init-param>
  </filter>
  <!-- Apply LateAccessFilter to the home page. -->
  <filter-mapping>
    <filter-name>LateAccessFilter</filter-name>
    <url-pattern>/index.jsp</url-pattern>
  </filter-mapping>
</web-app>
```

5.7   Blocking the Response

Up to now, all the filters discussed have concluded their doFilter methods by calling the doFilter method of the FilterChain object. This approach is the normal one—the call to doFilter invokes the next resource in the chain (another filter or the actual servlet or JSP page).

But what if your filter detects an unusual situation and wants to prevent the original resource from being invoked? How can it block the normal response? The answer is quite simple: Just omit the call to the doFilter method of the FilterChain object. Instead, the filter can redirect the user to a different page (e.g., with a call to response.sendRedirect) or generate the response itself (e.g., by calling get-Writer on the response and sending output, just as with a regular servlet). Just remember that the first two arguments to the filter's main doFilter method are declared to be of type ServletRequest and ServletResponse. So, if you want to use methods specific to HTTP, cast these arguments to HttpServletRequest and HttpServletResponse, respectively. Here is a brief example:

```
public void doFilter(ServletRequest request,
                     ServletResponse response,
                     FilterChain chain)
    throws ServletException, IOException {
  HttpServletRequest req = (HttpServletRequest)request;
  HttpServletResponse res = (HttpServletResponse)response;
  if (isUnusualCondition(req)) {
    res.sendRedirect("http://www.somesite.com");
  } else {
    chain.doFilter(req,res);
  }
}
```

5.8 Example: A Prohibited-Site Filter

Suppose you have a competitor that you want to ban from your site. For example, this competing company might have a service that accesses your site, removes advertisements and information that identify your organization, and displays them to their customers. Or, they might have links to your site that are in framed pages, thus making it appear that your page is part of their site. You'd like to prevent them from accessing certain pages at your site. However, every time their Web hosting company boots them off, they simply change domain names and register with another ISP. You thus want the ability to easily change the domain names that should be banned.

The solution is to make a filter that uses initialization parameters to obtain a list of banned sites. Requests originating or referred from these sites result in a warning message. Other requests proceed normally. To accomplish this functionality, we implement the following.

1. **A class that implements the Filter interface.** This class is called BannedAccessFilter and is shown in Listing 5.12. The init method of this class first obtains a list of sites from an initialization parameter called bannedSites. The filter parses the entries in the resultant String using the String.split method and stores each individual site name in a HashSet that is accessible through an

instance variable (i.e., field) of the filter. The `String.split` method is supplied with the regular expression for one or more white space characters to serve as the delimiter. For more details on Java regular expressions, see http://java.sun.com/j2se/1.5.0/docs/api/java/util/regex/Pattern.html. Finally, `BannedAccessFilter` provides an empty body for the `destroy` method.

2. **Filtering behavior in the `doFilter` method.** This method looks up the requesting and referring hosts by using the `getRemoteHost` method of `ServletRequest` and parsing the `Referer` HTTP request header, respectively.

3. **A conditional call to the `doFilter` method of the `Filter-Chain`.** The filter checks to see if the requesting or referring host is listed in the `HashMap` of banned sites. If so, it calls the `showWarning` method, which sends a custom response to the client. If not, the filter calls `doFilter` on the `FilterChain` object to let the request proceed normally.

4. **Registration with the daily special servlet; definition of initialization parameters.** First, the `filter` element associates the name `BannedAccessFilter` with the class `coreservlets.filters.BannedAccessFilter`. The `filter` element also includes an `init-param` subelement that specifies the prohibited sites (separated by white space). Because the resource that the competing sites abuse is the servlet that shows the daily special, the `filter-mapping` element uses a `servlet-name` of `Todays-Special`. The `servlet` element assigns the name `TodaysSpecial` to `coreservlets.TodaysSpecialServlet`. See Listing 5.13.

5. **Disablement of the invoker servlet.** This operation is shown in Section 5.2 (Example: A Reporting Filter) and is not repeated here.

Listing 5.14 shows a very simple page that contains little but a link to the daily special servlet. When that page is hosted on a normal site (Figure 5–3), the link results in the expected output (Figure 5–4). However, when the page that contains the link is hosted on a banned site (Figure 5–5), the link results only in a warning page (Figure 5–6)—access to the real servlet is blocked.

Figure 5–3   A page that links to the daily special servlet. This version is hosted on the desktop development server.

Figure 5–4   You can successfully follow the link from the page of Figure 5–3. The `BannedAccess-Filter` does not prohibit access from localhost.

Figure 5–5   A page that links to the daily special servlet. This version is hosted on www.tbiq.com.

Figure 5–6   You cannot successfully follow the link from the page of Figure 5–5. The `BannedAccessFilter` prohibits access from **www.tbiq.com** (an unscrupulous competitor to filtersRus.com).

Listing 5.12	BannedAccessFilter.java

```
package coreservlets.filters;

import java.io.*;
import java.net.*;
import java.util.*;
import javax.servlet.*;
import javax.servlet.http.*;

/** Filter that refuses access to anyone connecting directly
 *  from or following a link from a banned site.
 */
public class BannedAccessFilter implements Filter {
  private HashSet<String> bannedSiteTable;

  /** Deny access if the request comes from a banned site
   *  or is referred here by a banned site.
   */
  public void doFilter(ServletRequest request,
                       ServletResponse response,
                       FilterChain chain)
      throws ServletException, IOException {
    HttpServletRequest req = (HttpServletRequest)request;
    String requestingHost = req.getRemoteHost();
    String referringHost =
      getReferringHost(req.getHeader("Referer"));
    String bannedSite = null;
    boolean isBanned = false;
    if (bannedSiteTable.contains(requestingHost)) {
      bannedSite = requestingHost;
      isBanned = true;
```

Listing 5.12   BannedAccessFilter.java *(continued)*

```java
      } else if (bannedSiteTable.contains(referringHost)) {
        bannedSite = referringHost;
        isBanned = true;
    if (bannedSiteTable.contains(requestingHost)) {
        bannedSite = requestingHost;
        isBanned = true;
      } else if (bannedSiteTable.contains(referringHost)) {
        bannedSite = referringHost;
        isBanned = true;
      }
      if (isBanned) {
        showWarning(response, bannedSite);
      } else {
        chain.doFilter(request,response);
      }
  }

  /** Create a table of banned sites based on initialization
   *  parameters.
   */
  public void init(FilterConfig config)
      throws ServletException {
    bannedSiteTable = new HashSet<String>();
    String bannedSites =
      config.getInitParameter("bannedSites");
    if (bannedSites == null) {
    return;
    }
    // Split using one or more white spaces
    String[] sites = bannedSites.split("\\s++");
    for (String bannedSite: sites) {
      bannedSiteTable.add(bannedSite);
      System.out.println("Banned " + bannedSite);
    }
  }

  public void destroy() {}

  private String getReferringHost(String refererringURLString) {
    try {
      URL referringURL = new URL(refererringURLString);
      return(referringURL.getHost());
    } catch(MalformedURLException mue) { // Malformed or null
      return(null);
    }
  }
}
```

Listing 5.12 BannedAccessFilter.java *(continued)*

```java
// Replacement response that is returned to users
// who are from or referred here by a banned site.

private void showWarning(ServletResponse response,
                         String bannedSite)
    throws ServletException, IOException {
  response.setContentType("text/html");
  PrintWriter out = response.getWriter();
  String docType =
    "<!DOCTYPE HTML PUBLIC \"-//W3C//DTD HTML 4.0 " +
    "Transitional//EN\">\n";
  out.println
    (docType +
     "<HTML>\n" +
     "<HEAD><TITLE>Access Prohibited</TITLE></HEAD>\n" +
     "<BODY BGCOLOR=\"WHITE\">\n" +
     "<H1>Access Prohibited</H1>\n" +
     "Sorry, access from or via " + bannedSite + "\n" +
     "is not allowed.\n" +
     "</BODY></HTML>");
  }
}
```

Listing 5.13 web.xml (Excerpt for prohibited-site filter)

```xml
<?xml version="1.0" encoding="ISO-8859-1"?>
<web-app xmlns="http://java.sun.com/xml/ns/j2ee"
  xmlns:xsi="http://www.w3.org/2001/XMLSchema-instance"
  xsi:schemaLocation=
  "http://java.sun.com/xml/ns/j2ee
  http://java.sun.com/xml/ns/j2ee/web-app_2_4.xsd"
  version="2.4">
<!-- Give a name to the Today's Special servlet so that filters
     can be applied to it. -->
<servlet>
  <servlet-name>TodaysSpecial</servlet-name>
  <servlet-class>
    coreservlets.TodaysSpecialServlet
  </servlet-class>
</servlet>
<!-- Make /TodaysSpecial invoke the servlet
     named TodaysSpecial (i.e., coreservlets.TodaysSpecial).
     -->
```

Listing 5.13 web.xml (Excerpt for prohibited-site filter) *(continued)*

```xml
<servlet-mapping>
  <servlet-name>TodaysSpecial</servlet-name>
  <url-pattern>/TodaysSpecial</url-pattern>
</servlet-mapping>
<!-- Register the name "BannedAccessFilter" for
     coreservlets.filter.BannedAccessFilter.
     Supply an initialization parameter:
     bannedSites. -->
<filter>
  <filter-name>BannedAccessFilter</filter-name>
  <filter-class>
    coreservlets.filters.BannedAccessFilter
  </filter-class>
  <init-param>
    <param-name>bannedSites</param-name>
    <param-value>
      www.tbiq.com
      www.bettersite.com
      www.coreservlets.com
    </param-value>
  </init-param>
</filter>
<!-- Apply BannedAccessFilter to the servlet named
     "TodaysSpecial". -->
<filter-mapping>
  <filter-name>BannedAccessFilter</filter-name>
  <servlet-name>TodaysSpecial</servlet-name>
</filter-mapping>
</web-app>
```

Listing 5.14 linker.html

```html
<!DOCTYPE HTML PUBLIC "-//W3C//DTD HTML 4.0 Transitional//EN">
<HTML>
<HEAD>
<TITLE>Link to Filter Company</TITLE>
</HEAD>
<BODY>
<H2 ALIGN="CENTER">Link to Filter Company</H2>
Click <A HREF="http://localhost/filtersrus/TodaysSpecial">
here</A>
to see the daily special at filtersRus.com.
</BODY>
</HTML>
```

5.9   Modifying the Response

So filters can block access to resources or invoke them normally. But what if filters want to change the response that a resource generates? There don't appear to be any methods that provide access to the response that a resource generates. The second argument to doFilter (the ServletResponse) gives the filter a way to send new output to a client, but it doesn't give the filter access to the output of the servlet or JSP page. How could it? When the doFilter method is first invoked, the servlet or JSP page hasn't even executed yet. Once you call the doFilter method of the FilterChain object, it appears to be too late to modify the response—data has already been sent to the client. Hmm, a quandary.

The solution is to change the response object that is passed to the doFilter method of the FilterChain object. You create a response object that looks like an ordinary HttpServletResponse object to the servlet or JSP page. However, when the servlet or JSP page calls response.getWriter or response.getOutputStream and starts sending output, the output doesn't really get sent to the client. Instead, it gets buffered up into a large string where the filter can examine or modify it before really sending it to the client. The servlet API provides a useful resource for this purpose: the HttpServletResponseWrapper class. Use of this class involves five steps:

1. **Create a response wrapper.** Extend javax.servlet.http.HttpServletResponseWrapper.

2. **Provide a PrintWriter and a ServletOutputStream that buffer output.** Override the getWriter and getOutputStream methods to return a PrintWriter and a ServletOutputStream that save everything sent to them and store that result in a field that can be accessed later. The reason we need to override both getWriter and getOutputStream is because the servlet providing the actual output is free to use either getWriter or getOutputStream methods. However, remember that it is illegal to call both of those methods on the same response object, so we are guaranteed that only one of those methods will be called.

3. **Pass that wrapper to doFilter.** This call is legal because HttpServletResponseWrapper implements HttpServletResponse.

4. **Extract and modify the output.** After the call to the doFilter method of the FilterChain, the output of the original resource is available to you through whatever mechanism you provided in Step 2. You can modify or replace it as appropriate for your application.

5. **Send the modified output to the client.** Because the original resource no longer sends output to the client (the output is stored in your response wrapper instead), you have to send the output. Your filter needs to obtain the PrintWriter or ServletOutputStream from the original response object and pass the modified output to that stream.

A Reusable Response Wrapper

Listing 5.15 presents a wrapper that can be used in most applications where you want filters to modify a resource's output. The StringWrapper class overrides the get-Writer and getOutputStream methods to return a PrintWriter or a Serv-letOutputStream, respectively, that accumulate everything in a large string. This result is available to the developer through the toStringBuffer or toString methods. We need to do a bit more work to override the getOutputStream method. The ServletOutputStream, which getOutputStream must return, happens to be an abstract class, so there is no way for us to create it right away. Instead, we have to provide our own implementation of it so it does what we want, namely, buffer up the output instead of sending it straight to the client. Listing 5.16 shows the StringOutputStream class, which does just that. Now, we are able to return an instance of type StringOutputStream from the getOutputStream method because StringOutputStream extends ServletOutputStream.

Sections 5.10 (Example: A Replacement Filter) and 5.11 (Example: A Compression Filter) give two examples of use of this class.

Listing 5.15   StringWrapper.java

```
package coreservlets.filters;

import java.io.*;
import javax.servlet.*;
import javax.servlet.http.*;

/** A response wrapper that takes everything the client
 *  would normally output and saves it in one large string.
 */
public class StringWrapper
          extends HttpServletResponseWrapper {
  private StringWriter stringWriter;

  /** Initializes wrapper.
   *  <P>
   *  First, this constructor calls the parent
   *  constructor. That call is crucial so that the response
   *  is stored and thus setHeader, setStatus, addCookie,
   *  and so forth work normally.
   *  <P>
   *  Second, this constructor creates a StringWriter
   *  that will be used to accumulate the response.
   */
```

Listing 5.15 StringWrapper.java *(continued)*

```java
public StringWrapper(HttpServletResponse response) {
  super(response);
  stringWriter = new StringWriter();
}

/** When servlets or JSP pages ask for the Writer,
 *  don't give them the real one. Instead, give them
 *  a version that writes into the StringBuffer.
 *  The filter needs to send the contents of the
 *  buffer to the client (usually after modifying it).
 */

public PrintWriter getWriter() {
  return(new PrintWriter(stringWriter));
}
 /** Similarly, when resources call getOutputStream,
  * give them a phony output stream that just
  * buffers up the output.
  */

public ServletOutputStream getOutputStream() {
  return(new StringOutputStream(stringWriter));
}

/** Get a String representation of the entire buffer.
 *   <P>
 *   Be sure <I>not</I> to call this method multiple times
 *   on the same wrapper. The API for StringWriter
 *   does not guarantee that it "remembers" the previous
 *   value, so the call is likely to make a new String
 *   every time.
 */

public String toString() {
  return(stringWriter.toString());
}

/** Get the underlying StringBuffer. */

public StringBuffer getBuffer() {
  return(stringWriter.getBuffer());
}
}
```

Listing 5.16   StringOutputStream.java

```
package coreservlets.filters;

import java.io.*;
import javax.servlet.*;
import javax.servlet.http.*;

/** StringOutputStream is a stub for ServletOutputStream which
 *  buffers up the output in a string buffer instead of sending it
 *  straight to the client.
 */
public class StringOutputStream
            extends ServletOutputStream {
  private StringWriter stringWriter;

  public StringOutputStream(StringWriter stringWriter) {
    this.stringWriter = stringWriter;
  }

  public void write(int c) {
    stringWriter.write(c);
  }
}
```

5.10 Example: A Replacement Filter

This section presents one common application of the StringWrapper shown in the previous section: a filter that changes all occurrences of a target string to some replacement string.

A Generic Modification Filter

Listing 5.17 presents a filter that wraps the response in a StringWrapper, passes that wrapper to the doFilter method of the FilterChain object, extracts a String that represents all of the resource's output, and calls the doModification method, passing it the original output string. The doModification method makes changes to the original output and returns the modified output string. It is the modified output that gets actually sent to the client.

There is one thing to note about this filter—it is an abstract class. To use it, you must create a subclass that provides the implementation of the doModification method. This setup allows us to adapt this generic modification filter to whatever our response modification needs might be in the future, preparing the setup for better code reuse. The next subsection includes an example of this process.

Listing 5.17	ModificationFilter.java

```java
package coreservlets.filters;

import java.io.*;
import javax.servlet.*;
import javax.servlet.http.*;

/** Generic modification filter that buffers the output and lets
 *  doModification method change the output string before sending
 *  it to the real output, i.e., the client. This is an abstract
 *  class: you <I>must</I> override doModification in a subclass.
 */
public abstract class ModificationFilter implements Filter {
  protected FilterConfig config;
  private HttpServletRequest request;
  private HttpServletResponse response;

  public void doFilter(ServletRequest req,
                       ServletResponse resp,
                       FilterChain chain)
      throws ServletException, IOException {
    request = (HttpServletRequest)req;
    response = (HttpServletResponse)resp;
    StringWrapper responseWrapper = new StringWrapper(response);
    // Invoke resource, accumulating output in the wrapper.
    chain.doFilter(request, responseWrapper);
    // Turn entire output into one big String.
    String modifiedResponse =
      doModification(responseWrapper.toString());
    // Send modified response to the client
    PrintWriter out = response.getWriter();
    out.write(modifiedResponse);
  }

  /** Classes extending from ModificationFilter must
   *  override this method.
   */
  public abstract String doModification(String origResponse)
    throws IOException;

  /** Saving off the request object for potential use by the child
   *  class.
   */
```

Listing 5.17	ModificationFilter.java *(continued)*

```
  public HttpServletRequest getRequest() {
    return(request);
  }

  /** Saving off the response object for potential use by the child
   *   class.
   */
  public HttpServletResponse getResponse() {
    return(response);
  }

  public void init(FilterConfig config) {
    // Save FilterConfig object for later use by subclasses
    this.config = config;
  }

  public void destroy() {}
}
```

A Specific Modification Filter

Oh no! A competitor bought out filtersRus.com. All the Web pages that refer to the company name are now obsolete. However, the developers hate to change all their Web pages because another takeover could occur anytime (this company is a hot commodity, after all). No problem—Listing 5.18 presents a filter that replaces all occurrences of filtersRus.com with weBefilters.com. Figure 5–7 shows a page (Listing 5.20) that promotes the filtersRus.com site name. Figure 5–8 shows the page after the filter is applied.

To accomplish this functionality, we implement the following capabilities.

1. **A class that implements the `Filter` interface.** This class is called `ReplaceSiteNameFilter` and is shown in Listing 5.18. It extends the generic `ModificationFilter` of Listing 5.17. The inherited init method stores the `FilterConfig` object in a field. The private `getInitParameter` method uses the `FilterConfig` object to retrieve the values of the init parameters `target` and `replacement` from web.xml. The `doModification` method uses the regular expression-based `String.replaceAll` method to replace every occurrence of the `target` string with the `replacement` string. The parent class also provides an empty body for the `destroy` method.

2. **A wrapped response object.** The `doFilter` method, inherited from `ModificationFilter`, wraps the `ServletResponse` object in a `StringWrapper` and passes that wrapper to the `doFilter`

method of the `FilterChain` object. After this call completes, all other filters and the final resource have executed and the output is inside the wrapper. So, the original `doFilter` extracts a `String` that represents all of the resource's output and passes it to the `doModifi-cation` method, which performs some modifications of the output. Finally, `doFilter` sends that modified result to the client by supplying the modified `String` to the `write` method of the `PrintWriter` that is associated with the original response.

3. **Registration with the JSP page that promotes filtersRus.com.** First, the `filter` element of web.xml (Listing 5.19) associates the name `ReplaceSiteNameFilter` with the class `coreservlets.filters.ReplaceSiteNameFilter`, specifying two init parameters: `target` and `replacement`. Next, the `filter-mapping` element uses a `url-pattern` of `/plugSite/page2.jsp` (see Listing 5.20) so that the filter fires each time that JSP page is requested.

4. **Disablement of the invoker servlet.** This operation is shown in Section 5.2 (Example: A Reporting Filter) and is not repeated here.

Figure 5–7   A page that promotes the filtersRus.com site.

Figure 5–8   The page that promotes the filtersRus.com site after its output is modified by the ReplaceSiteNameFilter.

Listing 5.18 | ReplaceSiteNameFilter.java

```
package coreservlets.filters;

/** Filter that replaces all occurrences of the target
 *  string with the replacement string. The target and
 *  replacement strings are provided as init parameters
 *  to the filter in the web.xml file.
 */
public class ReplaceSiteNameFilter extends ModificationFilter {
  private boolean isCaseInsensitive = false;
```

Listing 5.18 ReplaceSiteNameFilter.java *(continued)*

```java
/** The string that needs replacement.
 */
public String getTarget() {
  return getInitParameter("target");
}

/** The string that replaces the target.
 */
public String getReplacement() {
  return getInitParameter("replacement");
}

/** Returns the init parameter value specified by 'param' or
 *  null if it is not present or an empty string
 */
private String getInitParameter(String param) {
  String value = config.getInitParameter(param);
  if ((value == null) || (value.trim().equals(""))) {
    value = null;
  }
  return value;
}

/** Sets whether the search for the target string
 *  will be case sensitive.
 */
public void setCaseInsensitive(boolean flag) {
  isCaseInsensitive = flag;
}
/** Returns true or false, indicating if the search
 *  for the target string is case sensitive.
 */
public boolean isCaseInsensitive() {
  return(isCaseInsensitive);
}

/** Replaces all strings matching the target string
 *  with the replacement string.
 */
public String doModification(String orig) {
  if ((getTarget() == null) || (getReplacement() == null)) {
    return(orig);
  } else {
```

Listing 5.18 ReplaceSiteNameFilter.java *(continued)*

```java
    String target = getTarget();
    if (isCaseInsensitive()) {
      target = "(?i)" + target;
    }
    String replacement = getReplacement();
    return(orig.replaceAll(target, replacement));
  }
 }
}
```

Listing 5.19 web.xml (Excerpt for site name replacement filter)

```xml
<?xml version="1.0" encoding="ISO-8859-1"?>
<web-app xmlns="http://java.sun.com/xml/ns/j2ee"
  xmlns:xsi="http://www.w3.org/2001/XMLSchema-instance"
  xsi:schemaLocation=
  "http://java.sun.com/xml/ns/j2ee
  http://java.sun.com/xml/ns/j2ee/web-app_2_4.xsd"
  version="2.4">
  <!-- Register the name "ReplaceSiteNameFilter" for
       coreservlets.filters.ReplaceSiteNameFilter. -->
  <filter>
    <filter-name>ReplaceSiteNameFilter</filter-name>
    <filter-class>
      coreservlets.filters.ReplaceSiteNameFilter
    </filter-class>
    <init-param>
      <param-name>target</param-name>
      <param-value>filtersRus.com</param-value>
    </init-param>
    <init-param>
      <param-name>replacement</param-name>
      <param-value>weBefilters.com</param-value>
    </init-param>
  </filter>
  <!-- Apply ReplaceSiteNameFilter to page2.jsp page
       in the plugSite directory -->
  <filter-mapping>
    <filter-name>ReplaceSiteNameFilter</filter-name>
    <url-pattern>/plugSite/page2.jsp</url-pattern>
  </filter-mapping>
</web-app>
```

Listing 5.20 page1.jsp (Identical to page2.jsp)

```
<!DOCTYPE HTML PUBLIC "-//W3C//DTD HTML 4.0 Transitional//EN">
<HTML>
<HEAD>
<TITLE>filtersRus.com</TITLE>
<LINK REL=STYLESHEET
      HREF="../filter-styles.css"
      TYPE="text/css">
</HEAD>
<BODY>
<CENTER>
<TABLE BORDER=5>
  <TR><TH CLASS="TITLE">filtersRus.com</TABLE>
<P>
<TABLE>
  <TR>
    <TH><IMG SRC="../images/air-filter.jpg"
            ALT="Air Filter">
    <TH><IMG SRC="../images/coffee-filter.gif"
            ALT="Coffee Filter">
    <TH><IMG SRC="../images/pump-filter.jpg"
            ALT="Pump Filter">
</TABLE>
<H3>filtersRus.com specializes in the following:</H3>
<UL>
  <LI>Air filters
  <LI>Coffee filters
  <LI>Pump filters
  <LI>Camera lens filters
  <LI>Image filters for Adobe Photoshop
  <LI>Web content filters
  <LI>Kalman filters
  <LI>Servlet and JSP filters
</UL>
Check out <A HREF="../TodaysSpecial">Today's Special</A>.
</CENTER>
</BODY></HTML>
```

5.11 Example: A Compression Filter

Most recent browsers can handle gzipped content, automatically uncompressing documents that have gzip as the value of the Content-Encoding response header and then treating the result as though it were the original document. Sending such compressed content can be a real time saver because the time required to compress the document on the server and then uncompress it on the client is typically dwarfed by the savings in download time, especially when dial-up connections are used. For example, Listing 5.22 shows a servlet that has very long, repetitive, plain-text output: a ripe candidate for compression. If gzip could be applied, it could compress the output by a factor of over 300!

However, although most browsers support this type of encoding, a few do not. Sending compressed content to browsers that don't support gzip encoding produces a totally garbled result. Browsers that support content encoding include most versions of Netscape for UNIX, most versions of Internet Explorer for Windows, Netscape 4.7 and later for Windows, Firefox, and Opera 5.12 and above. Therefore, this compression cannot be done blindly—it is only valid for clients that use the Accept-Encoding request header to specify that they support gzip.

We demonstrate very similar functionality in *Core Servlets and JavaServer Pages, Volume 1: Core Technologies*, compressing the output right in the servlet. However, because we would like to be able to apply this behavior to multiple resources, a filter is a much more appropriate place for it. The compression filter can use the String-Wrapper of Section 5.9 (Modifying the Response) to compress content when the browser supports such a capability. Accomplishing this task requires the following:

1. **A class that implements the `Filter` interface.** This class is called CompressionFilter and is shown in Listing 5.21. The init method stores the FilterConfig object in a field in case subclasses need access to the servlet context or filter name. The body of the destroy method is left empty.

2. **A wrapped response object.** The doFilter method checks if the client indicates that it supports compression (i.e., has gzip as one of the values of its Accept-Encoding header). If it doesn't, we invoke the doFilter method of the FilterChain object with the original response and request objects. If the client supports gzip compression, the doFilter method wraps the ServletResponse object in a StringWrapper and passes that wrapper to the doFilter method of the FilterChain object. After this call completes, all other filters and the final resource have executed and the output is inside the wrapper. So the original doFilter extracts a String that represents all of the resource's output. We then wrap a ByteArray-

OutputStream in a GZIPOutputStream. We wrap the resultant GZIPOutputStream in an OutputStreamWriter, enabling us to pass a String through the compression mechanism. Using the toString method of the StringWrapper, we copy the original buffered output into the OutputStreamWriter. Finally, doFilter sends the compressed output to the client by writing the entire underlying byte array of our stream chain (e.g., ByteArrayOutputStream, GZIPOutputStream, and OutputStreamWriter) to the OutputStream that is associated with the original response object.

3. **Registration with long servlet.** First, the filter element of web.xml (Listing 5.23) associates the name CompressionFilter with the class coreservlets.filters.CompressionFilter. Next, the filter-mapping element uses a servlet-name of LongServlet so that the filter fires each time that long servlet (Listing 5.22) is requested. The servlet and servlet-mapping elements assign the name LongServlet to the servlet and specify the URL that corresponds to the servlet.

4. **Disablement of the invoker servlet.** This operation is shown in Section 5.2 (Example: A Reporting Filter) and is not repeated here.

When the filter is attached, the body of the servlet is reduced 300 times and the time to access the servlet on a 28.8K modem is reduced by more than a factor of 10 (more than 50 seconds uncompressed; less than 5 seconds compressed), a huge savings. Figure 5–9 shows the page that the compression filter was used on. However, two small warnings are in order here.

First, there is a saying in the software industry that there are three kinds of lies: lies, darn lies, and benchmarks. The point of this maxim is that people always rig benchmarks to cast their point in the most favorable light possible. We did the same thing by using a servlet with long simple output and using a slow modem connection. So, we're not promising that you will always get a tenfold performance gain, but it is a simple matter to attach or detach the compression filter. That's the beauty of filters. Try it yourself and see how much it buys you in typical usage conditions.

Second, although the specification does not officially mandate that you set response headers before calling the doFilter method of the FilterChain, some servers require you to do so. This is to prevent you from attempting to set a response header after a resource has sent content to the client. So, for portability, be sure to set response headers before calling chain.doFilter.

Core Warning

If your filter sets response headers, be sure it does so before calling the doFilter method of the FilterChain object.

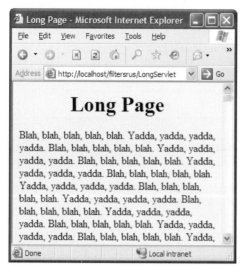

Figure 5–9   The `LongServlet`. The content is more than 300 times smaller when gzip is used, resulting in more than a tenfold speed increase when the servlet is accessed with a 28.8K modem.

Listing 5.21   CompressionFilter.java

```
package coreservlets.filters;

import java.io.*;
import java.util.zip.*;
import javax.servlet.*;
import javax.servlet.http.*;

/** Filter that compresses output with gzip
 *  (assuming that browser supports gzip).
 */
public class CompressionFilter implements Filter {
  private FilterConfig config;

  /** If browser does not support gzip, invoke resource
   *  normally. If browser <I>does</I> support gzip,
   *  set the Content-Encoding response header and
   *  invoke resource with a wrapped response that
   *  collects all the output. Extract the output
   *  and write it into a gzipped byte array. Finally,
   *  write that array to the client's output stream.
   */
```

Listing 5.21 CompressionFilter.java *(continued)*

```java
public void doFilter(ServletRequest request,
                     ServletResponse response,
                     FilterChain chain)
    throws ServletException, IOException {
  HttpServletRequest req = (HttpServletRequest)request;
  HttpServletResponse res = (HttpServletResponse)response;
  if (!isGzipSupported(req)) {
    // Invoke resource normally.
    chain.doFilter(req,res);
  } else {
    // Tell browser we are sending it gzipped data.
    res.setHeader("Content-Encoding", "gzip");

    // Invoke resource, accumulating output in the wrapper.
    StringWrapper responseWrapper =
      new StringWrapper(res);
    chain.doFilter(req,responseWrapper);

    // Make a writer that compresses data and puts
    // it into a byte array.
    ByteArrayOutputStream byteStream =
      new ByteArrayOutputStream();
    GZIPOutputStream zipOut =
      new GZIPOutputStream(byteStream);
    OutputStreamWriter tempOut =
      new OutputStreamWriter(zipOut);

    // Compress original output and put it into byte array.
    tempOut.write(responseWrapper.toString());

    // Gzip streams must be explicitly closed.
    tempOut.close();

    // Send compressed result to client.
    OutputStream realOut = res.getOutputStream();
    byteStream.writeTo(realOut);
  }
}

/** Store the FilterConfig object in case subclasses
 *  want it.
 */
```

Listing 5.21 CompressionFilter.java *(continued)*

```java
public void init(FilterConfig config)
    throws ServletException {
  this.config = config;
}

protected FilterConfig getFilterConfig() {
  return(config);
}

public void destroy() {}

private boolean isGzipSupported(HttpServletRequest req) {
  String browserEncodings =
    req.getHeader("Accept-Encoding");
  return((browserEncodings != null) &&
         (browserEncodings.indexOf("gzip") != -1));
}
}
```

Listing 5.22 LongServlet.java

```java
package coreservlets;

import java.io.*;
import javax.servlet.*;
import javax.servlet.http.*;

/** Servlet with <B>long</B> output. Used to test
 *  the effect of the compression filter of Chapter 9.
 */
public class LongServlet extends HttpServlet {
  public void doGet(HttpServletRequest request,
                    HttpServletResponse response)
      throws ServletException, IOException {
    response.setContentType("text/html");
    PrintWriter out = response.getWriter();
    String docType =
      "<!DOCTYPE HTML PUBLIC \"-//W3C//DTD HTML 4.0 " +
      "Transitional//EN\">\n";
    String title = "Long Page";
```

Listing 5.22   LongServlet.java *(continued)*

```
    out.println
      (docType +
       "<HTML>\n" +
       "<HEAD><TITLE>" + title + "</TITLE></HEAD>\n" +
       "<BODY BGCOLOR=\"#FDF5E6\">\n" +
       "<H1 ALIGN=\"CENTER\">" + title + "</H1>\n");
    String line = "Blah, blah, blah, blah, blah. " +
                  "Yadda, yadda, yadda, yadda.";
    for(int i=0; i<10000; i++) {
      out.println(line);
    }
    out.println("</BODY></HTML>");
  }
}
```

Listing 5.23   web.xml (Excerpt for compression filter)

```
<?xml version="1.0" encoding="ISO-8859-1"?>
<web-app xmlns="http://java.sun.com/xml/ns/j2ee"
  xmlns:xsi="http://www.w3.org/2001/XMLSchema-instance"
  xsi:schemaLocation=
  "http://java.sun.com/xml/ns/j2ee
  http://java.sun.com/xml/ns/j2ee/web-app_2_4.xsd"
  version="2.4">
  <!-- Register the name "CompressionFilter" for
       coreservlets.filters.CompressionFilter. -->
  <filter>
    <filter-name>CompressionFilter</filter-name>
    <filter-class>
      coreservlets.filters.CompressionFilter
    </filter-class>
  </filter>
  <!-- Apply CompressionFilter to the servlet named
       "LongServlet". -->
  <filter-mapping>
    <filter-name>CompressionFilter</filter-name>
    <servlet-name>LongServlet</servlet-name>
  </filter-mapping>
  <!-- Give a name to the servlet that generates long
       (but very exciting!) output. -->
  <servlet>
    <servlet-name>LongServlet</servlet-name>
    <servlet-class>coreservlets.LongServlet</servlet-class>
  </servlet>
```

Listing 5.23 **web.xml (Excerpt for compression filter)** *(continued)*

```
<!-- Make /LongServlet invoke the servlet
     named LongServlet (i.e., coreservlets.LongServlet). -->
<servlet-mapping>
  <servlet-name>LongServlet</servlet-name>
  <url-pattern>/LongServlet</url-pattern>
</servlet-mapping>
<!-- Disable the invoker servlet. -->
<servlet>
  <servlet-name>NoInvoker</servlet-name>
  <servlet-class>coreservlets.NoInvokerServlet</servlet-class>
</servlet>
<servlet-mapping>
  <servlet-name>NoInvoker</servlet-name>
  <url-pattern>/servlet/*</url-pattern>
</servlet-mapping>
</web-app>
```

5.12 Configuring Filters to Work with RequestDispatcher

Version 2.3 of the servlet specification only allowed us to configure filters for requests that came directly from the client. Filters did not apply to requests that were made as a result of the `forward` or `include` methods of `RequestDispatcher`. Version 2.4 introduced a new deployment descriptor element, `dispatcher`, which allows us to configure filters to do just that.

The optional `dispatcher` element must be placed inside the `filter-mapping` element after the `url-pattern` or `servlet-name` element. It can be assigned one of the following values: REQUEST, FORWARD, INCLUDE, or ERROR. If you want to apply the filter to different types of requests, you can do so by repeating the dispatcher element with a different value. Here is a simple example:

```
<!-- ... -->
<filter-mapping>
  <filter-name>MyFilter</filter-name>
  <url-pattern>/index.jsp</url-pattern>
  <dispatcher>REQUEST</dispatcher>
  <dispatcher>INCLUDE</dispatcher>
</filter-mapping>
```

Each value of the `dispatcher` element represents a different type of request. The filter mapping will apply only to the types of requests specified. Details follow.

REQUEST

When the `dispatcher` element is assigned REQUEST, the filter mapping will apply to any request coming directly from the client for the Web resources matching the `url-pattern` or `servlet-name` element. If the resource specified by the `filter-mapping` element is invoked using methods of `RequestDispatcher` (i.e., `forward` or `include`), the filter mapping will not apply and the associated filter will not be invoked. If the `dispatcher` element is omitted, the server assumes the REQUEST setting and configures the filter mapping accordingly. However, if any other setting is specified (e.g., INCLUDE), the filter mapping will not automatically apply to requests coming directly from the client. In such situations, you must specify an additional `dispatcher` element with the value of REQUEST if you want to intercept direct client requests as well.

Core Warning

If the `dispatcher` element is omitted, the REQUEST setting is assumed. However, if any other setting is specified (e.g., INCLUDE), you must specify the REQUEST setting for the filter mapping to apply to direct client requests.

FORWARD

When the `dispatcher` element is assigned FORWARD, the filter mapping will apply to any request made as a result of the `RequestDispatcher.forward` method call to the Web resources matching the `url-pattern` or `servlet-name` element.

INCLUDE

When the `dispatcher` element is assigned INCLUDE, the filter mapping will apply to any request made as a result of the `RequestDispatcher.include` method call to the Web resources matching the `url-pattern` or `servlet-name` element.

ERROR

When the `dispatcher` element is assigned ERROR, the filter mapping will apply to any request that was forwarded by the server to the Web resource matching the `url-pattern` or `servlet-name` element using the error page mechanism. For example, suppose the NotFound.jsp error page was designated in web.xml to serve as an HTTP 404 custom error page as follows:

```
<error-page>
  <error-code>404</error-code>
  <location>/NotFound.jsp</location>
</error-page>
```

Now, suppose we specify a `filter-mapping` element as follows:

```
<filter-mapping>
  <filter-name>SomeFilter</filter-name>
  <url-pattern>/NotFound.jsp</url-pattern>
  <dispatcher>ERROR</dispatcher>
<filter-mapping>
```

The server will forward any request to a nonexisting resource to NotFound.jsp as part of the error page mechanism. Because we specified `SomeFilter` to intercept a request to NotFound.jsp when the request is being made as part of the error page mechanism, `SomeFilter` will be invoked before the request reaches NotFound.jsp. For more information on the error page mechanism, see Section 2.9 (Designating Pages to Handle Errors).

5.13 Example: Plugging a Potential Security Hole

In Chapter 3 (Declarative Security), when discussing declarative security, we mentioned that the security constraints only apply to clients that access the resources directly. They do not apply to resources that are accessed through the MVC architecture with a `RequestDisplatcher` or by the similar means of `jsp:forward` or `jsp:include`. This asymmetry can catch developers off guard and allow them to accidentally provide unrestricted access to resources that should be protected.

In this section, we configure a filter that ensures that even if one of the developers makes a mistake, our secure resources remain safe from unauthorized access. Normally, you use the forward or the include mechanism because the servlet creates some data that the JSP page will use. There is almost never a good reason to forward to a regular HTML page. The real solution to this problem would therefore be to conduct regular code reviews, weed out the "bad apple" developer, and either get rid of this developer or arrange for a nice training class. However, that's not always up you, so you are stuck with implementing a safety net. To accomplish this functionality, we implement the following capabilities.

1. **A class that implements the `Filter` interface.** This class is called `SecurityHolePlugFilter` and is shown in Listing 5.24. The init and destroy methods of this class do nothing and thus are provided empty bodies.

2. **Filtering behavior in the `doFilter` method.** This method forces the client to directly invoke the requested resource by calling the `sendRedirect` method. This setup will trigger the server's security mechanism, preventing unauthorized access to the protected resource. Because this filter is configured to only intercept the `RequestDis-patcher` and error page calls and we do not intend to let any such requests pass, we never call the `doFilter` method of the `FilterChain`.

3. **Configuration of security constraints, roles, and login mechanism.** Using the `security-constraint` element, we restrict access to any resource inside the **secure** directory to users in the `executive` role only. Using the `security-role` element, we declare the `executive` role. Finally, using the `login-config` element, we specify the type of user authentication as `BASIC`. See Listing 5.26. For more details on defining security constraints, roles, login mechanism, and associating usernames with passwords, see Section 3.1 (Form-Based Authentication).

4. **Registration with URLs that attempt to invoke a resource inside the secure directory.** First, the `filter` element associates the name `SecurityHolePlugFilter` with the class `coreserv-lets.filters.SecurityHolePlugFilter`. The `filter-mapping` element uses the same `url-pattern` as the `security-onstraint` element (i.e., `/secure/*`). We specify three dispatcher elements—one with `INCLUDE`, one with `FORWARD`, and another with `ERROR` values. Because security constraints already apply to direct requests, we need to safeguard the **secure** directory from the other types of requests. Our filter intercepts those types of requests and essentially converts them into direct client requests, forcing the security constraints to apply. See Listing 5.26.

5. **A servlet to test the `SecurityHolePlugFilter`.** We write a simple servlet called `SecurityHoleServlet`, which uses the `RequestDispatcher.forward` method in an attempt to access job-openings.html inside the **security** directory, bypassing the security constraints. We associate the name `SecurityHole` with the class `core-servlets.SecurityHoleServlet` using the `servlet` element. We assign `/SecurityHole` as the URL that will invoke the `Security-Hole` servlet using the `servlet-mapping` element. See Listing 5.25.

6. **Disablement of the invoker servlet.** This operation is shown in Section 5.2 (Example: A Reporting Filter) and is not repeated here.

Listing 5.24 and Listing 5.25 show the complete code for SecurityHolePlugFil-ter.java and SecurityHoleServlet.java, respectively. Listing 5.26 shows the excerpt from the deployment descriptor with all the configurations needed for this example. If the `SecurityHolePlugFilter` is disabled, the `SecurityHoleServlet` is able to bypass the security constraint and access the protected resource (i.e., /secure/job-openings.html) without being authorized to do so. Because we are using the RequestDispatcher.forward method, the originally requested URL is shown in the browser's address bar (Figure 5–10). If the SecurityHolePlugFilter is enabled, it intercepts and converts the RequestDispatcher.forward call into a direct client request using the response.sendRedirect method. This invocation becomes no different than trying to directly invoke http://localhost/filtersrus/secure/job-openings.html, therefore the server asks for username and password to proceed (Figure 5–11). If the user successfully logs in with a username belonging to the executive role, the screen captured in Figure 5–12 is shown. Note that even though the originally requested URL was http://localhost/filtersrus/SecurityHole, the filter forced the client to directly request the resource, thus changing the requested URL to http://localhost/filtersrus/secure/job-openings.html. Listing 5.27 shows the complete code for job-openings.html.

Listing 5.24 SecurityHolePlugFilter.java

```
package coreservlets.filters;

import java.io.*;
import javax.servlet.*;
import javax.servlet.http.*;

/** This filter converts any request that it is configured to
 *  intercept into a direct client request. This prevents
 *  developers from making a mistake by dynamically forwarding
 *  the client to a secure resource, bypassing the
 *  declarative security mechanism.
 */
public class SecurityHolePlugFilter implements Filter {
  public void doFilter(ServletRequest request,
                       ServletResponse response,
                       FilterChain chain)
      throws ServletException, IOException {
    HttpServletRequest req = (HttpServletRequest) request;
    HttpServletResponse res = (HttpServletResponse) response;
    res.sendRedirect(req.getRequestURI());
  }

  public void init(FilterConfig config)
      throws ServletException {
  }

  public void destroy() {}
}
```

Listing 5.25 SecurityHoleServlet.java

```java
package coreservlets;

import java.io.*;
import javax.servlet.*;
import javax.servlet.http.*;

/** This servlet is used to demonstrate forwarding to a
 *  protected resource.
 */
public class SecurityHoleServlet extends HttpServlet {
  public void doGet(HttpServletRequest request,
                    HttpServletResponse response)
      throws ServletException, IOException {
    RequestDispatcher dispatcher =
    request.getRequestDispatcher("/secure/job-openings.html");
    dispatcher.forward(request, response);
  }

  public void doPost(HttpServletRequest request,
                     HttpServletResponse response)
      throws ServletException, IOException {
    doGet(request, response);
  }
}
```

Listing 5.26 Excerpt from web.xml

```xml
<?xml version="1.0" encoding="ISO-8859-1"?>
<web-app xmlns="http://java.sun.com/xml/ns/j2ee"
  xmlns:xsi="http://www.w3.org/2001/XMLSchema-instance"
  xsi:schemaLocation=
  "http://java.sun.com/xml/ns/j2ee
  http://java.sun.com/xml/ns/j2ee/web-app_2_4.xsd"
  version="2.4">
  <!-- Only executives are allowed to view internal job
       descriptions -->
  <security-constraint>
    <web-resource-collection>
      <web-resource-name>
        Job openings, internal
      </web-resource-name>
      <url-pattern>/secure/*</url-pattern>
    </web-resource-collection>
```

Listing 5.26 Excerpt from web.xml *(continued)*

```
  <auth-constraint>
    <role-name>executive</role-name>
  </auth-constraint>
</security-constraint>
<security-role>
  <role-name>executive</role-name>
</security-role>
<login-config>
  <auth-method>BASIC</auth-method>
  <realm-name>Internal</realm-name>
</login-config>
<!-- Servlet that erroneously forwards to a secure
     resource. -->
<servlet>
  <servlet-name>SecurityHole</servlet-name>
  <servlet-class>
    coreservlets.SecurityHoleServlet
  </servlet-class>
</servlet>
<servlet-mapping>
  <servlet-name>SecurityHole</servlet-name>
  <url-pattern>/SecurityHole</url-pattern>
</servlet-mapping>
<!-- Register the name "SecurityHolePlugFilter" for
     coreservlets.filters.SecurityHolePlugFilter. -->
<filter>
  <filter-name>SecurityHolePlugFilter</filter-name>
  <filter-class>
    coreservlets.filters.SecurityHolePlugFilter
  </filter-class>
</filter>
<!-- Apply SecurityHolePlugFilter any resource
     inside the secure directory -->
<filter-mapping>
  <filter-name>SecurityHolePlugFilter</filter-name>
  <url-pattern>/secure/*</url-pattern>
  <!-- Only invoke this filter as a result of
       RequestDispatcher's forward/include methods or as a
       result of error page mechanism. -->
  <dispatcher>FORWARD</dispatcher>
  <dispatcher>INCLUDE</dispatcher>
  <dispatcher>ERROR</dispatcher>
</filter-mapping>
...
</web-app>
```

Listing 5.27 job-openings.html located in the secure directory

```
<!DOCTYPE HTML PUBLIC "-//W3C//DTD HTML 4.01 Transitional//EN">
<HTML>
<HEAD>
<TITLE>Job Openings at FiltersRUs</TITLE>
</HEAD>
<BODY>
<H1 ALIGN="CENTER">Job Openings at FiltersRUs</H1>
This page contains descriptions of positions within our company
that we are looking to fill. These descriptions are not to be
shared with the commoners, i.e., regular employees, under any
circumstances. Only executives are allowed to access this page.<P>
<B>Position:</B> Manager<BR>
<B>Description:</B> A person in charge of making crucial
decisions and providing his subordinates with the right tools to
do their jobs in a timely manner.<BR/>
<B>Salary:</B> $50,000<P>
<B>Position:</B> Boss<BR>
<B>Description:</B> A person who knows very little about anyone's
job
or how to support it, but is good at looking important, parading
around the office, and especially prolonging meetings by listening
to
himself talk.<BR>
<B>Salary:</B> $300,000<P>
FiltersRUs Management
</BODY></HTML>
```

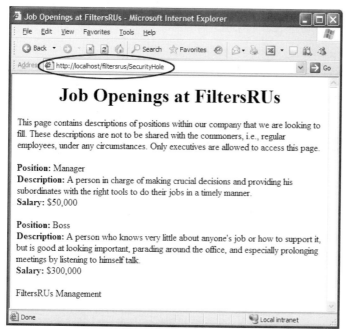

Figure 5–10 If the `SecurityHolePlugFilter` is disabled, the `SecurityHoleServlet` is able to bypass the security constraint and access the protected resource (i.e., /secure/ job-openings.html) without being authorized to do so. Because we are using the `RequestDispatcher.forward` method, the originally requested URL is showing in the browser's address bar.

Figure 5–11 If the `SecurityHolePlugFilter` is enabled, it converts the `RequestDispatcher.forward` call into a direct client request. This invocation becomes no different than trying to directly invoke http://localhost/filtersrus/secure/ job-openings.html, therefore the server asks for username and password to proceed.

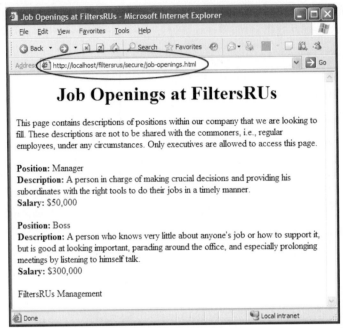

Figure 5–12 Even though the originally requested URL was http://localhost/filtersrus/ SecurityHole, the filter forced the client to directly request the resource, thus changing the requested URL to http://localhost/filtersrus/secure/job-openings.html. This screen is shown if the user successfully logs in with a username belonging to the executive role.

5.14 The Complete Filter Deployment Descriptor

The previous sections showed various excerpts of the web.xml file for filtersRus.com. Listing 5.28 shows the file in its entirety.

Listing 5.28	web.xml (Complete version for filter examples)

```xml
<?xml version="1.0" encoding="ISO-8859-1"?>
<web-app xmlns="http://java.sun.com/xml/ns/j2ee"
  xmlns:xsi="http://www.w3.org/2001/XMLSchema-instance"
  xsi:schemaLocation=
  "http://java.sun.com/xml/ns/j2ee
  http://java.sun.com/xml/ns/j2ee/web-app_2_4.xsd"
  version="2.4">
  <!-- Give a name to the Today's Special servlet so that filters
       can be applied to it. -->
  <servlet>
    <servlet-name>TodaysSpecial</servlet-name>
    <servlet-class>
      coreservlets.TodaysSpecialServlet
    </servlet-class>
  </servlet>
  <!-- Make /TodaysSpecial invoke the servlet
       named TodaysSpecial (i.e., coreservlets.TodaysSpecial).
       -->
  <servlet-mapping>
    <servlet-name>TodaysSpecial</servlet-name>
    <url-pattern>/TodaysSpecial</url-pattern>
  </servlet-mapping>
  <!-- Register the name "Reporter" for ReportFilter. -->
  <filter>
    <filter-name>Reporter</filter-name>
    <filter-class>
      coreservlets.filters.ReportFilter
    </filter-class>
  </filter>
  <!-- Apply the Reporter filter to home page. -->
  <filter-mapping>
    <filter-name>Reporter</filter-name>
    <url-pattern>/index.jsp</url-pattern>
  </filter-mapping>
  <!-- Also apply the Reporter filter to the servlet named
       "TodaysSpecial". -->
  <filter-mapping>
    <filter-name>Reporter</filter-name>
    <servlet-name>TodaysSpecial</servlet-name>
  </filter-mapping>
  <!-- Register the name "BannedAccessFilter" for
       coreservlets.filter.BannedAccessFilter.
       Supply an initialization parameter:
       bannedSites. -->
```

Listing 5.28 web.xml
(Complete version for filter examples) *(continued)*

```xml
<filter>
  <filter-name>BannedAccessFilter</filter-name>
  <filter-class>
    coreservlets.filters.BannedAccessFilter
  </filter-class>
  <init-param>
    <param-name>bannedSites</param-name>
    <param-value>
      www.tbiq.com
      www.bettersite.com
      www.coreservlets.com
    </param-value>
  </init-param>
</filter>
<!-- Apply BannedAccessFilter to the servlet named
     "TodaysSpecial". -->
<filter-mapping>
  <filter-name>BannedAccessFilter</filter-name>
  <servlet-name>TodaysSpecial</servlet-name>
</filter-mapping>
<!-- Give a name to the servlet that generates long
     (but very exciting!) output. -->
<servlet>
  <servlet-name>LongServlet</servlet-name>
  <servlet-class>coreservlets.LongServlet</servlet-class>
</servlet>
<!-- Make /LongServlet invoke the servlet
     named LongServlet (i.e., coreservlets.LongServlet). -->
<servlet-mapping>
  <servlet-name>LongServlet</servlet-name>
  <url-pattern>/LongServlet</url-pattern>
</servlet-mapping>
<!-- Register the name "CompressionFilter" for
     coreservlets.filters.CompressionFilter. -->
<filter>
  <filter-name>CompressionFilter</filter-name>
  <filter-class>
    coreservlets.filters.CompressionFilter
  </filter-class>
</filter>
<!-- Apply CompressionFilter to the servlet named
     "LongServlet". -->
<filter-mapping>
  <filter-name>CompressionFilter</filter-name>
  <servlet-name>LongServlet</servlet-name>
</filter-mapping>
```

Listing 5.28 web.xml
(Complete version for filter examples) *(continued)*

```xml
<!-- Register the name "Logger" for LogFilter. -->
<filter>
  <filter-name>Logger</filter-name>
  <filter-class>
    coreservlets.filters.LogFilter
  </filter-class>
</filter>
<!-- Apply the Logger filter to all servlets and
     JSP pages. -->
<filter-mapping>
  <filter-name>Logger</filter-name>
  <url-pattern>/*</url-pattern>
</filter-mapping>
<!-- Register the name "LateAccessFilter" for
     coreservlets.filter.LateAccessFilter.
     Supply two initialization parameters:
     startTime and endTime. -->
<filter>
  <filter-name>LateAccessFilter</filter-name>
  <filter-class>
    coreservlets.filters.LateAccessFilter
  </filter-class>
  <init-param>
    <param-name>startTime</param-name>
    <param-value>2</param-value>
  </init-param>
  <init-param>
    <param-name>endTime</param-name>
    <param-value>10</param-value>
  </init-param>
</filter>
<!-- Apply LateAccessFilter to the home page. -->
<filter-mapping>
  <filter-name>LateAccessFilter</filter-name>
  <url-pattern>/index.jsp</url-pattern>
</filter-mapping>
<!-- Register the name "ReplaceSiteNameFilter" for
     coreservlets.filters.ReplaceSiteNameFilter. -->
<filter>
  <filter-name>ReplaceSiteNameFilter</filter-name>
  <filter-class>
    coreservlets.filters.ReplaceSiteNameFilter
  </filter-class>
```

Listing 5.28	web.xml (Complete version for filter examples) *(continued)*

```
    <init-param>
      <param-name>target</param-name>
      <param-value>filtersRus.com</param-value>
    </init-param>
    <init-param>
      <param-name>replacement</param-name>
      <param-value>weBefilters.com</param-value>
    </init-param>
  </filter>
  <!-- Apply ReplaceSiteNameFilter to page1.jsp and page2.html
       pages in the plugSite directory -->
  <filter-mapping>
    <filter-name>ReplaceSiteNameFilter</filter-name>
    <url-pattern>/plugSite/page2.jsp</url-pattern>
  </filter-mapping>
  <!-- Only executives are allowed to view internal job
       descriptions -->
  <security-constraint>
    <web-resource-collection>
      <web-resource-name>
        Job openings, internal
      </web-resource-name>
      <url-pattern>/secure/*</url-pattern>
    </web-resource-collection>
    <auth-constraint>
      <role-name>executive</role-name>
    </auth-constraint>
  </security-constraint>
  <security-role>
    <role-name>executive</role-name>
  </security-role>
  <login-config>
    <auth-method>BASIC</auth-method>
    <realm-name>Internal</realm-name>
  </login-config>
  <!-- Servlet that erroneously forwards to a secure
       resource. -->
  <servlet>
    <servlet-name>SecurityHole</servlet-name>
    <servlet-class>
      coreservlets.SecurityHoleServlet
    </servlet-class>
  </servlet>
```

Listing 5.28 web.xml
(Complete version for filter examples) *(continued)*

```
<servlet-mapping>
  <servlet-name>SecurityHole</servlet-name>
  <url-pattern>/SecurityHole</url-pattern>
</servlet-mapping>
<!-- Register the name "SecurityHolePlugFilter" for
     coreservlets.filters.SecurityHolePlugFilter. -->
<filter>
  <filter-name>SecurityHolePlugFilter</filter-name>
  <filter-class>
    coreservlets.filters.SecurityHolePlugFilter
  </filter-class>
</filter>
<!-- Apply SecurityHolePlugFilter any resource
     inside the secure directory -->
<filter-mapping>
  <filter-name>SecurityHolePlugFilter</filter-name>
  <url-pattern>/secure/*</url-pattern>
  <!-- Only invoke this filter as a result of
       RequestDispatcher's forward/include methods or as a
       result of error page mechanism. -->
  <dispatcher>FORWARD</dispatcher>
  <dispatcher>INCLUDE</dispatcher>
  <dispatcher>ERROR</dispatcher>
</filter-mapping>
<!-- If URL gives a directory but no filename, try index.jsp
     first and index.html second. If neither is found,
     the result is server specific (e.g., a directory
     listing).  Order of elements in web.xml matters.
     welcome-file-list needs to come after servlet but
     before error-page. -->
<welcome-file-list>
  <welcome-file>index.jsp</welcome-file>
  <welcome-file>index.html</welcome-file>
</welcome-file-list>
<!-- Disable the invoker servlet. -->
<servlet>
  <servlet-name>NoInvoker</servlet-name>
  <servlet-class>coreservlets.NoInvokerServlet</servlet-class>
</servlet>
<servlet-mapping>
  <servlet-name>NoInvoker</servlet-name>
  <url-pattern>/servlet/*</url-pattern>
</servlet-mapping>
</web-app>
```

THE APPLICATION
EVENTS FRAMEWORK

Topics in This Chapter

- Understanding the general event-handling strategy
- Monitoring servlet context initialization and shutdown
- Setting application-wide values
- Detecting changes in attributes of the servlet context
- Packaging listeners in JSP tag libraries
- Recognizing creation and destruction of HTTP sessions
- Analyzing overall session usage
- Watching for changes in session attributes
- Tracking purchases at an e-commerce site
- Identifying request creation and destruction
- Tracking server request load
- Monitoring request attribute addition and change
- Using multiple cooperating listeners

Chapter 6

Developers have many tools at their disposal for handling the life cycle of individual servlets or JSP pages. The servlet `init` method (Section 2.6) fires when a servlet is first instantiated. JSP pages use the nearly identical `jspInit` method (Section 2.6). Both methods can use initialization parameters that are specified with the `init-param` subelement of the **web**.xml `servlet` element (Section 2.6). Requests are handled with `service` and `_jspService`, and destruction is handled with `destroy` and `jspDestroy`.

This is all fine for individual resources, but what if you want to respond to major events in the life cycle of the Web application itself? What if you want to create application-wide connection pools, locate resources, or set up shared network connections? For example, suppose you want to record the e-mail address of the support group at your company, an address that will be used by many different servlets and JSP pages. Sure, you can use the following to store the information:

```
context.setAttribute("supportAddress", "balmer@microsoft.com");
```

Better yet, you could use the **web**.xml `context-param` element (Section 2.6) to designate the address, then read it with the `getInitParameter` method of `ServletContext`. Fine. But which servlet or JSP page should perform this task? Or you could read the address from a database. Fine. But which servlet or JSP page should establish the database connection? There is no good answer to this question; you don't know which resources will be accessed first, so the code that performs these tasks would have to be repeated many different places. You want more global control than any one servlet or JSP page can provide. That's where application life-cycle event listeners come in.

There are eight kinds of event listeners that respond to Web application life-cycle events.

- **Servlet context listeners.** These listeners are notified when the servlet context (i.e., the Web application) is initialized and destroyed.
- **Servlet context attribute listeners.** These listeners are notified when attributes are added to, removed from, or replaced in the servlet context.
- **Session listeners.** These listeners are notified when session objects are created, invalidated, or timed out.
- **Session attribute listeners.** These listeners are notified when attributes are added to, removed from, or replaced in any session.
- **Session migration listeners.** These listeners are notified when the session objects are serialized and deserialized by the container. Usually, the serialization and deserialization of session objects occurs when the container migrates the session objects from one machine to another.
- **Session object binding listeners.** These listeners are notified when the implementing object is added or removed from the session object.
- **Request listeners.** These listeners are notified when request objects are initialized and destroyed.
- **Request attribute listeners.** These listeners are notified when attributes are added to, removed from, or replaced in any request.

Using these listeners involves six basic steps. We'll give a general outline here, then provide listener-specific details in the following sections.

1. **Implement the appropriate interface.** Use `ServletContext-Listener`, `ServletContextAttributeListener`, `HttpSessionListener`, `HttpSessionAttributeListener`, `HttpSessionActivationListener`, `HttpSessionBinding-Listener`, `ServletRequestListener`, or `ServletRequest-AttributeListener`. The interfaces without the Http prefix in their name reside in the `javax.servlet` package and the interfaces with the Http prefix reside in the `javax.servlet.http` package.

2. **Implement the methods needed to respond to the events of interest.** Provide empty bodies for the other methods in the interface. For example, the `ServletContextListener` interface defines two methods: `contextInitialized` (the Web application was just loaded and the servlet context was initialized) and

contextDestroyed (the Web application is being shut down and the servlet context is about to be destroyed). If you wanted to define an application-wide servlet context entry, you could provide a real implementation for contextInitialized and an empty body for contextDestroyed.

3. **Obtain access to the important Web application objects.** There are nine important objects that you are likely to use in your event-handling methods: the servlet context, the name of the servlet context attribute that changed, the value of the servlet context attribute that changed, the session object, the name of the session attribute that changed, the value of the session attribute that changed, the request object, the name of the request attribute that changed, and the value of the request attribute that changed.

4. **Use these objects.** This process is application specific, but there are some common themes. For example, with the servlet context, you are most likely to read initialization parameters (getInitParameter), store data for later access (setAttribute), and read previously stored data (getAttribute).

5. **Declare the listener.** You do this with the listener and listener-class elements of the general Web application deployment descriptor (web.xml) or of a TLD file.

6. **Provide any needed initialization parameters.** Servlet context listeners commonly read context initialization parameters to use as the basis of data that is made available to all servlets and JSP pages. You use the context-param web.xml element to provide the names and values of these initialization parameters.

Note, however, that the ServletRequestListener and the Servlet-RequestAttributeListener are new additions to version 2.4 of the servlet specification. If your Web application needs to support servers compliant only with version 2.3, you cannot use the aforementioned listeners.

Core Warning

ServletRequestListener and ServletRequestAttribute-Listener fail in servers that are compliant only with version 2.3 of the servlet specification.

6.1 Monitoring Creation and Destruction of the Servlet Context

The `ServletContextListener` class responds to the initialization and destruction of the servlet context. These events correspond to the creation and shutdown of the Web application itself. The `ServletContextListener` is most commonly used to set up application-wide resources like database connection pools and to read the initial values of application-wide data that will be used by multiple servlets and JSP pages. Using the listener involves the following six steps.

1. **Implement the `ServletContextListener` interface.** This interface is in the `javax.servlet` package.
2. **Implement `contextInitialized` and `contextDestroyed`.** The first of these (`contextInitialized`) is triggered when the Web application is first loaded and the servlet context is created. The two most common tasks performed by this method are creating application-wide data (often by reading context initialization parameters) and storing that data in an easily accessible location (often in attributes of the servlet context). The second method (`contextDestroyed`) is triggered when the Web application is being shut down and the servlet context is about to be destroyed. The most common task performed by this method is the releasing of resources. For example, `context-Destroyed` can be used to close database connections associated with a now-obsolete connection pool. However, because the servlet context will be destroyed (and garbage collected if the server itself continues to execute), there is no need to use `contextDestroyed` to remove normal objects from servlet context attributes.
3. **Obtain a reference to the servlet context.** The `context-Initialized` and `contextDestroyed` methods each take a `ServletContextEvent` as an argument. The `ServletContextEvent` class has a `getServletContext` method that returns the servlet context.
4. **Use the servlet context.** You read initialization parameters with `getInitParameter`, store data with `setAttribute`, and make log file entries with `log`.
5. **Declare the listener.** Use the `listener` and `listener-class` elements to simply list the fully qualified name of the listener class, as shown here:

```
<listener>
  <listener-class>somePackage.SomeListener</listener-class>
</listener>
```

For now, assume that this declaration goes in the web.xml file. However, keep in mind that if you package listeners with tag libraries, you can use the identical declaration within the TLD file of the tag library. This technique is discussed in Section 6.5 (Packaging Listeners with Tag Libraries).

6. **Provide any needed initialization parameters.** Once you have a reference to the servlet context (see Step 3), you can use the get-InitParameter method to read context initialization parameters as the basis of data that will be made available to all servlets and JSP pages. You use the context-param web.xml element to provide the names and values of these initialization parameters, as follows:

```
<context-param>
  <param-name>name</param-name>
  <param-value>value</param-value>
</context-param>
```

6.2 Example: Initializing Commonly Used Data

Suppose that you are developing a Web site for a dot-com company that is a hot commodity. So hot, in fact, that it is constantly being bought out by larger companies. As a result, the company name keeps changing. Rather than changing zillions of separate servlets and JSP pages each time you change the company name, you could read the company name when the Web application is loaded, store the value in the servlet context, and design all your servlets and JSP pages to read the name from this location. To prevent confusion among customers, the site can also prominently display the former company name, initializing and using it in a manner similar to the current company name.

The following steps summarize a listener that accomplishes this task.

1. **Implement the ServletContextListener interface.** Listing 6.1 shows a class (InitialCompanyNameListener) that implements this interface.

2. **Implement contextInitialized and contextDestroyed.** The InitialCompanyNameListener class uses context-Initialized to read the current and former company names and store them in the servlet context. Because the contextDestroyed method is not needed, an empty body is supplied.

3. **Obtain a reference to the servlet context.** The context-Initialized method calls getServletContext on the ServletContextEvent argument and stores the result in the context local variable.

4. **Use the servlet context.** The listener needs to store the company-Name and formerCompanyName initialization parameters in a globally accessible location, so it calls getInitParameter on the context variable, checks for missing values, and uses setAttribute to store the result in the servlet context.

5. **Declare the listener.** The listener is declared in the deployment descriptor with the listener and listener-class elements, as shown here:

```
<listener>
  <listener-class>
    coreservlets.listeners.InitialCompanyNameListener
  </listener-class>
</listener>
```

The web.xml file is shown in Listing 6.2.

6. **Provide any needed initialization parameters.** The company-Name and formerCompanyName init parameters are defined in web.xml (Listing 6.2) as follows:

```
<context-param>
  <param-name>companyName</param-name>
  <param-value>not-dot-com.com</param-value>
</context-param>
<context-param>
  <param-name>formerCompanyName</param-name>
  <param-value>hot-dot-com.com</param-value>
</context-param>
```

Listings 6.3 and 6.4 present two JSP pages that use the predefined JSP EL variable applicationScope (i.e., the servlet context) to access the companyName and formerCompanyName attributes. Figures 6–1 and 6–2 show the results.

Listing 6.1	InitialCompanyNameListener.java

```
package coreservlets.listeners;

import javax.servlet.ServletContext;
import javax.servlet.ServletContextEvent;
import javax.servlet.ServletContextListener;
```

Listing 6.1   InitialCompanyNameListener.java *(continued)*

```
/** Listener that looks up the name of the company when
 *  the Web application is first loaded. Stores this
 *  name in the companyName servlet context attribute.
 *  Various servlets and JSP pages will extract it
 *  from that location.
 */

public class InitialCompanyNameListener
    implements ServletContextListener {
  private static final String DEFAULT_NAME =
    "MISSING-COMPANY-NAME";

  /** Looks up the companyName and formerCompanyName
   *  init parameters and puts them into the servlet context.
   */
  public void contextInitialized(ServletContextEvent event) {
    ServletContext context = event.getServletContext();
    setInitialAttribute(context,
                        "companyName",
                        DEFAULT_NAME);
    setInitialAttribute(context,
                        "formerCompanyName",
                        "");
  }

  public void contextDestroyed(ServletContextEvent event) {}

  // Looks for a servlet context init parameter with a
  // given name. If it finds it, it puts the value into
  // a servlet context attribute with the same name. If
  // the init parameter is missing, it puts a default
  // value into the servlet context attribute.
  private void setInitialAttribute(ServletContext context,
                                   String initParamName,
                                   String defaultValue) {

    String initialValue =
      context.getInitParameter(initParamName);
    if (initialValue != null) {
      context.setAttribute(initParamName, initialValue);
    } else {
      context.setAttribute(initParamName, defaultValue);
    }
  }
}
```

Listing 6.2 web.xml (Excerpt for initial company name listener)

```xml
<?xml version="1.0" encoding="ISO-8859-1"?>
<web-app xmlns="http://java.sun.com/xml/ns/j2ee"
  xmlns:xsi="http://www.w3.org/2001/XMLSchema-instance"
  xsi:schemaLocation=
  "http://java.sun.com/xml/ns/j2ee
  http://java.sun.com/xml/ns/j2ee/web-app_2_4.xsd"
  version="2.4">

  <!-- Because the company name changes so frequently,
       supply it as a servlet context parameter instead
       of embedding it into lots of different servlets and
       JSP pages. The InitialCompanyNameListener will
       read this value and store it in the servlet context. -->
  <context-param>
    <param-name>companyName</param-name>
    <param-value>not-dot-com.com</param-value>
  </context-param>

  <!-- Also store the previous company name. -->
  <context-param>
    <param-name>formerCompanyName</param-name>
    <param-value>hot-dot-com.com</param-value>
  </context-param>

  <!-- Register the listener that sets up the
       initial company name. -->
  <listener>
    <listener-class>
      coreservlets.listeners.InitialCompanyNameListener
    </listener-class>
  </listener>

  <!-- If URL gives a directory but no file name, try index.jsp
       first and index.html second. If neither is found,
       the result is server specific (e.g., a directory
       listing).  Order of elements in web.xml matters.
       welcome-file-list needs to come after servlet but
       before error-page.
  -->
  <welcome-file-list>
    <welcome-file>index.jsp</welcome-file>
    <welcome-file>index.html</welcome-file>
  </welcome-file-list>
  <!-- ... -->

</web-app>
```

Listing 6.3 index.jsp

```
<!DOCTYPE HTML PUBLIC "-//W3C//DTD HTML 4.0 Transitional//EN">
<HTML>
<HEAD>
<TITLE>${applicationScope.companyName}</TITLE>
<LINK REL=STYLESHEET
      HREF="events-styles.css"
      TYPE="text/css">
</HEAD>

<BODY>
<TABLE BORDER=5 ALIGN="CENTER">
  <TR><TH CLASS="TITLE">
      ${applicationScope.companyName}<BR>
      (formerly ${applicationScope.formerCompanyName})
</TABLE>
<P>
Welcome to the home page of <B>
${applicationScope.companyName}</B> (formerly
${applicationScope.formerCompanyName})
<P>
<B>${applicationScope.companyName}</B> is a high-flying,
fast-growing, big-potential company. A perfect choice for your
retirement portfolio!
<P>
Click <A HREF="company-info.jsp">here</A> for more information.
</BODY>
</HTML>
```

Listing 6.4 company-info.jsp

```
<!DOCTYPE HTML PUBLIC "-//W3C//DTD HTML 4.0 Transitional//EN">
<HTML>
<HEAD>
<TITLE>${applicationScope.companyName}</TITLE>
<LINK REL=STYLESHEET
      HREF="events-styles.css"
      TYPE="text/css">
</HEAD>

<BODY>
```

Listing 6.4	company-info.jsp *(continued)*

```
<TABLE BORDER=5 ALIGN="CENTER">
  <TR><TH CLASS="TITLE">
      ${applicationScope.companyName}<BR>
      (formerly ${applicationScope.formerCompanyName})
</TABLE>
<P>
Learn more about <B>${applicationScope.companyName}</B>
(formerly ${applicationScope.formerCompanyName})
<UL>
  <LI><A HREF="products.jsp">${applicationScope.companyName}
  products</A>
  <LI><A HREF="services.jsp">${applicationScope.companyName}
  services</A>
  <LI><A HREF="history.jsp">${applicationScope.companyName}
  history</A>
  <LI><A HREF="invest.jsp">investing in
  ${applicationScope.companyName}</A>
  <LI><A HREF="contact.jsp">contacting
  ${applicationScope.companyName}</A>
</UL>

</BODY>
</HTML>
```

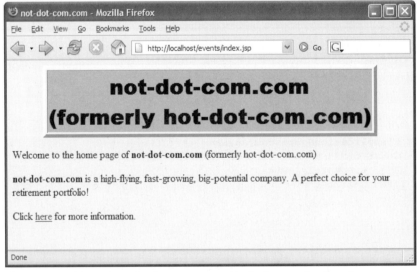

Figure 6–1   Home page for the company with the frequently changing name.

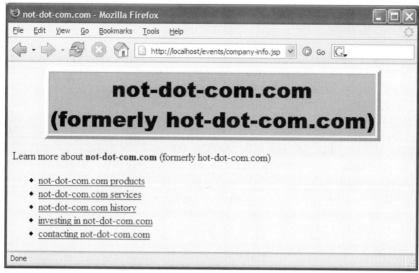

Figure 6–2   Informational page for the company with the frequently changing name.

6.3   Detecting Changes in Servlet Context Attributes

When the Web application is loaded, you can set up initial values of resources and store references to them in the servlet context, but what if you want to be notified whenever these resources change? For example, what if the value of resource B depends on the value of resource A? If resource A changes, you need to automatically update the value of resource B. Handling this situation is the job of servlet context attribute listeners. Using them involves the following steps.

1. **Implement the `ServletContextAttributeListener` interface.** This interface is in the `javax.servlet` package.
2. **Implement `attributeAdded`, `attributeReplaced`, and `attributeRemoved`.** The `attributeAdded` method is triggered when a new attribute is added to the servlet context. When a new value is assigned to an existing servlet context attribute, `attribute-Added` is triggered with the new value and `attributeReplaced` is triggered with the old value (i.e., the value being replaced). The `attributeRemoved` method is triggered when a servlet context attribute is removed altogether.

3. **Obtain references to the attribute name, attribute value, and servlet context.** Each of the three `ServletContextAttribute-Listener` methods takes a `ServletContextAttributeEvent` as an argument. The `ServletContextAttributeEvent` class has three useful methods: `getName` (the name of the attribute that was changed), `getValue` (the value of the changed attribute—the new value for `attributeAdded` and the previous value for `attribute-Replaced` and `attributeRemoved`), and `getServletContext` (the servlet context).

4. **Use the objects.** You normally compare the attribute name to a stored name to see if it is the one you are monitoring. The attribute value is used in an application-specific manner. The servlet context is usually used to read previously stored attributes (`getAttribute`), store new or changed attributes (`setAttribute`), and make entries in the log file (`log`).

5. **Declare the listener.** Use the `listener` and `listener-class` elements to simply list the fully qualified name of the listener class, as shown here:

```
<listener>
  <listener-class>somePackage.SomeListener</listener-class>
</listener>
```

The following section gives an example.

6.4 Example: Monitoring Changes to Commonly Used Data

Section 6.2 (Example: Initializing Commonly Used Data) shows how to read the current and former company names when the Web application is loaded and how to make use of those values in JSP pages. But what if you want to change the company name during the execution of the Web application? It is reasonable to expect a routine that makes this change to modify the `companyName` servlet context attribute. After all, in this context, that's what it means to change the company name. It is not reasonable, however, to expect that routine to modify (or even know about) the `formerCompanyName` attribute. However, if the company name changes, the former company name must change as well. Enter servlet context attribute listeners!

The following steps summarize a listener that automatically updates the former company name whenever the current company name changes.

1. **Implement the `ServletContextAttributeListener` interface.** Listing 6.5 shows a class (ChangedCompanyNameListener) that implements this interface.
2. **Implement `attributeAdded`, `attributeReplaced`, and `attributeRemoved`.** The attributeReplaced method is used to detect modification to context attributes. Empty bodies are supplied for the attributeAdded and attributeRemoved methods.
3. **Obtain references to the attribute name, attribute value, and servlet context.** The attributeReplaced method calls getName and getValue on its ServletContextAttributeEvent argument to obtain the name and value of the modified attribute. The method also calls getServletContext on its argument to get a reference to the servlet context.
4. **Use the objects.** The attribute name is compared to "companyName". If the name matches, the attribute value is used as the new value of the formerCompanyName servlet context attribute.
5. **Declare the listener.** The listener is declared in the deployment descriptor with the listener and listener-class elements, as shown here:

```
<listener>
  <listener-class>
    coreservlets.listeners.ChangedCompanyNameListener
  </listener-class>
</listener>
```

The web.xml file is shown in Listing 6.6.

Listing 6.7 presents a JSP page containing a form that displays the current company name, lets users enter a new name, and submits the new name to the Change-CompanyName servlet (Listing 6.8). Because changing the company name is a privileged operation, access to the form and the servlet should be restricted.

So, the form is placed in the admin directory and the servlet and servlet-mapping elements are used to assign the servlet a URL that also starts with /admin. See Section 2.4 (Assigning Names and Custom URLs) for details on servlet and servlet-mapping; see the deployment descriptor in Listing 6.6 for the usage in this example.

Next, the security-constraint element is used to stipulate that only authenticated users in the ceo role can access the admin directory. The ceo role is declared using the security-role element. Then, the login-config element is used to specify that form-based authentication be used, with login.jsp (Listing 6.9) collecting usernames and passwords and login-error.jsp (Listing 6.10) displaying messages to users who failed authentication. Listing 6.11 shows a Tomcat-specific password file used to designate a user who is in the ceo role. See Section 3.1

(Form-Based Authentication) for details on these types of security settings; see the deployment descriptor in Listing 6.6 for the usage in this example.

Figures 6–3 through 6–8 show the results of logging in, changing the company name, and revisiting the pages that display the current and former company names.

Listing 6.5 ChangedCompanyNameListener.java

```java
package coreservlets.listeners;

import javax.servlet.ServletContext;
import javax.servlet.ServletContextAttributeEvent;
import javax.servlet.ServletContextAttributeListener;

/** Listener that monitors changes in the company
 *  name (which is stored in the companyName attribute
 *  of the servlet context).
 */
public class ChangedCompanyNameListener
    implements ServletContextAttributeListener {

  /** When the companyName attribute changes, put
   *  the previous value into the formerCompanyName
   *  attribute.
   */
  public void attributeReplaced
                  (ServletContextAttributeEvent event) {
    if (event.getName().equals("companyName")) {
      String oldName = (String)event.getValue();
      ServletContext context = event.getServletContext();
      context.setAttribute("formerCompanyName", oldName);
    }
  }

  public void attributeAdded
                  (ServletContextAttributeEvent event) {}

  public void attributeRemoved
                  (ServletContextAttributeEvent event) {}
}
```

Listing 6.6	web.xml (Excerpt for changed company name listener)

```xml
<?xml version="1.0" encoding="ISO-8859-1"?>
<web-app xmlns="http://java.sun.com/xml/ns/j2ee"
  xmlns:xsi="http://www.w3.org/2001/XMLSchema-instance"
  xsi:schemaLocation=
  "http://java.sun.com/xml/ns/j2ee
  http://java.sun.com/xml/ns/j2ee/web-app_2_4.xsd"
  version="2.4">

  <!-- Disable the invoker servlet. -->
  <servlet>
    <servlet-name>NoInvoker</servlet-name>
    <servlet-class>coreservlets.NoInvokerServlet</servlet-class>
  </servlet>
  <servlet-mapping>
    <servlet-name>NoInvoker</servlet-name>
    <url-pattern>/servlet/*</url-pattern>
  </servlet-mapping>

  <!-- Because the company name changes so frequently,
       supply it as a servlet context parameter instead
       of embedding it into lots of different servlets and
       JSP pages. The InitialCompanyNameListener will
       read this value and store it in the servlet context. -->
  <context-param>
    <param-name>companyName</param-name>
    <param-value>not-dot-com.com</param-value>
  </context-param>

  <!-- Also store the previous company name. -->
  <context-param>
    <param-name>formerCompanyName</param-name>
    <param-value>hot-dot-com.com</param-value>
  </context-param>

  <!-- Register the listener that sets up the
       initial company name. -->
  <listener>
    <listener-class>
      coreservlets.listeners.InitialCompanyNameListener
    </listener-class>
  </listener>
  <!-- Register the listener that monitors changes to
       the company name.
  -->
```

Listing 6.6   web.xml (Excerpt for changed company name listener) *(continued)*

```
<listener>
  <listener-class>
    coreservlets.listeners.ChangedCompanyNameListener
  </listener-class>
</listener>

<!-- Assign the name ChangeCompanyName to
     coreservlets.ChangeCompanyName. -->
<servlet>
  <servlet-name>ChangeCompanyName</servlet-name>
  <servlet-class>coreservlets.ChangeCompanyName</servlet-class>
</servlet>
<!-- Assign the URL /admin/ChangeCompanyName to the
     servlet that is named ChangeCompanyName. -->
<servlet-mapping>
  <servlet-name>ChangeCompanyName</servlet-name>
  <url-pattern>/admin/ChangeCompanyName</url-pattern>
</servlet-mapping>

<!-- Protect everything within the "admin" directory.
     Direct client access to this directory requires
     authentication. -->
<security-constraint>
  <web-resource-collection>
    <web-resource-name>Admin</web-resource-name>
    <url-pattern>/admin/*</url-pattern>
  </web-resource-collection>
  <auth-constraint>
    <role-name>ceo</role-name>
  </auth-constraint>
</security-constraint>

<!-- Declare security roles. -->
<security-role>
  <role-name>ceo</role-name>
</security-role>

<!-- Tell the server to use form-based authentication. -->
<login-config>
  <auth-method>FORM</auth-method>
  <form-login-config>
    <form-login-page>/admin/login.jsp</form-login-page>
    <form-error-page>/admin/login-error.jsp</form-error-page>
  </form-login-config>
</login-config>
</web-app>
```

Listing 6.7 change-company-name.jsp

```
<!DOCTYPE HTML PUBLIC "-//W3C//DTD HTML 4.0 Transitional//EN">
<HTML>
<HEAD>
<TITLE>Changing Company Name</TITLE>
<LINK REL=STYLESHEET
      HREF="../events-styles.css"
      TYPE="text/css">
</HEAD>

<BODY>
<TABLE BORDER=5 ALIGN="CENTER">
  <TR><TH CLASS="TITLE">Changing Company Name
</TABLE>
<P>

<FORM ACTION="ChangeCompanyName">
New name:
<INPUT TYPE="TEXT" NAME="newName" VALUE="${companyName}">
<P>
<CENTER><INPUT TYPE="SUBMIT" VALUE="Submit Change"></CENTER>
</FORM>
</BODY></HTML>
```

Listing 6.8 ChangeCompanyName.java

```
package coreservlets;

import java.io.IOException;
import java.io.PrintWriter;

import javax.servlet.ServletException;
import javax.servlet.http.HttpServlet;
import javax.servlet.http.HttpServletRequest;
import javax.servlet.http.HttpServletResponse;

/** Servlet that changes the company name. The web.xml
 *  file specifies that only authenticated users in the
 *  ceo role can access the servlet. A servlet context
 *  attribute listener updates the former company name
 *  when this servlet (or any other program) changes
 *  the current company name.
 */
```

Listing 6.8   ChangeCompanyName.java *(continued)*

```java
public class ChangeCompanyName extends HttpServlet {
  public void doGet(HttpServletRequest request,
                    HttpServletResponse response)
     throws ServletException, IOException {
    boolean isNameChanged = false;
    String newName = request.getParameter("newName");
    if ((newName != null) && (!newName.equals(""))) {
      isNameChanged = true;
      getServletContext().setAttribute("companyName",
                                       newName);
    }
    response.setContentType("text/html");
    PrintWriter out = response.getWriter();
    String docType =
      "<!DOCTYPE HTML PUBLIC \"-//W3C//DTD HTML 4.0 " +
      "Transitional//EN\">\n";
    String title = "Company Name";
    out.println
      (docType +
       "<HTML>\n" +
       "<HEAD><TITLE>" + title + "</TITLE></HEAD>\n" +
       "<BODY BGCOLOR=\"#FDF5E6\">\n" +
       "<H2 ALIGN=\"CENTER\">" + title + "</H2>");
    if (isNameChanged) {
      out.println("Company name changed to " + newName + ".");
    } else {
      out.println("Company name not changed.");
    }
    out.println("</BODY></HTML>");
  }
}
```

Listing 6.9 login.jsp

```
<!DOCTYPE HTML PUBLIC "-//W3C//DTD HTML 4.0 Transitional//EN">
<HTML>
<HEAD>
<TITLE>Log In</TITLE>
<LINK REL=STYLESHEET
      HREF="../events-styles.css"
      TYPE="text/css">
</HEAD>

<BODY>
<TABLE BORDER=5 ALIGN="CENTER">
  <TR><TH CLASS="TITLE">Log In</TABLE>
<P>
<H3>Sorry, you must log in before accessing this resource.</H3>
<FORM ACTION="j_security_check" METHOD="POST">
<TABLE>
<TR><TD>User name: <INPUT TYPE="TEXT" NAME="j_username">
<TR><TD>Password: <INPUT TYPE="PASSWORD" NAME="j_password">
<TR><TH><INPUT TYPE="SUBMIT" VALUE="Log In">
</TABLE>
</FORM>

</BODY>
</HTML>
```

Listing 6.10 login-error.jsp

```
<!DOCTYPE HTML PUBLIC "-//W3C//DTD HTML 4.0 Transitional//EN">
<HTML>
<HEAD>
<TITLE>Begone!</TITLE>
<LINK REL=STYLESHEET
      HREF="../events-styles.css"
      TYPE="text/css">
</HEAD>

<BODY>
<TABLE BORDER=5 ALIGN="CENTER">
  <TR><TH CLASS="TITLE">Begone!</TABLE>

<H3>Begone, ye unauthorized peon.</H3>

</BODY>
</HTML>
```

Listing 6.11   tomcat-users.xml (Excerpt for events examples)

```xml
<?xml version='1.0' encoding='utf-8'?>
<tomcat-users>
  <!-- ... -->
  <role rolename="ceo"/>
  <user username="kennethLay" password="enron" roles="ceo"/>
</tomcat-users>
```

Figure 6–3   Only users who are in the ceo role can access the form that changes the company name.

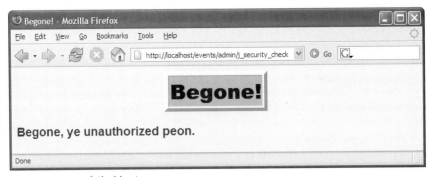

Figure 6–4   A failed login attempt.

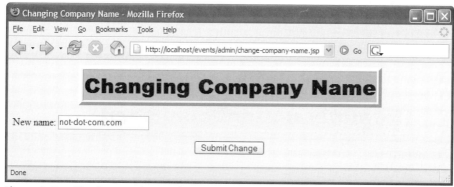

Figure 6–5   The form to change the company name when the page is accessed by an authenticated user who is in the ceo role.

Figure 6–6   The name change confirmation page.

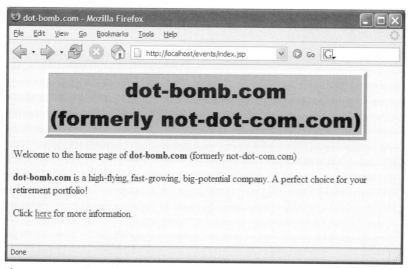

Figure 6–7   When the company name changes, the company home page (Listing 6.3) is automatically updated.

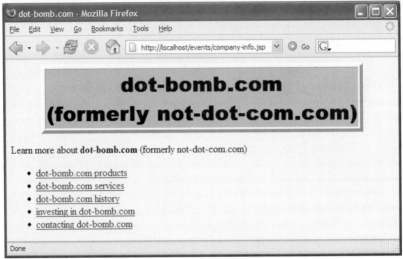

Figure 6–8   When the company name changes, the company information page (Listing 6.4) is also updated automatically.

6.5   Packaging Listeners with Tag Libraries

JSP tag libraries, discussed in Chapter 7 (Tag Libraries: The Basics), provide a great way of encapsulating content that will be accessed by multiple JSP pages. But what if that content depends on life-cycle event listeners? If the listener and listener-class elements of web.xml were the only option for declaring listeners, tag library maintenance would be much more difficult. Normally, the user of a tag library can deploy it by simply dropping a JAR file in WEB-INF/lib and putting a TLD file in WEB-INF. Users of the tag libraries need no knowledge of the individual classes within the library, only of the tags that the library defines. However, if the tag libraries used listeners, users of the libraries would need to discover the name of the listener classes and make web.xml entries for each one. This would be significantly more work.

Fortunately, the JSP specification version 1.2 and above lets you put the listener declarations in the TLD file instead of in the deployment descriptor. But, wait! Event listeners need to run when the Web application is first loaded, not just the first time a JSP page that uses a custom library is accessed. How does the system handle this? When the Web application is loaded, the system automatically searches WEB-INF and its subdirectories for files with .tld extensions and uses all

listener declarations that it finds. Because starting with version 1.2 of the JSP specification it is required that you place all your TLD files inside WEB-INF, all listeners
declared in TLD files will be found.

Version 2.0 of the JSP specification switched to using XML Schema instead of
Document Type Definition (DTD) for validation of TLD files. Besides replacing
the DOCTYPE with the new XML Schema-compliant declaration, the order of some
of the elements has changed as well. Listing 6.12 shows a template for a TLD file
in JSP 2.0.

Listing 6.12 JSP 2.0 Tag Library Descriptor (Template)

```xml
<?xml version="1.0" encoding="UTF-8" ?>
<taglib xmlns="http://java.sun.com/xml/ns/j2ee"
  xmlns:xsi="http://www.w3.org/2001/XMLSchema-instance"
  xsi:schemaLocation="http://java.sun.com/xml/ns/j2ee
  http://java.sun.com/xml/ns/j2ee/web-jsptaglibrary_2_0.xsd"
  version="2.0">

  <description>
    Tag library documentation.
  </description>
  <tlib-version>1.0</tlib-version>
  <short-name>some name</short-name>
  <uri>some uri</uri>

  <listener>
    <listener-class>somePackage.someListener</listener-class>
  </listener>

  <tag>
    <description>Tag documentation</description>
    <name>agName</name>
    <tag-class>somePackage.someTagHandler</tag-class>
    <body-content>...</body-content>
  </tag>
</taglib>
```

6.6 Example: Packaging the Company Name Listeners

Listings 6.13 and 6.14 show custom tags that print out the current and former company names, respectively. The first tag simply prints the current company name. The second tag uses a fullDescription attribute to decide whether to simply print the former company name (e.g., some-company.com) or the company name inside parentheses (e.g., (formerly some-company.com)). Listing 6.15 shows the TLD file for this library: The listener elements of Sections 6.2 and 6.4 are moved out of the web.xml file and into the TLD file, which is then placed in the WEB-INF directory.

Listings 6.16 and 6.17 show the company home page (see Listing 6.3) and company information page (see Listing 6.4) reworked with the new custom tags. The augmented InitialCompanyNameListener is shown in Listing 6.18. Figures 6–9 and 6–10 show the results—identical to those shown earlier in Figures 6–1 and 6–2.

Listing 6.13 CompanyNameTag.java

```
package coreservlets.tags;
import java.io.*;
import javax.servlet.*;
import javax.servlet.jsp.*;
import javax.servlet.jsp.tagext.*;
import coreservlets.listeners.*;

/**
 * The InitialCompanyNameListener class has static methods that
 * permit access to the current and former company names. But,
using
 * these methods in JSP requires explicit Java code, and creating
 * beans that provided the information would have yielded a
 * cumbersome result. So, we simply move the code into a custom
tag.
 */
public class CompanyNameTag extends SimpleTagSupport {
  public void doTag() throws JspException, IOException {
    PageContext pageContext = (PageContext) getJspContext();
    ServletContext context = pageContext.getServletContext();
    String companyName =
      InitialCompanyNameListener.getCompanyName(context);
    JspWriter out = pageContext.getOut();
    out.print(companyName);
  }
}
```

Listing 6.14   FormerCompanyNameTag.java

```java
package coreservlets.tags;
import java.io.*;
import javax.servlet.*;
import javax.servlet.jsp.*;
import javax.servlet.jsp.tagext.*;
import coreservlets.listeners.*;

/** The InitialCompanyNameListener class has static
 *  methods that permit access to the current and former
 *  company names. But, using these methods in JSP requires
 *  explicit Java code, and creating beans that provided
 *  the information would have yielded a cumbersome result.
 *  So, we simply move the code into a custom tag.
 */

public class FormerCompanyNameTag extends SimpleTagSupport {
  private boolean useFullDescription = false;
  public void doTag() throws JspException, IOException {
    PageContext pageContext = (PageContext) getJspContext();
    ServletContext context = pageContext.getServletContext();
    String formerCompanyName =
     InitialCompanyNameListener.getFormerCompanyName(context);
    JspWriter out = pageContext.getOut();
    if (useFullDescription) {
      String formerCompanyDescription = "";
      if (!formerCompanyName.equals("")) {
        formerCompanyDescription =
          "(formerly " + formerCompanyName + ")";
      }
      out.print(formerCompanyDescription);
    } else {
      out.print(formerCompanyName);
    }
  }

  /** If the user supplies a fullDescription attribute
   *  with the value "true" (upper, lower, or mixed case),
   *  set the useFullDescription instance variable to true.
   *  Otherwise, leave it false.
   */
  public void setFullDescription(String flag) {
    if (flag.equalsIgnoreCase("true")) {
      useFullDescription = true;
    }
  }
}
```

Listing 6.15   company-name-taglib.tld

```xml
<?xml version="1.0" encoding="UTF-8" ?>
<taglib xmlns="http://java.sun.com/xml/ns/j2ee"
  xmlns:xsi="http://www.w3.org/2001/XMLSchema-instance"
  xsi:schemaLocation="http://java.sun.com/xml/ns/j2ee
  http://java.sun.com/xml/ns/j2ee/web-jsptaglibrary_2_0.xsd"
  version="2.0">
<description>
   A tag library to print out the ever-changing current
   and former company names (which are monitored by event
   listeners). From Core Servlets and JavaServer Pages Volume 2,
   http://volume2.coreservlets.com/.
</description>
<tlib-version>1.0</tlib-version>
<short-name>company-name-tags</short-name>
<uri>http://coreservlets.com/listeners</uri>
<!-- Register the listener that sets up the
     initial company name. -->
<listener>
  <listener-class>
    coreservlets.listeners.InitialCompanyNameListener
  </listener-class>
</listener>
<!-- Register the listener that monitors changes to
     the company name.
-->
<listener>
  <listener-class>
    coreservlets.listeners.ChangedCompanyNameListener
  </listener-class>
</listener>
<!-- Define a tag that prints out the current name. -->
<tag>
  <description>The current company name</description>
  <name>companyName</name>
  <tag-class>coreservlets.tags.CompanyNameTag</tag-class>
  <body-content>empty</body-content>
</tag>
<!-- Define a tag that prints out the previous name. -->
<tag>
  <description>The previous company name</description>
  <name>formerCompanyName</name>
  <tag-class>coreservlets.tags.FormerCompanyNameTag</tag-class>
  <body-content>empty</body-content>
  <attribute>
    <name>fullDescription</name>
    <required>false</required>
  </attribute>
</tag>
</taglib>
```

Listing 6.16 index2.jsp

```
<!DOCTYPE HTML PUBLIC "-//W3C//DTD HTML 4.0 Transitional//EN">
<HTML>
<HEAD>
<%@ taglib uri="http://coreservlets.com/listeners" prefix="csajsp"
%>
<TITLE><csajsp:companyName/></TITLE>
<LINK REL=STYLESHEET
      HREF="events-styles.css"
      TYPE="text/css">
</HEAD>
<BODY>
<TABLE BORDER=5 ALIGN="CENTER">
  <TR><TH CLASS="TITLE">
      <csajsp:companyName/><BR>
      <csajsp:formerCompanyName fullDescription="true"/>
</TABLE>
<P>
Welcome to the home page of <B><csajsp:companyName/></B>
<csajsp:formerCompanyName fullDescription="true"/>
<P>
<B><csajsp:companyName/></B> is a high-flying, fast-growing,
big-potential company. A perfect choice for your
retirement portfolio!
<P>
Click <A HREF="company-info2.jsp">here</A> for more information.
</BODY></HTML>
```

Listing 6.17 company-info2.jsp

```
<!DOCTYPE HTML PUBLIC "-//W3C//DTD HTML 4.0 Transitional//EN">
<HTML>
<HEAD>
<%@ taglib uri="http://coreservlets.com/listeners"
        prefix="csajsp" %>
<TITLE><csajsp:companyName/></TITLE>
<LINK REL=STYLESHEET
      HREF="events-styles.css"
      TYPE="text/css">
</HEAD>
<BODY>
<TABLE BORDER=5 ALIGN="CENTER">
  <TR><TH CLASS="TITLE">
      <csajsp:companyName/><BR>
      <csajsp:formerCompanyName fullDescription="true"/>
```

Listing 6.17   company-info2.jsp *(continued)*

```
</TABLE>
<P>
Learn more about <B><csajsp:companyName/></B>
<csajsp:formerCompanyName fullDescription="true"/>
<UL>
  <LI><A HREF="products.jsp"><csajsp:companyName/> products</A>
  <LI><A HREF="services.jsp"><csajsp:companyName/> services</A>
  <LI><A HREF="history.jsp"><csajsp:companyName/> history</A>
  <LI><A HREF="invest.jsp">investing in <csajsp:companyName/></A>
  <LI><A HREF="contact.jsp">contacting <csajsp:companyName/></A>
</UL>
</BODY></HTML>
```

Listing 6.18   InitialCompanyNameListener.java

```
package coreservlets.listeners;
import javax.servlet.*;

/** Listener that looks up the name of the company when
 *  the Web application is first loaded. Stores this
 *  name in the companyName servlet context attribute.
 *  Various servlets and JSP pages will extract it
 *  from that location.
 *  <P>
 *  Also looks up and stores the former company name and
 *  stores it in the formerCompanyName attribute.
 */

public class InitialCompanyNameListener
    implements ServletContextListener {
  private static final String DEFAULT_NAME =
    "MISSING-COMPANY-NAME";

  /** Looks up the companyName and formerCompanyName
   *  init parameters and puts them into the servlet context.
   */
  public void contextInitialized(ServletContextEvent event) {
    ServletContext context = event.getServletContext();
    setInitialAttribute(context,
                        "companyName",
                        DEFAULT_NAME);
    setInitialAttribute(context,
                        "formerCompanyName",
                        "");
  }
```

Listing 6.18 InitialCompanyNameListener.java *(continued)*

```java
public void contextDestroyed(ServletContextEvent event) {}
  /** Looks for a servlet context init parameter with a
   *  given name. If it finds it, it puts the value into
   *  a servlet context attribute with the same name. If
   *  the init parameter is missing, it puts a default
   *  value into the servlet context attribute.
   */
private void setInitialAttribute(ServletContext context,
                                 String initParamName,
                                 String defaultValue) {
    String initialValue =
      context.getInitParameter(initParamName);
    if (initialValue != null) {
      context.setAttribute(initParamName, initialValue);
    } else {
      context.setAttribute(initParamName, defaultValue);
    }
  }


  /** Static method that returns the servlet context
   *  attribute named "companyName" if it is available.
   *  Returns a default value if the attribute is
   *  unavailable.
   */
public static String getCompanyName(ServletContext context) {
    String name =
      (String)context.getAttribute("companyName");
    if (name == null) {
      name = DEFAULT_NAME;
    }
    return(name);
  }


  /** Static method that returns the servlet context
   *  attribute named "formerCompanyName" if it is available.
   *  Returns an empty string if the attribute is
   *  unavailable.
   */
public static String getFormerCompanyName
                             (ServletContext context) {
    String name =
      (String)context.getAttribute("formerCompanyName");
    if (name == null) {
      name = "";
    }
    return(name);
  }
}
```

Figure 6–9   Reworking the company home page to use custom tags results in an identical appearance (compare Figure 6–1).

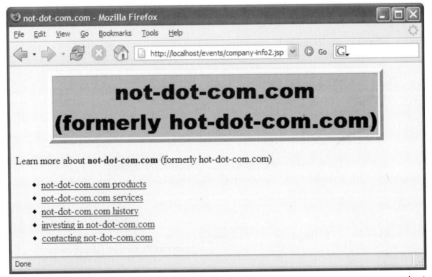

Figure 6–10   Reworking the company information page to use custom tags results in an identical appearance (compare Figure 6–2).

6.7 Recognizing Session Creation and Destruction

Classes that implement the `ServletContextListener` and `ServletContext-AttributeListener` interfaces respond to creation, destruction, and changes in the servlet context, which is shared by all servlets and JSP pages in the Web application. But, with session tracking (Chapter 9 of Volume 1), data is stored in per-user `HttpSession` objects, not in the servlet context. What if you want to monitor changes to this user-specific data? That's the job of the `HttpSessionListener` and `HttpSessionAttributeListener` interfaces. This section discusses `HttpSessionListener`, the listener that is notified when a session is created or destroyed (either deliberately with `invalidate` or by timing out). Section 6.9 (Watching for Changes in Session Attributes) discusses `HttpSessionAttributeListener`, the listener that is notified when session attributes are added, replaced, or removed.

Using `HttpSessionListener` involves the following steps.

1. **Implement the `HttpSessionListener` interface.** This interface is in the `javax.servlet.http` package.

2. **Implement `sessionCreated` and `sessionDestroyed`.** The first of these (`sessionCreated`) is triggered when a new session is created. The second method (`sessionDestroyed`) is triggered when a session is destroyed. This destruction could be due to an explicit call to the `invalidate` method or because the elapsed time since the last client access exceeds the session timeout.

3. **Obtain a reference to the session and possibly to the servlet context.** Each of the two `HttpSessionListener` methods takes an `HttpSessionEvent` as an argument. The `HttpSessionEvent` class has a `getSession` method that provides access to the session object. You almost always want this reference; you occasionally also want a reference to the servlet context. If so, first obtain the session object and then call `getServletContext` on it.

4. **Use the objects.** Surprisingly, one of the only methods you usually call on the session object is the `setAttribute` method. You do this in `sessionCreated` if you want to guarantee that all sessions have a certain attribute. Wait! What about `getAttribute`? You don't use it. In `sessionCreated`, there is nothing in the session yet, so `getAttribute` is pointless. In addition, all attributes are removed before `sessionDestroyed` is called, so calling `getAttribute` is also pointless there. If you want to clean up attributes that are left in sessions that time out, you use the `attributeRemoved` method of

`HttpSessionAttributeListener` (Section 6.9). Consequently, `sessionDestroyed` is mostly reserved for listeners that are simply keeping track of the number of sessions in use.

5. **Declare the listener.** In the web.xml or TLD file, use the `listener` and `listener-class` elements to simply list the fully qualified name of the listener class, as shown here:

```
<listener>
  <listener-class>somePackage.SomeListener</listener-class>
</listener>
```

6.8   Example: A Listener That Counts Sessions

Session tracking can significantly increase the server's memory load. For example, if a site that uses session tracking has 1,000 unique visitors per hour and the server uses a two-hour session timeout, the system will have approximately 2,000 sessions in memory at any one time. Reducing the timeout to one hour would cut the session memory requirements in half but would risk having active sessions prematurely time out. You need to track typical usage before you can decide on the appropriate solution.

So, you need a listener that will keep track of how many sessions are created, how many are destroyed, and how many are in memory at any one time. Assuming that you have no explicit calls to `invalidate`, the session destructions correspond to expired timeouts.

The following steps summarize a listener that accomplishes this task.

1. **Implement the `HttpSessionListener` interface.** Listing 6.19 shows a class (`SessionCounter`) that implements this interface.
2. **Implement `sessionCreated` and `sessionDestroyed`.** The first of these (`sessionCreated`) increments two counters: `total-SessionCount` and `currentSessionCount`. If the current count is greater than the previous maximum count, the method also increments the `maxSessionCount` variable. The second method (`session-Destroyed`) decrements the `currentSessionCount` variable.
3. **Obtain and use the servlet context.** In this application, no specific use is made of the session object. The only thing that matters is the fact that a session was created or destroyed, not any details about the session itself. However, the session counts have to be placed in a location that is easily accessible to servlets and JSP pages that will display

the counts. So, the first time `sessionCreated` is called, it obtains the session object, calls `getServletContext` on it, and then calls `setAttribute` to store the listener object in the servlet context.

4. **Declare the listener.** Listing 6.20 shows the web.xml file. It declares the listener with the `listener` and `listener-class` elements, as follows:

```
<listener>
  <listener-class>
    coreservlets.listeners.SessionCounter
  </listener-class>
</listener>
```

Listing 6.21 shows a JSP page that displays the session counts. Figure 6–11 shows a typical result.

To test session creation and timeout, we made three temporary changes.

First, we disabled cookies in the browser. Because the servers can either use cookies, which we disabled, or URL rewriting for session tracking, and we did not dynamically rewrite the source URL for each frame, this had the result of making each request be a new session. See the following subsection for information on disabling cookies in Firefox and Internet Explorer.

Second, we created an HTML page (Listing 6.22, Figure 6–12) that used frames with four rows and four columns to request the same JSP page (Listing 6.23) 16 times. This JSP page uses the `colorUtil.randomColor` method (Listing 6.24) to choose a random color as a background color for the page. In an environment that has cookies disabled, a request for the framed page results in 16 new sessions being created on the server (recall that JSP pages perform session tracking automatically unless the `session` attribute of the `page` directive is set to `false`—see Section 12.4 of Volume 1).

Third, we chose an extremely low session timeout: two minutes. This saved us from waiting for hours to test the session-counting listener. Changing the default session timeout is discussed in Section 2.11 (Controlling Session Timeouts), but it simply amounts to creating a `session-config` entry in web.xml, as follows:

```
<session-config>
  <session-timeout>2</session-timeout>
</session-config>
```

Listing 6.19	SessionCounter.java

```java
package coreservlets.listeners;

import javax.servlet.*;
import javax.servlet.http.*;

/** Listener that keeps track of the number of sessions
 *  that the Web application is currently using and has
 *  ever used in its life cycle.
 */
public class SessionCounter implements HttpSessionListener {
  private int totalSessionCount = 0;
  private int currentSessionCount = 0;
  private int maxSessionCount = 0;
  private ServletContext context = null;

  public void sessionCreated(HttpSessionEvent event) {
    totalSessionCount++;
    currentSessionCount++;
    if (currentSessionCount > maxSessionCount) {
      maxSessionCount = currentSessionCount;
    }
    if (context == null) {
      storeInServletContext(event);
    }
  }

  public void sessionDestroyed(HttpSessionEvent event) {
    currentSessionCount--;
  }

  /** The total number of sessions created. */
  public int getTotalSessionCount() {
    return(totalSessionCount);
  }

  /** The number of sessions currently in memory. */
  public int getCurrentSessionCount() {
    return(currentSessionCount);
  }

  /** The largest number of sessions ever in memory
   *  at any one time.
   */
```

Listing 6.19   SessionCounter.java *(continued)*

```java
  public int getMaxSessionCount() {
    return(maxSessionCount);
  }

 /** Register self in the servlet context so that
  *  servlets and JSP pages can access the session counts.
  */
  private void storeInServletContext(HttpSessionEvent event) {
    HttpSession session = event.getSession();
    context = session.getServletContext();
    context.setAttribute("sessionCounter", this);
  }
}
```

Listing 6.20   web.xml (Excerpt for session counting listener)

```xml
<?xml version="1.0" encoding="ISO-8859-1"?>
<web-app xmlns="http://java.sun.com/xml/ns/j2ee"
  xmlns:xsi="http://www.w3.org/2001/XMLSchema-instance"
  xsi:schemaLocation=
  "http://java.sun.com/xml/ns/j2ee
  http://java.sun.com/xml/ns/j2ee/web-app_2_4.xsd"
  version="2.4">
  <!-- Register the session counting event listener. -->
  <listener>
    <listener-class>
      coreservlets.listeners.SessionCounter
    </listener-class>
  </listener>
  <!-- Set the default session timeout to two minutes. -->
  <session-config>
    <session-timeout>2</session-timeout>
  </session-config>
</web-app>
```

Listing 6.21   session-counts.jsp

```
<!DOCTYPE HTML PUBLIC "-//W3C//DTD HTML 4.0 Transitional//EN">
<HTML>
<HEAD>
<TITLE>Session Info</TITLE>
<LINK REL=STYLESHEET
      HREF="events-styles.css"
      TYPE="text/css">
</HEAD>
<BODY>
<TABLE BORDER=5 ALIGN="CENTER">
  <TR><TH CLASS="TITLE">Session Info</TABLE>
<P>
<UL>
<LI>Total number of sessions in the life of this
    Web application: ${sessionCounter.totalSessionCount}.
<LI>Number of sessions currently in memory:
      ${sessionCounter.currentSessionCount}.
<LI>Maximum number of sessions that have ever been in
    memory at any one time: ${sessionCounter.maxSessionCount}.
</UL>
</BODY></HTML>
```

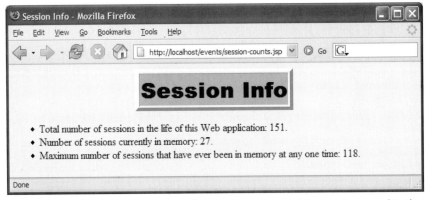

Figure 6–11   The SessionCounter listener keeps track of the sessions used in the Web application.

Listing 6.22 make-sessions.html

```html
<!DOCTYPE HTML PUBLIC "-//W3C//DTD HTML 4.0 Frameset//EN">
<HTML>
<HEAD>
  <TITLE>Session Testing...</TITLE>
</HEAD>
<FRAMESET ROWS="*,*,*,*" COLS="*,*,*,*">
  <FRAME SRC="test.jsp">
  <FRAME SRC="test.jsp">
  <FRAME SRC="test.jsp">
  <FRAME SRC="test.jsp">
  <FRAME SRC="test.jsp">
  <FRAME SRC="test.jsp">
  <FRAME SRC="test.jsp">
  <FRAME SRC="test.jsp">
  <FRAME SRC="test.jsp">
  <FRAME SRC="test.jsp">
  <FRAME SRC="test.jsp">
  <FRAME SRC="test.jsp">
  <FRAME SRC="test.jsp">
  <FRAME SRC="test.jsp">
  <FRAME SRC="test.jsp">
  <FRAME SRC="test.jsp">
  <NOFRAMES><BODY>
    This example requires a frame-capable browser.
  </BODY></NOFRAMES>
</FRAMESET>
</HTML>
```

Listing 6.23 test.jsp

```jsp
<!DOCTYPE HTML PUBLIC "-//W3C//DTD HTML 4.0 Transitional//EN">
<!-- The purpose of this page is to force the system
     to create a session. -->
<HTML>
<HEAD><TITLE>Test</TITLE></HEAD>
<%@ page import="coreservlets.*" %>
<BODY BGCOLOR="<%= ColorUtils.randomColor() %>">
</BODY></HTML>
```

Listing 6.24 ColorUtils.java

```java
package coreservlets;

/** Small utility to generate random HTML color names. */
public class ColorUtils {
  /** The official HTML color names. */
  private static String[] htmlColorNames =
    { "AQUA", "BLACK", "BLUE", "FUCHSIA", "GRAY", "GREEN",
      "LIME", "MAROON", "NAVY", "OLIVE", "PURPLE", "RED",
      "SILVER", "TEAL", "WHITE", "YELLOW" };

  public static String randomColor() {
    int index = randomInt(htmlColorNames.length);
    return(htmlColorNames[index]);
  }

  /** Returns a random number from 0 to n-1 inclusive. */
  private static int randomInt(int n) {
    return((int)(Math.random() * n));
  }
}
```

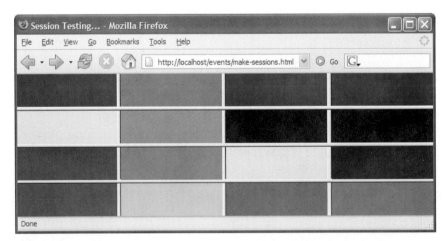

Figure 6–12 Session management was tested with a frame-based page that was invoked after cookies were disabled, so each request resulted in 16 different sessions.

Disabling Cookies

Figures 6–13 through 6–14 summarize the approach to disabling cookies in Firefox 1.5, and Internet Explorer 6.0. As discussed in the previous subsection, temporarily disabling cookies is useful for testing session usage.

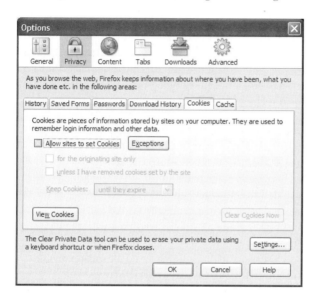

Figure 6–13   To disable cookies in Firefox 1.5, choose the Tools menu, then Options, then Privacy, then the Cookies tab. Make sure the "Allow sites to set Cookies" checkbox is not checked. Reset the browser after you are done testing; our preferred setting is to also check "for the originating site only."

Figure 6–14   To disable cookies in Internet Explorer 6.0, choose the Tools menu, then Internet Options, then Privacy, then move the slider all the way up to the "Block All Cookies" setting. Be aware that some versions of Internet Explorer ignore custom cookie settings when the host is localhost, so you should use the loopback IP address 127.0.01 instead.

6.9 Watching for Changes in Session Attributes

So `HttpSessionListener` lets you detect when a session is created or destroyed. But, because session attributes can't be placed into the session before its creation and are removed before its destruction, this listener does not provide appropriate hooks to monitor the life of the session attributes. That's the job of the `HttpSession-AttributeListener` interface. It gets notified when an object is placed into the session scope for the first time, replaced by another object, or removed from the session scope altogether. Use of this interface involves the following steps.

1. **Implement the `HttpSessionAttributeListener` interface.** This interface is in the `javax.servlet.http` package.

2. **Implement `attributeAdded`, `attributeReplaced`, and `attributeRemoved`.** The `attributeAdded` method is triggered when a new attribute is added to a session. When a new value is assigned to an existing session attribute, `attributeAdded` is triggered with the new value and `attributeReplaced` is triggered with the old value (i.e., the value being replaced). The `attributeRemoved` method is triggered when a session attribute is removed altogether.

3. **Obtain references to the attribute name, attribute value, session, and servlet context.** Each of the three `HttpSession-AttributeListener` methods takes an `HttpSessionBinding-Event` as an argument. The `HttpSessionBindingEvent` class has three useful methods: `getName` (the name of the attribute that was changed), `getValue` (the value of the changed attribute—the new value for `attributeAdded` and the previous value for `attribute-Replaced` and `attributeRemoved`), and `getSession` (the `HttpSession` object). If you also want access to the servlet context, first obtain the session and then call `getServletContext` on it.

4. **Use the objects.** The attribute name is usually compared to a stored name to see if it is the one you are monitoring. The attribute value is used in an application-specific manner. The session is usually used to read previously stored attributes (`getAttribute`) or to store new or changed attributes (`setAttribute`).

5. **Declare the listener.** In the web.xml or TLD file, use the `listener` and `listener-class` elements to simply list the fully qualified name of the listener class, as shown here:

```
<listener>
  <listener-class>somePackage.SomeListener</listener-class>
</listener>
```

6.10 Example: Monitoring Yacht Orders

Suppose you want to track buying patterns for a specific item (a yacht, in this case). Of course, you could try to find all servlets and JSP pages that process orders and change each one to record yacht purchases. That's an awful lot of work for what sounds like a simple request, though, and pretty hard to maintain, anyhow.

A much better option is to create a session attribute listener that monitors the attributes corresponding to order reservations or purchases and that records the information in the log file for later perusal by the sales manager.

The following steps summarize a listener that accomplishes this task.

1.   **Implement the `HttpSessionAttributeListener` interface.** Listing 6.25 shows a class (`YachtWatcher`) that implements this interface.

2.   **Implement `attributeAdded`, `attributeReplaced`, and `attributeRemoved`.** The first of these (`attributeAdded`) is used to log the fact that a yacht was reserved (tentative) or purchased (permanent). The other two methods are used to print retractions of order reservations (but not purchases—all sales are final).

3.   **Obtain references to the attribute name, attribute value, session, and servlet context.** Each of the three methods calls `getName` and `getValue` on its `HttpSessionBindingEvent` argument to obtain the name and value of the modified attribute. The methods also call `getServletContext` on the session object (obtained with `getSession`) to get a reference to the servlet context.

4.   **Use the objects.** The attribute name is compared to `"orderedItem"` (attribute addition, replacement, and removal) and `"purchasedItem"` (attribute addition only). If the name matches, then the attribute value is compared to `"yacht"`. If that comparison also succeeds, then the `log` method of the servlet context is called.

5.   **Declare the listener.** Listing 6.26 shows the web.xml file. It declares the listener with the `listener` and `listener-class` elements, as shown here:

```
<listener>
  <listener-class>
    coreservlets.listeners.YachtWatcher
  </listener-class>
</listener>
```

Listings 6.27 and 6.28 show a servlet that handles orders and an HTML form that sends it data, respectively. Figures 6–15 through 6–18 show the results. Listing 6.29 shows a portion of the resultant log file.

Listing 6.25   YachtWatcher.java

```java
package coreservlets.listeners;

import javax.servlet.*;
import javax.servlet.http.*;

/** Listener that keeps track of yacht purchases
 *  by monitoring the orderedItem and purchasedItem
 *  session attributes.
 */
public class YachtWatcher
    implements HttpSessionAttributeListener {
  private String orderAttributeName = "orderedItem";
  private String purchaseAttributeName = "purchasedItem";
  private String itemName = "yacht";

  /** Checks for initial ordering and final purchase of
   *  yacht. Records "Customer ordered a yacht" if the
   *  orderedItem attribute matches "yacht".
   *  Records "Customer finalized purchase of a yacht" if the
   *  purchasedItem attribute matches "yacht".
   */
  public void attributeAdded(HttpSessionBindingEvent event) {
    checkAttribute(event, orderAttributeName, itemName,
                   " ordered a ");
    checkAttribute(event, purchaseAttributeName, itemName,
                   " finalized purchase of a ");
  }

  /** Checks for order cancellation: was an order for "yacht"
   *  cancelled?  Records "Customer cancelled an order for
   *  a yacht" if the orderedItem attribute matches "yacht".
   */
  public void attributeRemoved(HttpSessionBindingEvent event) {
    checkAttribute(event, orderAttributeName, itemName,
                   " cancelled an order for a ");
  }

  /** Checks for item replacement: was "yacht" replaced
   *  by some other item? Records "Customer changed to a new
   *  item instead of a yacht" if the orderedItem attribute
   *  matches "yacht".
   */
  public void attributeReplaced(HttpSessionBindingEvent event) {
    checkAttribute(event, orderAttributeName, itemName,
                   " changed to a new item instead of a ");
  }
```

Listing 6.25 YachtWatcher.java *(continued)*

```java
private void checkAttribute(HttpSessionBindingEvent event,
                           String orderAttributeName,
                           String keyItemName,
                           String message) {
    String currentAttributeName = event.getName();
    String currentItemName = (String)event.getValue();
    if (currentAttributeName.equals(orderAttributeName) &&
        currentItemName.equals(keyItemName)) {
      ServletContext context =
        event.getSession().getServletContext();
      context.log("Customer" + message + keyItemName + ".");
    }
  }
}
```

Listing 6.26 web.xml (Excerpt for yacht-watching listener)

```xml
<?xml version="1.0" encoding="ISO-8859-1"?>
<web-app xmlns="http://java.sun.com/xml/ns/j2ee"
  xmlns:xsi="http://www.w3.org/2001/XMLSchema-instance"
  xsi:schemaLocation=
  "http://java.sun.com/xml/ns/j2ee
  http://java.sun.com/xml/ns/j2ee/web-app_2_4.xsd"
  version="2.4">
  <!-- Register the yacht-watching event listener. -->
  <listener>
    <listener-class>
      coreservlets.listeners.YachtWatcher
    </listener-class>
  </listener>
  <!-- Assign the name OrderHandlingServlet to
    coreservlets.OrderHandlingServlet. -->
  <servlet>
    <servlet-name>OrderHandlingServlet</servlet-name>
    <servlet-class>
      coreservlets.OrderHandlingServlet
    </servlet-class>
  </servlet>
  <!-- Assign the URL /HandleOrders to the
    servlet that is named OrderHandlingServlet. -->
  <servlet-mapping>
    <servlet-name>OrderHandlingServlet</servlet-name>
    <url-pattern>/HandleOrders</url-pattern>
  </servlet-mapping>
</web-app>
```

```
package coreservlets;
import java.io.*;
import javax.servlet.*;
import javax.servlet.http.*;

/** Servlet that handles submissions from the order form.
 *  If the user selects the "Reserve Order" button, the
 *  selected item is put into the orderedItem attribute.
 *  If the user selects the "Cancel Order" button, the
 *  orderedItem attribute is deleted.
 *  If the user selects the "Purchase Item" button, the
 *  selected item is put into the purchasedItem attribute.
 */
public class OrderHandlingServlet extends HttpServlet {
  private String title, picture;

  public void doGet(HttpServletRequest request,
                    HttpServletResponse response)
      throws ServletException, IOException {
    HttpSession session = request.getSession(true);
    String itemName = request.getParameter("itemName");
    if ((itemName == null) || (itemName.equals(""))) {
      itemName = "<B>MISSING ITEM</B>";
    }
    String message;
    if (request.getParameter("order") != null) {
      session.setAttribute("orderedItem", itemName);
      message = "Thanks for ordering " + itemName + ".";
    } else if (request.getParameter("cancel") != null) {
      session.removeAttribute("orderedItem");
      message = "Thanks for nothing.";
    } else {
      session.setAttribute("purchasedItem", itemName);
      message = "Thanks for purchasing " + itemName + ".";
    }
    response.setContentType("text/html");
    PrintWriter out = response.getWriter();
    String docType =
      "<!DOCTYPE HTML PUBLIC \"-//W3C//DTD HTML 4.0 " +
      "Transitional//EN\">\n";
    out.println
      (docType +
       "<HTML>\n" +
       "<HEAD><TITLE>" + message + "</TITLE></HEAD>\n" +
       "<BODY BGCOLOR=\"#FDF5E6\">\n" + "<H2 ALIGN=\"CENTER\">" +
       message + "</H2>\n" + "</BODY></HTML>");
  }
}
```

Listing 6.28   orders.html

```
<!DOCTYPE HTML PUBLIC "-//W3C//DTD HTML 4.0 Transitional//EN">
<HTML>
<HEAD>
<TITLE>Orders</TITLE>
<LINK REL=STYLESHEET
      HREF="events-styles.css"
      TYPE="text/css">
</HEAD>
<BODY>
<TABLE BORDER=5 ALIGN="CENTER">
  <TR><TH CLASS="TITLE">Orders
</TABLE>
<P>
Choose a valuable item below.
<P>
Select "Reserve Order" to hold the order for 30 days. Due to
unprecedented demand, you can only reserve a single item:
selecting another item will replace the previous choice.
<P>
Select "Purchase Item" to finalize your purchase. After
finalizing a purchase, you can reserve a new item.
<FORM ACTION="HandleOrders">
<DL>
  <DT><B>Item:</B>
  <DD><INPUT TYPE="RADIO" NAME="itemName" VALUE="yacht">Yacht
  <DD><INPUT TYPE="RADIO" NAME="itemName" VALUE="chalet">Chalet
  <DD><INPUT TYPE="RADIO" NAME="itemName" VALUE="car">Lamborghini
  <DD><INPUT TYPE="RADIO" NAME="itemName" VALUE="csajspVolI"
CHECKED>
      <I>Core Servlets and JavaServer Pages Volume I</I>
  <DD><INPUT TYPE="RADIO" NAME="itemName" VALUE="csajspVolII">
      <I>Core Servlets and JavaServer Pages Volume II</I>
</DL>
<CENTER>
<INPUT TYPE="SUBMIT" NAME="order" VALUE="Reserve Order">
<INPUT TYPE="SUBMIT" NAME="cancel" VALUE="Cancel Order">
<INPUT TYPE="SUBMIT" NAME="purchase" VALUE="Purchase Item">
</CENTER>
</FORM>
</BODY></HTML>
```

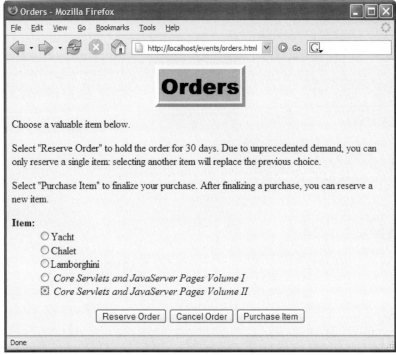

Figure 6–15 The order form that sends data to the order handling servlet (Listing 6.27). That servlet adds, replaces, and removes values in the `orderedItem` and `purchasedItem` session attributes, which in turn triggers the yacht-watching listener (Listing 6.25).

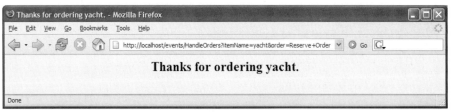

Figure 6–16 Result of reserving an order for a yacht. The yacht-watching listener makes an entry in the log file (Listing 6.29) saying that a customer ordered a yacht.

Figure 6–17   Result of cancelling an order. If the user had previously reserved an order for a yacht, the yacht-watching listener makes an entry in the log file (Listing 6.29) saying that a customer replaced a yacht order with something else.

Figure 6–18   Result of purchasing a yacht. The yacht-watching listener makes an entry in the log file (Listing 6.29) saying that a customer purchased a yacht.

Listing 6.29   Sample Log File Entries

```
Mar 27, 2006 8:29:07 PM
org.apache.catalina.core.ApplicationContext log
INFO: Customer ordered a yacht.
Mar 27, 2006 8:29:17 PM
org.apache.catalina.core.ApplicationContext log
INFO: Customer cancelled an order for a yacht.
Mar 27, 2006 8:29:30 PM
org.apache.catalina.core.ApplicationContext log
INFO: Customer ordered a yacht.
Mar 27, 2006 8:29:36 PM
org.apache.catalina.core.ApplicationContext log
INFO: Customer changed to a new item instead of a yacht.
Mar 27, 2006 8:29:52 PM
org.apache.catalina.core.ApplicationContext log
INFO: Customer finalized purchase of a yacht.
```

6.11 Identifying Servlet Request Initialization and Destruction

We use `ServletContextListener` (see Section 6.1) and `SessionListener` (see Section 6.7) to monitor creation and destruction of the `ServletContext` and `HttpSession`, respectively. Version 2.4 of the servlet specification introduced a new listener, `ServletRequestListener`, which allows us to detect creation and destruction of each `ServletRequest`.

The steps that involve using `ServletRequestListener` are very similar to the steps for using `ServletContextListener` and `SessionListener`.

1. **Implement the `ServletRequestListener` interface.** This interface is located in the `javax.servlet` package.
2. **Implement `requestInitialized` and `requestDestroyed`.** The first of these (`requestInitialized`) is triggered right before a new `ServletRequest` is processed by a Web component (e.g., a servlet or a filter). The second method (`requestDestroyed`) is triggered when a `ServletRequest` object is about to go out of scope of the processing Web component and become eligible for garbage collection.
3. **Obtain a reference to the request and possibly to the servlet context and session.** Each of the two `ServletRequestListener` methods takes a `ServletRequestEvent` as an argument. The `ServletRequestEvent` class has a `getServletRequest` method that provides access to the request object. Note that the return type of the `getServletRequest` method is `ServletRequest`, not `HttpServletRequest`. So, to use the HTTP-related methods you need to cast it down to `HttpServletRequest`. Once you get a reference to the `HttpServletRequest`, you can use it to obtain `HttpSession` object. The `ServletRequestEvent` class also has a `getServletContext` method that provides access to the `ServletContext`.
4. **Use the objects.** Obviously, this is the part that is very specific to what you are trying to accomplish. As with other similar listeners, it is most likely that you would want to store some objects as attributes of either `ServletContext`, `HttpSession`, or `ServletRequest` using the `setAttribute` method. You can also use the `getAttribute` method to retrieve previously stored attributes from the `ServletContext` and `HttpSession` objects. However, it would usually be pointless to try to use the `getAttribute` method on the `ServletRequest` in either `requestInitialized` or `request-`

`Destroyed` methods. The `requestInitialized` method is invoked before any other Web component (e.g., servlet or JSP page), so no attributes are available for retrieval yet. The `requestDestroyed` method is called after all of the attributes are removed, so calling `getAttribute` would be useless there as well. We say "usually" because it is possible to declare multiple `ServletRequestListener` classes. In such a case, the listener that gets invoked first can set attributes on the `ServletRequest` and those attributes would be available for retrieval by the other `ServletRequestListener` classes.

5. **Declare the listener.** In the web.xml or TLD file, use the `listener` and `listener-class` elements to simply list the fully qualified name of the listener class, as shown here:

```
<listener>
  <listener-class>somePackage.SomeListener</listener-class>
</listener>
```

6.12 Example: Calculating Server Request Load

In Section 6.8 (Example: A Listener That Counts Sessions) we count the number of session objects that are active at the same time. This helps us understand the server's memory load. However, knowing the number of simultaneously active sessions is only a part of the picture. Perhaps even more important is to know how many request objects get created at the same time. Unlike the session objects that get created only once per user session, the request objects get created every time the client (i.e., the browser) requests a resource from the server. So, one user will create one session object and could potentially create hundreds of request objects per hour. Besides using up extra memory for each newly created request, object creation is also an expensive operation as far as the CPU cycles are concerned. Therefore, it would be beneficial to know the server load in terms of the ratio of requests per second. Perhaps it's high enough for you to consider upgrading your server hardware or adding another server altogether, or perhaps it's so low that you can afford to cohost another Web application on the same machine without hurting the response time of either.

We accomplish this task by creating a listener that will keep track of when each request was made. Later on (using a servlet), we can retrieve the recorded data and calculate the request frequency.

The following steps summarize a listener that accomplishes this task.

1. **Implement the `ServletRequestListener` interface.** Listing 6.30 shows a class (RequestCounter.java) that implements this interface.

2. **Implement `requestInitialized` and `requestDestroyed`.** The `requestInitialized` method will be called before any other resource within our Web application is invoked for every request made by the client. We can insert our request counting code into this method. However, note that this method is called for every client request, not merely for every connection the client makes to the server, which is not always the same thing. For example, if a JSP page contains a stylesheet declaration, the browser will most likely keep the connection open for both requests—one retrieving the HTML code of the page and another retrieving the stylesheet file. Therefore, even though to the user of the browser a page retrieval looks like one request, in actuality two requests are made by the browser and therefore two separate request objects are created. The `requestDestroyed` method is not used and therefore its implementation is left empty.

3. **Obtain a reference to the request and possibly to the servlet context and session.** Because we need to store our request records where any user can retrieve the statistics at a later time, we need to obtain a reference to the `ServletContext`. We accomplish this by passing the `ServletRequestEvent` object to the helper method called `getRequestRecords` and calling `getServletContext` on it.

4. **Use the objects.** The helper `getRequestRecords` method is called by another helper method called `recordRecord` from the `requestInitialized` method. The `getRequestRecords` method retrieves an `ArrayList` as an attribute with the key of `requestRecords` from the `ServletContext` (or creates a new one if such an attribute doesn't already exist). The `recordRecord` method adds the current system time in milliseconds as an item to the list. This approach allows us to record the total number of requests (e.g., total number of items in the list) together with the time the first request and the last request are made (e.g., first item's value in the list and last item's value in the list). Using this information we are able to calculate request frequency as a number of requests per second.

   We use the `ProcessRequestStats` servlet together with the req-stats.jsp page to display the statistics we have gathered over time. Listing 6.31 and Listing 6.32 show the code for ProcessRequestStats.java and req-stats.jsp, respectively. The `doGet` method of the `ProcessRequestStats` servlet retrieves the `ServletContext` attribute with the key of `requestRecords`, which is the `ArrayList` that contains the request records gathered over some time. We calculate the request statistics (e.g., requests per seconds) and store them in the RequestStatsBean (shown in Listing 6.33), storing the bean in the request scope with the key of stats. We then use the Request-Dispatcher to forward to req-stats.jsp for displaying the information. The result is shown in Figure 6–19.

5. **Declare the listener.** Listing 6.34 shows the web.xml file. It declares the listener with the listener and listener-class elements, as well as the declaration and mapping of the ProcessRequestStats servlet.

Listing 6.30 RequestCounter.java

```java
package coreservlets.listeners;
import java.util.*;
import javax.servlet.*;

/** Listener that keeps track of the number of requests and
 *  the time each request was made. This data is later used
 *  to calculate request frequency per second.
 */
public class RequestCounter implements ServletRequestListener {
  private ArrayList<Long> requestRecords = null;
  private static boolean countingFinished = false;

  public void
        requestInitialized(ServletRequestEvent requestEvent) {
    if (countingFinished) {
      return;
    }
    recordRequest(requestEvent, System.currentTimeMillis());
  }

  private void recordRequest(ServletRequestEvent requestEvent,
                             Long time) {
    // Retrieve request records and record time
    ArrayList<Long> records = getRequestRecords(requestEvent);
    records.add(time);
  }

  private ArrayList<Long>
        getRequestRecords(ServletRequestEvent requestEvent) {
    // Check if it's already cached
    if (this.requestRecords != null) {
      return this.requestRecords;
    }
```

Listing 6.30 RequestCounter.java *(continued)*

```java
    // Initialize requestRecords and store it in ServletContext
    ServletContext context = requestEvent.getServletContext();
    requestRecords = new ArrayList<Long>();
    context.setAttribute("requestRecords", requestRecords);
    return requestRecords;
  }
  /** Allow outside classes to stop collection of request
   *  statistics.
   */
  public static void
              setCountingFinished(boolean countingFinished) {
    RequestCounter.countingFinished = countingFinished;
  }

  public void
        requestDestroyed(ServletRequestEvent requestEvent) {}
}
```

Listing 6.31 ProcessRequestStats.java

```java
package coreservlets;
import java.io.*;
import java.util.*;
import javax.servlet.*;
import javax.servlet.http.*;

/** Servlet that calculates request frequency as the number
 *  of requests made per second and forwards those results
 *  to a page that displays them.
 */
public class ProcessRequestStats extends HttpServlet {
  protected void doGet(HttpServletRequest request,
                       HttpServletResponse response)
        throws ServletException, IOException {
    // Retrieve requestRecords
    ServletContext context = this.getServletContext();
    ArrayList<Long> requestRecords =
      (ArrayList<Long>) context.getAttribute("requestRecords");
    long firstMillis = requestRecords.get(0);
    int totalRequests = requestRecords.size();
    long lastMillis = requestRecords.get(totalRequests - 1);
    // Calculate total seconds elapsed
    long totalSeconds = (lastMillis - firstMillis) / 1000;
```

Listing 6.31 ProcessRequestStats.java *(continued)*

```
    // Calculate ration of requests per second
    double ratio = totalRequests / (double) totalSeconds;
    ratio = ((int)(ratio * 100) / (double) 100);
    // Populate RequestStats bean;
    // store it in the request scope and
    // forward it to stats page
    RequestStatsBean requestStats =
      new RequestStatsBean(totalSeconds, totalRequests, ratio);
    request.setAttribute("stats", requestStats);
    RequestDispatcher dispatcher =
      request.
        getRequestDispatcher("/WEB-INF/pages/req-stats.jsp");
    dispatcher.forward(request, response);
  }
}
```

Listing 6.32 req-stats.jsp

```html
<!DOCTYPE HTML PUBLIC "-//W3C//DTD HTML 4.0 Transitional//EN">
<HTML>
<HEAD>
<TITLE>Request Frequency Statistics</TITLE>
<LINK REL=STYLESHEET
      HREF="events-styles.css"
      TYPE="text/css">
</HEAD>
<BODY>
<TABLE BORDER=5 ALIGN="CENTER">
  <TR><TH CLASS="TITLE">Request Frequency Statistics</TABLE>
<P>
<UL>
<LI>Total number of requests in the life of this
    Web application: ${stats.totalRequests}.
<LI>Web application has been up for
    ${stats.totalSeconds} seconds.
<LI>This means that our request load is about
    ${stats.ratio} requests per second.
</UL>
</BODY></HTML>
```

Listing 6.33   RequestStatsBean.java

```
package coreservlets;

/** Bean used to store the collected request frequency data.
 */
public class RequestStatsBean {
  private long totalSeconds;
  private int totalRequests;
  private double ratio;

  public RequestStatsBean() {}
  public RequestStatsBean(long totalSeconds,
                          int totalRequests,
                          double ratio) {
    this.totalSeconds = totalSeconds;
    this.totalRequests = totalRequests;
    this.ratio = ratio;
  }
  public double getRatio() {
    return ratio;
  }
  public void setRatio(double ratio) {
    this.ratio = ratio;
  }
  public int getTotalRequests() {
    return totalRequests;
  }
  public void setTotalRequests(int totalRequests) {
    this.totalRequests = totalRequests;
  }
  public long getTotalSeconds() {
    return totalSeconds;
  }
  public void setTotalSeconds(long totalSeconds) {
    this.totalSeconds = totalSeconds;
  }
}
```

Listing 6.34 web.xml (Excerpt for RequestCounter listener)

```xml
<?xml version="1.0" encoding="ISO-8859-1"?>
<web-app xmlns="http://java.sun.com/xml/ns/j2ee"
  xmlns:xsi="http://www.w3.org/2001/XMLSchema-instance"
  xsi:schemaLocation=
  "http://java.sun.com/xml/ns/j2ee
  http://java.sun.com/xml/ns/j2ee/web-app_2_4.xsd"
  version="2.4">
  <!-- Register the RequestCounter listener. -->
  <listener>
    <listener-class>
      coreservlets.listeners.RequestCounter
    </listener-class>
  </listener>

  <!-- Declare ProcessRequestStats servlet -->
  <servlet>
    <servlet-name>ProcessRequestStats</servlet-name>
    <servlet-class>
      coreservlets.ProcessRequestStats
    </servlet-class>
  </servlet>
  <!-- Assign the URL /processStats to ProcessRequestStats
       servlet. -->
  <servlet-mapping>
    <servlet-name>ProcessRequestStats</servlet-name>
    <url-pattern>/processStats</url-pattern>
  </servlet-mapping>
</web-app>
```

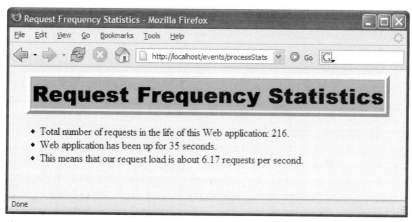

Figure 6–19   Sample request frequency result.

6.13 Watching Servlet Request for Attribute Changes

The ServletContextAttributeListener monitors the life cycle of application scope attributes and the HttpSessionAttributeListener monitors the life cycle of session scope attributes. Likewise, version 2.4 of the servlet specification introduced a listener that monitors the request scope attributes: Servlet-RequestAttributeListener. The container notifies this listener when an object is placed into the request scope for the first time, replaced by another object, or removed from the request scope altogether. The use of the ServletRequest-AttributeListener interface is almost identical to the use of its "sister" listener interfaces: ServletContextAttributeListener and HttpSession-AttributeListener. Details follow.

1. **Implement the ServletRequestAttributeListener interface.** This interface is in the javax.servlet package.
2. **Implement attributeAdded, attributeReplaced, and attributeRemoved.** The attributeAdded method is triggered when a new attribute is added to a request. When a new value is assigned to an existing request attribute, attributeAdded is triggered with the new value and attributeReplaced is triggered with the old value (i.e., the value being replaced). The attribute-Removed method is triggered when a request attribute is removed altogether.
3. **Obtain references to the attribute name, attribute value, request, and servlet context.** Each of the three ServletRequestAttributeListener methods takes a ServletRequestAttributeEvent as an argument. The ServletRequestAttributeEvent class has four useful methods: getName (the name of the attribute that was changed), getValue (the value of the changed attribute—the new value for attribute-Added and the previous value for attributeReplaced and attributeRemoved), getServletRequest, and getServlet-Context.
4. **Use the objects.** The attribute name is usually compared to a stored name to see if it is the one you are monitoring. The attribute value is used in an application-specific manner. The request and servlet context objects are usually used to read previously stored attributes (get-Attribute) or to store new or changed attributes (setAttribute).

5. **Declare the listener.** In the web.xml or TLD file, use the listener and listener-class elements to simply list the fully qualified name of the listener class, as shown here:

```
<listener>
  <listener-class>somePackage.SomeListener</listener-class>
</listener>
```

6.14 Example: Stopping Request Frequency Collection

In Section 6.12 (Example: Calculating Server Request Load), we use the Process-RequestStats servlet (Listing 6.31) to display the request frequency statistics. We do this by retrieving the raw collected data from the ServletContext, populating the RequestStatsBean (Listing 6.33) with the calculated statistics, adding the results bean to the request scope as an attribute with the key of stats, and dynamically forwarding the request to the req-stats.jsp page (Listing 6.32). Let's assume that we want to stop collecting the data once anyone looks at the results. We can use our newly acquired request attribute listener to notify us when an attribute with the key of stats is added to the request scope and signal a stop to further request frequency data collection. We signal the stop by calling the RequestCounter.setCountingFinished method.

The following steps summarize this task.

1. **Implement the ServletRequestAttributeListener interface.** Listing 6.35 shows a class (StopRequestCounter.java) that implements this interface.
2. **Implement attributeAdded, attributeReplaced, and attributeRemoved.** The attributeAdded method is used to watch for the newly added attribute with the key of stats. The other two methods are not used and therefore are left with an empty implementation.
3. **Obtain references to the attribute name, attribute value, request, and servlet context.** We use the getName method of the ServletRequestAttributeEvent to retrieve the name of the attribute that was added to the request scope.
4. **Use the objects.** If the attribute retrieved in Step 3 is equal to stats, we call RequestCounter.setCountingFinished(true) to prevent further data collection.

5. **Declare the listener.** Listing 6.36 shows the web.xml file. It declares the listener with the listener and listener-class elements.

Listing 6.35	StopRequestCounter.java

```java
package coreservlets.listeners;
import javax.servlet.*;

/** Listener that looks for 'stats' as the added attribute
 *  to the request scope. If such an attribute is added, it
 *  signals RequestCounter to stop collecting request
 *  frequency data.
 */
public class StopRequestCounter
         implements ServletRequestAttributeListener {
  /** If the attribute added to the request scope is "stats",
   *  signal to the ServletRequestListener to stop recording
   *  request statistics.
   */
  public void attributeAdded(ServletRequestAttributeEvent event) {
    String attributeName = event.getName();
    if (attributeName.equals("stats")) {
      RequestCounter.setCountingFinished(true);
    }
  }

  public void attributeRemoved(ServletRequestAttributeEvent event)
  {}
  public void
         attributeReplaced(ServletRequestAttributeEvent event)
  {}
}
```

Listing 6.36	web.xml (Excerpt for StopRequestCounter listener)

```xml
<?xml version="1.0" encoding="ISO-8859-1"?>
<web-app xmlns="http://java.sun.com/xml/ns/j2ee"
  xmlns:xsi="http://www.w3.org/2001/XMLSchema-instance"
  xsi:schemaLocation=
  "http://java.sun.com/xml/ns/j2ee
  http://java.sun.com/xml/ns/j2ee/web-app_2_4.xsd"
  version="2.4">
```

Listing 6.36	web.xml (Excerpt for StopRequestCounter listener) *(continued)*

```xml
<!-- Register the RequestCounter listener. -->
<listener>
  <listener-class>
    coreservlets.listeners.RequestCounter
  </listener-class>
</listener>

<!-- Register the StopRequestCounter listener -->
<listener>
  <listener-class>
    coreservlets.listeners.StopRequestCounter
  </listener-class>
</listener>

<!-- Declare ProcessRequestStats servlet -->
<servlet>
  <servlet-name>ProcessRequestStats</servlet-name>
  <servlet-class>
    coreservlets.ProcessRequestStats
  </servlet-class>
</servlet>
<!-- Assign the URL /processStats to ProcessRequestStats
     servlet. -->
<servlet-mapping>
  <servlet-name>ProcessRequestStats</servlet-name>
  <url-pattern>/processStats</url-pattern>
</servlet-mapping>
</web-app>
```

6.15 Using Multiple Cooperating Listeners

Now, the listeners discussed in this chapter are all well and good. There are plenty of applications where one of them is useful. However, there are also plenty of applications where no single listener can, in isolation, accomplish the necessary tasks. Multiple listeners need to work together.

For example, suppose that your yacht-watching listener was so successful that you are asked to expand it. Rather than tracking buying patterns of a fixed item such as a yacht, you should track orders for the current daily special to let management discover if their specials are effective. Accomplishing this task requires three listeners to cooperate: a `ServletContextListener` to set up application-wide information about the session attributes that store daily specials, a `ServletContextAttributeListener` to monitor changes to the attributes that store the information, and an `HttpSessionAttributeListener` to keep a running count of orders for the daily special.

The three listeners are described in more detail in the following subsections.

Tracking Orders for the Daily Special

As the first step in creating an order-tracking system, you need a servlet context listener to read initialization parameters that specify which session attributes correspond to orders and which items are the current daily specials. These values should be stored in the servlet context so other resources can determine what the daily specials are. Listing 6.37 shows this listener.

Second, you need a session attribute listener to keep a running count of orders for the daily special. The count will be incremented every time a designated attribute name is added with any of the daily specials as its value. The count will be decremented every time a designated attribute is replaced or removed and the previous value is one of the daily specials. Listing 6.38 shows this listener.

Listing 6.39 shows the deployment descriptor that registers the two listeners and sets up the servlet context initialization parameters that designate the names of order-related session attributes and the names of the daily specials.

Listing 6.40 shows a JSP page that prints the current order count. Figures 6–20 through 6–22 show some typical results.

Listing 6.37   DailySpecialRegistrar.java

```
package coreservlets.listeners;

import java.util.*;
import javax.servlet.*;

/** Listener that records how to detect orders
 *  of the daily special. It reads a list of attribute
 *  names from an init parameter: these correspond to
 *  session attributes that are used to record orders.
 *  It also reads a list of item names: these correspond
 *  to the names of the daily specials. Other listeners
 *  will watch to see if any daily special names appear
 *  as values of attributes that are hereby designated
 *  to refer to orders.
 */
```

Listing 6.37 DailySpecialRegistrar.java *(continued)*

```
public class DailySpecialRegistrar
    implements ServletContextListener {

  /** When the Web application is loaded, record the
   *  attribute names that correspond to orders and
   *  the attribute values that are the daily specials.
   *  Also set to zero the count of daily specials that have
   *  been ordered.
   */
  public void contextInitialized(ServletContextEvent event) {
    ServletContext context = event.getServletContext();
    addContextEntry(context, "order-attribute-names");
    addContextEntry(context, "daily-special-item-names");
    context.setAttribute("dailySpecialCount", new Integer(0));
  }

  public void contextDestroyed(ServletContextEvent event) {}

  /** Read the designated context initialization parameter,
   *  put the values into an ArrayList, and store the
   *  list in the ServletContext with an attribute name
   *  that is identical to the initialization parameter name.
   */
  private void addContextEntry(ServletContext context,
                               String initParamName) {
    ArrayList<String> paramValues = new ArrayList<String>();
    String attributeNames =
      context.getInitParameter(initParamName);
    if (attributeNames != null) {
      String[] params = attributeNames.split("\\s++");
      for (String value : params) {
        paramValues.add(value);
      }
      context.setAttribute(initParamName, paramValues);
    }
  }

  /** Returns a string containing the daily special
   *  names. For insertion inside an HTML text area.
   */
  public static String dailySpecials(ServletContext context) {
    String attributeName = "daily-special-item-names";
    ArrayList itemNames =
      (ArrayList)context.getAttribute(attributeName);
```

Listing 6.37 DailySpecialRegistrar.java *(continued)*

```
    String itemString = "";
    for(int i=0; i<itemNames.size(); i++) {
      itemString = itemString + (String)itemNames.get(i) + "\n";
    }
    return(itemString);
  }

  /** Returns a UL list containing the daily special
   *  names. For insertion within the body of a JSP page.
   */
  public static String specialsList(ServletContext context) {
    String attributeName = "daily-special-item-names";
    ArrayList itemNames =
      (ArrayList)context.getAttribute(attributeName);
    String itemString = "<UL>\n";
    for(int i=0; i<itemNames.size(); i++) {
      itemString = itemString + "<LI>" +
                   (String)itemNames.get(i) + "\n";
    }
    itemString = itemString + "</UL>";
    return(itemString);
  }
}
```

Listing 6.38 DailySpecialWatcher.java

```
package coreservlets.listeners;

import java.util.*;
import javax.servlet.*;
import javax.servlet.http.*;

/** Listener that keeps track of orders of the
 *  current daily special.
 */
public class DailySpecialWatcher
    implements HttpSessionAttributeListener {
  private static int dailySpecialCount = 0;
```

Listing 6.38 DailySpecialWatcher.java *(continued)*

```
/** If the name of the session attribute that was added
 *  matches one of the stored order-attribute-names AND
 *  the value of the attribute matches one of the
 *  stored daily-special-item-names, then increment
 *  the count of daily specials ordered.
 */
public void attributeAdded(HttpSessionBindingEvent event) {
  checkForSpecials(event, 1);
}

/** If the name of the session attribute that was removed
 *  matches one of the stored order-attribute-names AND
 *  the value of the attribute matches one of the
 *  stored daily-special-item-names, then decrement
 *  the count of daily specials ordered.
 */
public void attributeRemoved(HttpSessionBindingEvent event) {
  checkForSpecials(event, -1);
}

/** If the name of the session attribute that was replaced
 *  matches one of the stored order-attribute-names AND
 *  the value of the attribute matches one of the
 *  stored daily-special-item-names, then increment
 *  the count of daily specials ordered. Note that the
 *  value here is the old value (the one being replaced);
 *  the attributeAdded method will handle the new value
 *  (the replacement).
 */
public void attributeReplaced(HttpSessionBindingEvent event) {
  checkForSpecials(event, -1);
}

/** Check whether the attribute that was just added or removed
 *  matches one of the stored order-attribute-names AND
 *  the value of the attribute matches one of the
 *  stored daily-special-item-names. If so, add the delta
 *  (+1 or -1) to the count of daily specials ordered.
 */
private void checkForSpecials(HttpSessionBindingEvent event,
                              int delta) {
  ServletContext context =
    event.getSession().getServletContext();
  ArrayList<String> attributeNames =
    getList(context, "order-attribute-names");
```

Listing 6.38 DailySpecialWatcher.java *(continued)*

```
  ArrayList<String> itemNames =
    getList(context, "daily-special-item-names");
  synchronized(attributeNames) {
    for(int i=0; i<attributeNames.size(); i++) {
      String attributeName = attributeNames.get(i);
      for(int j=0; j<itemNames.size(); j++) {
        String itemName = itemNames.get(j);
        if (attributeName.equals(event.getName()) &&
            itemName.equals((String)event.getValue())) {
          dailySpecialCount = dailySpecialCount + delta;
        }
      }
    }
  }
  context.setAttribute("dailySpecialCount",
                       new Integer(dailySpecialCount));
}

/** Get either the order-attribute-names or
 *  daily-special-item-names list.
 */
private ArrayList<String> getList(ServletContext context,
                          String attributeName) {
  ArrayList<String> list =
    (ArrayList)context.getAttribute(attributeName);
  return(list);
}

/** Reset the count of daily specials that have
 *  been ordered. This operation is normally performed
 *  only when the daily special changes.
 */
public static void resetDailySpecialCount() {
  dailySpecialCount = 0;
}
}
```

Listing 6.39 web.xml (Excerpt for tracking daily special orders)

```
<?xml version="1.0" encoding="ISO-8859-1"?>
<web-app xmlns="http://java.sun.com/xml/ns/j2ee"
  xmlns:xsi="http://www.w3.org/2001/XMLSchema-instance"
  xsi:schemaLocation=
  "http://java.sun.com/xml/ns/j2ee
  http://java.sun.com/xml/ns/j2ee/web-app_2_4.xsd"
  version="2.4">
  <!-- Register the listener that sets up the entries
    that will be used to monitor orders for the daily
    special. -->
  <listener>
    <listener-class>
      coreservlets.listeners.DailySpecialRegistrar
    </listener-class>
  </listener>
  <!-- Register the listener that counts orders for the daily
    special. -->
  <listener>
    <listener-class>
      coreservlets.listeners.DailySpecialWatcher
    </listener-class>
  </listener>
  <!-- Declare the names of the session attributes that
    are used to store items that customers are
    purchasing. The daily special listener will
    track changes to the values of these attributes. -->
  <context-param>
    <param-name>order-attribute-names</param-name>
    <param-value>
      orderedItem
      purchasedItem
    </param-value>
  </context-param>
  <!-- The item names of the current daily specials. -->
  <context-param>
    <param-name>daily-special-item-names</param-name>
    <param-value>
      chalet
      car
    </param-value>
  </context-param>
</web-app>
```

Listing 6.40   track-daily-specials.jsp

```
<!DOCTYPE HTML PUBLIC "-//W3C//DTD HTML 4.0 Transitional//EN">
<HTML>
<HEAD>
<TITLE>Tracking Daily Special Orders</TITLE>
<LINK REL=STYLESHEET
      HREF="events-styles.css"
      TYPE="text/css">
</HEAD>
<BODY>
<CENTER>
<TABLE BORDER=5>
  <TR><TH CLASS="TITLE">Tracking Daily Special Orders
</TABLE>
<H2>Current Specials:</H2>
<%@ page import="coreservlets.listeners.*" %>
<%= DailySpecialRegistrar.specialsList(application) %>
<H2>Number of Orders:
${applicationScope.dailySpecialCount}
</H2>
</CENTER>
</BODY></HTML>
```

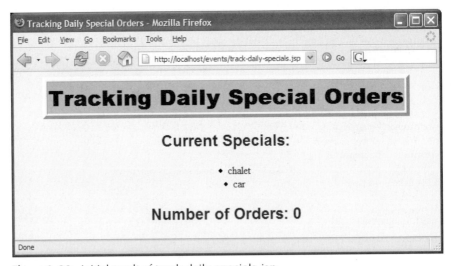

Figure 6–20   Initial result of track-daily-specials.jsp.

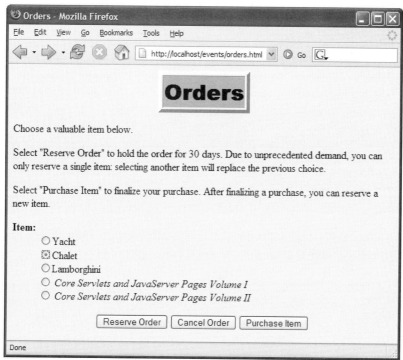

Figure 6–21   Ordering the daily special.

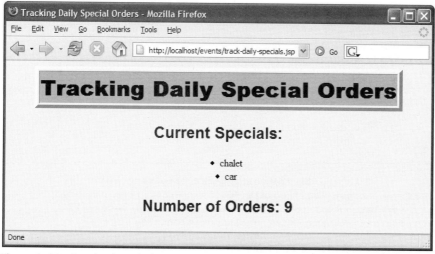

Figure 6–22   Result of track-daily-specials.jsp after several clients placed orders.

Resetting the Daily Special Order Count

The two listeners shown in the previous subsection are sufficient if you restart the server every time you change the daily specials.

However, if you change the daily specials while the server is running, you need a servlet context attribute listener to detect changes in the attribute that stores the names of the daily specials. In particular, when the daily specials change, you need to reset the running count of orders for the specials. Listing 6.41 shows this listener.

Listing 6.42 shows a JSP page that displays the current daily specials in a text area. It lets the user change the values and send them to a servlet (Listing 6.43) that records the changes in the servlet context. The JSP page is in the admin directory and the servlet is assigned a URL beginning with /admin (see the web.xml file in Listing 6.44), so the security restrictions discussed in Chapter 3 (Declarative Security) apply.

When an authorized user changes the names of the daily specials, the order count is reset. Figures 6–23 through 6–27 show some representative results.

Listing 6.41   ChangedDailySpecialListener.java

```
package coreservlets.listeners;

import javax.servlet.*;

/** Listener that monitors changes to the names
 *  of the daily specials (which are stored in
 *  the daily-special-item-names attribute of
 *  the servlet context). If the names change, the
 *  listener resets the running count of the number
 *  of daily specials being ordered.
 */
public class ChangedDailySpecialListener
    implements ServletContextAttributeListener {

  /** When the daily specials change, reset the
   *  order counts.
   */
  public void attributeReplaced
                  (ServletContextAttributeEvent event) {
    if (event.getName().equals("daily-special-item-names")) {
      ServletContext context = event.getServletContext();
      context.setAttribute("dailySpecialCount",
                           new Integer(0));
      DailySpecialWatcher.resetDailySpecialCount();
    }
  }
}
```

Listing 6.41   ChangedDailySpecialListener.java *(continued)*

```
  public void attributeAdded
              (ServletContextAttributeEvent event) {}

  public void attributeRemoved
              (ServletContextAttributeEvent event) {}
}
```

Listing 6.42   change-daily-specials.jsp

```
<!DOCTYPE HTML PUBLIC "-//W3C//DTD HTML 4.0 Transitional//EN">
<HTML>
<HEAD>
<TITLE>Changing Daily Specials</TITLE>
<LINK REL=STYLESHEET
      HREF="../events-styles.css"
      TYPE="text/css">
</HEAD>
<BODY>
<CENTER>
<TABLE BORDER=5>
  <TR><TH CLASS="TITLE">Changing Daily Specials
</TABLE>
<P>
<FORM ACTION="ChangeDailySpecial">
New specials:<BR>
<%@ page import="coreservlets.listeners.*" %>
<TEXTAREA NAME="newSpecials" ROWS=4 COLS=30>
<%= DailySpecialRegistrar.dailySpecials(application) %>
</TEXTAREA>
<P>
<INPUT TYPE="SUBMIT" VALUE="Submit Change">
</FORM>
</CENTER>
</BODY></HTML>
```

Listing 6.43 ChangeDailySpecial.java

```java
package coreservlets;

import java.io.*;
import java.util.*;
import javax.servlet.*;
import javax.servlet.http.*;

/** Servlet that changes the daily specials. The web.xml
 *  file specifies that only authenticated users in the
 *  ceo role can access the servlet. A servlet context
 *  attribute listener resets the count of daily special
 *  orders when this servlet (or any other program) changes
 *  the daily specials.
 */
public class ChangeDailySpecial extends HttpServlet {
  public void doGet(HttpServletRequest request,
                    HttpServletResponse response)
      throws ServletException, IOException {
    String dailySpecialNames =
      request.getParameter("newSpecials");
    if ((dailySpecialNames == null) ||
        (dailySpecialNames.equals(""))) {
      dailySpecialNames = "MISSING-VALUE";
    }
    ArrayList<String> specials = new ArrayList<String>();
    String[] dailySpecials = dailySpecialNames.split("\\s++");
    for (String special : dailySpecials) {
      specials.add(special);
    }
    ServletContext context = getServletContext();
    context.setAttribute("daily-special-item-names",
                          specials);
    response.setContentType("text/html");
    PrintWriter out = response.getWriter();
    String docType =
      "<!DOCTYPE HTML PUBLIC \"-//W3C//DTD HTML 4.0 " +
      "Transitional//EN\">\n";
    String title = "New Daily Specials";
    out.println
      (docType +
       "<HTML>\n" +
       "<HEAD><TITLE>" + title + "</TITLE></HEAD>\n" +
       "<BODY BGCOLOR=\"#FDF5E6\">\n" +
       "<H2 ALIGN=\"CENTER\">" + title + "</H2>\n" +
       "<UL>");
```

Listing 6.43   ChangeDailySpecial.java *(continued)*

```
    String special;
    for(int i=0; i<specials.size(); i++) {
      special = (String)specials.get(i);
      out.println("<LI>" + special);
    }
    out.println("</UL>\n" +
                "</BODY></HTML>");
  }
}
```

Listing 6.44   web.xml (Excerpt for resetting order counts)

```
<?xml version="1.0" encoding="ISO-8859-1"?>
<web-app xmlns="http://java.sun.com/xml/ns/j2ee"
  xmlns:xsi="http://www.w3.org/2001/XMLSchema-instance"
  xsi:schemaLocation=
  "http://java.sun.com/xml/ns/j2ee
  http://java.sun.com/xml/ns/j2ee/web-app_2_4.xsd"
  version="2.4">
  <!-- Register the listener that resets the order counts
    when the names of the daily specials change. -->
  <listener>
    <listener-class>
      coreservlets.listeners.ChangedDailySpecialListener
    </listener-class>
  </listener>
  <!-- Assign the name ChangeDailySpecial to
    coreservlets.ChangeDailySpecial.  -->
  <servlet>
    <servlet-name>ChangeDailySpecial</servlet-name>
    <servlet-class>
      coreservlets.ChangeDailySpecial
    </servlet-class>
  </servlet>
  <!-- Assign the URL /admin/ChangeDailySpecial to the
    servlet that is named ChangeDailySpecial. -->
  <servlet-mapping>
    <servlet-name>ChangeDailySpecial</servlet-name>
    <url-pattern>/admin/ChangeDailySpecial</url-pattern>
  </servlet-mapping>
</web-app>
```

Figure 6–23   Requests by unauthenticated users for change-daily-specials.jsp get sent to the login page (Listing 6.9).

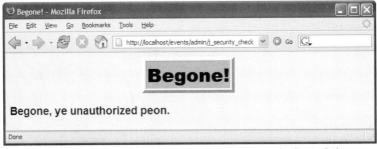

Figure 6–24   Users who fail authentication are shown the login-failure page (Listing 6.10).

Figure 6–25   Users who pass authentication and are in the designated role (ceo) are shown the form for changing the daily specials (Listing 6.42). The current daily specials are displayed as the initial value of the text area.

Figure 6–26   Result of submitting the form for changing daily specials after `yacht` and `chalet` are entered in the text area.

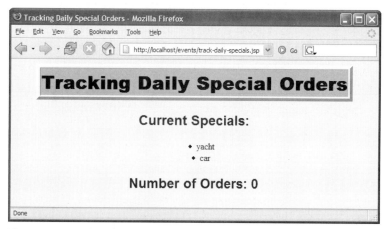

Figure 6–27   When the daily specials are changed, the servlet context attribute listener (Listing 6.41) resets the order count.

6.16 The Complete Events Deployment Descriptor

The previous sections showed various excerpts of the web.xml file for the application events examples. Listing 6.45 shows the file in its entirety.

Listing 6.45	web.xml (Complete version for events examples)

```xml
<?xml version="1.0" encoding="ISO-8859-1"?>
<web-app xmlns="http://java.sun.com/xml/ns/j2ee"
  xmlns:xsi="http://www.w3.org/2001/XMLSchema-instance"
  xsi:schemaLocation=
  "http://java.sun.com/xml/ns/j2ee
  http://java.sun.com/xml/ns/j2ee/web-app_2_4.xsd"
  version="2.4">

  <!-- Because the company name changes so frequently,
       supply it as a servlet context parameter instead
       of embedding it into lots of different servlets and
       JSP pages. The InitialCompanyNameListener will
       read this value and store it in the servlet context. -->
  <context-param>
    <param-name>companyName</param-name>
    <param-value>not-dot-com.com</param-value>
  </context-param>

  <!-- Also store the previous company name. -->
  <context-param>
    <param-name>formerCompanyName</param-name>
    <param-value>hot-dot-com.com</param-value>
  </context-param>

  <!-- Register the listener that sets up the
       initial company name. -->
  <listener>
    <listener-class>
      coreservlets.listeners.InitialCompanyNameListener
    </listener-class>
  </listener>


  <!-- Register the listener that monitors changes to
       the company name.
  -->
  <listener>
    <listener-class>
      coreservlets.listeners.ChangedCompanyNameListener
    </listener-class>
  </listener>
```

Listing 6.45   web.xml (Complete version for events examples) *(continued)*

```xml
<!-- Register the session counting event listener. -->
<listener>
  <listener-class>
    coreservlets.listeners.SessionCounter
  </listener-class>
</listener>

<!-- Set the default session timeout to two minutes. -->
<session-config>
  <session-timeout>2</session-timeout>
</session-config>

<!-- Assign the name ChangeCompanyName to
     coreservlets.ChangeCompanyName. -->
<servlet>
  <servlet-name>ChangeCompanyName</servlet-name>
  <servlet-class>coreservlets.ChangeCompanyName</servlet-class>
</servlet>
<!-- Assign the URL /admin/ChangeCompanyName to the
     servlet that is named ChangeCompanyName. -->
<servlet-mapping>
  <servlet-name>ChangeCompanyName</servlet-name>
  <url-pattern>/admin/ChangeCompanyName</url-pattern>
</servlet-mapping>

<!-- Protect everything within the "admin" directory.
     Direct client access to this directory requires
     authentication. -->
<security-constraint>
  <web-resource-collection>
    <web-resource-name>Admin</web-resource-name>
    <url-pattern>/admin/*</url-pattern>
  </web-resource-collection>
  <auth-constraint>
    <role-name>ceo</role-name>
  </auth-constraint>
</security-constraint>

<!-- Declare security roles. -->
<security-role>
  <role-name>ceo</role-name>
</security-role>
```

Listing 6.45	web.xml (Complete version for events examples) *(continued)*

```
<!-- Tell the server to use form-based authentication. -->
 <login-config>
   <auth-method>FORM</auth-method>
   <form-login-config>
     <form-login-page>/login/login.jsp</form-login-page>
     <form-error-page>/login/login-error.jsp</form-error-page>
   </form-login-config>
 </login-config>

 <!-- Register the listener that sets up the entries
   that will be used to monitor orders for the daily
   special. -->
 <listener>
   <listener-class>
      coreservlets.listeners.DailySpecialRegistrar
   </listener-class>
 </listener>

 <!-- Declare the names of the session attributes that
   are used to store items that customers are
   purchasing. The daily special listener will
   track changes to the values of these attributes. -->
 <context-param>
   <param-name>order-attribute-names</param-name>
   <param-value>
     orderedItem
     purchasedItem
   </param-value>
 </context-param>

 <!-- The item names of the current daily specials. -->
 <context-param>
   <param-name>daily-special-item-names</param-name>
   <param-value>
     chalet
     car
   </param-value>
 </context-param>

 <!-- Register the listener that counts orders for the daily
   special. -->
 <listener>
   <listener-class>
      coreservlets.listeners.DailySpecialWatcher
   </listener-class>
 </listener>
```

Listing 6.45	web.xml (Complete version for events examples) *(continued)*

```xml
<!-- Register the listener that resets the order counts
  when the names of the daily specials change. -->
<listener>
  <listener-class>
    coreservlets.listeners.ChangedDailySpecialListener
  </listener-class>
</listener>

<!-- Register the yacht-watching event listener. -->
<listener>
  <listener-class>
    coreservlets.listeners.YachtWatcher
  </listener-class>
</listener>

<!-- Assign the name OrderHandlingServlet to
  coreservlets.OrderHandlingServlet. -->
<servlet>
  <servlet-name>OrderHandlingServlet</servlet-name>
  <servlet-class>
    coreservlets.OrderHandlingServlet
  </servlet-class>
</servlet>
<!-- Assign the URL /HandleOrders to the
  servlet that is named OrderHandlingServlet. -->
<servlet-mapping>
  <servlet-name>OrderHandlingServlet</servlet-name>
  <url-pattern>/HandleOrders</url-pattern>
</servlet-mapping>

<!-- Assign the name ChangeDailySpecial to
  coreservlets.ChangeDailySpecial.  -->
<servlet>
  <servlet-name>ChangeDailySpecial</servlet-name>
  <servlet-class>
    coreservlets.ChangeDailySpecial
  </servlet-class>
</servlet>

<!-- Register the RequestCounter listener. -->
<listener>
  <listener-class>
    coreservlets.listeners.RequestCounter
  </listener-class>
</listener>
```

| Listing 6.45 | web.xml (Complete version for events examples) *(continued)* |

```
<!-- Register the StopRequestCounter listener -->
<listener>
  <listener-class>
    coreservlets.listeners.StopRequestCounter
  </listener-class>
</listener>

<!-- Declare ProcessRequestStats servlet -->
<servlet>
  <servlet-name>ProcessRequestStats</servlet-name>
  <servlet-class>
    coreservlets.ProcessRequestStats
  </servlet-class>
</servlet>
<!-- Assign the URL /processStats to ProcessRequestStats
  servlet. -->
<servlet-mapping>
  <servlet-name>ProcessRequestStats</servlet-name>
  <url-pattern>/processStats</url-pattern>
</servlet-mapping>

<!-- Assign the URL /admin/ChangeDailySpecial to the
  servlet that is named ChangeDailySpecial. -->
<servlet-mapping>
  <servlet-name>ChangeDailySpecial</servlet-name>
  <url-pattern>/admin/ChangeDailySpecial</url-pattern>
</servlet-mapping>

<!-- Disable the invoker servlet. -->
<servlet>
  <servlet-name>NoInvoker</servlet-name>
  <servlet-class>coreservlets.NoInvokerServlet</servlet-class>
</servlet>
<servlet-mapping>
  <servlet-name>NoInvoker</servlet-name>
  <url-pattern>/servlet/*</url-pattern>
</servlet-mapping>
```

Listing 6.45	web.xml (Complete version for events examples) *(continued)*

```
<!-- If URL gives a directory but no file name, try index.jsp
   first and index.html second. If neither is found,
   the result is server specific (e.g., a directory
   listing).  Order of elements in web.xml matters.
   welcome-file-list needs to come after servlet but
   before error-page.
-->
<welcome-file-list>
  <welcome-file>index.jsp</welcome-file>
  <welcome-file>index.html</welcome-file>
</welcome-file-list>
</web-app>
```

TAG LIBRARIES: THE BASICS

Topics in This Chapter

- Identifying tag library components
- Creating simple custom tags
- Handling attributes in custom tags
- Outputting tag bodies
- Creating JSP-based custom tags with tag files

Chapter 7

As discussed in Volume 1 (Section 11.2) of *Core Servlets and JavaServer Pages*, you have many options when it comes to generating dynamic content inside the JSP page. These options are as follows:

- Scripting elements calling servlet code directly
- Scripting elements calling servlet code indirectly (by means of utility classes)
- Beans
- Servlet/JSP combo (MVC)
- MVC with JSP expression language
- Custom tags

The options at the top of the list are much simpler to use and are just as legitimate as the options at the bottom of the list. However, industry has adopted a best practice to avoid placing Java code inside the JSP page. This best practice stems from it being much harder to debug and maintain Java code inside the JSP page. In addition, JSP pages should concentrate only on the presentation logic. Introducing Java code into the JSP page tends to divert its purpose and, inevitably, business logic starts to creep in. To enforce this best practice, version 2.4 of the servlet specification went so far as to provide a way to disable any type of JSP scripting for a group of JSP pages. We discuss how to disable scripting in Section 2.14 (Configuring JSP Pages).

That said, there are cases where the presentation logic itself is quite complex and using the non-Java code options in the JSP page to express that logic becomes either too clunky and unreadable or, sometimes, just impossible to achieve. This is where logic through the familiar HTML-like structures.

This chapter discusses how to create and use custom tags utilizing the new `SimpleTag` API, which was introduced in version 2.4 of the servlet specification. As its name suggests, `SimpleTag` API is very easy to use in comparison to its predecessor, now known as the classic tag API.

Although the `SimpleTag` API completely replaces the classic tag API, you should keep in mind that it works only in containers compliant with servlet specification 2.4 and above. Because there are still a lot of applications running on servlet 2.3-compliant containers, you should consider avoiding the `SimpleTag` API if you are not sure what type of container your code will end up on.

7.1   Tag Library Components

To use custom JSP tags, you need to define three separate components:

- The tag handler class that defines the tag's behavior
- The TLD file that maps the XML element names to the tag implementations
- The JSP file that uses the tag library

The rest of this section gives an overview of each of these components, and the following sections give details on how to build these components for various styles of tags. Most people find that the first tag they write is the hardest—the difficulty being in knowing where each component should go, not in writing the components. So, we suggest that you start by just downloading the simplest of the examples of this chapter from http://volume2.coreservlets.com/ and getting those examples to work on your machine. After that, you can move on and try creating some of your own tags.

The Tag Handler Class

When defining a new tag, your first task is to define a Java class that tells the system what to do when it sees the tag. This class must implement the `SimpleTag` interface. In practice, you extend `SimpleTagSupport`, which implements the `SimpleTag` interface and supplies standard implementations for some of its methods. Both the `SimpleTag` interface and the `SimpleTagSupport` class reside in the `javax.servlet.jsp.tagext` package.

The very first action the container takes after loading the tag handler class is instantiating it with its no-arg constructor. This means that every tag handler must have a no-arg constructor or its instantiation will fail. Remember that the Java compiler provides one for you automatically unless you define a constructor with arguments. In that case, be sure to define a no-arg constructor yourself.

The code that does the actual work of the tag goes inside the `doTag` method. Usually, this code outputs content to the JSP page by invoking the `print` method of the `JspWriter` class. To obtain an instance of the `JstWriter` class you call `getJspContext().getOut()` inside the `doTag` method. The `doTag` method is called at request time. It's important to note that, unlike the classic tag model, the Simple-Tag model never reuses tag handler instances. In fact, a new instance of the tag handler class is created for every tag occurrence on the page. This alleviates worries about race conditions and cached values even if you use instance variables in the tag handler class.

You place the compiled tag handler in the same location you would place a regular servlet, inside the WEB-INF/classes directory, keeping the package structure intact. For example, if your tag handler class belongs to the `mytags` package and its class name is `MyTag`, you would place theMyTag.class file inside the WEB-INF/classes/mytags/ directory.

Listing 7.1 shows an example of a tag handler class.

Listing 7.1 Example Tag Handler Class

```
package somepackage;

import javax.servlet.jsp.*;
import javax.servlet.jsp.tagext.*;
import java.io.*;

public class ExampleTag extends SimpleTagSupport {
  public void doTag() throws JspException, IOException {
    JspWriter out = getJspContext().getOut();
    out.print("<b>Hello World!</b>");
  }
}
```

The Tag Library Descriptor File

Once you have defined a tag handler, your next task is to identify this class to the server and to associate it with a particular XML tag name. This task is accomplished by means of a TLD file in XML format. This file contains some fixed information (e.g., XML Schema instance declaration), an arbitrary short name for your library, a short description, and a series of tag descriptions. Listing 7.2 shows an example TLD file.

Listing 7.2   Example Tag Library Descriptor File

```
<?xml version="1.0" encoding="UTF-8" ?>
<taglib xmlns="http://java.sun.com/xml/ns/j2ee"
   xmlns:xsi="http://www.w3.org/2001/XMLSchema-instance"
   xsi:schemaLocation="http://java.sun.com/xml/ns/j2ee
   http://java.sun.com/xml/ns/j2ee/web-jsptaglibrary_2_0.xsd"
   version="2.0">
   <tlib-version>1.0</tlib-version>
   <short-name>csajsp-taglib</short-name>
   <tag>
      <description>Example tag</description>
      <name>example</name>
      <tag-class>package.TagHandlerClass</tag-class>
      <body-content>empty</body-content>
   </tag>
</taglib>
```

We describe the details of the contents of the TLD file in later sections. For now, just note that the `tag` element through the following subelements in their required order defines the custom tag.

- **description.** This optional element allows the tag developer to document the purpose of the custom tag.
- **name.** This required element defines the name of the tag as it will be referred to by the JSP page (really tag suffix, as will be seen shortly).
- **tag-class.** This required element identifies the fully qualified name of the implementing tag handler class.
- **body-content.** This required element tells the container how to treat the content between the beginning and ending occurrence of the tag, if any. The value that appears here can be either `empty`, `scriptless, tagdependent,` or `JSP`.

  The value of `empty` means that no content is allowed to appear in the body of the tag. This would mean that the declared tag can only appear in the form:

  ```
  <prefix:tag/>
  ```

  or

  ```
  <prefix:tag></prefix:tag>
  ```

  (without any spaces between the opening and closing tags). Placing any content inside the tag body would generate a page translation error.

The value of `scriptless` means that the tag body is allowed to have JSP content as long as it doesn't contain any scripting elements like `<% ... %>` or `<%= ... %>`. If present, the body of the tag would be processed just like any other JSP content.

The value of `tagdependent` means that the tag is allowed to have any type of content as its body. However, this content is not processed at all and completely ignored. It is up to the developer of the tag handler to get access to that content and do something with it. For example, if you wanted to develop a tag that would allow the JSP page developer to execute an SQL statement, providing the SQL in the body of the tag, you would use `tagdependent` as the value of the `body-content` element.

Finally, the value of `JSP` is provided for backward compatibility with the classic custom tag model. It is not a legal value when used with the `SimpleTag` API.

Note that there is no legal way of allowing any scripting elements to appear as the tag body under the new `SimpleTag` API model.

Core Warning

When using the `SimpleTag` API, it is illegal to include scripting elements in the body of the tag.

The TLD file must be placed inside the WEB-INF directory or any subdirectory thereof.

Core Note

The TLD file must be placed inside the WEB-INF directory or a subdirectory thereof.

We suggest that you don't try to retype the TLD every time you start a new tag library, but start with a template. You can download such a template from http://volume2.coreservlets.com/.

The JSP File

Once you have a tag handler implementation and a TLD, you are ready to write a JSP file that makes use of the tag. Listing 7.3 gives an example. Somewhere in the JSP page you need to place the `taglib` directive. This directive has the following form:

```
<%@ taglib uri="..." prefix="..." %>
```

The required `uri` attribute can be either an absolute or relative URL referring to a TLD file like the one shown in Listing 7.2. For now, we will use a simple URL relative to the Web application's root directory. This makes it easy to refer to the same TLD file from multiple JSP pages in different directories. Remember that the TLD file must be placed somewhere inside the WEB-INF directory. Because this URL will be resolved on the server and not the client, it is allowed to refer to the WEB-INF directory, which is always protected from direct client access.

The required `prefix` attribute specifies a prefix to use in front of any tag name defined in the TLD of this `taglib` declaration. For example, if the TLD file defines a tag named `tag1` and the `prefix` attribute has a value of `test`, the JSP page would need to refer to the tag as `test:tag1`. This tag could be used in either of the following two ways, depending on whether it is defined to be a container that makes use of the tag body:

```
<test:tag1>Arbitrary JSP</test:tag1>
```

or just

```
<test:tag1 />
```

Listing 7.3   Example JSP File

```
<!DOCTYPE HTML PUBLIC "-//W3C//DTD HTML 4.0 Transitional//EN">
<HTML>
<HEAD>
<TITLE>Example JSP page</TITLE>
<LINK REL=STYLESHEET
      HREF="JSP-Styles.css"
      TYPE="text/css">
</HEAD>
<BODY>
<%@ taglib uri="/WEB-INF/tlds/example.tld"
          prefix="test" %>
<test:example/>
<test:example></test:example>
</BODY></HTML>
```

7.2   Example: Simple Prime Tag

In this example we create a simple custom tag that would output a random 50-digit prime number to the JSP page (a real treat!). We accomplish this task with the help of the `Primes` class shown in Listing 7.4.

We define a tag handler class `SimplePrimeTag` that extends the `SimpleTag-Support` class. In its `doTag` method, we obtain a reference to the `JspWriter` by calling `getJspContext().getOut()`. Then, by using the static method `Primes.nextPrime` we generate our random 50-digit prime number. We output this number to the JSP page by invoking the `print` method on the `JspWriter` object reference. The code for SimplePrimeTag.java is shown in Listing 7.5.

Listing 7.4   Primes.java

```java
package coreservlets;
import java.math.BigInteger;

/** A few utilities to generate a large random BigInteger,
 *  and find the next prime number above a given BigInteger.
 */
public class Primes {
  private static final BigInteger ZERO = BigInteger.ZERO;
  private static final BigInteger ONE = BigInteger.ONE;
  private static final BigInteger TWO = new BigInteger("2");

  // Likelihood of false prime is less than 1/2^ERR_VAL
  // Presumably BigInteger uses the Miller-Rabin test or
  // equivalent, and thus is NOT fooled by Carmichael numbers.
  // See section 33.8 of Cormen et al.'s Introduction to
  // Algorithms for details.
  private static final int ERR_VAL = 100;

  public static BigInteger nextPrime(BigInteger start) {
    if (isEven(start))
      start = start.add(ONE);
    else
      start = start.add(TWO);
    if (start.isProbablePrime(ERR_VAL))
      return(start);
    else
      return(nextPrime(start));
  }
```

Listing 7.4   Primes.java *(continued)*

```java
private static boolean isEven(BigInteger n) {
  return(n.mod(TWO).equals(ZERO));
}

private static StringBuffer[] digits =
  { new StringBuffer("0"), new StringBuffer("1"),
    new StringBuffer("2"), new StringBuffer("3"),
    new StringBuffer("4"), new StringBuffer("5"),
    new StringBuffer("6"), new StringBuffer("7"),
    new StringBuffer("8"), new StringBuffer("9") };
private static StringBuffer randomDigit(boolean isZeroOK) {
  int index;
  if (isZeroOK) {
    index = (int)Math.floor(Math.random() * 10);
  } else {
    index = 1 + (int)Math.floor(Math.random() * 9);
  }
  return(digits[index]);
}

/** Create a random big integer where every digit is
 *  selected randomly (except that the first digit
 *  cannot be a zero).
 */
public static BigInteger random(int numDigits) {
  StringBuffer s = new StringBuffer("");
  for(int i=0; i<numDigits; i++) {
    if (i == 0) {
      // First digit must be non-zero.
      s.append(randomDigit(false));
    } else {
      s.append(randomDigit(true));
    }
  }
  return(new BigInteger(s.toString()));
}

/** Simple command-line program to test. Enter number
 *  of digits, and it picks a random number of that
 *  length and then prints the first 50 prime numbers
 *  above that.
 */

public static void main(String[] args) {
  int numDigits;
```

Listing 7.4   Primes.java *(continued)*

```
    try {
      numDigits = Integer.parseInt(args[0]);
    } catch (Exception e) { // No args or illegal arg.
      numDigits = 150;
    }
    BigInteger start = random(numDigits);
    for(int i=0; i<50; i++) {
      start = nextPrime(start);
      System.out.println("Prime " + i + " = " + start);
    }
  }
}
```

Listing 7.5   SimplePrimeTag.java

```
package coreservlets.tags;
import javax.servlet.jsp.*;
import javax.servlet.jsp.tagext.*;
import java.io.*;
import java.math.*;
import coreservlets.Primes;

/**
 * SimplePrimeTag output a random 50-digit prime number
 * to the JSP page.
 */
public class SimplePrimeTag extends SimpleTagSupport {
  protected int length = 50;

  public void doTag() throws JspException, IOException {
    JspWriter out = getJspContext().getOut();
    BigInteger prime = Primes.nextPrime(Primes.random(length));
    out.print(prime);
  }
}
```

Now that we have our tag handler class, we need to describe our tag to the container. We do this using the TLD csajsp-taglib.tld shown in Listing 7.6. Because all our tag does is output a prime number, we don't need to allow the tag to include a body, and so we specify empty as the value of the body-content element. We place the csajsp-taglib.tld file in the WEB-INF/tlds folder.

Listing 7.6	Excerpt from csajsp-taglib.tld

```
<?xml version="1.0" encoding="UTF-8" ?>
<taglib xmlns="http://java.sun.com/xml/ns/j2ee"
  xmlns:xsi="http://www.w3.org/2001/XMLSchema-instance"
  xsi:schemaLocation="http://java.sun.com/xml/ns/j2ee
  http://java.sun.com/xml/ns/j2ee/web-jsptaglibrary_2_0.xsd"
  version="2.0">
  <tlib-version>1.0</tlib-version>
  <short-name>csajsp-taglib</short-name>

  <tag>
    <description>Outputs 50-digit primes</description>
    <name>simplePrime</name>
    <tag-class>coreservlets.tags.SimplePrimeTag</tag-class>
    <body-content>empty</body-content>
  </tag>
  ...
</taglib>
```

Listing 7.7 shows the simple-primes-1.jsp page, which uses the simple prime tag. We assign csajsp as the prefix for all tags (so far just simplePrime) in the /WEB-INF/tlds/csajsp-taglib.tld library. Also note that it is perfectly legal to use a closing tag with the body-content of empty as long as there is nothing, not even a space, between the opening tag and the closing tag, as shown by the last occurrence of the tag in the simple-primes-1.jsp page; that is, <csajsp:simple-Prime></csajsp:simplePrime>. The resulting output is shown in Figure 7–1.

Listing 7.7	simple-primes-1.jsp

```
<!DOCTYPE HTML PUBLIC "-//W3C//DTD HTML 4.0 Transitional//EN">
<HTML>
<HEAD>
<TITLE>Some 50-Digit Primes</TITLE>
<LINK REL=STYLESHEET
      HREF="JSP-Styles.css"
      TYPE="text/css">
</HEAD>
<BODY>
<H1>Some 50-Digit Primes</H1>
<%@ taglib uri="/WEB-INF/tlds/csajsp-taglib.tld"
           prefix="csajsp" %>
```

Listing 7.7	simple-primes-1.jsp *(continued)*

```
<UL>
  <LI><csajsp:simplePrime />
  <LI><csajsp:simplePrime />
  <LI><csajsp:simplePrime />
  <LI><csajsp:simplePrime></csajsp:simplePrime>
</UL>
</BODY></HTML>
```

Figure 7–1   Result of simple-primes-1.jsp.

7.3   Assigning Attributes to Tags

Allowing tags like

```
<prefix:name attribute1="value1" attribute2="value2"... />
```

adds significant flexibility to your tag library because the attributes allow us to pass information to the tag. This section explains how to add attribute support to your tags.

Tag Attributes: Tag Handler Class

Providing support for attributes is straightforward. Use of an attribute called attribute1 simply results in a call to a method called setAttribute1 in your class that extends SimpleTagSupport (or that otherwise implements the Simple-Tag interface). Consequently, adding support for an attribute named attribute1 is merely a matter of implementing the following method in your tag handler class:

```
public void setAttribute1(String value1) {
  doSomethingWith(value1);
}
```

Note that an attribute with the name of `attributeName` (lowercase a) corresponds to a method called `setAttributeName` (uppercase A).

One of the most common things to do in the attribute handler is to simply store the attribute in a field for later use by the `doTag` method. For example, the following is a code snippet of a tag implementation that adds support for the `message` attribute:

```
private String message = "Default Message";
public void setMessage(String message) {
  this.message = message;
}
```

If the tag handler is accessed from other classes, it is a good idea to provide a `getAttributeName` method in addition to the `setAttributeName` method. Only `setAttributeName` is required, however.

Tag Attributes: Tag Library Descriptor

Tag attributes must be declared inside the `tag` element by means of an `attribute` element. The `attribute` element has three nested elements that can appear between `<attribute>` and `</attribute>`.

- **name.** This is a required element that defines the case-sensitive attribute name.
- **required.** This is an optional element that stipulates whether the attribute must always be supplied, `true`, or is optional, `false` (default). If `required` is `false` and the JSP page omits the attribute, no call is made to the `setAttributeName` method, so be sure to give default values to the fields that the method sets if the attribute is not declared as required. Omitting a tag attribute, which is declared with the `required` element equal to `true`, results in an error at page translation time.
- **rtexprvalue.** This is an optional element that indicates whether the attribute value can be either a JSP scripting expression like `<%= expression %>` or JSP EL like `${bean.value}` (true), or whether it must be a fixed string (`false`). The default value is `false`, so this element is usually omitted except when you want to allow attributes to have values determined at request time. Note that even though it is never legal for the body of the tag to contain JSP scripting expressions like `<%= expression %>`, they are nevertheless legal as attribute values.

Tag Attributes: JSP File

As before, the JSP page has to declare the tag library using the `taglib` directive. This is done in the following form:

```
<%@ taglib uri="..." prefix="..." %>
```

The usage of the tag is very similar, except now we are able to specify a custom attribute as well. Remember that just like tag names, the attribute names are case-sensitive and have to appear in the JSP page exactly as they were declared inside the TLD file. Because custom tags are based on XML syntax, the value of an attribute has to be enclosed by either single or double quotes. For example:

```
<some-prefix:tag1 attribute1="value" />
```

7.4   Example: Prime Tag with Variable Length

In this example, we modify the previous prime number example, shown in Section 7.2 (Example: Simple Prime Tag), to provide an attribute for specifying the length of the prime number. Listing 7.8 shows the `PrimeTag` class, a subclass of `SimpleP-rimeTag` that adds support for the `length` attribute. This change is achieved by supplying an additional method, `setLength`. When this method is called, it attempts to convert its `String` argument into an `int` and store it in an instance variable `length`. If it fails, the originally initialized value for the instance variable `length` is used.

The TLD, shown in Listing 7.9, declares the optional attribute `length`. It is this declaration that tells the container to call the `setLength` method if the attribute `length` appears in the tag when it's used in the JSP page.

The JSP page, shown in Listing 7.10, declares the tag library with the `taglib` directive as before. However, now we are able to specify how long our prime number should be. If we omit the `length` attribute, the prime tag defaults to 50. Figure 7–2 shows the result of this page.

Listing 7.8   PrimeTag.java

```java
package coreservlets.tags;

/** PrimeTag outputs a random prime number
 *  to the JSP page. The length of the prime number is
 *  specified by the length attribute supplied by the JSP
 *  page. If not supplied, it defaults to 50.
 */
public class PrimeTag extends SimplePrimeTag {
  public void setLength(String length) {
    try {
      this.length = Integer.parseInt(length);
    } catch(NumberFormatException nfe) {
      // Do nothing as length is already set to 50
    }
  }
}
```

Listing 7.9   Excerpt from csajsp-taglib.tld

```xml
<?xml version="1.0" encoding="UTF-8" ?>
<taglib xmlns="http://java.sun.com/xml/ns/j2ee"
  xmlns:xsi="http://www.w3.org/2001/XMLSchema-instance"
  xsi:schemaLocation="http://java.sun.com/xml/ns/j2ee
  http://java.sun.com/xml/ns/j2ee/web-jsptaglibrary_2_0.xsd"
  version="2.0">
  <tlib-version>1.0</tlib-version>
  <short-name>csajsp-taglib</short-name>

  <tag>
    <description>Outputs an N-digit prime</description>
    <name>prime</name>
    <tag-class>coreservlets.tags.PrimeTag</tag-class>
    <body-content>empty</body-content>
    <attribute>
      <description>N (prime number length)</description>
      <name>length</name>
      <required>false</required>
    </attribute>
  </tag>
</taglib>
```

Listing 7.10   primes-1.jsp

```
<!DOCTYPE HTML PUBLIC "-//W3C//DTD HTML 4.0 Transitional//EN">
<HTML>
<HEAD>
<TITLE>Some N-Digit Primes</TITLE>
<LINK REL=STYLESHEET
      HREF="JSP-Styles.css"
      TYPE="text/css">
</HEAD>
<BODY>
<H1>Some N-Digit Primes</H1>
<%@ taglib uri="/WEB-INF/tlds/csajsp-taglib.tld"
           prefix="csajsp" %>
<UL>
  <LI>20-digit: <csajsp:prime length="20" />
  <LI>40-digit: <csajsp:prime length="40" />
  <LI>80-digit: <csajsp:prime length="80" />
  <LI>Default (50-digit): <csajsp:prime />
</UL>
</BODY></HTML>
```

Figure 7–2   Result of primes-1.jsp.

7.5   Including Tag Body in the Tag Output

Up to this point, all of the custom tags you have seen did not allow a body and thus were always used as standalone tags of the following form:

```
<prefix:tagname/>
<prefix:tagname></prefix:tagname>
```

Note that the second tag shown does not have any space between the opening and closing tags. The fact that these tags were not allowed to include a body was a direct result of supplying the element body-content with the value of empty.

In this section, we see how to define tags that use their body content and are thus written in the following matter:

```
<prefix:tagname>scriptless JSP content</prefix:tagname>
```

Tag Bodies: Tag Handler Class

Supporting tag bodies does not introduce any structural changes to the tag handler class. You still need to include setter methods for any attributes you are planning to declare and use. You still need to override the doTag method. To output the body content of the tag, inside the doTag method you need to acquire the JspFragment instance representing the body of the tag by calling the getJspBody method, then using its invoke method passing it null as its argument. Usually, this is done in a single step as follows:

```
getJspBody().invoke(null);
```

The container processes the JSP content found in the body of the tag just like any other JSP page content. If the invoke method is passed null as its argument, the resulting output of that JSP content is passed verbatim to the client. Therefore, the doTag method has no way of accessing the tag body output. All it can do is pass it along. We show how to access and modify the output of the tag body content before it's sent to the client in Section 8.1 (Manipulating Tag Body). It's important to stress, however, that it is the output resulting from the execution of the JSP code in the tag body, not the JSP code itself, that is passed to the client.

Core Note

When getJspBody().invoke(null) is called, it is the output resulting from the execution of the tag body's JSP content that gets passed to the client, not the JSP code itself.

In practice, you almost always output something before or after outputting the tag body as follows:

```
JspWriter out = getJspContext().getOut();
out.print("...");
getJspBody().invoke(null);
out.print("...");
```

Note that because sending the JSP content of the tag body boils down to a simple method invocation, it is very easy to create a tag that conditionally sends the JSP content to the client by surrounding the method call with an `if` statement. We show an example of this in Section 7.7 (Example: Debug Tag). It is also trivial to output the tag body content several times, as the method call can be placed inside a `for` loop and invoked many times. We show an example of this in Section 8.4 (Example: Simple Looping Tag).

Tag Bodies: Tag Library Descriptor

The change to the TLD is trivial. Instead of the value of `empty` for the required `body-content` element, we need to provide the value of `scriptless`.

Tag Bodies: JSP File

There are no changes to the JSP file. You still need to declare and assign a `prefix` to the TLD through the `taglib` directive. However, now we can use our tags with nonempty bodies.

Remember, however, that the `body-content` was declared as `scriptless`, and that `scriptless` means we are allowed to place JSP content into the body of the tag, but are not allowed to place JSP scriptlets there. So, the following is a legal usage of the tag:

```
<prefix:tagname>
  some content with ${bean.property}
</prefix:tagname>
```

The following would be illegal:

```
<prefix:tagname>
  some content with <%= bean.property %>
</prefix:tagname>
```

7.6 Example: Heading Tag

Listing 7.11 shows HeadingTag.java, which defines a tag for a heading element that is more flexible than the standard HTML H1 through H6 elements. (Yes, we know that the entire problem could be solved more elegantly with Cascading Style Sheets [CSS] and without the use of a custom tag, but this is for demonstration purposes only, so work with us.) This new element allows a precise font size, a list of preferred font names (the first entry that is available on the client system will be used), a foreground color, a background color, a border, and an alignment (LEFT, CENTER, RIGHT). Only the alignment capability is available with the H1 through H6 elements. The heading is implemented through use of a one-cell table enclosing a SPAN element that has embedded stylesheet attributes.

The doTag method first generates the <TABLE> and <SPAN> start tags, then invokes getJspBody().invoke(null) to instruct the system to include the tag body, and then generates the </SPAN> and </TABLE> tags. We use various setAttributeName methods to handle the attributes like bgColor and fontSize.

Listing 7.12 shows the excerpt from the csajsp-taglib.tld file that defines the heading tag. Listing 7.13 shows heading-1.jsp, which uses the heading tag. Figure 7–3 shows the resulting JSP page.

Listing 7.11 HeadingTag.java

```
package coreservlets.tags;
import javax.servlet.jsp.*;
import javax.servlet.jsp.tagext.*;
import java.io.*;

/** Heading tag allows the JSP developer to create
 *  a heading and specify alignment, background color,
 *  foreground color, font, etc. for that heading.
 */
public class HeadingTag extends SimpleTagSupport {
  private String align;
  private String bgColor;
  private String border;
  private String fgColor;
  private String font;
  private String size;

  public void setAlign(String align) {
    this.align = align;
  }
```

Listing 7.11   HeadingTag.java *(continued)*

```java
  public void setBgColor(String bgColor) {
    this.bgColor = bgColor;
  }
  public void setBorder(String border) {
    this.border = border;
  }
  public void setFgColor(String fgColor) {
    this.fgColor = fgColor;
  }
  public void setFont(String font) {
    this.font = font;
  }
  public void setSize(String size) {
    this.size = size;
  }

public void doTag() throws JspException, IOException {
    JspWriter out = getJspContext().getOut();
    out.print("<TABLE ALIGN=\"" + align + "\"\n" +
              "         BGCOLOR=\"" + bgColor + "\"\n" +
              "         BORDER=" + border + "\">\n");
    out.print("<TR><TH>");
    out.print("<SPAN STYLE=\"color: " + fgColor + ";\n" +
              "              font-family: " + font + ";\n" +
              "              font-size: " + size + "px; " +
              "\">\n");
    // Output content of the body
    getJspBody().invoke(null);
    out.println("</SPAN></TH></TR></TABLE>" +
                "<BR CLEAR=\"ALL\"><BR>");
  }
}
```

Listing 7.12   Excerpt from csajsp-taglib.tld

```xml
<?xml version="1.0" encoding="UTF-8" ?>
<taglib xmlns="http://java.sun.com/xml/ns/j2ee"
  xmlns:xsi="http://www.w3.org/2001/XMLSchema-instance"
  xsi:schemaLocation="http://java.sun.com/xml/ns/j2ee
  http://java.sun.com/xml/ns/j2ee/web-jsptaglibrary_2_0.xsd"
  version="2.0">
  <tlib-version>1.0</tlib-version>
  <short-name>csajsp-taglib</short-name>
```

Listing 7.12   Excerpt from csajsp-taglib.tld *(continued)*

```
<tag>
    <description>Formats enclosed heading</description>
    <name>heading</name>
    <tag-class>coreservlets.tags.HeadingTag</tag-class>
    <body-content>scriptless</body-content>
    <attribute>
      <name>align</name>
      <required>true</required>
    </attribute>
    <attribute>
      <name>bgColor</name>
      <required>true</required>
    </attribute>
    <attribute>
      <name>border</name>
      <required>true</required>
    </attribute>
    <attribute>
      <name>fgColor</name>
      <required>true</required>
    </attribute>
    <attribute>
      <name>font</name>
      <required>true</required>
    </attribute>
    <attribute>
      <name>size</name>
      <required>true</required>
    </attribute>
  </tag>
</taglib>
```

Listing 7.13   heading-1.jsp

```
<!DOCTYPE HTML PUBLIC "-//W3C//DTD HTML 4.0 Transitional//EN">
<HTML>
<HEAD><TITLE>Headings</TITLE>
<LINK REL=STYLESHEET
      HREF="JSP-Styles.css"
      TYPE="text/css">
</HEAD>
<BODY>
<%@ taglib uri="/WEB-INF/tlds/csajsp-taglib.tld"
           prefix="csajsp" %>
```

| Listing 7.13 | heading-1.jsp *(continued)* |

```
<csajsp:heading align="LEFT" bgColor="CYAN"
                border="10" fgColor="BLACK"
                font="Arial Black" size="78">
  First Heading
</csajsp:heading>

<csajsp:heading align="RIGHT" bgColor="RED"
                border="1" fgColor="YELLOW"
                font="Times New Roman" size="50">
  Second Heading
</csajsp:heading>

<csajsp:heading align="CENTER" bgColor="#C0C0C0"
                border="20" fgColor="BLUE"
                font="Arial Narrow" size="100">
  Third Heading
</csajsp:heading>
</BODY></HTML>
```

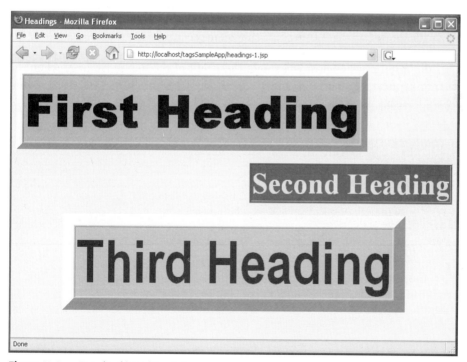

Figure 7–3   Result of heading-1.jsp.

7.7 Example: Debug Tag

In Section 7.5 (Including Tag Body in the Tag Output), we explained that to send the JSP content of the tag body to the client, one need only call the `getJsp-Body().invoke(null)` method inside the `doTag` method of the tag handler class. This simplicity allows us to easily create tags that output their bodies conditionally. This functionality can be achieved by simply surrounding the `getJsp-Body().invoke(null)` invocation within an `if` statement.

In this section, we present an example of a custom tag that conditionally outputs its tag body. It's quite often the case when the output of the JSP page is something other than what you expected. In such a case, it's useful to have the option of seeing some debugging information right on the page without having to resort to embedding `System.out.print` statements throughout the page. However, we do not want the user to see the debugging information in the production system. To solve this problem, we create a custom tag that conditionally outputs its body based on the presence of the `debug` request parameter. If the `debug` request parameter is present, it would signal to the JSP page to output the debugging information.

Listing 7.14 shows the `DebugTag.java` file. In its `doTag` method, we output the tag body if the `debug` request parameter is present and skip the body of the tag if it's not. Inside the JSP page, shown in Listing 7.16, we surround the debugging information with our `debug` tag. Listing 7.15 shows the excerpt from the **csajsp-taglib.tld** file declaring the `debug` tag to the container. Listing 7.16 shows the **debug.jsp** page that uses the `debug` tag. Figure 7–4 shows the result of the **debug.jsp** page when the `debug` request parameter is not present. Figure 7–5 shows the result of the **debug.jsp** page when the `debug` request parameter is supplied.

Listing 7.14	DebugTag.java

```
package coreservlets.tags;
import javax.servlet.jsp.*;
import javax.servlet.jsp.tagext.*;
import java.io.*;
import javax.servlet.http.*;

/**
 *  DebugTag outputs its body if the request parameter
 *  'debug' is present and skips it if it's not.
 */
```

Listing 7.14   DebugTag.java *(continued)*

```java
public class DebugTag extends SimpleTagSupport {
  public void doTag() throws JspException, IOException {
    PageContext context = (PageContext) getJspContext();
    HttpServletRequest request =
      (HttpServletRequest) context.getRequest();
    // Output body of tag only if debug param is present.
    if (request.getParameter("debug") != null) {
      getJspBody().invoke(null);
    }
  }
}
```

Listing 7.15   Excerpt from csajsp-taglib.tld

```xml
<?xml version="1.0" encoding="UTF-8" ?>
<taglib xmlns="http://java.sun.com/xml/ns/j2ee"
  xmlns:xsi="http://www.w3.org/2001/XMLSchema-instance"
  xsi:schemaLocation="http://java.sun.com/xml/ns/j2ee
  http://java.sun.com/xml/ns/j2ee/web-jsptaglibrary_2_0.xsd"
  version="2.0">
  <tlib-version>1.0</tlib-version>
  <short-name>csajsp-taglib</short-name>

  <tag>
    <description>Conditionally outputs enclosed body</description>
    <name>debug</name>
    <tag-class>coreservlets.tags.DebugTag</tag-class>
    <body-content>scriptless</body-content>
  </tag>
</taglib>
```

Listing 7.16   debug.jsp

```html
<!DOCTYPE HTML PUBLIC "-//W3C//DTD HTML 4.0 Transitional//EN">
<HTML>
<HEAD>
<TITLE>Some Hard-to-Debug Page</TITLE>
<LINK REL=STYLESHEET
      HREF="JSP-Styles.css"
      TYPE="text/css">
</HEAD>
```

Listing 7.16   debug.jsp *(continued)*

```
<BODY>
<H1>Some Hard-to-Debug Page</H1>
<%@ taglib uri="/WEB-INF/tlds/csajsp-taglib.tld"
          prefix="csajsp" %>
Top of regular page. Blah, blah, blah.
Yadda, yadda, yadda.
<csajsp:debug>
<H2>Debug Info:</H2>
********************<BR>
-Remote Host: ${pageContext.request.remoteHost}<BR>
-Session ID: ${pageContext.session.id}<BR>
-The foo parameter: ${param.foo}<BR>
********************<BR>
</csajsp:debug>
<P>
Bottom of regular page. Blah, blah, blah.
Yadda, yadda, yadda.
</BODY></HTML>
```

Figure 7–4   Result of **debug.jsp** page without supplying the debug request parameter.

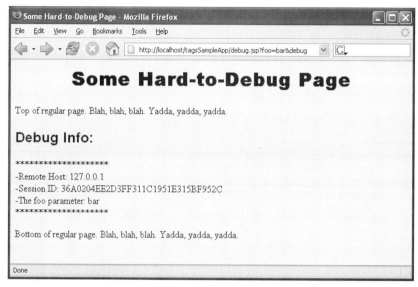

Figure 7–5   Result of **debug.jsp** page when the debug request parameter is supplied.

7.8   Creating Tag Files

JSP specification version 2.0 introduced a JSP-based way to create custom tags using tag files. One of the key differences between what we talk about in the beginning of this chapter, Java-based custom tags, and tag files (or JSP-based custom tags) is that with Java-based tags the tag handler is a Java class, whereas with JSP-based tags the tag handler is a JSP page. Tag files are also a bit simpler to write because they don't require you to provide a TLD.

The guidelines for when to develop a JSP-based custom tag versus a Java-based custom tag are analogous to the guidelines for when to use a JSP page versus a servlet. When there is a lot of logic, use Java to create output. When there is a lot of HTML formatting, use tag files to create output. To review the general benefits of JSPs versus servlets, please see Section 10.2 of Volume 1.

There is one caveat that might force your choice between tag files and Java-based custom tags. Tag files run only in JSP 2.0, whereas Java-based custom tags have a "classic" version that does not rely on the new `SimpleTag` API. So, if the container you are targeting is only compliant with earlier versions of the specification, you have to use classic Java-based custom tag development. The bad news is that classic

Java-based custom tag development is quite more complicated than the `SimpleTag` API and we do not cover classic tags in this book. The good news is that almost all mainstream containers have been updated to be compliant with servlet specification 2.4 and JSP specification 2.0, so chances are you won't need to develop the classic Java-based custom tags.

In general, there are two steps to creating a JSP-based custom tag.

- **Create a JSP-based tag file.** This file is a fragment of a JSP page with some special directives and a .tag extension. It must be placed inside the WEB-INF/tags directory or a subdirectory thereof.
- **Create a JSP page that uses the tag file.** The JSP page points to the directory where the tag file resides. The name of the tag file (minus the .tag extension) becomes the name of the custom tag and therefore no TLD connecting the implementation of the tag with its name is needed.

In the next few sections, we reproduce the same custom tags we developed earlier in this chapter, but we use tag files to accomplish it.

7.9 Example: Simple Prime Tag Using Tag Files

Let's rewrite the simple prime custom tag example using tag files. Listing 7.17 shows simplePrime2.tag. It consists of just one line invoking the static method `nextPrime` of the `Primes` class. The `Primes.java` file is shown in Listing 7.4. We place the simplePrime2.tag file into the WEB-INF/tags directory. Listing 7.18 shows simple-primes-2.jsp, which uses our JSP-based custom tag. Note that the `taglib` directive no longer has a `uri` attribute, but uses a `tagdir` attribute instead. This attribute tells the container which directory contains the tag files. Figure 7–6 shows the result of simple-primes-2.jsp.

Listing 7.17   simplePrime2.tag

```
<%= coreservlets.Primes.nextPrime
       (coreservlets.Primes.random(50)) %>
```

Listing 7.18 simple-primes-2.jsp

```
<!DOCTYPE HTML PUBLIC "-//W3C//DTD HTML 4.0 Transitional//EN">
<HTML>
<HEAD>
<TITLE>Some 50-Digit Primes</TITLE>
<LINK REL=STYLESHEET
      HREF="JSP-Styles.css"
      TYPE="text/css">
</HEAD>
<BODY>
<H1>Some 50-Digit Primes</H1>
<%@ taglib tagdir="/WEB-INF/tags" prefix="csajsp" %>
<UL>
  <LI><csajsp:simplePrime2 />
  <LI><csajsp:simplePrime2 />
  <LI><csajsp:simplePrime2 />
  <LI><csajsp:simplePrime2 />
</UL>
</BODY></HTML>
```

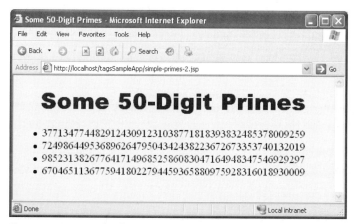

Figure 7–6   Result of simple-primes-2.jsp.

7.10 Example: Prime Tag with Variable Length Using Tag Files

In this section, we rewrite the example of Section 7.4 (Example: Prime Tag with Variable Length) with a JSP-based custom tag. To use attributes with a JSP-based custom tag, each attribute must be declared inside the tag file. This declaration is accomplished by the `attribute` directive. The `attribute` directive itself has attributes that provide the same information that the `attribute` subelements inside the TLD would provide. For example, you can specify whether an attribute is required or not by supplying a `required` attribute with a value of either `true` or `false`. When the value is passed through an attribute to the tag file, it is automatically stored into a scoped variable for access from the JSP EL and into a local variable for access from Java code (scriptlets and scripting expressions). Note once again that because the tag file has the ability to describe itself to the container, no TLD is required.

Listing 7.19 shows `prime2.tag` declaring an optional attribute called `length`. Note that we are able to refer to that attribute just like to any other local variable inside the Java code. The JSP page, `primes-2.jsp`, shown in Listing 7.20, uses our tag file to output prime numbers of different lengths. Figure 7–7 shows the result of `primes-2.jsp`.

Listing 7.19   prime2.tag

```
<%@ attribute name="length" required="false" %>
<%
int len = 50;
try {
  len = Integer.parseInt(length);
} catch(NumberFormatException nfe) {}
%>
<%= coreservlets.Primes.nextPrime
      (coreservlets.Primes.random(len)) %>
```

Listing 7.20   primes-2.jsp

```
<!DOCTYPE HTML PUBLIC "-//W3C//DTD HTML 4.0 Transitional//EN">
<HTML>
<HEAD>
<TITLE>Some N-Digit Primes</TITLE>
<LINK REL=STYLESHEET
      HREF="JSP-Styles.css"
      TYPE="text/css">
</HEAD>
<BODY>
<H1>Some N-Digit Primes</H1>
<%@ taglib tagdir="/WEB-INF/tags" prefix="csajsp" %>
<UL>
  <LI>20-digit: <csajsp:prime2 length="20" />
  <LI>40-digit: <csajsp:prime2 length="40" />
  <LI>80-digit: <csajsp:prime2 length="80" />
  <LI>Default (50-digit): <csajsp:prime2 />
</UL>
</BODY></HTML>
```

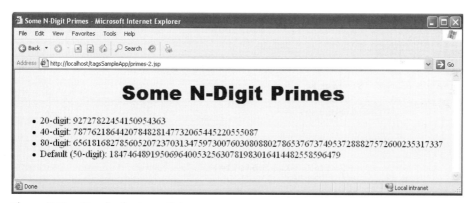

Figure 7–7   Result of primes-2.jsp.

7.11 Example: Heading Tag Using Tag Files

In this section, we rewrite the heading example of Section 7.6 (Example: Heading Tag) with a JSP-based custom tag. Outputting the tag body inside a tag file is as simple as providing a `<jsp:doBody/>` tag. That's it! No additional configurations, no TLD file, and the access to attributes is still the same simple process described in Section 7.10 (Example: Prime Tag with Variable Length Using Tag Files). Just place `<jsp:doBody/>` where you want the tag body to appear in the final output and you are done.

Listing 7.21 shows the `heading2.tag` file. It declares quite a number of required attributes and then proceeds to use them as regular scoped variables. We use `<jsp:doBody/>` to output the body of the tag to the client. Listing 7.22 shows the `headings-2.jsp` file, which uses the `heading2.tag` custom tag. Figure 7–8 shows the result of `headings-2.jsp`.

Listing 7.21 heading2.tag

```
<%@ attribute name="align" required="true" %>
<%@ attribute name="bgColor" required="true" %>
<%@ attribute name="border" required="true" %>
<%@ attribute name="fgColor" required="true" %>
<%@ attribute name="font" required="true" %>
<%@ attribute name="size" required="true" %>
<TABLE ALIGN="${align}"
       BGCOLOR="${bgColor}"
       BORDER="${border}">
  <TR><TH>
      <SPAN STYLE="color: ${fgColor};
                   font-family: ${font};
                   font-size: ${size}px;">
      <jsp:doBody/></SPAN>
</TABLE><BR CLEAR="ALL"><BR>
```

Listing 7.22 headings-2.jsp

```
<!DOCTYPE HTML PUBLIC "-//W3C//DTD HTML 4.0 Transitional//EN">
<HTML>
<HEAD><TITLE>Headings</TITLE>
<LINK REL=STYLESHEET
      HREF="JSP-Styles.css"
      TYPE="text/css">
</HEAD>
```

Listing 7.22   headings-2.jsp *(continued)*

```
<BODY>
<%@ taglib tagdir="/WEB-INF/tags" prefix="csajsp" %>
<csajsp:heading2 align="LEFT" bgColor="CYAN"
                 border="10" fgColor="BLACK"
                 font="Arial Black" size="78">
  First Heading
</csajsp:heading2>
<csajsp:heading2 align="RIGHT" bgColor="RED"
                 border="1" fgColor="YELLOW"
                 font="Times New Roman" size="50">
  Second Heading
</csajsp:heading2>
<csajsp:heading2 align="CENTER" bgColor="#C0C0C0"
                 border="20" fgColor="BLUE"
                 font="Arial Narrow" size="100">
  Third Heading
</csajsp:heading2>
</BODY></HTML>
```

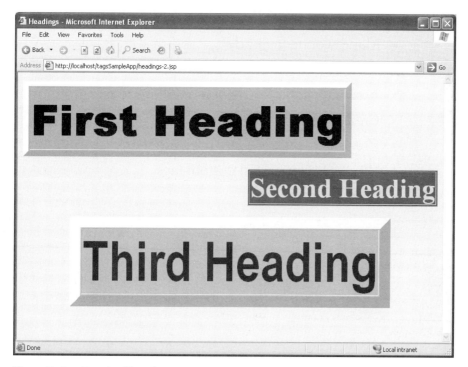

Figure 7–8   Result of headings-2.jsp.

TAG LIBRARIES: ADVANCED FEATURES

Topics in This Chapter

- Manipulating tag body
- Assigning dynamic values to tag attributes
- Assigning complex objects as values to tag attributes
- Creating looping tags
- Creating expression language functions
- Working with nested custom tags

Chapter 8

As we mention throughout the book, the JSP page should, under normal circumstances, contain no business logic of any kind. The JSP page is there to present the output of some business logic operation, nothing more. Crowding the JSP page with anything else makes it harder to write the code for the page and introduces maintenance headaches down the line. In other words, the JSP page should contain only the presentation logic.

However, it is quite often the case that the presentation logic itself is very complex and would require use of straightforward Java code to implement. Java code is something we try to avoid inside the JSP pages. What we want to do is write tag-based code inside the JSP pages and write the Java code inside regular Java classes. Java-based custom tags allow us to do just that.

In Chapter 7 (Tag Libraries: The Basics), we discussed the basics of creating and working with Java-based as well as JSP-based custom tags. In this chapter, we continue talking about Java-based custom tags while looking at some of the more advanced applications.

8.1 Manipulating Tag Body

In Section 7.5 (Including Tag Body in the Tag Output), we discussed how to include the body of the tag in the output of the Java-based custom tag. To review, there are essentially two things you need to do.

- Specify `scriptless` in the `body-content` element of the TLD for the tag. This allows the page author to insert JSP content between the opening and closing elements of the tag. Remember that this JSP content is not allowed to have any scripting elements like `<% ... %>` or `<%= ... %>`.
- Invoke the output of the tag body by calling `getJspBody().invoke(null)` inside the `doTag` method of the tag handler class. Remember that this statement passes the output of the JSP content to the client, not the actual JSP code itself.

The `invoke` method takes a `Writer` as its argument. If `null` is passed to the invoke method, the container directs the output of the tag body to the `JspWriter` object. The server obtains a reference to this object by calling methods similar to `getJspContext().getOut()`. In other words, the statements

```
getJspBody().invoke(null);
```

and

```
getJspBody().invoke(getJspContext().getOut());
```

accomplish exactly the same result.

This construct lets us pass a different `Writer` to the `invoke` method. Using the new `Writer`, we can buffer up the output of the JSP content, extract it from the `Writer`, manipulate it, and output the new content to the client.

The following are the steps of how this can be accomplished.

1. Create an instance of a convenient `Writer`. Any class that inherits from `java.io.Writer` class is acceptable. Because the output to the client is usually HTML, which is just a string, the `java.io.String-Writer` class is the most common `Writer` to use. For example:

   ```
   StringWriter myWriter = new StringWriter();
   ```

2. Pass the newly created `StringWriter` as an argument to the `invoke` method. For example:

   ```
   getJspBody().invoke(myWriter);
   ```

   Note that now the output of the tag body is not sent to the client but buffered up inside `myWriter`.

3. Extract the buffered output from the `Writer`, modify it, and send the modified version to the client like so:

```
String modified = modify(myWriter.toString());
getJspContext().getOut().print(modified);
```

8.2   Example: HTML-Filtering Tag

There are two types of tags in HTML that affect the style of the characters as they are rendered by the browsers: physical and logical style tag types. For example, the physical style tag `<b>` always means bold, but the logical tag `<strong>` can be bold or some other browser interpretation of strong.

In this example, we create a custom tag, `filterhtml`, that allows us to see our particular browser's interpretation of these logical style tags. We accomplish this task by creating a custom tag that filters out the HTML code, converting it to regular text, thus preventing the browser from interpreting it as HTML code. We are now able to see the actual unrendered HTML code alongside its rendered version, which is convenient for demonstration of this idea.

We define a tag handler class `HtmlFilterTag`, shown in Listing 8.1, which extends the `SimpleTagSupport` class. In its `doTag` method we pass a newly created `StringWriter` to the `getJspBody().invoke(stringWriter)` method and buffer up the output of the JSP content that the `filterhtml` tag surrounds. We extract the output from the `StringWriter`, modify it using the `ServletUtilities.filter` method, shown in Listing 8.2, and send the modified output to the client. We describe the tag to the container using the TLD csajsp-taglib-adv.tld. The excerpt of the `htmlfilter` tag TLD description is shown in Listing 8.3. The JSP page using the `htmlfilter` tag is shown in Listing 8.4. The result is shown in Figure 8–1.

| Listing 8.1 | HtmlFilterTag.java |

```
package coreservlets.tags;
import javax.servlet.jsp.*;
import javax.servlet.jsp.tagext.*;
import java.io.*;
import coreservlets.ServletUtilities;

/** Tag that replaces special HTML characters (like less than
 *  and greater than signs) with their HTML character entities.
 */
public class HtmlFilterTag extends SimpleTagSupport {
  public void doTag() throws JspException, IOException {
```

Listing 8.1 HtmlFilterTag.java *(continued)*

```
    // Buffer tag body's output
    StringWriter stringWriter = new StringWriter();
    getJspBody().invoke(stringWriter);

    // Filter out any special HTML characters
    // (e.g., "<" becomes "&lt;")
    String output =
      ServletUtilities.filter(stringWriter.toString());

    // Send output to the client
    JspWriter out = getJspContext().getOut();
    out.print(output);
  }
}
```

Listing 8.2 Excerpt from ServletUtilities.java

```
package coreservlets;
import javax.servlet.*;
import javax.servlet.http.*;

/** Some simple time-savers. Note that most are static methods.
 */
public class ServletUtilities {

  /** Replaces characters that have special HTML meanings
   *  with their corresponding HTML character entities.
   */
  public static String filter(String input) {
    if (!hasSpecialChars(input)) {
      return(input);
    }
    StringBuffer filtered = new StringBuffer(input.length());
    char c;
    for(int i=0; i<input.length(); i++) {
      c = input.charAt(i);
      switch(c) {
        case '<': filtered.append("&lt;"); break;
        case '>': filtered.append("&gt;"); break;
        case '"': filtered.append("&quot;"); break;
        case '&': filtered.append("&amp;"); break;
        default: filtered.append(c);
      }
    }
```

Listing 8.2   Excerpt from ServletUtilities.java *(continued)*

```
      return(filtered.toString());
  }

  private static boolean hasSpecialChars(String input) {
    boolean flag = false;
    if ((input != null) && (input.length() > 0)) {
      char c;
      for(int i=0; i<input.length(); i++) {
        c = input.charAt(i);
        switch(c) {
          case '<': flag = true; break;
          case '>': flag = true; break;
          case '"': flag = true; break;
          case '&': flag = true; break;
        }
      }
    }
    return(flag);
  }
}
```

Listing 8.3   Excerpt from csajsp-taglib-adv.tld

```
<?xml version="1.0" encoding="UTF-8" ?>
<taglib xmlns="http://java.sun.com/xml/ns/j2ee"
  xmlns:xsi="http://www.w3.org/2001/XMLSchema-instance"
  xsi:schemaLocation="http://java.sun.com/xml/ns/j2ee
  http://java.sun.com/xml/ns/j2ee/web-jsptaglibrary_2_0.xsd"
  version="2.0">

  <tlib-version>1.0</tlib-version>
  <short-name>csajsp-taglib-adv</short-name>
  <uri>http://coreservlets.com/csajsp-taglib-adv</uri>

  <tag>
    <description>
      Converts special HTML characters such as less than
      and greater than signs to their corresponding HTML
      character entities such as &lt; and &gt;.
    </description>
    <name>filterhtml</name>
    <tag-class>coreservlets.tags.HtmlFilterTag</tag-class>
    <body-content>scriptless</body-content>
  </tag>

</taglib>
```

Listing 8.4   html-filter.jsp

```
<!DOCTYPE HTML PUBLIC "-//W3C//DTD HTML 4.0 Transitional//EN">
<HTML>
<HEAD>
<TITLE>HTML Logical Character Styles</TITLE>
<LINK REL=STYLESHEET
      HREF="JSP-Styles.css"
      TYPE="text/css">
</HEAD>
<BODY>
<H1>HTML Logical Character Styles</H1>
Physical character styles (B, I, etc.) are rendered consistently
in different browsers. Logical character styles, however,
may be rendered differently by different browsers.
Here's how your browser renders the HTML 4.0 logical character
styles:
<P>
<TABLE BORDER=1 ALIGN="CENTER">
<TR CLASS="COLORED"><TH>Example<TH>Result

<%@ taglib uri="/WEB-INF/tlds/csajsp-taglib-adv.tld"
           prefix="csajsp" %>
<TR>
<TD><PRE><csajsp:filterhtml>
<EM>Some emphasized text.</EM><BR>
<STRONG>Some strongly emphasized text.</STRONG><BR>
<CODE>Some code.</CODE><BR>
<SAMP>Some sample text.</SAMP><BR>
<KBD>Some keyboard text.</KBD><BR>
<DFN>A term being defined.</DFN><BR>
<VAR>A variable.</VAR><BR>
<CITE>A citation or reference.</CITE>
</csajsp:filterhtml></PRE>

<TD>
<EM>Some emphasized text.</EM><BR>
<STRONG>Some strongly emphasized text.</STRONG><BR>
<CODE>Some code.</CODE><BR>
<SAMP>Some sample text.</SAMP><BR>
<KBD>Some keyboard text.</KBD><BR>
<DFN>A term being defined.</DFN><BR>
<VAR>A variable.</VAR><BR>
<CITE>A citation or reference.</CITE>

</TABLE>
</BODY></HTML>
```

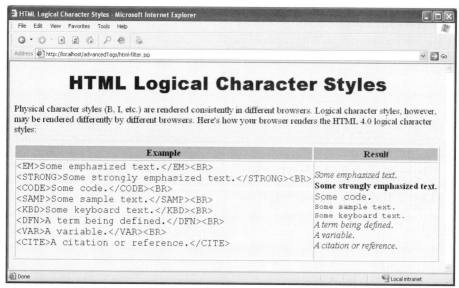

Figure 8–1   The HTML code on the left is shown unrendered by the browser because it was surrounded with the `filterhtml` tag, which converted the HTML tags to its text equivalent.

8.3 Assigning Dynamic Values to Tag Attributes

In Section 7.3 (Assigning Attributes to Tags), we discussed how to add attribute support to your custom tags. However, because of our setup we were limited to static strings as the values the JSP page was allowed to provide for those attributes. In this section, we show you how to change that so the author of the JSP page is free to pass dynamic values to your tag. In other words, we would like to be able to call our custom tag with a construct like the following:

```
<prefix:name attribute1="${bean.value}"
             attribute2="<%= bean.getValue() %>" />
```

Dynamic Attribute Values: Tag Handler Class

There is nothing that you need to do differently in the tag handler class for dynamic values than if the values for the attributes were just static strings placed into the page during development time. As far as the tag handler class is concerned, there is no difference. You still need to provide a setter method for the attribute in the form of setXxx(`String value`), where Xxx is the name of the attribute with the first character capitalized. So, if we have `attribute1` as our attribute in the tag, we would have to provide a setter method in the tag handler class like the following:

```
public void setAttribute1(String value1) {
  doSomethingWith(value1);
}
```

As before, the most common thing to do with the actual value in the setter method is to store it in a private instance variable for later use.

Dynamic Attribute Values: Tag Library Descriptor

As before, each attribute needs to be declared inside the TLD. However, because we want to allow the JSP author to specify dynamic (or runtime) expressions as values for the attributes, we must specify `rtexprvalue` to be `true`, like in the following:

```
<tag>
  <description>...</description>
  <name>mytag</name>
  <tag-class>package.TagHandler</tag-class>
  <body-content>...</body-content>
  <attribute>
    <description>...</description>
    <name>attribute1</name>
    <rtexprvalue>true</rtexprvalue>
  </attribute>
</tag>
```

Dynamic Attribute Values: JSP File

As before, the JSP page has to declare the tag library using the `taglib` directive. This is done in the following form:

```
<%@ taglib uri="..." prefix="..." %>
```

The usage of the tag is very much the same, except now you are able to specify JSP expressions as values for the attributes that are declared in the TLD with `rtexprvalue` of `true`. Note, however, that this does not mean that only JSP expressions are allowed to be placed as values for those attributes. Good old static string values, placed there during the authoring of the page, are still allowed. Also note that unlike the content of the tag body, the values of the attributes that accept runtime content are allowed to be JSP scripting expressions and JSP EL. In other words, the following tag, which combines JSP EL and JSP scripting expression, is perfectly legal.

```
<prefix:name attribute1="${bean.value}"
              attribute2="<%= bean.getValue() %>" />
```

8.4 Example: Simple Looping Tag

In this example, we create a simple `for` loop tag that outputs its tag body the number of times that the `count` attribute specifies. The `count` attribute is declared to accept runtime expressions, so we let its value be a JSP scripting expression that produces a random number every time the page is accessed.

Listing 8.5 shows the CoinBean.java class that produces a result of a random coin flip. Because we are allowed to use JSP EL inside the tag body, we use it to simulate a random number of coin flips inside the `for` loop by invoking its `getFlip()` method through the JSP EL notation `${coin.flip}`. This is exhibited in the simple-loop-test.jsp page, shown in Listing 8.8.

The ForTag.java class, shown in Listing 8.6, has a `setCount` method that stores the randomly produced value of the `count` attribute in the instance variable `count`. This value is then used in the `doTag` method as the number of times to loop the invocation code that outputs the tag body. Listing 8.7 shows the SimpleLoopTest.java class, which is the servlet mapped to `/simpleLoopTest` URL pattern in web.xml (Listing 8.9). The servlet creates an instance of the `CoinBean` class and stores it as a request scope attribute. The request is then dispatched to /WEB-INF/results/simple-loop-test.jsp, shown in Listing 8.8. Listing 8.10 shows an excerpt from csa-jsp-taglib-adv.tld, which defines the `for` tag. The result is shown in Figure 8–2.

Listing 8.5	CoinBean.java

```
package coreservlets;
import java.io.*;

/** Bean that represents a coin. It has a single method that
 *  simulates a random coin flip.
 */
public class CoinBean implements Serializable {
  public String getFlip() {
    if (Math.random() < 0.5) {
      return("Heads");
    } else {
      return("Tails");
    }
  }
}
```

Listing 8.6	ForTag.java

```java
package coreservlets.tags;
import javax.servlet.jsp.*;
import javax.servlet.jsp.tagext.*;
import java.io.*;

/** Simple for loop tag. It outputs the its tag body the
 *  number of times specified by the count instance
 *  variable.
 */
public class ForTag extends SimpleTagSupport {
  private int count;
  public void setCount(int count) {
    this.count = count;
  }
  public void doTag() throws JspException, IOException {
    for(int i=0; i<count; i++) {
      getJspBody().invoke(null);
    }
  }
}
```

Listing 8.7	SimpleLoopTest.java

```java
package coreservlets;
import java.io.*;
import javax.servlet.*;
import javax.servlet.http.*;

/** Simple servlet that creates a CoinBean bean, stores it
 *  in the request scope as an attribute, and forwards the
 *  request on to a JSP page. This servlet is used to
 *  demonstrate a simple looping tag.
 */
public class SimpleLoopTest extends HttpServlet {
  public void doGet(HttpServletRequest request,
                    HttpServletResponse response)
      throws ServletException, IOException {
    CoinBean coin = new CoinBean();
    request.setAttribute("coin", coin);
    String address =
      "/WEB-INF/results/simple-loop-test.jsp";
    RequestDispatcher dispatcher =
      request.getRequestDispatcher(address);
    dispatcher.forward(request, response);
  }
}
```

Listing 8.8 simple-loop-test.jsp

```
<!DOCTYPE HTML PUBLIC "-//W3C//DTD HTML 4.0 Transitional//EN">
<HTML>
<HEAD>
<TITLE>Simple Loop Test</TITLE>
<LINK REL=STYLESHEET
      HREF="JSP-Styles.css"
      TYPE="text/css">
</HEAD>
<BODY>
<H1>Simple Loop Test</H1>
<P>
<%@ taglib uri="/WEB-INF/tlds/csajsp-taglib-adv.tld"
           prefix="csajsp" %>
<H2>A Very Important List</H2>
<UL>
  <csajsp:for count="<%=(int)(Math.random()*10)%>">
    <LI>Blah
  </csajsp:for>
</UL>
<H2>Some Coin Flips</H2>
<UL>
  <csajsp:for count="<%=(int)(Math.random()*10)%>">
    <LI>${coin.flip}
  </csajsp:for>
</UL>
</BODY></HTML>
```

Listing 8.9 Excerpt from web.xml

```
<?xml version="1.0" encoding="ISO-8859-1"?>
<web-app xmlns="http://java.sun.com/xml/ns/j2ee"
         xmlns:xsi="http://www.w3.org/2001/XMLSchema-instance"
         xsi:schemaLocation=
         "http://java.sun.com/xml/ns/j2ee
          http://java.sun.com/xml/ns/j2ee/web-app_2_4.xsd"
         version="2.4">
  <servlet>
    <servlet-name>SimpleLoopTester</servlet-name>
    <servlet-class>coreservlets.SimpleLoopTest</servlet-class>
  </servlet>
  <servlet-mapping>
    <servlet-name>SimpleLoopTester</servlet-name>
    <url-pattern>/simpleLoopTest</url-pattern>
  </servlet-mapping>
</web-app>
```

Listing 8.10	Excerpt from csajsp-taglib-adv.tld

```xml
<?xml version="1.0" encoding="UTF-8" ?>
<taglib xmlns="http://java.sun.com/xml/ns/j2ee"
  xmlns:xsi="http://www.w3.org/2001/XMLSchema-instance"
  xsi:schemaLocation="http://java.sun.com/xml/ns/j2ee
  http://java.sun.com/xml/ns/j2ee/web-jsptaglibrary_2_0.xsd"
  version="2.0">
  <tlib-version>1.0</tlib-version>
  <short-name>csajsp-taglib-adv</short-name>
  <uri>http://coreservlets.com/csajsp-taglib-adv</uri>
  <tag>
    <description>
      Loops specified number of times.
    </description>
    <name>for</name>
    <tag-class>coreservlets.tags.ForTag</tag-class>
    <body-content>scriptless</body-content>
    <attribute>
      <description>
        Number of times to repeat body.
      </description>
      <name>count</name>
      <required>true</required>
      <rtexprvalue>true</rtexprvalue>
    </attribute>
  </tag>
</taglib>
```

Figure 8–2 Result of simple loop test. The number of times the word "blah" displays, as well as the number of simulated coin flips, is random.

8.5   Assigning Complex Objects as Values to Tag Attributes

In Section 8.3 (Assigning Dynamic Values to Tag Attributes), we showed how to set up your custom tag to accept dynamic values from the JSP page. After that setup, we are able to pass JSP EL as well as JSP scripting expressions as values of the tag attributes, like the following:

```
<prefix:name attribute1="${bean.value}"
             attribute2="<%= bean.getValue() %>" />
```

However, the value produced by `${bean.value}` was still just a string. What if you wanted to pass a `Collection` of `Orders` or some other complex object structure? What would we have to change to accommodate that?

Luckily, the answer to this question is: very little.

Complex Dynamic Attribute Values: Tag Handler Class

We still need to provide the setter for the attribute as before. However, the type of the argument in the setter would now be the complex object type instead of `String`, like the following:

```
public void setAttribute1(SomeComplexObject value1) {
  doSomethingWith(value1);
}
```

That's it! The container takes care of the rest. Again, as before, the most common thing to do with the actual value in the setter method is to store it in a private instance variable for later use.

Complex Dynamic Attribute Values: Tag Library Descriptor

The TLD stays the same as in Section 8.3 (Assigning Dynamic Values to Tag Attributes), making sure to provide the `rtexprvalue` element with a value of `true`, as follows:

```
<tag>
  <description>...</description>
  <name>mytag</name>
```

```
<tag-class>package.TagHandler</tag-class>
<body-content>...</body-content>
<attribute>
  <description>...</description>
  <name>attribute1</name>
  <rtexprvalue>true</rtexprvalue>
</attribute>
</tag>
```

Complex Dynamic Attribute Values: JSP File

As before, the JSP page has to declare the tag library using the `taglib` directive. This is done in the following form:

```
<%@ taglib uri="..." prefix="..." %>
```

The usage of the tag is very much the same as when we had dynamic values that were strings.

```
<prefix:name attribute1="${bean.value}"
            attribute2="<%= bean.getValue() %>" />
```

However, you must make sure that the type of the runtime expression is either the type declared in the setter method's argument or a subtype of that type. For example, if the setter method looks like this:

```
public void setAttribute1(SuperClass value1) {
  doSomethingWith(value1);
}
```

Then, inside the JSP page, the expression `${bean.value}` must evaluate to either an instance of `SuperClass` or an instance of any class that inherits from `SuperClass`. If the expression `${bean.value}` evaluates to anything else, the container-generated servlet code, produced as a result of this JSP page, will not compile because of the type mismatch.

8.6 Example: Table Formatting Tag

In this example, we list the three most recent swimming world records, as listed in the FINA (Fédération Internationale de Natation) database. To list the records, we employ the use of a custom table-formatting tag that lets the JSP author pass the entire record set to the tag as a two-dimensional array object.

We start off with the ShowRecords servlet, shown in Listing 8.11. This servlet is mapped inside web.xml (Listing 8.12) to the /showRecords URL. The servlet retrieves the records to be displayed using the WorldRecords class, shown in Listing 8.13. We store the records as a request scope attribute and forward the request to the show-records.jsp page shown in Listing 8.14. The show-records.jsp page utilizes the makeTable tag to display the records in a neatly formatted table. The tag handler class for this tag is MakeTableTag, which is shown in Listing 8.15. We declared the makeTable tag in the csajsp-taglib-adv.tld as shown in Listing 8.16. The result is shown in Figure 8–3.

Listing 8.11   ShowRecords.java

```
package coreservlets;

import java.io.*;
import javax.servlet.*;
import javax.servlet.http.*;

/** Servlet retrieves the records, stores them in the request
 *  scope, and forwards the request to show-records.jsp.
 */
public class ShowRecords extends HttpServlet {
  public void doGet(HttpServletRequest request,
                    HttpServletResponse response)
      throws ServletException, IOException {
    Object[][] records = WorldRecords.getRecentRecords();
    request.setAttribute("records", records);
    String address = "/WEB-INF/results/show-records.jsp";
    RequestDispatcher dispatcher =
      request.getRequestDispatcher(address);
    dispatcher.forward(request, response);
  }
}
```

Listing 8.12   Excerpt from web.xml

```xml
<?xml version="1.0" encoding="ISO-8859-1"?>
<web-app xmlns="http://java.sun.com/xml/ns/j2ee"
         xmlns:xsi="http://www.w3.org/2001/XMLSchema-instance"
         xsi:schemaLocation=
         "http://java.sun.com/xml/ns/j2ee
          http://java.sun.com/xml/ns/j2ee/web-app_2_4.xsd"
         version="2.4">
  <servlet>
    <servlet-name>RecordDisplayer</servlet-name>
    <servlet-class>coreservlets.ShowRecords</servlet-class>
  </servlet>
  <servlet-mapping>
    <servlet-name>RecordDisplayer</servlet-name>
    <url-pattern>/showRecords</url-pattern>
  </servlet-mapping>
</web-app>
```

Listing 8.13   WorldRecords.java

```java
package coreservlets;

/** This class simulates the retrieval of world records
 *  from the FINA database.
 */
public class WorldRecords {
  public static Object[][] getRecentRecords() {
    Object[][] records = {
      { "Event", "Name", "Time" },
      { "400 IM", "Michael Phelps", "4:08.25"},
      { "100 Br", "Lindsay Hall", "1:05.08"},
      { "200 IM", "Katie Hoff", "2:09.71"}};
    return(records);
  }
}
```

Listing 8.14   show-records.jsp

```
<!DOCTYPE HTML PUBLIC "-//W3C//DTD HTML 4.0 Transitional//EN">
<HTML>
<HEAD>
<TITLE>Recent World Records</TITLE>
<LINK REL=STYLESHEET
      HREF="JSP-Styles.css"
      TYPE="text/css">
</HEAD>
<BODY>
<H1>Recent World Records</H1>
Following are the three most recent swimming
world records, as listed in the FINA database.
<P>
<%@ taglib uri="/WEB-INF/tlds/csajsp-taglib-adv.tld"
           prefix="csajsp" %>
<CENTER>
<csajsp:makeTable rowItems="${records}"
                  headerClass="COLORED" />
</CENTER>
</BODY></HTML>
```

Listing 8.15   MakeTableTag.java

```java
package coreservlets.tags;

import javax.servlet.jsp.*;
import javax.servlet.jsp.tagext.*;
import java.io.*;

/** Tag handler class for the makeTable tag. It builds an
 *  HTML table and outputs the records of the two-dimensional
 *  array provided as one of the attributes of the tag in
 *  the JSP page.
 */
public class MakeTableTag extends SimpleTagSupport {
  private Object[][] rowItems;
  private String headerClass;
  private String bodyClass;

  public void setRowItems(Object[][] rowItems) {
    this.rowItems = rowItems;
  }
```

Listing 8.15   MakeTableTag.java *(continued)*

```java
  public void setHeaderClass(String headerClass) {
    this.headerClass = headerClass;
  }

  public void setBodyClass(String bodyClass) {
    this.bodyClass = bodyClass;
  }

  public void doTag() throws JspException, IOException {
    if (rowItems.length > 0) {
      JspContext context = getJspContext();
      JspWriter out = context.getOut();
      out.println("<TABLE BORDER=1>");
      Object[] headingRow = rowItems[0];
      printOneRow(headingRow, getStyle(headerClass), out);
      for(int i=1; i<rowItems.length; i++) {
        Object[] bodyRow = rowItems[i];
        printOneRow(bodyRow, getStyle(bodyClass), out);
      }
      out.println("</TABLE>");
    }
  }

 }
 private void printOneRow(Object[] columnEntries,
                          String style,
                          JspWriter out)
     throws IOException {
    out.println("  <TR" + style + ">");
    for(int i=0; i<columnEntries.length; i++) {
      Object columnEntry = columnEntries[i];
      out.println("    <TD>" + columnEntry + "</TD>");
    }
    out.println("  </TR>");
  }

  private String getStyle(String className) {
    if (className == null) {
      return("");
    } else {
      return(" CLASS=\"" + headerClass + "\"");
    }
  }
}
```

Listing 8.16   Excerpt from csajsp-taglib-adv.tld

```xml
<?xml version="1.0" encoding="UTF-8" ?>
<taglib xmlns="http://java.sun.com/xml/ns/j2ee"
  xmlns:xsi="http://www.w3.org/2001/XMLSchema-instance"
  xsi:schemaLocation="http://java.sun.com/xml/ns/j2ee
  http://java.sun.com/xml/ns/j2ee/web-jsptaglibrary_2_0.xsd"
  version="2.0">
  <tlib-version>1.0</tlib-version>
  <short-name>csajsp-taglib-adv</short-name>
  <uri>http://coreservlets.com/csajsp-taglib-adv</uri>

  <tag>
    <description>
      Given an array of arrays, puts values into a table
    </description>
    <name>makeTable</name>
    <tag-class>coreservlets.tags.MakeTableTag</tag-class>
    <body-content>scriptless</body-content>
    <attribute>
      <description>
        An array of arrays. The top-level arrays
        represents the rows, the sub-arrays represent
        the column entries.
      </description>
      <name>rowItems</name>
      <required>true</required>
      <rtexprvalue>true</rtexprvalue>
    </attribute>
    <attribute>
      <description>
        Style sheet class name for table header.
      </description>
      <name>headerClass</name>
      <required>false</required>
    </attribute>
    <attribute>
      <description>
        Style sheet class name for table body.
      </description>
      <name>bodyClass</name>
      <required>false</required>
    </attribute>
  </tag>
</taglib>
```

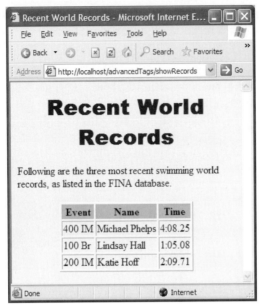

Figure 8–3   Result of `show-records.jsp`.

8.7   Creating Looping Tags

In Section 8.1 (Manipulating Tag Body), we discussed how to manipulate the content of the tag body. That approach boils down to buffering up all of the output of the JSP content surrounded by the tag, modifying it in some way, and sending the modified version to the client. But what if we wanted to control only a small part of the tag body with the rest of it unchanged?

Consider the following typical Java looping structure. In it, we use a `for` loop to iterate through an array of strings.

```
for (int i; i < someArray.length; i++) {
  System.out.print("Object at position " + i + "is: ");
  System.out.print(someArray[i]);
}
```

The looping index variable, `i`, is what makes each iteration through the loop unique. The `for` loop construct exposes the looping index `i` to its body. However, no code outside of the `for` loop body is able to access `i` because its scope is limited to the body of the loop, delimited by the curly braces.

This construct is very useful inside a JSP page as well. In this case, the looping structure would be the custom tag. This tag would create some bean with appropriate values and pass it to the JSP content inside the body of the tag. This is done inside the `doTag` method with the use of the `tag body` scope attribute. The `tag body` scope is similar to the `request` or `application` scope in nature, except that its attributes are only visible to the tag body. Any JSP code outside of the custom tag's beginning and ending elements would not be able to access it. You use the following code inside the `doTag` method to place an object as an attribute of the `tag body` scope:

```
getJspContext().setAttribute(key, object);
```

You then use JSP EL inside the body of the custom tag to access this attribute. This is no different than accessing any other scoped bean. You just have to remember that this attribute is not available outside the confines of the tag body.

```
<prefix:custom-tag>
  some text ${someBean.someValue}
</prefix:custom-tag>
```

When creating a looping tag, it is also very common to provide the author of the JSP page with an attribute they can set, which lets them pass the name of the attribute they will later access in the tag body; that is, let them specify the string value of the `key` argument that gets passed into `getJspContext().setAttribute(key, object)`. For example:

```
<mytags:for beanKeyValue="arrayValue" iterateOver="${someArray}">
  Value is: ${arrayValue}
</mytags:for>
```

Section 8.8 (Example: ForEach Tag) shows an example of creating a `foreach` looping tag that utilizes this approach.

8.8 Example: ForEach Tag

In this example, we create a `forEach` custom tag that can iterate over arrays of any objects. The array is passed to the tag handler class through the tag's `items` attribute. Because we are interested in outputting the contents of the array to the page, we let the users of our tag (i.e., the page authors) designate a key through which they can refer to the current element in the loop iteration inside the body of the tag. This feature makes the tag very generic in nature because we are no longer dictating how the output should look. We are not sending back any HTML from the tag, just the values. The page authors are free to represent the collection of data in the array any way they choose.

To demonstrate the usage of the forEach tag, we create a servlet called LoopTest, shown in Listing 8.17. This servlet creates two arrays. The first is a one-dimensional array containing names of J2EE Web servers. The second is a two-dimensional array we used in Section 8.6 (Example: Table Formatting Tag), containing recent world swimming records from the FINA database. We use the getRecentRecords method of the WorldRecords class (Listing 8.13) to populate the two-dimensional array. Once the arrays are created, they are placed into the request scope, and the request is forwarded onto the loop-test.jsp page, shown in Listing 8.18. The JSP page uses the forEach tag to loop through the two arrays. Note that in the case of the two-dimensional array, we are able to nest the looping tags just like we would in regular Java code. Using the var attribute of the forEach tag, we assign a key that we use to refer to the current element of the array inside the body of the tag as the elements of the array are being looped over.

The tag handler class of the forEach tag is implemented by the ForEachTag class, shown in Listing 8.19. The TLD definition of the forEach tag is listed in csajsp-taglib-adv.tld, shown in Listing 8.20. The servlet declaration and mapping is shown in the excerpt of the web.xml file of Listing 8.21. The resultant page is shown in Figure 8–4.

Listing 8.17 LoopTest.java

```java
package coreservlets;
import java.io.*;
import javax.servlet.*;
import javax.servlet.http.*;

/** This servlet creates two arrays and stores them in the
 *  request scope as attributes and forwards the request
 *  to the loop-test.jsp page.
 */
public class LoopTest extends HttpServlet {
  public void doGet(HttpServletRequest request,
                    HttpServletResponse response)
     throws ServletException, IOException {
    String[] servers =
      {"Tomcat", "Resin", "JRun", "WebLogic",
       "WebSphere", "Oracle 10g", "JBoss" };
    request.setAttribute("servers", servers);
    Object[][] records = WorldRecords.getRecentRecords();
    request.setAttribute("records", records);
    String address = "/WEB-INF/results/loop-test.jsp";
    RequestDispatcher dispatcher =
      request.getRequestDispatcher(address);
    dispatcher.forward(request, response);
  }
}
```

Listing 8.18 loop-test.jsp

```
<!DOCTYPE HTML PUBLIC "-//W3C//DTD HTML 4.0 Transitional//EN">
<HTML>
<HEAD>
<TITLE>Loop Test</TITLE>
<LINK REL=STYLESHEET
      HREF="JSP-Styles.css"
      TYPE="text/css">
</HEAD>
<BODY>
<H1>Loop Test</H1>
<P>
<%@ taglib uri="/WEB-INF/tlds/csajsp-taglib-adv.tld"
           prefix="csajsp" %>
<H2>Some Java-Based Servers</H2>
<UL>
  <csajsp:forEach items="${servers}" var="server">
    <LI>${server}
  </csajsp:forEach>
</UL>
<H2>Recent World Records</H2>
<TABLE BORDER=1>
<csajsp:forEach items="${records}" var="row">
  <TR>
  <csajsp:forEach items="${row}" var="col">
    <TD>${col}</TD>
  </csajsp:forEach>
  </TR>
</csajsp:forEach>
</TABLE>
</BODY></HTML>
```

Listing 8.19 ForEachTag.java

```
package coreservlets.tags;
import javax.servlet.jsp.*;
import javax.servlet.jsp.tagext.*;
import java.io.*;

/** This class is a tag handler class for the forEach custom
 *  tag. It is able to iterate over an array of objects.
 */
```

Listing 8.19   ForEachTag.java *(continued)*

```java
public class ForEachTag extends SimpleTagSupport {
  private Object[] items;
  private String attributeName;

  public void setItems(Object[] items) {
    this.items = items;
  }

  public void setVar(String attributeName) {
    this.attributeName = attributeName;
  }

  public void doTag() throws JspException, IOException {
    for(int i=0; i<items.length; i++) {
      getJspContext().setAttribute(attributeName, items[i]);
      getJspBody().invoke(null);
    }
  }
}
```

Listing 8.20   Excerpt from csajsp-taglib-adv.tld

```xml
<?xml version="1.0" encoding="UTF-8" ?>
<taglib xmlns="http://java.sun.com/xml/ns/j2ee"
  xmlns:xsi="http://www.w3.org/2001/XMLSchema-instance"
  xsi:schemaLocation="http://java.sun.com/xml/ns/j2ee
  http://java.sun.com/xml/ns/j2ee/web-jsptaglibrary_2_0.xsd"
  version="2.0">
  <tlib-version>1.0</tlib-version>
  <short-name>csajsp-taglib-adv</short-name>
  <uri>http://coreservlets.com/csajsp-taglib-adv</uri>

  <tag>
    <description>
      Loops down each element in an array
    </description>
    <name>forEach</name>
    <tag-class>coreservlets.tags.ForEachTag</tag-class>
    <body-content>scriptless</body-content>
    <attribute>
      <description>
        The array of elements.
      </description>
    </attribute>
```

Listing 8.20 Excerpt from csajsp-taglib-adv.tld *(continued)*

```
      <name>items</name>
      <required>true</required>
      <rtexprvalue>true</rtexprvalue>
    </attribute>
    <attribute>
      <description>
        The name of the scoped variable to which
        each entry is assigned.
      </description>
      <name>var</name>
      <required>true</required>
    </attribute>
  </tag>
</tablib>
```

Listing 8.21 Excerpt from web.xml

```
<?xml version="1.0" encoding="ISO-8859-1"?>
<web-app xmlns="http://java.sun.com/xml/ns/j2ee"
         xmlns:xsi="http://www.w3.org/2001/XMLSchema-instance"
         xsi:schemaLocation=
         "http://java.sun.com/xml/ns/j2ee
          http://java.sun.com/xml/ns/j2ee/web-app_2_4.xsd"
         version="2.4">
  <servlet>
    <servlet-name>LoopTester</servlet-name>
    <servlet-class>coreservlets.LoopTest</servlet-class>
  </servlet>
  <servlet-mapping>
    <servlet-name>LoopTester</servlet-name>
    <url-pattern>/loopTest</url-pattern>
  </servlet-mapping>
</web-app>
```

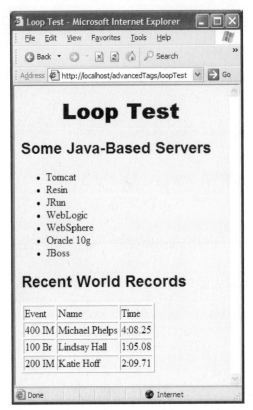

Figure 8–4   Resultant view of the page that uses the `foreach` custom tag.

8.9   Creating Expression Language Functions

In Section 7.7 (Example: Debug Tag), we showed an example of creating a `debug` tag. This simple tag surrounds some debugging information inside the JSP page. If the `debug` request parameter is present, the contents of the `debug` tag are allowed to be processed and output to the JSP page. This provides a very convenient mechanism for outputting debugging information while developing a Web page.

There is, however, one pretty significant limitation to our `debug` tag. As with all custom tags based on the `SimpleTag` API, the body of the tag is not allowed to contain any JSP scripting. The only way we can output something is through JSP EL, which requires that the object has bean-like getter methods. No doubt, we can create such a bean in the `doTag` method of the `debug` tag handler class, but this would require us to update the tag handler class code every time we need to output some new debugging information or modify the current output. Furthermore, we would like to reuse the same `debug` tag on multiple JSP pages. Placing the information we want to see for one page into the tag handler class would require us to create multiple `debug` tags for different JSP pages. In other words, the `debug` tag would be very tightly coupled with the particular JSP page.

There are two sensible solutions to this dilemma. One would involve the usage of nested custom tags. The nested custom tag would output the debugging information specific to one JSP page. If the inner custom tag does not need to communicate with the outer custom tag, there wouldn't be anything different you would need to do to create it from what we discussed throughout Chapter 7 (Tag Libraries: The Basics). You still need to implement a tag handler class, declare the tag in some TLD, and use it inside the JSP page. The situation where the inner tag needs to communicate with the outer tag and vice versa is discussed in Section 8.11 (Handling Nested Custom Tags).

The second solution, and the topic of this section, is to use an EL function. EL functions are a new feature to the JSP specification 2.0. EL functions allow the developer to call a static method inside the JSP page, but instead of using JSP scripting to do it, which is illegal inside the tag body, EL functions allow the developer to use EL notation to invoke the function. Inside the JSP page, an EL function invocation would look like the following:

```
${prefix:someFunction(package.ClassName argument)}
```

The steps for creating an EL function are very similar to those required to create a custom Java-based tag.

1. **Create a class with a** `public static` **method.** This class should be placed into the WEB-INF/classes directory just like any servlet, filter, and so on. If this class has to come as part of a JAR file, the JAR file has to be placed inside the WEB-INF/lib directory. The return type of the method can be any type, but usually it is either a `String` or void.

```
public class SomeClass {
  public static void someMethod() {...}
}
```

2. **Declare the method inside a TLD file.** This step is very similar to declaring a tag inside a TLD file. The fully qualified class name and one of its methods gets mapped to some name that will be used inside the JSP page to invoke that method. However, instead of the `tag` element, which declares a tag, EL functions use the `function` element and its related elements as follows:

```
<function>
  <name>run</name>
  <function-class>somePackage.SomeClass</function-class>
  <function-signature>void someMethod()</function-signature>
</function>
```

There are a couple of things that are important to emphasize here. The value of the `function-class` element must be the fully qualified name of the Java class that implements the method. The value of the `function-signature` element should contain the signature of the method with all the specified types using their fully qualified class notation. In other words, if `someMethod` takes an argument of type `String`, the TLD must use `java.lang.String` to declare it, as follows:

```
. . .
<function-signature>
  void someMethod(java.lang.String)
</function-signature>
. . .
```

Core Warning

The values of `function-class` *and* `function-signature` *have to contain fully qualified Java classes.*

3. **Declare tag library inside the JSP page.** This step is identical to declaring a TLD that contains declarations of custom tags exclusively. Just like before you use the `taglib` directive, assign a prefix to be used throughout the JSP page. For example:

```
<%@ taglib prefix="myfunc" uri="someURI" %>
```

4. **Use JSP EL to invoke the method.** The invocation of the method is done in the following form:

```
${myfunc:run()}
```

The `myfunc` part is the prefix that comes from the `taglib` declaration mentioned in Step 3. The `run` part comes from the name element inside the `function` element declaration in the TLD. Note that the function name used inside the JSP page does not have to be the same as the method name inside the implementing class.

8.10 Example: Improved Debug Tag

In Section 7.7 (Example: Debug Tag), we introduced a debug tag. To review, the debug tag lets us output part of the JSP page designated as debugging information. If one of the request parameters sent to the page is debug, the contents of the JSP page containing the debugging information, which are surrounded by the debug tag, are allowed to be output to the client. If no debug request parameter is present, the page executes without outputting the debugging information.

However, because the debugging information is inside a custom tag, we are very limited in the type of content we are allowed to output. Namely, we are only allowed to use JSP EL. For example, we can't use JSP scripting to invoke a utility method. However, now that we know how to use JSP EL functions, we can get around this limitation.

The debug tag itself does not need to be changed at all. Therefore, in this example, the DebugTag class, shown in Listing 8.22, remains unchanged. Instead, we define a Util class (Listing 8.23) with a public static method called information. We map this method inside the csajsp-taglib-adv.tld file (Listing 8.24) to a JSP EL function named info. Then, we are able to use JSP EL inside the debug.jsp page (Listing 8.25) to invoke the info function as part of the debug tag body. Figure 8–5 shows the result of invoking the debug.jsp page with a number of request parameters.

Listing 8.22 DebugTag.java

```
package coreservlets.tags;
import javax.servlet.jsp.*;
import javax.servlet.jsp.tagext.*;
import java.io.*;
import javax.servlet.http.*;

/** DebugTag outputs its body if the request parameter
 *  'debug' is present and skips it if it's not.
 */
public class DebugTag extends SimpleTagSupport {
  public void doTag() throws JspException, IOException {
    PageContext context = (PageContext)getJspContext();
    HttpServletRequest request =
      (HttpServletRequest)context.getRequest();
    // Output body of tag only if debug param is present.
    if (request.getParameter("debug") != null) {
      getJspBody().invoke(null);
    }
  }
}
```

Listing 8.23   Util.java

```java
package coreservlets.jsp;
import java.util.Enumeration;
import javax.servlet.http.HttpServletRequest;

/** Utility class whose method is used as an JSP EL function. */
public class Util {
  public static String information(HttpServletRequest request) {
    String result = "";
    result += "Agent Header: " + request.getHeader("User-Agent");
    result += "<BR>";
    result += "Parameters:<BR>";
    Enumeration paramNames = request.getParameterNames();
    while (paramNames.hasMoreElements()) {
        String paramName = (String) paramNames.nextElement();
        result += paramName + "<BR>";
    }
    return result;
  }
}
```

Listing 8.24   Excerpt from csajsp-tablib-adv.tld

```xml
<?xml version="1.0" encoding="UTF-8" ?>
<taglib xmlns="http://java.sun.com/xml/ns/j2ee"
  xmlns:xsi="http://www.w3.org/2001/XMLSchema-instance"
  xsi:schemaLocation="http://java.sun.com/xml/ns/j2ee
  http://java.sun.com/xml/ns/j2ee/web-jsptaglibrary_2_0.xsd"
  version="2.0">
  <tlib-version>1.0</tlib-version>
  <short-name>csajsp-taglib-adv</short-name>
  <uri>http://coreservlets.com/csajsp-taglib-adv</uri>

  <tag>
    <description>Conditionally outputs debug info</description>
    <name>debug</name>
    <tag-class>coreservlets.tags.DebugTag</tag-class>
    <body-content>scriptless</body-content>
  </tag>
```

Listing 8.24   Excerpt from csajsp-tablib-adv.tld *(continued)*

```
<function>
  <name>info</name>
  <function-class>coreservlets.jsp.Util</function-class>
  <function-signature>
    java.lang.String
    information(javax.servlet.http.HttpServletRequest)
  </function-signature>
</function>
</taglib>
```

Listing 8.25   debug.jsp

```
<!DOCTYPE HTML PUBLIC "-//W3C//DTD HTML 4.0 Transitional//EN">
<HTML>
<HEAD>
<TITLE>Some Hard-to-Debug Page</TITLE>
<LINK REL=STYLESHEET
      HREF="JSP-Styles.css"
      TYPE="text/css">
</HEAD>
<BODY>
<H1>Some Hard-to-Debug Page</H1>
<%@ taglib uri="/WEB-INF/tlds/csajsp-taglib-adv.tld"
           prefix="csajsp" %>
Top of regular page. Blah, blah, blah.
Yadda, yadda, yadda.
<csajsp:debug>
<H2>Debug Info:</H2>
********************<BR>
-Remote Host: ${pageContext.request.remoteHost}<BR>
-Session ID: ${pageContext.session.id}<BR>
-${csajsp:info(pageContext.request)}
********************<BR>
</csajsp:debug>
<P>
Bottom of regular page. Blah, blah, blah.
Yadda, yadda, yadda.
</BODY></HTML>
```

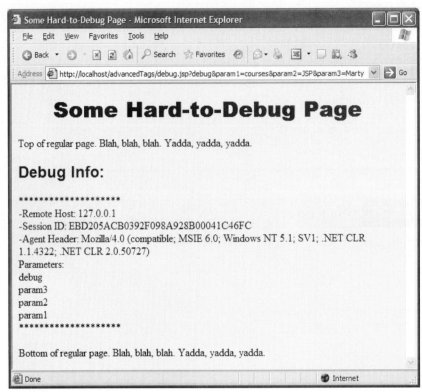

Figure 8–5   Result of invoking the debug.jsp page, specifying the debug request parameter.

8.11 Handling Nested Custom Tags

So far we have seen custom tags whose bodies contained ordinary JSP content. Of course, as discussed in Section 7.5 (Including Tag Body in the Tag Output), we take care to use only JSP EL and EL functions in the tag body. However, the tag body of a custom tag can also contain other custom tags, as follows:

```
<prefix:tagOuter>
  <prefix:tagInner>
  ...
  </prefix:tagInner>
</prefix:tagOuter>
```

Note that, just like in XML, the inner tag has to be closed before the outer tag. There is really nothing different about constructing these tags if the inner tag and outer tags don't depend on each other; that is, the inner tag can appear some other place without the presence of the outer tag and vice versa, and neither tag needs to share data with the other. However, frequently, these tags need to interact in some way. The `SimpleTag` API provides two methods that let an inner tag get a hold of the outer tag. The first method is `getParent()`. It is called on the instance of the inner tag. It returns an object of type `JspTag`, which can be cast to the type of the outer tag's handler class. If this method is called on the most outer tag in the hierarchy, it returns `null`.

Although you can keep calling the `getParent` method over and over until you either reach the tag instance you are seeking or `null`, if at the top of the tag hierarchy, the `SimpleTag` API provides another convenient method that lets you avoid repeat calls with `getParent()`. This is a static method that is provided as part of the `SimpleTagSupport` class called `findAncestorWithClass(JspTag fromTag, Class toBeMatchedClass)`. This method starts searching the hierarchy of tags from a given tag instance, `fromTag`, looking at its parent tag up until it finds a tag instance that matches the type of `toBeMatchedClass`. If the search takes it all the way to the top of the hierarchy with no results, it returns `null`. If this method finds the right instance of the tag class, it returns it as a `JspTag` instance, which needs to be cast to the proper type. There is another advantage to using the `findAncestorWithClass` method over the `getParent` method. With the `get-Parent` method, you need to anticipate a `ClassCastException` because you don't know the parent tag's type in advance. With `findAncestorWithClass`, however, this is not an issue. If it returns anything other than `null`, you are guaranteed that that you can successfully cast down the instance it returns using the class type that was passed in as a second argument to the `findAncestorWithClass` method.

So, if you are working inside of some inner tag, you have a way to get at the outer tag instance. What about the other way around? What method does the API provide to get at the inner tag from the outer tag? None.

If you remember our discussion about the tag life cycle from Section 7.1 (Tag Library Components), this should make perfect sense. Remember that a new instance of the tag handler class is created for every tag occurrence on the page. This rule means that after completing the instantiation of the outer tag, the inner tag instance doesn't yet exist. It would therefore be impossible to create a method that gets a hold of an instance that hasn't been created yet.

All these reasons are great, but the question still remains: How do we get the outer tags to communicate with the inner tags? The answer is to store some information in the outer tag that the inner tag can later retrieve and act on, as follows:

```
public class OuterTag extends SimpleTagSupport {
    public void setSomeValue(SomeClass arg) { ... }
    public SomeClass getSomeValue() { ... }
```

```
  public void doTag() { ... }
}

public class InnerTag extends SimpleTagSupport {
  public int doTag() throws JspException, IOException {
    OuterTag parent =
      (OuterTag)findAncestorWithClass(this, OuterTag.class);
    if (parent == null) {
      throw new JspTagException("nesting error");
    }
    SomeClass value = parent.getSomeValue();
    DoSomethingWithValue(value);
  }
  ...
}
```

Similarly, an inner tag can affect other inner tags by getting a hold of an instance of the outer tag and setting some value in it that can later be read by some other inner tag and dealt with accordingly.

8.12 Example: If-Then-Else Tag

In this example, we are going to create three custom tags: if, then, and else. Obviously, these tags have to work together to produce a meaningful result. The if tag has an attribute, test, that evaluates to true or false. This condition is stored in an instance variable of the IfTag class, shown in Listing 8.26, for which we provide the required setter method as well as the getter method. These methods are used by the nested tag handler classes.

The then tag gets a hold of the if tag instance, acquires the test attribute value, and allows its body to be processed if the value is true. The else tag also gets a hold of the if tag instance and reads the test attribute value, but allows its body to be processed if the value is false. In both ThenTag and ElseTag classes, shown in Listing 8.27 and Listing 8.28, we make sure that the result of the getParent method is actually an instance of the IfTag class. If the call to the getParent method does not return an instance of the IfTag class, a ClassCastException will occur. This means that the author of the JSP page made a mistake in the nesting order. We catch the ClassCastException and rethrow it as a JspTagException with the appropriate message. Likewise, the getParent method will return null if either the then or the else tags are outside of the if tag. Again, in such a case, we throw a JspTagException.

Note that in our example we use the `getParent` method and not the `find-AncestorWithClass` method. In the case of the `if-then-else` construct, it is not appropriate to have other custom tags in the tag hierarchy between either the `then` or `else` tags and the `if` tag. If we used the `findAncestorWith-Class` method, it would return an instance of the `if` tag even if it wasn't a direct parent of either the `then` or `else` tags. Therefore, its use in our example would be inappropriate.

The declaration of these tags is inside the csajsp-tablib-adv.tld file shown in Listing 8.29. We use the if-test.jsp file, shown in Listing 8.30, to demonstrate their use. The result is shown in Figure 8–6.

Listing 8.26   IfTag.java

```
package coreservlets.tags;
import javax.servlet.jsp.*;
import javax.servlet.jsp.tagext.*;
import java.io.*;

/** Tag handler class for the if tag. It relies on the
 *  required 'test' attribute and stores the evaluated
 *  condition in the test instance variable to be later
 *  accessed by the ThenTag.java and ElseTag.java.
 */
public class IfTag extends SimpleTagSupport {
  private boolean test;

  public void setTest(boolean test) {
    this.test = test;
  }

  public boolean getTest() {
    return(test);
  }

  public void doTag() throws JspException, IOException {
    getJspBody().invoke(null);
  }
}
```

Listing 8.27 ThenTag.java

```java
package coreservlets.tags;
import javax.servlet.jsp.*;
import javax.servlet.jsp.tagext.*;
import java.io.*;

/** Tag handler class for the then tag. It gets a hold of
 *  the IfTag instance and processes its body if the value
 *  test attribute of the IfTag is true. It also throws
 *  a JspTagException if the parent of this tag is anything
 *  other than an instance of the IfTag class.
 */
public class ThenTag extends SimpleTagSupport {
  public void doTag() throws JspException, IOException {
    // Get parent tag (if tag)
    IfTag ifTag = null;
    try {
      ifTag = (IfTag)getParent();
    }
    catch (ClassCastException cce) {
      String msg = "Error: 'then' must be inside 'if'.";
      throw new JspTagException(msg);
    }
    if (ifTag != null) {
      // Decide whether to output body of then
      if (ifTag.getTest()) {
        getJspBody().invoke(null);
      }
    } else {
      String msg = "Error: 'then' must be inside 'if'.";
      throw new JspTagException(msg);
    }
  }
}
```

Listing 8.28 ElseTag.java

```java
package coreservlets.tags;
import javax.servlet.jsp.*;
import javax.servlet.jsp.tagext.*;
import java.io.*;
```

Listing 8.28 ElseTag.java *(continued)*

```java
/** Tag handler class for the else tag. It gets a hold of
 *  the IfTag instance and processes its body if the value
 *  test attribute of the IfTag is false. It also throws
 *  a JspTagException if the parent of this tag is anything
 *  other than an instance of the IfTag class.
 */
public class ElseTag extends SimpleTagSupport {
  public void doTag() throws JspException, IOException {
    // Get parent tag (if tag)
    IfTag ifTag = null;
    try {
      ifTag = (IfTag)getParent();
    }
    catch (ClassCastException cce) {
      String msg = "Error: 'else' must be inside 'if'.";
      throw new JspTagException(msg);
    }
    if (ifTag != null) {
      // Decide whether to output body of else
      if (!ifTag.getTest()) {
        getJspBody().invoke(null);
      }
    } else {
      String msg = "Error: 'else' must be inside 'if'.";
      throw new JspTagException(msg);
    }
  }
}
```

Listing 8.29 Excerpt from csajsp-taglib-adv.tld

```xml
<?xml version="1.0" encoding="UTF-8" ?>
<taglib xmlns="http://java.sun.com/xml/ns/j2ee"
  xmlns:xsi="http://www.w3.org/2001/XMLSchema-instance"
  xsi:schemaLocation="http://java.sun.com/xml/ns/j2ee
  http://java.sun.com/xml/ns/j2ee/web-jsptaglibrary_2_0.xsd"
  version="2.0">
  <tlib-version>1.0</tlib-version>
  <short-name>csajsp-taglib-adv</short-name>
  <uri>http://coreservlets.com/csajsp-taglib-adv</uri>
```

Listing 8.29   Excerpt from csajsp-taglib-adv.tld *(continued)*

```
<tag>
  <description>If tag</description>
  <name>if</name>
  <tag-class>coreservlets.tags.IfTag</tag-class>
  <body-content>scriptless</body-content>
  <attribute>
    <description>Condition of the if</description>
    <name>test</name>
    <required>true</required>
    <rtexprvalue>true</rtexprvalue>
  </attribute>
</tag>
<tag>
  <description>Then tag (goes with If tag)</description>
  <name>then</name>
  <tag-class>coreservlets.tags.ThenTag</tag-class>
  <body-content>scriptless</body-content>
</tag>
<tag>
  <description>Else tag (goes with If tag)</description>
  <name>else</name>
  <tag-class>coreservlets.tags.ElseTag</tag-class>
  <body-content>scriptless</body-content>
</tag>
</taglib>
```

Listing 8.30   if-test.jsp

```
<!DOCTYPE HTML PUBLIC "-//W3C//DTD HTML 4.0 Transitional//EN">
<HTML>
<HEAD>
<TITLE>If Test</TITLE>
<LINK REL=STYLESHEET
      HREF="JSP-Styles.css"
      TYPE="text/css">
</HEAD>
<BODY>
<H1>If Test</H1>
<P>
<%@ taglib uri="/WEB-INF/tlds/csajsp-taglib-adv.tld"
           prefix="csajsp" %>
```

Listing 8.30	if-test.jsp *(continued)*

```
<H2>SSL Usage</H2>
<csajsp:if
    test="${pageContext.request.protocol==https}">
  <csajsp:then>Using SSL.</csajsp:then>
  <csajsp:else>Not using SSL.</csajsp:else>
</csajsp:if>
<H2>Coin Tosses</H2>
<UL>
  <csajsp:for count="5">
    <LI><csajsp:if test="<%=Math.random()<0.5%>">
        <csajsp:then>Heads</csajsp:then>
        <csajsp:else>Tails</csajsp:else>
      </csajsp:if>
  </csajsp:for>
</UL>
</BODY></HTML>
```

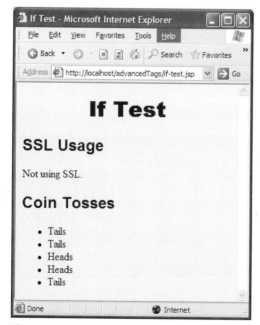

Figure 8–6   Result of if-test.jsp.

JSP Standard Tag Library (JSTL)

Topics in This Chapter

- Installing JSP Standard Tag Library (JSTL)
- out Tag
- forEach and forTokens Tags
- if Tag
- choose, when, and otherwise Tags
- set and remove Tags
- import Tag
- url and param Tags
- redirect Tag
- catch Tag

Chapter 9

It's easy to see why the standard JSP actions and JSP EL are usually not powerful enough when it comes to implementing a complex presentation logic. They lack basic features such as looping and storing scoped variables, and they have limited conditional logic, among many others. However, the ability to create custom tags and functions more than compensates for this drawback.

However, it would be a terrible waste of time for every developer to have to write his or her own `if` tags, `for` loop tags, and so on. This is where the JSP Standard Tag Library (JSTL) comes to the rescue. JSTL provides many useful tag libraries and has been universally excepted by the Java community, so much so that it became its own specification. Although this specification is not part of the JSP specification, it's very closely related and the Sun Certified Web Component Developer (SCWCD) certification requires the knowledge of its `core` tag library to pass the exam.

The most commonly used JSTL tag library is the `core` library. This library is also the only one you need to know to pass the SCWCD certification exam. Version 1.1 of this library is the focus of this chapter. It contains the following tags: `out`, `if`, `forEach`, `forTokens`, `choose`, `when`, `otherwise`, `set`, `remove`, `import`, `url`, `param`, `redirect`, and `catch`.

9.1   Installation of JSTL

Because JSTL is a specification, more than one implementation of this specification is possible. Apache Foundation's Jakarta Taglibs project provides a very popular implementation of JSTL and that's the one we use in this chapter.

To import JSTL into a Web application, follow these steps.

1. **Download JSTL.** You can download the implementation by following this URL: http://jakarta.apache.org/site/downloads/downloads_taglibs-standard.cgi. The Web page offers you two options for download, either a .zip format or .tar.gz format. Usually, users of Windows download the .zip format file and users of UNIX-based systems download the .tar.gz format file.

2. **Unzip it to a directory.** The directory can be any directory on your hard drive. Because Apache implementation ships with some supporting material (e.g., a sample Web application), we don't need to copy all of it into our Web app.

3. **Copy standard.jar and jstl.jar into the WEB-INF/lib of your application.** These JAR files are located in the directory to which you unzipped the downloaded file in the jakarta-taglibs-standard-1.1.2/lib directory. You need both of these JARs because jstl.jar contains only the interfaces that the JSTL specification requires these tags to implement and standard.jar contains the actual implementations along with the TLD files.

4. **Import the library into your JSP page with the taglib directive.** We discuss how to import any tag library into your JSP page in Chapter 7 (Tag Libraries: The Basics). There is nothing different about importing the JSTL tag library. It uses the same `taglib` directive mechanism as in the following. Note the `uri` value shown. This is the URI that imports the `core` JSTL tag library.

   ```
   <%@ taglib prefix="c"
           uri="http://java.sun.com/jsp/jstl/core" %>
   ```

5. **(Optional) Download the JSTL tag library documentation.** It is also very useful to save a link to or download the JSTL tag library documentation, its TLDDoc. TLDDoc is HTML-based documentation that is similar to JavaDoc, but it's specially formatted for displaying information about Java-based custom tags. It's generated from the TLD file. The documentation for the JSTL 1.1, which is what we are covering in this chapter, can be found at http://java.sun.com/products/jsp/jstl/1.1/docs/tlddocs/index.html

Note that the prefix we assigned to the core JSTL tag library in Step 4 is "c". As we explained in Chapter 7 (Tag Libraries: The Basics), this prefix can be anything you want. However, it's a known convention that the JSTL core tag library is assigned "c" as the prefix and you should stick to that whenever possible. Following universally accepted conventions makes the code easier to read. In fact, from this point on in the chapter we refer to the tags together with their standard prefix, as in c:out tag.

9.2   c:out Tag

The c:out tag is very similar to JSP scripting expressions like <%= ... %> and standard JSP EL use like ${...}, but it has many advantages. Unlike the JSP scripting, it's a regular tag, so it makes the HTML look cleaner. However, the cleaner look can be accomplished with JSP EL as well. However, unlike JSP EL, the c:out tag lets the JSP developer specify a default value to output if the resulting expression evaluates to null. It also has an attribute that allows the tag to automatically escape any XML type characters like <, >, &, ", '. If the result of some expression contains any of the characters mentioned, it might break the rendering of the HTML page. This is because the browsers will try to interpret those characters as part of HTML markup. Much nastier problems could arise if a malicious user inserts some HTML markup into an input field that is output to the screen unfiltered, which is known as a cross-site scripting (CSS) attack. The c:out tag avoids all these problems by providing the escapeXml attribute that is set to true by default. This feature means that the c:out tag converts those special characters into the HTML equivalent characters. For example, the character < would be converted to <.

Because the old containers, pre-JSP 2.0, do not understand the JSP EL, the c:out tag can also be used as a portable alternative to JSP EL, if support for older containers is important to your application.

Listing 9.1 shows a JSP page, out.jsp, which uses the c:out tag. We import the JSTL core library using the standard taglib directive at the top of the page. Note that the title and the heading of the page use the c:out tag to output special characters, namely < and >. Also, because the bean specified by the key account doesn't really exist in any scope, the expression evaluates to null. However, because we are able specify a default value using the c:out tag, the user will see the word none instead. Figure 9–1 shows the resultant page view.

Listing 9.1   out.jsp

```
<%@ taglib prefix="c" uri="http://java.sun.com/jsp/jstl/core"%>
<!DOCTYPE HTML PUBLIC "-//W3C//DTD HTML 4.01 Transitional//EN">
<HTML>
<HEAD>
<TITLE><c:out value="<c:out> Tag"/></TITLE>
</HEAD>
<BODY>
<H1 ALIGN="center"><CODE><c:out value="<c:out> Tag"/></CODE></H1>
<UL>
 <LI>Subscription ID:
     <c:out value="${account}" default="none"/></LI>
</UL>
</BODY></HTML>
```

Figure 9–1   Result of out.jsp.

9.3   c:forEach and c:forTokens Tags

The c:forEach tag provides basic iteration, accepting many different collection types. It can also function as a counter-based for loop, specifying a begin, end, and a step index. It uses the var attribute to allow the JSP developer to specify a key with which to refer to the current element through the iteration. The c:forTokens tag functions much like c:forEach except it is designed to iterate over a string of tokens separated by delimiters. What is considered a delimiter is customized through its required delims attribute.

Listing 9.2 shows a JSP page, for.jsp, which demonstrates several uses of both c:forEach and c:forTokens tags. Figure 9–2 shows the resultant page view.

Listing 9.2   for.jsp

```jsp
<%@ taglib prefix="c" uri="http://java.sun.com/jsp/jstl/core"%>
<!DOCTYPE HTML PUBLIC "-//W3C//DTD HTML 4.01 Transitional//EN">
<HTML>
<HEAD>
<TITLE><c:out value="<c:foreach>, <c:forTokens> Tags"/></TITLE>
</HEAD>
<BODY>
<H1 ALIGN="center"><CODE><c:out value="<c:foreach>, <c:forTokens>
Tags"/></CODE></H1>
<TABLE>
<TR><TD>
<UL>
 <c:forEach var="i" begin="1" end="10" step="2">
 <LI>i = ${i}</LI>
 </c:forEach>
</UL>
</TD>
<TD>
<%
java.util.List list = new java.util.ArrayList();
list.add("One");
list.add("Two");
list.add("Three");
list.add("Four");
list.add("Five");
request.setAttribute("list", list);
%>
<UL>
 <c:forEach var="item" items="${list}">
 <LI>${item}</LI>
 </c:forEach>
</UL>
</TD>
<TD>
<UL>
 <c:forTokens var="item"
    items="<Once)Upon,A(Time%There...>"
    delims="<),(%>">
 <LI>${item}</LI>
 </c:forTokens>
</UL>
</TD>
</TR>
</TABLE>
</BODY></HTML>
```

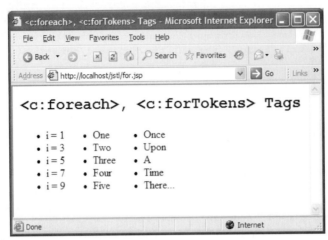

Figure 9–2   Result of for.jsp.

9.4   c:if Tag

The c:if tag is a simple conditional tag that evaluates its body if the supplied condition is true. The condition is evaluated through its required attribute test.

Listing 9.3 shows the forif.jsp page that uses the c:forEach tag to loop through a set of numbers. We use the c:if tag inside the loop to conditionally output the words greater than 3 if the current index of the loop is in fact greater than 3. Figure 9–3 shows the result.

Listing 9.3   forif.jsp

```
<%@ taglib prefix="c" uri="http://java.sun.com/jsp/jstl/core"%>
<!DOCTYPE HTML PUBLIC "-//W3C//DTD HTML 4.01 Transitional//EN">
<HTML>
<HEAD>
<TITLE><c:out value="<c:if> Tags"/></TITLE>
</HEAD>
<BODY>
<H1 ALIGN="center"><CODE><c:out value="<c:if> Tag"/></CODE></H1>
<UL>
```

Listing 9.3   forif.jsp *(continued)*

```
<c:forEach var="i" begin="1" end="10" step="2">
<LI>
  i = ${i}
  <c:if test="${i > 3}">
  (greater than 3)
  </c:if>
</LI>
</c:forEach>
</UL>
</BODY></HTML>
```

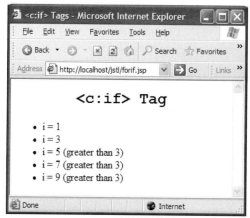

Figure 9–3   Result of forif.jsp.

9.5   c:choose Tag

The c:choose tag is a conditional tag that establishes a context for mutually exclusive conditional operations, marked by the c:when and c:otherwise tags. These three tags work much in the same way as the standard Java switch-case-default statements. The c:choose tag itself does not have any attributes. Its sole purpose is to provide the context to the other two tags (i.e., c:when and c:otherwise). The c:when tag functions in exactly the same way as the c:if tag. It has a test attribute that allows the JSP developer to specify a condition, which if evaluated to true, would signal to the container to evaluate the body of the c:when tag. If a particular c:when tag's condition evaluates to true, no other c:when tags below it are evaluated and the processing jumps to the line after the closing c:choose tag. If the optional c:otherwise tag is specified and no c:when tag evaluates to true, the body of the c:otherwise tag is evaluated.

Listing 9.4 shows the forchoose.jsp page. In it, we iterate through numbers 1 through 10 and output different messages depending on what the current iteration index is. This is nothing exciting, but it illustrates the point. Figure 9–4 shows the result.

Listing 9.4   forchoose.jsp

```
<%@ taglib prefix="c" uri="http://java.sun.com/jsp/jstl/core"%>
<!DOCTYPE HTML PUBLIC "-//W3C//DTD HTML 4.01 Transitional//EN">
<HTML>
<HEAD>
<TITLE><c:out value="<c:choose>, <c:when>, <c:otherwise> Tags"/>
</TITLE>
</HEAD>
<BODY>
<H1 ALIGN="center"><CODE>
<c:out value="<c:choose>, <c:when>, <c:otherwise> Tags"/></CODE></
H1>
<UL>
 <c:forEach var="i" begin="1" end="10">
 <LI>
  i = ${i}
  <c:choose>
    <c:when test="${i < 3}">(less than 3)</c:when>
    <c:when test="${i < 5}">(less than 5)</c:when>
    <c:when test="${i == 5}">(It IS 5! SO exciting!)</c:when>
    <c:otherwise>(greater than 5)</c:otherwise>
  </c:choose>
 </LI>
 </c:forEach>
</UL>
</BODY></HTML>
```

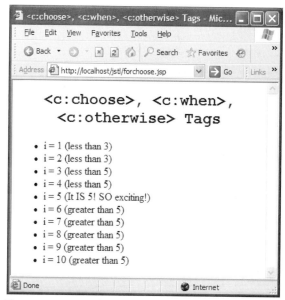

Figure 9–4 Result of forchoose.jsp.

9.6 c:set and c:remove Tags

The c:set tag is used either for setting a scoped attribute or updating and creating bean properties and map values. The following are some of the common forms in which the c:set tag is used.

```
<c:set var="attributeName" value="someValue" />
<c:set target="map" property="elementKey" value="elementValue" />
<c:set target="bean" property="name">John Dow</c:set>
```

Notice that the last c:set tag does not specify the value attribute. Its value comes from the body of the c:set tag. It's often the case that the value we want to set contains characters or dynamic expressions that are either difficult or sometimes simply impossible to place inside a tag attribute (i.e., value) in a legal way. This is why the c:set tag allows the value to come from either its value attribute or the body of the c:set tag.

Core Note

You can specify the value of the `c:set` *tag either using its* `value` *attribute or placing the value as the body of the* `c:set` *tag.*

The `c:set` tag provides two attributes, `var` and `target`, of which at least one is required. However, these attributes are not allowed to appear at the same time.

The `var` attribute is used to specify the name of an attribute to set. This attribute is set in the scope specified by the optional `scope` attribute. If the `scope` attribute is not specified, it defaults to `page` scope.

The `target` attribute must be an expression that evaluates to some object. If the object implements the `Map` interface, the `property` attribute of the `c:set` tag is treated as a key with which to create a new map entry with the value specified. If the `target` evaluates to a JavaBean, the value of the `c:set` tag is passed to the property of the target JavaBean specified by the `property` attribute.

When the value of the `c:set` tag evaluates to `null`, the effect is no different then invoking `someScopeReference.setAttribute(null)`, where `some-ScopeReference` is one of request, response, session, and so on, which essentially removes the attribute from that scope. For convenience, JSTL provides an explicit `c:remove` tag. The `c:remove` tag allows the JSP author to specify the name of the attribute to remove using the required `var` attribute and the scope to remove it from using the optional `scope` attribute. Unlike the `c:set` tag, if the `scope` attribute is not specified, the `c:remove` tag will remove the attribute from all scopes.

Listing 9.5 shows **set.jsp** as an example of how **c:set** and **c:remove** can be used. First, we use the `c:set` tag to create an attribute called map (of type `HashMap`) and store it in the `request` scope. We populate the map using the `c:set` tag as well. The first element in the map is `partialTitle`, which contains only part of this book's title. The `fullTitle` element is comprised from the `partialTitle` element plus the second part of the title. Note that because the value of the `partial-Title` contains special characters, which can be interpreted by the browser as HTML, we are forced to use the `c:out` tag for output. The convenience provided by the `c:set` tag in allowing its body to be utilized as the value to set comes in very handy because it would be illegal to place a custom tag as the value of another custom tag's attribute. We use the regular JSP EL to output the title inside the `H1` tag. We proceed to set the `authors` attribute using the `c:set` tag in the `request` scope. Then, we set another `authors` attribute omitting the `scope` attribute, which defaults to the `page` scope. Using JSP EL, we output the label for the list of authors, which is stored in the `authors` attribute contained in the `page` scope, and the list of authors itself, which is stored in the `authors` attribute contained in the `request` scope. Next, we demonstrate how the c:remove tag works by instructing it to remove the authors attribute from every scope by omitting the scope attribute. Outputting both authors attributes, in the page and request scopes, we observe that they are no longer there. Figure 9–5 shows the result of invoking the set.jsp page.

Listing 9.5	set.jsp

```
<%@ taglib prefix="c" uri="http://java.sun.com/jsp/jstl/core"%>
<!DOCTYPE HTML PUBLIC "-//W3C//DTD HTML 4.01 Transitional//EN">
<HTML>
<HEAD>
<TITLE><c:out value="<c:set>, <c:remove> Tags"/></TITLE>
</HEAD>
<BODY>
<H1 ALIGN="CENTER"><CODE><c:out value="<c:set>, <c:remove> Tags"/>
</CODE></H1>
<c:set var="map" value="<%= new java.util.HashMap() %>"
       scope="request"/>
<c:set target="${map}" property="partialTitle"
       value="<read-it>Core</read-it>"/>
<c:set target="${map}" property="fullTitle">
 <c:out value="${map.partialTitle}"/> <BR> Servlets and
 JSP Volume 2
</c:set>
<H1 ALIGN="CENTER">${map.fullTitle}</H1>

<c:set var="authors"
       value="Marty Hall, Larry Brown, Yaakov Chaikin"
       scope="request"/>
<c:set var="authors">Authors</c:set>
<H2 ALIGN="CENTER">${authors}: ${requestScope.authors}</H2>
<c:remove var="authors"/>
<H2 ALIGN="CENTER">${pageScope.authors}: ${requestScope.authors}
</H2>
</BODY></HTML>
```

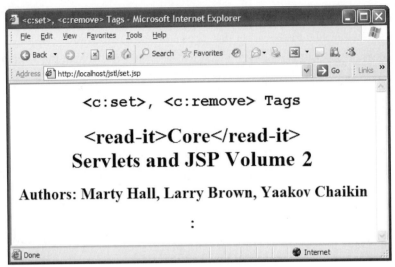

Figure 9–5   Result of invoking set.jsp.

9.7   c:import Tag

The JSP framework provides a couple of ways to include content from the same container. We can use the static inclusion by employing the include directive, which includes the referenced content at page translation time. We can also use the dynamic inclusion by employing the jsp:include standard action, which includes the referenced content at request time. Remember that with both of these types of inclusion mechanisms the included content cannot be a complete HTML page unless the including page is nothing more than the inclusion statement itself. Usually, therefore, the included content has to provide only a snippet of HTML that can fit in with the rest of the including page's HTML markup without invalidating it.

However, what if the content we want to include resides on a different server? The include directive as well as the jsp:include standard action can't help us there, but the c:import JSTL tag can. This tag can include the content, pointed to by the required attribute url, even if the content resides on a different Web server.

The default behavior of c:import is to output the included content into the including page at the place where c:import appears. However, if the optional var and the likewise optional scope attributes are specified, the included content can be saved as a scoped attribute instead. If the scope attribute is omitted, it defaults to the page scope.

Again, be aware that whatever you import into your existing JSP page better not be a complete HTML page by itself. The imported content has to be a snippet of HTML that has to fit into the structure of your existing HTML page. Also remember that if the imported content contains relative links they will most likely not work anymore because the links will be interpreted relative to the location of the importing page. This issue is just as relevant to the other aforementioned ways of inclusion, but even more so to the `c:import` tag because it is able to import content from other Web sites on the Internet over which you probably have even less control.

Core Warning

The imported content has to be a snippet of HTML that fits into the structure of your existing HTML page. The links inside the imported content have to be absolute.

The `c:import` tag can just as easily import content from the same container. In such cases, you can use the `c:param` tag in the exact same way as you would use the `jsp:param` with the `jsp:include` standard action. For more details on the `jsp:include` standard action, see Volume 1, Chapter 13..

Listing 9.6 shows the import.jsp page. In this page we use `c:import` to pull down two different HTML snippets from http://volume2.coreservlets.com. The snippets are snake.html and marty-with-snake.html, shown in Listing 9.7 and Listing 9.8, respectively. Note two important things about these snippets. The first is that they are just HTML snippets; that is, they are not valid HTML pages by themselves. The second is that the IMG tag's SRC attribute specifies the source of the image by its absolute URL, not a relative one. If it didn't, we would not be able to import it into our page and still see the images. The first `c:import` tag in the page does not output the included content, but caches it into a scoped attribute `martyWithSnake`, using the `c:import` tag's optional `var` attribute. Because we do not specify the scope attribute, it defaults to `page` scope, which is good enough for our example. Later on in the page we display this content by simply accessing the martyWith-Snake attribute with the JSP EL expression `${martyWithSnake}`. The second `c:import` tag does not specify a `var` attribute, so the included content is output into the place where the `c:import` tag appears. Figure 9–6 shows the result of invoking import.jsp.

Listing 9.6 import.jsp

```
<%@ taglib prefix="c" uri="http://java.sun.com/jsp/jstl/core"%>
<!DOCTYPE HTML PUBLIC "-//W3C//DTD HTML 4.01 Transitional//EN">
<HTML>
<HEAD>
<TITLE>Marty playing with snakes</TITLE>
</HEAD>
<BODY>
<c:import
    url="http://volume2.coreservlets.com/marty-with-snake.html"
    var="martyWithSnake"/>
<TABLE ALIGN="CENTER">
<TR>
 <TD COLSPAN="2" ALIGN="CENTER"><H1>Travels to Far East</H1></TD>
</TR>
<TR>
 <TD>
 <c:import url="http://volume2.coreservlets.com/snake.html"/>
 </TD>
 <TD>${martyWithSnake}</TD>
</TR>
</TABLE>
</BODY></HTML>
```

Listing 9.7 snake.html

```
<DIV>
<IMG SRC="http://volume2.coreservlets.com/images/snake.jpg">
<BR>
A snake
</DIV>
```

Listing 9.8 marty-with-snake.html

```
<DIV>
<IMG
 SRC="http://volume2.coreservlets.com/images/MartyWithSnake.jpg">
<BR>
Marty holding a snake
</DIV>
```

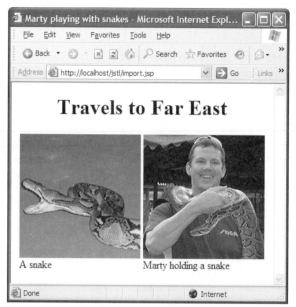

Figure 9–6   Result of invoking import.jsp.

9.8   c:url and c:param Tags

Recall from Volume 1, Chapter 9 that with the `HttpSession` object provided by the container, session tracking is taken care of for you. There is, however, one task that you cannot escape with automatic session tracking alone: links in your pages that point back to other pages in your own Web application. Automatic session tracking will work whether the client has cookies enabled or not. In case the cookies are disabled the session tracking is done through URL rewriting; that is, the container reads the session ID straight from the URL without using a session cookie. However, the container will not automatically append the session ID to the URLs that are sent back to the client inside your JSP pages. Every URL within your application needs to be encoded if it is to retain the session ID information. This is usually done with the `encodeURL` method of the `HttpServletResponse` class. However, it would be great if we didn't need to insert Java code inside our JSP pages just to encode URLs. This is where JSTL's `c:url` tag is very handy. Just like the `encodeURL` method, it encodes the URL specified in its required `value` attribute, appending the session ID if the client browser is not using cookies, and leaves the URL as it was if the client browser is able to accept a session cookie. For more information on encoding URLs, please see Volume 1, Section 9.5.

Just like the c:import tag, the c:url tag is able to hold off on outputting the URL string if the optional var attribute is present. In such a case, the resulting URL gets stored in a scoped attribute. The scope can be specified by the optional scope attribute. If omitted, the scope defaults to page scope, as usual.

The c:url tag in combination with the c:param tag solves yet another problem. What if you need to append some parameters at the end of the URL you are constructing? Sure, you can do something like this:

```
<c:url value="myurl?fullName=${fullNameParam}"/>
```

However, what if the fullNameParam turns out to be John Dow, with the space character in it? Spaces are illegal inside URLs, so we need to encode the parameters as well. This is quite easily done with one or more c:param tags nested inside the c:url tag. The c:param tag supplies the c:url tag with the name and value of request parameters for the URL with its required attributes called name and value.

Listing 9.9 shows url.jsp as a simple example of using the c:url and c:param tags. We disabled cookies in the browser to force the c:url tag to append the session ID to the resulting URL. First, we use the c:url tag just to output a URL and see the session ID appended. Next, we use the c:url tag in conjunction with the c:param tag to encode a value with a space in it, John Dow. Instead of outputting the resulting URL right away, we store it in a scoped attribute inputUrl and output it later in the page using JSP EL. Because we omitted the scope attribute, it defaults to the page scope. Figure 9–7 shows the result of invoking url.jsp. We observe that the URL strings output in the page contain the session ID and that the value of the request parameter has been encoded as well, replacing the space character with the + character.

Listing 9.9	url.jsp

```
<%@ taglib prefix="c" uri="http://java.sun.com/jsp/jstl/core"%>
<!DOCTYPE HTML PUBLIC "-//W3C//DTD HTML 4.01 Transitional//EN">
<HTML>
<HEAD>
<TITLE><c:out value="<c:url>, <c:param> Tags"/></TITLE>
</HEAD>
<BODY>
<H1 ALIGN="center"><CODE><c:out value="<c:url>, <c:param> Tags"/>
</CODE></H1>
<H4>URL without parameters: <c:url value="/out.jsp"/></H4>
<c:url value="/out.jsp" var="inputUrl">
  <c:param name="name" value="John Dow"/>
</c:url>
<H4>URL with parameters: ${inputUrl}</H4>
</BODY></HTML>
```

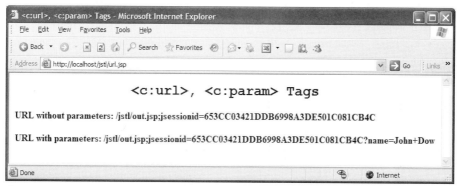

Figure 9–7   Result of invoking url.jsp.

9.9   c:redirect Tag

The c:redirect tag could be called the one-stop shop for redirecting URLs in JSP pages. If its required url attribute specifies an absolute URL, the c:redirect tag acts just like the sendRedirectURL method of the HttpServletResponse class. This results in the browser making an additional request to the new URL, and in fact is no different than if the user were to type the URL by hand. If, however, the URL specified in the url attribute is a relative URL, a dynamic forward occurs, which is equivalent to the forward method of the RequestDispatcher class. In this case, the browser address bar still shows the original URL and not the URL of the forwarded to page.

Just like c:url and c:import, the c:redirect tag can take advantage of the automatic encoding provided by nesting one or more c:param tags in its body.

The following two examples show the usage of c:redirect. Listing 9.10 shows redirect1.jsp. This page consists of just the taglib directive and the c:redirect tag. In this instance we use a relative URL. Figure 9–8 shows that the URL in the browser address bar stays the same (i.e., redirect1.jsp) but the page shown is, in fact, out.jsp, which is where the forward was directed. Listing 9.11 shows redirect2.jsp. Similarly, this page consists of only the taglib directive and the c:redirect tag. However, this time, the url attribute specifies an absolute URL. We also nest two c:param tags in the body of the c:redirect tag to supply the URL with some encoded request parameters. Figure 9–9 shows the result of invoking redirect2.jsp. Note that not only is the content of the page different, but the URL shown in the browser is different from the originally typed in URL (i.e., http://localhost/jstl/redirect2.jsp).

Listing 9.10 redirect1.jsp

```
<%@ taglib prefix="c" uri="http://java.sun.com/jsp/jstl/core"%>
<c:redirect url="out.jsp"/>
```

Listing 9.11 redirect2.jsp

```
<%@ taglib prefix="c" uri="http://java.sun.com/jsp/jstl/core"%>
<c:redirect url="http://www.google.com/search">
<c:param name="hl" value="en"/>
<c:param name="q">Core Servlets</c:param>
</c:redirect>
```

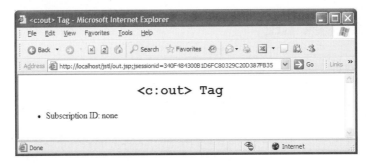

Figure 9–8
Result of invoking
redirect1.jsp.

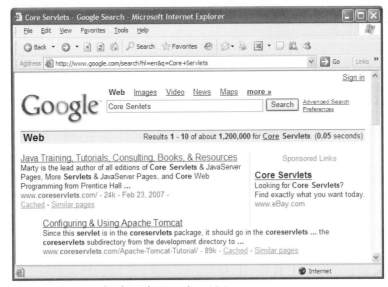

Figure 9–9   Result of invoking redirect2.jsp.

9.10 c:catch Tag

The c:catch tag acts like the try/catch construct in Java, except in the case of c:catch, there is no try. If you surround part of the page that may throw an exception with the c:catch tag, and an exception occurs, the page will still render up until the point where the exception occurred and then continue rendering from the c:catch end tag on. You can store the thrown exception in a page scoped attribute specified by the optional var attribute.

We strongly discourage you from using this tag for anything other than debugging or experimentation. Exception handling is not the job of the JSP page. Exceptions should be handled by the business logic before the control ever gets to the JSP page.

Core Warning

Avoid using the c:catch tag for anything other than debugging or experimentation. Exception handling should be part of the business logic code, not the JSP page.

Listing 9.12 shows catch.jsp as an example of how to use the c:catch tag. We trigger a java.lang.ArithmeticException, which gets caught and stored in an attribute called myException. We display the message of this exception using JSP EL. Note that even though the exception occurred, that page still completed rendering. Figure 9–10 shows the result of invoking catch.jsp.

Listing 9.12 catch.jsp

```
<%@ taglib prefix="c" uri="http://java.sun.com/jsp/jstl/core"%>
<!DOCTYPE HTML PUBLIC "-//W3C//DTD HTML 4.01 Transitional//EN">
<HTML>
<HEAD>
<TITLE><c:out value="<c:catch> Tag"/></TITLE>
</HEAD>
<BODY>
<H1 ALIGN="center"><CODE><c:out value="<c:catch> Tag"/></CODE>
</H1>
<H3>Before illegal operation</H3>
<c:catch var="myException">
```

Listing 9.12 catch.jsp *(continued)*

```
<% int x = 1 / 0; %>
</c:catch>
<H3>After illegal operation</H3>
Exception message: ${myException.message}
</BODY></HTML>
```

Figure 9–10   Result of invoking catch.jsp.

THE STRUTS FRAMEWORK: BASICS

Topics in This Chapter

- Downloading and installing Struts
- Weighing the pros and cons of Struts
- Understanding the Struts flow of control
- Learning the six basic steps in using Struts
- Writing `Actions` to process requests
- Using form beans to handle request parameters
- Prepopulating input forms
- Redisplaying input forms

Chapter 10

In Chapter 15 of *Core Servlets and JavaServer Pages, Volume 1*, we presented the MVC architecture. By using `RequestDispatcher` in the servlets and the JSP 2.0 EL in the JSP pages, you can create a nice separation between the code that creates the data (Java) and the code that presents the data (HTML/JSP). Although this is a simple and powerful approach, in many applications it does not go far enough. The Apache Struts framework is a powerful framework for applications that use the MVC approach. It adds many capabilities on top of the ones provided by `Request-Dispatcher` and the JSP EL, has become very popular in the developer community, and is used in a number of well-known Web sites such as travelocity.com, Enterprise Rent-a-Car, the Internal Revenue Service, imax.com, circuitcity.com, and mastercard.com.

10.1 Understanding Struts

What is Struts all about? What are the pros and cons of using it? Where do I get it? How do I install it? This section answers all of these questions.

Different Views of Struts

Although Struts is very popular, nobody can agree on exactly what Struts is. Here are the most common views:

- **An MVC framework.** Struts provides a unified framework for deploying servlet and JSP applications that use the MVC architecture. This view is the way Struts is billed on its Web site, and the way Struts is presented in almost all Struts books.
- **A collection of utilities.** Struts provides utilities to simplify many of the most common tasks in Web application development. Many of these utilities are not directly tied to MVC. Historically, many people have downloaded Struts because they want Tiles (a page layout facility built on top of `jsp:include`) or a file upload facility, neither of which have anything specifically to do with MVC.
- **A set of JSP custom tag libraries.** Struts provides custom tag libraries for outputting bean properties, generating HTML forms, iterating over various types of data structures, and conditionally outputting HTML. Especially before the advent of the JSTL (which was derived from the Struts iteration and logic libraries), many people got Struts just for those tag libraries.

Which is the proper way to view Struts? The answer depends on what you are going to use it for. All three viewpoints are legitimate. However, the most common way of looking at Struts is as an MVC framework.

Next, we discuss the pros and cons of Struts.

Advantages of Apache Struts (Compared to MVC with RequestDispatcher and the EL)

Many Struts books and tutorials start like this: "Here is a Web application with JSP pages jam packed with explicit Java code. Tut, tut, isn't it hard to create, debug, and maintain? Here is the same application redone in Struts. Isn't it so much better? This shows that Struts is good." What nonsense. Yes, of course tons of Java code in JSP pages is bad, and of course Struts would be a huge improvement. That proves nothing; practically anything would be an improvement. Showing how Struts improves things over a lousy, badly designed JSP application is hardly relevant; the question is what Struts provides for applications that are designed properly (e.g., using MVC and the JSP EL). The answer, fortunately, is quite a lot. These advantages are the ones worth paying attention to.

Compared to the standard MVC approach, here are the main additional benefits that Struts provides.

- **Centralized file-based configuration.** Rather then hard-coding information into Java programs, many Struts values are represented in XML or property files. This loose coupling means that many changes can be made without modifying or recompiling Java code, and that wholesale changes can be made by editing a single file. This approach also lets Java and Web developers focus on their specific tasks (implementing business logic, presenting certain values to clients, etc.) without needing to know very much about the overall system design.

- **Form beans.** In JSP, you can use `property="*"` with `jsp:setProperty` to automatically populate a JavaBean component based on incoming request parameters. Obviously, behind the scenes, there is Java code that takes a bean and a request object, matches up the request parameters with the bean property names, and calls the appropriate setter methods. However, this Java API is not exposed. The specification exposed the API in exactly the place where you don't want to use it (you want access to the request parameters long before you get to the presentation layer), and failed to expose it in the place where you do want to use it. Aargh! This annoying reversal has been known to drive developers (well, the authors of this book, anyhow) to apoplexy. Apache Struts provides a straightforward facility for populating a bean based on request parameters, and accessing that bean from Java code. This capability is so useful that it is almost impossible to live without it once you have been spoiled by trying it. In fact, in *Core Servlets and JavaServer Pages, Volume 1*, we showed how to steal this code from Struts and use it in regular applications.

- **Bean tags.** Apache Struts provides a set of custom JSP tags (`bean:write`, in particular) that let you easily output the properties of JavaBeans components. Basically, these are concise and powerful variations of the standard `jsp:useBean` and `jsp:getProperty` tags. In applications that use JSP 1.2 and earlier, this is a huge advantage. These Struts tags also provide some capabilities not supported by the JSP EL (e.g., filtering of HTML characters), but they are also longer and more verbose than the JSP EL. Therefore, the Struts `bean:` tags are less of an advantage in newer servers.

- **HTML tags.** Apache Struts provides a set of custom JSP tags to create HTML forms that are associated with JavaBeans components. This bean/form association lets you get initial form field values from Java objects and lets you redisplay forms with some or all previously entered values intact. Form redisplay is one of the single most tedious and poorly supported tasks in the standard servlet and JSP API, and Struts provides a clean and simple way to do it.

- **Form field validation.** Apache Struts has built-in capabilities for checking that form values are in the required format. If values are missing or in an improper format, the form can be automatically redisplayed with error messages and with the previously entered values maintained. This validation can be performed on the server (in

Java), or both on the server and on the client (in JavaScript). This saves hours of work in most applications.

- **Consistent approach.** MVC is a pretty general idea: Separate the code that creates the data from the code that presents the results to the end user. However, there are many different ways of implementing this general strategy. Struts encourages a consistent way of implementing MVC, so developers always know where page navigation rules go, where request parameters are stored, where the request controller starts, and so on.

Disadvantages of Apache Struts (Compared to MVC with RequestDispatcher and the EL)

The advantages of Struts are very significant, even when you consider only the advantages compared to a good design within the standard servlet/JSP APIs. Even the books and papers that don't present bogus advantages of Struts ("look how great Struts is compared to 10 million lines of Java code in JSP pages!") almost always stop after the advantages. But are there any disadvantages? Yes, and some very significant ones. If you consider only the advantages of Struts, you will be disappointed when you use it on a real project and are unprepared for the complexity and spinup time. On the other hand, if you have realistic expectations, carefully weigh the advantages and disadvantages, and use Struts only in the projects and with the teams for which it makes sense, you will find Struts an extremely useful weapon in your development arsenal.

Here are the main disadvantages:

- **Bigger learning curve.** To use MVC with the standard `RequestDispatcher`, you need to be comfortable with the standard JSP and servlet APIs. To use MVC with Struts, you have to be comfortable with the standard JSP and servlet APIs and a large and elaborate framework that is almost equal in size to the core servlet and JSP specification. This drawback is especially significant with smaller projects, near-term deadlines, and less experienced developers; you could spend as much time learning Struts as building your actual system. Struts is complicated, takes a long time to learn, and is hard for new developers to work with. On larger and more complex projects, the additional complexity is often more than compensated for by the additional power, but this is not always true. Far from it. Count the cost before committing to Struts.
- **Worse documentation.** Guess who pays the Struts developers to work on Struts? Nobody! So guess what parts of the system they spend the most time working on? The parts that are fun. Raise your hand if

your favorite task is writing documentation. See our point? Compared
to the standard servlet and JSP APIs, Struts has fewer online
resources, and many new users find the online Apache documentation
confusing and poorly organized.

- **Less transparent.** With Struts applications, there is a lot more going
  on behind the scenes than with normal servlet-and-JSP-based Web
  applications. In some ways, this is good: Struts performs many of the
  tasks you normally would have to do yourself. In other ways, this is
  bad: When there is an error or a performance bottleneck in a Struts
  application, it is often more difficult to pinpoint the source of the
  problem.
- **Rigid approach.** If you like the Struts spin on MVC, you would say
  that struts "encourages" a "consistent" approach to MVC. If you don't
  like the Struts slant on MVC, you will feel that Struts "forces" a "rigid"
  approach. If you use Struts, you need to do things the Struts way, at
  least for the most part.
- **Community fragmentation.** Until the end of 2005, there was one
  Struts framework. Now, however, there are three: the Struts 1
  framework (formally simply "Struts"), the reengineered Struts 2
  framework (currently under development), and a new and different
  framework called Struts Shale (built around JavaServer Faces). And,
  speaking of JavaServer Faces (JSF), it is a competing framework that is
  rapidly growing in popularity. Which framework will dominate in the
  future? We certainly don't know, and this uncertainty is a serious
  problem, because you hate to invest in learning a framework if you will
  switch to another one next year. Nevertheless, given the huge head start
  of the classic Struts framework, it is unlikely that JSF or Struts Shale will
  replace the Struts framework in the short term. As empirical evidence,
  we compared advertised job openings for Struts jobs and JSF jobs in the
  first quarter of 2007, and got the results shown in Table 10.1.

Table 10.1   Advertised Struts and JSF Job Openings for Q1 2007

	dice.com	hotjobs.yahoo.com	monster.com
Struts jobs	2,079	1,052	more than 1,000 (monster.com limits matches to 1,000)
JSF jobs	458	232	335
Ratio of Struts jobs for each JSF job	4.5:1	4.5:1	at least 3:1

10.2 Setting Up Struts

This section walks you through the process of downloading the Struts software, setting up your environment, and testing a simple application. Following, we cover Struts 1, specifically Struts 1.3. At the time of this writing, Struts 2 was still under development.

Core Note

This material covers the popular Apache Struts 1. At the time of this writing, Struts 2, based on WebWork, was still under development.

Installing Struts

In the following list, we quickly summarize the steps to install and configure Struts.

1. **Download the Struts code.** You can get the latest release build at http://struts.apache.org/downloads.html. You can get the source code, example applications, or the documentation, but all that is absolutely required is the struts-blank Web application. If you want to use the same Struts subrelease as our examples, just grab struts-blank.zip from the book's source code archive.
2. **Update your CLASSPATH.** To compile your Struts-based Web applications, add struts-core-1.3.5.jar to the CLASSPATH used by your compiler or IDE.
3. **Bookmark the Struts documentation.** You can access the documentation online at http://struts.apache.org/1.x/learning.html. Alternatively, you can download a copy of the documentation for local access.

The following subsections give details on each of these steps.

Downloading Struts

To use Struts, all you really need is a blank Web application to use as the starting point for your Struts-based apps. Struts is a library that works within a regular servlet and JSP environment; it is not a server or a new programming language. Therefore, if you have a template Web application with the appropriate JAR files, supporting files, and web.xml settings, you have Struts. That means that all you absolutely need to download is the struts-blank template Web application; nothing else is required. You can find the struts-blank template in the examples distribution, struts-1.3.5-apps.zip.

The Apache Struts Web site also has a fuller distribution that includes a local copy of the documentation, examples, and source code, but this fuller distribution is optional, not required.

Grab the struts-blank-1.3.5 template from struts-1.3.5-app.zip or from the fuller distribution, struts-1.3.5-all.zip, at http://struts.apache.org/downloads.html. After downloading the .zip file, unzip it into a directory of your choice.

Updating Your CLASSPATH

To compile your Web applications, add struts-core-1.3.5.jar to the CLASSPATH used by your compiler or IDE (not by your server). This JAR file can be found in the lib directory of struts-blank-1.3.5, and is also in the lib directory of the fuller distribution.

Following are three possible ways to set your CLASSPATH.

- **Set the CLASSPATH in the startup file.** For example, on Microsoft Windows, you would put the following lines in C:\autoexec.bat:

```
set CLASSPATH=some-path\struts-core-1.3.5.jar;CLASSPATH%
```

On UNIX or Linux, use your .cshrc, .bashrc, or .profile instead. For example, you would place the following in your .cshrc file (note that this all goes on one line with no spaces—it is broken here for readability):

```
setenv CLASSPATH .:some-path/struts-core-1.3.5.jar:
                 $CLASSPATH
```

- **Set the CLASSPATH through a system setting.** On Microsoft Windows XP, go to the Start menu and select Control Panel, then System, then click the Advanced tab, then click the Environment Variables button. On Microsoft Windows 2000, go to the Start menu and select Settings, then Control Panel, then System, then Environment. Either way, enter the CLASSPATH value from the previous bullet.
- **Set the CLASSPATH in your editor or IDE.** Most IDEs have a way of specifying the JAR files needed to compile projects. Or, you could make a small .bat file (Microsoft Windows) or shell script (UNIX/ Linux) that supplies the struts-core-1.3.5.jar file as the argument to -classpath for javac.

Bookmarking the Struts Documentation

You can access Struts documentation on the Apache Web site or you can download a local copy from struts-1.3.5-docs.zip. The documentation includes a user's guide, FAQs, examples, and the API in Javadoc format. From the Apache Web site, you can find the documentation online at http://struts.apache.org/1.x/learning.html. If you downloaded the fuller Struts distribution, struts-1.3.5-all.zip, you can find the Struts documentation at *struts_install_dir*/docs. Either way, we strongly recommend you bookmark the documentation for easy access.

Testing Struts

After downloading Struts, you should test it with your servlet engine. To do so, all you need to do is install the struts-blank Web application. Here are the basic steps:

1. **Install struts-blank on your server.** Put a copy of struts-blank-1.3.5.war in your server's Web application autodeploy directory. For Apache Tomcat, you can install the application by copying the file to *tomcat_install_dir*/webapps/. Alternatively, use jar -xvf (or WinZip) to extract the files and copy them *tomcat_install_dir*/webapps/.

2. **Start the server.** Most servers automatically recognize newly deployed Web applications and do not require a restart if they are already running when you deploy struts-blank.

3. **Access the struts-blank application.** Access the application through http://localhost/struts-blank-1.3.5/. This URL assumes you are running the server on your desktop and the server is using port 80. In general, you would access the application through http://*hostname:port*/struts-blank-1.3.5/ (for Struts version 1.3.5). If successful, you should see a Web page similar to the one shown in Figure 10–1.

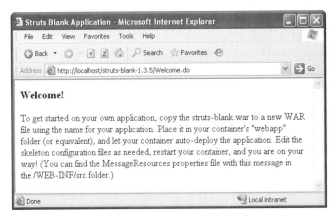

Figure 10–1   Test of the struts-blank Web application.

Making Your Own Struts Applications

To make your own Struts application, you need the appropriate JAR files, TLD files, XML files, properties files, and web.xml entries. Because struts-blank-1.3.5 already has all of these files, the simplest strategy is to copy and rename struts-blank-1.3.5 or some previous Web application that was derived from struts-blank. So, your development process typically looks like this:

1. Copy the struts-blank-1.3.5 directory to your development area.
2. Rename it whatever you want to call your Web application (say, my-struts-app).
3. Add code for your application. Remove index.jsp and pages/ Welcome.jsp. Remove any commented out or irrelevant entries in struts-config.xml.
4. Copy to your server's Web application deployment directory (e.g., the webapps directory for Tomcat).
5. Start the server and access http://localhost/my-struts-app/*path*, where *path* corresponds to a file or .do address you created in the application.

Adding Struts to an Existing Web Application

Adding Struts capabilities to existing Web applications is a huge undertaking and will probably require several attempts to get it right. Assuming that your Web application is in the directory *your_web_app*, here is a quick summary of the steps you would take.

1. **Copy the JAR files.** Copy the JAR files from struts-blank-1.3.5/ WEB-INF/lib to *your_web_app*/WEB-INF/lib. There should be about 10 of them, but this can vary in Struts subreleases.
2. **Copy the Struts configuration file.** Copy struts-config.xml from struts-blank-1.3.5/WEB-INF to *your_web_app*/WEB-INF.
3. **Copy the properties file.** Copy MessageResources.properties from struts-blank-1.3.5/WEB-INF/classes to *your_web_app*/WEB-INF/ classes.
4. **Copy the Tiles and Validator configuration file.** If you plan on using the Validator plug-in, copy validation.xml from struts-blank-1.3.5/ WEB-INF to *your_web_app*/WEB-INF. If you plan on using the Tiles plug-in, copy tiles-def.xml from struts-blank-1.3.5/WEB-INF to *your_web_app*/WEB-INF.
5. **Copy the deployment descriptor declarations.** Copy the declarations out of struts-blank-1.3.5/WEB-INF/web.xml into *your_web_app*/ WEB-INF/web.xml.

This is a huge pain; don't bother! Start with struts-blank-1.3.5 (or a previously created Web app based on struts-blank) instead.

10.3 The Struts Flow of Control and the Six Steps to Implementing It

In this section, we give the big picture of how a basic Struts application works. First, we examine the typical flow of a request through the Struts framework. Then, we present the six basic steps needed to implement this flow. In the rest of the chapter, we give details and examples of the control flow and the steps for implementing it.

Struts Flow of Control

Before writing your first Struts application, you need to understand the normal flow of execution through the Struts framework. Figure 10–2 illustrates the apparent execution flow of the request through the Struts framework. We use the word *apparent* because, behind the scenes, the Struts system handles numerous internal steps. However, from the point of view of the developer, this flow diagram should suffice.

The following list summarizes the flow, and the subsequent subsections explain it in more detail.

1. **The user requests a form.** The input form is built with the Struts `html:` tags. These tags associate a bean with the form so that you can prepopulate the form with values from your application, so that you can redisplay incorrectly filled out forms, and so that Struts knows where to store the request parameters when the form is submitted.

2. **The form is submitted to a URL of the form *blah*.do.** The form contains an `ACTION` ending in *blah*.do. The Struts system receives the request, where an `action` mapping in `struts-config.xml` associates the address with an `Action` object.

3. **The `execute` method of the `Action` object is invoked.** One of the arguments to `execute` is a form bean that is automatically created and whose properties are automatically populated with the incoming form data. Once it examines the user input data in the bean, the `execute` method invokes business logic and data-access logic, placing the results in normal beans stored in the `request`, `session`, or `application` scope. Finally, the `execute` method uses `mapping.findForward` to return various conditions that are mapped by `struts-config.xml` to JSP pages.

4. **Struts forwards the request to the appropriate JSP page.** Struts normally invokes the results page with `RequestDispatcher.forward`, although `request.sendRedirect` is occasionally used (e.g., with session-scoped data). In most real applications, the results page uses `bean:write` or the JSP 2.0 EL to output bean properties.

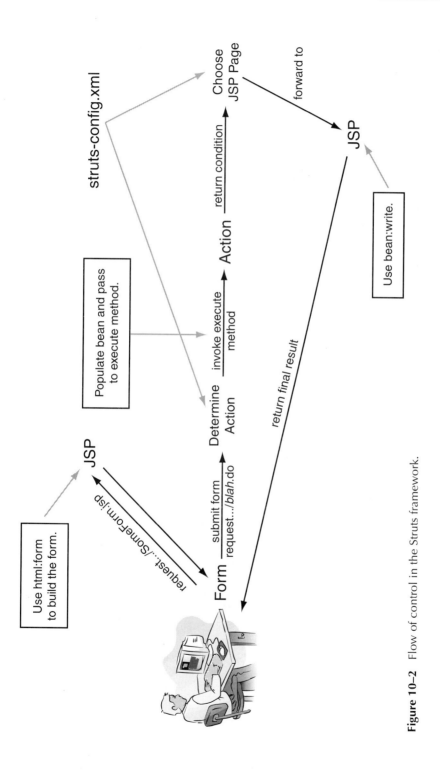

Figure 10–2 Flow of control in the Struts framework.

The User Requests a Form

You use the `html:form` and `html:text` tags to create the form, like this:

```
<html:form action="/blah">
  <html:text property="someBeanPropertyName"
</html:form>
```

When Struts sees the `html:form` tag, it creates or finds a bean that corresponds to the /blah address in the Struts configuration file, `struts-config.xml`. The `html:text` line indicates two things: first, that the value of the bean's `someBean-PropertyName` property (i.e., the result of calling `getSomeBeanPropertyName`) should be the initial value of the text field, and second, that when the form is submitted, the text field value is stored in the `someBeanPropertyName` property (i.e., the request parameter will be passed to `setSomeBeanPropertyName`). Finally, the `action` of the `html:form` tag indicates that the submitted address will be http://*hostname*/*webappname*/blah.do.

In the first few examples, we focus on the most fundamental parts of Struts (editing `struts-config.xml` and defining `Action` and bean classes), and use ordinary static HTML for the input form. We introduce the `html:` tags in Section 10.6 (Prepopulating and Redisplaying Input Forms).

The Form Is Submitted to a URL of the Form *blah*.do

The form submits data to a URL of the form *blah*.do; any request ending in .do is handled by the Struts controller. The deployment descriptor file, web.xml, contains a servlet mapping that associates URLs ending with .do with the Struts `ActionServlet`. See the following web.xml fragment:

```
<servlet>
  <servlet-name>action</servlet-name>
  <servlet-class>
    org.apache.struts.action.ActionServlet
  </servlet-class>
  ...
</servlet>
<servlet-mapping>
  <servlet-name>action</servlet-name>
  <url-pattern>*.do</url-pattern>
</servlet-mapping>
```

The controller looks at the incoming URL for an `action` mapping in struts-config.xml to process the request. Here is an example:

```
<action-mappings>
  <action path="/register"
          type="coreservlets.RegisterAction"
```

```
            name="someFormBeanName"
            scope="request">
       <forward name="success"
                path="/WEB-INF/results/confirm-registration.jsp"/>
    </action>
 </action-mappings>
```

This particular mapping says that if the URL http://*hostname/webappname/*
register.do is received, the execute method of coreservlets.Register-
Action should be invoked. Notice that the .do extension is implied in the path definition of the action; this fact is quite useful because it lets you change the extension
from .do to anything you want, without having to change lots of separate addresses.

The execute Method of the Action Object Is Invoked

Once Struts determines the URL mapping, it sends the request to the execute
method of the appropriate Action object. One of the arguments to the execute
method is a form bean that is automatically created and whose properties are automatically populated with the incoming form data.

After examining the form data, the Action object then invokes business logic and
data-access logic, placing the results in normal beans stored in the request,
session, or application scope. In this manner, the Action can share the
results beans with the output page (request scope), with subsequent requests by
the same user (session scope), or with requests from all users (application
scope). In practice, the request scope is the most common place for storing the
result beans, because the data is usually needed only for presentation on the output
JSP page.

Finally, the execute method returns a condition (technically an ActionFor-
ward object). Based on the user input and business logic, more than one output JSP
page may be possible, so the execute method must determine which condition or
situation applies. The struts-config.xml file uses forward elements to map these
return conditions to the associated JSP pages. Next we show a fragment of a
struts-config.xml file with a forward definition. Specifically, the forward entry
says that if the execute method of RegisterAction returns mapping.find-
Forward("success"), the system should forward the result to /WEB-INF/results/
confirm-registration.jsp.

```
 <action-mappings>
   <action path="/register"
           type="coreservlets.RegisterAction"
           name="someFormBeanName"
           scope="request">
      <forward name="success"
               path="/WEB-INF/results/confirm-registration.jsp"/>
    </action>
 </action-mappings>
```

We cover the basics of the `action` element, `forward` element, and `Action` class in Section 10.4 (Processing Requests with Action Objects); we introduce form beans in Section 10.5 (Handling Request Parameters with Form Beans).

Struts Forwards the Request to the Appropriate JSP Page

Based on the condition returned from the `Action`'s execute method, the Struts system invokes the appropriate JSP results page. Unless you designate otherwise, the system uses `RequestDispatcher.forward` to invoke the page. In most real applications, the results page uses `bean:write` or the JSP 2.0 EL to output bean properties. In Section 10.4 (Processing Requests with Action Objects) we focus on `struts-config.xml` and the `Action` definition, and we introduce beans in Section 10.5 (Handling Request Parameters with Form Beans).

The Six Basic Steps in Using Struts

There are six basics steps needed to implement the control flow just described. We give a quick summary first, then provide more details. The sections in the rest of the chapter flesh out even more details and give examples.

1. **Modify struts-config.xml.** For basic Struts usage, this file should contain three main sections: a table that maps incoming addresses to `Action` objects (`action` entries), a table that maps return conditions to JSP pages (`forward` entries), and a list of the beans used to handle request parameters (`form-bean` entries). The next two chapters introduce some more advanced features (properties files, Tiles, validation) that also use information from `struts-config.xml`.

2. **Define a form bean.** Rather than requiring you to call `request.getParameter` for each incoming piece of query data, Struts can instantiate and populate a bean representing the incoming form data. This is one of the single most useful features of the Struts framework.

3. **Create the results beans.** If the JSP page needs data resulting from the business logic, then create results beans to hold the data. These beans are nothing Struts-specific, but are normal beans as used in the basic MVC architecture presented in Chapter 15 of *Core Servlets and JavaServer Pages, Volume 1.*

4. **Define an `Action` class to handle the request**. Struts automatically invokes the execute method of the `Action` object specified in the `action` entry of `struts-config.xml`. The execute method typically uses the form bean to access request data submitted by the user, invokes business logic and data-access logic, stores results beans based on that logic, and calls `mapping.findForward` to designate the result condition.

5. **Create a form that invokes *blah*.do.** Create an HTML form for the user's input. Use `html:form` to associate the form with a bean and to specify the address that should handle the form submission. Use `html:text` and related elements to gather user data and to associate bean properties with the input elements.

6. **Display the results in a JSP page.** Write a JSP page to display the results. Depending on the user input and business logic, you could have more than one possible results page. Use `bean:write` or the JSP EL to output bean properties.

Details follow.

Step 1: Modify struts-config.xml

The main thing new Struts developers should focus on is the Struts configuration file, struts-config.xml. In general, you must make the following changes to the WEB-INF/struts-config.xml file.

- **Use `action` entries to map incoming .do address to `Action` classes.** For example,

```
<action path="/someAddress"
        type="somePackage.SomeAction"
        name="someFormBeanName"
        scope="request">
```

means that when the URL http://hostname/webappname/someAddress.do is received, the system should instantiate the bean given by someFormBeanName, populate it based on matching request parameter names to bean property names, and pass it to the execute method of the SomeAction class.

- **Use `forward` entries to map return conditions to JSP pages.** For example,

```
<forward name="condition1"
         path="/WEB-INF/results/page1.jsp">
```

means that when the Action returns "condition1", the system should invoke page1.jsp.

- **Declare form beans.** For example,

```
<form-bean name="someFormBeanName"
           type="package.SomeActionFormSubclass"/>
```

associates the given name with the given class. You can choose any name you want, but the action entry (from the first bullet) must use the same name.

Whenever you modify struts-config.xml, you must restart your server. Unless you tell your server to treat struts-config.xml specially (e.g., by adding struts-config.xml to the WatchedResource list in Tomcat's context.xml file), the struts-config.xml file is read only when the Web application is first loaded.

Also, the struts-config.xml included in struts-blank-1.3.5 is full of commented-out examples. Leaving these examples in real applications clutters your configuration file and makes changes difficult. Remove everything except for the action and forward entries that are specific to your application.

Core Approach

Only include the entries in struts-config.xml that your application needs. Delete all the examples and comments from struts-config.xml in struts-blank-1.3.5. After you make changes to struts-config.xml, restart the server.

Step 2: Define a Form Bean

A form bean is a class that extends ActionForm and has accessor methods for each field of the input form submitted by the user. Instead of calling request.get-Parameter for each form field entry, the system automatically populates and gives you a form bean with all the query data.

We cover the basics of form beans in Section 10.5 (Handling Request Parameters with Form Beans); we cover more advanced usage (in particular, the reset and validate methods) in Chapter 12 (The Struts Framework: Validating User Input).

Step 3: Create the Results Beans

In the MVC architecture, the business logic and data-access code create the results without regard to the presentation, and the JSP page presents the data without regard to where it came from. To transfer the results from the Action (or the business logic that the Action invokes) to the presentation layer, the results are stored in beans. These beans differ from form beans in that they need not extend a particular class, and they represent the output of the computational process, not the input to the process.

In general, you may need to create results beans for each output JSP page. Depending on how you design your beans, you may be able to use them for more than one output JSP page.

We cover beans in Section 10.5 (Handling Request Parameters with Form Beans).

Step 4: Define an Action Class to Handle the Request

The struts-config.xml file designates the Action object with an execute method that handles the request for each URL submission. The Action objects themselves do the real work in the Web application. Each Action has the following important roles:

- Read the user data from the form bean supplied as the second argument to execute.
- Invoke the appropriate business and data-access logic.
- Store the results in scoped beans.
- Designate the type of situation that is appropriate for the results (missing data, database error, success category 1, success category 2, etc.).

Step 5: Create a Form That Invokes *blah*.do

Use the Struts html: tags to create an input form whose ACTION corresponds to one of the .do addresses listed in your struts-config.xml and whose input fields are associated with bean properties. You typically have something like this:

```
<html:form action="/blah">
  <html:text property="someBeanPropertyName">
</html:form>
```

We postpone the discussion of html:form until Section 10.6 (Prepopulating and Redisplaying Input Forms). The next two sections use the standard HTML FORM element.

Step 6: Display the Results in a JSP Page

The last step is to display the results in a JSP page. Because Struts is built around the MVC design pattern, these JSP pages should avoid JSP scripting elements whenever possible. Because the dynamic content of the JSP page is generally located in results beans, the most common Struts approach is to use the bean:write custom tag to display properties of the bean.

If the servlet engine supports the JSP 2.0 API, then using the JSP 2.0 EL is a viable alternative. Also, in complex cases, using JSTL or the Struts looping and logic tags is suitable.

In most cases, the JSP pages only make sense when the request is funneled through the Action object, because it is the Action that stores the data that the JSP pages will present. If the user were to access the JSP pages directly, the data would be missing and the pages would crash or display incorrectly. So, just as with standard RequestDispatcher-based MVC, the results pages are usually stored somewhere under WEB-INF. This prevents direct user access to the pages, but still lets the system forward to them.

Core Approach

To prevent direct access to your results pages, place them in a directory within WEB-INF.

However, if the JSP pages make sense independently of the data just created by the `Action` object (e.g., if they display session data), then place the JSP pages in a regular directory of the Web application, not under WEB-INF. In this case, the `forward` entries in struts-config.xml should specify a `redirect` of `true`, as illustrated here:

```
<forward ... redirect="true"/>
```

This entry instructs the system to invoke the page using `response.send-Redirect` instead of `RequestDispatcher.forward`.

10.4 Processing Requests with Action Objects

You downloaded struts-blank-1.3.5 to use as the starting point for your apps, and updated your `CLASSPATH` to include struts-core-1.3.5.jar so that your editor or IDE will let you compile Struts-specific code. You understand the basic flow of control in Struts. You are now ready to try a real Struts application.

The Struts framework is quite complicated, and learning all the pieces at once is an overwhelming task. In this section, we focus on two pieces: first, using `Action` objects to handle requests, and second, using the struts-config.xml file to map incoming .do addresses to these `Action` objects and to map the return conditions of the `Action` objects to JSP pages. In later sections of in this chapter, we look at using form beans and the Struts `html:` tags.

Understanding Actions

Before looking at a couple of examples, we need to understand the requirements for using the `Action` class in Struts. First, in struts-config.xml you need to define `action` and `forward` entries. Second, you need to write the `Action` class itself.

We discuss each of these requirements in the following subsections.

Defining Actions in struts-config.xml

In general, when defining an `Action`, you need to make three modifications to struts-config.xml.

- Use `action` entries to map incoming .do addresses to `Action` classes.
- Use `forward` entries to map return conditions to JSP pages.
- Declare form beans.

The upcoming example illustrates the first two modifications. We postpone the third step until Section 10.5 (Handling Request Parameters with Form Beans).

Map Incoming .do Addresses to Action Classes

To designate an `Action` class to handle a request, add an `action` entry to action-mappings in struts-config.xml. A representative `action` is given here:

```
<action-mappings>
  <action path="/register"
          type="coreservlets.RegisterAction">
    <forward name="success"
             path="/WEB-INF/results/confirm-registration.jsp"/>
  </action>
  ...
</action-mappings>
```

This `action` entry associates the URL http://*hostname*/*webappname*/register.do with the `Action` class coreservlets.RegisterAction. Notice that .do is implied automatically, so the path attribute is "/register", not "/register.do". When the Struts controller sees an incoming URL of http://*hostname*/*webappname*/register.do, it invokes the execute method of coreservlets.Register-Action. In Section 10.5 (Handling Request Parameters with Form Beans), we see that the system may also instantiate, populate, and validate form beans before the execute method is called.

Table 10.2 summarizes the common attributes of the action element. For a complete list of action attributes, see http://struts.apache.org/dtds/struts-config_1_3.dtd.

Table 10.2   Common Attributes of the `action` Element in `struts-config.xml`

Attribute	Description
path	The relative path that should trigger the `Action`. This is the incoming URL, minus the host and Web app names at the front and minus .do at the end. For example, `path="/foo/bar"` refers to http://hostname/webappname/foo/bar.do. This attribute is required.
type	The fully qualified class name of the `Action` whose execute method is invoked when Struts receives a request for the specified path. This attribute is required.
name	The alias of the form bean associated with the `Action`. The value for this attribute must match a form bean defined in the `form-beans` section. See Section 10.5 for details on form beans.
scope	The scope of the form bean associated with the `Action`. By default, the form bean has `session` scope, but can be `request` or `application`. See Section 10.5 for details on form beans. This attribute is optional, but it is good practice to always explicitly state the scope.
input	The relative path to the input form. If validation of the form data fails, the system can route the request back to the input page. See Chapter 12 (The Struts Framework: Validating User Input) for more information.

Map Return Conditions to JSP Pages

The execute method uses `mapping.findForward` to return different conditions based on various results of the business logic. Typically, you specify a different JSP page for each of the various return values. To specify a response page, add a `forward` entry to the `action` element in `struts-config.xml`. The name should match one of the conditions returned by the execute method of the `Action` object. An example is shown here:

```
<action path="/register"
        type="coreservlets.RegisterAction">
  <forward name="success"
           path="/WEB-INF/results/confirm-registration.jsp"/>
  ...
</action>
```

If the execute method of `RegisterAction` returns `mapping.find-Forward("success")`, the Struts system uses `RequestDispatcher.forward` to invoke /WEB-INF/results/confirm-registration.jsp. You define a different `forward` element for each of the possible return values.

Table 10.3 summarizes the common `forward` attributes. The default behavior is to invoke the JSP page with `RequestDispatcher.forward`, which means that forwarding occurs within the servlet container, and the URL in the browser will be the original .do address, not the address of the output JSP page.

Alternatively, if you use `redirect="true"`, the JSP page will be invoked with `response.sendRedirect`. As discussed in Chapter 6 of *Core Servlets and JavaServer Pages, Volume 1*, a redirect means that a 302 status code and a `Location` response header are sent to the browser, and then the browser connects to the URL specified in the `Location` header. This means that a redirect results in two round trips from the browser to the server, and the URL displayed in the browser will reflect the output JSP page. You only use `redirect="true"` with session or application scoped data.

Table 10.3 Common Attributes of the `forward` Element in **struts-config.xml**

Attribute	Description
name	The return condition that this entry corresponds to. This attribute is required.
path	The URL of the JSP page that is invoked if the return condition matches `name`. Except when using `redirect="true"`, the page should be in a subdirectory of **WEB-INF** to prevent the user from accessing the page before the data the page displays is ready. This attribute is required.
redirect	By default, the `redirect` attribute is `false`, meaning that the Struts system uses `RequestDispatcher.forward` to invoke the page. Use `true` to tell Struts to use `response.sendRedirect` instead.

Declare the Use of Any Form Beans

The Struts system automatically populates the form bean with the user form data before sending the request to the `Action`. We discuss how to declare form beans in **struts-config.xml** in Section 10.5 (Handling Request Parameters with Form Beans).

Writing an Action

The `execute` method of the `Action` processes the request, applies business and data-access logic, creates data representing the results (usually stored in the form of beans), and designates which return condition applies. When writing an `Action`, you should adhere to the following guidelines.

- **Place it in a package.** Place all your classes, not just your `Action` classes, in packages. You then refer to the fully qualified class name (i.e., `packagename.classname`) in the `type` attribute of the `action` element.

- **Add Struts-specific import statements.** In particular, your class needs to import `javax.servlet.http.*` (standard servlet import) and `org.apache.struts.action.*` (Struts-specific import). You would add these imports to the list of your other imports.
- **Extend the `Action` class.** Your class must inherit from the Struts `Action` class, as shown here:

```
public class YourAction extends Action {
  ...
}
```

- **Override the `execute` method.** The Struts system determines which `Action` class to run based on the requesting URL. Once determined, the Struts system calls the `execute` method of that class. The `execute` method is defined as follows:

```
public ActionForward execute(ActionMapping mapping,
                             ActionForm form,
                             HttpServletRequest request,
                             HttpServletResponse response)
    throws Exception {
  ...
}
```

The first argument, `ActionMapping`, is used to designate a condition that should match a `forward` entry in struts-config.xml. The second argument, `ActionForm`, is a form bean associated with the input page. We discuss form beans in Section 10.5 (Handling Request Parameters with Form Beans). The third and fourth arguments are the familiar `HttpServletRequest` and `HttpServletResponse` objects, respectively.

- **Return `mapping.findForward`.** The `execute` method should return an `ActionForward` based on conditions determined by the business logic. Each condition is mapped to a JSP page by a named `forward` entry in struts-config.xml. To designate the return condition, call `mapping.findForward` with the name of the condition, as illustrated here:

```
public ActionForward execute(ActionMapping mapping,
                             ActionForm form,
                             HttpServletRequest request,
                             HttpServletResponse response)
    throws Exception {
  ...
  return(mapping.findForward("someCondition"));
}
```

Example: One Result Mapping

Next, we present a very simple example that illustrates the six basic steps in using Struts. For this example, an input form submits to an `Action`, the `execute` method always yields the same result condition (regardless of user input), and then through a mapping in struts-config.xml, the flow routes to a single, static, output page.

This example presents a simplified version of the Struts flow of control, but defers many of the parts until later sections. Even this "simplified" example requires many steps. If all these steps seem like more trouble than they are worth, you are right: For this simple application, Struts is overkill. However, as we work our way toward more complex examples, you will eventually see that all the extra effort is often more than worth the bother.

Figure 10–3 shows a simplified Struts flow of control for this example. Following, we outline the general flow of this example.

- The user completes the form and submits the page. Struts, based on the URL, http://*hostname*/struts-actions/register1.do, determines to handle the action by the class `RegisterAction1`. The `RegisterAction1` class extends `Action` and is located in the `coreservlets` package.
- The `execute` method causes an action, returning a result condition. Specifically, the action of `RegisterAction1` returns only one condition, `"success"`; regardless of the user input, the result is always `"success"`.
- Based on information in struts-config.xml, Struts forwards the request to a result JSP for display to the user. Specifically, the configuration file struts-config.xml has a single `forward` entry for the `"success"` condition. The single return condition results in the display of /WEB-INF/results/confirm-registration.jsp. Because the system uses `RequestDispatcher.forward` to invoke the JSP page, the URL shown in the browser will always show register1.do.

Next, we review the six steps in using Struts in the context of this simple example.

Step 1: Modify struts-config.xml

As presented earlier, the struts-config.xml file supports two main tasks: mapping incoming addresses to `Action` objects, and mapping return condition to JSP pages. We need to add `action` entries for the first task and `forward` entries for the second.

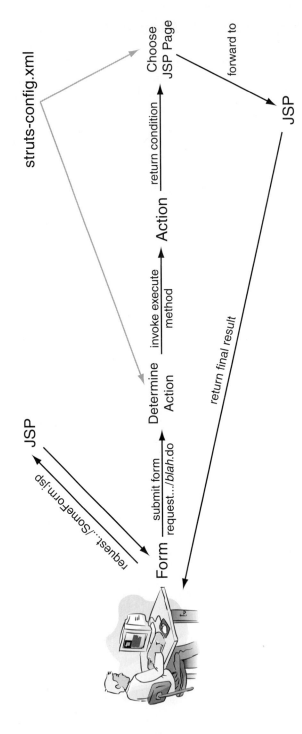

Figure 10–3 Simplified flow of control in Struts.

Map Incoming .do Address to Action Classes

In this example, we define an the action element in struts-config.xml to designate that RegisterAction1 should handle requests for register1.do. To accomplish this step, we add an action entry to action-mappings in struts-config.xml, as shown in the following code fragment:

```
<action path="/register1"
        type="coreservlets.RegisterAction1">
   ...
</action>
```

Remember that .do is implied automatically in the path, so the actual incoming URL will be http://*hostname*/*webappname*/register1**.do**.

The type attribute designates the fully qualified class name of the Action object, coreservlets.RegisterAction1. We omit the other common action attributes in this example (name, scope, and input); we use name and scope in Section 10.5 (Handling Request Parameters with Form Beans) and use input in Chapter 12 (The Struts Framework: Validating User Input).

Map Return Conditions to JSP Pages

In this example, we have only one forward element, for the "success" condition. The forward entry in struts-config.xml is given here:

```
<forward name="success"
         path="/WEB-INF/results/confirm-registration.jsp"/>
```

Placing the result page within /WEB-INF means the user cannot directly access it. This may not seem important in this highly simplified example where the JSP pages consist of static content, but it is extremely important in later examples where the JSP pages output the properties of beans that do not even exist until the Action object is invoked.

The struts-config.xml is given in Listing 10.1. Note that in this file, all of the examples and comments from the version in struts-blank have been removed. We strongly recommend you follow the same practice: Keep the commented version around for reference, but in your actual applications omit all irrelevant entries.

Listing 10.1 struts-actions/WEB-INF/struts-config.xml

```
<?xml version="1.0" encoding="ISO-8859-1" ?>
<!DOCTYPE struts-config PUBLIC
  "-//Apache Software Foundation//DTD Struts Configuration 1.3//EN"
  "http://struts.apache.org/dtds/struts-config_1_3.dtd">
<struts-config>
  <action-mappings>
    <action path="/register1"
            type="coreservlets.RegisterAction1">
      <forward name="success"
               path="/WEB-INF/results/confirm-registration.jsp"/>
    </action>
    ...
  </action-mappings>
</struts-config>
```

Step 2: Define a Form Bean

In the simplified example, we pay no attention to the user input on the registration page. Regardless, the user always sees the same output for a "success" condition. Thus, this example uses no form bean.

Step 3: Create the Results Beans

In this simplified example, we are concentrating on the basic flow of control, so the final JSP pages show simple static content and use no results beans.

Step 4: Create an Action Object to Handle the Request

To create an Action object, we follow the guidance outlined earlier.

- **Place in a package.** For this example, we place the class in the coreservlets package:

```
package coreservlets;
```

  Because we use a Web application name of struts-actions, we need to place the class file in the /struts-actions/WEB-INF/classes/coreservlets directory.

- **Add Struts-specific import statements.** For this example, we add the following to our Action class:

```
import javax.servlet.http.*;
import org.apache.struts.action.*;
```

- **Extend the `Action` class.** For this example, we define a RegisterAction1 class that extends Action.

  ```
  public class RegisterAction1 extends Action {
      ...
  }
  ```

- **Override the `execute` method.** In this example, we override the execute method to do nothing more than produce a "success" condition. There is no other business logic.

  ```
  public ActionForward execute(ActionMapping mapping,
                               ActionForm form,
                               HttpServletRequest request,
                               HttpServletResponse response)
      throws Exception {
    return(mapping.findForward("success"));
  }
  ```

- **Return `mapping.findForward`.** In this example, only a "success" return condition is possible. The mapping is given here:

  ```
  mapping.findForward("success")
  ```

The complete Action class is given in Listing 10.2.

Listing 10.2	struts-actions/WEB-INF/classes/coreservlets/ RegisterAction1.java

```java
package coreservlets;

import javax.servlet.http.*;
import org.apache.struts.action.*;

/** An action that always returns a mapping to a "success"
 *  page.
 */

public class RegisterAction1 extends Action {
  public ActionForward execute(ActionMapping mapping,
                               ActionForm form,
                               HttpServletRequest request,
                               HttpServletResponse response)
      throws Exception {
    return(mapping.findForward("success"));
  }
}
```

Step 5: Create a Form That Invokes *blah*.do

For this example, we need an input form that invokes http://*hostname*/struts-actions/register1.do. We place the input form in the top-level directory of the struts-actions Web app, and use a relative URL for the ACTION. Normally, the input form is built from Struts tags. Rather than overwhelm you with everything in the framework at once, we delay discussing the Struts html: tags until Section 10.6 (Prepopulating and Redisplaying Input Forms). Thus, for now, we build the form using normal HTML elements.

The registration JSP page, register1.jsp, is given in Listing 10.3.

Listing 10.3   struts-actions/register1.jsp

```
<!DOCTYPE HTML PUBLIC "-//W3C//DTD HTML 4.0 Transitional//EN">
<HTML>
<HEAD><TITLE>New Account Registration</TITLE></HEAD>
<BODY BGCOLOR="#FDF5E6">
<CENTER>
<H1>New Account Registration</H1>
<FORM ACTION="register1.do" METHOD="POST">
  Email address: <INPUT TYPE="TEXT" NAME="email"><BR>
  Password: <INPUT TYPE="PASSWORD" NAME="password"><BR>
  <INPUT TYPE="SUBMIT" VALUE="Sign Me Up!">
</FORM>
</CENTER>
</BODY></HTML>
```

Step 6: Display the Results in a JSP Page

For this example, we have only one output JSP page for the "success" condition. As the output makes no use of the user input, the page simply has static content.

The results page, confirm-registration.jsp, is given in Listing 10.4. Notice that this output JSP is located in /struts-actions/WEB-INF/results and thus is not directly accessible by the user.

Finally, the complete directory structure of the files for this example is shown in Figure 10–4.

Listing 10.4	struts-actions/WEB-INF/results/confirm-registration.jsp

```
<!DOCTYPE HTML PUBLIC "-//W3C//DTD HTML 4.0 Transitional//EN">
<HTML>
<HEAD><TITLE>Success</TITLE></HEAD>
<BODY BGCOLOR="#FDF5E6">
<CENTER>
<H1>You have registered successfully.</H1>
Congratulations
</CENTER>
</BODY></HTML>
```

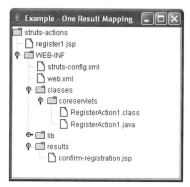

Figure 10–4   Complete file structure for "One Result Mapping" example.

Results

Now, we present the results for this example, reviewing the processing flow through the Struts framework.

- The user first invokes the input form through the URL http://localhost/struts-actions/register1.jsp. This initial JSP page is shown in Figure 10–5.
- The user completes the form and submits it. The form's ACTION results in the URL http://localhost/struts-actions/register1.do.
- The URL is mapped by struts-config.xml to the RegisterAction1 class. The Struts system invokes the execute method of RegisterAction1.
- The execute method returns a mapping.findForward for the single condition, "success". This condition maps to /WEB-INF/results/confirm-registration.jsp in struts-config.xml. Finally, the request is forwarded to the output JSP page. See Figure 10–6. Notice in the figure that the URL displayed to the user remains register1.do.

Figure 10–5   Initial registration page. The ACTION submits to register1.do.

Figure 10–6   Successful registration page.

Example: Multiple Result Mappings

Next, we expand on the previous example, but now, instead of displaying a single output JSP page, more than one output JSP page is possible. Which page is displayed depends on the input the user provides on the registration page. This example is more realistic, incorporating business logic in the Action. It also illustrates the simplicity of setting up multiple return pages in the Struts configuration file.

Following, we outline the general flow of this example.

- The URL http://*hostname*/struts-actions/register2.do is handled by the class RegisterAction2.
- The execute method of RegisterAction2 returns one of three conditions: "success", "bad-address", or "bad-password".

- The three return conditions result in the following JSP pages displayed to the user, respectively:

  /WEB-INF/results/bad-address.jsp
  /WEB-INF/results/bad-password.jsp
  /WEB-INF/results/confirm-registration.jsp

  Because the system uses RequestDispatcher.forward to invoke the JSP page, the URL shown in the browser will always show register2.do.
- The configuration file struts-config.xml has a forward entry for each of the three possible output pages.

Next, we review the six steps in using Struts in the context of this modified example.

Step 1: Modify struts-config.xml

As discussed earlier, the struts-config.xml file supports two main tasks: mapping incoming addresses to Action objects, and mapping return condition to JSP pages.

Map Incoming .do Addresses to Action Classes

As before, we define an the action element in struts-config.xml to designate that RegisterAction2 should handle requests for register2.do. Thus, we add an action entry to action-mappings in struts-config.xml, as shown in the following code fragment:

```
<action path="/register2"
        type="coreservlets.RegisterAction2">
  ...
</action>
```

Again, remember that .do is implied automatically in the path, so the actual incoming URL will be http://*hostname*/*struts-actions*/register2.**do**.

Map Return Conditions to JSP Pages

In this modified example, we use multiple forward elements, one for each of the possible return conditions ("success", "bad-address", and "bad-password"). The forward entries are defined in struts-config.xml as follows:

```
<forward name="bad-address"
        path="/WEB-INF/results/bad-address.jsp"/>
<forward name="bad-password"
        path="/WEB-INF/results/bad-password.jsp"/>
<forward name="success"
        path="/WEB-INF/results/confirm-registration.jsp"/>
```

We place all the results pages within the /WEB-INF directory structure. Thus, the user cannot directly access them through the browser. The complete struts-config.xml file is given in Listing 10.5.

Listing 10.5 struts-actions/WEB-INF/struts-config.xml

```xml
<?xml version="1.0" encoding="ISO-8859-1" ?>
<!DOCTYPE struts-config PUBLIC
   "-//Apache Software Foundation//DTD Struts Configuration 1.3//EN"
   "http://struts.apache.org/dtds/struts-config_1_3.dtd">
<struts-config>
  <action-mappings>
    ...
    <action path="/register2"
             type="coreservlets.RegisterAction2">
      <forward name="bad-address"
               path="/WEB-INF/results/bad-address.jsp"/>
      <forward name="bad-password"
               path="/WEB-INF/results/bad-password.jsp"/>
      <forward name="success"
               path="/WEB-INF/results/confirm-registration.jsp"/>
    </action>
  </action-mappings>
</struts-config>
```

Step 2: Define a Form Bean

In general, the `execute` method uses a form bean to access the incoming request parameters. For experienced Struts developers, this approach is easier and more robust than repeatedly calling `request.getParameter`. However, this example is complicated enough already, so we postpone form beans until a later example, and call the familiar `request.getParameter` method instead.

Note that although you rarely call `request.getParameter` in real Struts applications, you frequently use the `HttpServletRequest` object for other purposes. In particular, Struts provides no built-in facility for accessing cookies or standard HTTP request headers, so `request.getCookies` and `request.getHeader` are still used in Struts.

Step 3: Create the Results Beans

In this simplified example, we are concentrating on the basic flow of control, so the final JSP pages show simple static content and use no results beans.

Step 4: Create an Action Object to Handle the Request

To create an `Action` object, we follow the guidance outlined earlier. We place this new `RegisterAction2` class in the `coreservlets` package. In addition, we override the `execute` method to first use `request.getParameter` explicitly to look up form input values and then specify a return condition based on the values of those parameters. Later, in Section 10.5 (Handling Request Parameters with Form Beans) we let Struts automatically populate a bean with the request data.

The logic for our `execute` method is shown here:

```
public ActionForward execute(ActionMapping mapping,
                             ActionForm form,
                             HttpServletRequest request,
                             HttpServletResponse response)
    throws Exception {
  String email = request.getParameter("email");
  String password = request.getParameter("password");
  if ((email == null) ||
      (email.trim().length() < 3) ||
      (email.indexOf("@") == -1)) {
    return(mapping.findForward("bad-address"));
  } else if ((password == null) ||
             (password.trim().length() < 6)) {
    return(mapping.findForward("bad-password"));
  } else {
    return(mapping.findForward("success"));
  }
}
```

Three return conditions are possible:

- **bad-address.** If the e-mail address is missing, is less than three characters long, or does not contain an @ sign, then return `mapping.findForward("bad-address")`.
- **bad-password.** If the password is missing or is less than six characters long, then return `mapping.findForward("bad-password")`.
- **success.** Otherwise, return `mapping.findForward("success")`.

The complete `RegisterAction2` class is given in Listing 10.6.

Listing 10.6	struts-actions/WEB-INF/classes/coreservlets/ RegisterAction2.java

```java
package coreservlets;

import javax.servlet.http.*;
import org.apache.struts.action.*;

/** An action that has three possible mapping conditions:
 *      bad-address  if the e-mail address is missing or doesn't
 *                   contain @
 *      bad-password if the password is missing or is less than 6
 *                   characters
 *      success      if e-mail address and password are OK
 */

public class RegisterAction2 extends Action {
  public ActionForward execute(ActionMapping mapping,
                               ActionForm form,
                               HttpServletRequest request,
                               HttpServletResponse response)
      throws Exception {
    String email = request.getParameter("email");
    String password = request.getParameter("password");
    if ((email == null) ||
        (email.trim().length() < 3) ||
        (email.indexOf("@") == -1)) {
      return(mapping.findForward("bad-address"));
    } else if ((password == null) ||
               (password.trim().length() < 6)) {
      return(mapping.findForward("bad-password"));
    } else {
      return(mapping.findForward("success"));
    }
  }
}
```

Step 5: Create a Form That Invokes *blah*.do

This example requires an input form that invokes http://*hostname*/struts-actions/ register2.do. As before, we place the input form in the top-level directory of the struts-actions Web app, and use a relative URL for the ACTION. The registration JSP page, register2.jsp, is given in Listing 10.7.

| Listing 10.7 | struts-actions/register2.jsp |

```
<!DOCTYPE HTML PUBLIC "-//W3C//DTD HTML 4.0 Transitional//EN">
<HTML>
<HEAD><TITLE>New Account Registration</TITLE></HEAD>
<BODY BGCOLOR="#FDF5E6">
<CENTER>
<H1>New Account Registration</H1>
<FORM ACTION="register2.do" METHOD="POST">
  Email address: <INPUT TYPE="TEXT" NAME="email"><BR>
  Password: <INPUT TYPE="PASSWORD" NAME="password"><BR>
  <INPUT TYPE="SUBMIT" VALUE="Sign Me Up!">
</FORM>
</CENTER>
</BODY></HTML>
```

Step 6: Display the Results in a JSP Page

For this example, we have three possible output JSP pages, depending on whether the user completed the input form correctly.

- **bad-address.jsp.** For condition `"bad-address"`.
  See Listing 10.8.
- **bad-password.jsp.** For condition `"bad-password"`.
  See Listing 10.9.
- **confirm-registration.jsp.** For condition `"success"`.
  See Listing 10.10.

Each output JSP page is located in /struts-actions/WEB-INF/results and thus is not directly accessible by the user.

Also note that there are some significant problems in our validation logic. First, we have weak rules about what constitutes a valid e-mail address. Second, the error pages do not show the actual input values. Third, if the user enters an invalid e-mail address and an invalid password, only one error is flagged. For now, we can live with these deficiencies because our goal is to show the basic way to structure struts-config.xml and define an `Action` object. However, all of these deficiencies are addressed with more advanced Struts features in Chapter 12 (The Struts Framework: Validating User Input).

Finally, the complete file structure for this example is shown in Figure 10–7.

Listing 10.8   struts-actions/WEB-INF/results/bad-address.jsp

```
<!DOCTYPE HTML PUBLIC "-//W3C//DTD HTML 4.0 Transitional//EN">
<HTML>
<HEAD><TITLE>Illegal Email Address</TITLE></HEAD>
<BODY BGCOLOR="#FDF5E6">
<CENTER>
<H1>Illegal Email Address</H1>
Address must be of the form username@host.
Please <A HREF="register2.jsp">try again</A>.
</CENTER>
</BODY></HTML>
```

Listing 10.9   struts-actions/WEB-INF/results/bad-password.jsp

```
<!DOCTYPE HTML PUBLIC "-//W3C//DTD HTML 4.0 Transitional//EN">
<HTML>
<HEAD><TITLE>Illegal Password</TITLE></HEAD>
<BODY BGCOLOR="#FDF5E6">
<CENTER>
<H1>Illegal Password</H1>
Password must contain at least six characters.
Please <A HREF="register2.jsp">try again</A>.
</CENTER>
</BODY></HTML>
```

Listing 10.10   struts-actions/WEB-INF/results/confirm-registration.jsp

```
<!DOCTYPE HTML PUBLIC "-//W3C//DTD HTML 4.0 Transitional//EN">
<HTML>
<HEAD><TITLE>Success</TITLE></HEAD>
<BODY BGCOLOR="#FDF5E6">
<CENTER>
<H1>You have registered successfully.</H1>
Congratulations
</CENTER>
</BODY></HTML>
```

Figure 10–7 File structure for "Multiple Result Mappings" example.

Results

Now, we present the results for this example, reviewing the processing flow through the Struts framework.

- The user first invokes the input form through the URL http://localhost/struts-actions/register2.jsp. This initial JSP page is shown in Figure 10–8.
- The user completes the form and submits it. The form's ACTION results in the URL http://localhost/struts-actions/register2.do.
- The URL is mapped by struts-config.xml to the RegisterAction2 class. The Struts system invokes the execute method of RegisterAction2.
- The execute method returns a mapping.findForward condition corresponding to three possible situations, based on the user input.
- If the user fills in an incorrect e-mail address, then the execute method returns a "bad-address" condition. This condition maps to /WEB-INF/results/bad-address.jsp in struts-config.xml. See Figure 10–9.
- If the user fills in a correct e-mail address, but the password is incorrect (fewer than six characters), the execute method returns a "bad-password" condition. This condition maps to /WEB-INF/results/bad-password.jsp in struts-config.xml. See Figure 10–10.
- If the user correctly fills in the e-mail address and password, then a "success" condition is returned and the request is forwarded to /WEB-INF/results/confirm-registration.jsp. See Figure 10–11.

Regardless of which final JSP page is displayed, the URL displayed to the user remains register2.do.

Figure 10–8   Initial registration page. The ACTION submits to register2.do.

Figure 10–9   Registration form with an illegal e-mail address–one that doesn't contain an @ symbol (left). Response for a "bad-address" condition (right).

Figure 10–10   Registration form with an illegal password—one that doesn't contain six characters (left). Response for a "bad-password" condition (right).

Figure 10–11 Successful registration page.

Combining Shared Condition (Forward) Mappings

Suppose that you had several different `action` entries, all of which mapped `"success"` to /WEB-INF/results/confirm-registration.jsp. Listing identical `forward` entries within all the `action` elements is repetitive and requires you to make changes to multiple `forward` entries if you rename the confirmation page. Therefore, if the same result condition maps to the same JSP page in more than one `action` entry, Struts lets you replace all the separate `forward` entries with a single `forward` entry in a `global-forwards` section. Note that the `global-forwards` section goes before `action-mappings`, not within it. The `forward` entries within `global-forwards` have the same syntax and behavior as `forward` entries within `action`, but they apply to any action. However, a `forward` entry within an `action` always takes precedence over a `forward` entry in `global-forwards`. So, for example, the following code fragment says "unless an `action` says otherwise, if the return condition is `"success"`, invoke confirm-registration.jsp."

```
<global-forwards>
  <forward name="success"
          path="/WEB-INF/results/confirm-registration.jsp"/>
</global-forwards>
```

To further illustrate the use of global forwards, Listing 10.11 presents a `struts-config.xml` file with two actions, `RegisterAction1` and `RegisterAction2`. Both actions have a `forward` entry that maps `"success"` to /WEB-INF/results/confirm-registration.jsp for the condition `"success"`. As this `forward` is common, it can be moved to a `global-forward` entry as shown in Listing 10.12.

Listing 10.11 Two actions with a duplicate forward entry

```xml
<?xml version="1.0" encoding="ISO-8859-1" ?>
<!DOCTYPE struts-config PUBLIC
  "-//Apache Software Foundation//DTD Struts Configuration 1.3//EN"
  "http://struts.apache.org/dtds/struts-config_1_3.dtd">
<struts-config>
  <action-mappings>
    <action path="/register1"
            type="coreservlets.RegisterAction1">
      <forward name="success"
               path="/WEB-INF/results/confirm-registration.jsp"/>
    </action>
    <action path="/register2"
            type="coreservlets.RegisterAction2">
      <forward name="bad-address"
               path="/WEB-INF/results/bad-address.jsp"/>
      <forward name="bad-password"
               path="/WEB-INF/results/bad-password.jsp"/>
      <forward name="success"
               path="/WEB-INF/results/confirm-registration.jsp"/>
    </action>
    ...
  </action-mappings>
</struts-config>
```

Listing 10.12 Two actions with a common global-forward entry

```xml
<?xml version="1.0" encoding="ISO-8859-1" ?>
<!DOCTYPE struts-config PUBLIC
  "-//Apache Software Foundation//DTD Struts Configuration 1.3//EN"
  "http://struts.apache.org/dtds/struts-config_1_3.dtd">
<struts-config>
  <global-forwards>
    <forward name="success"
             path="/WEB-INF/results/confirm-registration.jsp"/>
  </global-forwards>
  <action-mappings>
    <action path="/register1"
            type="coreservlets.RegisterAction1">
    </action>
    <action path="/register2"
            type="coreservlets.RegisterAction2">
```

Listing 10.12	Two actions with a common global-forward entry *(continued)*

```
        <forward name="bad-address"
                  path="/WEB-INF/results/bad-address.jsp"/>
        <forward name="bad-password"
                  path="/WEB-INF/results/bad-password.jsp"/>
    </action>
    ...
  </action-mappings>
</struts-config>
```

10.5 Handling Request Parameters with Form Beans

In the previous example, we explicitly called `request.getParameter` to obtain the form data. We used this manual approach because we wanted to concentrate only on the `action` mappings, `forward` entries, and structure of the `Action` class. In a real application, however, making repeated `request.getParameter` calls is tedious and error prone. Fortunately, Struts has a very convenient and powerful facility that simplifies this process: form beans.

Basically, a form bean is little more than a JavaBean with property names that correspond to request parameter names. When a user submits a request, the system instantiates the bean; populates it based on the incoming request parameters (i.e., if any incoming parameter name matches a bean property name, it calls the corresponding setter method); stores it in `request`, `session`, or `application` scope; and passes it to the `execute` method of your `Action`. That way, you don't have to call `request.getParameter` a zillion times, but instead get all of the form data in one fell swoop. This idea is sort of what `jsp:setProperty` with `property="*"` does (see Chapter 14 of *Core Servlets and JavaServer Pages, Volume 1*), except that `jsp:setProperty` is exactly backward. It lets you do the process in a JSP page (where you don't want to), but doesn't expose the underlying Java API (so you can call it from Java code). In addition, Struts form beans have two additional capabilities: a `reset` method that gets called before any of the setter methods is called, and a `validate` method that is called after all of the setter methods is called. In this section we concentrate on the main use of form beans to represent form data; in Chapter 12 (The Struts Framework: Validating User Input) we see how the `reset` and `validate` methods come in handy.

Struts Flow of Control: Updates for Bean Use

In Section 10.3 (The Struts Flow of Control and the Six Steps to Implementing It), we presented the flow of the request through the Struts framework. Let's review that flow, but concentrate on the parts related to bean usage. See Figure 10–12 for a diagram of the request flow.

- **The user requests a form.** In real applications, the input form is almost always built with the Struts `html:` tags. Until we get to Section 10.6 (Prepopulating and Redisplaying Input Forms), however, we use normal HTML.
- **The form is submitted to a URL of the form *blah*.do.** The form contains an `ACTION` of the form *blah*.do. The Struts system receives the request, where a mapping in struts-config.xml associates the address with an `Action` object.
- **The `execute` method of the `Action` object is invoked.** Struts instantiates a form bean; calls all setter methods for form parameter names that match bean property names; stores the bean in `request`, `session`, or `application` scope; and passes the bean to `execute` as the second argument. Rather than calling `request.getParameter` explicitly, the `execute` method just uses the form bean. The `execute` method also invokes business logic and data-access logic, placing the results in normal beans stored in `request`, `session`, or `application` scope. The `execute` method then uses `mapping.findForward` to return various conditions that are mapped by struts-config.xml to various JSP pages.
- **Struts forwards the request to the appropriate JSP page.** Struts invokes the JSP page given in the forward entry. That JSP page uses `bean:write` or the JSP 2.0 EL to output the properties of either the results beans or the form bean.

Next, we review the six basic steps in using Struts, emphasizing the bean-related parts.

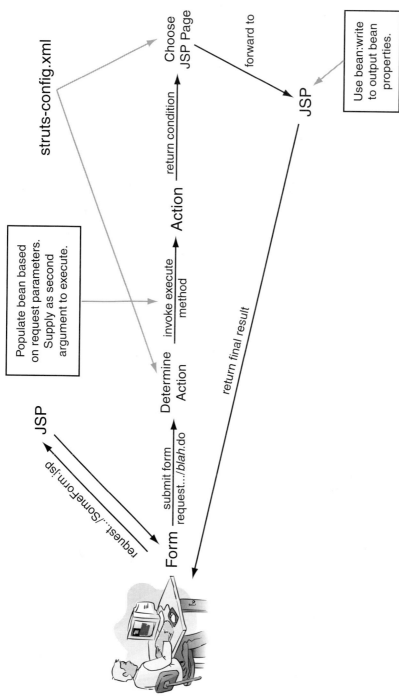

Figure 10–12   Flow of request through the Struts framework. Boxed entries show updates for using beans.

The Six Basic Steps in Using Struts

In Section 10.4 (Processing Requests with Action Objects), we showed the six basic steps in using Struts in the context of a working application. In that section, we focused on the simplest possible usage of the `Action` class; in this section, the emphasis is on form beans and results beans.

Step 1: Modify struts-config.xml

You need to add three main entries to WEB-INF/struts-config.xml.

- **Use `action` entries to map incoming .do addresses to `Action` classes.** This step is mostly done the same way as in the previous examples, but now you also list the name and scope of the form bean, as shown here:

```
<action path="..." type="..."
        name="beanName" scope="request">
```

Unfortunately, the default `scope` in Struts is `session`, so always specify `scope="request"` unless you have a specific need for session tracking.

- **Use `forward` entries to map return conditions to JSP pages.** This is done exactly the same way as in the previous examples.

- **Declare form beans.** Put a `form-bean` entry in the `form-beans` section for each bean that is associated with an `Action`. Give each form bean a name.

```
<form-beans>
  <form-bean name="beanName" type="package.Class"/>
</form-beans>
```

In Section 10.4 (Processing Requests with Action Objects) we covered the first two bullets; now we focus on the third.

Step 2: Define a Form Bean

A form bean is a class that extends `ActionForm` and represents the data submitted by the user. It should have a bean property for each incoming request parameter. For instance, if the input form has `firstName` and `lastName` parameters, the bean must have `setFirstName` and `setLastName` methods, and usually also has `get-FirstName` and `getLastName` methods.

When the user requests the URL corresponding to the `Action`, the bean is automatically instantiated, the setter methods that match any nonempty parameters are called, the bean is stored in the appropriate scope, and the bean is passed to the `execute` method.

Step 3: Create the Results Beans

In the MVC architecture, results beans are just normal beans that hold data that the presentation-layer JSP pages will display. The form bean represents the input data, the data that came from the HTML form. In most applications, the more important type of data is the result data, the data created by the business logic to represent the results of the computation or database lookup.

For the beans to be available to the output JSP, you need to store them in the request, session, or application scope. Simply call the setAttribute method on the corresponding scope object (HttpServletRequest, HttpSession, ServletContext) just as in normal non-Struts applications. It is also possible to create extra properties in the form bean to be used to store the results. Both approaches are common, although we usually find it slightly clearer to have separate beans for the results.

Step 4: Define an Action Class to Handle the Requests

As presented in Section 10.4 (Processing Requests with Action Objects), each incoming URL needs an Action object to handle the request. In Section 10.4, we used request.getParameter in the execute method to retrieve the form data. When using form beans, however, all you need to do is cast the ActionForm to your specific class, then access the already fully populated bean. For example:

```
public ActionForward execute(ActionMapping mapping,
                             ActionForm form,
                             HttpServletRequest request,
                             HttpServletResponse response)
        throws Exception {
    MyFormBean myBean = (MyFormBean)form;
    accessInputData(myBean);
    ...
}
```

Step 5: Create a Form That Invokes *blah*.do

In a real Struts application, you would use the Struts html:form custom tag to build the input form. We postpone the discussion of html:form until Section 10.6 (Prepopulating and Redisplaying Input Forms) and for now, use the standard HTML FORM element.

Step 6: Display the Results in a JSP Page

Finally, you need to present the results in the JSP page specified in the forward element. Use the Struts bean:write tag to output the bean properties.

```
<bean:write name="beanName" property="beanProperty"/>
```

Also, if the servlet engine supports the JSP 2.0 API, then you may consider using the JSP 2.0 EL as an alternative to the bean:write tag.

Understanding Form Beans

Form beans play a critical role in the Struts framework. As we see in this section, form beans represent the incoming user data. As we will see in the next section, form beans let you prepopulate and redisplay input forms. As we see in Chapter 12 (The Struts Framework: Validating User Input), form beans support validation of the input data. In all cases, you need to define a form-bean element in struts-config.xml and write an ActionForm class.

Defining Form Beans in struts-config.xml

To use form beans, you have to perform two new tasks in struts-config.xml.

- **Declare the form beans.** Give each a name and a type.
- **Update the action declarations.** Use name to refer to the form-bean name, and use scope="request" (usually), scope="session" (when the bean needs to persist between requests), or scope="application" (in the rare cases when the bean needs to be accessible to any user).

We discuss each of these tasks in the following subsections.

Declare the Form Beans

To designate a form bean (i.e., an ActionForm object) to handle input data, add a form-bean entry to the form-beans element in struts-config.xml. Place the form-beans element before the action-mappings element.

Core Note

The form-beans *section goes before the* action-mappings *element in struts-config.xml, not inside* action-mappings.

If supporting an existing application that uses global-exceptions and global-forwards elements, place the form-bean entry before these.
We give an example of a form-bean declaration here:

```
<form-beans>
   <form-bean name="someFormBean"
            type="coreservlets.SomeFormBean"/>
</form-beans>
```

The name attribute is an alias for the form bean. Choose any name you want, but use the same name in the action declaration. When defining the bean, you must also identify the fully qualified class name of the bean. Use the type attribute for this part. For a complete list of all form-bean attributes, see http://struts.apache.org/dtds/struts-config_1_3.dtd.

Update the Action Declarations to Use Form Beans

After using form-bean to give your bean a name, you need to update your action element so that Struts knows which ActionForm bean to instantiate and populate for which Action.

Specifically, you need to add name and scope attributes to the action element. For example,

```
<action path="/register"
        type="coreservlets.ActionWithBean"
        name="userFormBean"
        scope="request">
```

The name attribute must match a bean name from the form-beans section of struts-config.xml. The scope specifies the location to both find and store the form bean. If no bean of the given name is found in the specified scope, Struts instantiates a new bean, populates it based on matching request parameter names to bean property names, stores it in the specified scope, and passes it to the execute method. If a bean of the given name is found in the specified scope (which could easily happen with session-scoped data), Struts uses the existing bean instead of creating a new one.

The scope can be request, session, or application. Surprisingly, session is the default, but the request scope is the more common place to store the bean. If you do use the session scope for your bean, we recommend stating the scope in the action, even though session is the default.

Writing an ActionForm

When writing a form bean, the class should adhere to the following guidelines.

- **Extend the ActionForm class.** All form beans must extend the ActionForm class. In this section, it is not clear why Struts makes you extend any particular class, but in Chapter 12 (The Struts Framework: Validating User Input), we see that the ActionForm class has two important inherited methods: reset (which is called before any of the bean properties are set—i.e., setter methods called) and validate (which is called after all the bean properties are set).

- **Have a zero-argument constructor.** When instantiating the bean, the system always calls the default constructor. Remember that Java gives you a zero-argument constructor automatically when no constructors are defined, so there is often no need to explicitly define a constructor.
- **Have settable bean properties that correspond to request parameter names.** The bean must have a `setBlah` method corresponding to each incoming request parameter named `blah`. The properties should be of type `String` (i.e., each `setBlah` method should take a `String` as an argument).
- **Have gettable bean properties for each property that you want to output in the JSP page.** That is, the bean must have a `getBlah` method corresponding to each bean property that you want to display in JSP using `bean:write` or the JSP EL. In practice, form beans almost always have getter and setter methods for every request parameter, but sometimes have additional getter methods for computed properties.

Displaying Bean Properties

Typically, after the `Action` processes the request, the system routes the request to the output JSP page, where you display the results. In principle, you can use any of the following approaches to display the bean properties in the JSP page. In practice, the last two are the usual ones in Struts applications.

- **Use JSP scripting elements.** This approach is out of the question; it is precisely what Struts is designed to avoid.
- **Use `jsp:useBean` and `jsp:getProperty`.** This approach is possible, but these tags are a bit clumsy and verbose.
- **Use the JSTL `c:out` tag.** This approach is not a bad idea, but it is hardly worth the bother using JSTL just for this situation. Unless you are using JSTL in your application anyhow, don't bother with `c:out`.
- **Use JSP 2.0 EL.** This is perhaps the best option if the server supports JSP 2.0. For example:

```
Email Address:   ${userFormBean.email}
```

However, if the application needs to run on multiple servers, some of which support only JSP 1.2, this won't be an option.
- **Use the Struts `bean:write` tag.** Because Struts was developed before the JSP EL, and because the other options for bean access are poor, Struts developed a custom tag library just for this purpose. The `bean:write` tags are more succinct and readable than the

jsp:useBean tags (although not as succinct as the JSP EL), and using them is by far the most common approach when using Struts. For example:

Email Address: **<bean:write name="userFormBean"
                              property="email"/>**

Note that, unlike c:out and the JSP 2.0 EL, bean:write automatically filters special HTML characters, replacing < with < and > with >. You can disable this behavior by specifying false for the filter attribute, as in the following:

```
<bean:write name="userFormBean"
            property="email"
            filter="false"/>
```

Table 10.4 summarizes the common attributes of the bean:write tag. For a complete listing of attributes, see http://struts.apache.org/1.x/struts-taglib/tlddoc/bean/write.html.

Table 10.4   Common Attributes of bean:write

Attribute	Description
name	The name of the bean. For form beans, this is the name given in the form-bean entry. For regular beans, this is the key supplied to setAttribute. This attribute is required.
property	The bean property to retrieve. Interestingly, this attribute is optional. If you don't specify a property, the tag calls toString on the bean object.
scope	The location in which to find the bean. The scope can be page, request, session, or application. This attribute is optional, so if you don't specify it, Struts searches the scopes in the following order: page, request, session, application. Most developers omit this attribute.
filter	Indicates if the bean property should be filtered for HTML characters, for example, replacing < with < and replacing > with >. The default value is true, so to turn filtering off, set to false.

Example: Form and Results Beans

Now, we present an example using form and results beans. This example is similar to the one presented in Section 10.4 (Processing Requests with Action Objects), but uses both a form bean and a result bean.

This example further illustrates the processing flow of a request in the Struts framework: An input form submits to a URL ending in *something*.do; the system instantiates a form bean and populates it based on the request parameters; the form bean is stored in `request` or `session` scope and then passed to the `execute` method of the `Action` that matches the incoming URL; the `execute` method applies business logic to create results beans and to determine a result condition; the system invokes the JSP page that corresponds to the result condition; and the JSP page outputs properties of both the form bean and the results beans.

Here is how that flow looks in this example:

- The URL http://*hostname*/struts-beans/register.do should be handled by the class `BeanRegisterAction`.
- Instead of reading form data explicitly with `request.getParameter`, the `execute` method of `BeanRegisterAction` uses a form bean that is automatically populated with the request data.
- The `execute` method of `BeanRegisterAction` creates and stores a results bean with a suggested correct e-mail address or password, and returns one of three possible return conditions: `"bad-address"`, `"bad-password"`, or `"success"`.
- These three return values result in /WEB-INF/results/bad-address.jsp, /WEB-INF/results/bad-password.jsp, and /WEB-INF/results/confirm-registration.jsp, respectively.
- The JSP pages use `bean:write` to output bean properties.

Here are the new features of this example:

- **The use of a bean to represent the incoming form data.** This form bean extends the `ActionForm` class, is declared in struts-config.xml with the `form-bean` tag, and is referenced in the `action` element with `name` and `scope` attributes.
- **The use of a regular bean to represent custom results.** As with beans used with regular MVC, this bean need not extend any particular class and requires no special struts-config.xml declarations.
- **The use of the Struts `bean:write` tags to output bean properties in the JSP page that displays the final results.** This approach is basically a more powerful and concise alternative to the standard `jsp:getProperty` tag. Before we use `bean:write`, we have to import the bean tag library as follows:

```
<%@ taglib uri="http://struts.apache.org/tags-bean"
           prefix="bean" %>
```

Now, with this design in mind, we review the six steps in using Struts.

Step 1: Modify struts-config.xml

In Section 10.4 (Processing Requests with Action Objects) we showed how to modify struts-config.xml to map incoming .do requests to Action classes and to map return conditions to JSP pages. In this example we also declare a form bean (by using form-bean) and associate it with the Action (by using name and scope in action).

Map Incoming .do Addresses to Action Classes

As before, we use the action element in struts-config.xml. Here, we designate that BeanRegisterAction should handle requests for /register.do. A fragment of the action element is shown here:

```
<action path="/register
        type="coreservlets.BeanRegisterAction"
        ...
/>
```

Map Return Conditions to JSP Pages

As before, we use multiple forward elements, one for each possible return value of the execute method. The three forward entries are shown here:

```
<forward name="bad-address"
         path="/WEB-INF/results/bad-address.jsp"/>
<forward name="bad-password"
         path="/WEB-INF/results/bad-password.jsp"/>
<forward name="success"
         path="/WEB-INF/results/confirm-registration.jsp"/>
```

Declare the Use of Any Form Beans

Next, we define a form-bean entry in struts-config.xml (within the forms-beans element) with a name attribute of userFormBean and a type attribute of core-servlets.UserFromBean, as shown here:

```
<form-beans>
  <form-bean name="userFormBean"
             type="coreservlets.UserFormBean"/>
</form-beans>
```

Update action Declaration

After declaring the `form-bean` element, we add two new attributes to the `action` element so that Struts knows about the form bean. Specifically, we add a `name` attribute that matches the name from `form-bean`, and a `scope` attribute that specifies `request`, `session`, or `application` (usually `request`). Here is the updated action:

```
<action path="/register"
        type="coreservlets.BeanRegisterAction"
        name="userFormBean"
        scope="request">
```

The complete listing for **struts-config.xml** is given in Listing 10.13.

Listing 10.13   struts-beans/WEB-INF/struts-config.xml

```
<?xml version="1.0" encoding="ISO-8859-1" ?>
<!DOCTYPE struts-config PUBLIC
  "-//Apache Software Foundation//DTD Struts Configuration 1.3//EN"
  "http://struts.apache.org/dtds/struts-config_1_3.dtd">
<struts-config>

  <form-beans>
    <form-bean name="userFormBean"
               type="coreservlets.UserFormBean"/>
  </form-beans>

  <action-mappings>
    <action path="/register"
            type="coreservlets.BeanRegisterAction"
            name="userFormBean"
            scope="request">
      <forward name="bad-address"
               path="/WEB-INF/results/bad-address.jsp"/>
      <forward name="bad-password"
               path="/WEB-INF/results/bad-password.jsp"/>
      <forward name="success"
               path="/WEB-INF/results/confirm-registration.jsp"/>
    </action>
  </action-mappings>
</struts-config>
```

Step 2: Define a Form Bean

The form bean is automatically instantiated, filled in with the incoming form parameters, stored in the `request` scope, and passed to the `execute` method of the `Action` object. To create an `ActionForm` bean, we follow the guidance given earlier.

- **Extend `ActionForm` class.** For this example, we define a `UserFormBean` that extends `ActionForm`.

  ```
  public class UserFormBean extends ActionForm {
      ...
  }
  ```

- **Have a zero argument constructor.** We rely on the no-argument constructor provided by the Java compiler. The instance variables (`email` and `password`) are set to default values when the bean is instantiated.
- **Have settable bean properties that correspond to request parameters.** The bean has `String` setter methods for the two request parameters, `email` and `password`.
- **Have gettable bean properties for each property that you want to output in the JSP page.** The form bean has getter methods for the `email` and `password` bean properties, `getEmail` and `getPassword`, respectively.

The complete listing for `UserFormBean` is given in Listing 10.14.

Listing 10.14	struts-beans/WEB-INF/classes/coreservlets/ UserFormBean.java

```
package coreservlets;

import org.apache.struts.action.*;

/** A FormBean for registration information. When the user
 *  submits the input form, the Struts system automatically
 *  populates the bean with the values from the email and
 *  password request parameters.
 */

public class UserFormBean extends ActionForm {
  private String email = "Missing address";
  private String password = "Missing password";
```

Listing 10.14	struts-beans/WEB-INF/classes/coreservlets/ UserFormBean.java *(continued)*

```java
  public String getEmail() {
    return(email);
  }

  public void setEmail(String email) {
    this.email = email;
  }

  public String getPassword() {
    return(password);
  }

  public void setPassword(String password) {
    this.password = password;
  }
}
```

Step 3: Create the Results Beans

Results beans are the normal type of beans used in the MVC architecture (i.e., implemented with RequestDispatcher), need extend no particular class, and require no definitions in the **struts-config.xml** file. Of course, results beans need to have getter and setter methods like normal JavaBeans. In particular, they need getter methods for each property that you want to output using bean:write or the JSP EL.

For this example, we define a single results bean, SuggestionBean, to hold a suggested e-mail address and password. If the user does not complete the input form correctly, then we use a result bean on the output page to suggest alternative values.

To create the SuggestionBean, we use a very simple business logic class, SuggestionUtils, that generates a bean with one of four possible candidate e-mail addresses and a random password with a length of eight characters.

Listings 10.15 and 10.16 present our SuggestionBean and SuggestionUtils classes, respectively.

Listing 10.15 struts-beans/WEB-INF/classes/coreservlets/ SuggestionBean.java

```
package coreservlets;

/** JavaBean to hold a candidate email and address to
 *  suggest to the user.
 */

public class SuggestionBean {
  private String email;
  private String password;

  public SuggestionBean(String email, String password) {
    this.email = email;
    this.password = password;
  }

  public String getEmail() {
    return(email);
  }

  public String getPassword() {
    return(password);
  }
}
```

Listing 10.16 struts-beans/WEB-INF/classes/coreservlets/ SuggestionUtils.java

```
package coreservlets;

/** Utility class to generate a SuggestionBean with
 *  candidate email and password values.
 */

public class SuggestionUtils {
  private static String[] suggestedAddresses =
    { "president@whitehouse.gov",
      "gates@microsoft.com",
      "palmisano@ibm.com",
      "ellison@oracle.com" };
  private static String chars =
    "abcdefghijklmnopqrstuvwxyz0123456789#@$%^&*?!";
```

Listing 10.16	struts-beans/WEB-INF/classes/coreservlets/ SuggestionUtils.java *(continued)*

```java
public static SuggestionBean getSuggestionBean() {
  String address = randomString(suggestedAddresses);
  String password = randomString(chars, 8);
  return(new SuggestionBean(address, password));
}

public static int randomInt(int range) {
  return((int)(Math.random() * range));
}

public static String randomString(String[] strings) {
  return(strings[randomInt(strings.length)]);
}

public static char randomChar(String string) {
  return(string.charAt(randomInt(string.length())));
}

public static String randomString(String string,
                                  int length) {
  StringBuffer result = new StringBuffer();
  for(int i=0; i<length; i++) {
    result.append(randomChar(string));
  }
  return(result.toString());
}
}
```

Step 4: Define an Action Class to Handle the Requests

This Action is similar to the one in Section 10.4 (Processing Requests with Action Objects), except that we do not call request.getParameter explicitly. Instead, we extract the request parameters from the already populated form bean.

Specifically, in our BeanRegisterAction, we take the ActionForm argument supplied to the execute method, cast it to UserFormBean (our concrete class that extends ActionForm), and then call getter methods on that bean, as shown here:

```java
UserFormBean userBean = (UserFormBean)form;
String email = userBean.getEmail();
String password = userBean.getPassword();
```

Also, in our BeanRegisterAction, we create a SuggestionBean and store it in request scope for later display of the bean properties in a JSP page.

```
SuggestionBean suggestionBean =
  SuggestionUtils.getSuggestionBean();
request.setAttribute("suggestionBean", suggestionBean);
```

The complete code for BeanRegisterAction is given in Listing 10.17.

Listing 10.17 struts-beans/WEB-INF/classes/coreservlets/
BeanRegisterAction.java

```java
package coreservlets;

import javax.servlet.http.*;
import org.apache.struts.action.*;

/** An action that uses an ActionForm bean to hold the HTML
 *  form parameters. Upon submission of the HTML form, the
 *  Struts system automatically populates the email and
 *  password fields of the UserFormBean.
 */

public class BeanRegisterAction extends Action {
  public ActionForward execute(ActionMapping mapping,
                               ActionForm form,
                               HttpServletRequest request,
                               HttpServletResponse response)
      throws Exception {
    UserFormBean userBean = (UserFormBean)form;
    String email = userBean.getEmail();
    String password = userBean.getPassword();
    SuggestionBean suggestionBean =
      SuggestionUtils.getSuggestionBean();
    request.setAttribute("suggestionBean", suggestionBean);
    if ((email == null) ||
        (email.trim().length() < 3) ||
        (email.indexOf("@") == -1)) {
      return(mapping.findForward("bad-address"));
    } else if ((password == null) ||
               (password.trim().length() < 6)) {
      return(mapping.findForward("bad-password"));
    } else {
      return(mapping.findForward("success"));
    }
  }
}
```

Step 5: Create a Form That Invokes *blah*.do

For this example, we need an input form that invokes http://*hostname*/struts-beans/register.do. This form is given in Listing 10.18.

Listing 10.18	struts-beans/register.jsp

```
<!DOCTYPE HTML PUBLIC "-//W3C//DTD HTML 4.0 Transitional//EN">
<HTML>
<HEAD><TITLE>New Account Registration</TITLE></HEAD>
<BODY BGCOLOR="#FDF5E6">
<CENTER>
<H1>New Account Registration</H1>
<FORM ACTION="register.do" METHOD="POST">
  Email address: <INPUT TYPE="TEXT" NAME="email"><BR>
  Password: <INPUT TYPE="PASSWORD" NAME="password"><BR>
  <INPUT TYPE="SUBMIT" VALUE="Sign Me Up!">
</FORM>
</CENTER>
</BODY></HTML>
```

Step 6: Display the Results in a JSP Page

We have three possible output pages, depending on the input provided by the user. All three output pages rely on beans in the `request` scope.

To display the bean properties, we use the Struts `bean:write` tag. To use this tag, however, we have to import the `bean` tag library in our JSP pages as follows:

```
<%@ taglib uri="http://struts.apache.org/tags-bean"
           prefix="bean" %>
```

Here is a summary of the three output pages.

- **bad-address3.jsp.** This page is displayed if the user did not provide a legal e-mail address. We use `bean:write` to display the bad e-mail address from the form bean and to display a suggested e-mail address from the suggestion bean. See bad-address.jsp in Listing 10.19.
- **bad-password.jsp.** This page is displayed if the user did not provide a legal password. Again, we use `bean:write` to display the bad password from the form bean and to display a suggested password from the suggestion bean. See bad-password.jsp in Listing 10.20.
- **confirm-registration.jsp.** This page is displayed if the user provided both a legal e-mail and password. The `bean:write` tag displays the registration information from the form bean. See confirm-registration.jsp in Listing 10.21.

We place each output JSP page in **/struts-beans/WEB-INF/results** so that the user cannot access the page directly (which would result in an error due to missing beans).

The file structure for this example is shown in Figure 10–13.

Listing 10.19 struts-beans/WEB-INF/results/bad-address.jsp

```
<!DOCTYPE HTML PUBLIC "-//W3C//DTD HTML 4.0 Transitional//EN">
<HTML>
<HEAD><TITLE>Illegal Email Address</TITLE></HEAD>
<BODY BGCOLOR="#FDF5E6">
<CENTER>
<H1>Illegal Email Address</H1>
<%@ taglib uri="http://struts.apache.org/tags-bean"
          prefix="bean" %>
The address
"<bean:write name="userFormBean" property="email"/>"
is not of the form username@hostname (e.g.,
<bean:write name="suggestionBean" property="email"/>).
<P>
Please <A HREF="register.jsp">try again</A>.
</CENTER>
</BODY></HTML>
```

Listing 10.20 struts-beans/WEB-INF/results/bad-password.jsp

```
<!DOCTYPE HTML PUBLIC "-//W3C//DTD HTML 4.0 Transitional//EN">
<HTML>
<HEAD><TITLE>Illegal Password</TITLE></HEAD>
<BODY BGCOLOR="#FDF5E6">
<CENTER>
<H1>Illegal Password</H1>
<%@ taglib uri="http://struts.apache.org/tags-bean"
          prefix="bean" %>
The password
"<bean:write name="userFormBean" property="password"/>"
is too short; it must contain at least six characters.
Here is a possible password:
<bean:write name="suggestionBean" property="password"/>.
<P>
Please <A HREF="register.jsp">try again</A>.
</CENTER>
</BODY></HTML>
```

Listing 10.21 struts-beans/WEB-INF/results/confirm-registration.jsp

```
<!DOCTYPE HTML PUBLIC "-//W3C//DTD HTML 4.0 Transitional//EN">
<HTML>
<HEAD><TITLE>Success</TITLE></HEAD>
<BODY BGCOLOR="#FDF5E6">
<CENTER>
<H1>You have registered successfully.</H1>
<%@ taglib uri="http://struts.apache.org/tags-bean"
           prefix="bean" %>
<UL>
  <LI>Email Address:
      <bean:write name="userFormBean" property="email"/>
  <LI>Password:
      <bean:write name="userFormBean" property="password"/>
</UL>
Congratulations.
</CENTER>
</BODY></HTML>
```

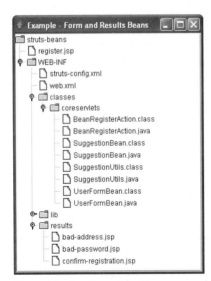

Figure 10–13 Complete file structure for "Form and Results Beans" example.

Results

Finally, we present the results for this example.

- The user invokes the input form with the URL http://localhost/struts-beans/register.jsp. The initial JSP page is shown in Figure 10–14.
- The user completes this form and submits it to the server. The form's ACTION results in the URL http://localhost/struts-beans/register.do.
- Based on the form-bean associated with the action in struts-config.xml, the Struts system populates a UserFormBean with the request parameters and automatically places the bean in the request scope.
- This URL address maps to the BeanRegisterAction class in struts-config.xml. The Struts system then invokes the execute method of BeanRegisterAction, passing the form bean as an argument.
- The execute method creates a suggestion bean and places it in the request scope. Then, it uses mapping.findForward to return one of three possible conditions ("bad-address", "bad-password", or "success").
- If the user fills in an invalid e-mail address, the execute method returns a "bad-address" condition. This condition maps to /WEB-INF/results/bad-address.jsp in struts-config.xml. The output JSP page uses the bean:write tag to display properties from the form bean and suggestion bean. See Figure 10–15.
- If the user fills in a valid e-mail address, but the password is invalid, the execute method returns a "bad-password" condition. This condition maps to /WEB-INF/results/bad-password.jsp in struts-config.xml. The JSP page uses the bean:write tag to display properties from the form bean and suggestion bean. See Figure 10–16.
- If the user correctly fills in the e-mail address and password, then a "success" condition is reached and system invokes /WEB-INF/results/confirm-registration.jsp. The bean:write tag displays the user's registration information from the form bean located in the request scope. See Figure 10–17.

Regardless of the final JSP page displayed, because the page is invoked with RequestDispatcher.forward and not response.sendRedirect, the URL displayed to the user remains register.do.

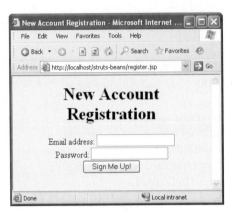

Figure 10–14 Initial registration page. The ACTION submits to register.do.

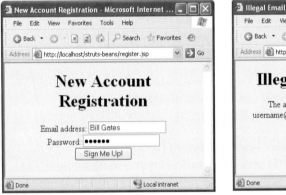

Figure 10–15 Registration form with an illegal e-mail address—doesn't contain an @ symbol (left). Response for a "bad-address" condition (right). The bean:write tag displays both the bad address (from the form bean) and suggested address (from the suggestion bean).

Figure 10–16 Registration form with an illegal password—one that doesn't contain six characters (left). Response for a `"bad-password"` condition (right). The `bean:write` tag displays both the bad password (from the form bean) and suggested password (from the suggestion bean).

Figure 10–17 Successful registration page displayed to user. The legal address and password, properties of the form bean in the `request` scope, are displayed in the response page through the `bean:write` custom tag.

10.6 Prepopulating and Redisplaying Input Forms

In the previous section, we showed how to create form beans that the system instantiates and populates automatically. We also showed how to output bean properties in results pages. In this section, we show how to associate form beans with the input page using the Struts `html:` tags. Associating form beans with input forms provides three advantages:

- **It guarantees that the request parameter names and the bean property names stay in sync.** If you write the form by hand, you might change the parameter names but forget to change the bean. When using the `html:` tags, you explicitly refer to the bean property names when defining text fields or other input elements, so if you use the wrong name, you get an immediate error message.
- **It lets you prepopulate text fields with initial values.** By associating a bean with the input page, the initial text field values can come from your application. So, for example, if the available health plans change in your database, you don't have to separately remember to change hard-coded HTML on the page that asks employees to choose a health plan.
- **It lets you redisplay values in the text fields.** If you send the user back to the original form, the originally entered values are automatically filled in. That's because the form is already associated with a bean, but now the bean is the one that was just created from the request.

In the remainder of this chapter, we examine the `html:` tags in detail and explain how you can use them to build your input pages.

Struts Flow of Control

First, we review the Struts flow of control, emphasizing use of the `html:` tags and form beans to prepopulate fields of the input page. See Figure 10–18 for a diagram of the Struts flow. Then, we give details on the syntax of the `html:` tags and provide an example of their use.

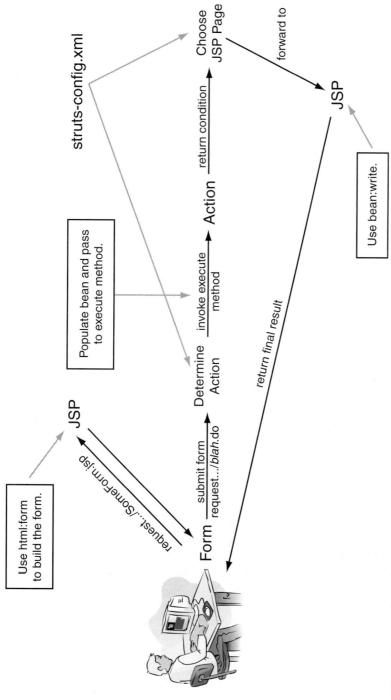

Figure 10–18 Flow of control in the Struts framework.

- **The user requests a form.** This form is built with `html:form`, `html:text`, and similar elements. These tags keep input field names in sync with bean property names and let initial values of text fields and other input elements come from the application.
- **The form is submitted to a URL of the form *blah*.do.** The `html:form` tag automatically prepends the Web application name and appends .do. That way, the action listed in the form and the path listed in `action` match exactly. The URL is mapped in struts-config.xml to an `Action` class.
- **The `execute` method of the `Action` object is invoked.** One of the arguments to `execute` is a form bean that is automatically created and whose properties are automatically populated based on incoming request parameters of the same name. The `Action` invokes business logic and data-access logic, placing the results in normal beans stored in the `request`, `session`, or `application` scope. The `Action` uses `mapping.findForward` to return a condition, and the conditions are mapped by struts-config.xml to various JSP pages.
- **Struts forwards request to the appropriate JSP page.** The page can use `bean:write` or the JSP 2.0 EL to output bean properties.

The Six Basic Steps in Using Struts

Now, we review the six steps in using Struts, but emphasize the use of the `html:` tags to associate beans with input forms.

1. **Modify struts-config.xml.** Map incoming URLs to `Action` objects, map return conditions to JSP pages, and declare form beans.
2. **Define a form bean.** Define a class that extends `ActionForm` and has properties that match the request parameter names. Declare the bean in the `form-beans` section of struts-config.xml.
3. **Create the results beans.** If the output JSP pages need data resulting from the business logic, then create results beans to hold the data. These beans need extend no special class and need not be declared in struts-config.xml.
4. **Define an `Action` class to handle the request**. Create an `Action` class with an `execute` method to process the request. Obtain input data from the second argument to `execute` (the form bean). Call business logic and data-access logic and store the results in beans. Use `mapping.findForward` to return a result condition.

5. **Create a form that invokes *blah*.do.** Create a form to collect the user's input. Use

```
<html:form action="/path-as-in-struts-config">
```

to instantiate a form bean and associate it with the form. Then, use various input elements such as

```
<html:text name="beanPropertyName" />
```

   The text field is prepopulated with the result of the getter method corresponding to `beanPropertyName`, and, when the form is submitted, the text field value is stored in a form bean by calling the setter method corresponding to `beanPropertyName`.

6. **Display the results in a JSP page.** Use `bean:write` or the JSP expression language to output bean properties.

Details follow.

Step 1: Modify struts-config.xml

You need three main entries in struts-config.xml.

- **Use `action` entries to map incoming .do addresses to `Action` classes.** The `path` attribute should exactly match the `action` of `html:form`, the `type` attribute should be the fully qualified `Action` class name, the `name` attribute should match a name from a `form-bean` element, and the `scope` attribute should be `request` or `session`.
- **Use `forward` entries to map return conditions to JSP pages.** The `name` attribute should match a return condition from the `execute` method of the `Action` and the `path` attribute should list a JSP page in WEB-INF. If the same `forward` entry appears in more than one `action`, you can move the entry to the `global-forwards` section.
- **Declare form beans.** Put a `form-bean` entry in the `form-beans` section for each bean that is associated with an `Action`. Give each form bean a name.

Remember to restart the server after modifying struts-config.xml.

Step 2: Define a Form Bean

Your bean will extend `ActionForm` and have a bean property for each incoming request parameter. In addition to using the bean in the `execute` method of the `Action` and in the final JSP pages, use the bean in the input form to give names and values to the various input elements.

Step 3: Create the Results Beans

Results beans are normal beans as used in the MVC approach when implemented directly with `RequestDispatcher`, and are created and used in the same way as described in the previous section.

Step 4: Define an Action Class to Handle the Request

As in the previous section, rather than calling `request.getParameter` explicitly, use the form bean passed as the second argument of the `execute` method. Cast the `ActionForm` argument to the specific form bean class, then use the appropriate getter methods to access the properties of the object.

Step 5: Create a Form That Invokes *blah*.do

Rather than using the standard HTML `FORM` and `INPUT` tags, use `html:form` and `html:text` (and related tags). The `html:form` tag associates a bean with the form. The `html:text` tag automatically uses bean property names for each text field `NAME` and bean property values for each text field `VALUE`.

Step 6: Display the Results in a JSP Page

As before, the JSP page uses `bean:write` or the JSP EL to output properties of the form and result beans.

Using Struts html: Tags

In this subsection, we examine the use of Struts `html:` tags. To effectively use these tags, you need to understand the following techniques:

- Using the Struts `html:form` element instead of the standard HTML `FORM` element to declare the form.
- Using `html:text` elements to declare the input fields of the form.

Before you use any of the `html:` tags, you must declare the tag library:

```
<%@ taglib uri="http://struts.apache.org/tags-html"
           prefix="html" %>
```

Using html:form to Declare the Form

The `action` attribute of the `html:form` tag should start with a slash and exactly match the `path` attribute of the `action` element in struts-config.xml. For example, if the `path` in struts-config.xml is given by

```
<action path="/actions/blah" ... >
   ...
</action>
```

then `action` in `html:form` should similarly be given by

```
<html:form action="/actions/blah">
```

Using the Struts `html:form` element instead of the standard HTML `FORM` element yields these four results:

- **A bean is associated with the form.** Struts first finds an action whose path matches the URL, then finds a form bean whose name matches the name attribute of the action. Struts then instantiates a bean of that type (or uses an existing one if such a bean is already in the proper scope).
- **The Web application prefix is prepended automatically.** The `html:form` tag understands the context path of the Web application. Thus, you say

  ```
  <html:form action="/actions/...">
  ```

  to get

  ```
  <FORM ACTION="/webAppPrefix/actions/..." ...>
  ```

- **The .do suffix is appended automatically.** As with the `path` in struts-config.xml, the .do is implied in the `action` attribute. Thus, say

  ```
  <html:form action="/actions/blah">
  ```

  to get

  ```
  <FORM ACTION="/webAppPrefix/actions/blah.do" ...>
  ```

- **The default METHOD is POST, not GET.** You say

  ```
  <html:form action="/actions/blah">
  ```

  to get

  ```
  <FORM ACTION="/webAppPrefix/actions/blah.do"
        METHOD="POST">
  ```

Using html:text to Declare the Input Fields of the Form

Use the `html:text` element and similar elements to declare the input fields of the form. The NAME of each input field is taken from the bean property name, and the VALUE is taken from the bean property value. For example, using

```
<html:text property="firstName"/>
```

is equivalent to first declaring a bean of the appropriate type, then doing

```
<INPUT TYPE="TEXT" NAME="firstName"
       VALUE="<%= theBean.getFirstName() %>">
```

If the default bean property is `null` or an empty string, the text field is left blank.

Core Note

If the default value for the bean property is `null` or an empty string, then the `html:text` tag leaves the text field empty.

Prepopulating Forms

In many cases, you want the values in the initial form to be derived from data in your application. If the application data changes, you want the initial values of the form fields to change automatically. Using the `html:` tags to associate a bean with the form makes this process simple.

First, we summarize how to use the `html:` tags to prepopulate forms, then present an example. The critical idea here is that for each input page you associate a form bean that defines default values for each property. Through the right `html:` tags, when the user first accesses the page, the system creates the bean and then populates the input fields with the values from the bean properties.

To prepopulate forms, follow these steps:

- **Use `html:form` for the main form.** In the input form, you should use `html:form`, and should specify

  ```
  <html:form action="/path/blah">
  ```

  not

  ```
  <html:form action="/webAppPrefix/path/blah.do">
  ```

  Also, POST is the default method for `html:form`.

- **Use `html:text` for text fields.** In your input form, you should use

  ```
  <html:text property="propertyName" />
  ```

  to declare input text fields. Each text field NAME is taken from the bean property name, and each text field VALUE is taken from the bean property value. If the bean property value is `null` or an empty string, the text field is initially empty.
- **Use `html:xxxx` for other input elements.** In your input form, use `html:button`, `html:checkbox`, `html:textarea`, and so on, to declare submit buttons, checkboxes, text areas, and so on. For details, see http://struts.apache.org/1.x/struts-taglib/ tagreference.html#struts-html.tld.

Example: Prepopulating Forms

In this example, we present a Web application with a registration page that uses a form bean to prepopulate the input fields.

Here is the specific flow:

- The URL http://hostname/signup/actions/signup1.do is handled by the `Action` class `SignupAction1`.
- The `Action` uses a `ContactFormBean` whose properties are automatically filled with the registration page fields. The `execute` method returns either a `"missing-value"` condition (if the first name or last name is not provided) or a `"success"` condition (if both fields are properly filled in).
- The two return conditions result in the display of either /WEB-INF/ results/missing-value.jsp or /WEB-INF/results/signup-confirmation.jsp. The two JSP pages use `bean:write` to output values from both the form bean (`ContactFormBean`) and the results bean (`MessageBean`).

We next review the six steps in using Struts in this context.

Step 1: Modify struts-config.xml

The changes to struts-config.xml are very similar to the other examples already presented in this chapter.

Map Incoming .do Addresses to Action Classes

We use the `action` element to designate that `SignupAction1` should handle requests for signup1.do, as follows:

```
<action path="/actions/signup1"
        type="coreservlets.SignupAction1" ...>
...
</action>
```

Map Return Conditions to JSP Pages

We use multiple `forward` elements, one for each possible return value of the execute method. However, because two different `Actions` eventually use the same condition to indicate the same JSP page (a later example in this section builds on this example), the repeated mapping goes in `global-forwards` as shown here:

```
<global-forwards>
   <forward name="success"
            path="/WEB-INF/results/signup-confirmation.jsp"/>
</global-forwards>
```

Declare the Use of Any Form Beans

As before, we use name and type attributes within `form-bean`, as shown next. We also add `name` (the bean name as given in `form-bean`) and `scope` (request) attributes to the `action` declaration.

```
<form-beans>
   <form-bean name="contactFormBean"
              type="coreservlets.ContactFormBean"/>
</form-beans>
```

The complete listing of struts-config.xml is given in Listing 10.22.

Listing 10.22 signup/WEB-INF/struts-config.xml

```
<?xml version="1.0" encoding="ISO-8859-1" ?>
<!DOCTYPE struts-config PUBLIC
   "-//Apache Software Foundation//DTD Struts Configuration 1.3//EN"
   "http://struts.apache.org/dtds/struts-config_1_3.dtd">
<struts-config>
  <form-beans>
    <form-bean name="contactFormBean"
               type="coreservlets.ContactFormBean"/>
  </form-beans>
  <global-forwards>
    <forward name="success"
             path="/WEB-INF/results/signup-confirmation.jsp"/>
  </global-forwards>
  <action-mappings>
```

Listing 10.22 signup/WEB-INF/struts-config.xml *(continued)*

```
    <action path="/actions/signup1"
            type="coreservlets.SignupAction1"
            name="contactFormBean"
            scope="request">
      <forward name="missing-value"
               path="/WEB-INF/results/missing-value.jsp"/>
    </action>
    ...
  </action-mappings>
</struts-config>
```

Step 2: Define a Form Bean

The form bean is similar to the earlier examples. Specifically, the form bean extends
ActionForm, is automatically filled in with the incoming form parameters, and is
passed to the execute method of the Action.

However, in this example, the input form also uses the form bean. The
html:form and html:text tags instruct Struts to create a new instance of the
form bean and use it to fill in the fields of the input form. The NAME of each input
field comes from the bean property name and the VALUE comes from the bean property value.

Listing 10.23 presents a form bean corresponding to contact information for a
person who registers with our application. The bean contains properties for first
name, last name, e-mail address, and fax number.

Listing 10.23   signup/WEB-INF/classes/coreservlets/
ContactFormBean.java

```
package coreservlets;

import javax.servlet.http.*;
import org.apache.struts.action.*;

/** Form bean for signup information. Struts will automatically
 *  populate the bean with the incoming form parameters. The
 *  class provides default values for input fields.
 */
```

Listing 10.23   signup/WEB-INF/classes/coreservlets/
ContactFormBean.java *(continued)*

```java
public class ContactFormBean extends ActionForm {
  private String firstName = "First name";
  private String lastName = "Last name";
  private String email = "user@host";
  private String faxNumber = "xxx-yyy-zzzz";
  private String[] defaultValues =
    { firstName, lastName, email, faxNumber };
  private String warning = "";

  public String getFirstName() {
    return(firstName);
  }

  public void setFirstName(String firstName) {
    this.firstName = firstName;
  }

  public String getLastName() {
    return(lastName);
  }

  public void setLastName(String lastName) {
    this.lastName = lastName;
  }

  public String getEmail() {
    return(email);
  }

  public void setEmail(String email) {
    this.email = email;
  }

  public String getFaxNumber() {
    return(faxNumber);
  }

  public void setFaxNumber(String faxNumber) {
    this.faxNumber = faxNumber;
  }

  public String getWarning() {
    return(warning);
  }
```

Listing 10.23	signup/WEB-INF/classes/coreservlets/ ContactFormBean.java *(continued)*

```
public void setWarning(String baseWarning) {
  this.warning =
    "<H2><FONT COLOR=RED>Missing or invalid " +
    baseWarning + "!</FONT></H2>";
}

public void clearWarning() {
  warning = "";
}

// The reset method below is ONLY needed if you make
// the bean session-scoped. See the chapter on validation
// for more details.

public void reset(ActionMapping mapping,
                  HttpServletRequest request) {
  clearWarning();
}

public boolean isMissing(String value) {
  if ((value == null) || (value.trim().equals(""))) {
    return(true);
  } else {
    for(int i=0; i<defaultValues.length; i++) {
      if (value.equals(defaultValues[i])) {
        return(true);
      }
    }
    return(false);
  }
}
}
```

Step 3: Create the Results Beans

As a reminder, the form bean represents the input data that came from the HTML form. The results beans represent the results of any computations or database look-ups. Results beans need not extend any particular class, and are not declared in struts-config.xml.

For this example, we have a single results bean to hold any error messages for the output pages. Listing 10.24 presents our simple MessageBean.

Listing 10.24 | signup/WEB-INF/classes/coreservlets/MessageBean.java

```
package coreservlets;

/** Simple bean to hold a message. */

public class MessageBean {
  private String message = "";

  public String getMessage() {
    return(message);
  }

  public void setMessage(String message) {
    this.message = message;
  }
}
```

Step 4: Define an Action Class to Handle the Requests

In this example, we check each of the required input parameters (first name, last name, e-mail address, and fax number) to see if the value is missing. In this case, our definition of "missing" is null, whitespace only, or unchanged from the default value. If any values are missing, we use mapping.findForward to return a "missing-value" condition, which is mapped by struts-config.xml to an error page that contains a message saying which parameter was missing. If all parameters are present, we return "success", which results in a signup confirmation page.

The execute method is similar to that of the previous example. Again, we do not call request.getParameter explicitly, but instead extract the request parameters from the already populated form bean. Specifically, we take the ActionForm argument supplied to execute, cast it to ContactFormBean (our concrete class that extends ActionForm), and then call getter methods on that bean.

Also, we pass the error message to the JSP page by creating a MessageBean and storing it in the request scope. We put this code in a separate method (makeWarning) because in the next example we will override this method and store the error message in the form bean instead of in a separate bean.

The full class definition is given in Listing 10.25.

```java
package coreservlets;

import javax.servlet.http.*;
import org.apache.struts.action.*;

/** Action that receives the user input through a form bean.
 *  If there is a problem with the input data, a description
 *  of the problem is placed in a message bean.
 */

public class SignupAction1 extends Action {
  public ActionForward execute(ActionMapping mapping,
                               ActionForm form,
                               HttpServletRequest request,
                               HttpServletResponse response)
      throws Exception {
    ContactFormBean userBean = (ContactFormBean)form;
    String firstName = userBean.getFirstName();
    String lastName = userBean.getLastName();
    String email = userBean.getEmail();
    String faxNumber = userBean.getFaxNumber();
    if (userBean.isMissing(firstName)) {
      makeWarning(request, "first name");
      return(mapping.findForward("missing-value"));
    } else if (userBean.isMissing(lastName)) {
      makeWarning(request, "last name");
      return(mapping.findForward("missing-value"));
    } else if ((userBean.isMissing(email)) ||
               (email.indexOf("@") == -1)) {
      makeWarning(request, "email address");
      return(mapping.findForward("missing-value"));
    } else if (userBean.isMissing(faxNumber)) {
      makeWarning(request, "fax number");
      return(mapping.findForward("missing-value"));
    } else {
      return(mapping.findForward("success"));
    }
  }

  protected void makeWarning(HttpServletRequest request,
                             String message) {
    MessageBean messageBean = new MessageBean();
    messageBean.setMessage(message);
    request.setAttribute("messageBean", messageBean);
  }
}
```

Step 5: Create a Form That Invokes *blah*.do

This form is very different from earlier ones in this chapter. Instead of using the standard HTML FORM tag, we import and use the Struts html:form tag. This tag automatically generates the Web application prefix, appends the .do suffix, and sets the default request method to POST. Here, we use

```
<%@ taglib uri="http://struts.apache.org/tags-html"
           prefix="html" %>
<html:form action="/actions/signup1">
  ...
</html:form>
```

to get something equivalent to

```
<FORM ACTION="/signup/actions/signup1.do METHOD="POST">
  ...
</FORM>
```

Even more important, html:form causes the system to find or instantiate a bean corresponding to the action. Because the action of html:form matches the path attribute of the action declaration in struts-config.xml, a bean is automatically created when the input page is accessed. The system determines the type of bean to create by looking at the name that goes with the action, and finding the form-bean with the same name. In this case, the bean is a ContactFormBean.

Next, the bean properties are used for the form fields. After declaring the form and associating it with a bean, we use html:text to build input elements whose NAME and VALUE are taken from the names and values of the form bean's properties.

In essence, the code fragment

```
First name: <html:text property="firstName"/>
```

results in something similar to

```
<jsp:useBean id="contactBean" scope="request"
             class="coreservlets.ContactFormBean"/>
First name:
<INPUT TYPE="TEXT" NAME="firstName"
       VALUE="${contactBean.firstName}">
```

assuming that JSP 2.0 were available.

Listing 10.26 shows our complete input form.

Listing 10.26	signup/forms/signup1.jsp

```
<!DOCTYPE HTML PUBLIC "-//W3C//DTD HTML 4.0 Transitional//EN">
<HTML>
<HEAD><TITLE>Sign Up</TITLE></HEAD>
<BODY BGCOLOR="#FDF5E6">
<H1 ALIGN="CENTER">Sign Up</H1>
Looking to receive late-breaking unverified virus alerts,
unknown ebay secrets, can't miss stock tips, works-in-your-sleep
diet plans, and all sorts of medications? Want to get them both
by email <I>and</I> by fax? Look no further: the Single Provider
of Alert Memos system lets you sign up for them all in one easy
request!
<P>
<CENTER>
<%@ taglib uri="http://struts.apache.org/tags-html"
           prefix="html" %>
<html:form action="/actions/signup1">
  First name: <html:text property="firstName"/><BR>
  Last name: <html:text property="lastName"/><BR>
  Email address: <html:text property="email"/><BR>
  Fax number: <html:text property="faxNumber"/><BR>
  <html:submit value="Sign Me Up!"/>
</html:form>
</CENTER>
</BODY></HTML>
```

Step 6: Display the Results in a JSP Page

In this example, there are two possible result JSP pages: one for missing input (missing-value.jsp in Listing 10.27) and one for success (signup-confirmation.jsp in Listing 10.28).

We use the MessageBean to customize error messages for the output page in the event of any missing input. That way, a separate page is not needed for each type of error. As in earlier examples, we use bean:write to output bean properties without having to resort to explicit Java code.

Listing 10.27 signup/WEB-INF/results/missing-value.jsp

```
<!DOCTYPE HTML PUBLIC "-//W3C//DTD HTML 4.0 Transitional//EN">
<HTML>
<%@ taglib uri="http://struts.apache.org/tags-bean"
           prefix="bean" %>
<HEAD><TITLE>Missing or invalid
<bean:write name="messageBean" property="message"/>
</TITLE></HEAD>
<BODY BGCOLOR="#FDF5E6">
<CENTER>
<H2>Missing or invalid
<bean:write name="messageBean" property="message"/>!</H2>
Please <A HREF="../forms/signup1.jsp">try again</A>.
</CENTER>
</BODY></HTML>
```

Listing 10.28 signup/WEB-INF/results/signup-confirmation.jsp

```
<!DOCTYPE HTML PUBLIC "-//W3C//DTD HTML 4.0 Transitional//EN">
<HTML>
<HEAD><TITLE>Confirmation</TITLE></HEAD>
<BODY BGCOLOR="#FDF5E6">
<CENTER>
<H1>Confirmation</H1>
Congratulations. You are now signed up for the
Single Provider of Alert Memos network!
<%@ taglib uri="http://struts.apache.org/tags-bean"
           prefix="bean" %>
<UL>
  <LI>First name:
  <bean:write name="contactFormBean" property="firstName"/>
  <LI>Last name:
  <bean:write name="contactFormBean" property="lastName"/>
  <LI>Email address:
  <bean:write name="contactFormBean" property="email"/>
  <LI>Fax number:
  <bean:write name="contactFormBean" property="faxNumber"/>
</UL>
To be removed from the network, send email
<A HREF="mailto:blackhole@spam-network.com">here</A>.
</CENTER>
</BODY></HTML>
```

Results

Finally, we present the results, pointing out the central ideas of this example.

- The user first invokes the HTML form through the URL http://localhost/ signup/forms/signup1.jsp. The initial JSP page is shown in Figure 10–19. Notice that Struts prepopulates the text fields with the values of the `ContactFormBean` properties.
- The page uses `html:form` to build the `FORM` element. The `action` in the `html:form` element is `"/actions/signup1"`, resulting in the URL http://localhost/signup/actions/signup1.do.
- Based on the `action` mapping in struts-config.xml, the system invokes the `execute` method the `SignupAction1`. This method examines the first name, last name, e-mail address, and fax number to see if any are missing. If so, it calls `makeWarning` to store an error message in a request-scoped bean and returns `mapping.findForward` with a value of `"missing-value"`. Otherwise it returns `"success"`.
- The return values are mapped by struts-config.xml to /WEB-INF/results/ missing-value.jsp or /WEB-INF/results/signup-confirmation.jsp. In the case of an error, the `MessageBean` stores the specific error message so that the error page output is different in each of the error cases. See Figure 10–20 for examples of a missing first name and missing last name. Figure 10–21 shows the output page when the user provides complete registration information.

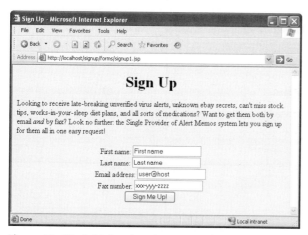

Figure 10–19 Initial registration page. The initial values for the fields are derived from a form bean.

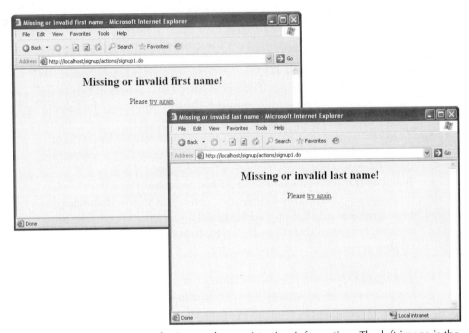

Figure 10–20   Output pages for incomplete registration information. The left image is the response for a missing first name, and the right image is the response for a missing last name. In both cases, the page uses the Struts `bean:write` tag to output the properties of a message bean.

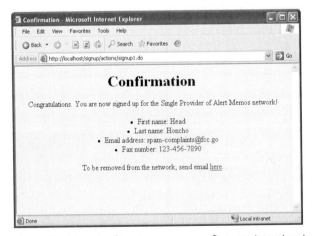

Figure 10–21   Confirmation page, `confirm-registration.jsp`.

URL Design Strategies for Actions

When writing a Struts application, you have two general options for the URLs of your forms and your actions: simple addresses (without subdirectories) and addresses with subdirectories. Next, we examine both options.

Option 1: Designing Action URLs without Subdirectories

The first design option is to use simple URLs (without subdirectories) for the action of html:form and for the input forms. For this option, you would place the input forms in the top-level directory of the Web application. Also, for the action of html:form (and thus the path of the action definitions in **struts-config.xml**), you would use a slash followed by a simple name. Table 10.5 provides examples of this approach.

Table 10.5   Designing URLs without Subdirectories

Design Element	Approach
HTML form location	Form placed in top-level Web application directory: http://*hostname*/signup/**signup1.jsp**
action of html:form	Form specifies top-level name: <html:form **action="/signup1"**...>
action in struts-config.xml	Action path gives a name only (no subdirectory): <action **path="/signup1"**.../>

Option 2: Designing Action URLs with Subdirectories

The second design option is to place your input forms in subdirectories and to use a pseudo-directory for each action. The pseudo-directory for the action does not physically exist; it is simply a virtual mapping understood by **struts-config.xml**. Table 10.6 gives examples of this design strategy.

Table 10.6 Designing URLs with Subdirectories

Design Element	Approach
HTML form location	Form placed in Web application subdirectory: http://*hostname*/signup/**forms**/signup1.jsp
action of `html:form`	Form specifies path with pseudo-directory name: `<html:form action="/actions/signup1"...>`
action in `struts-config.xml`	Action `path` gives a pseudo-directory name: `<action path="/actions/signup1"...>`

Advantages of Using Subdirectories

Using subdirectories has advantages both for the `actions` and the input forms.

Advantages for Actions

- **Similar path for all `action` URLs.** If all the `action` URLs start with a similar path (`/actions` in this case) it is much easier to distinguish `action` URLs from other URLs.
- **Easier to apply filtering and security settings.** If all the `action` URLs start with a similar path, it is much easier to use web.xml to apply filters or Web application security settings.

Advantages for Forms

- **Simplifies organization and editing of forms.** If the forms are in a directory different than the other HTML or JSP pages, it simplifies organization and editing of the forms.
- **Improves filtering and security setting for forms.** If all the forms start with a similar path (/forms in this case), it is much easier to use web.xml to apply filters or Web application security settings to the forms.

Disadvantages of Using Subdirectories

Probably the biggest disadvantage to using subdirectories is that it confuses beginning Struts developers. A common question for beginners is: "Where is the actions directory?" There is no such directory! It simply is a part of the URL that is understood by the Struts system. However, that is not so strange. After all, the main address (*blah*.do) is also a mapping, not a virtual file (just as the URL pattern of normal servlets is just a mapping, not a real file).

Redisplaying Forms

In the last subsection we examined the use of the `html:` tags to prepopulate form input fields. The initial values came from a newly created bean.

Now, we show how to redisplay a form and base its values on bean whose properties have been filled in from a previous request. This second technique lets you submit a form, check if all the required data is supplied, and redisplay the form if any of the data is missing or in the wrong format. Most important, when you redisplay the form, you can maintain the previous values that the user entered and give an error message indicating what values had problems. This section shows the basic idea, and shows how the `html:` tags simplify the process. However, in Chapter 12 (The Struts Framework: Validating User Input), we show how to take this idea even further. Whether you do it the simple way shown in this section or the more advanced way shown later, it is the `html:` tags that are the key to the redisplay process.

Figure 10–22 shows the control flow in the Struts framework, with updates for redisplaying input forms. For now, we assume that the `Action` contains logic that determines whether a problem exists with the submitted input parameters. If there is such a problem, the `execute` method returns a condition that forwards the response back to the input page. When the form is redisplayed, the input fields are populated with their previous submitted values. The redisplayed input page should also summarize the errors so that the user understands what corrections to make to the input.

Implementing this behavior involves two tasks:

1. **Mapping an error condition back to the input page.** In struts-config.xml, provide a `forward` element that maps back to the input page.
2. **Storing and displaying an error message.** Place a message in the form bean to display on the input page. Given what we know so far, placing an error message in a bean and displaying it on the input page is the best we can do. However, in Chapter 12 (The Struts Framework: Validating User Input), we cover many more options for validating input values and displaying error messages.

Details of these two tasks follow.

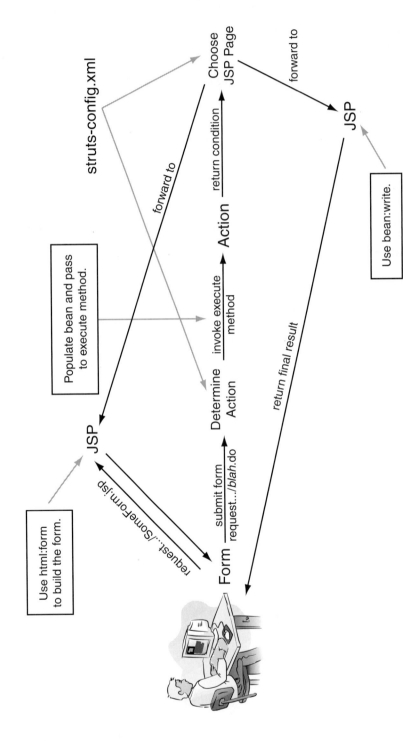

Figure 10–22   Flow of request through the Struts framework showing updates for redisplaying forms. If there is a problem with the input data, the `Action` returns a condition to forward the request back to the input page. When redisplaying the input pages, the system fills the input fields from the previous values stored in the from bean.

Task 1: Mapping Error Condition Back to Input Form

In struts-config.xml, the `forward` entry corresponding to missing data should supply the address of the input form, rather than supplying the address of a new JSP page as before. For instance, instead of

```
<forward name="missing-value"
         path="/WEB-INF/results/missing-value.jsp"/>
```

you would say

```
<forward name="missing-value"
         path="/forms/originalInputPage.jsp"/>
```

Task 2: Creating and Displaying Error Messages

When redisplaying your input form, you should display an error message that tells the user which data was incorrect. The `Action` can store this message in a separate bean, or, more simply, in a special property of the form bean designed for storing error messages. By making the default value of this bean property an empty string, you can avoid logic that requires you to distinguish the initial display of the form from a redisplay.

Listing 10.29 presents a template for a form bean that can hold error messages. To display the errors on the input page, use `bean:write`, as shown here:

```
<bean:write name="someFormBean"
            property="warning"
            filter="false"/>
```

Notice that we use `filter="false"` because the error message contains HTML tags. Also, note that this statement must come after the `html:form` tag on the input page, because on the initial request, the bean does not exist until after `html:form` is encountered.

Core Approach

Unless you use more advanced Struts validation features (see Chapter 12), use your form bean to hold any error messages. Then on your input page, place the `bean:write` tag inside the `html:form` tag. In this manner, on the initial request, the bean exists before execution of the `bean:write` tag.

Listing 10.29	Form bean template for supporting error messages

```
package coreservlets;

import javax.servlet.http.*;
import org.apache.struts.action.*;

/** Form bean that can hold warning messages. Use bean:write
 *  to display the warnings.
 */

public class SomeFormBean extends ActionForm {
  ...
  private String warning = "";

  ...
  public void setWarning(String baseWarning) {
    this.warning =
      "<H2><FONT COLOR=RED>Missing or invalid " +
      baseWarning + "!</FONT></H2>";
  }

  public String getWarning() {
    return(warning);
  }

  public void clearWarning() {
    warning = "";
  }
}
```

Example: Redisplaying Forms

Next, we present an example that, when the input is incomplete, redisplays the input form with correctly entered values maintained and missing values flagged with an error message. This example is similar to the earlier one on prepopulating forms, but instead of using a separate output page to display errors, the input page is redisplayed with the errors. Also, this example is different in that the messages are held in the form bean instead of a separate results bean.

We outline the design strategy of this example next.

- The URL http://hostname/signup/actions/signup2.do is handled by the Action class SignupAction2.
- We inherit the execute method of SignupAction1. That method uses a ContactFormBean whose properties are automatically filled

with the registration page fields. If the input data has any problems, the inherited method calls the `makeWarning` method. However, we override `makeWarning` so that it stores the error messages in the form bean instead of in a new bean. Finally, as before, the inherited `execute` method returns either a `"missing-value"` condition or a `"success"` condition.

- The two return conditions result in the display of either /signup/ forms/signup2.jsp or /WEB-INF/results/signup-confirmation.jsp. When redisplaying the input page, the `bean:write` tag displays any errors.

Given this design strategy, we go through the six steps in using Struts.

Step 1: Modify struts-config.xml

The modifications to struts-config.xml are similar to those in the earlier examples.

Map Incoming .do Addresses to Action Classes

We use the `action` element to designate that `SignupAction2` should handle requests for signup2.do.

```
<action path="/actions/signup2"
        type="coreservlets.SignupAction2" ...>
...
</action>
```

Map Return Conditions to JSP Pages

We use multiple `forward` elements, one for each possible return value of the execute method. We still map the `"success"` condition to /WEB-INF/results/ signup-confirmation.jsp. However, for the `"missing-value"` condition, we specify the location of the original input form, rather than the location of a new JSP page.

```
<forward name="missing-value"
        path="/forms/signup2.jsp"/>
```

Declare the Use of Any Form Beans

As before, we use name and type attributes within form-bean, as shown next. We also add name (the bean name as given in form-bean) and scope (request) attributes to the action declaration.

```
<form-bean name="contactFormBean"
        type="coreservlets.ContactFormBean"/>
```

The complete listing of struts-config.xml is given in Listing 10.30.

Listing 10.30 signup/WEB-INF/struts-config.xml

```xml
<?xml version="1.0" encoding="ISO-8859-1" ?>
<!DOCTYPE struts-config PUBLIC
  "-//Apache Software Foundation//DTD Struts Configuration 1.3//EN"
  "http://struts.apache.org/dtds/struts-config_1_3.dtd">
<struts-config>
  <form-beans>
    <form-bean name="contactFormBean"
               type="coreservlets.ContactFormBean"/>
  </form-beans>
  <global-forwards>
    <forward name="success"
             path="/WEB-INF/results/signup-confirmation.jsp"/>
  </global-forwards>
  <action-mappings>
  ...
    <action path="/actions/signup2"
            type="coreservlets.SignupAction2"
            name="contactFormBean"
            scope="request">
      <forward name="missing-value"
               path="/forms/signup2.jsp"/>
    </action>
  </action-mappings>
</struts-config>
```

Step 2: Define a Form Bean

This example uses the same ContactFormBean as before. However, in this example we make use of the warning property. This property does not correspond to a request parameter, but rather is used to send missing-entry warnings from the Action back to the input form.

Our ContactFormBean is given in Listing 10.31.

Listing 10.31 signup/WEB-INF/classes/coreservlets/ContactFormBean.java

```java
package coreservlets;

import javax.servlet.http.*;
import org.apache.struts.action.*;
```

Listing 10.31	signup/WEB-INF/classes/coreservlets/ ContactFormBean.java *(continued)*

```
/** Form bean for signup information. Struts will automatically
 *  populate the bean with the incoming form parameters. The
 *  class provides default values for input fields.
 */

public class ContactFormBean extends ActionForm {
  private String firstName = "First name";
  private String lastName = "Last name";
  private String email = "user@host";
  private String faxNumber = "xxx-yyy-zzzz";
  private String[] defaultValues =
    { firstName, lastName, email, faxNumber };
  private String warning = "";

  public String getFirstName() {
    return(firstName);
  }

  public void setFirstName(String firstName) {
    this.firstName = firstName;
  }

  public String getLastName() {
    return(lastName);
  }

  public void setLastName(String lastName) {
    this.lastName = lastName;
  }

  public String getEmail() {
    return(email);
  }

  public void setEmail(String email) {
    this.email = email;
  }

  public String getFaxNumber() {
    return(faxNumber);
  }
```

Listing 10.31 signup/WEB-INF/classes/coreservlets/ ContactFormBean.java *(continued)*

```
   this.faxNumber = faxNumber;
  }

  public void setFaxNumber(String faxNumber) {
  public String getWarning() {
    return(warning);
  }

  public void setWarning(String baseWarning) {
    this.warning =
      "<H2><FONT COLOR=RED>Missing or invalid " +
      baseWarning + "!</FONT></H2>";
  }

  public void clearWarning() {
    warning = "";
  }

  // The reset method below is ONLY needed if you make
  // the bean session-scoped. See the chapter on validation
  // for more details.

  public void reset(ActionMapping mapping,
                    HttpServletRequest request) {
    clearWarning();
  }

  public boolean isMissing(String value) {
    if ((value == null) || (value.trim().equals(""))) {
      return(true);
    } else {
      for(int i=0; i<defaultValues.length; i++) {
        if (value.equals(defaultValues[i])) {
          return(true);
        }
      }
      return(false);
    }
  }
}
```

Step 3: Create Results Beans

Because the confirmation page merely displays the data entered by the user (which is taken from the form bean), no results beans are needed.

The warning messages are shown in the original input form. Instead of using a separate warning-message bean, as in the previous example, the warning message is stored inside the form bean itself. This approach is convenient because the form already has access to the form bean, because the `html:form` tag creates it (for request-scoped beans) or verifies that it already exists (for session-scoped beans).

Step 4: Define an Action Class to Handle the Requests

Again, this example is very similar to the previous one. However, instead of storing any missing-value warning messages in a separate bean that are displayed in a separate JSP page, the warnings are stored in the form bean, which is used when the original input page is redisplayed.

For this example, we want the same behavior in the `execute` method as the previous example, so we extend the earlier `SignUpAction1` class and inherit `execute`, but we do need a new `makeWarning` method. Therefore we replace the original `makeWarning` method with a version that stores the warnings in the form bean (intended for the original input page) rather than in the `MessageBean` (intended for a custom error page).

`SignupAction2` is given in Listing 10.32.

Listing 10.32   signup/WEB-INF/classes/coreservlets/SignupAction2.java

```java
package coreservlets;

import javax.servlet.http.*;

/** Action that stores the warning messages in the form bean.
 *  This approach allows displaying the input form values
 *  along with error messages on the input page.
 */

public class SignupAction2 extends SignupAction1 {
  protected void makeWarning(HttpServletRequest request,
                             String message) {
    ContactFormBean contactFormBean =
      (ContactFormBean)request.getAttribute("contactFormBean");
    contactFormBean.setWarning(message);
  }
}
```

Step 5: Create a Form That Invokes *blah*.do

This form is very similar to the one in the previous example. Again, we use the `html:form` and `html:text` elements to build an HTML form whose form field values are derived from bean properties.

We output a warning message that reminds the user which field he or she omitted. The default warning message is an empty string, so rather than testing to see if the form is being initially displayed or redisplayed, we always output the error message (with `filter="false"` because the error message can contain HTML tags). If the user accesses the form directly, the warning message is empty; if the system forwards to the form, the warning message is filled in first.

Listing 10.33 shows the input form.

Listing 10.33 signup/forms/signup2.jsp

```
<!DOCTYPE HTML PUBLIC "-//W3C//DTD HTML 4.0 Transitional//EN">
<HTML>
<HEAD><TITLE>Sign Up</TITLE></HEAD>
<BODY BGCOLOR="#FDF5E6">
<H1 ALIGN="CENTER">Sign Up</H1>
Looking to receive late-breaking unverified virus alerts,
unknown ebay secrets, can't miss stock tips,
works-in-your-sleep diet plans, and
all sorts of medications? Want to get them both by email
<I>and</I> by fax? Look no further: the
Single Provider of Alert Memos
system lets you sign up for them all in one easy
request!
<P>
<CENTER>
<%@ taglib uri="http://struts.apache.org/tags-html"
           prefix="html" %>
<%@ taglib uri="http://struts.apache.org/tags-bean"
           prefix="bean" %>
<html:form action="/actions/signup2">
  <bean:write name="contactFormBean" property="warning"
              filter="false"/>
  First name: <html:text property="firstName"/><BR>
  Last name: <html:text property="lastName"/><BR>
  Email address: <html:text property="email"/><BR>
  Fax number: <html:text property="faxNumber"/><BR>
  <html:submit value="Sign Me Up!"/>
</html:form>
</CENTER>
</BODY></HTML>
```

Results

Finally, we present the results of this example.

- The user first invokes the form with the URL http://localhost/ signup/forms/signup2.jsp. As before, the text fields are prepopulated with values from the ContactFormBean properties. The page uses html:form to build the FORM element. Also, the warning property of the form bean is output, but the default value is an empty string. See Figure 10–23.
- The action in the html:form element is /actions/signup2, resulting in a URL of http://localhost/signup/actions/signup2.do when the form is submitted. Based on the action mapping in struts-config.xml, the system invokes the execute method the SignupAction2. The inherited execute method from SignupAction1 examines the input values to see if any are missing. If so, it calls makeWarning and returns mapping.findForward with a value of "missing-value". Otherwise it returns "success".
- As before, the "success" condition is mapped by struts-config.xml to /WEB-INF/results/signup-confirmation.jsp. However, the "missing-value" condition is mapped by struts-config.xml to /forms/signup2.jsp, the original input page. Because the makeWarning method stores the error message in the form bean, the input form can display it. Figures 10–24 and 10–25 show the redisplay of the input page with error messages for a missing first name and a missing last name, respectively. Figure 10–26 shows the output page when the registration information is complete.

Figure 10–23 Initial registration page. The form bean is instantiated and its properties are used to prepopulate the input fields.

Figure 10–24 Redisplay of the input page as the result of a missing first name. Not only does the form bean contain the previously submitted values (to redisplay in the input fields), the bean also contains warning messages.

Figure 10–25 Redisplay of the input page as a result of a missing last name. Again, the form bean contains the previously submitted values as well as the warning message.

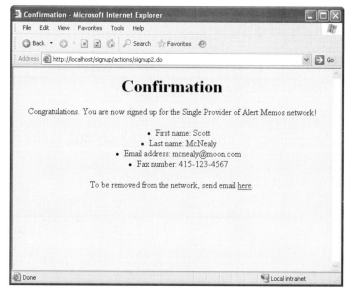

Figure 10–26 Result of a successful registration. The `bean:write` tag displays the registration properties stored in the form bean.

THE STRUTS FRAMEWORK: DOING MORE

Topics in This Chapter

- Using properties files for messages
- Creating parameterized messages
- Internationalizing Web sites
- Using Tiles to create a common layout
- Creating template files and layout pieces
- Using Definitions to create parent layouts and derived layouts
- Handling URLs correctly with `html:rewrite`

Chapter 11

In Chapter 10 (The Struts Framework: Basics), we covered the basics of the Struts framework for creating simple Web applications. However, Struts provides a lot more capabilities than controlling request flow and populating beans.

In this chapter, we dig deeper into Struts, explaining how to use properties files for messages in your JSP pages. The beauty of properties files is that you don't have to hard-code messages in your JSP files, but can place the messages in a common text file. Properties files also make it easy to internationalize your Web site. All you need to do is create local-specific properties files.

Also in this chapter, we introduce Struts Tiles, which is an excellent framework for building your Web pages with a common look and feel. Struts Tiles goes far beyond the `jsp:include` for including content in a page. Using the `tiles:` tags, you can easily create a basic layout for your site, defining stubbed out sections for headers, footers, and so on, and later create pages that provide definition for the stubbed out sections.

11.1 Using Properties Files

In the simplest terms, properties files are nothing more text files that contain name–value pairs, or rather, key–message pairs. By using `bean:message` from the Struts tag library, you can easily retrieve messages from your properties file and display them on your JSP pages.

Advantages of Properties Files

Nearly all Struts developers use properties files to simplify development of their Web applications. Following, we summarize the two greatest advantages of properties files.

- **Centralized updates.** If the application uses a message in several JSP pages, with properties files you can easily update a message with a single change. This capability is consistent with the Struts philosophy of making as many changes as possible in configuration files, not in Java or JSP code.
- **Internationalization (I18N).** If you use messages pervasively in your JSP pages, you can easily internationalize your application by having multiple properties files corresponding to the locale (as with standard I18N in Java). Simply create a file for each language that requires support. For instance, to support English, Japanese, and Spanish (Mexico dialect), you would create the following properties files, respectively:

```
MessageResources.properties
MessageResources_ja.properties
MessageResources_es_mx.properties
```

In Section 11.2 (Internationalizing Applications), we cover I18N in detail.

Struts Flow of Control— Updates for Properties Files

Figure 11–1 shows the Struts flow of control with updates for properties files. The main changes to the diagram are at the input and output pages. At the input page, you could use the `bean:message` tag to add fixed strings from the properties file to the JSP page. For instance, you might use fixed strings for the title or for labels of input fields. Similarly, on your output pages, along with using `bean:write` to display messages from your results beans, you could use `bean:message` to display fixed strings from the properties file.

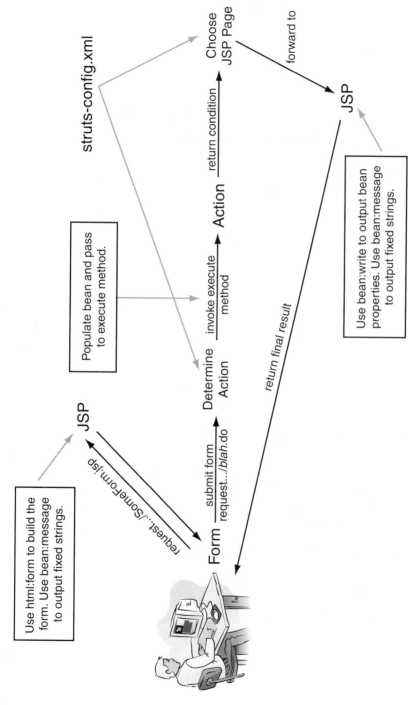

Figure 11–1 Flow of request through the Struts framework with updates for using properties files. In both the input page and output pages, the bean:message tag can display messages from the properties file.

Steps for Using Properties Files

Next, we summarize the changes needed in your application to support properties files. These changes have four essential steps.

1. **Create a properties file in WEB-INF/classes.** Place a properties file named MessageResources.properties in the WEB-INF/classes directory.
2. **Define strings in the properties file.** Add messages to your properties file for later display on your JSP pages.
3. **Load the properties file in struts-config.xml.** So that Struts knows about the properties file, you must place a resource file definition in struts-config.xml.
4. **Output the messages in JSP pages.** To display the messages in your JSP pages, load the Struts bean tag library and output the messages using bean:message.

Details follow.

Step 1: Create a Properties File in WEB-INF/classes

By default, Struts looks for a properties file in the WEB-INF/classes directory. This properties file should always end in .properties. The most common name for the properties file is MessageResources.properties.

Technically, you can have more than one properties file in your application; however, you must provide additional configuration information in struts-config.xml.

Step 2: Define Strings in the Properties File

In the properties file, provide key–message pairs. Each message must have a unique key. For instance,

```
some.key1=first message
some.key2=second message
some.key3=some parameterized message: {0}
```

As seen in the last key–message pair, some.key3, a message can have a parametric place holder. At run time, when the bean:message tag retrieves the message, you can provide a dynamic value to substitute for {0} in the message. We further discuss parameterized messages later in this section and in Chapter 12 (The Struts Framework: Validating User Input).

Step 3: Load the Properties File in struts-config.xml

To declare a properties file for your Struts application, add a `message-resources` entry in **struts-config.xml**. Place this entry after your `action-mappings`, unless maintaining an existing application with a `controller` section. In this case, place the `message-resources` entry after the `controller` entry.

An example is shown here:

```
<message-resources parameter="MessageResources"
                   null="false"/>
```

The `parameter` attribute refers to the `CLASSPATH` of the properties file, relative to the **WEB-INF/classes** directory. The file extension, **.properties**, is implied. Thus, the preceding example refers to the file, **WEB-INF/classes/MessageResources.properties**. The `null` attribute determines whether Struts should flag missing messages not found in the properties file. If set to `false`, a reference to a nonexistent message yields a warning message like *???keyName???*. Otherwise, a `null` string results when retrieving a nonexistent message.

We do not recommend setting the `null` attribute to `true`. If the `bean:message` tag sees a `null` for the message, then the tag may throw a `JspException`.

Core Approach

> In the `message-resources` element, we recommend always specifying *false* for the `null` attribute. This choice results in a warning message like *???keyName???* instead of a `null` return value and a possible *JspException* thrown by the `bean:message` tag.

By default, Struts assumes a single properties files for the application, but you can declare additional properties files. To declare these extra files, add a unique `key` attribute to identify each additional properties file. Two examples are shown here:

```
<message-resources parameter="MessageResources"/>
<message-resources parameter="LabelMessageResources"/>
                   key="labels"/>
```

The first declaration defines a default properties file, **MessageResources.properties**. The second declaration defines a supporting properties file, **LabelMessage-Resources.properties**, with a `key` identifier of `labels`. Later, when retrieving messages from the nondefault file, you would specify a `bundle` attribute in the `bean:message` tag that matches the `key` identifier, as in

```
<bean:message key="some.key" bundle="labels"/>
```

For reference, we summarize the common attributes of the message-resources element in Table 11.1. For a complete listing of all attributes, see http://jakarta.apache.org/struts/dtds/struts-config_1_3.dtd.

Table 11.1 Common Attributes of the `message-resources` Element in struts-config.xml

Attribute	Description
parameter	The CLASSPATH of the properties file relative to WEB-INF/classes directory. If you place the file in a subdirectory of classes, then use the dotted package notation in the parameter value. For example, if the properties file is located in WEB-INF/classes/resources/Messages.properties, then the parameter value must be `resources.Messages`. The file extension, .properties, is always implied.
null	Indicates whether a `null` string value or a warning message should be returned when a message is not found in the properties file. Set to `false` to return a warning message in the form `???keyName???`; otherwise, set to `true` (default) to return a `null`.
key	Specifies a unique identifier for the properties file. To retrieve messages from a nondefault properties file add a `bundle` attribute to the `bean:message` tag. The value for the `bundle` attribute must match the corresponding value for the resource `key` attribute.

Step 4: Output the Messages in JSP Pages

To display output messages in JSP pages, load the Struts bean tag library and access the message through `bean:message`. Details follow.

- **Load the tag library.** So that you can use the bean tag library, add the following `taglib` declaration to your JSP page:

```
<%@ taglib uri="http://struts.apache.org/tags-bean"
           prefix="bean" %>
```

- **Output the messages using `bean:message`.** To display a message from the properties file, use `bean:message` where the value of the key attribute corresponds to a key in the properties file. Some examples are given here:

```
First message is <bean:message key="some.key1"/>
Second: <bean:message key="some.key2"/>
Third: <bean:message key="some.key3" arg0="replacement"/>
```

In the last example, the tag has an arg0 attribute, which defines a parametric replacement value for {0} in the message. We cover parametric values later in this chapter.

If not using the default properties file for your messages, clarify the file through the bundle attribute, as shown here:

```
<bean:message bundle="otherPropertiesFile"
              key="some.key4"/>
```

Table 11.2 summarizes the common attributes for the bean:message tag. For a complete listing of all attributes, see http://struts.apache.org/1.x/ struts-taglib/ tlddoc/bean/message.html.

Be aware that unlike the bean:write custom tag, the bean:message tag provides no mechanism to filter the message for HTML characters. See *Core Servlets and JavaServer Pages, Volume 1,* for cross-site scripting attacks.

Core Warning

The bean:message tag does not filter the string for special HTML characters. If dynamically providing strings from user input as parametric values, the JSP page may be at risk to cross-site scripting attacks.

Table 11.2   Common Attributes of the bean:message Tag

Attribute	Description
key	The key identifies which message to retrieve from the properties file.
bundle	The bundle identifies which properties file to user for retrieve the message. This attribute is only necessary if not using the default properties file.
arg0 arg1 arg2 arg3 arg4	Replacement for the first through fifth parametric values in the message, respectively. For instance, the tag substitutes the value of arg0 for {0} in the message, the value for arg1 for {1} in the message, and so on. The tag does not filter the value for special HTML characters.

Example: Simple Messages

Next, we illustrate the use of a properties file to display messages in an application. In this example, we provide a simple registration page that, on submission, always routes to a results page. Both the registration page and results page build their output from messages in a properties file.

Following, we outline the design strategy for this example.

- The URL, http://hostname/struts-messages/actions/register.do, is handled by the class RegistrationAction.
- The RegistrationAction returns a "success" condition regardless of the user input.
- The "success" condition maps to a single results page, /WEB-INF/results/confirm-registration.jsp.
- The titles and text labels in the input and results pages come from a properties file.

Given this design strategy, we go through the six steps of using Struts.

Step 1: Modify struts-config.xml

As presented in Chapter 10 (The Struts Framework: Basics), we need to follow the general guidance of: mapping an incoming .do address to an Action class, mapping return conditions to JSP pages, and declaring any form beans. In addition, we now must also declare a properties file.

Map Incoming .do Addresses to Action Classes

The action element designates that RegistrationAction should handle requests from /actions/register.do, as shown in the following code fragment:

```
<action path="/actions/register"
        type="coreservlets.RegistrationAction"
        name="registrationBean"
        scope="request">
    ...
</action>
```

Map Return Conditions to JSP Pages

We use the forward element to map the single "success" condition to /WEB-INF/results/confirm-registration.jsp, as shown here:

```
<forward name="success"
         path="/WEB-INF/results/confirm-registration.jsp"/>
```

Declare the Use of Any Form Beans

Here, we declare a single `form-bean` entry with `name` and `type` attributes. The form bean, `registrationBean`, handles the submitted request parameters.

```
<form-beans>
  <form-bean name="registrationBean"
             type="coreservlets.RegistrationFormBean"/>
</form-beans>
```

Declare a Properties File

After the `action-mappings` entry, we declare a single properties file, as shown here:

```
<message-resources parameter="MessageResources"
                   null="false"/>
```

We place the `MessageResources.properties` file in the `WEB-INF/classes` directory. For the `null` attribute, we specify a value of `false`, requesting that any messages not found in the properties file yield a warning message like ???*keyName*???.

The complete listing of `struts-config.xml` is given in Listing 11.1 and the properties file for this example is given in Listing 11.2.

Listing 11.1 struts-messages/WEB-INF/struts-config.xml

```
<?xml version="1.0" encoding="ISO-8859-1" ?>
<!DOCTYPE struts-config PUBLIC
  "-//Apache Software Foundation//DTD Struts Configuration 1.3//EN"
  "http://struts.apache.org/dtds/struts-config_1_3.dtd">
<struts-config>
  <form-beans>
    <form-bean name="registrationBean"
               type="coreservlets.RegistrationFormBean"/>
  </form-beans>
  <action-mappings>
    <action path="/actions/register"
            type="coreservlets.RegistrationAction"
            name="registrationBean"
            scope="request">
      <forward name="success"
               path="/WEB-INF/results/confirm-registration.jsp"/>
    </action>
  </action-mappings>
  <message-resources parameter="MessageResources"
                     null="false"/>
</struts-config>
```

Listing 11.2	struts-messages/WEB-INF/classes/ MessageResources.properties

```
# -- Custom messages for struts-messages application --
form.title=Registration
form.firstName=First name
form.lastName=Last name
form.emailAddress=Email address
form.buttonLabel=Register Me
form.successString=Success
```

Step 2: Define a Form Bean

This example uses a single form bean, `RegistrationFormBean`, shown in Listing 11.3. The bean simply holds registration information (first name, last name, e-mail address).

Listing 11.3	struts-messages/WEB-INF/classes/ RegistrationFormBean.java

```java
package coreservlets;

import org.apache.struts.action.*;

/** A simple form bean for registration information. */

public class RegistrationFormBean extends ActionForm {
  private String firstName, lastName, emailAddress;

  public String getFirstName() {
    return(firstName);
  }

  public void setFirstName(String firstName) {
    this.firstName = firstName;
  }

  public String getLastName() {
    return(lastName);
  }

  public void setLastName(String lastName) {
    this.lastName = lastName;
  }
```

Listing 11.3	struts-messages/WEB-INF/classes/ RegistrationFormBean.java *(continued)*

```java
  public String getEmailAddress() {
    return(emailAddress);
  }

  public void setEmailAddress(String emailAddress) {
    this.emailAddress = emailAddress;
  }
}
```

Step 3: Create the Results Beans

This example does not use results beans.

Step 4: Define an Action Class to Handle Requests

Our `RegistrationAction` always returns a `"success"` condition, regardless of the registration information entered by the user.

The code for `RegistrationAction` is given in Listing 11.4.

Listing 11.4	struts-messages/WEB-INF/classes/RegistrationAction.java

```java
package coreservlets;

import javax.servlet.http.*;
import org.apache.struts.action.*;

/** A simple Action that always routes to a single
 *  output page corresponding to a success condition.
 */

public class RegistrationAction extends Action {
  public ActionForward execute(ActionMapping mapping,
                               ActionForm form,
                               HttpServletRequest request,
                               HttpServletResponse response)
      throws Exception {
    return(mapping.findForward("success"));
  }
}
```

Step 5: Create a Form That Invokes *blah*.do

For this example, we define an input form, register.jsp, that invokes http://*hostname*/struts-messages/actions/register.do. The registration page is given in Listing 11.5.

Instead of directly listing headings, prompts, and textual messages for the registration page, they are taken from the properties file using `bean:message`. That way, if we later decide to change the messages (or if we have multiple versions in different languages), we can update the messages without modifying the actual JSP pages. Furthermore, as we use some of the prompts in more than one page, extracting the prompts from the properties file limits changes to one location, even though the prompts are used in multiple locations.

Listing 11.5   struts-messages/forms/register.jsp

```
<%@ taglib uri="http://struts.apache.org/tags-html"
           prefix="html" %>
<%@ taglib uri="http://struts.apache.org/tags-bean"
           prefix="bean" %>
<!DOCTYPE HTML PUBLIC "-//W3C//DTD HTML 4.0 Transitional//EN">
<HTML>
<HEAD><TITLE><bean:message key="form.title"/></TITLE></HEAD>
<BODY BGCOLOR="#FDF5E6">
<CENTER>
<H1><bean:message key="form.title"/></H1>
<CENTER>
<html:form action="/actions/register">
  <bean:message key="form.firstName"/>:
  <html:text property="firstName"/><BR>
  <bean:message key="form.lastName"/>:
  <html:text property="lastName"/><BR>
  <bean:message key="form.emailAddress"/>:
  <html:text property="emailAddress"/><BR>
  <html:submit>
    <bean:message key="form.buttonLabel"/>
  </html:submit>
</html:form>
</CENTER>
</BODY></HTML>
```

Step 6: Display the Results in a JSP Page

We have a single results page, WEB-INF/results/confirm-registration.jsp. This output page relies on the `RegistrationFormBean` passed to it through the `request` scope. The JSP page uses `bean:write` to display the registration information. In addition, the page uses bean:message to display the title, the heading, and registration labels from the properties file.

The results page, confirm-registration.jsp, is given in Listing 11.6.

Listing 11.6 WEB-INF/results/confirm-registration.jsp

```
<%@ taglib uri="http://struts.apache.org/tags-bean"
           prefix="bean" %>
<!DOCTYPE HTML PUBLIC "-//W3C//DTD HTML 4.0 Transitional//EN">
<HTML>
<HEAD><TITLE>
<bean:message key="form.title"/>:
<bean:message key="form.successString"/>
</TITLE></HEAD>
<BODY BGCOLOR="#FDF5E6"><CENTER>
<H1>
<bean:message key="form.title"/>:
<bean:message key="form.successString"/>
</H1>
<UL>
  <LI><bean:message key="form.firstName"/>:
      <bean:write name="registrationBean"
                  property="firstName"/>
  <LI><bean:message key="form.lastName"/>:
      <bean:write name="registrationBean"
                  property="lastName"/>
  <LI><bean:message key="form.emailAddress"/>:
      <bean:write name="registrationBean"
                  property="emailAddress"/>
</UL>
</CENTER>
</BODY></HTML>
```

Results

Figure 11–2 presents both the registration page and results page. In both cases, the browser title, heading, and field labels are retrieved from a single properties file, WEB-INF/classes/MessageResources.properties.

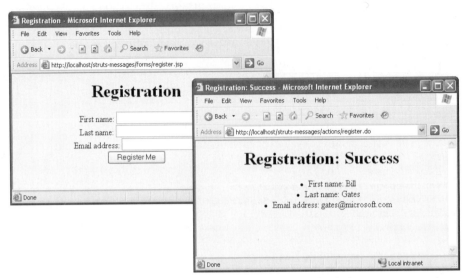

Figure 11–2   Result of `struts-message` Web application. For both the input page and results page, `bean:message` retrieves the title, heading, and field labels from the default properties file.

Dynamic Keys

With the `bean:message` tag, you can dynamically provide the value for the `key` attribute; the `key` value need not be hard-coded.

Following is an example of a properties file that contains key–message pairs for three different colleges. The key is the acronym for the college, whereas the message is the full college name.

```
# Properties File
jhu=Johns Hopkins University
upenn=University of Pennsylvania
umbc=University of Maryland Baltimore County
```

In a JSP page, assuming that a variable or a bean contains information about the school of interest, you could provide the key dynamically when retrieving the message. Two examples follow, the first using the JSP 2.0 EL and the second using a traditional JSP scripting expression.

```
<bean:message key="${user.school}"/>
<bean:message key="<%= school %>"/>
```

Parameterized Messages

With properties files, you can parameterize any message. Parameterization allows you, during run time, to dynamically substitute a text value into the message at a desired location, thus creating a customized message.

To support parameterized messages, you first need to modify your messages to indicate where the parameterized substitution should occur and then to provide the parametric replacements in the JSP pages. Details follow.

- **Add parametric notation to messages in properties file.** Use `{n}` notation in each message to indicate the location of the *n*th parametric substitution. Up to five substitutions are allowed, `{0}` ... `{4}`. Two examples are shown here:

```
error.missing=You must enter {0}, you idiot!
error.number={0} and {1} are not whole numbers!
```

- **Provide parametric replacements in JSP pages.** On the JSP page use the `bean:message` tag to retrieve the parameterized message from the properties file. For each `{n}` in the message, provide a corresponding `argN` attribute in the tag. During execution, the tag substitutes the value for the `arg` attribute in the message at the proper location. Examples follow.

```
<bean:message key="error.missing"
              arg0="your first name"/>
<bean:message key="error.number"
              arg0="<%= Math.random() %>"
              arg1="${user.firstName}"/>
```

As seen, you can provide the value for the attribute using JSP scripting expressions or the JSP 2.0 EL. Unfortunately, you cannot take the argument value directly from the properties file itself, so parameterized messages may not work well with I18N.

Remember that when providing values for the parameterized messages, the `bean:message` tag does not filter the argument for special HTML characters.

Later in Chapter 12 (The Struts Framework: Validating User Input), we present a Struts application that uses parameterized messages in conjunction with input validation.

11.2 Internationalizing Applications

With Struts, creating an I18N application is easy! Well, maybe. If you're willing to pull all the titles, labels, and text messages from a properties file, then you can easily I18N your application. Just create a properties file for each language (locale) you would like to support.

Loading Locale-Specific Properties Files

Struts attempts to use a properties file that corresponds to the browser language setting. When requesting a page, the browser sends an `Accept-Language` request header, listing the language preferences. If no corresponding language (locale) file is found, then Struts uses the default properties file.

- **Default properties file.** To establish a default properties file, use the `message-resource` element in struts-config.xml. Thus, when you say

  ```
  <message-resources parameter="someName" ...>
  ```

  the file, WEB-INF/classes/someName.properties, is loaded and treated as the default language file.
- **Locale-specific properties file.** Based on the languages accepted by the browser, Struts automatically looks for specialized files corresponding to the locale. A locale-specific file has the same name as the default properties file, but is augmented with local information, for example, someName_es.properties (Spanish locale) or someName_fr.properties (French locale). Entries from a more specific file override entries from the default file. The locale can also be set explicitly (e.g., based on incoming checkbox value) in an `Action` with `setLocale`.

Setting Language Preferences in Browsers

Once you have created a locale-specific properties file, you will want to test it in your Web application. To test the new properties file, change the language settings in the browser.

We next explain how to change the language setting in Internet Explorer and Firefox.

- **Internet Explorer.** For Internet Explorer, select Tools from the menu, then Internet Options, then Languages. Click the Add button to select other languages for the browser. To change the language preference order, use the Move Up button. See the Internet Explorer screen in Figure 11–3.
- **Firefox.** For Firefox, select Tools from the menu, then Options, then Languages. Click the Add button to select other languages for the browser. To change the language preference order, use the Move Up button. See the Firefox screen in Figure 11–3.

 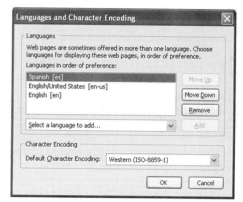

Figure 11–3 Changing language preferences in Internet Explorer (left) and in Firefox (right).

Example: Internationalizing for English, Spanish, and French

Now, we present an example where we internationalize the earlier registration application (Example: Simple Message) from Section 11.1 (Using Properties Files). For our modified application to support English, Spanish, and French, all we need to do is create two new properties files, MessageResources_es.properties for the Spanish locale and MessageResources_fr.properties for the French locale. The assumption is that the original file, MessageResources.properties, supports the English locale.

The two new locale files contain all the same messages as Message-Resources.properties (Listing 11.2), but translated to the appropriate language. The keys remain the same. This change is all that is needed to internationalize the application for Spanish and French—there are no changes to any configuration files or code!

Listing 11.7 presents our `MessageResources_es` properties file, with the messages translated to Spanish, and Listing 11.8 presents our `MessageResources_fr` properties file, with the messages translated to French.

Listing 11.7	struts-messages/WEB-INF/classes/ MessageResources_es.properties

```
# -- Custom messages for struts-messages application --
form.title=Registro
form.firstName=Primer nombre
form.lastName=Apellido
form.emailAddress=Dirección de email
form.buttonLabel=Colóqueme
form.successString=Éxito
```

Listing 11.8	struts-messages/WEB-INF/classes/ MessageResources_fr.properties

```
# -- Custom messages for struts-messages application --
form.title=Enregistrement
form.firstName=Prénom
form.lastName=Nom
form.emailAddress=Adresse électronique
form.buttonLabel=Enregistrez Moi
form.successString=Succès
```

Results

To test our application for Spanish users, we first changed the language preference in Internet Explorer to "Spanish (International Sort) [es]", restarted the browser, and then accessed the registration page. Figure 11–4 shows the result for a Spanish locale.

Similarly, for French users, we changed the language setting in Internet Explorer to "French (France) [fr]". Figure 11–5 shows the result for a French locale.

Figure 11–4   Result of the registration application with the browser language preference set to Spanish.

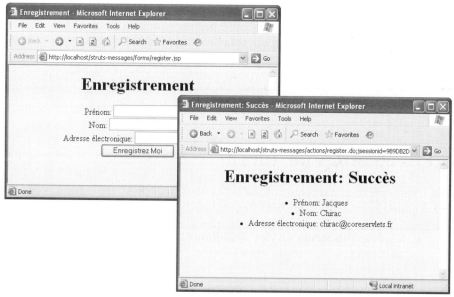

Figure 11–5   Result of the registration application with the browser language preference set to French.

11.3 Laying Out Pages with Tiles

Many Web sites contain pages with a common header, footer, and menu. If you would like to build your site with a common look and feel, starting with Struts Tiles is an excellent choice.

With the Tiles framework, you create a common page layout for your site, and then, based on the layout, use Struts `tiles:` tags to include JSP fragments and Strings for the main pages of the site. The Tiles approach is much more powerful than the traditional `jsp:include` for including files in a JSP page. In fact, some developers find themselves using Struts just for the Tiles capability, as the servlet/JSP community has very few equivalents. In future versions of Tiles, you'll be able to use the technology outside of Struts.

Tiles Motivations

We summarize three main reasons to choose Tiles for your site design.

- **Reuse (not rewrite) repeated sections of pages.** For similar content, you need only write sections once and then use Tiles to easily add those sections to your JSP pages.
- **Simplify the creation of similar pages.** With templates you can easily lay out similar pages in your site. Then, with the layout template, provide specific content for the layout pieces.
- **Increase flexibility and ease of maintenance.** With Tiles you get a lot more flexibility than with the traditional `<jsp:include .../>` tag. Plus, the supporting elements for Tiles (handling relative URLs, inheritance) eases the overall maintenance of the site.

Prerequisites for Tiles

Next we cover three prerequisites for using Tiles in a Struts application. For complete information on Tiles, see http://struts.apache.org/1.x/struts-tiles/.

- **Update the Struts servlet definition in web.xml.** To support Tiles add a `chainConfig` parameter for the `ActionServlet` in web.xml, as shown here:

```
<servlet>
  <servlet-name>action</servlet-name>
  <servlet-class>
     org.apache.struts.action.ActionServlet
  </servlet-class>
```

```
  <init-param>
    <param-name>chainConfig</param-name>
    <param-value>
      org/apache/struts/tiles/chain-config.xml
    </param-value>
  </init-param>
  ...
</servlet>
```

An example of a complete `servlet` entry in web.xml is given in
Listing 11.9

- **Add Tiles plug-in to struts-config.xml.** After your
  `message-resources` element in struts-config.xml, add an entry for
  the Tiles plug-in, as shown here:

```
<plug-in className="org.apache.struts.tiles.TilesPlugin" >
  <!-- Path to XML definition file -->
  <set-property property="definitions-config"
                value="/WEB-INF/tiles-defs.xml" />
  <!-- Set Module-awareness to true -->
  <set-property property="moduleAware" value="true" />
</plug-in>
```

If you started with struts-blank-1.3.5, then this change already exists
in struts-config.xml. You just need to uncomment out the plug-in
element.

- **Add Tiles JAR file to application.** From either the full distribution
  of Struts, struts-1.3.5-all.zip, or the examples file, struts-1.3.5-apps.zip,
  add struts-tiles-1.3.5.jar to your WEB-INF/lib directory. Note that this
  JAR file is already included with struts-blank-1.3.5.

If you download the struts-blank application from the book's source code archive,
http://volume2.coreservlets.com/, we include all the necessary changes for Tiles.

Listing 11.9 Struts servlet entry in web.xml supporting Tiles

```
<!-- Standard Action Servlet Configured for Tiles -->
<servlet>
  <servlet-name>action</servlet-name>
  <servlet-class>
    org.apache.struts.action.ActionServlet
  </servlet-class>
  <init-param>
    <param-name>config</param-name>
    <param-value>/WEB-INF/struts-config.xml</param-value>
  </init-param>
```

Listing 11.9 Struts servlet entry in web.xml supporting Tiles *(continued)*

```
<init-param>
  <param-name>chainConfig</param-name>
  <param-value>
    org/apache/struts/tiles/chain-config.xml
  </param-value>
</init-param>
<load-on-startup>2</load-on-startup>
</servlet>
```

The Four Basic Steps in Using Tiles

Next, we outline the four basic steps in using Tiles. Afterward, we cover these steps in detail and present a simple example.

1. **Sketch out the desired page layout.** Before you start writing a template file for your Tiles layout, we recommend that you first sketch the page layout on a piece of paper.
2. **Make a template file that represents the layout.** In your template file, use `tiles:insert` wherever a layout piece should go. Also, use `tiles:getAsString` wherever changeable text goes. Both of these `tiles:` tags act as stubs that are later filled in by other pieces. To prevent direct access of the template file, place the file in WEB-INF or a subdirectory.
3. **Create JSP pages that define the layout pieces.** Create JSP pages that contain HTML fragments for the stubbed-out layout. To prevent direct access to these fragments, also put them in WEB-INF or a subdirectory.
4. **Create JSP pages that populate the layout.** Use `tiles:insert` to refer to the layout from Step 1. Use `tiles:put` to specify the layout pieces that apply to each specific page. Unless forwarding the request to the output pages through `RequestDispatcher`, place these JSP files in a directory normally accessible by the user (do not place them in WEB-INF).

Details follow.

Step 1: Sketch the Desired Layout

Many Web sites have groups of pages that have a common general layout, for instance, a common header, title, menu, body, and footer. Often only one or two parts (e.g., the body) changes from page to page.

Before you create a template file for your site layout, sketch the layout on one or more pieces of paper. On the sketches, identify those areas that are consistent throughout the pages. Each one of these identified areas will most likely become part of your template layout.

Step 2: Make a Template File That Represents the Layout

The template file captures the general layout of your Web site. In the template file you use various `tiles:` tags to indicate where a layout piece (JSP fragment) or changeable text should go. Layout pieces are for larger sections of the page, whereas a changeable text section may be for a title or header.

With the template file you establish stubs (`tiles:` tags) that are later filled in by other pieces (file or text string). A loose analogy of Tiles is to think of a layout template as an interface. The layout page has abstract methods or rather stubs, that define the pieces of the layout. Later, you provide pages with definitions that populate the layout. These pages implement the layout interface and provide concrete definitions for each stub.

When creating template files, follow this general guidance:

- **Use regular HTML for parts that never change.** Static parts should remain in HTML.
- **Declare the Struts tiles tag library.** Before you use any of the `tiles:` tags in your JSP pages, you must declare the Tiles tag library, as shown here:

```
<%@ taglib uri="http://struts.apache.org/tags-tiles"
           prefix="tiles" %>
```

- **Use `tiles:insert` to stub out sections that will be filled in by layout pieces.** The `tiles:insert` tag stubs out replacement sections in the template. As example is shown here:

```
<tiles:insert attribute="header"/>
```

  The `attribute` names the stubbed section. Later, a JSP page using the template will reference the `header` stub and provide a JSP fragment to insert at that location.

- **Use `tiles:getAsString` to stub out locations that will be replaced by simple text.** Similarly, the `tiles:getAsString` allows you to stub out locations for String substitutions (versus a stub for a file). For instance, the following `tiles:getAsString` tag creates a String stub named `title`:

```
<tiles:getAsString name="title"/>
```

The JSP page using the template will later provide a real string to substitute at the layout location.

- **Template files should never be accessed directly.** Template files simply define a layout for use by other pages. The user should not be able to access template files directly. Put template files in WEB-INF to avoid accidental access.

Core Approach

Place the template files that represent your site layout in WEB-INF or a subdirectory. In this manner, the user cannot access these template files directly.

For more information on `tiles:` tags, see `http://struts.apache.org/1.x/struts-tiles/tagreference.html`.

Step 3: Create JSP Pages That Define the Layout Pieces

After you create the layout template, then create the JSP pages that define the layout pieces to apply to the template. These are regular JSP page fragments that define portions of an HTML page. When creating these pieces, keep the following in mind.

- **Do not repeat HTML header elements.** The layout pieces are HTML fragments inserted into a parent JSP page. Be sure not to repeat HTML elements such as DOCTYPE, HEAD, BODY, and so on, that are defined in the template file from Step 2.
- **They can themselves be tiles.** The pieces could themselves also be tiles, defining additional layouts.
- **Pages can use the `bean:` and `html:` Struts tags.** As the layout pieces are simply JSP page fragments, they can use the familiar `bean:` and `html:` tags. Furthermore, these layout pieces can access any beans stored in the `request` scope.
- **Layout pieces should never be accessed directly.** As with the layout template file, the layout pieces (JSP fragments) should not be directly accessible by the user. Put the layout pieces in WEB-INF or a subdirectory to avoid accidental access by the user.

Step 4: Create JSP Pages That Populate the Layout

The last step is to create the Web pages that populate the layout. These pages specify which layout template file to use and which layout pieces to apply to the template. To create these pages, perform the following steps:

- **Declare the Struts Tiles tag library.** So you can use the `tiles:` tags, declare the tag library, as shown.

  ```
  <%@ taglib uri="http://struts.apache.org/tags-tiles"
             prefix="tiles" %>
  ```

- **Use `tiles:insert` to refer to the layout template file.** With the `tiles:insert` tag, provide a `page` attribute to specify the layout template to use (the template file you created in Step 2). An example is shown here:

  ```
  <tiles:insert page="/WEB-INF/tiles/layout.jsp">
    ...
  </tiles:insert>
  ```

- **Use `tiles:put` to specify the layout pieces.** With the `tiles:put` tag, specify which specific layout pieces (JSP page fragments or strings) to substitute into the template stubs for this particular page. Use the `name` attribute to reference the stubbed `tile` element in the template. Use the `value` attribute to provide the substitution file or string. See the following example:

  ```
  <tiles:insert page="/WEB-INF/tiles/layout.jsp">
    <tiles:put name="title" value="Page 1 Title"/>
    <tiles:put name="header"
               value="/WEB-INF/tiles/header.jsp"/>
  </tiles:insert>
  ```

Example: Simple Tiles

Next, we present a simple Tiles example. Even though this example doesn't contain much page content, it does demonstrate the four basic steps in using Tiles.

Step 1: Sketch Out the Desired Layout

Figure 11–6 shows a sketch of two representative pages for our Web site. We want a similar look and feel for our pages and, as seen, both pages have five common areas suitable for a Tiles design: header, footer, title, menu, and body.

Header

Title

Menu

Body

Footer

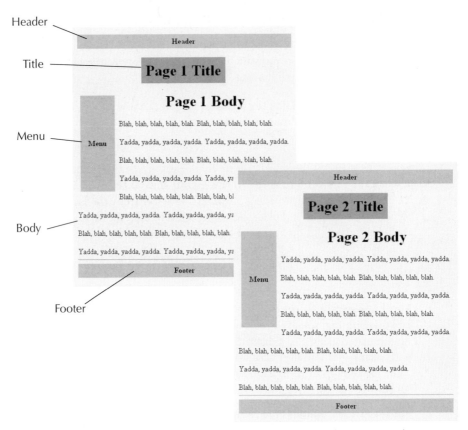

Figure 11–6 Initial sketch of pages for a Web site to help identify a common layout.

Step 2: Make a Template File That Represents the Layout

Listing 11.10 presents our template file for the page layout. This template file sets up the structure for each page in our Web site. We use the `tiles:getAsString` tag to stub out the title of the page and use the `tiles:insert` tag to stub out the header, body, menu, and footer. To prevent access by the user, we place this layout template file in the WEB-INF/tiles directory.

Listing 11.10 tiles-test/WEB-INF/tiles/layout.jsp

```
<%@ taglib uri="http://struts.apache.org/tags-tiles"
           prefix="tiles" %>
<!DOCTYPE HTML PUBLIC "-//W3C//DTD HTML 4.0 Transitional//EN">
<HTML>
<HEAD><TITLE><tiles:getAsString name="title"/></TITLE></HEAD>
<BODY BGCOLOR="#FDF5E6">
<tiles:insert attribute="header"/>
<P>
<TABLE BORDER=5 ALIGN="CENTER" BGCOLOR="#EF8429">
  <TR><TH><FONT SIZE="+3">
    <tiles:getAsString name="title"/>
</FONT></TH></TR></TABLE>
<P>
<TABLE WIDTH=75 ALIGN="LEFT" CELLSPACING="5">
<TR><TD><tiles:insert attribute="menu"/></TD></TR>
</TABLE>
<tiles:insert attribute="body"/>
<BR CLEAR="ALL">
<HR>
<tiles:insert attribute="footer"/>
</BODY></HTML>
```

Step 3: Create JSP Pages That Define the Layout Pieces

Listings 11.11 through 11.15 present our JSP fragments for each stubbed-out section in the template file. As these are page fragments and not a full HTML page, they contain no DOCTYPE, HEAD, or BODY sections. Like the template file, we place these page fragments in the WEB-INF/tiles directory so that the user can't access them directly.

Listing 11.11 tiles-test/WEB-INF/tiles/header.jsp

```
<TABLE BORDER=1 WIDTH="100%" BGCOLOR="#C0C0C0">
  <TR><TH>Header</TH></TR>
</TABLE>
```

Listing 11.12 tiles-test/WEB-INF/tiles/menu.jsp

```
<TABLE BORDER=1 BGCOLOR="#C0C0C0" WIDTH=75 HEIGHT=200>
  <TR><TH>Menu</TH></TR>
</TABLE>
```

Listing 11.13 tiles-test/WEB-INF/tiles/body1.jsp

```
<H1 ALIGN="CENTER">Page 1 Body</H1>
Blah, blah, blah, blah, blah.
Blah, blah, blah, blah, blah.
<P>
Yadda, yadda, yadda, yadda.
Yadda, yadda, yadda, yadda.
<P>
...
```

Listing 11.14 tiles-test/WEB-INF/tiles/body2.jsp

```
<H1 ALIGN="CENTER">Page 2 Body</H1>
Blah, blah, blah, blah, blah.
Blah, blah, blah, blah, blah.
<P>
Yadda, yadda, yadda, yadda.
Yadda, yadda, yadda, yadda.
<P>
...
```

Listing 11.15 tiles-test/WEB-INF/tiles/footer.jsp

```
<TABLE BORDER=1 WIDTH="100%" BGCOLOR="#C0C0C0">
  <TR><TH>Footer</TH></TR>
</TABLE>
```

Step 4: Create JSP Pages That Populate the Layout

Finally, we create the two pages that use the layout template created in Step 2. See Listings 11.16 and 11.17. Both these JSP pages initially use the `tiles:insert` tag to declare that WEB-INF/tiles/layout.jsp is the template file for the JSP page. Within the `tiles:insert` tag we add `tiles:put` tags to specify the content for each stub in the template file.

We place both these pages in the root directory of the Web application for direct access by the user (whereas the layout template file and JSP fragments are placed under WEB-INF).

Listing 11.16 tiles-test/page1.jsp

```
<%@ taglib uri="http://struts.apache.org/tags-tiles"
          prefix="tiles" %>
<tiles:insert page="/WEB-INF/tiles/layout.jsp">
  <tiles:put name="title" value="Page 1 Title"/>
  <tiles:put name="header" value="/WEB-INF/tiles/header.jsp"/>
  <tiles:put name="menu" value="/WEB-INF/tiles/menu.jsp"/>
  <tiles:put name="body" value="/WEB-INF/tiles/body1.jsp"/>
  <tiles:put name="footer" value="/WEB-INF/tiles/footer.jsp"/>
</tiles:insert>
```

Listing 11.17 tiles-test/page2.jsp

```
<%@ taglib uri="http://struts.apache.org/tags-tiles"
          prefix="tiles" %>
<tiles:insert page="/WEB-INF/tiles/layout.jsp">
  <tiles:put name="title" value="Page 2 Title"/>
  <tiles:put name="header" value="/WEB-INF/tiles/header.jsp"/>
  <tiles:put name="menu" value="/WEB-INF/tiles/menu.jsp"/>
  <tiles:put name="body" value="/WEB-INF/tiles/body2.jsp"/>
  <tiles:put name="footer" value="/WEB-INF/tiles/footer.jsp"/>
</tiles:insert>
```

Results

Figure 11–7 presents the results for page1.jsp and page2.jsp. Even though both pages have a similar layout (same template), each page uniquely defines which file and text fragments to substitute into the template stubs.

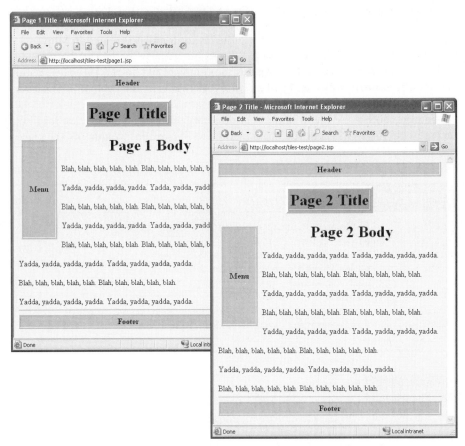

Figure 11–7   Result of `page1.jsp` and `page2.jsp`. Both pages use Tiles with a common layout template file for the header, footer, title, menu, and body.

Handling Relative URLs

In a JSP page, many elements are referenced with relative URLs, for instance images, style sheets, and simple hypertext links. However, with Tiles, JSP fragments cannot use URLs that refer to page elements relative to the location of the layout pieces (i.e., the JSP fragments). That's because the layout pieces are actually located in WEB-INF, not in a location immediately accessible by the browser.

Often to resolve this issue, you use a URL beginning with a slash, for instance, /images/pic.jpg. However, depending on how the page is built, such a URL may be rendered relative to the host (http://host/) and not the application context (http://host/webApp/). For the earlier situation, you could use `request.getContextPath` to prefix the URL with the application context, but then you need to add a scriptlet.

Using html:rewrite

To properly handle relative URLs from a layout page or JSP fragment, use the `html:rewrite` tag. The `html:rewrite` tag lets you use URLs beginning with slashes. You simply list the path relative to Web application home, then the tag automatically prefixes the Web application (context path) to the front of the URL. For instance,

```
<html:rewrite page="/dir/somePage.html"/>
```

produces a result similar to

```
/webApp/dir/somePage.html;jsessionid=72C6D63791839
```

Be aware that the tag also appends the session ID to the address. Remember that to use the `html:rewrite` tag, you must import the Struts `html:` tag library.

```
<%@ taglib uri="http://struts.apache.org/tags-html"
           prefix="html" %>
```

Here are a couple of practical examples.

- From layout template:

  ```
  <LINK REL="STYLESHEET"
        HREF="<html:rewrite page='/css/styles.css'/>"
        TYPE="text/css">
  ```

- From JSP fragment or layout template:

  ```
  <IMG SRC="<html:rewrite page='/images/pic.jpg'/>" ...>
  ```

When calling an `Action` class, use the `action` attribute instead of the `page` attribute. For instance, instead of

```
<html:rewrite page='/actions/logout.do'/>
```

use

```
<html:rewrite action='/actions/logout'/>
```

For more details on `html:rewrite`, see http://struts.apache.org/1.x/struts-taglib/tlddoc/html/rewrite.html.

Example: e-boats Application

Now, we present a more detailed Tiles example based on an online store that sells boats. Our design approach is the following:

- Uses Tiles for pages that have similar layouts. For this Web site, only the title and body changes from page to page.
- Uses stylesheet to control look and feel. The stylesheet controls the background colors for different areas of the pages, as well as the font and font size for various titles.
- Uses images on multiple pages. Each page references an image from the /images directory. So that the image URL is referenced correctly, we use the html:rewrite tag.

Next, we cover the four basic steps in using Tiles for this example.

Step 1: Sketch Out the Desired Layout

Figure 11–8 presents the desired page layout for our e-boats application. Annotations indicate the various sections of the page that are suitable for a Tiles layout, as described in the list that follows the figure.

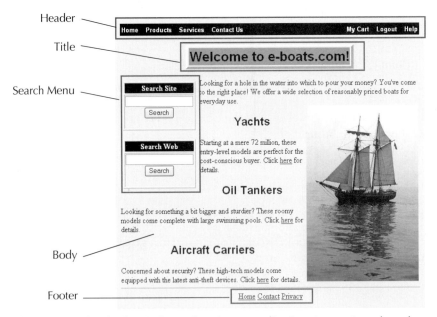

Figure 11–8 Sketch of typical page for e-boats application. Annotations show the various sections of the page suitable for a Tiles layout.

- **Header.** This section provides basic site navigation and is the same for all pages.
- **Title.** This section provides the title for the page. Even though each page has a title section, the actual title is unique to each particular page.
- **Search menu.** This section provides search capabilities for either the Web site or the Internet. The search menu is present on all pages.
- **Body.** This section provides the main content for the page. In addition to basic text information, each page presents an image of a boat.
- **Footer.** This section provides supplementary links to site information and is present on all pages.

Step 2: Make a Template File That Represents the Layout

Listing 11.18 presents our template file, main-layout.jsp, that captures the general layout of all the pages for our site. We place this file in the WEB-INF/tiles directory so that the user does not have direct access to the template.

This layout template file sets the stage for all the main pages in the site and defines the locations for the Tiles sections identified earlier in Step 1. Specifically, we use the `tiles:insert` tag to stub out the header, search menu, body, and footer sections. For the title section, we use the `tiles:getAsString` tag.

Listing 11.18   e-boats/WEB-INF/tiles/main-layout.jsp

```
<%@ taglib uri="http://struts.apache.org/tags-tiles"
           prefix="tiles" %>
<%@ taglib uri="http://struts.apache.org/tags-html"
           prefix="html" %>
<!DOCTYPE HTML PUBLIC "-//W3C//DTD HTML 4.0 Transitional//EN">
<HTML>
<HEAD><TITLE><tiles:getAsString name="title"/></TITLE>
<LINK REL="STYLESHEET"
      HREF="<html:rewrite page='/css/styles.css'/>"
      TYPE="text/css">
</HEAD>
<BODY>
<tiles:insert attribute="header"/>
<P>
<TABLE BORDER=5 ALIGN="CENTER">
  <TR><TH CLASS="TITLE"><tiles:getAsString name="title"/>
</TH></TR></TABLE>
```

Listing 11.18 e-boats/WEB-INF/tiles/main-layout.jsp *(continued)*

```
<P>
<TABLE WIDTH=75 ALIGN="LEFT" CELLSPACING="5">
<TR><TD><tiles:insert attribute="search-menu"/></TD></TR>
</TABLE>
<tiles:insert attribute="body"/>
<BR CLEAR="ALL">
<HR>
<tiles:insert attribute="footer"/>
</BODY></HTML>
```

Step 3: Create JSP Pages That Define the Layout Pieces

Next, we create the individual layout pieces (JSP fragments) for each of the stubbed-out sections in the layout template. Listings 11.19 through 11.21 present the layout pieces for the header, search menu, and footer sections, respectively. We place all of these pages in the WEB-INF/tiles directory. So that included URLs are correct in the rendered pages, we use the `html:rewrite` tag throughout the layout pieces. In this manner, we don't have to hard-code the Web application name, e-boats, in the URL links.

In Listings 11.22 through 11.25, we present the JSP fragments for each of the four body sections in the site. The body-index.jsp section contains the opening body content for the site. The other three body sections, body-yachts.jsp, body-tankers.jsp, and body-carriers.jsp, are for the three various boats types available for purchase. As with the other JSP pieces, we place these body sections in the WEB-INF/tiles directory.

Listing 11.19 e-boats/WEB-INF/tiles/header.jsp

```
<%@ taglib uri="http://struts.apache.org/tags-html"
           prefix="html" %>
<TABLE WIDTH="100%" CLASS="DARK">
  <TR>
    <TH ALIGN="LEFT">
      <A HREF="<html:rewrite page='/index.html'/>"
         CLASS="WHITE">
      Home</A>   
      <A HREF="<html:rewrite page='/products.html'/>"
         CLASS="WHITE">
      Products</A>   
```

Listing 11.19 e-boats/WEB-INF/tiles/header.jsp *(continued)*

```
      <A HREF="<html:rewrite page='/services.html'/>"
         CLASS="WHITE">
      Services</A>   
      <A HREF="<html:rewrite page='/contact.html'/>"
         CLASS="WHITE">
      Contact Us</A>
    </TH>
    <TH ALIGN="RIGHT">
      <A HREF="<html:rewrite action='/actions/showCart'/>"
         CLASS="WHITE">
      My Cart</A>   
      <A HREF="<html:rewrite action='/actions/logout'/>"
         CLASS="WHITE">
      Logout</A>   
      <A HREF="<html:rewrite page='/help.html'/>"
         CLASS="WHITE">
      Help</A>
    </TH>
  </TR>
</TABLE>
```

Listing 11.20 e-boats/WEB-INF/tiles/search-menu.jsp

```
<%@ taglib uri="http://struts.apache.org/tags-html"
           prefix="html" %>
<CENTER>
<TABLE BORDER=1>
  <TR BGCOLOR="BLACK"><TH>
    <FONT COLOR="WHITE">Search Site</FONT>
  </TH></TR>
  <TR><TH>
    <FORM ACTION=
        "<html:rewrite action='/actions/siteSearch'/>">
      <INPUT TYPE="TEXT" NAME="query"><BR>
      <INPUT TYPE="SUBMIT" VALUE="Search">
    </FORM>
  </TH></TR>
</TABLE>
<P>
<TABLE BORDER=1>
  <TR BGCOLOR="BLACK">
    <TH><FONT COLOR="WHITE">Search Web</FONT></TH>
  </TR>
```

Listing 11.20 e-boats/WEB-INF/tiles/search-menu.jsp *(continued)*

```
  <TR><TH>
    <FORM ACTION="http://google.com/search">
      <INPUT TYPE="HIDDEN" NAME="hl" VALUE="en">
      <INPUT TYPE="TEXT" NAME="q"><BR>
      <INPUT TYPE="SUBMIT" VALUE="Search">
    </FORM>
  </TH></TR>
</TABLE>
</CENTER>
```

Listing 11.21 e-boats/WEB-INF/tiles/footer.jsp

```
<%@ taglib uri="http://struts.apache.org/tags-html"
           prefix="html" %>
<CENTER>
<A HREF="<html:rewrite page='/index.html'/>">Home</A>
<A HREF="<html:rewrite page='/contact.html'/>">Contact</A>
<A HREF="<html:rewrite page='/privacy.html'/>">Privacy</A>
</CENTER>
```

Listing 11.22 e-boats/WEB-INF/tiles/body-index.jsp

```
<%@ taglib uri="http://struts.apache.org/tags-html"
           prefix="html" %>
<P>
Looking for a hole in the water into which to pour your money?
You've come to the right place! We offer a wide selection of
reasonably priced boats for everyday use.
<IMG SRC="<html:rewrite page='/images/yacht.jpg'/>"
     WIDTH=240 HEIGHT=367
     ALIGN="RIGHT" ALT="Base-model yacht">

<H2>Yachts</H2>
Starting at a mere 72 million, these entry-level models are
perfect for the cost-conscious buyer.
Click <A HREF="<html:rewrite page='/yachts.jsp'/>">
here</A> for details.
```

Listing 11.22 e-boats/WEB-INF/tiles/body-index.jsp *(continued)*

```
<H2>Oil Tankers</H2>
Looking for something a bit bigger and sturdier? These
roomy models come complete with large swimming pools.
Click <A HREF="<html:rewrite page='/tankers.jsp'/>">
here</A> for details.

<H2>Aircraft Carriers</H2>
Concerned about security? These high-tech models come
equipped with the latest anti-theft devices.
Click <A HREF="<html:rewrite page='/carriers.jsp'/>">
here</A> for details.
```

Listing 11.23 e-boats/WEB-INF/tiles/body-yachts.jsp

```
<%@ taglib uri="http://struts.apache.org/tags-html"
          prefix="html" %>
Luxurious models for the <S>wasteful</S>
wealthy buyer.
<H2>Available Models</H2>
Choose a model to see a picture along with price and
availability information.
<FORM ACTION="<html:rewrite action='/actions/displayItem'/>">
<INPUT TYPE="RADIO" NAME="itemNum" VALUE="BM1">
Base Model -- Includes 4-car garage<BR>
<INPUT TYPE="RADIO" NAME="itemNum" VALUE="MR1">
Mid Range -- Has 15 bedrooms and a helipad<BR>
<INPUT TYPE="RADIO" NAME="itemNum" VALUE="HE1">
High End -- Free tropical island nation included
<P>
<CENTER>
<INPUT TYPE="SUBMIT" VALUE="Get Details">
</CENTER>
</FORM>
<CENTER>
<IMG SRC="<html:rewrite page='/images/yacht.jpg'/>"
     ALT="Yacht"></CENTER>
```

Listing 11.24 e-boats/WEB-INF/tiles/body-tankers.jsp

```
<%@ taglib uri="http://struts.apache.org/tags-html"
           prefix="html" %>
Stable and roomy models for the <S>uninformed</S>
innovative buyer.
<H2>Available Models</H2>
Choose a model to see a picture along with price and
availability information.
<FORM ACTION="<html:rewrite action='/actions/displayItem'/>">
<INPUT TYPE="RADIO" NAME="itemNum" VALUE="Valdez">
Valdez -- Slightly damaged model available at discount<BR>
<INPUT TYPE="RADIO" NAME="itemNum" VALUE="BigBertha">
Big Bertha -- Includes 10 million gallon swimming pool<BR>
<INPUT TYPE="RADIO" NAME="itemNum" VALUE="EcoDisaster">
ED I -- For those who don't mind political incorrectness
<P>
<CENTER>
<INPUT TYPE="SUBMIT" VALUE="Get Details">
</CENTER>
</FORM>
<CENTER>
<IMG SRC="<html:rewrite page='/images/tanker.jpg'/>"
     ALT="Tanker"></CENTER>
```

Listing 11.25 e-boats/WEB-INF/tiles/body-carriers.jsp

```
<%@ taglib uri="http://struts.apache.org/tags-html"
           prefix="html" %>
High-security models for the <S>paranoid</S> careful buyer.
<H2>Available Models</H2>
Choose a model to see a picture along with price and
availability information.
<FORM ACTION="<html:rewrite action='/actions/displayItem'/>">
<INPUT TYPE="RADIO" NAME="itemNum" VALUE="SafeT-1A">
SafeT-1A -- Our Most Popular Model<BR>
<INPUT TYPE="RADIO" NAME="itemNum" VALUE="SafeT-1B">
SafeT-1B -- 1000-man crew included<BR>
<INPUT TYPE="RADIO" NAME="itemNum" VALUE="Lubber-1">
Land Lubber I -- Land-based replica; no water to worry about!
<P>
<CENTER>
<INPUT TYPE="SUBMIT" VALUE="Get Details">
</CENTER>
</FORM>
<CENTER>
<IMG SRC="<html:rewrite page='/images/carrier.jpg'/>"
     ALT="Carrier"></CENTER>
```

Step 4: Create JSP Pages That Populate the Layout

Now, we create the main pages for the site. As we are using Tiles, these main pages rely on the layout template file created in Step 2. After using the `tiles:insert` tag to specify which layout template file to use, each page then uses the `tiles:put` tag to specify which file fragments from Step 3 to use for the stubbed-out sections in the template.

Listings 11.26 through 11.29 present the four main pages for our e-boats application, `index.jsp`, `yachts.jsp`, `tankers.jsp`, and `carriers.jsp`, respectively. The `tiles:put` elements for the header, search menu, and footer sections are the same for all four pages. The main differences between these pages are the values for the title and body sections.

As these are the main pages for the site and accessible by the user, we place these files in the default (root) directory for the site, e-boats, and not in the WEB-INF subdirectory (as with the template file and layout pieces).

The complete file structure of the e-boats application is shown in Figure 11–9.

Listing 11.26 e-boats/index.jsp

```
<%@ taglib uri="http://struts.apache.org/tags-tiles"
          prefix="tiles" %>
<tiles:insert page="/WEB-INF/tiles/main-layout.jsp">
  <tiles:put name="title" value="Welcome to e-boats.com!"/>
  <tiles:put name="header" value="/WEB-INF/tiles/header.jsp"/>
  <tiles:put name="search-menu"
          value="/WEB-INF/tiles/search-menu.jsp"/>
  <tiles:put name="body" value="/WEB-INF/tiles/body-index.jsp"/>
  <tiles:put name="footer" value="/WEB-INF/tiles/footer.jsp"/>
</tiles:insert>
```

Listing 11.27 e-boats/yachts.jsp

```
<%@ taglib uri="http://struts.apache.org/tags-tiles"
          prefix="tiles" %>
<tiles:insert page="/WEB-INF/tiles/main-layout.jsp">
  <tiles:put name="title" value="E-boats.com Yachts!"/>
  <tiles:put name="header" value="/WEB-INF/tiles/header.jsp"/>
  <tiles:put name="search-menu"
          value="/WEB-INF/tiles/search-menu.jsp"/>
  <tiles:put name="body" value="/WEB-INF/tiles/body-yachts.jsp"/>
  <tiles:put name="footer" value="/WEB-INF/tiles/footer.jsp"/>
</tiles:insert>
```

Listing 11.28 e-boats/tankers.jsp

```
<%@ taglib uri="http://struts.apache.org/tags-tiles"
           prefix="tiles" %>
<tiles:insert page="/WEB-INF/tiles/main-layout.jsp">
  <tiles:put name="title" value="E-boats.com Oil Tankers!"/>
  <tiles:put name="header" value="/WEB-INF/tiles/header.jsp"/>
  <tiles:put name="search-menu"
             value="/WEB-INF/tiles/search-menu.jsp"/>
  <tiles:put name="body" value="/WEB-INF/tiles/body-tankers.jsp"/>
  <tiles:put name="footer" value="/WEB-INF/tiles/footer.jsp"/>
</tiles:insert>
```

Listing 11.29 e-boats/carriers.jsp

```
<%@ taglib uri="http://struts.apache.org/tags-tiles"
           prefix="tiles" %>
<tiles:insert page="/WEB-INF/tiles/main-layout.jsp">
  <tiles:put name="title" value="E-boats.com Aircraft Carriers!"/>
  <tiles:put name="header" value="/WEB-INF/tiles/header.jsp"/>
  <tiles:put name="search-menu"
             value="/WEB-INF/tiles/search-menu.jsp"/>
  <tiles:put name="body" value="/WEB-INF/tiles/body-carriers.jsp"/
>
  <tiles:put name="footer" value="/WEB-INF/tiles/footer.jsp"/>
</tiles:insert>
```

Figure 11–9   Complete file structure of e-boats application.

Results

Figures 11–10 though 11–13 present the results for our e-boats application. Figure 11–10 is the opening page for the site, index.jsp (Listing 11.26). Figures 11–11 through 11–13 are the results for the yachts.jsp (Listing 11.27), tankers.jsp (Listing 11.28), and carriers.jsp (Listing 11.29) pages, respectively. All four pages use the same template file, WEB-INF/titles/main-layout.jsp (Listing 11.18) to achieve a similar layout.

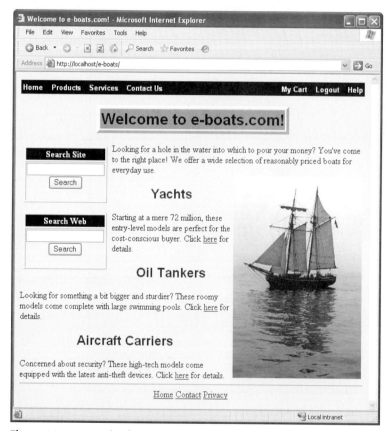

Figure 11–10   Result of e-boats/index.jsp.

Figure 11–11 Result of e-boats/yachts.jsp.

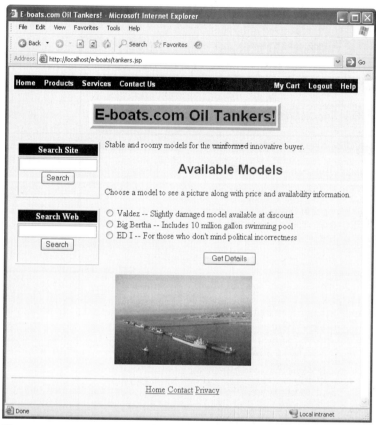

Figure 11–12 Result of e-boats/tankers.jsp.

Figure 11–13   Result of e-boats/carriers.jsp.

11.4 Using Tiles Definitions

Earlier we showed you how to use Tiles to design a Web site that has a common look and feel. Basically, with this approach, you first created a layout template file with stubbed-out sections, created JSP fragments for each stubbed section, and then created pages main that defined which fragments to substitute for the stubs.

With Tiles Definitions you can design your Web site with a slightly different approach. Initially, you create a definition file, WEB-INF/tiles-def.xml, that defines a top-level layout. The top-level layout can reference a template file and provide information about the stubbed-out sections in the template. In the same definition file, you create additional layouts derived from the top-level layout. These derived layouts can substitute new content for sections in the top-level layout. To create the final pages of the Web site, you simply refer to the derived layouts in WEB-INF/ tiles-def.xml.

You can think of Tiles Definitions as a loose form of inheritance. First you create a top-level layout for the overall design of your pages, and then you create derived layouts that override sections of the top-level layout.

Tiles Definitions Motivations

You don't have to use Tiles Definitions for your Web site. You could design your site using the initial Tiles approach presented in Section 11.3 (Laying Out Pages with Tiles). However, in the following list, we summarize the main reasons why you may want to use Tiles Definitions instead.

- **Avoiding repetition.** In the previous example (e-boats application), each final JSP page repeated the definition of all the elements. Even though only the title and body changed, each final JSP page still had to do tiles:put for the header, search menu, and footer. With Tiles Definitions, you don't have to repeat common elements.
- **Centralized changes.** The locations of the various layout pieces (JSP fragments) are scattered around multiple JSP pages, so if locations change, multiple files need to be edited. With Tiles Definitions, you have fewer layout pieces scattered throughout your site and less editing.
- **Usage of config files.** Struts philosophy is to put as much as possible in config files and as little as possible in JSP and Java code. Tiles Definitions permits you to define most of your layout in a single file.

The Five Basic Steps in Using Tiles Definitions

Next, we outline the five basic steps in using Tiles Definitions. The first three steps are the same as for basic Tiles. The last two steps are new.

1. **Sketch out the desired layout.** As with the previous Tiles approach, we recommend that you sketch the basic page layout for your site on a piece of paper.
2. **Make a template file that represents the layout.** Use tiles:insert wherever a layout piece (JSP fragment) should go. Also, use tiles:getAsString wherever changeable text goes. Both these tiles: tags act as stubs that are later filled in by other pieces.

3. **Create JSP pages that define the layout pieces.** Create JSP pages that contain HTML fragments for the stubbed-out layout.

4. **Define layouts in WEB-INF/tiles-defs.xml.** In the definition file, define a top-level layout and any derived layouts.

5. **Create JSP pages that use the layouts.** Create the main pages for the site. These JSP pages typically have nothing more than a line to import the Tiles tag library and a line with `tiles:insert` to specify which layout definition in tiles-defs.xml to use.

Details follow.

Step 1: Sketch Out the Desired Layout

This step is the same as with basic Tiles (see Section 11.3).

Step 2: Make a Template File That Represents the Layout

Again, this step is the same as with basic Tiles (see Section 11.3).

Step 3: Create JSP Pages That Define the Layout Pieces

Also, this step is the same as with basic Tiles (see Section 11.3).

Step 4: Define Layouts in WEB-INF/tiles-defs.xml

For Tiles Definitions, you need to define a top-level layout and derived layouts in WEB-INF/tiles-defs.xml. In general, the format for tiles-def.xml is the following:

```
<?xml version="1.0" encoding="ISO-8859-1" ?>
<!DOCTYPE tiles-definitions PUBLIC
 "-//Apache Software Foundation//DTD Tiles Configuration 1.3//EN"
 "http://jakarta.apache.org/struts/dtds/tiles-config_1_3.dtd">
<tiles-definitions>
  <definition name=".mainLayout"
            path="/WEB-INF/tiles/main-layout.jsp">
    ...
  </definition>
  <definition name="somePage" extends=".mainLayout">
    ...
  </definition>
  <definition name="anotherPage" extends=".mainLayout">
    ...
  </definition>
  ...
</tiles-definitions>
```

Typically, the first definition is the main layout of your pages and references a template file. The remaining definitions are derived from the main layout.

Note that the struts-blank-1.3.5 application does contain a tiles-def.xml file. If needed, as a starting point, you can download a blank tiles-def.xml file from the book's source code archive at http://volume2.coreservlets.com/.

Top-Level Layouts

Initially, in tiles-def.xml, define the top-level layout for your site in a `definition` element. Each `definition` element must provide a `name` attribute to uniquely identify the layout. Use the path `attribute` to specify the top-level template file for your site. A representative example is shown here:

```
<definition name="top-level-layout-name"
            path="/WEB-INF/.../some-layout.jsp">
  <put name="title"
       value="Some Page Title" />
  <put name="menu"
       value="/WEB-INF/.../some-menu.jsp" />
  <put name="body"
       value="/WEB-INF/.../some-body.jsp" />
  ...
</definition>
```

Within the `definition` element, use the `put` element to specify any initial pages to populate the parent layout. With this initial top-level definition, you can easily set up common elements (titles, headers, footers, etc.) for all your pages. You need only specify these common elements once in the first definition. Then, in derived definitions you can clarify additional changes to the main layout.

Derived Layouts

After creating your top-level layouts in WEB-INF/tiles-def.xml, provide any derived layouts that you also need for your site. These derived layouts specify only the changes from the parent layout. The structure of the parent layout is automatically inherited by the derived layout.

To create a derived layout, use the `definition` element with a name attribute to uniquely identify the layout. However, add an `extends` attribute to clarify from which parent layout to build the new one. Within the `definition` element, provide put elements to override any definitions in the parent layout. A representative example follows:

```
<definition name="derived-layout-name"
            extends="top-level-layout-name">
  <put name="title"
       value="Another Page Title" />
</definition>
```

In this example, if the parent layout provides a definition for the title, then the derived layout would override the parent title and provide a new value. All other defined stubs in the parent layout would convey to the derived layout.

Step 5: Create JSP Pages That Use the Layouts

The last step is to create the main Web pages accessed by the user. These pages specify which layout to use from WEB-INF/tiles-defs.xml. Typically, these pages have only two lines in them, as described next.

- **Declare the Struts tiles tag library.** To use the `tiles:` tags, declare the tag library.

  ```
  <%@ taglib uri="http://struts.apache.org/tags-tiles"
             prefix="tiles" %>
  ```

- **Use `tiles:insert` to refer to the definition layout.** With the `tiles:insert` tag, use the `definition` attribute to specify which derived layout to use from WEB-INF/tiles-defs.xml. The following is an example:

  ```
  <tiles:insert definition="some-layout-name" />
  ```

Example: e-boats Application with Tiles Definitions

Next, we rework the e-boats example from Section 11.3 (Laying Out Pages with Tiles), but use Tiles Definitions instead. The following is our new design approach.

- Use the same look for the Web site and keep the JSP page names the same. Also, uses the same template file to represent the general layout of pages and keep the same layout pieces (JSP fragments) for the header, menu, footer, and so on.
- Use WEB-INF/tiles-def.xml to specify the parent layout and derived layouts.
- In the final JSP pages, use the `tiles:insert` tag to refer to a derived layout in WEB-INF/tiles-def.xml.

Now, for this example, we cover the five basic steps in using Tiles Definitions.

Step 1: Sketch Out the Desired Layout

The general layout is the same as the previous e-boats application in Section 11.3 (Laying Out Pages with Tiles). For convenience, the layout is shown again in Figure 11–14.

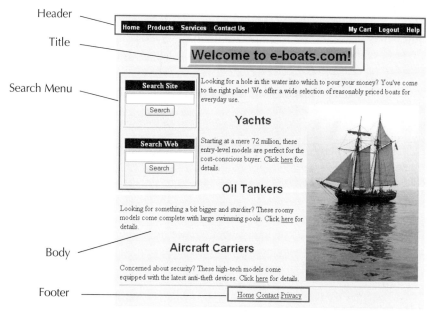

Figure 11–14 Sketch of a typical page for **e-boats2** application. Annotations indicate the various Tiles sections.

Step 2: Make a Template File That Represents the Layout

The template file, WEB-INF/tiles/main-layout.jsp, is the same as the previous e-boats application in Section 11.3 (Laying Out Pages with Tiles). See Listing 11.18.

Step 3: Create JSP Pages That Define the Layout Pieces

The layout pieces (JSP fragments) are no different from previous example. See Listings 11.19 through 11.25, for the following layout pieces, respectively.

- WEB-INF/tiles/header.jsp
- WEB-INF/tiles/search-menu.jsp
- WEB-INF/tiles/footer.jsp
- WEB-INF/tiles/body-index.jsp
- WEB-INF/tiles/body-yachts.jsp
- WEB-INF/tiles/body-tankers.jsp
- WEB-INF/tiles/body-carriers.jsp

Step 4: Define Layouts in WEB-INF/tiles-defs.xml

In WEB-INF/tiles-defs.xml, we first specify the top-level layout definition, .main-Layout, as given here:

```
<definition name=".mainLayout"
              path="/WEB-INF/tiles/main-layout.jsp">
  <put name="title" value=""/>
  <put name="header" value="/WEB-INF/tiles/header.jsp"/>
  <put name="search-menu"
      value="/WEB-INF/tiles/search-menu.jsp"/>
  <put name="body" value=""/>
  <put name="footer" value="/WEB-INF/tiles/footer.jsp"/>
</definition>
```

This definition states that the template file, main-layout.jsp, is the main layout page for the site. For each stub in main-layout.jsp, we use the put element to specify each layout piece for the corresponding tiles:insert or tiles:getAsString. Initially, the title and body stubs have no value; inherited layouts will provide values for these stubs.

Next, we specify derived layout definitions in WEB-INF/tiles-defs.xml for each of the four pages in the e-boats2 application. Each derived layout extends the .mainLayout and provides a replacement definition for the title and body stubs. The index.page layout is shown here:

```
<definition name="index.page" extends=".mainLayout">
  <put name="title" value="Welcome to e-boats.com!"/>
  <put name="body" value="/WEB-INF/tiles/body-index.jsp"/>
</definition>
```

For the remaining derived layouts, see the complete WEB-INF/tiles-defs.xml in Listing 11.30.

Listing 11.30   e-boats2/WEB-INF/tiles-defs.xml

```
<?xml version="1.0" encoding="ISO-8859-1" ?>
<!DOCTYPE tiles-definitions PUBLIC
  "-//Apache Software Foundation//DTD Tiles Configuration 1.3//EN"
  "http://jakarta.apache.org/struts/dtds/tiles-config_1_3.dtd">
<tiles-definitions>
  <definition name=".mainLayout"
              path="/WEB-INF/tiles/main-layout.jsp">
    <put name="title" value=""/>
    <put name="header" value="/WEB-INF/tiles/header.jsp"/>
```

Listing 11.30 e-boats2/WEB-INF/tiles-defs.xml *(continued)*

```
    <put name="search-menu"
         value="/WEB-INF/tiles/search-menu.jsp"/>
    <put name="body" value=""/>
    <put name="footer" value="/WEB-INF/tiles/footer.jsp"/>
  </definition>
  <definition name="index.page" extends=".mainLayout">
    <put name="title" value="Welcome to e-boats.com!"/>
    <put name="body" value="/WEB-INF/tiles/body-index.jsp"/>
  </definition>
  <definition name="yachts.page" extends=".mainLayout">
    <put name="title" value="E-boats.com Yachts!"/>
    <put name="body" value="/WEB-INF/tiles/body-yachts.jsp"/>
  </definition>
  <definition name="tankers.page" extends=".mainLayout">
    <put name="title" value="E-boats.com Oil Tankers!"/>
    <put name="body" value="/WEB-INF/tiles/body-tankers.jsp"/>
  </definition>
  <definition name="carriers.page" extends=".mainLayout">
    <put name="title" value="E-boats.com Aircraft Carriers!"/>
    <put name="body" value="/WEB-INF/tiles/body-carriers.jsp"/>
  </definition>
</tiles-definitions>
```

Step 5: Create JSP Pages That Use the Layouts

The last step is to create the main JSP pages that use the layouts. These files simply use the `tiles:insert` tag to apply the appropriate layout definition, from WEB-INF/tiles-defs.xml, when rendering the page.

Listings 11.31 through 11.34 show the four main pages for our e-boats2 application, index.jsp, yachts.jsp, tankers.jsp, and carriers.jsp, respectively. Again, as these are the main pages for the site and accessible by the user, we place these files in the default (root) directory of the site.

Listing 11.31 e-boats2/index.jsp

```
<%@ taglib uri="http://struts.apache.org/tags-tiles"
           prefix="tiles" %>
<tiles:insert definition="index.page"/>
```

Listing 11.32 e-boats2/yachts.jsp

```
<%@ taglib uri="http://struts.apache.org/tags-tiles"
          prefix="tiles" %>
<tiles:insert definition="yachts.page"/>
```

Listing 11.33 e-boats2/tankers.jsp

```
<%@ taglib uri="http://struts.apache.org/tags-tiles"
          prefix="tiles" %>
<tiles:insert definition="tankers.page"/>
```

Listing 11.34 e-boats2/carriers.jsp

```
<%@ taglib uri="http://struts.apache.org/tags-tiles"
          prefix="tiles" %>
<tiles:insert definition="carriers.page"/>
```

Results

The results for our reworked **e-boats** application are the same as before. See Figures 11–10 though 11–13 in Section 11.3 (Laying Out Pages with Tiles), for the representative output pages.

THE STRUTS
FRAMEWORK:
VALIDATING
USER INPUT

Topics in This Chapter

- Manually validating input fields in an `Action` or `ActionForm`
- Returning to the input page when errors occur
- Displaying messages with the `html:messages` tag
- Using rules in validation.xml to check input fields
- Adding client-side JavaScript validation

Chapter 12

Probably the most tedious and time-consuming part of developing a Web site is validation of the input data. There is no easy way of getting around it—you *have* to check for missing or poorly formatted input values. Unfortunately, the servlet and JSP APIs provide no mechanism for easily validating input data!

To the rescue come the Struts Validation framework. The framework is incredibly flexible and easy to use, supporting both server-side and client-side validation.

For validating form fields, Struts gives you the following options:

- **Do validation in the `Action`.** This is the most powerful and flexible approach. Validation in the `Action` has access to business logic, databases, and so on. However, this validation approach may require repetition of code in multiple `Actions` and requires you to write the validation rules yourself. Also, you need to manually map conditions back to the input page.
- **Do validation in the form bean.** You can do validation in individual setter methods—not really validation, but useful to modify values. Better, you can use the `validate` method in `ActionForm`. This approach does not require repetition of code in multiple `Actions`, but still requires you to write validation rules. Based on the return value from `validate`, Struts can automatically redisplay the input page.

- **Use automatic validator.** Automatic validation is the most powerful approach. The Struts Validation framework includes many rules for automatically checking input values (missing data, phone number format, e-mail format, etc.). In addition, the automatic validator can incorporate client-side JavaScript for field validation.

12.1 Validating in the Action Class

In this section, we cover manual validation of input fields in the `Action` class. Did we say *manual* validation? As you'll discover, manual validation of data gives you the most power, the greatest flexibility, and complete control of your validation code. However, you have to write the code. Yuck!

Later in this chapter, we cover other approaches that take advantage of the validation techniques automatically built into the Struts framework.

For simple input validation—missing data, wrong format—using the Struts framework is a great time saver. However, if you have to do more complicated validation, like checking values against a database, then you have to write code. Thus, we first show you how to perform manual validation of input fields in the `Action` class.

Struts Flow of Control

Figure 12–1 illustrates the Struts flow of control, with updates for manual validation of input data in the `Action` class.

As presented in Chapter 10 (The Struts Framework: Basics), when the user submits an input page to the server, the Struts system populates the form bean with the input data and then passes the bean to the `execute` method of the `Action` class. Here, the `execute` method can apply business logic to manually validate the input data, and depending on the result, return a condition to forward the request back to the input page or to a results page.

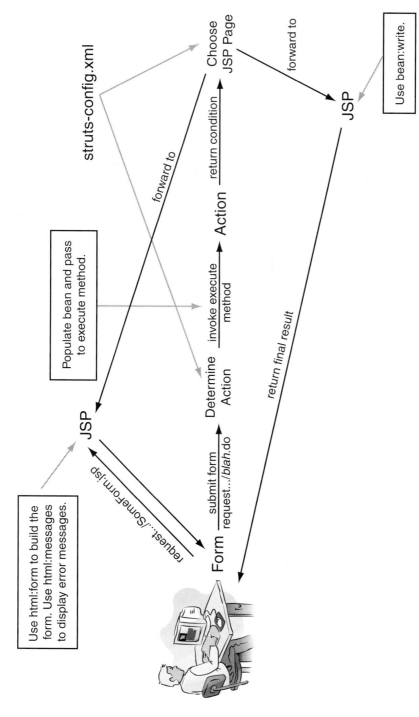

Figure 12–1 Flow of the request through the Struts framework with manual validation of the input fields in the Action. If there are errors with the input data, the Action can return a condition to forward the request back to the input page.

Performing Validation in the Action

When performing manual validation of the input fields in an `Action`, we recommend the following approach.

- **Access input fields from bean.** Proceed as normal by casting the `ActionForm` bean (second argument to `execute` method) to the specific class type. Then, call the appropriate getter methods to retrieve the field values.
- **Add error messages to `ActionMessages` and place in the `request` scope.** For each missing or incorrect value add an error message to `ActionMessages`. Place the `ActionMessages` in the `request` scope for access by the input page.
- **Return error code and map error code to input form.** Use `mapping.findForward` to return an error code that maps back to the input form. In **struts-config.xml**, define a `forward` element that maps the error code back to the input form.
- **Use `html:messages` to output error messages in input form.** On the input JSP page, use the `html:messages` tag to display any error messages.

Details follow.

Access Input Fields from Bean

As presented in Chapter 10 (The Struts Framework: Basics), access the `Action-Form` bean from the second argument of the `ActionForm`'s `execute` method. Remember to cast the bean to the specific class type. Then, call the appropriate getter methods to retrieve the field values.

Add Error Messages to ActionMessages and Place in the request Scope

For each missing or incorrect input field, add an error message to `Action-Messages`. To accomplish this step, first create an `ActionMessages` object in the `execute` method of `Action`. Then, check each input field (property) of the form bean. If an error is identified, create an error message and add it to the `Action-Messages` object. An example is shown here:

```
ActionMessages messages = new ActionMessages();
String value = someFormBean.getItem();
if ((value==null) || (value.trim().equals(""))) {
  String warning = "Item missing value"
  messages.add("item", new ActionMessage(warning, false));
}
...
```

When creating the `ActionMessage`, provide a literal string for the error or warning message in the first argument of the constructor and specify a value of `false` for the second argument. The `false` value indicates that the message is a literal and not a key referencing a message in a properties files. Later in Section 12.2 (Validating in the Form Bean), we cover accessing messages from properties files.

Finally, place the `ActionMessages` in the `request` scope for access by the input page, as shown here:

```
if (!messages.isEmpty()) {
   addMessages(request, messages);
}
```

Return Error Code and Map Error Code to Input Form

As presented in Chapter 10 (The Struts Framework: Basics), use `mapping.find-Forward` to return an error code that maps back to the input form.

Use html:messages to Output Error Messages in the Input Form

Use `html:messages` on the input page to list errors found with the input fields. This tag checks the `request` scope for an `ActionMessages` (or `ActionErrors`) object. If messages are present, use `bean:write` to display each message. An example of the `html:messages` tag is given here:

```
<html:messages id="msg" message="true">
   <bean:write name="msg"/>
</html:messages>
```

Specifically, the `id` attribute is required and identifies which variable to place in each message as the `html:messages` tag iterates over a collection of messages. The tag places the individual messages in `page` scope. Then, by using `bean:write`, you can access and display each message.

The `message` attribute indicates whether the collection of messages is stored in an `ActionMessages` object (`true`) or `ActionErrors` object (`false`). We cover `ActionErrors` in Section 12.2 (Validating in the Form Bean). If there are no messages to display, the `html:messages` tag produces no output.

Table 12.1 summarizes the common attributes of the `html:messages` tag. For a complete listing of attributes, see http://struts.apache.org/1.x/struts-taglib/tagreference.html#messages.

Table 12.1   Common Attributes of the `html:messages` Tag

Attribute	Description
id	The name of the bean in which to store each message. The tag places the bean in `page` scope.
message	Indicates if the messages are stored in an `ActionMessages` object (`true`) or an `ActionErrors` object (`false`).
property	Specifies which messages to display. The value would have to match the name of the `ActionMessage` when added to `ActionMessages` or `ActionErrors`. If not specified, the default behavior is to display all messages.
header	To display text before all messages, use the `header` attribute to specify the key of the text message in the properties file. See Section 12.2 for properties files.
footer	To display text after all the messages, use the `footer` attribute to specify the key of the text message in the properties file. See Section 12.2 for properties files.

Instead of listing all the messages, you can target only those messages for a particular input field. To achieve this result, use `<html:messages property="name" .../>`, where the `"name"` matches the one given to the `ActionMessage` when it was added to `ActionMessages` (or `ActionErrors`).

For instance, suppose that you used the following names when adding messages to `ActionMessages`:

```
messsages.add("someName", new ActionMessage("message1", false));
messsages.add("someOtherName",
                new ActionMessage("message2", false));
messsages.add("someName", new ActionMessage("message3", false));
```

Then, on the input page, you could display only someName messages with this:

```
<html:messages id="msg" message="true"
                property="someName">
  <bean:write name="msg"/>
</html:messages>
```

Next, we present a simple example that illustrates manual validation of input data in the `Action` class.

Example: Choosing Colors and Font Sizes for Resume

In this example, we produce a sample online resume. The user, through an input page, can specify the fonts and colors to use when generating the resume. If the user doesn't complete all the fields, or makes some poor choices for values (same background color and foreground color), the application returns the user to the input page, displaying any relevant error messages.

We outline our design strategy for this example here.

- Use the input form to collect font sizes and colors. The user can specify font sizes for the resume title, heading, and body. The user can also specify a resume foreground color and background color.
- Use `html:messages` to print out error messages on the input page.
- Use `ActionForm` for input data. The `ActionForm` bean performs no error checking, as validation is done in the `Action`. When the user submits the request, Struts populates the bean with the input data before handing it to the `Action`.
- Use `Action` to manually validate the input fields. The `execute` method checks if any parameters are missing (font sizes, colors). If so, the `execute` method adds warning messages to `ActionMessages` and returns an error code to map back to the input page.
- Use struts-config.xml to map an error code back to the input form.

Listing 12.1 presents our input form, form1.jsp. The user has the choice of five input fields to create the perfect resume: title size, heading size, body size, foreground color, and background color. This form uses `html:form` and `html:text` tags from the Struts HTML tag library to build the form elements.

Before the `html:form` tag, we use the `html:messages` tag to display any error messages stored in the `request` scope. If no `ActionMessages` are found in the `request` scope (as would be the case on the first request of the page), then the tag yields no output.

Listing 12.2 gives our form bean, `FormatFormBean`. Aside from setter and getter methods for the bean properties, the bean has an `isMissing` method to check for missing values.

Our `Action` class, `ShowSampleAction`, is given in Listing 12.3. After retrieving the form bean, the `execute` method checks each input field (bean property) for potential problems. If a problem with a field is found, an `ActionMessage` is added to the collection of `ActionMessages` and the forward condition is set to `"missing-data"`. After checking all the fields, the `execute` method places the `ActionMessages` in the `request` scope and returns a forward condition.

Listing 12.4 presents struts-config.xml for this example. The action element defines two forwards, one for a "success" condition and one for a "missing-data" condition. The forward elements are given here:

```
<forward name="success"
         path="/WEB-INF/results/resume.jsp"/>
<forward name="missing-data"
         path="/forms/form1.jsp"/>
```

For a "missing-data" condition, Struts returns the user back to the input page, form1.jsp; otherwise, for a "success" condition, the user is sent to the resume for review, resume.jsp.

Finally, Listing 12.5 presents the output page for the sample resume. Basically, the page uses a stylesheet based on the user input to control the font sizes, background color, and foreground color. The bean:write tag,

```
<bean:write name="formatFormBean"
            property="styleSheet" filter="false"/>
```

retrieves the stylesheet information from the bean.

Listing 12.1 chooseFormat1/forms/form1.jsp

```
<!DOCTYPE HTML PUBLIC "-//W3C//DTD HTML 4.0 Transitional//EN">
<HTML>
<HEAD><TITLE>Choose Format</TITLE></HEAD>
<BODY BGCOLOR="#FDF5E6">
<H1 ALIGN="CENTER">Choose Format</H1>
Please select the font sizes and colors that you would
like used to display your resume.
<P>
<CENTER>
<%@ taglib uri="http://struts.apache.org/tags-html"
           prefix="html" %>
<%@ taglib uri="http://struts.apache.org/tags-bean"
           prefix="bean" %>
<UL>
<html:messages id="msg" message="true">
  <LI><B><FONT COLOR="RED">
    <bean:write name="msg"/>
  </FONT></B></LI>
</html:messages>
</UL>
```

Listing 12.1   chooseFormat1/forms/form1.jsp *(continued)*

```
<html:form action="/actions/showSample">
  Title size: <html:text property="titleSize"/><BR>
  Heading size: <html:text property="headingSize"/><BR>
  Body text size: <html:text property="bodySize"/><BR>
  Background color: <html:text property="bgColor"/><BR>
  Foreground color: <html:text property="fgColor"/><BR>
  <html:submit value="Show Sample"/>
</html:form>
</CENTER>
</BODY></HTML>
```

Listing 12.2   chooseFormat1/WEB-INF/classes/coreservlets/
FormatFormBean.java

```
package coreservlets;

import javax.servlet.http.*;
import org.apache.struts.action.*;

/** Bean with fields for formatting resume. Other than
 *  isMissing method, the bean provides no error checking
 *  of the input fields.
 */

public class FormatFormBean extends ActionForm {
  private String titleSize = "";
  private String headingSize = "";
  private String bodySize = "";
  private String bgColor = "";
  private String fgColor = "";

  public String getTitleSize() {
    return(titleSize);
  }

  public void setTitleSize(String titleSize) {
    this.titleSize = titleSize;
  }

  public String getHeadingSize() {
    return(headingSize);
  }
```

Listing 12.2	chooseFormat1/WEB-INF/classes/coreservlets/ FormatFormBean.java *(continued)*

```java
  public void setHeadingSize(String headingSize) {
    this.headingSize = headingSize;
  }

  public String getBodySize() {
    return(bodySize);
  }

  public void setBodySize(String bodySize) {
    this.bodySize = bodySize;
  }

  public String getBgColor() {
    return(bgColor);
  }

  public void setBgColor(String bgColor) {
    this.bgColor = bgColor;
  }

  public String getFgColor() {
    return(fgColor);
  }

  public void setFgColor(String fgColor) {
    this.fgColor = fgColor;
  }

  public String getStyleSheet() {
    return(
      "<STYLE TYPE=\"text/css\">\n" +
      "<!--\n" +
      "H1 { font-size: " + titleSize + "px; }\n" +
      "H2 { font-size: " + headingSize + "px; }\n" +
      "BODY { font-size: " + bodySize + "px;\n" +
      "       background-color: " + bgColor + ";\n" +
      "       color: " + fgColor + "; }\n" +
      "-->\n" +
      "</STYLE>");
  }

  public boolean isMissing(String value) {
    return((value == null) || (value.trim().equals("")));
  }
}
```

Listing 12.3 chooseFormat1/WEB-INF/classes/coreservlets/
ShowSampleAction.java

```java
package coreservlets;

import javax.servlet.http.*;
import org.apache.struts.action.*;

/** Action that performs manual validation of the form bean
 *  properties. If a problem exists with the user provided data,
 *  then the Action creates warning messages and place them in
 *  request scope.
 */

public class ShowSampleAction extends Action {
  public ActionForward execute(ActionMapping mapping,
                               ActionForm form,
                               HttpServletRequest request,
                               HttpServletResponse response)
      throws Exception {
    FormatFormBean formatBean = (FormatFormBean)form;
    ActionForward forward = mapping.findForward("success");
    ActionMessages messages = new ActionMessages();

    if (formatBean.isMissing(formatBean.getTitleSize())) {
      addMessage(messages, "title", "Missing Title Size");
      forward = mapping.findForward("missing-data");
    }
    if (formatBean.isMissing(formatBean.getHeadingSize())) {
      addMessage(messages, "headings", "Missing Heading Size");
      forward = mapping.findForward("missing-data");
    }
    if (formatBean.isMissing(formatBean.getBodySize())) {
      addMessage(messages, "body", "Missing Body Size");
      forward = mapping.findForward("missing-data");
    }
    if (formatBean.isMissing(formatBean.getBgColor())) {
      addMessage(messages, "bg", "Missing Background Color");
      forward = mapping.findForward("missing-data");
    }
    if (formatBean.isMissing(formatBean.getFgColor())) {
      addMessage(messages, "fg", "Missing Foreground Color");
      forward = mapping.findForward("missing-data");
    } else if (formatBean.getFgColor().equals
                  (formatBean.getBgColor())) {
```

Listing 12.3 chooseFormat1/WEB-INF/classes/coreservlets/ ShowSampleAction.java *(continued)*

```
      addMessage(messages, "fg",
                 "Foreground and Background Identical!");
      forward = mapping.findForward("missing-data");
    }
    if (!messages.isEmpty()) {
      addMessages(request, messages);
    }
    return(forward);
  }

  protected void addMessage(ActionMessages messages,
                            String property,
                            String warning) {
    messages.add(property, new ActionMessage(warning, false));
  }
}
```

Listing 12.4 chooseFormat1/WEB-INF/struts-config.xml

```
<?xml version="1.0" encoding="ISO-8859-1" ?>
<!DOCTYPE struts-config PUBLIC
  "-//Apache Software Foundation//DTD Struts Configuration 1.3//
EN"
  "http://struts.apache.org/dtds/struts-config_1_3.dtd">
<struts-config>
  <form-beans>
    <form-bean name="formatFormBean"
               type="coreservlets.FormatFormBean"/>
  </form-beans>
  <action-mappings>
    <action path="/actions/showSample"
            type="coreservlets.ShowSampleAction"
            name="formatFormBean"
            scope="request">
      <forward name="success"
               path="/WEB-INF/results/resume.jsp"/>
      <forward name="missing-data"
               path="/forms/form1.jsp"/>
    </action>
    ...
  </action-mappings>
</struts-config>
```

Listing 12.5	chooseFormat1/WEB-INF/classes/results/sample.jsp

```
<!DOCTYPE HTML PUBLIC "-//W3C//DTD HTML 4.0 Transitional//EN">
<HTML>
<HEAD><TITLE>Sample</TITLE>
<%@ taglib uri="http://struts.apache.org/tags-bean"
           prefix="bean" %>
<bean:write name="formatFormBean"
            property="styleSheet" filter="false"/>
</HEAD>
<BODY>
<H1 ALIGN="CENTER">Your Name Here</H1>
Intro. Blah blah blah. Yadda, yadda, yadda.
<H2>Professional Experience</H2>
<UL>
  <LI>Blah blah blah.
  <LI>Yadda, yadda, yadda.
</UL>
<H2>Education</H2>
Blah blah blah. Yadda, yadda, yadda.
</BODY></HTML>
```

Results

Figure 12–2 shows the input page containing the five fields to control the look of the sample resume. If the user submits the page without completing all the fields, the user is returned to the input page as shown Figure 12–3.

For the result shown, because the user did not provide a title size and foreground color, ShowSampleAction added two error messages to the ActionMessages and returned a "missing-data" condition, sending the request back to the input page. As seen, the html:messages tag displays the error messages above the input fields. Also, observe that the previously submitted values are redisplayed in their respective input fields (a benefit of using the Struts html: tags).

Note that the RequestDispatcher handles the forwarding of the request back to the input page. Thus, the browser address remains the submitted ACTION URL, /chooseFormat1/actions/showSample.do, not the original input page, /chooseFormat1/forms/form1.jsp.

Finally, Figure 12–4 presents a good resume with all the input fields completed correctly. The result shown is for a title size of 60 and a foreground color of red.

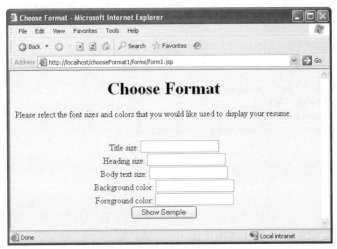

Figure 12–2 Input page for specifying text sizes, foreground color, and background color for sample resume.

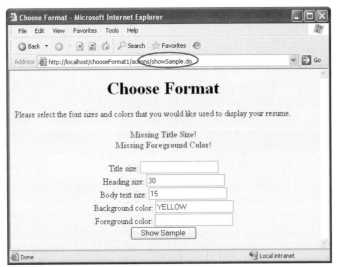

Figure 12–3 Result of not completing the input form correctly (missing title size and foreground color). On submission, the request is sent back to the input page using the RequestDispatcher. Thus, the URL remains the submitted .do action. Above the form fields, the html:messages tag displays the error messages.

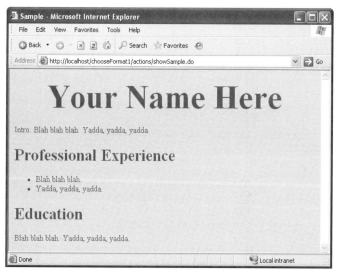

Figure 12–4 Good resume resulting from correctly completing all five input fields. The title size is 60 and the foreground color is red.

12.2 Validating in the Form Bean

In this section, instead of validating input fields in the `Action` class, we show you how to validate the input fields in the `ActionForm` bean. In practice, validation in the form bean is a better choice, as the input fields are immediately available to the bean. Moreover, the Struts framework is designed to support validation of input fields in the form bean.

Struts Flow of Control

Figure 12–5 illustrates the Struts flow of control, with updates for validation in the `ActionForm` bean. When the user submits the input page, Struts populates the form bean with the input fields and then calls `validate` on the bean. In the `validate` method, you can check the input fields for errors and return any associated error messages. If validation does return error messages, Struts automatically forwards the request back to the input page where you can display the messages back to the user. If the form bean returns no errors, then the Struts flow continues as normal, sending the request to the `Action`.

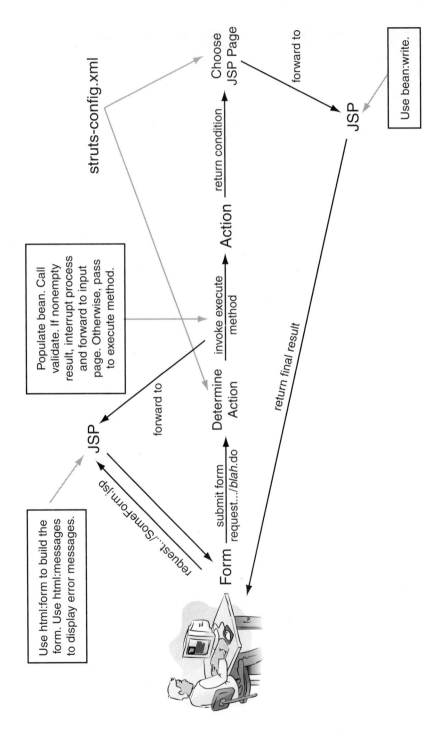

Figure 12–5 Flow of the request through the Struts framework with validation of the input fields in the `ActionForm` bean. After populating the bean with the input fields, Struts calls `validate` on the bean. If `validate` returns errors, the request is forwarded back to the input page.

Performing Validation in the ActionForm

As Struts automatically populates the form bean with the input fields, it seems only natural to check the input fields there. Simply add logic to the `validate` method for checking the fields, and if needed, add any error message for later display on the input page.

The following is our recommended approach for validating input fields in the `ActionForm`.

- **Create `validate` method in `ActionForm`.** Check each input field in the `validate` method of the `ActionForm`. If no errors are found return either a `null` or an empty `ActionErrors` object. Otherwise, for each error, add an `ActionMessage` entry to `ActionErrors`. Furthermore, instead of hard-coding messages directly in the bean, we recommend using a properties file for the messages.
- **Specify and input page in struts-config.xml.** If `validate` returns a nonempty `ActionErrors` object, the system automatically forwards the request back to an input page. Use the `input` attribute of `action` in struts-config.xml to specify to which page to return the user.
- **Create a property file with error messages.** When creating error messages, reference messages in a properties file. Each message should have a unique key for identification. Modify struts-config.xml to declare the properties file.
- **Use `html:messages` in input form.** Use the `html:messages` tag to list error messages on the input form. If no messages exist, the tag produces no output.

Details follow.

Creating a validate Method in the ActionForm

By default, Struts automatically calls `validate` on the form bean after populating the fields. An example of a `validate` method is shown in the following code fragment:

```
public ActionErrors validate(ActionMapping mapping,
                             HttpServletRequest request) {
  ActionErrors errors = new ActionErrors();
  if (isSomeProblem(getSomeProperty())) {
    errors.add("someName",
            new ActionMessage("some.key"));
    errors.add("someOtherName",
            new ActionMessage("literal message", false));
  }
```

```
   . . .
   return(errors);
}
```

In the `validate` method, first create an `ActionErrors` object. Then, check each property of the form bean. If the data has no errors, return `null` or an empty `ActionErrors` object. For each error, add an `ActionMessage` entry to `Action-Errors`.

Similar to `ActionMessages` (discussed in Section 12.1), the `add` method of `ActionErrors` takes a name and an `ActionMessage` argument. The name argument lets you associate a message to a particular input field.

When constructing an `ActionMessage`, provide a key that maps to a corresponding message in the properties file. If you would like to state the message directly (versus referencing a key in the properties file) in the `ActionMessage` constructor, simply provide the message as the first argument and `false` as the second argument.

Note, that in Struts 1.2, `ActionErrors` was depreciated; however it is still in use as the return value of the `validate` method in `ActionForm`. In later versions of Struts, we expect complete removal of `ActionErrors` in favor of `Action-Messages`. Except for the `ActionForm` class, use `ActionMessages` wherever possible to hold any error messages.

For more details on `ActionErrors` and `ActionMessages`, see the Struts API at http://struts.apache.org/1.x/struts-core/apidocs/.

Specifying Input Page in struts-config.xml

If `validate` returns a nonempty `ActionErrors` object, Struts forwards the request to an input form. Use the `input` attribute of `action` in **struts-config.xml** to specify the input page. The following is an `action` example with an `input` attribute stating that **original-form.jsp** is the input page to return the request if validation errors occur in the form bean.

```
<action path="/somePath/someActionName"
        type="somePackage.SomeClass"
        name="someFormBean"
        scope="request"
        input="/somePath/original-form.jsp"
        validate="true">
   <forward name="..." path"..."/>
</action>
```

Specifying the `validate` attribute is optional, as validation is the default behavior.

Core Note

When using form beans, the default behavior of Struts is to populate the form bean with the input fields and then call `validate` *on the bean. Specifying* `validate="true"` *is optional.*

Preventing Validation

In certain applications, you may use the same bean in multiple `actions`. What if you want some `actions` to perform validation, and other `actions` not to perform validation. The solution is to simply state `validate="false"` for `actions` that do not require validation.

Creating a Properties File with Messages

Each `ActionMessage` can refer to a message in the properties file. In the properties file, add key–message pairs for errors commonly encountered with the input fields. Then, when creating an `ActionMessage`, reference the key corresponding to the appropriate error message in the properties file.

A sample properties file is given here:

```
# -- Custom validation messages --
some.key=Some Message
some.other.key=Some Other Message
```

For more information on configuring Struts for properties files, see Section 11.1 (Using Properties Files).

Using html:messages in the Input Form

As covered in Section 12.1 (Validating in the Action Class), use `html:messages` on the input page to list all error messages returned by the form bean's `validate` method. However, in this case, because the error messages are stored in `Action-Errors`, specify `false` for the message attribute. False indicates that the messages were not placed in an `ActionMessages` object, but rather an `ActionErrors` object. An example illustrating the use of `html:messages` is given here:

```
<html:messages id="msg" message="false">
  <bean:write name="msg"/>
</html:messages>
```

As a reminder, the `html:messages` tag iterates over the error messages, placing each message in `page` scope (referenced by the variable identified by `id`). With `bean:write`, you can access and display the message.

Instead of listing all the messages in a single group, you can target only those messages for a particular field. Use the `property` attribute to indicate which messages to extract from the collection.

For instance, suppose that you used the following names when adding messages to `ActionMessages`:

```
messsages.add("someName", new ActionMessage("some.key1"));
messsages.add("someOtherName", new ActionMessage("some.key2"));
messsages.add("someName", new ActionMessage("some.key3"));
```

Then, on the input page, you could display only `someName` messages with

```
<html:messages id="msg" message="false"
               property="someName">
  <bean:write name="msg"/>
</html:messages>
```

Example: Choosing Colors and Font Sizes for a Resume (Take 2)

Now, we revisit the first example presented in this section—the online sample resume. However, instead of validating the input fields in the `Action`, we validate the input fields in the `ActionForm`.

As before, the user can specify the fonts and colors for generating a resume. If the user enters bad or missing data, validation in the form bean results in returning the request back to the input page, where `html:messages` displays any messages.

Next, we outline our general design strategy for this modified example.

- Use an input form to collect font sizes and colors. The user can specify font sizes for the resume title, heading, and body. The user can also specify a foreground and background color for the resume.
- Use `html:messages` to print out any messages on the input page.
- Use `ActionForm` for input data. The `validate` method checks if any parameters are missing. If so, `validate` creates an `ActionMessage` keyed to a named message in the properties file. Add each `ActionMessage` to the `ActionErrors` returned by the method.
- Use `Action` to always map to the output page. No validation is performed in `Action`, only in the form bean.
- In struts-config.xml, provide an `input` attribute in `action` that refers to the input form.

Listing 12.6 presents our new `FormatFormBean` with a `validate` method that checks each of the five input fields. If a field is missing, the method adds an `ActionMessage` to the `ActionErrors` collection. The `ActionMessage` constructor provides a key to the true message in the properties file.

The properties file for this example is given in Listing 12.7. We place this file in the WEB-INF/classes directory and add a `message-resources` element to struts-config.xml. Listing 12.8 shows our struts-config.xml file.

In struts-config.xml, we also add an `input` attribute to the `action` element, as shown in the following code fragment:

```
<action path="/actions/showSample"
        type="coreservlets.ShowSampleAction"
        name="formatFormBean"
        scope="request"
        input="/forms/index.jsp">
  <forward name="success"
           path="/WEB-INF/results/sample.jsp"/>
</action>
```

If `validate` returns any errors, Struts sends the request back to /forms/index.jsp.

The input page, /forms/index.jsp, is given in Listing 12.9. Essentially, this page is the same as Listing 12.1, except now `html:messages` finds the messages in an `ActionErrors` object (located in the `request` scope) instead of an `Action-Messages` object.

Listing 12.10 presents our modified `ShowSampleAction` class. The `Action` performs no validation (the input has to be good, as the `ActionForm` performs all the validation before Struts even invokes the `Action`). Thus, the execute method always returns a `"success"` condition that maps to /WEB-INF/results/sample.jsp.

Listing 12.6	chooseFormat2/WEB-INF/classes/coreservlets/FormatFormBean.java

```
package coreservlets;

import javax.servlet.http.*;
import org.apache.struts.action.*;

/** Bean with fields for formatting resume. The bean provides
 *  a validate method for checking the input fields. The Struts
 *  system calls the validate method after populating the fields.
 */

public class FormatFormBean extends ActionForm {
  private String titleSize = "";
  private String headingSize = "";
```

Listing 12.6   chooseFormat2/WEB-INF/classes/coreservlets/
FormatFormBean.java *(continued)*

```java
private String bodySize = "";
private String bgColor = "";
private String fgColor = "";

public String getTitleSize() {
  return(titleSize);
}

public void setTitleSize(String titleSize) {
  this.titleSize = titleSize;
}

public String getHeadingSize() {
  return(headingSize);
}

public void setHeadingSize(String headingSize) {
  this.headingSize = headingSize;
}

public String getBodySize() {
  return(bodySize);
}

public void setBodySize(String bodySize) {
  this.bodySize = bodySize;
}

public String getBgColor() {
  return(bgColor);
}

public void setBgColor(String bgColor) {
  this.bgColor = bgColor;
}

public String getFgColor() {
  return(fgColor);
}

public void setFgColor(String fgColor) {
  this.fgColor = fgColor;
}
```

Listing 12.6 chooseFormat2/WEB-INF/classes/coreservlets/
FormatFormBean.java *(continued)*

```java
  public String getStyleSheet() {
    return(
      "<STYLE TYPE=\"text/css\">\n" +
      "<!--\n" +
      "H1 { font-size: " + titleSize + "px; }\n" +
      "H2 { font-size: " + headingSize + "px; }\n" +
      "BODY { font-size: " + bodySize + "px;\n" +
      "       background-color: " + bgColor + ";\n" +
      "       color: " + fgColor + "; }\n" +
      "-->\n" +
      "</STYLE>");
  }

  public ActionErrors validate(ActionMapping mapping,
                               HttpServletRequest request) {
    ActionErrors errors = new ActionErrors();
    if (isMissing(getTitleSize())) {
      errors.add("title",
                 new ActionMessage("titleSize.required"));
    }
    if (isMissing(getHeadingSize())) {
      errors.add("heading",
                 new ActionMessage("headingSize.required"));
    }
    if (isMissing(getBodySize())) {
      errors.add("body",
                 new ActionMessage("bodySize.required"));
    }
    if (isMissing(getBgColor())) {
      errors.add("bg",
                 new ActionMessage("bgColor.required"));
    }
    if (isMissing(getFgColor())) {
      errors.add("fg",
                 new ActionMessage("fgColor.required"));
    } else if (getFgColor().equals(getBgColor())) {
      errors.add("fg",
                 new ActionMessage("colors.notMatch"));
    }
    return(errors);
  }

  private boolean isMissing(String value) {
    return((value == null) || (value.trim().equals("")));
  }
}
```

Listing 12.7 chooseFormat2/WEB-INF/classes/ MessageResources.properties

```
# -- Custom validation messages --
titleSize.required=Title size required.
headingSize.required=Heading size required.
bodySize.required=Body text size required.
bgColor.required=Background color required.
fgColor.required=Foreground color required.
colors.notMatch=Foreground and background colors must be different.
```

Listing 12.8 chooseFormat2/WEB-INF/struts-config.xml

```
<?xml version="1.0" encoding="ISO-8859-1" ?>
<!DOCTYPE struts-config PUBLIC
  "-//Apache Software Foundation//DTD Struts Configuration 1.3//EN"
  "http://struts.apache.org/dtds/struts-config_1_3.dtd">
<struts-config>
  <form-beans>
    <form-bean name="formatFormBean"
               type="coreservlets.FormatFormBean"/>
  </form-beans>
  <action-mappings>
    <action path="/actions/showSample"
            type="coreservlets.ShowSampleAction"
            name="formatFormBean"
            scope="request"
            input="/forms/index.jsp">
      <forward name="success"
               path="/WEB-INF/results/sample.jsp"/>
    </action>
  </action-mappings>
  <message-resources parameter="MessageResources"
                     null="false"/>
</struts-config>
```

Listing 12.9 chooseFormat2/forms/index.jsp

```
<!DOCTYPE HTML PUBLIC "-//W3C//DTD HTML 4.0 Transitional//EN">
<HTML>
<HEAD><TITLE>Choose Format</TITLE></HEAD>
<BODY BGCOLOR="#FDF5E6">
<H1 ALIGN="CENTER">Choose Format</H1>
Please select the font sizes and colors that you would
like used to display your resume.
```

| Listing12.9 | chooseFormat2/forms/index.jsp *(continued)* |

```
<P>
<CENTER>
<%@ taglib uri="http://struts.apache.org/tags-html"
           prefix="html" %>
<%@ taglib uri="http://struts.apache.org/tags-bean"
           prefix="bean" %>
<UL>
<html:messages id="msg" message="false">
  <LI><B><FONT COLOR="RED">
    <bean:write name="msg"/>
  </FONT></B></LI>
</html:messages>
</UL>
<html:form action="/actions/showSample">
  Title size: <html:text property="titleSize"/><BR>
  Heading size: <html:text property="headingSize"/><BR>
  Body text size: <html:text property="bodySize"/><BR>
  Background color: <html:text property="bgColor"/><BR>
  Foreground color: <html:text property="fgColor"/><BR>
  <html:submit value="Show Sample"/>
</html:form>
</CENTER>
</BODY></HTML>
```

| Listing 12.10 | chooseFormat2/WEB-INF/classes/coreservlets/ ShowSampleAction.java |

```java
package coreservlets;

import javax.servlet.http.*;
import org.apache.struts.action.*;

/** Validation if performed in FormBean, so Action
 *  simply forwards based on "success" condition.
 */

public class ShowSampleAction extends Action {
  public ActionForward execute(ActionMapping mapping,
                               ActionForm form,
                               HttpServletRequest request,
                               HttpServletResponse response)
      throws Exception {
    return(mapping.findForward("success"));
  }
}
```

Results

Figure 12–6 shows the input page for the sample resume builder. If the user submits the page without completing all the fields, validation in the `ActionForm` bean causes the request to return to the input page, as shown in Figure 12–7. Here, the user did not provide sizes for the title, heading, and body text, so the `validate` method of the `ActionForm` added three messages to the `ActionErrors` object. Because of the errors, Struts returned the request to the input page where the `html:messages` tag displays the three messages.

Notice that in Figure 12–7, the `RequestDispatcher` handles the request flow through forwarding. Thus, when Struts returns the request to the input page, the browser address remains the submitted .do address, not the input page address.

Figure 12–8 shows the resulting sample resume when the user completes all five input fields with valid values. The result shown is for a title size of 60, a heading size of 30, and a body text size of 15.

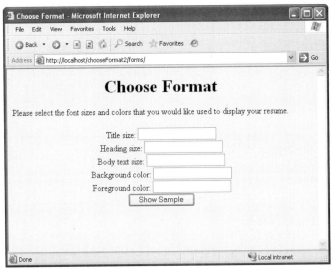

Figure 12–6   Input page for specifying text sizes, foreground color, and background color for our sample resume.

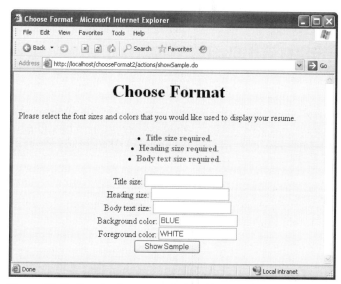

Figure 12–7   Result of not completing the input form correctly (missing title, heading, and body sizes). The `html:messages` tag displays the error messages created by the `validate` method of the `ActionForm` bean.

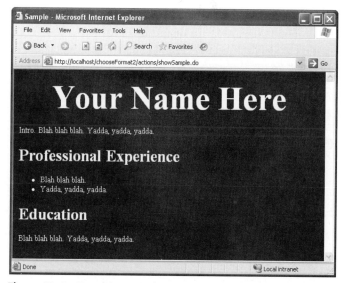

Figure 12–8   Resulting sample resume when the user completes all input fields correctly. As shown, the title size is 60, the heading size is 30, and the body text size is 15.

Using Parameterized Error Messages

In Section 11.1 (Using Properties Files), we explained how to parameterize messages in a properties file. The main benefit of parameterized messages is that they can reflect runtime values versus static values. If you parameterize messages wisely, your application can yield more descriptive messages with less repetition.

To support parameterized messages, you first need to modify your messages to indicate where the parameterized substitution should occur and then to add parametric arguments when you create your `ActionMessages`. We discuss the steps here.

- **Add parametric notation to messages in the properties file.** Use `{n}` notation in your messages to indicate the location of the *n*th parametric substitution. For instance,

  ```
  value.required={0} is required
  ```

- **Add parametric arguments to `ActionMessages`.** In the `validate` method of your `ActionForm`, add extra arguments to your `ActionMessage` constructors. Provide one argument for each parametric placeholder. The `ActionMessage` constructor allows up to four separate arguments. If you need more arguments, supply an array.

When displaying parameterized messages with `html:messages`, the message is filtered for HTML characters, removing the risk of cross-site scripting attacks. See *Core Servlets and JavaServer Pages, Volume 1* for more on cross-site scripting attacks.

Example: Validation with Parameterized Messages

Again, we revisit our earlier sample resume application, but now we modify the error messages to contain dynamic content through message parameterization. The following is our strategy for this example.

- Leave the input form, `Action`, and **struts-config.xml** file as before.
- Parameterize the custom error messages. Because each input field could have the common problem of a missing value, use a single parameterized message corresponding to `value.required` in the properties file.
- Modify each `ActionMessage` in the `ActionForm` to provide an argument for the parameterized message.

Listing 12.11 presents our new `FormatFormBean`. The only changes are in the `validate` method. In the `ActionMessage` constructors, we provide a parameter value for the message. The code for a missing title size is given here:

```
errors.add("titleSizeMissing",
           new ActionMessage("value.required", "Title size"));
```

By passing in `"Title Size"` for the {0}th argument in the message, `"{0} is required."`, the final message becomes `"Title size is required."`

Our parameterized properties file is given in Listing 12.12.

Listing 12.11   chooseFormat3/WEB-INF/classes/coreservlets/
FormatFormBean.java

```java
package coreservlets;

import javax.servlet.http.*;
import org.apache.struts.action.*;

/** Bean with fields for formatting resume. ActionMessages
 *  provide additional arguments for use with parameterized
 *  messages in properties file.
 */

public class FormatFormBean extends ActionForm {
  private String titleSize = "";
  private String headingSize = "";
  private String bodySize = "";
  private String bgColor = "";
  private String fgColor = "";
  ...

  public ActionErrors validate(ActionMapping mapping,
                               HttpServletRequest request) {
    ActionErrors errors = new ActionErrors();
    if (isMissing(getTitleSize())) {
      errors.add("titleSizeMissing",
              new ActionMessage("value.required",
                                "Title size"));
    } else if (!isInt(getTitleSize())) {
      errors.add("titleNotInt",
              new ActionMessage("value.int",
                                "title size",
                                getTitleSize()));
    }
    if (isMissing(getHeadingSize())) {
      errors.add("headingSizeMissing",
              new ActionMessage("value.required",
                                "Heading size"));
```

Listing 12.11   chooseFormat3/WEB-INF/classes/coreservlets/ FormatFormBean.java *(continued)*

```
    } else if (!isInt(getHeadingSize())) {
      errors.add("headingNotInt",
                new ActionMessage("value.int",
                                  "heading size",
                                   getHeadingSize()));
    }
    if (isMissing(getBodySize())) {
      errors.add("bodySizeMissing",
                new ActionMessage("value.required",
                                  "Body text size"));
    } else if (!isInt(getBodySize())) {
      errors.add("bodyNotInt",
                new ActionMessage("value.int",
                                  "body text size",
                                  getBodySize()));
    }
    if (isMissing(getBgColor())) {
      errors.add("bgColorMissing",
                new ActionMessage("value.required",
                                  "Background color"));
    }
    if (isMissing(getFgColor())) {
      errors.add("fgColorMissing",
                new ActionMessage("value.required",
                                  "Foreground color"));
    } else if (getBgColor().equals(getFgColor())) {
      errors.add("colorsIdentical",
                new ActionMessage("colors.match",
                                  getBgColor()));
    }
    return(errors);
  }

  private boolean isMissing(String value) {
      return((value == null) || (value.trim().equals("")));
  }

  private boolean isInt(String potentialInt) {
    boolean isInt = true;
    try {
      int x = Integer.parseInt(potentialInt);
    } catch(NumberFormatException nfe) {
      isInt = false;
    }
    return(isInt);
  }
}
```

Listing 12.12	chooseFormat3/WEB-INF/classes/ MessageResources.properties

```
# -- Custom validation messages --
value.required={0} is required.
value.int=Whole number required for {0}; "{1}" is not an integer.
colors.match=The foreground and background color are both "{0}".
```

Results

Except for the error messages, the results for this example are similar to the previous one. See Figure 12–6 for the input page. If the user fails to complete any input fields correctly, customized error messages result, as shown in Figure 12–9. See earlier Figure 12–8 for a representative resume based on a correctly completed input form.

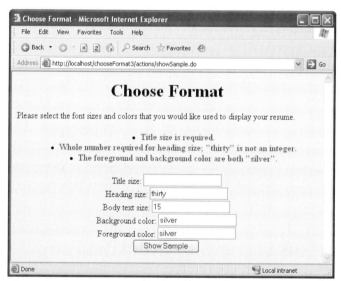

Figure 12–9   Result of the user not completing the input form correctly. After Struts routes the submission back to the input page, parameterized error messages help to clarify the problems with the submitted input.

12.3 Using the Automatic Validation Framework

Writing code to validate every input field on your Web site can become quite tedious, so the designers of Struts built in a complete automatic validation framework. With this framework, you can easily check for missing or badly formatted fields.

In this section, we show you how to add automatic validation of input fields to your Struts application. First, though, we review various validation approaches.

Manual versus Automatic Validation

We briefly discuss here the differences between manual and automatic validation.

- **Manual validation.** Manual validation of input fields is the most flexible. You have full access to beans, to business logic, and to the application database. Unfortunately, manual validation often results in repeated logic and often runs only on the server. If you also do client-side validation, then most likely, you're writing lots of tedious JavaScript code embedded in JSP code. This approach violates the Struts strategy of placing as much as possible in editable files versus in code that must be compiled.
- **Automatic validation.** Automatic validation typically consolidates the amount of validation code needed and lets you use standard validation rules. Also, automatic validation runs on the server, but can optionally include JavaScript that runs on the client. With automatic validation in Struts, instead of building code that requires compilation, you can easily describe the validation rules in XML files.

Client-Side versus Server-Side Validation

A common question for the new Web developer is this: Do I validate data on the client or on the server? For security reasons alone, you must always validate the data on the server—a hacker could simply bypass your input forms completely. However, along with server-side validation, you can obtain benefits through client-side validation.

Next, we discuss client-side and server-side validation.

- **Client-side validation.** For client-side validation, JavaScript code verifies the format of input fields. If any fields are bad, a dialog box can warn the user of any illegal values. If the input is bad, JavaScript can block the submission to the server.

Client-side validation with JavaScript tends to be very fast. The validation does not require a trip to the server. However, there are limitations. You cannot do validation that requires application logic, such as talking to a database server. Finally, with client-side validation, you need to consider the possibility of the user deliberately or accidentally bypassing JavaScript (i.e., turning it off).

- **Server-side validation.** For server-side validation, Java code on the server can validate the fields. Most likely, server-side validation performs similar checks as the client-side validation, but can invoke stronger application logic for additional checks. Instead of a pop-up dialog box, you can display warning messages back on the input form. Unfortunately, server-side validation is slower, but you really have no choice here. You must do server-side validation regardless of whether or not you do client-side validation.

Core Approach

Always perform server-side validation of input data. Don't simply rely on client-side validation as the user (or a hacker) can accidentally or deliberately bypass the JavaScript validation.

Struts Flow of Control

Figure 12–10 illustrates the Struts flow of control, with updates for the automated validation. When the user submits the input form, Struts first populates the form bean with input data and then calls the `validate` method inherited from `ValidatorForm`. At this point, Struts checks the field entries against the rules in validator.xml.

If the `validate` method returns an empty array of error messages, then the request is sent to the `execute` method of the `Action`. Otherwise, the Struts system interrupts the process and sends the request back to the input page. By using the `html:messages` tag on the input page, you can display any error messages.

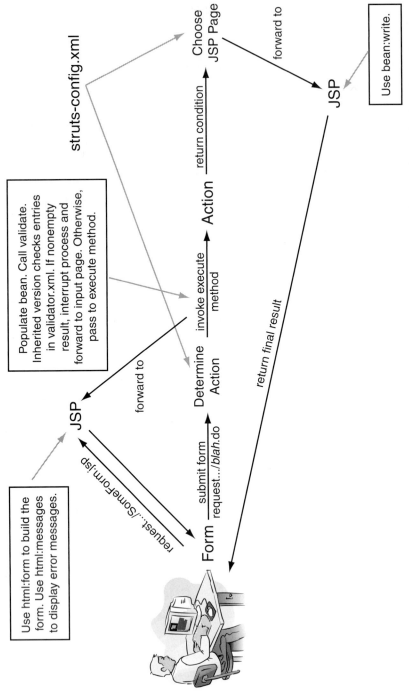

Figure 12–10 Flow of the request through the Struts framework with automatic validation. After populating the form bean, Struts checks the entries against the validation rules in validator.xml.

Steps in Using Automatic Validation

Successful incorporation of automatic validation in your Struts application requires a lot of changes. To help you configure Struts automatic validation, we recommend the following six steps.

1. **Configure struts-config.xml.** In struts-config.xml, indicate the URI of the input form, indicate the properties file, and turn on the automatic validator.
2. **Edit the properties file.** In the properties file, edit the standard validator messages (`errors.invalid`, etc.) and create names for replacements of parameterized arguments (`{0}`, `{1}`, etc.) in these standard messages.
3. **Put validation rules in validation.xml.** For each input field, specify one or more validation rules in validation.xml. Determine the name of the corresponding error message for the validation rule. Look in the properties file to see how many `args` are needed for the message and define `arg` values as necessary.
4. **Have form bean extend `ValidatorForm`.** Instead of Action-Form, the form bean should now extend `ValidatorForm`.
5. **Use `html:messages` tag.** As shown earlier in Section 12.2 (Validating in the Form Bean), use the `html:messages` tag on the input page to display any error messages.
6. **(Optional) Enable JavaScript validation.** If desired, modify the input page to support client-side validation of the input fields.

Details follow.

Step 1: Configure struts-config.xml

To support automatic validation of input fields, make the following three changes to struts-config.xml:

- **List the address of the input form.** In the `action` element, provide an `input` attribute for the input page. If errors are found in the input fields, Struts returns the request to this input page. An example is given here:

```
<action path="..."
        type="..."
        name="..."
        scope="request"
        input="/inputFormAddress.jsp">
```

- **List the the properties file.** After the `action-mapping` element in struts-config.xml, list the properties file with the `message-resource` element, as shown here:

```
<message-resources parameter="MessageResources"/>
```

  If supporting an existing application with a `controller` section, place the `message-resources` entry after the `controller` entry. Remember that Struts assumes a file extension of .properties and that the file is located in WEB-INF/classes. For more information on properties files, see Section 11.1 (Using Properties Files).

- **Turn on the automatic validator.** To turn on automatic validation add the validator plug-in to struts-config.xml, as given here:

```
<plug-in
  className="org.apache.struts.validator.ValidatorPlugIn">
  <set-property property="pathnames"
     value="/org/apache/struts/validator/validator-rules.xml,
            /WEB-INF/validation.xml"/>
</plug-in>
```

  Don't enter the `plug-in` element by hand. Uncomment and copy the entry from the struts-blank-1.3.5 application (bundled in struts-1.3.5-apps.zip at http://struts.apache.org/downloads.html).

Step 2: Edit the Properties File

Automatic validation relies heavily on error messages from the properties file. As a starting point, use the MessageResources.properties file from the struts-blank-1.3.5 application.

In the following list, we recommend changes to the properties file.

- **Edit the standard "validator" error messages.** As needed, edit the validator messages in the properties file. A couple of examples are given here:

```
errors.invalid={0} is invalid.
errors.maxlength={0} cannot be greater than {1} characters.
```

  The struts-blank-1.3.5 properties file has several typos in it, for instance, "an" long, "an" byte, "can not", etc. So, you will want to fix these typos.

- **Add prompts or messages to substitute into error messages.** For the error messages in your application, provide a key–message pair to substitute for {0}, {1}, and so on. Examples follow.

```
inputForm.firstName=First name
inputForm.lastName=Last name
inputForm.zipCode=5-digit ZIP Code
```

Later, in the validation rules, you can specify which prompts or messages to substitute in the error messages. Basically, the parameterized messages and the values (prompts) to substitute into the parameterized messages are all self-contained in the properties file. You just need to refer to the prompts in your validation rule.

Step 3: Put Validation Rules in validation.xml

We recommend starting with the validation.xml file provided with struts-blank-1.3.5 (bundled in struts-1.3.5-apps.zip at http://struts.apache.org/downloads.html).

When you first examine an existing validation file it may seem like a mystery. For instance, where are the validation rules? If the validation rule fails, what is the error message?

To help you understand validation files, we initially examine the overall structure of the validation.xml file and then, in the next section, we examine how to define individual validation rules.

Understanding the Structure of validation.xml

The overall structure of validation.xml has the following elements.

- **form-validation and formset elements.** These are the main enclosing elements for all the validation rules. The general structure of validation.xml is given here:

```
<!DOCTYPE form-validation PUBLIC
"-//Apache Software Foundation//DTD Commons Validator Rules
Configuration 1.3.0//EN"
"http://jakarta.apache.org/commons/dtds/validator_1_3_0.dtd">
<form-validation>
  <formset>
    <form ...> ... </form> // Rules for 1st HTML form
    <form ...> ... </form> // Rules for 2nd HTML form
    ...
  </formset>
</form-validation>
```

  The form-validation element is the root container for the XML file. The formset element defines one or more forms for a locale.

- **form elements.** The form element is an XML container for a set of field elements in a particular form, where each field element would correspond to an input field on the form. The general format for the form element is given here:

```
<form name="beanName">
    <field ...> ... </field>
    ...
</form>
```

The value of the name attribute must match the value of the corresponding form-bean in struts-config.xml.

- **field elements.** Each field element defines a set of validation rules for an input field (i.e., bean property). An example of a field definition is given here:

```
<field property="beanPropertyName"
       depends="required">
  <arg key="inputForm.firstName"/>
</field>
```

The value of the property attribute must match an input field (bean property). The depends attribute can contain a comma-separated list of standard validation rules as defined in validator-rules.xml. In the next subsection, we cover validation rules in more detail.

Defining Fields in validation.xml

The Struts Validation framework contains numerous built-in validation rules (see http://struts.apache.org/1.x/faqs/validator.html). Most likely, they're all you'll need. Following, we summarize the steps to set up individual validation rules for each of your input fields.

- **Specify dependency of validation rules.** For each field, specify one or more validation rules from the list of built-in choices (required, mask, email, etc.). Use

```
<field property="..." depends="...">
```

where property identifies the bean property to check and depends specifies which rule to check the field against. You can specify more than one validation rule by comma separating them, as in

```
<field property="propName"
       depends="ruleName1, ruleName2">
```

Table 12.2 on page 632 summarizes the built-in validation rules available from validation-rule.xml. For a complete listing of the available validation rules, see http://struts.apache.org/1.x/faqs/validator.html.

- **Determine name of error message.** Find the name of the error
  message generated when the rule fails. The name corresponds to a
  message in the properties file. Usually, the name of the error message
  is errors.*ruleName*, where *ruleName* is the name of the rule. To
  be sure, check the value given by the msg attribute for the validation
  rule in validator-rules.xml.

  Note that in Struts 1.3.5, the validator-rules.xml file is bundled in
  struts-core-1.3.5.jar. To examine this file, you may need to unjar the
  file

  ```
  jar xf struts-core-1.3.5.jar validator-rules.xml
  ```

  or use a standard decompression utility like WinZip.
- **Determine arguments for error message.** If starting with the
  struts-blank-1.3.5 application, examine the properties file,
  MessageResources.properties, to see what {} arguments the various
  error messages require. A couple of examples are given here:

  ```
  errors.invalid={0} is invalid.
  errors.maxlength={0} cannot be greater than {1} characters.
  ```

  The first error message, errors.invalid, takes one argument. The
  second error message, error.maxlength, takes two arguments.
- **Supply an arg element for each placeholder in error message.**
  Use the arg element to specify the text to substitute for each
  placeholder.

  ```
  field property="propName" depends="ruleName">
    <arg key="key.Name1"/>
    <arg key="key.Name2"/>
  </field>
  ```

  Struts substitutes text into the placeholders {} in the same order as
  listed in the validation rule. Instead of explicitly stating the text in the
  validation rule, use the key attribute to refer to a substitution value in
  the properties file. In this manner, all your error messages and substitution values for the {} arguments are contained in a single file.

  The following is an example:

  ```
  <field property="firstName"
         depends="required">
    <arg key="inputForm.firstName"/>
  </field>
  ```

This validation rule states that the `firstName` field is required in the form. If missing, the error message in the properties file, `errors.required`, should use the value from `inputForm.first-Name` to substitute into the error message. The properties file would contain the following two messages:

```
inputForm.firstName=First name
errors.required={0} is required.
```

Table 12.2   Common Validation Rules Defined in **validation-rules**.xml

Validator	Description
`required`	Field value must be nonempty (contains characters other than whitespace). Default error message in properties file is `errors.required`.
`mask`	Field value must match a regular expression given by a `mask` attribute. Default error message in properties file is `errors.invalid`.
`email`	Field value must have a valid e-mail address format. Default error message in properties file is `errors.email`.
`creditCard`	Field value should be a legal credit card number (based on Luhn checksum). Use 4111111111111111 for testing. Default error message in properties file is `errors.creditcard`.

Step 4: Have Form Bean Extend ValidatorForm

For automatic validation, instead of extending `ActionForm`, your form bean should extend `ValidatorForm`. See the following code fragment:

```
public class YourFormBean extends ValidatorForm {
    ...
}
```

The `ValidatorForm` class provides support for Struts to validate the bean properties against the rules in **validation**.xml.

Step 5: Put html:messages Tag in Input Page

As with manual validation (Section 12.2), add `html:messages` to your input page to display any error messages when the request is returned to the input page.

Step 6: (Optional) Enable JavaScript Validation

Struts has excellent support for client-side validation with JavaScript. To enable Java-Script validation on your input page, do the following.

- **Add `html:javascript` tag to JSP page.** Add a tag similar to

  ```
  <html:javascript formName="beanName"/>
  ```

  to the input page, where *beanName* is the name of the form bean for the page. The `html:javascript` tag adds all the necessary Java-Script code to validate the input fields on the client browser. You can place this tag anywhere on the input page. We typically place the tag after the closing `html:form` tag.

  This tag can produce hundreds of lines of JavaScript code in your input page (depending on which validation rules you select). Believe us, you don't want to write all this JavaScript code yourself!

- **Add the `onsubmit` attribute to `html:form` tag.** In your `html:form` tag, add an `onsubmit` attribute, as shown here:

  ```
  <html:form action="/actions/someAction"
             onsubmit="return validateBeanName(this);">
  ```

  where *BeanName* is the name of the form bean for the page. When the user submits the page, the browser automatically calls the JavaScript function, `validateBeanName`. If the function returns `false`, meaning that errors were found with the input fields, then the browser cancels the submission to the server. Otherwise, if the function returns `true` (the input fields are fine), the browser submits the page to the server.

Example: Automatic Validation

Next, using the Struts Validation framework, we create a Web site for ordering the famous Un-Divet tool. We incorporate both client-side and server-side validation to check the fields of the Un-Divet ordering form.

Next, we go through the six steps in using automatic validation.

Step 1: Configure struts-config.xml

Listing 12.13 presents our **struts-config.xml** file. We define an `action` that uses the bean, `orderFormBean`, to the hold the input fields of the ordering form. Then, to support automatic validation, we provide an `input` page attribute of **/forms/ order-form.jsp**. If validation fails, Struts routes the request back to this input page. We also add a `message-resources` element for the properties file that holds all the error messages. Finally, we enable the validator plug-in.

Listing 12.13	orders/WEB-INF/struts-config.xml

```xml
<?xml version="1.0" encoding="ISO-8859-1" ?>
<!DOCTYPE struts-config PUBLIC
  "-//Apache Software Foundation//DTD Struts Configuration 1.3//EN"
  "http://struts.apache.org/dtds/struts-config_1_3.dtd">
<struts-config>
  <form-beans>
    <form-bean name="orderFormBean"
               type="coreservlets.OrderFormBean"/>
  </form-beans>

  <action-mappings>
    <action path="/actions/order"
            type="coreservlets.Order"
            name="orderFormBean"
            scope="request"
            input="/forms/order-form.jsp">
      <forward name="success"
               path="/WEB-INF/results/order-confirmation.jsp"/>
    </action>
  </action-mappings>

  <message-resources parameter="MessageResources"/>

  <plug-in className="org.apache.struts.validator.ValidatorPlugIn">
    <set-property
        property="pathnames"
        value="/org/apache/struts/validator/validator-rules.xml,
               /WEB-INF/validation.xml"/>
  </plug-in>
</struts-config>
```

Step 2: Edit the properties File

Listing 12.14 presents our properties file, MessageResources.properties. To create this file, we started with the MessageResources.properties file from the struts-blank-1.3.5 application, then added the following custom messages to the beginning of the file:

```
inputForm.firstName=First name
inputForm.lastName=Last name
inputForm.address=Postal address
inputForm.zipCode=5-digit ZIP Code
inputForm.creditCardNumber=Credit card number
inputForm.email=Email address
```

Each one of these messages corresponds to an ordering field on the input form. When substituted into one of the generic validation messages, they tell the user which field failed validation.

Listing 12.14 orders/WEB-INF/classes/MessageResources.properties

```
# -- Custom messages for this application --
inputForm.firstName=First name
inputForm.lastName=Last name
inputForm.address=Postal address
inputForm.zipCode=5-digit ZIP Code
inputForm.creditCardNumber=Credit card number
inputForm.email=Email address
# -- validator --
errors.invalid={0} is invalid.
errors.maxlength={0} cannot be greater than {1} characters.
errors.minlength={0} cannot be less than {1} characters.
errors.range={0} is not in the range {1} through {2}.
errors.required={0} is required.
errors.byte={0} must be a byte.
errors.date={0} is not a date.
errors.double={0} must be a double.
errors.float={0} must be an float.
errors.integer={0} must be an integer.
errors.long={0} must be a long.
errors.short={0} must be a short.
errors.creditcard={0} is not a valid credit card number.
errors.email={0} is an invalid email address.
# -- other --
errors.cancel=Operation cancelled.
errors.detail={0}
errors.general=The process did not complete. Details should follow.
errors.token=Request could not be completed. Operation is not in
sequence.
```

Step 3: Put Validation Rules in validation.xml

Listing 12.15 presents our validation.xml file. We specify validation rules for each of the six input fields on the ordering form. Details follow.

- **firstName.** This field is validated against the Struts built-in required rule. If the firstname is only whitespace, then validation fails and the message corresponding to errors.required results. The error message has only one parameterized argument, {0}, for which we specify the substitution of inputForm.firstName from the properties file.
- **lastName.** Similarly, this field is also required. If the validation rule fails, Struts substitutes the value corresponding to inputForm.lastName in the properties file into the errors.required message.
- **address.** This field is also required. If validation fails, Struts substitutes the value corresponding to inputForm.address into the errors.required message.
- **zipCode.** The zipCode field has two validation rules. Not only is the field required, the field must also conform to the specified mask. For the mask, we provide a regular expression with the var element.

```
<var>
  <var-name>mask</var-name>
  <var-value>^\d{5}\d*$</var-value>
</var>
```

  The regular expression, ^\d{5}\d*$, requires that the value contain five decimal digits. If not, Struts substitutes the text corresponding to inputForm.zipCode into the errors.zipcode message.
- **creditCardNumber.** This field also has two validation rules, required and creditCard. If the value is missing or does not meet the algorithm for a legal credit card, Struts displays the corresponding error message, errors.required or errors.creditcard, respectively. In both cases, Struts substitutes the text corresponding to inputForm.creditCardNumber into the error message.
- **email.** This field also has two validation rules, required and email. If the value is missing or does not conform to the format of a legal e-mail address, Struts displays the corresponding error message, errors.required or errors.email, respectively. In both cases, Struts substitutes the text corresponding to inputForm.email into the error message.

Listing 12.15 | orders/WEB-INF/validation.xml

```xml
<?xml version="1.0" encoding="ISO-8859-1" ?>
<!DOCTYPE form-validation PUBLIC
    "-//Apache Software Foundation//DTD Commons Validator Rules
    Configuration 1.3.0//EN"
    "http://jakarta.apache.org/commons/dtds/validator_1_3_0.dtd">
<form-validation>
  <formset>
    <form name="orderFormBean">
      <field property="firstName"
             depends="required">
        <arg key="inputForm.firstName"/>
      </field>
      <field property="lastName"
             depends="required">
        <arg key="inputForm.lastName"/>
      </field>
      <field property="address"
             depends="required">
        <arg key="inputForm.address"/>
      </field>
      <field property="zipCode"
             depends="required,mask">
        <arg key="inputForm.zipCode"/>
        <var>
          <var-name>mask</var-name>
          <var-value>^\d{5}\d*$</var-value>
        </var>
      </field>
      <field property="creditCardNumber"
             depends="required,creditCard">
        <arg key="inputForm.creditCardNumber"/>
      </field>
      <field property="email"
             depends="required,email">
        <arg key="inputForm.email"/>
      </field>
    </form>
  </formset>
</form-validation>
```

Step 4: Have Form Bean Extend ValidatorForm

Listing 12.16 presents our form bean. Aside from extending `ValidatorForm`, the bean simply has setter and getter methods for each of the six input fields of the ordering form.

Listing 12.16	orders/WEB-INF/classes/coreservlets/ OrderFormBean.java

```java
package coreservlets;

import org.apache.struts.validator.*;

public class OrderFormBean extends ValidatorForm {
  private String firstName = "";
  private String lastName = "";
  private String address = "";
  private String zipCode = "";
  private String creditCardNumber = "";
  private String email = "";

  public String getFirstName() {
    return(firstName);
  }

  public void setFirstName(String firstName) {
    this.firstName = firstName;
  }

  public String getLastName() {
    return(lastName);
  }

  public void setLastName(String lastName) {
    this.lastName = lastName;
  }

  public String getAddress() {
    return(address);
  }

  public void setAddress(String address) {
    this.address = address;
  }
```

Listing 12.16	orders/WEB-INF/classes/coreservlets/ OrderFormBean.java *(continued)*

```java
  public String getZipCode() {
    return(zipCode);
  }

  public void setZipCode(String zipCode) {
    this.zipCode = zipCode;
  }

  public String getCreditCardNumber() {
    return(creditCardNumber);
  }

  public void setCreditCardNumber(String creditCardNumber) {
    this.creditCardNumber = creditCardNumber;
  }

  public String getEmail() {
    return(email);
  }

  public void setEmail(String email) {
    this.email = email;
  }
}
```

Step 5: Put html:messages Tag in Input Page

Listing 12.17 presents our input page for the amazing Un-Divet tool, order-form.jsp. We use the `html:messages` tag to display any error messages before the input fields.

Step 6: Enable JavaScript Validation

To support client-side validation of the input fields, we add

```
<html:javascript formName="orderFormBean"/>
```

after the `html:form` tag in order-form.jsp. This tag adds all the necessary JavaScript code to validate the six input fields based on various rules we defined in valida-tion.xml.

In addition to the `javascript` tag, we add an `onsubmit` attribute to the beginning `html:form` tag, as shown here:

```
<html:form action="/actions/order"
           onsubmit="return validateOrderFormBean(this);">
```

This `onsubmit` option invokes JavaScript validation when the user submits the form. If validation fails, the browser presents the user with a message dialog box summarizing the errors; otherwise, the browser submits the request to the server.

Listing 12.17	orders/forms/order-form.jsp

```
<!DOCTYPE HTML PUBLIC "-//W3C//DTD HTML 4.0 Transitional//EN">
<HTML>
<HEAD><TITLE>No More Divets</TITLE></HEAD>
<BODY BGCOLOR="#FDF5E6">
<H1 ALIGN="CENTER">No More Divets</H1>
Thanks for ordering the Fred Randall
Amazing Un-Divet for the bargain-basement
price of $199.95. To complete your
order, please fill out and submit the
following information.
<P>
<CENTER>
<%@ taglib uri="http://struts.apache.org/tags-html"
           prefix="html" %>
<%@ taglib uri="http://struts.apache.org/tags-bean"
           prefix="bean" %>
<UL>
<html:messages id="msg" message="false">
  <LI><B><FONT COLOR="RED">
    <bean:write name="msg"/>
  </FONT></B></LI>
</html:messages>
</UL>
<html:form action="/actions/order"
           onsubmit="return validateOrderFormBean(this);">
  First name: <html:text property="firstName"/><BR>
  Last name: <html:text property="lastName"/><BR>
  Mailing address: <html:text property="address"/><BR>
  ZIP Code: <html:text property="zipCode"/><BR>
  Credit Card Number:
  <html:text property="creditCardNumber"/><BR>
  Email address for confirmation:
  <html:text property="email"/><BR>
  <html:submit value="Order Now!"/>
</html:form>
<html:javascript formName="orderFormBean"/>
</CENTER>
</BODY></HTML>
```

Results

Figure 12–11 shows the initial ordering form for the amazing Un-Divet tool. On submission, if the user fails to complete the order form correctly, client-side JavaScript validation produces the message box shown in Figure 12–12.

If the user disables JavaScript on the browser, validation is still performed on the server. If an error occurs, Struts sends the request back to the input page, where the html:messages tag displays the error messages above the input fields, as in Figure 12–13.

To test that the server-side validation is working in this example, you need to disable JavaScript in the browser. Next, we explain how to make this change in Internet Explorer and Firefox.

- **Disabling JavaScript in Internet Explorer.** Go to Tools, Internet Options. Select the Security tab and click the Custom Level button. For the Setting, change Active Scripting to Disable. Then, click OK.
- **Disabling JavaScript in Firefox.** Go to Tools, Options. Select the Web Features option and clear the Enable JavaScript checkbox. Click OK.

Finally, if the user completes all six input fields correctly, he or she sees the order-confirmation.jsp page in Figure 12–14.

For the complete example code, go to the book's source code archive at http://volume2.coreservlets.com/.

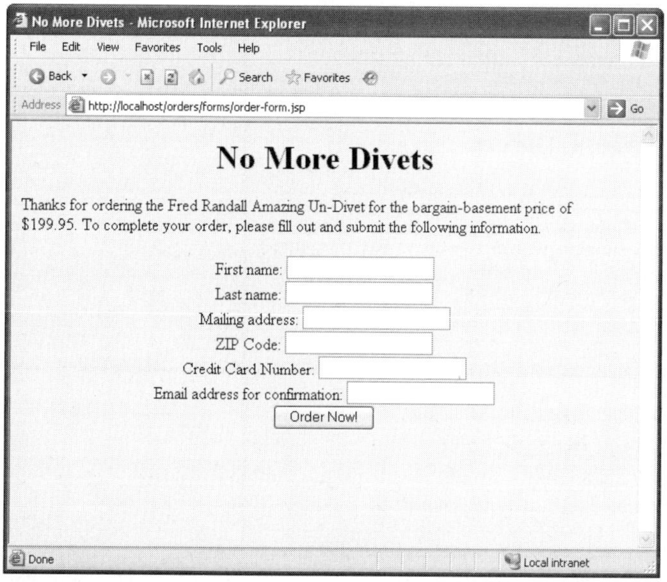

Figure 12–11 Ordering form for the amazing Un-Divet tool.

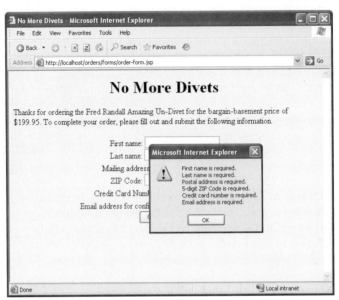

Figure 12–12 Results of submitting the order form with missing fields. Client-side JavaScript validation checks the fields against validation rules and displays a warning dialog box to the user.

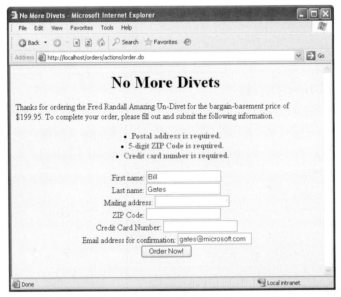

Figure 12–13 Results of submitting the order form with JavaScript disabled in the browser. In this case, Struts performs server-side validation. Any errors result in returning the request back to the input page where the html:messages tag displays the error messages.

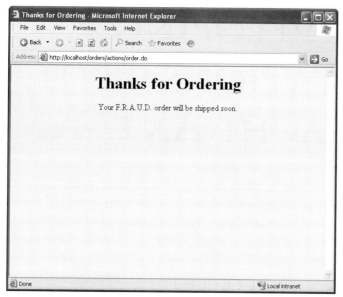

Figure 12–14   Result of a successful order request.

DEVELOPING APPLICATIONS WITH APACHE ANT

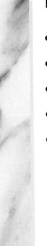

Topics in This Appendix

- Writing an Ant build file
- Understanding Ant targets and tasks
- Setting up an Ant directory structure
- Building a Web application for deployment
- Creating a WAR file

Appendix

Apache Ant is an open-source, cross-platform, development tool for building Java applications. Through Ant, you can completely control the build process of your Web application, from compiling source code to creating a WAR file.

In this appendix, we provide an introduction to Ant, where we focus on the build tasks that developers use for almost every Web application. Specifically, we first show you how to compile your application, then create a clean build of your application (create directory structure, copy files, and compile files), and finally, create a WAR file for deploying your application.

Each one of these common tasks is demonstrated through an example that provides a complete Ant build file that you can easily modify for your Web applications. The example build files, like all code shown in this book, are found at http://volume2.coreservlets.com/.

Once you're familiar with the basics, for advanced Ant capabilities, you might consider a book dedicated completely to Apache Ant. In addition, don't overlook the numerous examples found in the online documentation for Ant, located at http://ant.apache.org/manual/. For an open-source product, the online documentation is among the best that we have found.

If using Tomcat 5.5, you can find a general-purpose Ant build file located at http://tomcat.apache.org/tomcat-5.5-doc/appdev/sample/build.xml. This build file provides enhanced support for deploying your Web application directly to Tomcat through the Manager Web application (see http://tomcat.apache.org/tomcat-5.5-doc/manager-howto.html).

Finally, after you are comfortable with Apache Ant, you may want to further explore Apache Maven. Built on Ant, Maven is a complete framework for managing large-scale software projects. For more information on Maven, see http://maven.apache.org/.

A.1   Summarizing the Benefits of Ant

Ant is extremely popular with developers and is becoming the standard build tool for projects and Web applications. Many vendors now directly support Ant in their Java-based IDEs. For instance, jEdit, IBM Eclipse, Sun NetBeans, and JBuilder Enterprise Edition all support Ant as a build tool. Following, we summarize the main benefits of Ant.

- **Built for Java.** Ant is built from Java, for Java. Each command is executed within the JVM, instead of in a new process, thus improving performance. Also, Ant is a cross-platform tool, easily handling file paths and directory structures in both UNIX and Windows environments.
- **Based on XML.** An Ant project is completely written in XML. The XML syntax is simple and easy to learn. Compared to the traditional make files used with C and C++, Ant files are easier to read and maintain.
- **Easy to extend.** Each task in Ant originates from a Java class. Therefore, if needed, you can write your own custom tasks incorporating the build functionality you need. Once you've written the new task, you can add it to the Ant library.

A.2   Installing and Setting Up Ant

In the following list, we summarize the steps to install and configure Apache Ant 1.7.0. For additional installation instructions, see Apache's Web site at http://ant.apache.org/.

1. **Download the Ant implementation.** Apache Ant 1.7.0 is bundled as a ZIP file, apache-ant-1.7.0-bin.zip, located at http://ant.apache.org/bindownload.cgi. If you prefer, TAR files are also available. Extract the Ant files to a directory named apache-ant-1.7.0.

2. **Set the environment variables.** You should set your path to include the Ant bin directory. In addition, you should set environment variables for ANT_HOME and JAVA_HOME (if not already set). The ANT_HOME variable should list the base installation directory for Ant, not the bin subdirectory. Similarly, the JAVA_HOME variable should list the JDK installation directory, not the bin subdirectory. For example, if you installed Ant in C:\apache-ant-17.0 and the JDK in C:\j2sdk1.4.2_09, you might put the following lines in your C:\autoexec.bat file:

```
set PATH=C:\apache-ant-1.7.0\bin;%PATH%
set ANT_HOME=C:\apache-ant-1.7.0
set JAVA_HOME=C:\j2sdk1.4.2_09
```

   On Windows NT/2000/XP systems, instead of using the autoexec.bat file, you could also right-click My Computer, select Properties, then click the Advanced tab, then click the Environment Variables button. Then, you would enter the ANT_HOME and JAVA_HOME values, and click OK.
   On UNIX systems (Solaris, Linux, etc.), if Ant is installed in /usr/local/apache-ant-1.7.0, the SDK is installed in /usr/local/java1.4, and you use the C shell, you would put the following into your .cshrc file:

```
setenv PATH /usr/local/apache-ant-1.7.0/bin:$PATH
setenv ANT_HOME /usr/local/apache-ant-1.7.0
setenv JAVA_HOME /usr/local/java1.4
```

3. **Bookmark the Ant manual.** The Ant manual is included with the install download and is located in the *ANT_HOME*/docs/manual directory (see index.html). The manual is also available online at http://ant.apache.org/manual/. In addition, you should familiarize yourself with the Ant Tasks menu option, available through the manual's Table of Contents. This portion of the manual provides a complete summary of all the tasks available to build an Ant project.

To test that Ant is installed correctly, you can enter ant -version on the command line:

```
Prompt> ant -version
Apache Ant version 1.7.0 compiled on December 13 2006
```

A.3   Creating an Ant Project

Ant projects are written in XML. Because many developers are already familiar with XML, Ant is fairly easy to learn. In addition, XML has a well-defined structure, allowing you to easily organize the XML elements in your project.

An Ant project consists of targets and tasks, defined in a build file. Before examining the details of a build file, we first discuss the essential elements of an Ant project.

- **Targets.** An Ant project contains numerous targets to control the build process. A target logically groups one or more tasks for a particular step in the build process. For example, you might create a target in your project to group all the tasks to compile the source files in your application. You might create a target in your project, grouping all the tasks needed to generate a WAR file. Through the command line, you can ask Ant to run any one of the targets in the build file and execute all the tasks contained in the target group.

- **Core tasks.** Ant provides numerous core tasks that you can assign to your targets. These tasks execute a particular function available in the Ant library, for example, <mkdir> to create a new directory or <javac> to compile source code. Ant provides a rich library of core tasks with the default install.

- **Optional tasks.** Typically, the core tasks provide most of the functionality you need. However, on occasion you may require an optional task. These rarely used tasks are not all standard with Ant and can require installation of separate libraries or programs. Ant optional tasks are beyond the scope of this book and are not covered further.

We next present the details of an Ant project and the associated build file.

Defining the Ant Project

The basic structure for an Ant project contains a project definition and project targets, as shown here:

```
<?xml version="1.0" ?>
<project name="MyProj" basedir="projDir" default="defaultTarget">
  <description>My new Web application</description>
  <target name="targetName1">
    ...
  </target>
  <target name="targetName2">
    ...
```

```
    </target>
    . . .
</project>
```

The Ant project is defined in a file known as the build file. This file must contain a `<project>` root element, which functions as an XML container for declaring global properties and targets for the project.

The `<project>` element defines three attributes:

- **name.** The name attribute is optional, but we recommend using it to identify your project. In large Ant projects spanning multiple build files, the name attribute helps identify the particular project file.
- **basedir.** The basedir attribute is optional and defines the directory from which to make all path calculations. By default, basedir is the directory in which the build file is located. For clarity, developers often set the basedir attribute to . (period), explicitly stating that the directory is the current directory for the build file.
- **default.** The default attribute is required. This attribute specifies the default target to execute when running Ant on the build file.

When you declare an Ant `<project>` element, we strongly recommend that you add a `<description>` subelement to describe the Web application and build file.

Declaring Global Properties

With Ant, you can define properties for the project. In essence, these properties are constants that you can reference throughout the build file.

Ant supports six different approaches to define properties. For complete details, see the Ant manual under Table of Contents, Ant Tasks, Core Tasks, then Property. The property information is also available online at http://ant.apache.org/manual/CoreTasks/property.html.

The following are a couple of property declarations:

```
<property name="web.application" value="boats"/>

<property name="src.dir" location="src/boats"/>
```

The first declaration creates a property named web.application with an attribute value of boats. The second declaration creates a property named src.dir but contains a location attribute with a value of src/boats. A location refers to a file or directory resource. If a relative location is specified, then the full path to the file or directory is calculated from the project's basedir (as defined in the project element). Ant supports either UNIX or Windows separators in a location path.

To refer to the property value in the project file, simply place the property name inside the sequence `${...}`. You can refer to the property in any Ant element attribute or task, as shown in the following two examples:

```
<mkdir dir="${src.dir}/WEB-INF/classes"/>
<echo>Web application name: ${web.application}</echo>
```

In both cases, the referenced property is resolved at runtime.

In addition to declaring your own properties, you can access any of the Java system properties, using a similar notation as shown here:

```
<echo>User's current working directory: ${user.dir}</echo>.
```

The standard Java system properties are summarized at http://java.sun.com/j2se/1.4.2/docs/api/java/lang/System.html.

Writing Targets

Targets are a central concept to an Ant project. You use a target to group one or more tasks in the build file and invoke the target from the command line. The format for targets is shown here:

```
<target name="target-name1" description="Description of target.">
  <!-- Ant tasks. -->
  ...
</target>
<target name="target-name2" description="Description of target.">
  <!-- Ant tasks. -->
  ...
</target>
```

The required name attribute must be unique among all other targets in the project. When running Ant on your build file, you simply state as a command-line argument which target to invoke in the project.

For example, the following command prompts Ant to execute the target named `target-name` in the default build file, build.xml:

```
Prompt> ant target-name
```

The description attribute in the `<target>` element is optional, but we strongly recommend using this attribute to describe the tasks performed by the target.

More important, as the project becomes large with numerous targets, you can obtain a quick summary of the targets in the project by specifying the `-project-help` option when running Ant. Requesting `-projecthelp` outputs the name of each target, along with the description of the target.

Core Approach

Add a `description` *for the* `project` *and for each* `target` *in the build file. Then, by running* `ant -projecthelp`*, you can obtain a quick summary of the project and available targets.*

Assigning Tasks to Targets

You can assign multiple Ant tasks to each target in the project by placing the task inside the container of the `<target>` element. When Ant executes the target, each task is executed in the order in which it appears in the `<target>` element.

An example is shown here:

```
<target name="war" ...>
  <mkdir dir="${dist.dir}"/>
  <tstamp/>
  <jar destfile="${dist.dir}/${war.file}">
    <fileset dir="${build.dir}">
        <include name="**/*"/>
      </fileset>
      ...
  </jar>
</target>
```

This example `war` target contains three tasks: `<mkdir>`, `<tstamp>`, and `<jar>`.

The Ant library provides a rich set of core tasks for your targets, including `<mkdir>` to make directories, `<copy>` to copy files, and `<javac>` to compile files. Each library task has its own element name and set of attributes. For a complete listing of all available core tasks, see the online documentation at http://ant.apache.org/manual/ (from the Table of Contexts, select Ant Tasks, then Core Tasks).

Running an Ant Target

If you want Ant to execute one or more targets in your build file, specify the targets on the command line when invoking the Ant engine. Simply state the targets in the order of desired execution.

By default, Ant looks for the build file named build.xml. However, Ant also supports the `-buildfile`, `-file`, or `-f` command-line options to specify a different build file to process.

For instance, the Ant command

```
Prompt> ant compile
```

executes the `compile` target in the default build file, build.xml, where the build file is located in the working directory.

The next example,

```
Prompt> ant clean compile
```

lists two targets on the command line. Ant executes the tasks in the `clean` target first and then proceeds to execute the tasks in the `compile` target next.

If you don't state a target, as in

```
Prompt> ant
```

then Ant automatically invokes the `default` target as stated in the `<project>` element.

If you didn't use the default name for the build file, build.xml, you could specify the build file name through the `-f` option.

```
Prompt> ant -f MyProject.xml compile
```

Next, we cover the more common Ant tasks you would use in your build file.

A.4   Reviewing Common Ant Tasks

The Ant library provides numerous core tasks that you can add to a target. The online documentation for the core tasks is at http://ant.apache.org/manual/. From the Table of Contents menu, select Ant Tasks and then Core Tasks.

Next we summarize the following core tasks common to most build files: `<echo>`, `<tstamp>`, `<mkdir>`, `<delete>`, `<copy>`, and `<javac>`.

The echo Task

The `<echo>` task simply writes a message to `System.out` or a log file. The task requires a `message` attribute unless the message is stated in the body of the `<echo>` element (character section).

The following,

```
<echo message="Show me the money!"/>
<echo>Working directory: ${user.dir}</echo>
```

echo the messages shown here to the screen:

```
[echo] Show me the money!
[echo] Working directory: C:\ant-projects\boats
```

The property, `user.dir`, is the standard Java system property for the user's current working directory.

The next example,

```
<echo file="log.txt">
  Built by: ${user.name}
  Java version: ${java.version}
</echo>
```

writes the following message to the log.txt file, located in the working directory:

```
Built by: brownlm
Java version: 1.4.2_09
```

Both `user.name` and `java.version` are also standard Java system properties.

By default, the log file is overwritten unless you specify an `append` attribute with a value of `true`:

```
<echo file="log.txt" append="true"> ... </echo>
```

The tstamp Task

The `<tstamp>` task is handy for automatically setting the Ant time properties: DSTAMP, TSTAMP, and TODAY. The DSTAMP property is in the format "yyyymmdd," TSTAMP is in the format "hhmm," and TODAY is in the format "month day year."

For instance, the following,

```
<tstamp/>
<echo message="DSTAMP is ${DSTAMP}"/>
<echo message="TSTAMP is ${TSTAMP}"/>
<echo message="TODAY is ${TODAY}"/>
```

results in

```
[echo] DSTAMP is 20061231
[echo] TSTAMP is 1517
[echo] TODAY is December 31 2006
```

In addition, you can use the `<tstamp>` task in combination with the `<format>` subelement to create your own date and time formats.

This example creates a new property named `timestamp` in the ISO 8601 format (see http://www.w3.org/TR/NOTE-datetime):

```
<tstamp>
  <format property="timestamp"
          pattern="yyyy-MM-dd'T'HH:mm:ss"/>
</tstamp>
<echo message="Time is ${timestamp}"/>
```

That example produces the following Ant output:

```
[echo] Time is 2006-12-31T15:17:17
```

Also, developers commonly use the `<tstamp>` task to add a `Built-On` date to JAR manifest files. For details, see Section A.9 (Example: Creating a Web Application WAR File).

The mkdir Task

The `<mkdir>` task creates a new directory. The required (and only) attribute is `dir`, which specifies the directory to create. The following is an example of the `<mkdir>` task:

```
<mkdir dir="${build.dir}/WEB-INF/classes"/>
```

This task creates the `${build.dir}/WEB-INF/classes` directory, where the `build.dir` property is first resolved before the directory is created. If any parent directories are also missing, then Ant first creates the missing parent directories.

The delete Task

Another useful Ant task is `<delete>`, which can delete a file and a complete directory structure. The `<delete>` task supports multiple attributes. We summarize the more common attributes here.

- **file.** The `file` attribute specifies which file to delete. Either the `file` attribute or the `dir` attribute is required. The designated file can include a relative path (from the `basedir` directory) or an absolute path. If you want to specify multiple files or directories, use a `<fileset>` subelement. We discuss filesets in the next subsection.
- **dir.** The `dir` attribute specifies which directory to delete. If subdirectories exist, they are also deleted. Avoid `${base.dir}` or `.` for the `dir` value; otherwise, you will remove your complete Ant project and corresponding build file.
- **quiet.** If you don't want to receive a warning message when trying to delete a missing file or directory, specify `true` for the `quiet` attribute. The default value is `false`: display warning messages.

Core Note

For attributes that accept a boolean value, Ant treats all of the following as a true state: true, yes, *and* on. *All other values map to a false state.*

- **includeEmptyDirs.** The includeEmptyDirs attribute specifies whether to delete empty directories when using filesets. The default value is false: don't delete empty directories.
- **defaultexcludes.** Ant automatically excludes certain files from a fileset. This behavior prevents you from accidentally deleting your source code management files, for example, CVS or vssver.scc files. See http://ant.apache.org/manual/dirtasks.html#defaultexcludes for the complete list of files automatically excluded from a fileset. If you want to include source code management files in the fileset, specify an attribute value of false.

A couple of examples follow:

```
<delete dir="${build.dir}"/>
<delete file="${dist.dir}/${app.name}.war" quiet="true"/>
```

The first example deletes the directory specified by the build.dir property, as well as all subdirectories. The second example deletes the application's WAR file, located in the associated dist.dir directory.

The fileset Type

The <fileset> type is useful for indicating a group of files on which to operate. The <fileset> type is supported by many Ant tasks, including <delete> and <copy>.

You can select a single file through the file attribute. However, the more standard use is to state a directory through the dir attribute and then apply some rules to filter the set of selected files in the directory.

In the following, we use the <fileset> type to clarify which files to delete with the <delete> task:

```
<delete includeEmptyDirs="true" quiet="true">
  <fileset dir="temp"/>
</delete>

<delete>
  <fileset dir="${dist.dir}">
    <filename name="boats.war"/>
  </fileset>
</delete>
```

The first example deletes the temp directory and all subdirectories, even if empty. If the temp directory does not exist, all warning messages are quietly suppressed. The second example deletes the boats.war file from the directory determined by the dist.dir property.

With `<include>` and `<exclude>` subelements, you can control the grouping of files in a fileset. For example, the following deletes all `.class` files from the WEB-INF/classes directory and subdirectories.

```
<delete verbose="true">
  <fileset dir="WEB-INF/classes">
    <include name="**/*.class"/>
  </fileset>
</delete>
```

The next example deletes all but the `*.jsp` files from the html directory and subdirectories:

```
<delete>
  <fileset dir="html">
    <include name="**/*"/>
    <exclude name="**/*.jsp"/>
  </fileset>
</delete>
```

In both examples, the `**` acts as a wildcard to specify a search of all subdirectories when selecting files for the fileset. Remember though, source control files are not included in the fileset unless the `defaultincludes` attribute is set to `false`.

Core Note

*To include all subdirectories when grouping files in a fileset, use ** in the directory pattern.*

For more information on the `<delete>` task, see the Ant manual (Table of Contents, Ant Tasks, Core Tasks, then Delete) or the online documentation at http://ant.apache.org/manual/CoreTasks/delete.html. For information on the `<fileset>` type, see the manual (Table of Contents, Concepts and Types, FileSet) or the online documentation at http://ant.apache.org/manual/CoreTypes/fileset.html.

The copy Task

The `<copy>` task can copy either files or directories. The task supports numerous attributes. In the following list, we summarize the more important `<copy>` attributes.

- **file.** The `file` attribute specifies the file to copy. This attribute is required unless you use a `<fileset>` subelement.
- **tofile.** The `tofile` attribute specifies the name of the copied file. You must provide either a `tofile` or a `todir` attribute when using the `file` attribute.
- **todir.** The `todir` attribute specifies the directory into which the file should be copied. Typically, developers use the `todir` attribute in combination with a `<fileset>` subelement, as in

```
<copy todir="${backup.dir}">
  <fileset dir="${src.dir}"/>
</copy>
```

- **overwrite.** Ant only copies source files that are newer than the destination files. To overwrite existing files, regardless of their age, specify a value of `true` for the `overwrite` attribute. By default, the value is `false`: Newer destination files are not overwritten.
- **preservelastmodified.** If you want the copied files to have the same time stamp as the original files, provide a `preservelast-modified` attribute with a value of `true`. The default value is `false`: Give the copied files a new time stamp representing the current time.
- **includeEmptyDirs.** The `includeEmptyDirs` attribute specifies whether to copy empty directories when using filesets. The default value is `false`: Do not copy empty directories.
- **flatten.** The `flatten` attribute specifies whether to preserve the directory structure when copying a file. This attribute is helpful if you want to remove the hierarchy directory structure. A value of `true` removes the directory information from the file name. By default, the value is `false`.

The following example copies the file Welcome.jsp to index.jsp:

```
<copy file="${web.dir}/Welcome.jsp"
      tofile="${catalina.home}/webapps/${app.name}/index.jsp"/>
```

Before determining the full directory paths, Ant first resolves the property values for `web.dir`, `catalina.home`, and `app.name`.

The next example copies the MySQL JDBC drivers, bundled as a JAR file, to the build/WEB-INF/lib directory:

```
<copy file="mysql-connector-java-3.1.10-bin.jar"
      todir="build/WEB-INF/lib"/>
```

Developers often use the `<fileset>` type with the `<copy>` task to select a group of files or complete directories to copy. For this approach, you would use the `todir` attribute of the <copy> task to specify the destination directory and then use the <fileset> element to select files or directories to copy.

For example, the following <copy> task copies all the files in the directory defined by the `build.dir` property (and subdirectories) to the application's deployment directory in Tomcat:

```
<copy todir="${catalina.home}/webapps/${app.name}">
  <fileset dir="${build.dir}">
    <include name="**/*"/>
  </fileset>
</copy>
```

Again, Ant would first resolve the property values for `catalina.home` and `app.name` before determining the full directory paths and copying the files.

For more information on the <copy> task, see the Ant manual, Table of Contents, Ant Tasks, Core Tasks, then Copy, or the online documentation at http://ant.apache.org/manual/CoreTasks/copy.html.

The javac Task

Probably the most popular Ant task is <javac>, which compiles your source code to class files. The <javac> task is very robust and provides more than 30 attributes to select files and to control compiler options; most of the attributes map closely to the command-line options available in the SDK `javac` program.

In the following list, we cover the common <javac> attributes.

- **srcdir.** The `srcdir` attribute is the only required attribute. It specifies the directory to search for compiling `.java` files. Ant scans the `srcdir` and `destdir` directory recursively, compiling only those source files with a later time stamp than their corresponding `.class` files.
- **classpath.** The `classpath` attribute is optional and states where to find the class files. If not stated, Ant uses the CLASSPATH set for the operating environment. Instead of a `classpath` attribute, authors often use the <classpath> subelement to better clarify where to find the files. See the examples later in this section.

Core Note

If you don't specify a `classpath` attribute or <classpath> subelement for the <javac> task, then Ant uses the CLASSPATH as set for the operating system environment.

- **destdir.** The destdir attribute is optional and specifies the destination directory for the .class files (Ant preserves the package hierarchy). If you don't specify a destdir, then the .class files are placed in the same directories as their corresponding .java files.
- **debug.** The debug attribute specifies whether to include debug information in the .class files. The default value is false.
- **verbose.** The verbose attributes specifies whether to display messages output by the compiler. The default value is false.
- **listfiles.** If you want Ant to list the .java files to compile, specify true for the listfiles attribute. Otherwise, Ant won't tell you which files are compiled. The default is false: Don't list files.

The following is a simple <javac> task demonstrating use of the srcdir and destdir attributes:

```
<javac srcdir="${src.dir}"
       destdir="${build.dir}/WEB-INF/classes" />
```

This task performs an in-process compilation of the .java files located in the directory specified by the src.dir property. The task places the generated .class files in the WEB-INF/classes subdirectory, relative to the directory specified by the build.dir property.

For out-of-process compilation (execution of the SDK compiler externally as a separate process), add a fork attribute value with a value of true (the default is false).

Note that Ant scans the srcdir and destdir directories recursively, compiling only those source files that have a different time stamp than their corresponding .class files.

Ant automatically uses the CLASSPATH specified by your environment for the <javac> task, but you can explicitly state the CLASSPATH through an attribute.

For example, the following specifies a CLASSPATH containing the servlet-api.jar file (located in the directory specified by the lib.dir property):

```
<javac srcdir="${src.dir}"
       destdir="${build.dir}"
       debug="true"
       deprecation="true"
       verbose="true"
       classpath="${lib.dir}/servlet-api.jar"/>
```

Furthermore, the example sets attributes to generate debugging and deprecation information. The verbose attribute is also true, forcing a detailed summary of the compiler activity.

When specifying directory locations, don't go on a file exploration by using ../. Avoid constructs like the following:

```
// Poor directory path. Avoid!
classpath="../../../common/lib/servlet-api.jar"
```

Instead, move the JAR file to a common directory in the Ant project (see the recommended project directory structure in Section 3).

Ideally, you want all the files needed for your application located within the project area. This approach makes it easier to maintain the project with a version management system like Concurrent Versions System (CVS).

Core Approach

Place needed JAR files in the project directory structure. In this manner, all the files for the project are centrally located in the same area.

The classpath Element

If your project requires multiple files on the CLASSPATH, you could use a `<class-path>` subelement to specify the directories and files to include, as in

```
<javac srcdir="${src.dir}"
       destdir="${build.dir}"
   <classpath>
     <pathelement location="common/lib/classes"/>
     <pathelement location="lib/mail.jar"/>
   </classpath>
</javac>
```

Some developers choose to define a separate `<path>` element in the build file with an `id` attribute to identify the path group. Then, they create a `classpath` property to reference the group through the path `id`.

This approach is more clearly understood from the folowing example:

```
<path id="project.classpath">
  <pathelement location="common/lib/classes"/>
  <pathelement location="lib/mail.jar"/>
</path>
<property name="classpath" refid="project.classpath"/>
...
<javac srcdir="${src.dir}"
       destdir="${build.dir}"
   <classpath>
     <pathelement path="${classpath}"/>
   </classpath>
</javac>
```

Numerous other <classpath> constructs are possible; Ant provides extensive flexibility to select files and directories for establishing a CLASSPATH.

Regardless of your approach, explicitly provide the CLASSPATH information in your Ant project. That way, you're not relying on environment settings and your project is more portable.

Core Approach

Always declare the CLASSPATH information in your Ant project—don't rely on the default system environment setting for the CLASSPATH. This approach improves portability of your project to other platforms and improves documentation.

For a complete summary of the attributes supported by the <javac> task and other <classpath> constructs, go to the Ant manual, Table of Contents, Ant Tasks, Core Tasks, and then select Javac. The information is also available online at http://ant.apache.org/manual/CoreTasks/javac.html.

A.5   Example: Writing a Simple Ant Project

For our first Ant example, we use a small application (an online boat shop) that contains many aspects common to a Web site: JSP pages, images, servlets, and custom tags. Figure A–1 shows the files and directory structure for the boats Web application. The default page (index.jsp) for the boats application is shown in Figure A–2.

For Ant development, we provide this application bundled in a JAR file, boats-ant.jar, at http://volume2.coreservlets.com/. This JAR file contains the files and directory structure as recommended in Figure A–3 for our boats Web application.

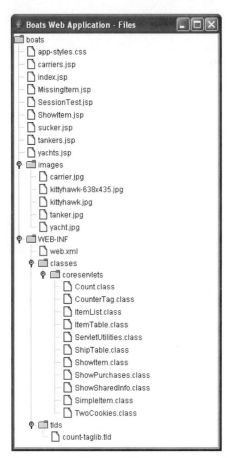

Figure A–1   Files and directory structure for **boats** Web application.

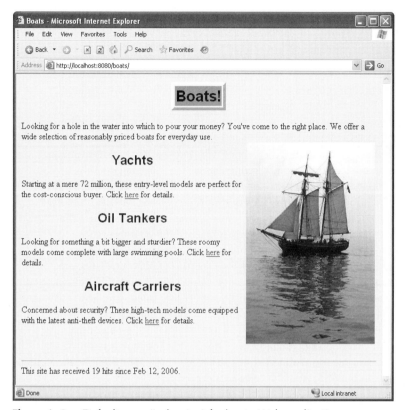

Figure A–2 Default page (index.jsp) for boats Web application.

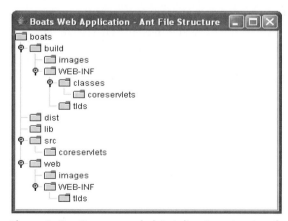

Figure A–3 Recommended Ant directory structure for boats Web application.

In general, you should organize your Web application into five subdirectories: src, lib, web, build, and dist. We explain the purpose of each directory in the following list.

- src. The src directory contains all Java source files normally compiled to the WEB-INF/classes directory. These files include your servlets, beans, listeners, tag classes, utility classes, and so on.
- lib. The lib directory contains JAR files that are normally located on your CLASSPATH and that are needed for compilation of your application; for example, the servlet API and the JSP API, bundled in servlet-api.jar and jsp-api.jar, respectively.
- web. The web directory contains all the files for your Web site, with the exception of the source files normally associated with the WEB-INF/classes subdirectory (the src directory contains the source files that get compiled to the classes directory). Thus, the web directory includes your HTML, JSP, and image files, along with all files contained in your WEB-INF directory structure (web.xml, TLDs, etc.).
- build. The build directory is the target for a clean build of the application before testing and deployment. The build directory contains all files for your Web application, including the compiled .class files.
  Typically, you don't manually create the build directory yourself. Instead you rely on Ant tasks (<mkdir>, <copy>) to automatically create the build directory structure and populate the directory with the appropriate content from the src, lib, and web directories.
- dist. The dist directory is the target directory for building a WAR file for distribution of your Web application.

In addition to the recommended directory structure, you should also use a source code management system like CVS that tracks all the files in your src, lib, and web directories.

The Ant build file for our application, boats1.xml, is given in Listing A.1. Place this file in the top-level boats directory shown in Figure A–3 (the directory above src).

The project contains two Ant targets, clean and compile. To see the available targets in the build file, use the -projecthelp option when running Ant on boats1.xml, as shown here:

```
// Run from boats directory.
Prompt> ant -projecthelp -f boats1.xml

Buildfile: boats1.xml
Web Application: Online Boat Shop
Main targets:
```

```
clean      Remove all .class files
compile  Compile files to WEB-INF/classes directory
Default target: compile
```

The first target, clean, removes all the .class files from the build area, where the property, build.webinf.classes.dir, is determined at runtime and has a value of build/WEB-INF/classes.

```
<target name="clean" ... >
  <delete quiet="true">
    <fileset dir="${build.webinf.classes.dir}">
      <filename name="**/*.class"/>
    </fileset>
  </delete>
</target>
```

We use a <fileset> type to select all the .class files in the directory structure for deletion. The directory structure itself is not deleted.

The second target is compile. This target compiles all the .java files in the src directory and places the resulting .class files in the build/WEB-INF/classes directory. If source files are located in subdirectories, then Ant compiles these files also.

```
<target name="compile" ... >
  <mkdir dir="${build.webinf.classes.dir}"/>
  <javac srcdir="${src.dir}"
         destdir="${build.webinf.classes.dir}"
         deprecation="${javac.deprecation}"
         listfiles="${javac.listfiles}">
    <classpath>
      <pathelement path="${classpath}"/>
    </classpath>
  </javac>
</target>
```

The target first defines a <mkdir> task to create the destination directory, build/WEB-INF/classes. Then, the target defines a <javac> task to compile the source files. Global properties provide values for the deprecation and listfiles attributes.

Instead of a classpath attribute, a <classpath> element defines the CLASS-PATH for the task. The <pathelement> references a path construct comprising the servlet API, servlet-api.jar, which is located in the lib directory. See the property and path definitions defined before the compile target in Listing A.1.

The compile target is the default target for this project. Thus, to compile the project source code, enter the following Ant command:

```
Prompt> ant -f boats1.xml

Buildfile: boats1.xml

compile:
    [mkdir] Created dir:
            C:\ant-projects\boats\build\WEB-INF\classes
    [javac] Compiling 11 source files to
            C:\ant-projects\boats\build\WEB-INF\classes

BUILD SUCCESSFUL
Total time: 3 seconds
```

The output shows that 11 source files were compiled and placed in the build area.

If you want information about which source files Ant compiled, change the global property `javac.listfiles` to `true`. For a detailed explanation of the Ant process, you can use the `-verbose` command-line option when running the target (see `-help` for a complete list of available Ant command-line options).

As mentioned earlier, Ant examines the time stamp of the files, compiling only those files modified since the previous compile. Thus, if you ran Ant a second time, you would see the following output:

```
Prompt> ant -f boats1.xml

Buildfile: boats1.xml

compile:

BUILD SUCCESSFUL
Total time: 1 seconds
```

Because the `.class` files are already up to date, Ant doesn't recompile the source files.

Now, to ensure that all source files are recompiled, you would first execute the `clean` target to remove all the existing `.class` files, then follow with the `compile` target to regenerate the `.class` files.

To accomplish this result, simply list both targets, in the desired order of execution, on the command line, as shown here:

```
Prompt> ant -f boats1.xml clean compile

Buildfile: boats1.xml

clean:
    [delete] Deleting 11 files from
      C:\ant-projects\boats\build\WEB-INF\classes
```

```
compile:
    [javac] Compiling 11 source files to
            C:\ant-projects\boats\build\WEB-INF\classes

BUILD SUCCESSFUL
Total time: 3 seconds
```

Listing A.1   ant-projects/boats/boats1.xml

```xml
<?xml version="1.0" ?>
<project name="Boats" default="compile" basedir=".">
  <description>Web Application: Online Boat Shop</description>
  <property name="javac.deprecation" value="true"/>
  <property name="javac.listfiles" value="false"/>

  <!-- Properties for project directories. -->
  <property name="src.dir" location="${basedir}/src"/>
  <property name="lib.dir" location="${basedir}/lib"/>
  <property name="build.dir" location="${basedir}/build"/>
  <property name="build.webinf.classes.dir"
    location="${build.dir}/WEB-INF/classes"/>

  <!-- The clean target removes all files from the
       WEB-INF/classes directory and subdirectories.
  -->
  <target name="clean"
          description="Remove all .class files">
    <delete quiet="true">
      <fileset dir="${build.webinf.classes.dir}">
        <filename name="**/*.class"/>
      </fileset>
    </delete>
  </target>

  <!-- Create a path element declaring the directories/files
       to include on the CLASSPATH. Then, define a property to
       the path information.
  -->
  <path id="project.classpath">
    <pathelement location="${lib.dir}/servlet-api.jar"/>
  </path>
  <property name="classpath" refid="project.classpath"/>
```

Listing A.1	ant-projects/boats/boats1.xml *(continued)*

```
<!-- Default target that compiles all the source files
     to the build/WEB-INF/classes directory. Ant compiles
     only those .class files that have a different time stamp
     than their corresponding .java files. To compile all
     classes, first run the "clean" target to delete all the
     .class files, then run the "compile" target to recreate
     them.
-->
<target name="compile"
    description="Compile files to WEB-INF/classes directory">
  <mkdir dir="${build.webinf.classes.dir}"/>
  <javac srcdir="${src.dir}"
         destdir="${build.webinf.classes.dir}"
         deprecation="${javac.deprecation}"
         listfiles="${javac.listfiles}">
    <classpath>
      <pathelement path="${classpath}"/>
    </classpath>
  </javac>
</target>
</project>
```

A.6   Using Ant to Build a Web Application

If all you ever did was compile your source code, you might not use Ant at all—you would simply run the standard `javac` program. The real benefit of Ant is its ability to nicely organize the build file to perform the various tasks common to preparing and deploying your Web application.

For instance, you might set up your build file with tasks to delete old files, create new directories, copy needed files, and compile source code. In some cases, one task might have dependencies on another, for instance, creating a directory structure before copying files.

With Ant, you can create dependencies between targets in the build file. Setting up target dependencies has two main benefits:

- **Process control.** By setting up dependencies, you can guarantee that certain tasks have completed in the build process before the application proceeds with subsequent tasks. Each target can have a specific task to perform in the build process.

- **Documentation.** By dividing the tasks into separate, dependent targets you can greatly improve the documentation and the life cycle of the build process.

We next explain how to define dependencies between targets in a build file.

Ant Dependencies

When you write a new `<target>` in your build file, you can use the `depends` attribute to specify another target on which your new target depends. If more than one dependency is required, you can use a comma-separated list. The order of the targets in the list determines the order of the dependencies and their order of execution.

A `<target>` with a `depends` attribute is shown here:

```
<target name="compile" depends="prepare"
  description="Compile files to WEB-INF/classes directory">
  // Ant tasks ...
</target>
```

In this example, the `compile` target depends on the `prepare` target. Thus, when

```
Prompt> ant compile
```

is run, the `prepare` target is executed first and then the `compile` target. The result would be the same as if you entered the following command:

```
Prompt> ant prepare compile
```

Often, developers create in their project a `build` or an `all` target that has no assigned tasks but simply defines dependencies on other targets that must complete to create a clean build of the application.

An example is shown here:

```
<target name="build" depends="clean, copy, compile"/>
```

Through dependencies, this target first cleans the build area (deleting existing files), then copies all necessary files for the Web application to the build area, and finally, compiles the source files.

Core Approach

To create a clean build of the Web application, add a `build` target to your Ant project to set up all the dependencies on other targets that must complete.

In the next section, we present an example that uses this approach to build a Web application before testing and deployment.

A.7   Example: Building a Web Application

In this example, we present an Ant project to completely build the **boats** Web application presented in Section A.5 (Example: Writing a Simple Ant Project).

The build file, boats2.xml, is given in Listing A.2. The build file contains five targets, briefly described here.

- **clean.** The clean target removes all files from the Web application's build directory.
- **prepare.** The prepare target creates the necessary directory structure to compile and build the Web application.
- **compile.** The compile target compiles the application source files, placing them in the build/WEB-INF/classes directory. The compile target is dependent on the prepare target.
- **copy.** The copy target copies all the Web application files from the web directory to the build directory. Unwanted files are not copied, for example, *.bak files.
- **build.** The build target creates a clean build of the application, with dependencies on the clean, copy, and compile targets.

The clean and compile targets are similar to the example presented earlier in Section A.5 (Example: Writing a Simple Ant Project). Therefore, in the following, we provide a detailed discussion only for the prepare, copy, and build targets.

The prepare Target

The prepare target sets up the necessary directory structure for the compile and copy targets. The prepare target is shown here. Global properties for the directories are defined at the beginning of the build file, boats2.xml.

```
<target name="prepare" ... >
  <mkdir dir="${build.dir}" />
  <mkdir dir="${build.images.dir}"/>
  <mkdir dir="${build.webinf.dir}"/>
  <mkdir dir="${build.webinf.classes.dir}"/>
  <mkdir dir="${build.webinf.tlds.dir}"/>
</target>
```

Specifically, the target uses the <mkdir> task to create the following directories:

```
build
build/images
build/WEB-INF
build/WEB-INF/classes
build/WEB-INF/tlds
```

Technically, the <mkdir> task creates any missing parent directories. Thus, we could achieve the same directory result with only three of the <mkdir> tasks shown:

```
<mkdir dir="${build.images.dir}"/>
<mkdir dir="${build.webinf.classes.dir}"/>
<mkdir dir="${build.webinf.tlds.dir}"/>
```

However, it's customary to use a separate <mkdir> task for each directory. Doing so improves the maintenance and readability of the build file over the life span of the project.

Core Approach

When setting up the build directory structure through an Ant target, add a separate <mkdir> task for each directory, instead of relying on Ant to automatically create the parent directory. This approach improves maintenance and readability of the build file.

The copy Target

The <copy> target simply mirrors the complete directory structure and files from the web directory to the build directory. The <copy> target is shown here:

```
<target name="copy" ... >
  <copy todir="${build.dir}"
        preservelastmodified="yes"
        overwrite="yes">
    <fileset dir="${web.dir}">
      <include name="**/*"/>
      <exclude name="**/*.bak"/>
    </fileset>
  </copy>
</target>
```

So as not to copy unwanted files, we use a <fileset> type to clarify the group of files to copy to the destination directory.

The fileset contains one `<include>` element and one `<exclude>` element. The `<include>` element,

```
<include name="**/*"/>
```

selects all files from the web directory and includes them in the set of files to copy. Remember that the ** acts as a wildcard to specify that all subdirectories be examined when looking for files to add to the fileset.

The `<exclude>` element,

```
<exclude name="**/*.bak"/>
```

states that any .bak files found throughout the directory structure should not be included in the set of files to copy.

After determining the final set of files, Ant copies them to the destination directory specified by the `todir` attribute. Again, only out-of-date files are copied unless you specify `true` for the `overwrite` attribute in the `<copy>` task.

The build Target

The `build` target is a convenience target to logically bundle together all the targets necessary to completely rebuild the Web application. You would use this target before deploying your Web application to a test or production server.

The `build` target is shown here:

```
<target name="build" depends="clean, prepare, copy, compile" ... />
```

The target depends on the `clean`, `prepare`, `copy`, and `compile` targets. The `copy` is performed before `compile` so that .class files accidentally located in the src directory don't overwrite newly compiled files.

Running the `build` target produces the following output. For the files to compile successfully, place the two API files, servlet-api.jar and jsp-api.jar, in the boats\lib directory.

```
Prompt> ant -f boats2.xml build

clean:
   [delete] Deleting directory C:\ant-projects\boats\build

prepare:
   [mkdir] Created dir: C:\ant-projects\boats\build
   [mkdir] Created dir: C:\ant-projects\boats\build\images
   [mkdir] Created dir: C:\ant-projects\boats\build\WEB-INF
   [mkdir] Created dir: C:\ant-projects\boats\build\WEB-INF\classes
   [mkdir] Created dir: C:\ant-projects\boats\build\WEB-INF\tlds
```

```
copy:
    [copy] Copying 16 files to C:\ant-projects\boats\build

compile:
   [javac] Compiling 11 source files to
           C:\ant-projects\boats\build\WEB-INF\classes

build:

BUILD SUCCESSFUL
Total time: 4 seconds
```

After running the `build` target, you are ready to test the Web application. If testing on the localhost, you could add another target to the project to copy the contents of the build directory to your server's Web application directory. Alternatively, you could create a WAR file as described in the next section.

Listing A.2 ant-projects/boats/boats2.xml

```xml
<?xml version="1.0" ?>
<project name="Boats" default="compile" basedir=".">
  <description>Web Application: Online Boat Shop</description>
  <property name="javac.deprecation" value="true"/>
  <property name="javac.listfiles" value="false"/>
  <property name="app.name" value="boats"/>

  <!-- Properties for project directories. -->
  <property name="src.dir" location="${basedir}/src"/>
  <property name="lib.dir" location="${basedir}/lib"/>
  <property name="web.dir" location="${basedir}/web"/>
  <property name="build.dir" location="${basedir}/build"/>

  <!-- Properties for build directories. -->
  <property name="build.images.dir"
          location="${build.dir}/images"/>
  <property name="build.webinf.dir"
          location="${build.dir}/WEB-INF"/>
  <property name="build.webinf.classes.dir"
          location="${build.webinf.dir}/classes"/>
  <property name="build.webinf.tlds.dir"
          location="${build.webinf.dir}/tlds"/>

  <!-- The clean target removes the complete build directory
       structure.
  -->
```

Listing A.2   ant-projects/boats/boats2.xml *(continued)*

```xml
<target name="clean"
        description="Remove all files from build directory">
  <delete dir="${build.dir}" quiet="true"/>
</target>

<!-- The prepare target to create the complete directory
     structure for the Web application. In particular, it
     creates a build/WEB-INF/classes directory
     necessary for compiling the source files.
-->
<target name="prepare"
    description="Create directory structure to build application">
  <mkdir dir="${build.dir}" />
  <mkdir dir="${build.images.dir}" />
  <mkdir dir="${build.webinf.dir}"/>
  <mkdir dir="${build.webinf.classes.dir}"/>
  <mkdir dir="${build.webinf.tlds.dir}"/>
</target>

<!-- The copy target copies all Web application files from
     the web directory and subdirectories to the build
     directory. Don't copy backup files (.bak extension).
-->
<target name="copy"
        description="Copy Web files to build directory">
  <copy todir="${build.dir}" preservelastmodified="true"
        overwrite="true">
    <fileset dir="${web.dir}">
      <include name="**/*"/>
      <exclude name="**/*.bak"/>
    </fileset>
  </copy>
</target>

<!-- Create a path element declaring the directories/files
     to include on the CLASSPATH. Then, define a property to
     the path information.
-->
<path id="project.classpath">
  <pathelement location="${lib.dir}/servlet-api.jar"/>
  <pathelement location="${lib.dir}/jsp-api.jar"/>
</path>
<property name="classpath" refid="project.classpath"/>
```

Listing A.2	ant-projects/boats/boats2.xml *(continued)*

```
<!-- Default target that compiles all the source files
     to the build/WEB-INF/classes directory. Ant compiles
     only those .class files that have a different time stamp
     than their corresponding .java files. To compile all
     classes, first run the "clean" target to delete all the
     .class files, then run the "compile" target to recreate
     them.
-->
<target name="compile" depends="prepare"
    description="Compile files to WEB-INF/classes directory">
  <javac srcdir="${src.dir}"
         destdir="${build.webinf.classes.dir}"
         listfiles="${javac.listfiles}"
         deprecation="${javac.deprecation}">
    <classpath>
      <pathelement path="${classpath}"/>
    </classpath>
  </javac>
</target>

<!-- Target to completely create a clean build of the Web
     application. This target has dependencies on the clean,
     copy, and compile targets to ensure that the built
     application contains new copies of the latest files.
-->
<target name="build" depends="clean, prepare, copy, compile"
    description="Creates a clean, complete build of project"/>
</project>
```

A.8 Using Ant to Create a WAR File

WAR (Web ARchive) files provide a convenient way of bundling Web applications in a single file. A WAR file contains the complete directory structure and files for the Web application.

Most J2EE containers allow you to auto-deploy a Web application through a WAR file. For instance, with Tomcat 5.5, you just place the .war file in the *tomcat_install_dir*/webapps directory, start the server, and Tomcat will deploy (expand) the WAR file.

We use the <jar> task to create WAR files—simply place all the Web application files in a build directory structure and then use the <jar> task to add the directory structure and file to a WAR file.

In addition to the Web application files, a WAR file must contain a manifest file, META-INF/MAINFEST.MF. Typically, a manifest contains version information but can also contain security information and define dependencies on libraries shared by the application. As a convenience, the `<jar>` task supports the `<manifest>` task as a subelement to help create a manifest file.

We next describe the `<jar>` and `<manifest>` tasks.

The jar Task

The `<jar>` task creates a JAR file in much the same manner as the SDK `jar` utility found in the JAVA_HOME/bin directory. To create a WAR file, simply give the JAR file a `.war` file name extension.

The following are the common attributes of the `<jar>` task.

- **destfile.** The `destfile` attribute specifies the location and name of the JAR file to create. This attribute is required.
- **basedir.** The `basedir` attribute specifies the source directory of the files to add to the JAR file. Alternatively, you can use the `dir` attribute of a `<fileset>` subelement to specify the source directory. See Section A.4 (Reviewing Common Ant Tasks) for details on the fileset type.
- **includes.** The `includes` attribute specifies which files to include in the archive. The value can be a comma- or space-separated list of files. By default, the `<jar>` task includes all files from the `basedir` directory.
- **excludes.** The `excludes` attribute specifies the files to exclude from the archive. The value can be a comma- or space-separated list of files. By default, Ant excludes only the code management files.
- **manifest.** The `manifest` attribute specifies the manifest file to add in the archive. This attribute is optional, so if you don't provide a manifest, Ant adds a minimal META-INF/MANIFEST.MF file to the archive. As an alternative to the `manifest` attribute, you can use a `<manifest>` subelement to dynamically create the manifest file.
- **update.** The `update` attribute indicates whether to update an existing JAR file or to create a new file. The default value is `false`: Create a new JAR file.
- **compress.** The `compress` attributes specifies whether to compress the archived files. The default value is `true`: Compress the files. Because uncompressed JAR files are faster to read, you might set this value to `false` for J2EE containers that don't expand deployed WAR files (i.e., containers that read the Web application files directly from the WAR file). Tomcat 5.5 automatically expands the WAR file into a directory structure.

- **index.** The index attribute specifies whether to create an index for the JAR file. Creating an index speeds the loading of class files directly from the archive. The default value is false: Do not create an index.

The following is a simple example of a `<jar>` task:

```
<jar destfile="${dist.dir}/myapp.war"
     basedir="${build.dir}"/>
```

This example creates a JAR file named myapp.war in the directory defined by the dist.dir property. The task adds all files from the directory specified by the build.dir property to the JAR file. All files located in subdirectories are also added.

The next example demonstrates the `<fileset>` and `<zipfileset>` types to explicitly select various files and directories to add to the JAR file:

```
<jar destfile="${dist.dir}/myapp.war"
     compress="false" index="true">
  <fileset dir="${build.dir}">
    <include name="**/*"/>
  </fileset>
  <zipfileset dir="${src.dir}" prefix="WEB-INF/classes">
    <include name="**/*.java"/>
    <exclude name="**/*.bak"/>
  </zipfileset>
</jar>
```

The `<fileset>` type selects all files in the directory tree structure at the location indicated by the build.dir property.

The `<zipfileset>` type operates similarly to the `<fileset>` type for selecting files; however, you can logically map the selected files to a new directory through the prefix attribute.

For instance, the `<zipfileset>` type in this example selects all the source files from the directory specified by the src.dir property, excluding any possible backup files ending in .bak. Because of the prefix attribute, when Ant adds the files to the set, each file is prefixed with the WEB-INF/classes directory information. This example effectively places the .java files in the same location as the .class files in the Web application.

Normally, you wouldn't place source code in WAR files that you deploy to production servers. The reasoning is that you want to protect your proprietary source code from potential hackers. Then again, a hacker good enough to compromise a server is probably good enough to reverse engineer the .class files (see http://jode.source-forge.net/ for a .class file decompiler).

The manifest Task

The `<manifest>` task dynamically creates a META-INF/MANIFEST.MF file. For a simple manifest file you might use this approach. However, for a complex manifest file, it's easier to first create a physical manifest file and then refer to the file through the `manifest` attribute of the `<jar>` task.

In general, a manifest file contains a main section for security and configuration information, along with optional sections to define various attributes for packages or files in the JAR file.

Manifest entries consist of name–value pairs. Use the `<attribute>` subelement to define the name–value pairs, as shown in this example:

```
<manifest file="MANIFEST.MF">
  <attribute name="Built-By" value="Larry Brown"/>
  <attribute name="Extension-List" value="javaMail"/>
  <attribute name="javaMail-Extension-Name" value="javax.mail"/>
  <attribute name="javaMail-Specification-Version"
             value="1.4"/>
  <attribute name="javaMail-Implementation-URL"
             value="http://www.coreservlets.com/javaMail.jar"/>
</manifest>
```

On our system, this example created a manifest file with the following contents:

```
Manifest-Version: 1.0
Ant-Version: Apache Ant 1.7.0
Created-By: 1.4.2_09-b05 (Sun Microsystems Inc.)
Built-By: Larry Brown
Extension-List: javaMail
javaMail-Extension-Name: javax.mail
javaMail-Specification-Version: 1.4
javaMail-Implementation-URL:
  http://www.coreservlets.com/javaMail.jar
```

This manifest, in addition to naming who built the file, contains information on the application's dependency on the JavaMail 1.4 JAR file.

When WAR files are deployed, J2EE-compliant containers are required to detect whether dependent library files are configured on the server and, if not, provide a warning.

For more details on creating a manifest file, see the online documentation at http://java.sun.com/j2se/1.4.2/docs/guide/jar/jar.html.

A.9   Example: Creating a Web Application WAR File

In this example, we use Ant to create a WAR file for deployment of our **boats** Web application presented in Section A.5 (Example: Writing a Simple Ant Project). The build file, **boats3.xml**, is given in Listing A.3 and extends the example presented in Section A.7 (Example: Building a Web Application).

Next, we discuss the `war` target for the build file. The build file does contain additional targets (not shown), but these targets are discussed in Section A.7 (Example: Building a Web Application). For a complete listing of the build file, see the online code at **http://volume2.coreservlets.com/**.

The war Target

The build file contains a `war` target to create the application WAR file. The target performs a sequence of steps to create the WAR file, as described in the following list.

- **Create a local property for the WAR file name.** Initially, the `war` target defines a local `property`, `war.file`, for the name of the WAR file.

  ```
  <property name="war.file" value="${app.name}.war"/>
  ```

  Ant builds the name from the `app.name` property by appending .war to the application name. Thus, when executed, the `war.file` property has a value of **boats.war**. This property is defined only within the scope of the `war` target.

- **Create the distribution directory.** Next, the target defines a `mkdir` task to create a distribution directory in which to place the WAR file.

  ```
  <mkdir dir="${dist.dir}"/>
  ```

  If the distribution directory and WAR file are already present, the default behavior is to re-create the WAR file. For clarity, you could add an `update` attribute with a value of `false` to the `<jar>` task.

- **Define a `timestamp` property for the manifest file.** After the `<mkdir>` task, the target defines the `<tstamp>` task. This task defines a property, named `timestamp`, that contains the date and time of task execution, expressed in the ISO 8601 format.

  ```
  <tstamp>
    <format property="timestamp"
            pattern="yyyy-MM-dd'T'HH:mm:ss"/>
  </tstamp>
  ```

The `timestamp` property is later used by the `<manifest>` task when it adds a `Built-On` attribute.

- **Use `jar` to create the distribution directory.** Finally, the target executes the `<jar>` task to create the WAR file and manifest file. The `<jar>` task, shown here, creates the WAR file named dist/boats.war, containing all the files from the build directory and subdirectories:

```
<jar destfile="${dist.dir}/${war.file}">
  <!-- Include all files in the build directory and
       subdirectories -->
  <fileset dir="${build.dir}">
    <include name="**/*"/>
  </fileset>
  <!-- Dynamically create the META/MANIFEST.MF file -->
  <manifest>
    <attribute name="Built-By" value="Larry Brown"/>
    <attribute name="Built-On" value="${timestamp}"/>
  </manifest>
</jar>
```

The manifest file, dynamically created, contains only two attributes: `Built-By` and `Built-On`. The `Built-By` attribute is set to Larry Brown. The `Built-On` value is set to the date assigned to the `timestamp` property.

The following shows the output from running the war target:

```
Prompt> ant -f boats3.xml war
Buildfile: boats3.xml

war:
    [jar] Building jar: C:\ant-projects\boats\dist\boats.war

BUILD SUCCESSFUL
Total time: 2 seconds
```

Before you distribute your Web application, you should check that the WAR file contains the directory structure and application files that you expect. You can list the contents of the WAR file through the `jar` utility by using the `tf` options.

The following is the list of contents for the boats.war file:

```
Prompt> jar tf dist/boats.war

META-INF/
META-INF/MANIFEST.MF
MissingItem.jsp
SessionTest.jsp
```

```
ShowItem.jsp
WEB-INF/
WEB-INF/classes/
WEB-INF/classes/coreservlets/
WEB-INF/classes/coreservlets/Count.class
WEB-INF/classes/coreservlets/CounterTag.class
WEB-INF/classes/coreservlets/ItemList.class
WEB-INF/classes/coreservlets/ItemTable.class
WEB-INF/classes/coreservlets/ServletUtilities.class
WEB-INF/classes/coreservlets/ShipTable.class
WEB-INF/classes/coreservlets/ShowItem.class
WEB-INF/classes/coreservlets/ShowPurchases.class
WEB-INF/classes/coreservlets/ShowSharedInfo.class
WEB-INF/classes/coreservlets/SimpleItem.class
WEB-INF/classes/coreservlets/TwoCookies.class
WEB-INF/tlds/
WEB-INF/tlds/count-taglib.tld
WEB-INF/web.xml
app-styles.css
carriers.jsp
images/
images/carrier.jpg
images/kittyhawk-638x435.jpg
images/kittyhawk.jpg
images/tanker.jpg
images/yacht.jpg
index.jsp
sucker.jsp
tankers.jsp
yachts.jsp
```

Listing A.3   ant-projects/boats/boats3.xml

```xml
<?xml version="1.0" ?>
<project name="Boats" default="compile" basedir=".">
  <description>Web Application: Online Boat Shop</description>
  <property name="javac.deprecation" value="true"/>
  <property name="javac.listfiles" value="false"/>
  <property name="app.name" value="boats"/>

  <!-- Properties for project directories. -->
  <property name="src.dir" location="${basedir}/src"/>
  <property name="web.dir" location="${basedir}/web"/>
  <property name="build.dir" location="${basedir}/build"/>
  <property name="dist.dir" location="${basedir}/dist"/>
```

Listing A.3   ant-projects/boats/boats3.xml *(continued)*

```xml
<!-- ... See online example at http://www.coreservlets.com/
         for complete source code listing.
         ... -->

<!-- Target to create a WAR file for deployment of the
     application. The manifest file is dynamically
     created.
-->
<target name="war"
         description="Create WAR file for deployment">
  <property name="war.file" value="${app.name}.war"/>
  <mkdir dir="${dist.dir}"/>
  <!-- Date for manifest file. -->
  <tstamp>
    <format property="timestamp"
             pattern="yyyy-MM-dd'T'HH:mm:ss"/>
  </tstamp>
  <!-- Build WAR file and manifest. -->
  <jar destfile="${dist.dir}/${war.file}"
       update="false" compress="true">
    <fileset dir="${build.dir}">
      <include name="**/*"/>
    </fileset>
    <manifest>
      <attribute name="Built-By" value="Larry Brown"/>
      <attribute name="Built-On" value="${timestamp}"/>
    </manifest>
  </jar>
</target>
</project>
```

Index